Kings of Jazz

KINGS OF JAZZ

Revised and Edited
by Stanley Green

Authors

Albert McCarthy	Martin Williams
Burnett James	Max Harrison
Michael James	Paul Oliver
G. E. Lambert	Charles Fox

South Brunswick and New York: A. S. Barnes and Co.
London: Thomas Yoseloff Ltd

"Louis Armstrong" © 1959 by Cassell & Co. Ltd.
"Bix Beiderbecke" © 1959 by Cassell & Co. Ltd.
"Miles Davs" © 1961 by Cassell & Co. Ltd.
"Johnny Dodds" © 1961 by Cassell & Co. Ltd.
"Duke Ellington" © 1959 by Cassell & Co. Ltd.
"Dizzy Gillespie" © 1959 by Cassell & Co. Ltd.
"Jelly Roll Morton" © 1962 by Cassell & Co. Ltd.
"King Oliver" © 1960 by Cassell & Co. Ltd.
"Charlie Parker" © 1960 by Cassell & Co. Ltd.
"Bessie Smith" © 1959 by Cassell & Co. Ltd.
"Fats Waller" © 1960 by Cassell & Co. Ltd.

New material © 1978 by A. S. Barnes and Co., Inc.

Library of Congress Catalogue Card Number: 74-30980

A. S. Barnes and Co., Inc.
Cranbury, New Jersey 08512

Thomas Yoseloff Ltd
Magdalen House
136–148 Tooley Street
London SE1 2TT, England

ISBN 0-498-01724-9

Printed in the United States of America

CONTENTS

Louis Armstrong

BY ALBERT J. McCARTHY

ACKNOWLEDGEMENTS

Acknowledgement is due to the following for permission to quote from their publications :

Peter Davies, Ltd   (*Just Jazz* 1);   *Jazz Review*

Maher Publications (*Down Beat*);   *Record Changer.*

INTRODUCTION

The problem that confronts any writer who takes Louis Armstrong for a subject is basically one of knowing what to select from the mass of available data. Armstrong is not only the most famous jazz musician in the world; he is also the most written about. Faced with the requirements of producing a book of some twenty thousand words that would need to satisfy both the newcomer and the more fully informed, the question of the form to be adopted became a paramount one. It is obvious that there must be a great deal of recapitulation of information which is well enough known to the long-term jazz enthusiast, and no matter how adroit one may be in cloaking established fact in a new guise, such matters as birth dates, years of joining and leaving different orchestras, highlights of a career and the listing of outstanding records can really only be presented in one fashion. In addition, it would be a fool rather than a brave man who could presume that he were able to say anything startlingly new about Armstrong and his playing. The hundreds of articles that have reviewed the great trumpeter's career, his style, his influence and his records from almost every conceivable viewpoint leave little room for anyone to come up with a completely fresh approach. In view of this I have tended to veer towards safety by keeping the less specialist reader in mind throughout.

As already indicated, source material on Armstrong is considerable. Two books have been published under his name, the first of which, *Swing that Music*, appeared in the thirties. In retrospect it seems unlikely that much of this was actually contributed by Armstrong himself and many of the views certainly do not agree with what he has expressed since. Although it also shows signs of editorial influence, *Satchmo— My Life in New Orleans*, first published in the U.S.A. in 1954,

seems reasonably authentic. It is the first of a projected series of volumes and only goes as far as Armstrong's trip to Chicago in 1922 to join King Oliver's band, but despite certain shortcomings it is a valuable documentation. As this book is readily available I have kept the section on the early days relatively short. To balance this brevity about the period prior to Armstrong's emergence as a performer of international renown I have dealt with more recent times in some detail. The reason for this is that there has been considerable controversy about Armstrong's later performances, particularly relating to his announcements and stage mannerisms. As several aspects of this matter touch on such subjects as the growth of the jazz audience as a whole and the relationship of the performer to his audience, I felt that a discussion of these points would have an interest beyond the point where they concern Armstrong himself.

To a considerable extent the development of Armstrong the artist is reflected in his recorded output. It was logical, therefore, to arrange the chapters in relationship to his records. This is made doubly necessary by the fact that there can hardly be any writer on jazz who was a witness of the events which took place during the early part of Armstrong's career. Quite by chance I had talked about certain aspects of the trumpeter's development during the thirties with some musicians who were in his bands. When their comments were not passed in private conversations, and where they are relevant, I have included them in the text.

A listing of some of the most important Armstrong records will be found at the end of this book. They are based on what is currently available at the time of writing.

ALBERT J. McCARTHY

I

1900-22 — THE EARLY DAYS

When, on New Year's Day in 1913, Louis Armstrong discharged a pistol which he had found at home, he little realized that the sequence of events which followed his action were to set him on the road to international fame. The immediate result was that he was arrested and sent to a reform school, but it was there that he received the first rudimentary training in music from one Captain Jones. Many years later he returned to that home as a celebrity and the bugle on which he first played is still preserved.

In his book *Satchmo—My Life in New Orleans* Armstrong gave a fascinating account of his early life. Because the book is generally available and is fairly well known I do not propose to devote a great deal of space to his early life, preferring to document later periods more fully. However, the picture that emerges from a reading of his autobiographical volume is an interesting one, and the sociologist as well as the jazz fan will find Armstrong's descriptions of New Orleans life worthy of study. He speaks of a society strictly governed by racial and economic discrimination with each racial group living in some degree of independence of others. It was also a society in which violence was never far from the surface and Armstrong tells of cases of murder with a nonchalance that could only arise from acceptance of such doings as part of the normal routine of life. He speaks with great affection of an early parade drummer 'Black Benny', who was reputed to be one of the toughest men in the area, and it is with awe that he relates that Benny was the only Negro who would go alone through the Irish quarter. In view of the lurid accounts he gives of the toughness of many of his companions, the Irish must have been ferocious indeed if they could cause those worthies to hesitate before stepping into their territory!

The early years of the twentieth century—Armstrong was born on 4 July 1900—found New Orleans flourishing as one of the widest open cities in the United States. It was to have a run of another seventeen years before the famous red light district was to close down and it catered for vice on a lavish scale. The famous New Orleans' *Blue Book* set out the attractions of the 'mansions' in glowing terms, stressing the high quality of the entertainment to be found within them and the culture of the madames who were in charge. Whatever one's taste in off-beat entertainment it could be found, for the American belief that the consumer is always right found its expression in a rather unexpected fashion in the red light district! It has been suggested that much of the history of New Orleans at this time has been romanticized and there may indeed be some truth in the criticism, but the guitarist Danny Barker has been gathering material for years on early New Orleans days, mainly from interviews with other musicians, and the parts of his manuscript that I have read would not suggest that much exaggeration would be needed to give a colourful picture of the era.

Armstrong accepted all that went on around him and was absorbed in the music he heard. He recalls listening to the legendary trumpeter Buddy Bolden, but says that he thought Bolden's playing was very rough. The parade bands fascinated him and he was first to take part in them as a member of the Waifs' Home band. However, his first musical experience in the form of actually entertaining others arose from his membership of a vocal quartet which included 'Kid Shots' Madison and 'Kid' Rena. This quartet used to wander around New Orleans singing in the streets for pennies. Its career was cut short when Louis was sent to the Waifs' Home.

In William Russell's article on Armstrong that appeared in the book *Jazzmen*, a story is related by Bunk Johnson which attempts to prove that Armstrong had played cornet before he was sent to the Waifs' Home. Johnson claimed: 'During that time (1911) Louis started after me to show him how to blow my cornet. When the band would not be playing I would have to let him carry it to please him.

'Now here is the time I began showing Louis. I took a job playing in a tonk for Dago Tony on Perdido and Franklin Street and Louis used to slip in there and get on the music stand behind the piano. He would fool with my cornet every chance he could get until he could get a sound out of it. Then I showed him just how to hold it and place it to his mouth and he did so and it wasn't long before he began getting a good tone out of my horn.'

The difficulty with the *Jazzmen* article is that Russell was far too uncritical of Johnson's claims, and in his autobiography Armstrong included a passage which is a flat contradiction of the above. It is worth quoting in full:

'The little brass band was very good, and Mr. Davis made the boys play a little of every kind of music. I had never tried to play cornet, but while listening to the band every day I remembered Joe Oliver, Bolden and Bunk Johnson. And I had an awful urge to learn the cornet. But Mr. Davis hated me. Furthermore I did not know how long they were going to keep me at the Home. The judge had condemned me for an indefinite period which meant that I would have to stay there until he set me free or until some important white person vouched for me and for my mother and father. That was my only chance of getting out of the Waifs' Home fast. So I had plenty of time to listen to the band and wish I could learn to play the cornet.'

It can be seen from this that Johnson's story was spurious. It is sometimes difficult to check information, but William Russell might have been a little more cautious in accepting a story which is at variance with claims made by Armstrong as early as 1935.

Armstrong was fourteen when he left the Home. He took a number of jobs during the day including that of coalman, milk roundsman and rag-and-bones man. He relates that his first job as a musician was obtained for him by one, Cocaine Buddy, and that it was in a honky tonk that catered for the good time girls when they were not working. Various jobs of this nature followed and around 1915 Armstrong formed his first band with drummer Joe Lindsey, patterned after 'Kid Ory's Brown Skinned Babies' in which King Oliver was the cornet player. In 1917 the band broke up and he again played with various groups which are now forgotten, but in the following year he got his first big break

when Kid Ory called on him to replace Oliver who had left for Chicago. From now on Armstrong was a full time musician, for Ory had a tremendous local reputation and obtained most of the good jobs that were going. While he was with Ory, Armstrong also joined the famous Tuxedo Brass Band, led by Oscar 'Papa' Celestin. His fame spread amongst the New Orleans musicians of the day and he could more or less take any job that he wanted. It is a matter of regret that the recording of jazz had not been started a decade earlier, for one can only speculate on the nature of the music played in New Orleans during the formative years of jazz. Many musicians have claimed that Oliver was long past his prime by the time he recorded in 1923.

It was in 1918 that Fate Marable called on Louis and offered him a job in his band on the S.S. *Sidney*. His offer was accepted and the experience proved a valuable one for the young musician. Marable, in his time, had some of the greatest jazz musicians in his various bands, and he played a more varied selection of material than most of the New Orleans bands. It was a hard routine on the riverboats, as Armstrong recalled in *Swing that Music*:

'Hot musicians throw a pack of energy into their work, and it takes a lot out of them. When we ran those all-day excursions, and we did that at most all the ports we touched at, it only left about two hours to rest up and get dressed and ready for the evening excursions.'

The other members of the band when Armstrong joined were Joe Howard, David Jones, Boyd Atkins, Johnny St. Cyr, Baby Dodds, George 'Pops' Foster and Marable himself. David Jones, the mellophone player, was the first person who really taught Armstrong how to read music and he soon became proficient enough not to need to sit out when a new orchestration was produced until such time as he could memorize the number by ear. It would appear from the testimony of Fletcher Henderson which is quoted in the next chapter that Armstrong's reading abilities were not all that impressive at the time he joined the Henderson band, but at least he had some rudimentary knowledge of the subject by 1924. The life of a travelling musician seems to have appealed to Armstrong and he made several trips with Marable, finally leaving him for good in 1921. During one of the excursions he first met Bix Beiderbecke at Davenport, Iowa.

11

When he was not working on the boats Armstrong took various jobs in New Orleans. In 1921 he was playing at the famous Tom Anderson's cabaret on Rampart Street with a quartet led by a fiddler, Paul Dominguez. This was an extremely remunerative engagement with the musicians earning much more from tips than from any regular salary. When Anderson's closed down for repairs Armstrong worked in a trio with drummer Zutty Singleton and pianist Udell Wilson at a club owned by Butsy Fernandez. During the daytime there were the jobs with the Tuxedo Brass Band, and Armstrong related his pleasure in being a member of that group in the following words:

'When I played with the Tuxedo Brass Band I felt just as proud as though I had been hired by John Philip Sousa or Arthur Pryor. It was a great thrill when they passed out the brass-band music on stiff cards that could be read as you walked along. I took great pains to play my part right and not miss a note. If I made a mistake I was brought down the whole day, but Celestin quickly saw how interested I was in my music. He appreciated that.'

In 1922 Armstrong was once more playing at Tom Anderson's in a group that included Albert Nicholas, Barney Bigard and Luis Russell. He was receiving frequent letters from King Oliver asking him to join his band in Chicago as second cornet player, and in the summer of that year decided that he would accept the invitation. He related that he had become convinced that Oliver was the only person for whom he would leave New Orleans, having witnessed too often the departure of other musicians with high hopes that were never to be fulfilled. He found the other members of the Tuxedo Brass Band anxious to dissuade him from leaving and they reported that Oliver was on the musicians' union's unfair list. This is a story that seems to have no basis in fact and was presumably an invention of those men who did not wish him to leave.

On 8 August 1922, Armstrong played at a funeral at Algiers in the afternoon. The funeral was for the father of Eddie Vincent, a trombone player of some local renown who later made a few records in Chicago. When it was over he went home, collected his clothes, and went to the Illinois Central Station to catch the 7 p.m. train to Chicago. The whole band and many friends and neighbours came to see him off. The musicians were glad that he was to have the opportunity of making a name for himself, but thought that he should have gone out on his own and not as the second cornet player to Oliver. Armstrong himself had no such qualms and the final sentence in his book, *Satchmo— My Life in New Orleans*, tells of his joy when he informed the porters on the train that he was going to Chicago 'to play with my idol, Papa Joe!' Although he was unaware of it his path to fame and international acclaim had begun.

2

1922-29 — THE EMERGENCE OF A JAZZ GIANT

Armstrong's arrival in Chicago has been described by him in the course of an article on Joe Oliver, characteristically titled 'Joe Oliver is still King', in the *Record Changer* of July–August 1950. The following are his own words on the subject:

'I'll never forget the night I joined the Oliver band. They were playing at the Lincoln Gardens, at 31st near Cottage Grove, an old, famous spot. They used to call it the Royal Gardens—that's where these blues came from. Then when Joe Oliver came up they changed the name to Lincoln Gardens, and it *still* jumped. Paul Whiteman, Louis Panico (they were fixtures in Chicago then), and all the cats from Friar's Inn used to come up there. Business was great. Well, I came up to Chicago then, and I didn't come in on the train that Joe was supposed to meet. So that makes me come in all by myself. I looked all around and I didn't see anybody. I said: "Lord, what's going to happen now?", and I wondered if I should go right back on the next train. I was just a youngster from New Orleans, and I felt real lost in Chicago. But a redcap told me: "Why don't you get a cab and go out to the Lincoln Gardens?"

'When I got there and got out of the cab, I heard this band. They were really jumping then, and I commenced to worry all over again. I wondered if I could ever fit into that band. Oh, those cats were blowing! Old Johnny Dodds was making those variations and Baby Dodds shimmying on the drums. Dutrey was good on that trombone, too. He played shallow parts, which made them pretty, and he had a beautiful tone and punctuation. When I walked in that night I just sat down and listened.'

Armstrong's reputation had preceded his arrival, spread mainly by New Orleans musicians who had come up to Chicago. There is considerable disagreement concerning Oliver's relationship to his young admirer, some claiming that he had sent for him as a safeguard against his going with any other band and thus ending Oliver's own reign as 'king'. It has even been said that the Dodds brothers and Dutrey were enraged with Oliver for not allowing Louis to play lead, but it seems unlikely that they could seriously have expected the leader to take a subordinate role in his own band. Louis himself seems to have no such ideas and is always quick to praise Oliver, although he did say, in the previously quoted *Record Changer* article, that Oliver was already past his prime. Against the suggestions advanced that Oliver was jealous of Louis must be laid the facts that he made him very welcome in Chicago, gradually allowed him to take more solos, and insisted that he studied music to fill in many gaps in his knowledge. The truth is probably that Oliver was well aware that Louis was the greater trumpeter and may have felt that he could do him less harm in his own band than with another leader, but that he also helped Armstrong to develop his talents is undeniable.

Whatever his failings might have been, the picture of Oliver that emerges from his series of tragic and moving letters that were printed in the book *Jazzmen*, is not that of a mean man. This view is supported on all sides, including the testimony of such an apparently unlikely witness as the late Lester Young who played with Oliver in his declining years.

The Oliver band acted as a catalyst on the development of jazz as a whole. The young men around Chicago who were becoming excited by the, to them, strange new music flocked to the Lincoln Gardens and in a very short while Armstrong's reputation had spread throughout the jazz world. There was little doubt in the minds of most of the listeners that Louis was the greatest member of the band and his acceptance as the most formidable soloist in the history of jazz dates from this period, although it was to be many years before he became known to the public at large.

On 31 March 1923 Armstrong entered the recording studio for the first time, as a member of the Oliver band. The session took place in Richmond, Indiana, and the acoustical recording apparatus was very crude by today's standards. It is also said that the studio which the Gennett Recording Company used for these sessions was very close to a railroad track and that every time a train passed the session had to come to an abrupt halt. The fifth and last title recorded that day was *Chimes Blues*, and on this Armstrong took his initial recorded solo, of twenty-four bars length. During 1923 the Oliver band took part in a total of ten sessions for four different labels—Gennett, Columbia, Okeh and Paramount—and these sides have become classics of their kind. Actually, despite the presence of Armstrong and Johnny Dodds, the emphasis is on the ensemble sound of the group and solos are used quite sparingly. It may well be that Oliver was now past his best, but there can be little doubt that it was his firm leadership and awareness of the exact type of performance he wanted that made the records as great as they are. Musicians who heard the band in person swear that they give no real idea of how it sounded at the Lincoln Gardens and insist that the records are a travesty of the reality. In jazz there is a tendency for the older musician to romanticize about the past, but the extremely poor recording, coupled with the arbitrary three-minute time limitation of a ten-inch disc, obviously resulted in a great deal of the music being lost. One is only left to marvel that so much has come across in spite of these deterring factors.

The playing of the Oliver band is a supreme example of the 'classic' New Orleans tradition. Since the nineteen-forties there have been dozens of attempts to emulate the band by young white 'revivalist' groups but none have come within measurable distance of its achievements. It is easy enough to point out that the musicians in the Oliver band were supreme of their kind, but this is only part of the story. For one thing, Oliver was particularly adept at selecting a tempo for the numbers played that did not strain the capabilities of his musicians. By comparison with the tempos chosen by many of the young white musicians who were influenced by the Oliver band, they seemed to be slower. It has been stated by fairly reliable witnesses that New Orleans musicians played blues at a much slower tempo in the early days than afterwards became fashionable and it is possible that this concept of tempo, presumably related to the needs of dancers, guided Oliver at the recording sessions. The beat of the band is even more important, for Oliver employed a straight four-four, whereas many of the revivalist rhythm sections have tended to accentuate the secondary beats. Perhaps the most impressive aspect of the Oliver records with Armstrong is the complete feeling of relaxation that comes across. There is none of the slightly uneasy feeling of effort that has become commonplace in the records of the revivalists: Oliver's music flows, or at least gives that impression, whereas the revivalists tend to sound jerky and this feeling destroys the effect of relaxation. This question has been well discussed by Larry Gushee, in a review of the Gennett Oliver recordings, in *Jazz Review* of November 1958. What he says is so relevant to the matter that I am quoting part of his review:

'The truly phenomenal rhythmic momentum generated by Oliver is just as much dependent on *continuity* of rhythmic pulse—only reinforced by uniformity of accentuation in the rhythm section and relaxed playing. One never hears the vertiginous excitement of Bix, or Tesch; one never feels that, with a little less control, a break or an entire chorus would fall into irrationality or musical *bizarrerie*. Oliver's swing is exciting after a different fashion: it is predictable, positive, and consistent. Only rarely is the total effect *manqué*, as in *Froggie Moore*, where the stop-and-go character of the tune makes consistency more difficult to achieve.

'Its consistency is, as I have said, largely the result of Oliver's personal conception of a band sound. How much he moulded the musicians to fit the ideal pattern of his own imagination, or how much he chose them with the knowledge that they would fit in, without trying to change

their personal style, is something we can't determine since we lack recordings by New Orleans bands before 1923.'

This discussion has more point than may at first appear, because the characteristics of much of Oliver's music in relationship to tempo, relaxation and rhythmic momentum are equally applicable to Armstrong's trumpet playing. Louis later spoke of this period as one of the happiest of his life and there is no stretching of credulity involved in the suggestion that the disciplined music of the Oliver band was to teach him lessons that were to stand him in good stead in the following years.

The pianist with Oliver's band when he joined was Lil Hardin. Miss Hardin had received a classical training and her main interest at the time was still in the classical field. However, it did not take her long to perceive the inherent brilliance of Armstrong's playing and she helped him in his studies. In an essay on Armstrong in the book *Jazzmen*, William Russell states that by the time Louis had left the Oliver band his initial studies with Dave Jones and those with Lil Hardin had resulted in his becoming a proficient sight-reader. As we shall see later, Fletcher Henderson's testimony on the subject suggests that this is something of an exaggeration. What is certain is that, under Lil's guidance, Louis was assimilating a great deal more theoretical knowledge of music. Early in 1924 Lil Hardin and Louis were married and Lil did much to further his career in the next few years. In the summer of 1924 she managed to persuade Louis to leave Oliver and to take a job at the Dreamland Café as first cornet. Her motives for doing this were probably a mixture of pique at what she considered to be Oliver's reluctance to feature Louis enough and a genuine desire for his success as an individual performer. In September of that year Louis recieved a telegram offering him a job in Fletcher Henderson's orchestra and he left for New York City to take up the offer.

Fletcher Henderson's orchestra at this time was a vastly different proposition from Oliver's. The *Chicago Defender*, the leading Negro newspaper in the U.S.A., said of Henderson's group that it was '. . . the greatest, not at all like the average Negro orchestra, but in a class with the good white orchestras, such as Paul Whiteman, Paul Ash, and Ted Lewis.' Of its music, it claimed that it was 'soft, sweet, and perfect, not the sloppy New Orleans hokum, but peppy blue syncopation.' This attitude on the part of the

Negro press to authentic jazz is not as uncommon as might be assumed, and a whole book could be devoted to the subject. Certain aspects of the matter will be touched on in the last chapter. However, it is clear enough from the above that it was more a popular dance orchestra at this time (the great period of the band, when it was packed with outstanding jazz musicians, was to come a year or two later) than a jazz group, and Louis found it very strange at first. That he was a success from the start is attested by the late Fletcher Henderson himself who, writing in the *Record Changer* of July–August 1950, said:

'Needless to say, Louis was a big success right from the start. About three weeks after he joined us, he asked me if he could sing a number. I know I wondered what he could possibly do with that big fish horn voice of his, but finally I told him to try it. He was great. The band loved it, and the crowd just ate it up. I believe that was the first time he ever sang anywhere. He didn't sing with Oliver, I'm sure.

'The band gained a lot from Louis, and he gained a lot from us. By that I mean that he *really* learned to read in my band, and to read in just about every key. Although it's common today, it wasn't usual at that time to write in such keys as E natural, or D natural, so that Louis had to learn, and did learn, much more about his own horn than he knew before he joined us.

'That's how we influenced him. But he influenced the band greatly, too, by making the men really swing-conscious with that New Orleans style of his. The same kind of effect that Coleman Hawkins had on the reeds, that right-down-to-earth swing, with punch and bounce. He surely was an asset to my orchestra; I have no hesitation at all in saying that.'

Listening to the records that Armstrong made with the Henderson orchestra during 1924–25 one is amazed by the freshness of his solos even after an interval of over fifty years. The records themselves are mostly pretty banal and were it not for the occasional Louis solo it is unlikely that they would be of interest to even the most starry-eyed collector of old dance items. A discovery by the American collector Walter C. Allen is a very important one. It concerns a very rare master of Henderson's *Everybody Loves My Baby* (take one) on the Regal label, on which there are vocal breaks by Louis. It has been assumed for years that the first vocal which Louis recorded was *Gut Bucket Blues*, made on 12 November 1925, but the Henderson side pre-dates this by nine months. It had been known that *Everybody Loves My Baby* was one of the numbers that Henderson featured during stage shows, complete with a vocal chorus by Louis, but that it was actually recorded with vocal breaks is an unexpected disclosure.

In addition to the records he made with the Henderson band, Louis also went into the studios as an accompanist to some of the great blues singers of the day, usually with companions from the full orchestra. The titles he made with Bessie Smith are available to this day, but others with such vocalists as Clara Smith and Maggie Jones are undeservedly obscure. As a blues accompanist Louis was superb, filling in between phrases and providing entirely apt background statements that enhanced the work of the vocalist without conflicting with it. Sensitivity and warmth are the basic requirements for a blues accompaniment, and Louis was only rivalled in this role by Joe Smith and Tommy Ladnier, both of them also members at one time or another of Henderson's trumpet team. Readers will find recommended records for most of the periods discussed in this book in a separate listing at the close. In addition to these blues items Louis also recorded with Clarence Williams's Blue Five during 1924–25. The Williams group often included another great New Orleans musician, the late Sidney Bechet, and the music was very much akin to that of the New Orleans pioneers. In these congenial surroundings Louis must often have felt more at home than when he was playing with Henderson. One of the titles he made with Williams was *Coal Cart Blues*, a reference to his early job driving a coal cart.

In 1925 Lil organized her own orchestra for an engagement at the Dreamland Café in Chicago and persuaded the owner to make Louis an offer of $75 a week if he would return from New York City and be featured with it. This was a very high salary at the time and at first Louis doubted the authenticity of the offer, but upon realizing that it was not a hoax he approached Henderson and obtained his release. The 14 November 1925 issue of the *Chicago Defender* carried an advertisement announcing that Lil's Dreamland Syncopators would include the 'World's Greatest Jazz Cornetist', Louis Armstrong. A week or two later the same paper carried a review of the band that asserted, of Louis, that 'This boy is in a class by himself.'

Within a few weeks of opening at the Dreamland, Erskine Tate booked Louis to appear with his Vendome Theatre Orchestra. For the first time Louis's extraordinary acting and singing ability was given full rein and it is said that many people came along to see the stage show and left before the film was shown. One of the routines Louis used here was the fairly common 'preaching' one during which he donned a frock-coat and delivered a mock sermon. A year or two later another famous trumpeter, the late 'Hot Lips' Page, stopped the show in Kansas City when, as a member of the Benny Moten band, he used the same routine. The Tate band had a large repertoire which included light classic pieces, but the only two titles which Armstrong recorded with them are stomps.

On 12 November 1925 Armstrong recorded for the first time as a leader in his own right. He used a pick-up group of himself, the famous New Orleans trombonist Edward 'Kid' Ory, and three members of the Oliver band—Johnny Dodds, Johnny St. Cyr and Lil Hardin, his wife. The first number he recorded was *My Heart* and the name of his band was the 'Hot Five'. From this time until the December of 1927 he recorded fairly frequently with this line-up, sometimes enlarging the group by adding Pete Briggs on tuba and Warren 'Baby' Dodds on drums. During the same period he made numerous records as an accompanist to various blues singers, including Bertha 'Chippie' Hill, Hociel Thomas, Sippie Wallace and Nolan Welsh. It is unfortunate that the latter have not been reissued except on an occasional 'bootleg' label, for they include some of his most moving playing, but it is some compensation that almost all of the 'Hot Five' and 'Hot Seven' records are currently obtainable on microgroove.

So much has been written about these records that there is very little that one can add at this late date. Within a short while of any person becoming interested in jazz they gain an awareness of their importance and their ranking as jazz classics would hardly be challenged by any rational critic. Louis's companions were ideal for performances of the kind he desired, with Johnny Dodds outstanding. Ory was a good ensemble man, but his solos were restricted by the tailgate style he used. Lil Hardin Armstrong was a

good musician but as has been already indicated her roots were not in jazz to the same extent as the others. Finally, the New Orleans banjoist Johnny St. Cyr has not always received his share of praise for his role in the 'Hot Five' recordings. It is an arduous task to make a two-piece rhythm section sound full and to give a powerful three-piece front line a solid support, but it is a remarkable commentary on St. Cyr's musicianship that one is never at all conscious of any thinness in the rhythm support on these numbers. It is no slight to some excellent musicians when one says that Dodds was the only man who could keep up with Louis as a soloist on these records and that even he had his work cut out at times, for this was the period when Armstrong was not only developing personally into a remarkable virtuoso soloist but was also setting the style for all jazz trumpeters in a fashion which was to dominate the field for a decade or more. In a more roundabout fashion his playing at this time has formed a link with the art of jazz trumpet playing down to this very day.

The mention in the last paragraph of the ability of the musicians as *soloists* is made necessary by the fact that the tight ensemble qualities of the Oliver band were gradually being replaced by a much looser conception. Although Armstrong retained the traditional New Orleans front line of trumpet, trombone and clarinet, and some of the ensemble work is excellent, the very nature of his individual development was bound to result, in the long run, in the breaking away from what was for him a restraining factor. Some purist critics have deplored this fact, and William Grossman and Jack Farrell, from the viewpoint of extreme New Orleans style partisanship, have devoted a chapter in their book *The Heart of Jazz* titled 'The Apostasy of Louis Armstrong' to a long jeremiad on Armstrong's refusal to keep within the 'pure' tradition. Leaving aside any disagreements with the position such purist critics maintain, it should be obvious to anyone familiar with Armstrong's work with Henderson, for example, that it must lead him towards the role of a virtuoso artist. The fact still remains that the 'Hot Five' and 'Hot Seven' records, despite more stress on solo playing, are amongst the greatest examples of New Orleans style jazz preserved.

The most casual listener cannot help but discern the increasing technical mastery and daringness of invention

Photo from Johnny St. Cyr
Louis Armstrong's Hot Five, *c.* 1926. Reading from left to right members are Johnny St. Cyr, Kid Ory, Louis Armstrong, Johnny Dodds, and Lil Hardin

which Armstrong displays on these records. The first few sessions are probably tighter as far as the ensembles are concerned, although there are many glimpses of the dazzling solos that were to come. By 1927 Armstrong had become bolder and embroidered the themes with solos of astonishing power and invention. The later 'Hot Seven' period included such masterpieces as *Melancholy Blues, Wild Man Blues, Gully Low Blues* and *Potato Head Blues* and it is a tribute to their worth that they still sound fresh today. Johnny Dodds was a perfect foil for Armstrong on this type of number. He certainly lacked Armstrong's total instrumental command, but as a blues clarinettist he has never been equalled. His thick tone with its blues-based inflections was the antithesis of the lighter and more pure toned Creole tradition, and on the numbers like *High Society* which called for an approach which combined rapid fingering and a fluent style he was certainly not at his best; but he was one of the few men who could hold his own with Louis in an ensemble and I can think of nobody at that time who could have followed the trumpet solo on *Wild Man Blues* without creating an effect of utter anti-climax. The French critic André Hodeir has tended to ridicule what he considers to be Dodds's 'corny' work on these records, but M. Hodeir seems startlingly insensitive to early blues forms and cannot be counted a reliable judge of such records.

It should be made clear that these records were made with a group which played together only in a recording

Pace photo by Gilbert Gaster

Armstrong and Trummy Young at an informal session at the
Humphrey Lyttelton club in Oxford Street, London, which some
members of the Armstrong All Stars visited during their tour of
England in 1956

studio. It made one public appearance, on 12 June 1926, when it took part in a mammoth concert of 'race' artists who recorded for the Okeh company (Negro artists were usually assigned to a series which was identified with the title of 'race' by the record companies at this time). Many years later Kid Ory recalled how easy these sessions were to make and it is still impossible to decide how much is owed to the Negro pianist Richard M. Jones who was in charge of this department of Okeh records at the time.

There can be no doubt that his giving the artists freedom to record what they wished without any irritating restrictions must have helped immeasurably in the quality of the music that resulted.

It was only natural that Armstrong's great reputation should tempt other trumpeters to try to defeat him in a battle of music, or 'cutting contest' as it was called. Kid Ory, in a discussion with Dick Hadlock in the *Down Beat* of 8 January 1959, refers to an attempt by another virtuoso trumpeter of the period, Jabbo Smith, to get the better of Armstrong. 'One time in Chicago', he recalled, 'Jabbo Smith came in with blood in his eyes for Louis, thinking he would blow him out. When Louis finished playing, Jabbo said, "I'm gonna get a trombone." Johnny Dunn tried to take Louis, too. Same thing.' An amusing story relates to the latter attempt. At this time Johnny Dunn was the great man in the north and it is said that when he arrived at a Chicago station, bearing a yard-long coach horn which he used during his stage shows, he ran into the flamboyant Jelly Roll Morton. Morton eyed the coach horn and advised Dunn 'to take that thing right back to New York. These Chicago boys will cut you to death!'

A final note on the 'Hot Seven' records is left to the modernist trumpeter Miles Davis in *Jazz Review*, dated December 1958. The U.S. critic Nat Hentoff played Davis the 1927 Armstrong version of *Potato Head Blues*. Davis commented as follows:

'Louis has been through all kinds of styles. That's good tuba by the way. You know you can't play anything on a horn that Louis hasn't played—I mean even modern. I love his approach to the trumpet; he never sounds bad. He plays on the beat and you can't miss when you play on the beat—with feeling. That's another phrase for swing.

'There's form there, and you take some of those early forms, play it today, and they'd sound good. I also like the little stops in his solo. We stop, but we often let the drums lay out altogether. If I had this record, I'd play it.'

To return to Louis's career during this period. During the spring of 1926 Armstrong left the Dreamland and joined Carroll Dickerson's orchestra at the Sunset Café, still retaining his other job with the Erskine Tate Vendome orchestra. By chance, just across the street was the Plantation Café and the band there was led by King Oliver. It was in Dickerson's band that Armstrong met the great pianist Earl Hines who was soon to be associated with him and to appear on many of his most famous records. He first recorded with Hines on 9 May 1927 when he made a single side, *Chicago Breakdown*, with a group other than his usual regular recording band. Early in 1927 Dickerson left the job and Armstrong took over the band and re-organized it. The manager and owner of the Sunset Café was Joe Glaser, now a famous booker and Armstrong's current manager. Sometime in 1927 Louis finally left the Vendome band, but became a regular attraction during the afternoon and evenings at the Metropolitan Theatre. When his band closed at the Sunset there came a little known interlude, told by William Russell in *Jazzmen*, when he hired the Warwick Hall and led his own group there. The venture was not successful and soon folded. In April 1928 Louis rejoined Carroll Dickerson's band at Chicago's Savoy Ballroom and gained more public acclaim than ever. Russell records that he left the Savoy for two nights to work a job in St. Louis which paid him a hundred dollars a night plus expenses—unheard of remuneration for that time. He received another offer from Fletcher Henderson at this time and the Savoy were forced to give him a considerable increase to prevent his acceptance. In addition to the regular patrons, musicians were flocking to hear Louis, and by word of mouth his fame spread across the country. It was, therefore, only natural that he should sooner or later go to New York City, and this move took place in 1929. But before writing of this it might be as well to mention some of the numbers that Louis recorded during 1928.

The last of the 'Hot Five' sessions took place in December 1927. On 26 June 1928 Louis was part of an instrumental quartet which accompanied the singer Lillie Delk Christian on four somewhat undistinguished titles. It is interesting to note that one of the musicians on this date was the great New Orleans clarinettist Jimmy Noone. The next day came the first of a series of recordings issued under the title of 'Louis Armstrong and his Hot Five' or 'Louis Armstrong and his Savoy Ballroom Five' which, despite the initial group name, were entirely different in character from anything he had done before. The front line instrumentation of trumpet, trombone and clarinet (now doubling on tenor saxophone) was retained but Fred Robinson and Jimmy Strong, who played trombone and clarinet respectively, were good competent musicians in a style that owed little to that of their predecessors Ory and Dodds. Mancy Cara was on banjo, but the real stars of the band apart from Armstrong himself, were Earl Hines and drummer Zutty Singleton. The latter had come up from New Orleans a year before and was a remarkably consistent drummer whose style suited the group Louis led at the time as almost no other drummer's could. He was much in advance in certain ways of most of the earlier drummers and until a disagreement some years later was Armstrong's constant companion for a lengthy period. If Zutty provided the firm foundation for the group, in Earl Hines Louis had found a musician who could match his own dazzling solos. Much has been made of Hines's supposed debt to Armstrong and the development of what has been called his 'trumpet style' of piano playing, but it is more likely true that Hines would have played the way he does even if he had never appeared with Armstrong at all in the twenties. Hines is himself a virtuoso performer whose nonchalance of approach can often lead one to miss the sheer technical command of his solos. He is a master at suspending the beat during a solo for a number of bars, causing the listener to suspect that he has lost it altogether, but invariably he returns to it with an unerring instinct at the appropriate bar. This device is one which creates tension in the best sense of the word, but it is a tension which is always resolved. His unflagging invention and his hard hit treble passages create great excitement for the listener and when I last heard him, in San Francisco during October 1958, although he was playing with an extremely indifferent band his own work was as scintillating as ever.

With companions of varying stature it was only natural that the records which Armstrong made should place even greater emphasis on the solo routines. As already indicated, Robinson and Strong were highly competent performers, but by comparison with Armstrong and Hines they were minor figures. One of the first titles that the six-piece group made is one of Armstrong's most famous, *West End Blues*. This is a slow, rather melancholy theme which includes a moving scat vocal by Louis and a solo that is justly renowned. The other numbers tended to be faster in tempo and gave scope for Hines and Armstrong to create solos of brilliance. A further departure from the New Orleans tradition was taken when Don Redman was added to the band as arranger and alto saxophonist. This was the first time that Armstrong had used an arranger but Redman's scores were simple and allowed plenty of scope for improvised solos. An example of Armstrong's increasing technical mastery and daring is *Tight Like This*, the last number he was to record with Hines for some years, where he builds up a solo of several choruses at the close which have an almost architectural solidity of structure. The logic of this particular solo is as remarkable as almost anything he has recorded. Although the overall impact of these records may not be quite as great as that of the earlier ones with Dodds and Ory, they show that Armstrong had now left the traditional New Orleans concept far behind.

The Savoy engagement was terminated in the spring of 1929 and the members of the band decided to remain together and, nominating Armstrong as the official leader, thought that the time had come to try their luck in New York. Their departure was somewhat eccentric. Louis owned a broken-down car which he used to drive himself, Hines and Singleton around in, and other members of the band possessed cars of equally dubious reliability. Lil managed to assemble a total of twenty dollars for each man, and they started the journey to New York. They did finally arrive there, most of them penniless, but there were various problems to face before they were out of trouble. Their first engagement was at the Aubudon Theatre in the Bronx, but when the time came for them to play the date there was great trouble in rounding up the various members of the band who had dispersed in search of other work. Jimmy Harrison had to be brought in on trombone, but when they finally played *St. Louis Blues* as their number at the theatre there was no doubt about their success. A week later they obtained a job at the famous Savoy Ballroom in Harlem and continuing success here led to a very good job at Connie's Inn. A short while afterwards Armstrong himself was booked to appear in the Broadway revue 'Hot Chocolates'. This resulted in his acceptance by a section of the general public who might never have heard of him otherwise, and it was a key event in his career. He sang and played *Ain't Misbehavin'* in the show and his record of this became one of his first popular sellers. From this time onwards Louis became a stage and show personality in his own right and in the years that followed he was gradually to break into all the fields that an entertainer finds open to him. Even so, he was still a long way from the international eminence that he enjoys today.

Soon after his arrival in New York he recorded with one of the first mixed groups to gather in a studio. The title that was issued from this session, *Knockin' a Jug*, is still highly regarded at the present time, and marked the first collaboration between Louis and the great white trombonist Jack Teagarden. He also recorded quite prolifically with a larger band and often used the Luis Russell group. The second 'Hot Five' made its last records on 10 June 1929, accompanying the blues singer Victoria Spivey on two numbers. Gene Anderson replaced Earl Hines, who had not left Chicago with the rest of the band. It was to be many years before Louis was again to record with a regular small group, and the next two decades were to see him fronting a number of large bands. On the records he was now making the band played a very subsidiary role in the main, the accent being strongly on Armstrong as a solo performer. His material was changing also, comprising a high proportion of popular hit songs of the day. It should be noted that the popular songs of the late 'twenties seem, in retrospect, to be considerably less inane than those of, say, thirty years later and many had a structure that was ideal for the improvising jazzman. On *Song of the Islands* Louis even added three violins to his recording band (Luis Russell's orchestra in this instance) and a few weeks later made his famous trumpet-piano duet with Buck Washington of *Dear Old Southland*. It says much for his popularity that he recorded steadily during the depression years when the sales of gramophone records touched rock bottom.

The engagement at Connie's Inn terminated in the early summer of 1930 and Louis left New York for California. He was now determined to exploit his success to date and the next few years were to see him travelling extensively. It was only eight years since he had come to Chicago to join King Oliver, but he had revolutionized the concept of jazz trumpet playing during that period.

3

1930-35 — THE VIRTUOSO PERIOD

Louis Armstrong arrived in Los Angeles in June 1930 and started a long engagement at the 'Sebastian New Cotton Club'. At this time he was booked as a single and fronted the house band. Some confusion exists as to the actual leader of the band when he first arrived, Louis himself claiming that the director was 'some old trumpet player named Elkins'. Whoever the mysterious Elkins might have been there is no evidence that he was in any group with whom Louis recorded at this time. Recent investigation has proved that the two bands with whom Louis recorded in Los Angeles were led by Leon Heriford and Les Hite, and both were the house bands at the 'New Cotton Club' during part of Louis's stay. Throughout the years Louis often left the selection of the musicians to others and was content to front a band that was already in existence. Orin Keepnews, in the *Record Changer* of July-August 1950, quoted him on the subject, as follows:

'I picked my own men to an extent, but I never did want to bother about all that other unnecessary business. So I always had a leader or a director—someone like Randolph, or Joe Garland, or Mike McKendrick—so when anybody was dissatisfied, they'd come to him to straighten it all out.'

The records Louis made in California are mostly of popular songs like *Body and Soul* and *Memories of You*. They contain excellent solos but are not great records overall. From about 1928 Louis had become enamoured of the sound of Guy Lombardo's saxophone section and in the issue of the *Record Changer* already mentioned he was tackled about the matter. For the benefit of readers unaware of Guy Lombardo it should be mentioned that he has been famous throughout the years as the purveyor of a brand of dance music noted for its extreme sentimentality and 'sweet' approach. Louis had the following to say about the Lombardo influence on his bands:

'Now you dig that *Sweethearts*, and that first chorus of *When You're Smiling*; it reminds you of Guy Lombardo. Crawford Wethington, who played with my band then, he was the nearest thing to Carmen Lombardo.

'When we were at the Savoy in Chicago, in 1928, every Sunday night we'd catch the Owl Club, with Guy Lombardo, and as long as he played we'd sit right there: Zutty,

Carroll Dickerson and all the band. We didn't go nowhere until after Lombardo signed off. That went on for months. Music for me, music that's good, you just want to hear it again!'

Jazz musicians show an obstinate refusal to conform to any purist notions that their fans may hold. Charlie Parker was a great admirer of Jimmy Dorsey, Lester Young liked a lot of somewhat dubious popular vocalists, and the list of apparently incompatible tastes could be lengthened to include many of the great jazz stars. Most jazz musicians see themselves as part of the larger field of entertainment and it is a comparatively recent development for many of them to take themselves seriously as 'artists'. If their own evaluation of themselves were more widely accepted many a disillusioned fan would be saved much anguish!

While in Los Angeles Louis recorded for the first time with Lionel Hampton—the solo in *Memories of You* was the first that the latter had recorded on vibraphone—and with Lawrence Brown who was later to become famous as a member of the Duke Ellington orchestra. At the end of the job at the 'Cotton Club' Louis went back to Chicago and formed a band there, the actual musical director being the trumpeter Zilner Randolph. On the whole this was a rather mediocre group, but some good records were made by it. Louis played around Chicago most of the time, but made one triumphant return to New Orleans, appearing at the Suburban Gardens. During 1930 and 1931 he also took part in a few short feature films and it would be interesting to have these shown again if there are copies still in existence.

In 1932 Louis made his first foreign tour, coming to England and playing at the London Palladium with a local group. The reactions were varied and it is apparent from reading the musical press of that time that even the critics were bewildered by much that they heard. Stories have grown up around this visit that are probably apocryphal, one such dealing with the time that he was challenged by another musician on the ground that he was attaining his high notes by the use of a freak instrument. The story has it that he smashed his instrument to pieces on the spot and went on with the show on a borrowed trumpet. The *Melody Maker* of the time does document his appearance, as a guest, at a brass band

rally! It is stated that the stolid brass bandsmen were unimpressed by what they heard of him.

Returning to America Louis took over the Chick Webb band and made one recording session with them. Early in 1933 he went back to Chicago and formed another band made up of local musicians. I talked to Teddy Wilson about this period during a visit to the U.S.A. and he told me that at the time Louis was studying quite hard and was generally of a quiet and studious disposition. Wilson thought that the showmanship that was so much a part of Louis's final period came much later, although this is contradicted by the testimony of other musicians. The truth is that there was always a large element of hokum in the New Orleans days—the great King Oliver was apparently not averse to placing a mute in his cornet and giving out imitations of a donkey braying—and it is natural for musicians from this era to exploit any talents that they may possess in this direction. The records which Louis made at this time for the Victor label are generally rated as amongst his least successful by collectors, and many people dislike the exhibitionism that is so much a part of them.

It seems certain that the batch of records made between January and April 1933 reflect Louis's performances of the period quite faithfully. We have the testimony of Milton 'Mezz' Mezzrow, in his book *Really the Blues*, that Louis often arrived at the studio without knowing what he was going to play and that the amount of time devoted to rehearsal was minimal in the extreme. The numbers performed included several very undistinguished, to put it no more strongly, pops. Yet, seen against Armstrong's career as a whole this was a phase through which it was more or less inevitable that he should pass. For several years he had been developing as an instrumentalist and he now had a command that would have been unthinkable to the earlier New Orleans men. It seems a corollary of technical advance that there will be a misuse of some element of it, and it also seems to be the case that even the greatest musicians are inclined to show lapses of taste, sometimes the greater the musician the more glaring their lapses are. By 1933 Armstrong had discovered that he could play in the upper register of his instrument with consummate ease. He also found that long high note codas went down well with the crowds that came to his stage shows. It became known that he featured these high note endings and what was more natural than that he should incorporate them into his records? At the same time there is a tendency to regard the use of high notes as being in poor taste under *any* circumstances. This is a ridiculous outlook, for occasionally they can be effective at the end of a logically developed solo or even as a means of increasing tension midway through a chorus. Even when used as a showy effect they can be quite a valid means to an end during a stage performance. It is only when they become an end in themselves, as on Charlie Barnet's *All the Things You Are* for example, that their use is entirely pointless. A good instance of the valid use of extreme high register notes can be heard in the closing bars of *Madness in Great Ones* from Duke Ellington's *Such Sweet Thunder* suite. It is unfortunate that the whole question has become confused by the puritanism that seems to accompany so much jazz criticism these days.

On the Victor records Louis sometimes used high notes to no good purpose, as in the coda of *Sittin' in the Dark*. On the other hand, on a number like *I Gotta Right to Sing the Blues* he used them quite logically and to telling effect. In fact, this latter performance is a remarkable one in every way. The solo that Louis builds here is one of the most powerful he has ever recorded and the rather poor band is forgotten when he begins to build his choruses. There are other numbers on which he plays very well indeed, but it would be true to say that the band is as ragged as any he has fronted and had few other soloists of any merit. The records as a whole are certainly not amongst Louis's great ones—although the strength of his solo on *I Gotta Right to Sing the Blues* is such that I rate this amongst his finest individual performances—but they are not as bad as many critics would have one believe. The fact is that Armstrong was such an extraordinary artist that very few of his considerable number of records are utterly without interest.

The thirties saw Louis influencing a whole new group of trumpeters and, indeed, musicians on all instruments. Although some critics have tended to write of nearly all this period as a time when he was more concerned with showy effects than playing what they like to consider real jazz, musicians saw it quite differently. Roy Eldridge, in the course of a conversation with the critic Nat Hentoff, reminisced about his early days and the time when he was

buying the 'Hot Seven' records. He went on to say:

'But Louis wasn't an influence on me until I saw him in person. Jabbo Smith didn't have Louis's sound, but he was faster. But Louis gave me something I couldn't get off Jabbo—continuity, which makes all the sense. Louis introduces the piece and sticks around the melody, but when he has it out, you know it's out, and you know he's going to finish a whole.

'In 1932, I first caught Louis at the Lafayette Theatre in New York, and he finally upset me. I was a young cat, and I was very fast, but I wasn't telling no kind of story. Well, I sat through the first show, and I didn't think Louis was so extraordinary. But in the second show, he played *Chinatown*. He started out like a new book, building and building, chorus after chorus, and finally reaching a full climax, ending on his high F. It was a real climax, right, clean, clear. The rhythm was rocking, and he had that sound going along with it. Everybody was standing up, including me. He was building the thing all the time instead of just playing in a straight line.'

Eldridge has touched here on an essential point of the high note controversy, for as often as not at this period Louis built to his upper register endings absolutely logically and, what is more, made them cleanly and clearly. One of the astonishing aspects of his playing is that his tone is as fine in the upper register as it is when he is playing in the medium range. In later years Louis was to feature high notes less and less, his style having become more simplified and the advance of age resulting in greater maturity. His influence on trumpet playing as a whole was mentioned by the ex-Ellington star Rex Stewart in *Down Beat* of 8 January 1950. He had the following to say:

'Seriously, I really feel that without his influence, I couldn't imagine what trumpet playing would be like. He showed that there was more range than high C, and more drive than the syncopation used before him. He did so many things. . . .'

The reason for bringing in a discussion of high note technique and the question of showmanship at this stage is that, despite the fact that many of the records that Louis made during the 'thirties are not counted amongst his finest work, it was probably at this time that he had the maximum influence on other musicians. It was quite common for the bigger bands of that period to carry a

Columbia Records photo by Don Hunstein
Louis Armstrong in 1959

trumpeter whose playing was modelled on Louis and, as often as not, one who would sing in the Armstrong style. Taft Jordan started out with Chick Webb as a pure Louis imitator and in this country there were people like Nat Gonella who modelled themselves on him. As is often the case, it is the technical side of a man's playing that has the greatest influence on others, but something of the spirit with which he approached a number was captured by some of the men who admired him. A trumpeter like Ruby Braff is playing today in a style very much influenced by Armstrong, but aside from the technical debt he owes to him he also captures a little of the spirit that made an Armstrong solo such a rewarding experience. Generally, though, apart from the revivalist musicians who have moved on to what is now called a 'mainstream' style, Armstrong's *direct* influence on other trumpeters is now slight. The reason is, of course, the almost complete enslavement of young modernist players to the concepts that arose out of the bop revolution. This will be briefly mentioned in the final section of the book.

Resuming the outline of Armstrong's career, it appears that the first trip to England had convinced him that the time was propitious for a longer tour, and in July 1933 he commenced his second European visit with a London appearance. This time he was again greeted with mixed reviews, for the more serious jazz followers who must have comprised a sizeable segment of his audiences found themselves unable to accept the high proportion of showmanship in his act and there were laments over his failure to size up the audiences to whom he would be playing. In his *Jazz in Britain* David Boulton suggests that one of the reasons might have been that British audiences had just had the opportunity of hearing the Duke Ellington band and were under the sway of Ellington's less flamboyant presentation, but Mr. Boulton forgets that Ellington himself had been criticized for the unadventurousness of *his* programmes and his tendency to play for safety by sticking to familiar material. History certainly does repeat itself in this connexion and virtually every tour undertaken by an American group in the past few years has been adversely reported on by some members of the jazz public for just such a failing. The *Melody Maker* of 5 August 1933 carried the following somewhat disillusioned report on an Armstrong concert:

'He seems to have come to the conclusion that a variety artist's only mission in life is to be sensational, to pander to the baser emotions, to sacrifice all art to crude showmanship.'

Apart from the matter of correctly gauging his audience, Armstrong had other troubles at this time. He was involved in a dispute with his manager, Jack Collins, and the partnership of some years was abruptly terminated, with Jack Hylton taking over his business management. After he had been here nearly a year, fronting various pick-up groups all the while, Coleman Hawkins arrived in London. Hawkins, who had revolutionized the playing of the tenor saxophone in jazz as Armstrong had, in his turn, the trumpet, was scheduled to join Louis for the final part

Louis Armstrong's dressing-room preparations prior to a public performance assume a ritualistic character. This photo was taken by Ken Palmer during Armstrong's British tour in 1959

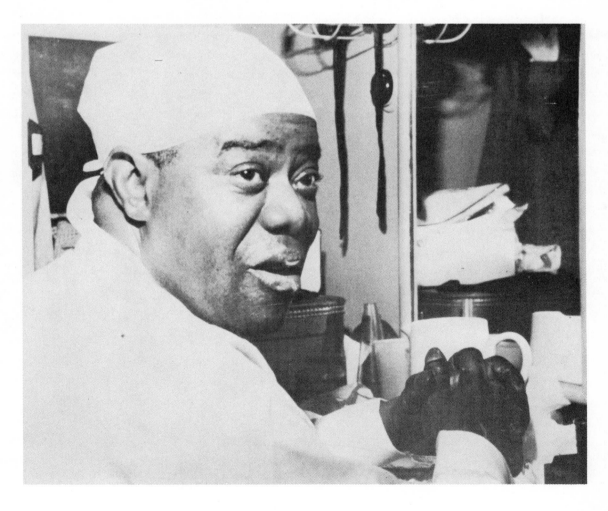

of his tour and arrangements were announced for the first of their joint appearances. Just a few days before it should have taken place Armstrong refused to go ahead and considerable ill-will was engendered as a result. It has never been explained why Armstrong acted as he did, but considering that it is quite contrary to all that is known of him to refuse to fulfil commitments to which he has already given assent, one must presume that he was reacting to pressures which he did not care to publicize. All this had little effect on his actual playing and he reverted to a less sensational presentation after the initial criticisms had been voiced. A very interesting comment by Harry Dial, drummer with the band that Louis was leading just prior to his coming to England, proves that Louis was well aware of the musical deficiencies of his normal stage routine, and are worth quoting in full. They were contained in an interview which the American collector Frank Driggs had with Dial which was reproduced in *Jazz Journal* of January 1959, as follows:

'When I got there the band was really putrid. I thought for a couple of years that the band was slipping because Louis had gone in for all the showmanship stuff, you know, high notes, gestures, and I thought he couldn't play any more. I soon lost that opinion when I began working with him. We used to get out in those little towns in the mid-west where people didn't know him too well and didn't pay much attention to the show, so he'd sit down and really play horn. He had special numbers for musicians who would drop by and listen to him. He'd play *High Society* and *Tiger Rag*, which used to work the stew out of any drummer, because he'd never stop where he'd say he was going to. He'd have a certain place where he'd want you to ride the cymbal. He'd hit as many as 350 high Cs on *Shine*, I used to count them. He'd make me so mad on *Tiger Rag* that I wouldn't know what to do. He'd want me to ride the cymbals on the last three choruses, and you'd swear he wasn't going to play more than ten choruses on *Tiger Rag*. I'd grab the cymbal around the 8th chorus and start riding it . . . 8 . . . 9 . . . 10 and by the end of the tenth chorus it would sound good to him. The end of the 11th, and he'd play ten more choruses!'

It is something of a mystery what the variety theatre patrons in this country really thought of Louis but to all intents and purposes he had a successful tour. He went over to the Continent after the English circuits had been exhausted and played two memorable concerts at the Salle Pleyel, Paris, in November 1934. While in Paris he recorded for the first time in eighteen months—one of the longest gaps in his recording career—and of the six titles made, *On the Sunny Side of the Street* has become something of a classic. Perhaps no other single recording gives so accurate a portrayal of the performances which Armstrong was featuring at this time. Two other titles from the session—*Song of the Vipers* and *Will You, Won't You Be My Baby*—were deleted within a day or two of the original issue and until they were reissued in the late 'forties remained amongst his rarest items. Upon hearing them now it is not apparent as to why they were withdrawn, unless exception was taken to the reference to vipers (marihuana smokers).

Armstrong was away from the United States for just over eighteen months, his longest absence ever, but homesickness at last caused him to return, and in January 1935 he arrived back in New York City. At that time nobody knew it, but this was to be the end of the pure virtuoso phase, and in the next year Armstrong's style was to undergo a change in the direction of greater simplicity, while his tone was to become less cloudy than it had been in the past five years. Whenever an artist varies a style there will be found those who regard it as proof of musical deterioration, and as we shall see, his new approach was poorly understood at first.

4

1935-47 —
JAZZ STAR AND ENTERTAINER

For the first few months of 1935 Armstrong was forced to rest as the result of a split lip. Strange rumours circulated in Europe about the nature of his illness and one newspaper reported his death! However, it was a comparatively short while before Louis was again ready to take to the road with a big band, and it was Luis Russell's orchestra that he fronted when he was once more completely fit. This association with Russell was to continue for over a decade and many famous musicians were to be members of the band during this period. A recording contract with the Decca company followed, and with only occasional breaks, has been renewed down to the present time.

To describe the period of the late 'thirties as an interim one for Armstrong does not imply that he was no longer playing well or making worthwhile records, but is meant to refer to the fact that his later eminence had not yet been attained, while the more purist jazz followers were somewhat dismayed by the 'commercial' records that he so often turned out. What so many of the objectors had not yet realized was that many of their most highly prized records were of popular tunes of the day, but that they themselves were far enough away from the period not to recognize them as such. The length of time it takes for a popular song to become a 'standard' has never been accurately measured, but one wonders how many people have denounced a number on its first appearance as just another hit song, only to enjoy it years afterwards and, quite probably, claim that it was proof of the superiority of the popular song in the past over that of the present!

In the decade now under review a very high proportion of Armstrong's records, and the stage and show presentations he took part in, featured popular song material and it might be as well to consider some of the viewpoints of the jazz follower in relationship to the popular number. My personal attitude is that Armstrong had such an ability to transform the *content* of a popular hit, both in his trumpet and vocal interpretation, that I am not usually disturbed by such considerations as an inane lyric or a song content that may be basically undesirable. This is not to say that I am never perturbed at Armstrong's material. In the period of which I write the popular song, although often banal, had not reached the depths of trashiness of the recent past and many made quite suitable vehicles for a jazz performer. Louis's unique vocal talents take the

sentimentality out of nearly all the popular songs he used on record and it is only occasionally that he selected, or had selected for him, a number so poor that even he could do nothing with it. That there are some jazz standards and popular songs, graced with the title of a standard through use over the years, that appear ideally suited to Armstrong I would not deny, but even this supposition is sometimes open to doubt in relationship to the real worth of the numbers. I think that one tends to overemphasize the merit of certain songs just because Armstrong has used them as the basis of an exceptional performance. Even the finest popular song shows up badly as against the best numbers of a Duke Ellington, for instance, but over the years the truly outstanding jazz musician has always had the ability to make routine material sound better than it really is. A performer of Armstrong's type can play a melody *almost* straight but it is the fractional differences of inflection that result in a performance that is outside the normal run of dance band routines. The whole problem cannot be seen clearly unless one takes into account the nature of the performer, for while one would be dismayed to hear a unique orchestra like Duke Ellington's confined to the popular song, great musicians like Armstrong, Hawkins and Earl Hines were always quite happy to use them and, in the process of their solos, strip them of over-sentimentality or banality. Collectors are apt to forget that even if one ignores the high proportion of popular material that Armstrong used from about 1929, the fact remains that quite a few of the earlier 'classic Hot Five' records use such material. It is, as I have already remarked, all a question of how far one is from the period when a song is current. It is also not inappropriate to mention that this is a period when 'original' compositions appear on nearly every new long playing record by jazz musicians, and the dullness of these themes is well enough known. Jazz has had very few exceptional composers and most jazz musicians write themes inferior to those of the better popular songwriters. The key to the problem lies in the treatment afforded to the songs, and it is certainly true that at the present time many vocalists are hailed as jazz performers when, in truth, they are above-average pop singers. However, I do not think that Armstrong could have been accused of excessive respect for popular material, and the use he made of it has nearly always been of a jazz nature. The reason why collectors were unhappy when Armstrong's

Decca recordings were first available is that the songs used were contemporaneous, not because they were popular songs as such.

It is somewhat interesting to note that one of the titles that Armstrong recorded at his first Decca session, in October 1935, was *On Treasure Island*, which he himself once said was one of his favourite records. The short but succinct reaction of one reviewer to the first Decca items to be issued in this country can be quoted from the January–February 1936 issue of *Swing Music*:

'The first titles are unbelievably bad. *Brand New Suit* has a grand swing opening, and Louis is Louis, but not at his best. The record just fades away towards the end.'

A few months later a reviewer in the same magazine, Eric Ballard, was expressing a different viewpoint and it is to his credit that he was one of the first critics apart from Hugues Panassié to realize that the changes that had taken place in Armstrong's playing were not necessarily for the worse. In the course of a review he had the following to say:

'This is not the old Armstrong. Louis is not playing the trumpet of his so-called "better" days, as I have heard it contended. He is playing trumpet in a way that we have never heard before. His tone is different; his ideas are new; only his method is the same.

'Harlem has been waiting a long time to hear Louis, and Harlem was reserving judgment until it had heard him. Ready to put him back on top if it thought fit, but just as ready to write him off as a back number if he failed to please. And what was Harlem's reception? You all know. Louis Armstrong is today more certainly the king of modern music than he ever was before. He is still so far ahead of the next best that any kind of comparison is impossible.'

This summary is actually a little extreme as far as the records are concerned, for while it is true that there are some very good solos by Armstrong on the records in question it was to be a year or two before the full flowering of the new style was to be heard. Of one fact there can be little doubt, and that is that the Luis Russell band at this period was at the lowest peak in its history. It had a sound rhythm section and one good soloist in Charlie Holmes, but the ensemble quality was deplorable, and rather understandably, such numbers as *Red Sails in the Sunset*, *Old*

Man Mose and *La Cucaracha* were hardly of the type to inspire any arranger. In addition the actual recording quality of many of the discs was poor, for it is a curious fact that many records made in 1927 and 1928 are much superior in this respect to those made a decade later when it might have been expected that advances in techniques would have ensured a higher quality of sound. If one looks down the list of titles Armstrong made during 1935 and 1936 there are few which one would unhesitatingly recommend for reissue today judged as overall performances.

Swing that Music, recorded in April 1936, was made to coincide with the appearance of a book bearing the same title and having Armstrong's name as the author. As already indicated in the introduction it seems somewhat unlikely that Armstrong in fact had much to do with the book. The style of writing is not his—and that style is as unique as his trumpet playing—while the impression the volume gives is of a not very competent hack job undertaken by a ghost writer. What is of interest is that by now Armstrong was a sufficiently established name to warrant a book being published under his nominal authorship. It was around the same time that Armstrong was first prominently credited in a film—he had previously made some now forgotten 'shorts' in the early 'thirties—the occasion being the Bing Crosby-Madge Evans feature *Pennies from Heaven*. Armstrong's role in this film was not a very lengthy one and it was typical of a Hollywood attitude to jazz musicians that prevailed through many years. It was a comic one hardly designed to show the Negro as other than buffoon, but it set Louis upon a film career that must have been personally lucrative if artistically somewhat barren. In the film he appeared as a vocalist and trumpeter during a number called *Skeleton In The Closet* (altered by the more prudish British record company to *Skeleton In The Cupboard* when it first appeared in England!) and in a couple of other scenes. In the following two years he had short scenes in four other films, *Artists and Models*, *Every Day's A Holiday*, (1937), *Doctor Rhythm*, *Goin' Places* (1938). In none of them was any real advantage taken of his unique abilities as a jazz musician or even of his natural flair for showmanship, but they did have the result of his becoming known to audiences throughout the world who were hardly interested in jazz as such. It is possible that Armstrong's roles in these films, and later ones, were to provide some of the basis for criticisms of his stage personality as representing 'Uncle Tomism' in the years to follow, although at this time the criticisms made were directed at the film companies and not at Armstrong himself.

The period from 1937 onwards saw Armstrong making records that were aimed at a wide public, with a miscellany of backings. Although he had recorded many popular titles in the past, as already discussed, it is unlikely that they sold much to the public who wanted a version of the latest hit, but from now on he became as much a popular entertainer as jazz musician. There is not the contradiction involved in the two roles that many jazz fans would have one believe, for it was to be a few years yet before there arose a whole group of musicians who thought of themselves primarily as artists. Whatever the position was amongst themselves as far as merit was concerned, jazz players from the earliest New Orleans days had accepted that their public role was essentially that of an entertainer. If they struck an indifferent audience they probably played less well than they would to an enthusiastic one, but it did not occur to them to berate the unresponsive ones as lacking awareness of their music. Also, it would be extraordinary if Armstrong was totally unaware of the financial rewards to be obtained from widening his audience, with its possibilities in the way of radio and film work. His first records made with an unusual backing were the four titles with Hawaiian bands recorded in August 1936. In April 1937 he made four numbers with the popular Mills Brothers vocal quartet, recording with them again in 1938 and 1940. In June 1938 he made four spiritual numbers with the Decca Mixed Chorus and these sides were popular for many years. Two months later he made two humorous monologues with Harry Mills, much to the horror of his purist followers.

However, it is apt to be forgotten that he still turned out consistently good jazz records during this time and only recently have a new generation of jazz record buyers begun to realize the quality of many of the Decca sides.

In 1937 there were changes in the Russell band and musicians of the calibre of J. C. Higginbotham, Albert Nicholas and Henry Allen were brought in to help raise the somewhat deplorable standard of the group. Armstrong himself seems to have been inspired by these changes, for his playing became much stronger and some of his solos, although more sober in style, have the majesty and power of his earlier classic performances. A really remarkable solo by him can be heard on his Decca version of *Struttin' With Some Barbecue*, where be builds chorus upon chorus at the close of the record in a most dazzling fashion. In the late 'thirties he began to re-record numbers which had been associated with him in the past, of the calibre of *Confessin'*, *West End Blues* and *Our Monday Date*. They formed a minority of his recordings at the time but a policy was inaugurated which in another decade was to be the cause of a great deal of argument amongst jazz fans in his concert audiences. It was at this time that I first heard the criticism that he was not improvising as much as he should and this is a matter which will be discussed in some detail in the next chapter.

In view of the lengthy period of fronting large bands it is interesting to note what Armstrong said on the subject in 1950 when asked if he preferred playing with a large or small group. The answer was printed in the *Record Changer* of July–August 1950:

'It don't really make no difference where I blow my horn as long as the guys behind me are playing right. But still and all I prefer the small band. I've had some good big bands; they were well rehearsed. But a leader's got to be able to instil himself into the band. Where there's too many men it's hard to get that *feeling*, like Joe Oliver and I had, like Jack (Teagarden) and I have.'

When I was in the U.S.A. in 1958 one musician who played in the big band Louis was fronting around 1939 intimated that he did not think that Louis was doing too well financially at the end of the 'thirties, but it is somewhat difficult to reconcile this with his film and radio appearances and the fact that the band worked steadily all the year round. This was still an era when the big band was supreme and there were theatres and dance halls throughout the U.S.A. booking them regularly. It is probable that the musician has confused the fact that Louis did not then have his vast public following, although his wide popularity by this time can hardly be denied. These years were comparatively tranquil ones for Armstrong compared with what was to happen in the next two decades, but he was fully employed moving from one city to another and taking the time out for the growing frequency of his film appearances.

In May 1940 Armstrong recorded with a small group again for an album of 'New Orleans Jazz' that Decca were planning. His companions included the great New Orleans veteran Sidney Bechet, and his drummer from the 'Savoy Ballroom Five' days, Zutty Singleton. One title he made was *Coal Cart Blues*, first recorded by him with Clarence Williams's Blue Five in 1924, and this is generally said to have been inspired by his youthful days when one of his jobs was delivering coal. In March and April of 1941 he recorded again with a group calling itself 'Louis Armstrong and his Hot Seven', but although one or two titles were good, the music was far below that of the original band of the same name. In 1942 a dispute between the American Federation of Musicians and the recording companies resulted in the former forbidding its members to make further records and, as a result, Armstrong was out of the studios for nearly three years. However, although he was not recording commercially, this was a period of intense activity for Armstrong.

Before dealing with the war years reference should be made to his one appearance as a stage actor, playing the role of Bottom in the play *Swingin' the Dream* at the Centre Theatre, New York City in 1939. The play had a very short run and although some of the theatre critics praised Armstrong it appears that the production as a whole was rather mediocre.

Following the bombing of Pearl Harbour the United States entered the war. The impact on the entertainment industry was drastic and the big bands were hit more badly than others. Key musicians were called up, touring became difficult and hazardous, while the quality of the music suffered as a result. Armstrong himself seems to have surmounted the difficulties very well and continued touring with a big band throughout the war years. The jazz world, however, was itself torn by the advent of a style of jazz initially called bop. This resulted from the searching experiments of musicians like Thelonious Monk, Clyde Hart, Dizzy Gillespie and Charlie Parker, and after at first meeting public hostility it was taken up enthusiastically by many critics and magazines of the time. In a decade and a half the work of the pioneers in the idiom was to lead to 'modern' jazz becoming the norm for most critics and

jazz followers in the U.S.A. At the time of its appearance it split the jazz fans into two warring factions, one of which heralded the new form as the answer to 'degenerate' swing while the other, largely influenced by the revival of interest in the New Orleans form, denied that it had any merit whatsoever. The group of musicians who suffered most were the great individualists of the swing era who found themselves caught between the embattled partisans. Today, many years after the event, many of the revivalist followers in the U.S.A. are recording modernists quite happily and there is a tendency to suggest that the *furor* was about nothing of lasting importance. This is hardly so, for certain elements of the bop phase cannot be accepted by many critics and jazz fans who were not revivalist partisans either, and who are now putting forward a strong case for the mid-period musicians. However, this discussion is not relevant in a study of Louis Armstrong except in so far as it is an important event in jazz history which had effects that were to cause the great trumpeter to face ill-conceived criticism from the musicians and admirers of the new school. Armstrong himself has been hostile to bop from the beginning, a reaction that is shared by many of his contemporaries and most musicians of the swing era. He recorded a skit on bop, using the melody of *The Whiffenpoof Song*, and has never retracted any of his acid comments on the new form. Many of the later criticisms concerning his stage behaviour have been made by followers of modern forms, although it is only fair to relate that musicians like Miles Davis and Dizzy Gillespie have maintained an attitude of praise for his actual playing throughout the years. Unlike some stars of the 'thirties, Armstrong made no attempt to alter his style, and as far as his playing was concerned bop might not have happened.

In 1943 the magazine *Esquire* held the first of a series of jazz polls and Armstrong won both the trumpet and vocal categories. *Esquire* presented the first jazz concert ever held at the Metropolitan Opera House in New York City, in January 1944, and Armstrong had a featured role. It is unfortunate that the recording ban was still in force at the time, but some numbers have been issued on the private wartime V-Discs (which were for the use of the American armed forces only) and these have found their way into collectors' hands in some instances. The concert was an all-star affair and apart from Armstrong included the late Art Tatum, Roy Eldridge, Jack Teagarden and Coleman Hawkins amongst the performers. The *Esquire* poll for 1945–46 saw Armstrong win the vocal section, while in 1947 be won both the trumpet and vocal categories. After this the magazine ceased to feature jazz to to any great extent.

In 1945 came the lifting of the recording ban and Armstrong was back in the studio by January 1945. A year elapsed before he recorded again, this time to make the first of many titles with Ella Fitzgerald. Both in personal appearances and on record the band behind him was becoming of less importance, for by now he was essentially the star performer and the orchestra's role was that of providing a suitable accompaniment. In any case, big bands were going through a very poor time as the result of many factors, one of which was the wartime-imposed entertainment tax which caused many club owners to fall back on smaller groups in the interest of economy. In 1946 Louis received an important acting part in the film *New Orleans*. This was a film that promised much but realized little, although there is some magnificent music in it by Armstrong and members of his pick-up group. The interesting aspect of this film from a musical viewpoint is that it resulted in Armstrong playing and recording with

a small group once more, including the New Orleans trombone veteran Edward 'Kid' Ory who had just made a most successful comeback and had a role in the film. After the film was made Louis did not reorganize a big band, instead assembling a small unit which he used, with personnel changes, until his death. This was the end of the big band era for Armstrong and apart from casual pick-up outfits in the recording studio he did not make any public appearances with one for well over a decade.

It has been said that jazz is a young man's music, but at the age of forty-six Armstrong was about to enter on the most hectic phase of his life and his fame was to grow throughout the next decade until his name became almost synonymous with jazz in the public mind. By now Joe Glaser had become his manager and Glaser, whatever his failings may be and some people insist that they are many, has handled Armstrong's business affairs astutely. He saw that the small group was both economically and artistically necessary to Armstrong if he was to continue to reach the widest possible public, and in 1946 he set about organizing one. The next ten years were to see Armstrong performing in many countries throughout the world and his fame grew equal to that of any concert virtuoso in the classical music field.

5

.

1947-59 — THE ALL STARS AND THE WORLD TRAVELLER

The story concerning the formation of the All Stars is told by Armstrong himself in the course of an interview with Sinclair Traill published in the book *Just Jazz* 1. He gives the credit to Glaser, as the following extract shows:

'Well the idea for the All Stars came from my manager, Joe Glaser. He knew that the days of big band bookings were fading out—that was in 1946—and so he formed the first All Stars to play at Billy Banks.

'Joe, he asked me what I'd like to do, would I like to come in, and I said it was up to him—to me it was just

like the rabbit and the briar patch. We rehearsed two days and went in there. Joe picked them and sent them out to me in California where I was just finishin' the film *Song is Born*. Let me see, we had that trumpet man on piano, Dick Cary, Barney Bigard played clarinet, Big Sid Catlett was on drums, Jack Teagarden, trombone and Morty Cobb, he played real good bass, came from out on the coast.

'No, I never pick my own bands—too many good musicians around, makes bad friends.'

Actually, some confusion exists as to exactly when the All Stars were formed. In his *Encyclopedia of Jazz* Leonard

Feather claims that it was formed after the filming of *New Orleans* and not *A Song is Born*. The latter certainly would seem to be correct, for the former film was made in 1946 and the All Stars was not formed until a year later. We have the additional evidence of Jack Teagarden who says that Joe Glaser approached him during the memorable Town Hall concert in New York City of 24 April 1947 and asked him to be a member of the new group. The American magazine *Record Changer* carries a photographic supplement on the opening of the All Stars in Los Angeles in its October 1947 issue and the first recording date featuring the band took place on 16 October 1947. What is probable is that Glaser had the idea for the smaller group sometime in 1946 but it was not formed until the autumn of 1947. It is as well to mention the Town Hall concert before starting on the history of the All Stars.

An English collector, Peter Tanner, was present at the concert and mentioned it in the *Record Changer* of September 1947, in the following terms:

'My first introduction to the real jazz was at one of the last of this season's concerts at Town Hall where the featured soloists were to have been Louis Armstrong and Sidney Bechet. Unfortunately Sidney was taken ill on the day of the concert and was unable to appear, and so the whole concert had to be carried by Louis. Not that I had any complaints to make about this and Louis gave a truly magnificent performance, singing and playing at his very best. Starting off with *Cornet Chop Suey*, Louis went through most of the fine numbers that he recorded for Okeh in the old days, including a magnificent trumpet solo (with piano) version of *Dear Old Southland*. Louis was accompanied by Jack Teagarden, with whom he sang *Rockin' Chair*, Bobby Hackett, Peanuts Hucko, Bob Haggart, Dick Cary and Big Sid Catlett. These musicians simply played background to Louis and gave him intelligent and very adequate support.'

The concert was actually recorded and a few numbers have been generally released on the Victor and RCA labels. One person who was particularly happy on the night of the concert was Jack Teagarden. The trombonist was just emerging from a period of extreme depression occasioned by the failure of his own big bands, and has related that he thought he played as well during the concert as at any time during his career. In retrospect, it seems very likely that the good reactions to the group which Armstrong used on this occasion may well have fortified Glaser in his view that a small band was the next step in promoting his charge.

The opening of the All Stars at Billy Bergs (not Billy Banks as is quoted in the extract from *Just Jazz*) resulted in enthusiastic press notices and Glaser's perspicacity was proved. A concert at Boston on 30 November 1947 was recorded and later issued in long playing record form. The one change in the personnel which opened at Bergs was the replacement of Cobb by Arvell Shaw. In addition, the group has carried the controversial vocalist Velma Middleton from its inception. January 1948 saw Cary leaving to be replaced by none other than Earl Hines. In February 1948 the All Stars took part in a jazz festival in Nice and a number of recordings of broadcasts were made available, presumably without Armstrong's authority. Failing health caused Sidney Catlett to leave the band a few months before his death, and he was replaced by Cozy Cole in 1950.

There can be little doubt that the period of the All Stars brought the greatest commercial success to Armstrong and made him the best known jazz musician in the world. His life, almost until his death, became one of constant travel. Before turning to the much debated questions of Armstrong's 'Uncle Tomism' and the repertoire which he used—questions which are relevant to his worth as a jazz musician at the present time—it is probably as well to bring the history of the All Stars up to the time of writing. In the summer of 1951 Teagarden was replaced by the ex-Jimmy Lanceford star, James 'Trummy' Young. In 1955 Barney Bigard was replaced by Edmond Hall, who was a member of the unit until 1958 when he left to free-lance. His place was taken by Michael 'Peanuts' Hucko until 1960. In 1953 Billy Kyle replaced Hines until his death in 1966, whilst from May 1954 until the summer of 1958 Barrett Deems was the drummer who succeeded Cozy Cole. He in turn was replaced by Danny Barcelona. Arvell Shaw left the band in early 1958 and several bass players were tried, before Mort Herbert came in as a permanent member. Velma Middleton was the permanent vocalist and entertainer until her death in 1961 while touring with Armstrong in Africa.

Foreign tours played an increasing part in the itinerary of the All Stars and they toured Europe in 1949 and again in 1952. In 1954 they appeared with great success in Japan and, in 1956, came the famous English appearances. After leaving England the band went on to France, Switzerland and other European countries, the tour culminating in a series of concerts in Ghana. This trip was the subject of an excellent documentary film, *The Satchmo Story*, directed by Ed Murrow, the well-known American television personality. In November 1956 Armstrong returned alone to play a single concert in aid of the Lord Mayor's Hungarian Relief Fund. The All Stars visited various South American countries in 1957 and, in March 1959, once more appeared in England and other European countries. Apart from the foreign trips the band constantly moved from city to city in the United States, playing concerts at the jazz festivals, night-club engagements, and various one-night appearances. Even when Armstrong was in his sixties this routine seemed not to disturb him, and when I took part in a panel discussion at the Monterey, California Jazz Festival in October 1958 he was scathing about those musicians who refuse to tour.

Throughout these years Armstrong recorded prolifically, both with his own group and with pick-up bands. His television and radio appearances were frequent and he took part in a number of films. Apart from the Ed Murrow documentary already mentioned, these films were very much in the stereotyped Hollywood convention and he never appeared to advantage in them. Honours af all types were heaped upon him, one of the most unusual being the citation presented to him by the House of Representatives at the State House in Boston in the early part of 1958. The citation read:

'Whereas, Louis Armstrong, the world's greatest trumpeter in the field of jazz music is about to celebrate his fiftieth year as a musician; and

'Whereas, Louis Armstrong has risen from humble origin to a pre-eminent position in the world of music and entertainment, and is a true exemplification of the strength of democratic principles and a shining example to all who aspire to greatness; and

'Whereas, Louis Armstrong by his artistry has through the universal language of music brought comfort, pleasure and understanding to people throughout the world, and is properly recognized as the outstanding ambassador of good will of our country; therefore be it

'Resolved, that the Massachusetts Senate extends its best wishes to Louis Armstrong and wishes him many years of health and happiness, so that he may continue to spread happiness for all people; and be it further

'Resolved, that copies of these resolutions be transmitted forthwith by the clerk of the Senate to Louis Armstrong.'

During the November 1956 concert a tribute was paid to Armstrong by Sir Laurence Olivier from the stage of the Royal Festival Hall. This concert was unusual in as far as Armstrong appeared with a small group of British musicians and also with the backing of the Royal Philharmonic Orchestra under the baton of Norman Del Mar. The results were curious to say the least. At one point Armstrong threw the orchestra into confusion by calling for an extra chorus which had not been pre-arranged. Mr. Del Mar was left conducting the air as the orchestra players scrambled to find the missing parts of the orchestration! This was not the first time that Louis had appeared with a symphony orchestra, for on the preceding June he had taken part in a concert at the Lewisohn Stadium in Chicago which featured a 'concert' arrangement of *St. Louis Blues*. On this occasion the conductor of the orchestra was Leonard Bernstein who has more than a casual acquaintance with jazz and was not likely to be disconcerted by any improvised additions to the score. The sequence when Armstrong played the number was shown in the film *Satchmo the Great* and one of the most moving moments in the film comes when the camera is swung on W. C. Handy, the composer, who was in the audience.

It might be assumed that these few years must be numbered amongst Armstrong's happiest, yet the situation was marred by a number of attacks on his stage mannerisms and by an insidious campaign against him as an 'Uncle Tom'. It would be as well to consider something of the background of the campaign.

The bop revolution of the early forties has already been mentioned. What has sometimes been overlooked is that the movement was not only a musical revolt but a sociological one as well. The young musicians who took up bop so enthusiastically had none of the background of the pioneers of the form, and tolerance of older musicians and styles was almost completely absent as far as they were concerned. The 'modern' jazz movement grew up at a time when the American Negro was making considerable advances in the economic and social spheres, mainly as a result of the need for the co-operation of the Negro population during the Second World War. Naturally, the younger Negroes had no intention of allowing the position to deteriorate after the war was over and there grew up a demand for equality in all fields. This in itself is highly commendable and no rational person could be other than sympathetic to such ideals. However, with it there developed an attitude of resentment against the past which found expression in a curious hostility to any characteristics which could be typed as essentially Negroid. On its lowest level it could be seen in the rather pathetic advertisements in the Negro newspapers for hair-straighteners and skin bleaches, but in the world of the modern jazz-men the reaction took the form of rejecting the musical past and in an attempt to dismiss all earlier styles as the expression of an unhappy period which would be best forgotten. At the heart of the matter was a complete acceptance of the norms of the dominant white capitalist society with its success equated with material gains. Such a viewpoint differs very considerably from the outlook of racial minorities in most countries who are usually proud of their heritage and would not for one moment consider complete 'assimilation' as anything but another form of subjection. Along with this attitude went a declaration that bop was a music of social revolt, yet upon examination it is seen that such claims are bogus. In actual fact, there is much less revolt in modern jazz than in earlier forms, for a spurious bohemianism and turning away from one's audience is an indication of neurosis not revolt.

Time might well have taken care of the situation, but the position was complicated by the acceptance of the new music and the propagation of a theory of continual progress in jazz by many of the American journalists who wrote regularly for the mass circulation journals. It was somehow inevitable that Armstrong should have been singled out for the brunt of the attacks. As I have mentioned in an earlier chapter Armstrong came from the era when musicians thought of themselves as entertainers and not as artists. It was perfectly natural that many of them should be excellent showmen who used comedy routines as part of their performance, and for two decades nobody had thought to question their right to do so. To the 'new' Negroes any suggestion of Southern Negro speech was tantamount to the worst sort of 'Uncle Tomming' (the definition of an Uncle Tom is a Negro who is obsequious to an exaggerated extent to white people) and, at the same time, the popularity of Armstrong shocked the more militant boppers. The 'progressive' critics mounted a campaign of hostility to Armstrong, his music and his personality that must be unparalleled in the history of jazz. It became routine to read that any concert by him was poor, that he clowned in an undignified manner on the stage and that, compared to the dignified modernists, he was a disgrace to his race. Curiously enough the same critics did not bother to hide their partisanship, as proved by their sympathetic writing, towards Charlie Parker, to give one example, who was involved in more disgraceful exhibitions in public than almost any other jazz performer. The fact is that Parker was a mentally sick man and I do not suggest that he should have been treated without sympathy, but the manner in which the same critics who would lean over backwards to present Parker in as agreeable a light as possible would seize every opportunity to belittle Armstrong showed that genuine concern for dignity was not involved in the polemics. In all, this was a disgraceful and shoddy campaign and people who knew Armstrong well say that he was much hurt by it. Perhaps the height of the criticisms were reached during the Armstrong concert at the Newport Jazz Festival in 1957.

The organizers of the Newport Festival had decided to make the opening night a birthday tribute to Armstrong. It had been claimed that he was to present a new programme and had agreed to certain other musicians making guest appearances with him. Exactly what did happen on that night it is impossible to decide, but there is no doubt that by the time Armstrong took the stage he was a very angry man. What should have been a happy occasion turned out to be something of a fiasco and the concert was abruptly concluded in an atmosphere of rancour. One of the musicians who was to have played with Armstrong on that occasion was Jack Teagarden, and when he was touring England a few months later he told me that Armstrong had been blamed unfairly in his opinion and that the real fault lay with the Newport Festival organizers. It does seem certain that there had been a considerable amount of provocation on the night of the concert and that by the time that the great trumpeter took the stage he had been goaded beyond the point of reasonableness. One story has it that two well-known critics had approached him and demanded that he present a new programme in a manner to which he took strong exception. In one way and another this unhappy episode reflects little credit on those who were dealing with the presentation of the programme.

The demand that Armstrong should speak out on social and racial matters is, in any case, a curious one. If the truth be told there have been very few jazz musicians who have cared to brand themselves as outspoken social critics and for all the sound and fury from the modernist camp these performers have not been noticeably less reticent in the matter. Many of the modernists have turned to Mohammedanism because of its racial tolerance but they have displayed no public militancy in social matters or, if they have, it has surprisingly not been reported. In September 1957 Armstrong dropped a bombshell amongst his critics. It was the period of Governor Faubus's defiance of the Supreme Court on the matter of racial integration, and in an angry interview Armstrong denounced President Eisenhower as 'two-faced', and said that he was permitting Faubus to 'run the country'. He cancelled his proposed tour of Russia for the State Department, 'because the way they are treating my people in the south, the government can go to hell'. This is probably the most widely publicized and outspoken comment on racial matters that a public entertainer has ever made, but the reaction of the critics who had been maligning Armstrong was as despicable as their former attacks. Not one publicly associated himself with Armstrong's remarks and in spite of their much boasted liberalism, the modernist musicians were not exactly headlong in their rush to support him. The campaign soon died down and one hopes that the motives of those conducting it were sufficiently discredited. The fact that anyone who ever met Armstrong could really consider him an 'Uncle Tom', as some critics maintained, is a sign of singular stupidity or sheer wilful antagonism.

Although it is an entirely different matter the critics who were involved in the 'Uncle Tom' campaign also took every opportunity to point out that the repertoire of Armstrong's concerts consisted of the same group of numbers and blasted Velma Middleton's antics on the stage. The charge of sameness of repertoire was partly justified, but Armstrong himself spoke on the subject in his interview with Sinclair Traill in *Just Jazz* 1. His comments are worth quoting:

'Lot of people say why don't we play more new tunes each night? Well y' know it's a real consolation always gettin' that same note—just hittin' it right. The public can get to know you better by them old tunes than by anything new. So, like Heifetz and Marian Anderson, we play the same tunes; every time they play the same solo they get the applause—so do we.'

The comparison with performers in another field might be considered ingenuousness but one has to remember that Armstrong always thought of himself primarily as an entertainer, and that the jazz fans as such formed a very slight segment of his audience. Armstrong was also in a somewhat similar position to the late Art Tatum in as far as he considered that, over the years, he evolved set solos that he was incapable of bettering. John McLellan has dealt with this point ably in the *Boston Traveler* of 29 July 1958:

'Louis is not trying to prove how fast he can run the chord changes of a tune. Nor how many choruses of variations he can string together. If, over a period of time, he has composed through improvisation a perfect solo—a solo with a rhythmic structure that swings, and a melodic structure that expresses beauty—why try to change it? And Louis plays plenty of perfect solos.'

In actual fact if one had the opportunity of hearing Armstrong on succeeding nights it was sometimes surprising to note just how much he did alter his solo within a pre-established framework. A comparison of versions of numbers that he recorded more than once during his latter years will show many variations. I feel that the problem is confused by the lingering belief of many fans that a true jazz performance should be completely improvised. The history of the music from the time of Oliver and Jelly Roll Morton gives the lie to this reasoning. I must admit, in all honesty, that I personally preferred to hear some new numbers at Armstrong's public performances, but a wish of this nature should not blind one to the quality of the music that one did hear. The antics of Velma Middleton on the stage were also not greatly to my liking and I had no great respect for her as a vocalist, but one accepted her as part of the show and it is essential to realize that a show was what it was in Armstrong's own mind.

Until illness forced him to abandon playing, Armstrong was as dedicated a performer as he ever was. He took considerable care of his health—his belief in a particular laxative must be known to all who ever met him!—and drank moderately and was only an occasional smoker. He had the attitude of a professional to his job and was not unaware of his own worth, although the latter attitude was an acceptance of reality rather than egotism. Armstrong the man was a blend of genuine humility and strength of character. He was also extremely generous to fellow musicians who had fallen on difficult times, but his charity was done unobtrusively. I found that all the musicians who came up in the 'twenties and early 'thirties idolized Armstrong both as a musician and man and in a curious sort of way they felt that his success was a vindication of their own attitude and style. Armstrong the public performer was one thing but the man as a private individual was probably only known to a few intimates. He had a considerable perspicacity in summing up a man's character and some of the musicians I met in New York reported some devastating comments on well-known critics and agents that he had made.

Until about the mid-1960s, Armstrong remained the greatest trumpeter in jazz and, indeed, the greatest creative genius in the history of the music. His records during the last two decades of his life were of a very variable quality, but the special occasion could still bring out the greatness in him. He had the habit of producing records that still all criticism after a succession of routine performances. The famous 'Louis Armstrong Plays W. C. Handy' LP of 1955 must rate amongst his greatest releases and there are many quite magnificent tracks in the four-volume set that he recorded during 1956–57 for Decca (released in England on the Brunswick label). This took the form of a musical autobiography with Armstrong himself commenting on the numbers which started with a group that he had first played with the King Oliver band. It is interesting to note that certain titles are superior to the original performances, notably *King of the Zulus, Georgia On My Mind* and *Lazy River*. The American writer Martin Williams summarized his reactions to some of these tracks in a review of the set in the December 1958 *Jazz Review*, and his remarks are so apt that I am quoting them here:

'It is all very well to talk about Armstrong's rhythmic conception, about his transformations of banal melodies, about the superb imagination of an harmonic variation like that in the 1938 *I Can't Give You Anything But Love*, about "the first great jazz soloist." It is also all very well to say that this *King of the Zulus* is not like the first. It happens to be better. On it, and on the other titles for which I have reserved comment, Armstrong is astonishing, and astonishing because he plays with such great power, authority, sureness, firmness, commanding presence as to be beyond style, beyond category, almost (as they say of Beethoven's last quartets) beyond music. When he plays the trumpet this way, all considerations of "schools", most other jazzmen, most other musicians simply drop away as we listen. The show biz personality act, the coasting, the forced jokes and sometimes forced geniality, the perpetual emotional content of much of Armstrong's music past and present (that of a marvellously exuberant but complex child)—all these drop away, and we are hearing a surpassing artist create for us—each of us—a surpassing art.'

Mr. Williams correctly summarized Armstrong. Quite often his shows were routine, although it was seldom that he did not play something of worth, and now and then the more commercial records sounded somewhat forced. If, in his advanced years, Armstrong sometimes decided to take it easy who is there to blame him? Although strongly expressed, his remarks that 'some of them modern trumpeters couldn't carry out my routine, why man, they would be carried away on stretchers!' has the ring of truth about it. Armstrong played so superbly for so many years that his lapses were understandable. The dawning of an adult appreciation of jazz, as of any art form, begins when one realizes that one's idols have their off-days and their moments of aberration. The truly astonishing factor in Armstrong's career is that out of the hundreds of records that he made there are so very few that are entirely without interest. If it was his decision to conserve some of the creativity for the special event or recording it seems entirely logical, yet the fact remains that in his sixties he could still show the same flashes of genius as he did when he was in his twenties. From a purely commercial point of view, he could still turn out such popular successes as *Mack the Knife* and *Hello, Dolly!* From the point of view of physical stamina, at the age of 65 he celebrated fifty years as a jazz performer by going on an extended tour of Eastern Europe. That year he also performed at President Lyndon Johnson's inaugural, was soloist with Leopold Stokowski and the American Symphony Orchestra at Carnegie Hall, and was awarded the Presidential Medal of Freedom.

Those of us who grew up with jazz for any length of time somehow developed the attitude of acceptance where Armstrong was concerned. Perhaps that is why his death at the age of 71 on 6 July 1971, was such a traumatic experience. Armstrong was with jazz almost from the beginning and as it grew so did he. The entertainment world in which he moved is a cynical, dishonest one, but he was much too big to be influenced by it. He remained one of the few artists who added something worthwhile to the lives of others and before his achievements the occasional failures seem unimportant. It would be fitting to let a musician who has played with him relate his feelings on Armstrong's importance, and I am concluding with the words, quoted in the 22 January 1959 issue of *Down Beat,* of one of the most thoughtful and literate musicians in jazz. In the course of an interview with Tom Scanlan, Teddy Wilson had the following to say about Armstrong:

'I think Louis is the greatest jazz musician that's ever been. He had a combination of all the factors that makes a good musician. He had balance . . . this most of all. Tone. Harmonic sense. Excitement. Technical skill. Originality. Every musician, no matter how good, usually has something out of balance, be it tone, too much imitativeness, or whatever. But in Armstrong everything was in balance. He had no weak point. Of course, I am speaking in terms of the general idiom of his day. Trumpet playing is quite different today than it was then.

'I don't think there has been a musician since Armstrong who has had all the factors in balance, all the factors equally developed. Such a balance was the essential thing about Beethoven, I think, and Armstrong, like Beethoven, had this high development of balance. Lyricism. Delicacy. Emotional outburst. Rhythm. Complete mastery of his horn.'

SELECTED DISCOGRAPHY

RECOMMENDED RECORDS BY OR FEATURING LOUIS ARMSTRONG

1923–33 "The Genius of Louis Armstrong"

Mandy Make Up Your Mind, Lonesome All Alone and Blue, Bridwell Blues, Cornet Chop Suey, Oriental Strut, Willie the Weeper, S.O.L. Blues, Wild Man Blues, Once in a While, Chicago Breakdown, Alligator Crawl, Potato Head Blues, Weary Blues, That's When I'll Come Back to You, Fireworks, St. Louis Blues, Monday Date, West End Blues, Sugar Foot Strut, Squeeze Me, Savoyageur's Stomp, Beau Koo Jack, Save It Pretty Mama, Mahogany Hall Stomp, I'm a Ding Dong Daddy from Dumas, You Rascal You, Lonesome Road, Kickin' the Gong Around, Lawd You Made the Nights Too Long

Columbia G30416

1923–24 *with* King Oliver's Creole Jazz Band

Snake Rag, Mabel's Dream, Room Rent Blues, Dippermouth Blues, I Ain't Gonna Tell Nobody, Working Man's Blues, High Society, Sweet Baby Doll, Sobbin' Blues, London Cafe Blues, My Sweet Lovin' Man, Camp Meeting Blues

Epic LN–3208 (deleted)

Chimes Blues, Just Gone, Canal Street Blues, Mandy Lee Blues, Weather Bird Rag, Dipper Mouth Blues, Froggie Moore, Snake Rag, Mabel's Dream, Southern Stomps, Riverside Blues

Riverside RLP12–122 (deleted)

1923–25 *with* King Oliver's Creole Jazz Band, Fletcher Henderson's Orchestra, Red Onion Jazz Babies, Ma Rainey, Trixie Smith

Alligator Hop, Krooked Blues, I'm Going Away To Wear You Off My Mind, Mandy Make Up Your Mind, Jelly Bean Blues, Countin' The Blues, Terrible Blues, Santa Claus Blues, Of All The Wrongs You've Done To Me, Nobody Knows The Way I Feel This Morning, Cake Walking Babies From Home, Railroad Blues

Riverside RLP12–101 (deleted)

1924–25 *with* Bessie Smith

St. Louis Blues, I Ain't Gonna Play No Second Fiddle, You've Been A Good Old Wagon, Sobbin' Hearted Blues, Reckless Blues, Careless Love

Blues, Cold In Hand Blues
included in Columbia CL–855

1925–27 Hot Five

Muskrat Ramble, Heebie Jeebies, Gut Bucket Blues, Skid-Dat-De-Dat, Yes! I'm In The Barrel, Cornet Chop Suey, Struttin' With Some Barbecue, I'm Not Rough, The Last Time, Got No Blues, Hotter Than That, Ory's Creole Trombone
Columbia CL–851

1925–27 *with* Erskine Tate's Vendome Orchestra, Red Onion Jazz Babies, Johnny Dodds, Lil's Hot Shots

Static Strut, Stomp Off Let's Go, Terrible Blues, Santa Claus Blues, Wild Man Blues, Melancholy, Georgia Bo Bo, Drop That Sack
Brunswick BL–58004 (deleted)

1927 Hot Seven

Potato Head Blues, Wild Man Blues, S.O.L. Blues, Gully Low Blues, Melancholy Blues, Weary Blues, Twelfth Street Rag, Willie The Weeper, Keyhole Blues, That's When I'll Come Back To You, Alligator Crawl, Chicago Breakdown
Columbia CL–852

1928 Savoy Ballroom Five

Basin Street Blues, Weather Bird, No, Papa, No, Muggles, St. James Infirmary, Tight Like This, West End Blues, Skip The Gutter, Two Deuces, Sugar Foot Strut, Squeeze Me, Don't Jive Me
Columbia CL–853

1929–31 *with* Orchestras under actual leadership of Les Hite, Carroll Dickerson, Leon Herriford and Luis Russell

Knockin' A Jug, Body And Soul, Stardust (two takes), Black And Blue, I Can't Give You Anything But Love, Lazy River, Dear Old Southland, If I Could Be With You, I'm Confessin', I'm A Ding Dong Daddy, Shine
Columbia CL–854

1932–33 "A Rare Batch of Satch"

I Gotta Right to Sing the Blues; Medley: When You're Smiling, St. James Infirmary, Dinah; There's a Cabin in the Pines; Basin Street Blues; I Hate to Leave You Now; Mahogany Hall Stomp; High Society; That's My Home; Medley: You Rascal You, When It's

Sleepy Time Down South, Nobody's Sweetheart; Snowball; Laughin' Louie; Hobo, You Can't Ride This Train
RCA Victor LPM2322 (deleted)

1932–56 "July 4, 1900–July 6, 1971"

You'll Wish You'd Never Been Born, Sittin' in the Dark, Hustlin' and Bustlin', He's a Son of the South, Some Sweet Day, Honey Don't You Love Me Anymore?, Dusky Stevedore, Mississippi Basin, Tomorrow Night, A Song Was Born, Lovely Weather We're Having, Please Stop Playing that Blues Boy, Ain't Misbehavin', Pennies from Heaven, Save It Pretty Mama, Rain Rain, I Never Saw a Better Day, I Wonder Who, Don't Play Me Cheap, Linger in My Arms a Little Longer, Whatta Ya Gonna Do?, Blues in the South, Joseph 'n His Brudders, Back o' Town Blues, No Variety Blues, I Want a Little Girl, Sugar, Blues Are Brewin', Why Doubt My Love, Endie, I Believe, You Don't Learn that in School, 50–50 Blues, Some Day You'll Be Sorry
RCA Victor VPM6044

1935–44 "Rare Items"

Thanks a Million, Lyin' to Myself, Swing that Music, Ev'ntide, Thankful, Skeleton in the Closet, Jubilee, Struttin' with Some Barbecue, I Double Dare You, 'S Wonderful, Hey Lawdy Mama, You're a Lucky Guy, Everything's Been Done Before, Groovin'
Decca 79225

1935–41 *with* Orchestra directed by Luis Russell

Shadrack, Jeepers Creepers, Old Man Mose, Shoe Shine Boy, Brother Bill, Now Do You Call That A Buddy, On The Sunny Side Of The Street, Confessin', Ain't Misbehavin', I Can't Give You Anything But Love, Sweethearts On Parade, Baby Won't You Please Come Home
Decca DL–8327 (deleted)

1937–39 *with* Orchestras under the actual leadership of Jimmy Dorsey and Luis Russell

When The Saints Go Marching In, Bye And Bye, West End Blues, Mahogany Hall Stomp, Dippermouth Blues, Save It Pretty Mama, You Rascal You, When It's Sleepy Time Down South, Hear Me Talkin' To Ya, Savoy Blues, Our Monday Date, Wolverine Blues
Decca DL–8284 (deleted)

1940 *with* pick-up group including Sidney Bechet

2.19 Blues, Perdido Street Blues, Coal Cart Blues, Down In Honky Tonk Town
included in Decca DL–8283 (deleted)

1947 Esquire's All-American Hot Jazz

Long Long Journey, Snafu; also *Blues for Yesterday* (Louis and his Hot Six)
included in Victor LPV 544

1950 All Stars

Panama, New Orleans Function, Flee As A Bird, Oh, Didn't He Ramble, Struttin' With Some Barbecue, Basin Street Blues, My Bucket's Got A Hole In It, Bugle Call Rag
Decca DL–8329 (deleted)

1954 All Stars—'Play W. C. Handy'

St. Louis Blues, Yellow Dog Blues, Loveless Love, Aunt Hagar's Blues, Long Gone, Memphis Blues, Beale Street Blues, Ole Miss, Chantez Les Bas, Hesitating Blues, Atlanta Blues
Columbia CL–591

1956 All Stars and Lewisohn Stadium Symphony Orchestra (valuable as a documentary)

When It's Sleepy Time Down South, Indiana, Interview In Paris With Edward R. Murrow, Flee As A Bird To The Mountain, Oh Didn't He Ramble, Mack The Knife, Mahogany Hall Stomp, All For You, Louis, Black And Blue, St. Louis Blues
Columbia CL–1077 (deleted)

1956–57 All Stars and studio group directed by Sy Oliver (This is a musical autobiography re-creating many of Armstrong's great hits of the period 1923–33, with spoken comments by Armstrong)

Dippermouth Blues, Canal Street Blues, High Society, Of All The Wrongs You've Done To Me, Everybody Loves My Baby, Mandy, Make Up Your Mind, Them There Eyes, Lazy River, Georgia On My Mind, That's My Home, Hobo, You Can't Ride This Train, On The Sunny Side Of The Street

See See Rider, Reckless Blues, Court House Blues, Trouble In Mind, New Orleans Function, Gut Bucket Blues, If I Could Be With You One Hour, Body and Soul, Memories Of You, You Rascal You, When It's Sleepy Time Down South, I Surrender Dear

Cornet Chop Suey, Heebie Jeebies, Georgia Grind, Muskrat Ramble, King of the Zulus, Snag It, Some Of These Days, When You're Smiling, Song of The Islands, I Can't Believe That You're In Love With Me, Dear Old Southland, Exactly Like You

Wild Man Blues, Potato Head Blues, Weary Blues, Gully Low Blues, Struttin' With Some Barbecue, Hotter Than That, Two Deuces, My Monday Date, Basin Street Blues, Knockin' A Jug, I Can't Give You Anything But Love, Mahogany Hall Stomp
Decca DXM 155

1957 "Ella and Louis" with Ella Fitzgerald and Oscar Peterson Group

Don't Be that Way, Let's Do It, Stompin' at the Savoy, I Won't Dance, Gee Baby Ain't I Good to You?, Can't We Be Friends?, Moonlight in Vermont, They Can't Take that Away From Me, Under a Blanket of Blue, A Foggy Day, Stars Fell on Alabama, The Nearness of You, Cheek to Cheek, Let's Call the Whole Thing Off, Love Is Here to Stay, I'm Putting All My Eggs in One Basket
Verve 6–8811

Bix Beiderbecke

BY BURNETT JAMES

I

Legends and myths grow with alarming swiftness round the memory of those who die young and, in their way, tragically, and before long become a species of distorting filters which in the end throw the entire picture out of focus. This, or something very like it, happened in the years following the death of Bix Beiderbecke. It is not simply that he was held in great personal affection by those who knew him and so wished to do all they could to perpetuate his memory; it is not even a matter of the esteem in which his colleagues held him as a musician. Far more than this or these it is a question of substantially extra-personal and non-musical circumstance which turned him into what has been not unjustly called the romantic legend of American jazz. Hence the 'Boy Meets Horn' type of memorial; hence the sentimentality and dewy-eyed adulation. Hence also the reaction against him, especially among those who did not fall under his personal spell and who remain more or less unaffected by his musical style. The situation is not by any means uncommon; but it does happen to have unusual relevance to the present case.

Neither of these attitudes, of course—breathless adoration or comprehensive disparagement—is a critical assessment of any value. The one, in fact, tends very often to be largely dependent on the other. The disparagement has arisen to a great extent out of the adulation: the adulation has reinforced itself against the disparagement. To let in some necessary fresh air it is, therefore, first of all essential to clear away the legend and look for the living man and artist who has become obscured behind it.

The biographical details of Bix's twenty-eight years of life are not copious. Much of it is inevitably anecdotal; most of the rest is tied up with the growth of jazz from local and particular beginnings to its position as, in one form or another, the characteristic popular music of the day during the nineteen-twenties. 'Read no history, no-thing but biography, for that is life without theory', is a celebrated dictum of Disraeli, and often a sound one. But it doesn't carry us all the way in the case of a jazz musician whose life and work were so essentially bound up with the times in which he lived and with currents of thought and feeling which he, to some extent, transcended, but without a basic knowledge of which he cannot be properly understood. His biography sets him clearly in time and space; but his lasting value as a creative artist has to be assessed on its own merit, apart alike from personal attachment and merely period significance.

He was born Leon Bismark Beiderbecke at Davenport, Iowa, on March 10th, 1903. Davenport lies beside the Mississippi River, and this environment was to have great influence on the boy's growing awareness of the world in which he was to live and the life he was subsequently to follow. The old riverboats with their jazz bands which used, in those days, to ply the great river, reached as far up the Mississippi Valley as Davenport, and, through early contact with them, the born musician in him was wakened into life and given direct stimulus while he was still a boy.

Bix's parents were well-to-do middle-class folk, not unmusical but with no immediate connexion with the musical profession. They were musical amateurs, after the frequent habit of their class and kind; but, also in keeping with their social background and standing, they tended to be resistant to the idea of a musical career for their offspring. A 'respectable' occupation was a matter of no less consequence for middle-class America of the day than for middle-class England; and a musical calling, let alone one devoted to the new-fangled jazz, hardly filled the bill. But that didn't, and in the end couldn't, deter Bix. Music was in his bloodstream (which in itself is no very astonishing phenomenon) and it had its way with him. He seems to have studied little:

his musical development, such as it was, appears to have been largely intuitive. He became an able pianist and later taught himself to play the cornet, as much as anything by accompanying the records of the Original Dixieland Jazz Band. Nick La Rocca, the O.D.J.B.'s renowned leader, had a good deal of influence on the young Bix's cornet style. In particular the round, clear, pure tone for which Bix subsequently became famous was in the first place a legacy of his studies of La Rocca.

The young Bix went to the Davenport High School in search of formal education. There he was undistinguished and more or less comprehensively disinterested. He paid small attention to his books and for two and a half years appears to have avoided academic study with determination and some skill. He was therefore dispatched to the Lake Forest Military Academy where it was hoped that a sterner discipline and more commanding authority would instil in him more orderly and respectable habits of mind and body. This was in 1921.

As it turned out, however, Bix found plenteous opportunities for further abstention from hard work and scholarly diligence, especially at the week-ends. He took his chances of escape and made the best of them. He found his way down to the South Side of Chicago and mixed freely and often with leading jazzmen of the day. Here many of the great New Orleans musicians were to be seen and heard, migrating northwards in search of regular employment. These new and exciting experiences settled Bix's future once for all. He determined to be a great trumpet player; he sat at the feet of the mighty and did not go away empty-handed. His family had moved to Chicago and the die was cast. He became so obsessed with his trumpet and so actively disinterested in anything else that the faculty at Lake Forest gave up the unequal battle after about a year and a half and sent him on his way—no doubt to their own as well as to Bix's heartfelt relief.

Just who among the great jazzmen of the day Bix did actually hear and learn from, both in Chicago and on the riverboats of his childhood, is not altogether certain. Certainly he came under the spell of King Oliver and Louis Armstrong, although it is doubtful if he actually heard Louis as early as some say—in the Davenport days, that is. There are stories, too, not entirely substantiated, that there was working around Davenport a fabulous trumpet player

(name of Emmett Hardy) who was the real originator of the style now entirely associated with Bix himself. But if it was so, the world has heard little more of him and will never know for sure just how much truth there was in it.

While Bix was at Lake Forest the pioneer white group known as the New Orleans Rhythm Kings came into Chicago, led by trumpeter Paul Mares and including George Brunies on trombone and Leon Rapollo on clarinet. Bix evidently learnt much from them and was enraptured anew. Some of the members of the New Orleans Rhythm Kings, notably Brunies and Don Murray, later appeared with Bix on his own recordings. He also heard Bessie Smith, Queen or Empress of the Blues, rightly so-called, and the legend has it that he was so overcome that he offered her a week's pay just to keep right on singing. This may have been a year or so later, when Bix returned to Chicago to join Charlie Straight's band after the break-up of the Wolverines, with whom he had his first active and professional job.

We can see these first years in Chicago when he was a young military cadet, and undergoing formal instruction to that end, as the significant formative years of Bix Beiderbecke the jazz musician. Whom he heard then and there and what precisely he did with such spare time as he legitimately or otherwise could find and make his own may be obscure. But it was obviously of the first importance for his subsequent career. Jazz fascinated and possessed him entirely. He had the great exemplars of the day constantly before him—the living witnesses of the music to which his life was henceforth to be dedicated. Whatever final conclusions we may in the light of our own judgment come to about Bix's contribution to the music we call jazz, it cannot be disputed that no man was more thoroughly immersed in his art or more completely possessed by it. It was necessary for him to be a jazz musician; jazz answered some deep need in his being; he could fulfil himself in no other way. No doubt this is true of many—it is certainly true of those like Armstrong and Ellington, Bessie Smith and Sidney Bechet, Johnny Hodges and Charlie Parker, who have created the true, enduring, and original styles in jazz. It is worth mentioning in the present context because jazz has always attracted those who have cynically exploited it and made a good thing out of a prevailing fashion, but for whom it has answered no urgent need, offered no genuine fulfilment. Bix Beiderbecke was not one of these; and it has no direct relationship to the contribution he actually made or to the manner in which he eventually brought his talent to fulfilment.

Bix's first professional engagement came when he joined the Wolverines in 1923. This group of college boys, led by their pianist, Dick Voynow, had been in a sort of sporadic existence for a year or two already. They did odd jobs on a more or less spare time basis, and Bix had played along with them. But towards the end of 1923 they began an engagement at the Stockton Club in Hamilton, Ohio, with a permanent booking. It was now that Bix laid the foundations of that glowing reputation that was to last until his death and long after.

The Wolverines were the first permanent white band composed entirely of non-New Orleans musicians. Their style was in effect an extension and, to some extent, a refinement of the style of the Original Dixieland Jazz Band. The revised 'Dixieland' style was in its heyday in these years and the Wolverines gave it fresh impetus. Concurrently there was another white group which had no permanent existence but which was assembled for various recording sessions under the name of the Original Memphis Five and led by another prominent white trumpet player, Phil Napoleon. They had nothing directly to do with Bix, who never played (or at least never recorded) with them. But they help to show the direction white jazz was taking and the particular refinements of style it was bringing to bear on the more rugged Dixieland ways.

The Wolverines were a huge and immediate success. They played with gusto, spirit and a sort of carefree *élan* which rocketed them to the dizzy heights of local popularity. Bix was their great star—he who led them in their revels and inspired them to their best efforts. This isn't yet the mature Bix, the Bix who left an indelible impression on the minds of those who knew and heard him and who is to-day honoured by many as the outstanding trumpeter in an essentially white style. This is just a happy young man with a natural gift for the music he played. But it is the beginning; and a beginning in which the end is not entirely unforeseen.

Apart from Bix none of the Wolverines who played regularly at the Stockton Club made a subsequent mark on jazz history, with the possible exception of Min Leibrook whose bass saxophone lumbered (I use the word deliberately) its way into many later recordings on which Bix himself was featured, not to their general advantage. The clarinettist Jimmy Hartwell was perhaps the best soloist along with Bix: his style had some affinities with that of the excellent Rapollo of the New Orleans Rhythm Kings. George Brunies, of the Rhythm Kings proper, sometimes sat in with the Wolverines; but Al Gandee, a lesser man, was their regular trombonist. George Johnson played some tenor saxophone solos which have a gorgeously period sound nowadays, but little else. For the most part he reveals only too well how necessary was the work done by Coleman Hawkins.

We should not let the collective and individual limitations of the Wolverines, plain enough though to today's ears they are, blind us to the fact that in their day they were pioneers and opened new paths. Compared to the great Negro bands from New Orleans and to King Oliver they probably didn't amount to much; but they were looking in another direction, exploring a different path.

The fame of the Wolverines spread far and fast. It was Hoagy Carmichael, then a student at Indiana University, who was responsible for the next move. Hoagy knew about the Wolverines, but he hadn't heard them play at first hand. However, he chanced his arm and on the strength of a reputation, invited them up for a spring dance. There is a charming and entirely characteristic story told of six young heathens turning up at the University for the big occasion in a fearful ramshackle old vehicle with battered instruments spilling out on all sides, to the momentary dismay, not only of Hoagy himself, but of others who feared that the sound might in the event prove as disconcerting as the sight. But the Wolverines in general and Bix in particular lived up to their fame. They played and were a sensation. They were acclaimed by everyone and caused heated excitement. Originally invited for a single week-end they came up for the next ten, always with the same result. And the association had its lasting consequences. Hoagy Carmichael and Bix struck a deep and immediate friendship which endured until Bix's death—a friendship mutually fruitful on the musical as well as on the personal plane. Hoagy wrote *Riverboat Shuffle* (originally *Free Wheeling*, but re-christened by Bix) for the Wolverines; and Bix

45

made his last records with a studio group organized by Hoagy—records which are especially interesting not only because they represent the last of Bix's playing to be perpetuated, but also because they find him playing in the company of his musical equals, including Jack Teagarden and, surprisingly perhaps, Bubber Miley.

The Wolverines went their energetic way, chancing their arm and enjoying themselves enormously in the process. The job at the Stockton Club came to an abrupt end after a New Year's Eve brawl, but it had been in its own way a historic engagement. While they were there the boys had settled into a compact unit and consolidated a style of their own. The personnel still wasn't settled, but the spadework was done. After the rowdy end of the Stockton Club the Wolverines went back to Chicago and took a job at Doyle's Dance Hall in the early weeks of 1924. Here Vic Moore joined them as drummer and Al Gandee came in on trombone because Bix wanted the front line to be the same as that of the Original Dixieland Jazz Band. Not everything went well at Doyle's. There were disagreements with the management which eventually resulted, if indirectly, in a walk-out. The dancers didn't go overboard for the band, but all the Chicago musicians adored it. In May, 1924, the Wolverines went over to Richmond, Indiana, and recorded four titles for Gennet. These were, *Oh Baby*, *Copenhagen*, *Susie* and Hoagy's *Riverboat Shuffle*. The latter had become a great feature with them, largely because the chorus—a 32-bar blues theme—offered the possibility of four breaks, which was a new idea at the time and caught the boys' fancy. Gandee doesn't appear on these sides, but he is there on a couple of others—*Fidgety Feet* and *Jazz Me Blues* —made around the same time.

During the summer of 1924 the Wolverines seem to have been at something of a loose end. At any rate Bix turned up for a while playing in a band led by Mezz Mezzrow at the Martinique Inn at Indiana Harbour. This was altogether an eccentric set-up with an eccentric management. Bix's association with it was brief but probably not unenjoyable.

In the autumn of 1924 the Wolverines moved over to New York and opened on September 5th at the Cinderella Ballroom. At the same time a band led by Sam Lanin and including Red Nichols was playing at the New York Roseland Ballroom. Red had already made some records of his own and begun to show his hand. Patterns were emerging; the way into the maturing of white jazz during the latter half of the nineteen-twenties was being pointed. The Wolverines made more records in New York, and Bix played on a recording session by a group called the Sioux City Six, led by Frankie Trumbauer, the famous saxophonist who was to be Bix's companion on so many of his later and most famous recordings. Also in the group was Miff Mole, the trombone player who effected something of a technical revolution on his instrument. The two sides made on October 10th, 1924, are not very distinguished. Little rapport had been established and no one really arouses interest. But they are interesting in that they represent the first recording Bix made away from the Wolverines and with 'Tram'.

Later in the year the Wolverines moved to the Roseland themselves; but things were beginning to change. Victor Berton, the drummer with Nichols' original Five Pennies, took over from Vic Moore, and the brilliant Eddie Lang joined on guitar. The changes resulted in a gradual breaking down of the old spirit of the band. New ideas were in the air, new men were at hand to implement them. Bix himself was progressing, maturing. Although he wasn't properly of, and never became intimately associated with it, the white jazz style that was to be predominant for the rest of the nineteen-twenties in the hands of such as Nichols, Venuti and Lang, and the Dorsey brothers, was establishing itself and the carefree Dixieland music on which the Wolverines had prospered was giving way before it. During 1925 they broke up; their day was over. Most of the original members faded into obscurity while the newer ones like Berton and Eddie Lang joined up with Red Nichols and explored fresh paths into the future.

Bix left the Wolverines in 1924 and went to join Charlie Straight's orchestra back in Chicago. For the rest of his life he was to work with the big white dance bands of the period—later with Jean Goldkette and lastly with Paul Whiteman. For a while towards the end of 1926 Bix played with a Goldkette group led by Frankie Trumbauer in St. Louis. The next year that band too came to an end. Bix and Trumbauer went into the main orchestra led by the French-born band leader, Jean Goldkette, in Detroit. At one time or another Goldkette had working with him most of the men who were later to be recognized as the leaders of white jazz. An earlier group had included Don Murray, Joe Venuti, and

46

Red Nichols. When Bix and Trumbauer joined him in 1926, they found themselves working alongside men who were later to be their colleagues on their most famous records—Murray, Bill Rank (trombone), Doc Ryker (saxes), Izzy Riskin (piano). Other leading jazzmen of the day joined the band for recording sessions.

Goldkette tried to keep up an all-star band—a band which played jazz as it was then known to and understood by the leader of a major white dance band. Bix found himself briefly still in congenial company. They played a good deal at the Ivy Ballroom, Philadelphia and at the Graystone Ballroom in Detroit, and did a good deal of touring. In 1927, however, Goldkette found the going too hard and was obliged to let the band go. The musicians themselves splintered off in different directions. Bix and 'Tram' went to Paul Whiteman and were joined there by Rank and others. Joe Venuti and Eddie Lang went to the orchestra led by Roger Wolfe Kahn, son of the millionaire Otto Kahn. It was with Kahn that Jack Teagarden made his first record—*She's a Great, Great Girl*—on a day when, as he himself tells, he was so nervous that Joe Venuti was obliged to use physical propulsion to get him up to the microphone. Bix spent the rest of his working life as a member of the Whiteman band—a figure of especial, not to say unique, status.

When he went back to Chicago to join Charlie Straight after the break-up of the Wolverines, Bix found himself mixing once more with the great Negro jazzmen who were pouring into the city. That he went among them freely and played with them when he could is not to be doubted. Nor is the continued influence they exercised on him. We see him growing in stature almost daily hereabouts. He had long since acquired such technique as he needed. Now he was deepening and ripening as an artist. The emotional warmth and subjective lyricism for which above all he was to become famous was without question the expression of his own deepest personality; but it was fostered and encouraged in Chicago by his constant mingling with and playing alongside on after-hours sessions, the great Negro musicians who were everywhere to be found. I do not propose here to analyse or discuss in particular detail Bix's personal style—that will come in a later section of this book. But it remains necessary here and now to insist on the importance of the frequent and varied associations.

Jazz at its best and contemporary greatest was everywhere around him. He soaked it up, took it into his musical bloodstream and so was immeasurably helped to find and eventually fulfil himself as a creative artist.

The Wolverines period was the happiest and most carefree known to the short life of Bix Beiderbecke. Thereafter, as we have seen, he was obliged to work in big commercial dance bands, even if they did make gestures on the side of breaking out into jazz properly so-called. But let it never be forgotten that for the most part these were gestures only. Even Goldkette was first of all a dance band leader in the accustomed manner of the day and age. Paul Whiteman, though called the 'King of Jazz', fronted an orchestra of semi-symphonic proportions. His jazzmen had their way from time to time, but in essence only as a sideline. He himself was a perceptive and experienced musician; he was also an astute business man. He knew Bix's worth and wasn't uncommunicative about it. But nothing can alter the fact that in his band Bix was a solitary figure—lonely and often frustrated, his life not a part of the life around him, his art private and personal.

Bix was not alone in this dilemma. Only his deep sensitivity and the precise nature of his temperament seem to have made it more acute for him than for others who could more readily acquiesce in necessity and regard it calmly and, let us say it, cynically. During this period it was necessary for a jazz musician to earn his living with the established dance bands, for that was where the money lay. He could join together with others of a like inclination for after-hours jam sessions or for recording dates; but the bread and butter had to come from elsewhere. The Negro musicians were in a rather different position. They were more or less completely debarred from the lucrative jobs in fashionable clubs and hotels, from the big radio programmes and suchlike. They were obliged to make their own music together in their own quarters—in Harlem and the coloured dives of New Orleans and Chicago. The recording studios were open to them, but not the gay, rich, and pleasure-loving world of the nineteen-twenties. For the most part the Negro jazzmen were neither obliged, nor indeed able, to pay solid homage to the more blatantly commercial side of popular entertainment. They had to keep to themselves and make their own way with the music of which they themselves were the legitimate progenitors. Of course, the segregation wasn't in any way complete. There was a good deal of intermingling, both ways. But while the white folk could and did go off down to the Negro quarters in search of what was widely regarded as a new form of exotic entertainment, the Negro couldn't reverse the process or provide that entertainment in the fashionable amusement palaces of the white society.

There is little doubt that these sociological considerations account to some considerable extent for the inflated reputations won by many of the early white jazz players. We needn't argue, as is too frequently done, that these men possessed no real talent or that their music was without merit; but it can hardly be questioned that the fame most of them achieved was not in direct proportion to their gifts as jazzmen, or that this was a good deal due to the superior opportunities that were theirs for other than strictly musical reasons. It has to be remembered that not until around 1935 did Benny Goodman break precedent by using mixed white and coloured groups for public performance. Even today a free mixing is not accepted without question in some parts of America. During the nineteen-twenties such a practice was to all intents impossible outside private sessions or the recording studios.

Bix joined Paul Whiteman in 1927, shortly after the break-up of the Goldkette band. At first he seems to have been not unhappy, and he found plenteous opportunities for the exercise of his particular talents. When Bix and Trumbauer accepted Whiteman's offer the orchestra was in the process of winning for itself a not undeserved reputation as a strongly rhythmic unit with recognizable jazz affiliations. Among their colleagues in the Whiteman ménage were, at one time or another, the Dorseys, Joe Venuti, Eddie Lang and Carl Kress, Bill Rank, Don Murray, and Izzy Friedman. These men made some mark as jazzmen, and in their company Bix played some of his best music. Frankie Trumbauer formed many small recording groups from contemporary Goldkette and Whiteman orchestras with Bix as the leading soloist and Bix himself furthered his own recording career by playing with other groups from the same sources under his own name. Those spirited, if rather rough and happy-go-lucky, records made by Bix and his 'Gang' belong to these years and derive from these resources.

Paul Whiteman's reputation, once so strong, has, since those now far-off days, suffered not so much deflation as near obliteration. As so often, the swing of the pendulum has passed from one extreme to the other. Historical perspective has been lost. Once set on a dizzy pinnacle of fame and esteem, Whiteman subsequently was dashed to the ground and his abilities and achievements set at nought. Exaggeration in one direction gave way to equal exaggeration in the opposite direction. The phenomenon is by no means without precedent. The truth, as always, lies somewhere between the two extremes.

I think it not unfair to say that Paul Whiteman was a very considerable figure in the development of modern dance music. His orchestra and his musicianship were alike superior to most of those working in the same field today. But he was not really involved, except incidentally, in the growth of jazz properly so-called. His championing of 'symphonic jazz' and the larger compositions of George Gershwin is a true indication as to where his real ambitions lay. He employed the leading white jazzmen of the day, Bix among them, and he evolved a particular style of what may best be termed 'hot dance music' which, if it couldn't be accepted as jazz, was at least heavily jazz-inflected.

When Bix joined him, then, Whiteman was playing a lot of music with a conscious jazz background. As time went on, however, and he became more and more involved in commercial entertainment, with radio programmes and vast tours where music other than jazz was required, Whiteman moved farther and farther away from the easy-going, rhythmically inclined style of his earlier days, his musical ideals becoming more and more subservient to his business sense. In these circumstances Bix found his situation growing less and less sympathetic until in the end it became next door to intolerable. He was constantly frustrated, unable to fulfil himself, and in the end it destroyed him.

In the dance-band world of the late nineteen-twenties, the life as well as the music was 'hot'. This was the era of Prohibition, of the hip flask and bathtub gin. It was the sort of thing that could only have been perpetrated by a jejune and adolescent society, wherein excessive drinking was inevitably turned from a social nuisance into a deadly menace. The gangsters and bootleggers who lived and thrived on it were the symptom of its basic idiocy. Bix always drank a lot—like most of his colleagues he had a liberal capacity and didn't take serious steps to curb his natural appetite. He was never one to resist temptation, and when the gin flowed Bix tended to take more than was good for him. So long as he was happy and found opportunities to play the music to which his life was dedicated it didn't do him much harm. Even if his lapses into excess were too frequent to be regarded with equanimity he generally kept his inclinations under control. But when things went hard against him and he began to feel himself lost and frustrated in an alien world, he gave way. Late in 1928 Bix had a breakdown. Whiteman, a solicitous and generous man, provided for him during his illness and enabled him to undergo a course of treatment for alcoholism. Bix might well have recovered completely if only on his return he had been able to find the sort of work that could have satisfied his deepest needs. But he couldn't do that. He became more and more unhappy as the new orientations of the Whiteman band caught him in a deadly grasp. He returned to drinking and irregular habits. His health got progressively worse, his stamina failed him, and his playing lost its pristine freshness and spontaneity.

What indirectly settled Bix's fate once for all was probably the great Wall Street 'crash' of October, 1929. This ominous occurrence marked the end of the extravagant pleasure-loving spree of the 'twenties, itself a reaction to the arduous years of the First World War. 'Boom' was succeeded by 'depression', and everyone felt the pinch, musicians as much as any. The band leaders were forced to contract, to conserve their resources and dispense with their more expensive attractions. In order to live at all they had to conform rigidly to the type of entertainment most likely to attract what little money there · left in circulation in a once-prosperous society. The world was shaken to the core.

Bix spent the winter of 1929–30 at his home in Davenport. He still hoped to rejoin Whiteman after a renewed spell of rest. Whether he actually did so is not finally established. He seems never to have become a regular member of the Whiteman band again; but it is probable that he did maintain some occasional association with it after his return to New York in 1930. What is more important is that the conditions which prevailed at the time of that return could offer him no hope of salvation, even if they had been able to offer him secure employment. The world had changed in his absence. He couldn't earn his living by playing the sort of jazz that was meat and drink to him, and without it he had no defence against the formidable encroachment of the alcoholism that was by now his mortal enemy. We can imagine the effect on a sensitive man like Bix of such a situation. It bit deep into his soul, destroyed his remaining confidence in himself, and drove him irrevocably back into a soul-destroying frustration. He made a few records with his old friend, Hoagy Carmichael, and a pick-up group. Then he went back to Davenport once again, physically ruined and in a state of acute mental depression. He played with various local bands for a while, and then made one last return to New York. But the result was the same. He got an engagement with a band on a radio show, but he wasn't even fit enough for that. He broke down many times: it was obvious that he was finished. His friends did their best to help him, both on the stand and off it. But it was no good. Bix had burnt himself out and the flame couldn't be rekindled.

It is a sad story, and to some extent an unnecessary one. His addiction to alcohol was partly innate, but under happier circumstances it probably would have been containable. He was clearly a man of great personal charm. Also, he was a strange character—a 'card'—wayward, loyal, and full of good intentions which never quite materialized. He left an indelible impression on the memory of all who knew and worked with him. Paul Whiteman, who knew a thing or two about men and musicians, said after his death: 'Bix was not only the greatest musician I have ever known, he was also the greatest gentleman.' Coming from such a source that is certainly a tribute worth setting down.

It was, indeed, Bix's characteristic courtesy and loyalty to his friends which precipitated his end. A dance was to be held at Princeton University and a scratch band had been engaged with Bix its star performer. The presence of Bix was the condition of employment. But shortly before the prescribed date Bix went down with a heavy cold and remained in his apartment in New York. He was not fit to turn out on the night. He sent word that he wouldn't be along. But the management was adamant: no Bix—no engagement for the band. When he learnt that his absence would cost his colleagues their jobs he defied common sense, put aside the advice of his friends, and went abroad in the cold night air. The result was fatal. He returned home and developed pneumonia. His never robust constitution could fight no more, and on August 6th, 1931, Bix Beiderbecke died.

His last act was, as I say, characteristic. He would not willingly disappoint his colleagues, and it proved his undoing. His end was in keeping with the rest of his life, in that it was directly brought about by an action and impulse at once generous and foolish. His biography offers many examples of his loyalty to his friends and the unfailing generosity of his nature. If at the end he perished because of that loyalty and that generosity it was at least fitting. In any case, one has the ineffable impression that he didn't care any more; that he was played out and knew it deep inside himself.

A study of Bix's essential personality would show that he was a man remarkable more for sensibility than for strength of character. He was only twenty-eight when he passed from the gaudy scene of this life's living; but it seems in retrospect as though into his short lifetime a whole world of vital experience had been packed. He passed rapidly from eager and buoyant youth to ripe maturity and then into decline. It is impossible to escape the conclusion that whatever had happened (short of a comprehensive, and impossible, mutation of his entire nature) he couldn't have lived much longer. Even if he had avoided the fateful ride to Princeton University, nothing that has been recorded about his last months on this earth gives the smallest hope that he would have survived. The story of those last months is pitiful. Bix could no longer keep to even the simplest routine. It can hardly be imagined what he must have suffered. To such a man the situation must have become rapidly intolerable. At the end he couldn't even play his instrument properly. That it was to a large extent his own doing will only be insisted on by those whose sense of a tragic destiny is so small that they habitually stand in self-righteous judgment on the sufferings and aspirations of those less fortunate than themselves. The perpetrators of the 'legend' are no better. Their sentimentality and mawkish adoration do scant justice to a man who had to pay the heaviest price for his shortcomings and who bore the inevitable heartbreak and spiritual despair with dignity and without bitterness to the end.

Had Bix been by nature and temperament other than in fact he was he would in all probability have pulled through

the times of difficulty and perplexity that were his as they were most other people's of the day. He needed strength of character and toughness of moral fibre to cope with the situation in which he found himself. But Bix simply didn't have that sort of strength. He couldn't rationalize his problems and so reduce them to manageable proportions. His sensibilities stuck out like exposed nerves, and when the times rubbed hard against them he had no protective shield. Most artists need a stimulating and propitious environment in which to do their true work, and ones like Bix find it almost essential if they are to live and thrive at all. He was simply unfortunate that although as an enthusiastic young stripling Bix found the right company and the right conditions they broke apart under his feet almost before he had grown to manhood and he couldn't find the means of keeping his balance under the subsidence.

We tread on dangerous ground if we express the wish that Bix had been a stronger character, had been altogether tougher and less susceptible to the temptations of the flesh so that he could have triumphed over his difficulties and so lived to give us the continued enjoyment of his art. Had Bix the man in fact been the sort of character implied by such a wish, he might well not have been the same artist we know and cherish. At bottom the man and the artist are one. You cannot really dissociate the two in any significant way. The type of sensibility which led Bix to play the trumpet as he did was the same that caused him to suffer defeat under the circumstances which beset him. Which is not, of course, to argue that a man's biography is reproduced in his work. That is a stupid and flabby notion against which criticism has to be constantly on its guard. On the other hand, artistic creation, though in itself autonomous, is the outcome of the deepest sources of personality, and personality embraces the whole man. Had he been a different man Bix would have played a different music; it might have been a more or a less valuable music, but it would not and could not have been the same as in the event it was, he being Bix Beiderbecke and no other, comprehensively considered. We may passionately regret that his innermost nature and temperament were such that he succumbed to the life he was obliged to live; but we can't wish him otherwise without at the same time undermining the quality of his artistry itself.

Bix simply did not possess the kind of temperamental

and moral equipment to enable him to survive in the jungle of popular entertainment. He had neither the cynicism which enables some men to compromise with it, nor the iron will which enables others to prevail in it without a major sacrifice of personal integrity. We get nowhere if we are content merely to point a finger in praise or blame. We have to make an imaginative attempt to understand the innermost nature of our particular subject; to balance weakness and strength in whatever form they may choose to manifest themselves as essential ingredients in the full complex of personality.

Bix's sensitive yet vigorous and enthusiastic cornet playing was a true reflection of his sensitive yet vigorous and enthusiastic nature. As a young man he was greatly addicted to sport. He was gay, pleasure-loving, fond of jokes and horse-play, and an appreciative conniver in the extravagant living of the times in which he lived. But he remained to the end courteous, considerate, and unasser-

The star of the Wolverines

51

Bix's first Goldkette assignment. The band led by Frankie Trumbauer at the Arcadia Ballroom, St. Louis, autumn 1925. Bix is in the middle at the back, Trumbauer is behind the bass sax and linking his arm is Pee Wee Russell. Other members of the group are Ray Thurston, Bud Hassler, Louis Feldman, Wayne Jacobson, Dan Gabey, Dee Orr and Morty Livingston

tive. And it is all there in his music. The style was the man.

When he died a local newspaper in Davenport offered the opinion that ' "Bixie" will be forgotten as quickly as the popular songs he played . . .' But he wasn't forgotten: his contemporary fame and the music he played have passed into jazz history. Later generations have argued and discussed his merits and failings with heat and passion. He has been extolled as one of the greatest of all jazzmen, or denigrated as one whose chief claim to immortality lay in the unfortunate circumstances of his later life and his early death. I have heard professional trumpet players say, simply and sincerely—'Bix was the daddy of them all.' And there are modern jazz critics who hold, with equal sincerity, that he was a gifted dance-band musician with a pretty melodic sense, no more. What is sure beyond dispute is that the expectation that his reputation would die with

him and his memory fade from the fickle slate of time has not been fulfilled. Precisely why that is so may perhaps become more apparent when we have made an attempt to discover once for all just what he did and what he did not do as a practising jazz musician; for it is there, and there alone, that we can hope to discern the lasting validity of his life and work. To that question it is now necessary that we address ourselves.*

* Since the writing of this brief biographical sketch, *Bugles for Beiderbecke*, by Charles H. Wareing and George Garlick, has been published (Sidgwick & Jackson, 25s.). This is quite the most detailed and fully documented account of Bix's life yet to appear. Although it does not alter the broad outlines it does throw fresh light on many hitherto obscure details and must be accepted as authoritative in the matter of the biography and the extremely comprehensive discography.

2

'Honest criticism and sensitive appreciation,' wrote T. S. Eliot, 'is directed not upon the poet but upon poetry.' Those wise and true words need to be kept constantly in mind by all critics and commentators, no matter what their subject of immediate interest. The more so do they have essential relevance in a case like the subject of our present study where romantic legends, personal reminiscence and non-artistic sympathies and antipathies have always risen up like spectres out of the past effectively to direct attention away from the poetry to the poet. Whatever we may think of Bix Beiderbecke as a man, however much we may feel sympathy or its reverse for his personal misfortunes and the difficulties he experienced during his short life, the basic question we have to ask ourselves is, did he play the trumpet well? We have, of course, to extend our inquiry after that. We have to try to discover how he played and what original contribution, if any, he made to the art which he practised. It may be argued that this is an austere doctrine, one to some extent lacking in warmth and sympathy; but it is the only one likely to lead us to the heart of the matter. And in the end it may well be the most personally satisfactory of all by directing inquiry to where it is most enduringly fruitful.

During the nineteen-twenties the three original trumpet stylists were Louis Armstrong, Bubber Miley, and Bix Beiderbecke. I do not say that they were, necessarily, the three greatest trumpet players of their day—although the pre-eminence of Louis Armstrong in any period would hardly be disputed. What matters is that each of these three men created original and personal styles in what were still the formative years of jazz history. It is doubly to be regretted that both Bix and Miley died before the new orientations taken by jazz during the nineteen-thirties had been more than generally indicated. Although both died during the early 'thirties their significant work was in an earlier age. Thus we were not only denied a proper continuation and development of their personal talents, but also the fructifying influence they might have exerted had

they lived longer than in fact they did. As it was it transpired that Louis Armstrong alone remained as the great exemplar of jazz trumpet playing for subsequent generations in an active and present capacity. Because they passed from the scene at an early stage both Miley and Bix were only able to exercise an influence at second hand, and have remained to a considerable extent bogged down in the welter of inevitable trivialities of the age in which they lived and worked. Miley, because he worked with Duke Ellington, the most genuinely progressive and exploring musical mind yet known to jazz, was in a better position than Bix who, as we have seen, was obliged to spend the better part of his active career in commercial dance bands which had the effect of frustrating rather than liberating his best abilities. But the important point is that, so far as active participation and living authority was concerned, Armstrong had to carry almost the full burden of developing jazz trumpet playing from its beginnings in the 'twenties. That he was perhaps the man most fitted to do just that is a piece of good fortune for which we can give constant thanks, but which does not alter the basic argument. If, of the three, Armstrong had been one of those who died young, the tragedy for the future of jazz would have been next to insupportable. On the other hand, if Miley and Bix had lived on alongside Louis Armstrong the development of jazz trumpet playing might well have run along three complementary lines, each reacting fruitfully on the others, instead of, as it had to, down a single channel.

It is said that Bix Beiderbecke exerted no great influence over his successors. This is the sort of statement, not at all uncommon, which contains at one and the same time a valuable truth and a dangerous half-truth proportionately mingled. Bix stands in no direct relationship to Louis Armstrong as one who created a style that became a sort of basic norm for subsequent generations—a great well or mine of inspiration out of which could grow and has grown great variety and wide-ranging individuality of style all stemming from a common source. This is partly due to

Armstrong's great personal stature and partly to the simple fact that he has remained creatively active throughout almost the whole of jazz's significant history.

It is true that a great artist tends to exert a potent influence over his contemporaries and his successors alike; but it is not true that his quality is in any way directly related to the degree of influence he establishes. Often quite minor artists exercise the greatest influence, especially over the technical aspects of their art. They discover for themselves some aspect of style, or some technical procedure, which only becomes fully significant when it has become incorporated into the more universally valid style of a major talent. But this is by the way. It is not relevant to the present discussion. Even if, as is frequently asserted with some confidence, Bix was essentially a minor figure in jazz, it cannot seriously be argued that his particular style was brought to fulfilment at a later date by one of more enduring significance than himself. Great or small in scope though it may in the end prove to be, Bix's style was original and personal—a precise way of thinking and feeling in music that has to this day remained unique and autonomous.

When we speak of an influence we have to be careful to think precisely what we mean. Imitation may or may not be the sincerest form of flattery, but it cannot be legitimately allowed into the category of an influence properly so-called. A true influence shows itself as at once deeper and less obvious. The haphazard taking over of a few external mannerisms cannot be said to constitute an influence. Every man, the greatest as well as the smallest, has his inevitable mannerisms which can be copied readily enough by anyone who takes the trouble to attend to them. But a mannerism is not the essential man—it is simply a by-product of the creative and technical process. It is a sort of personal cliché which tends to pop up every time habit is substituted for original thought. There are dozens of examples of this sort of thing in all the arts. They are neither significant nor interesting, and they have nothing whatever to do with the potency of genuine influence.

We come up against a particularly acute problem when discussing Bix Beiderbecke. He lived a good while ago, before the jazz world had sorted itself out conveniently into schools and coteries, and before anyone armed with a tape recorder could take down the smallest and most in-significant utterance from the smallest and most insignificant mouth, or hand. What, we may ask again, about the influence on Bix's formative years of the semi-legendary Emmett Hardy? Did this man really precede Bix in the trumpet style generally thought to be his alone? We shall never know for sure; but if we don't know we cannot possibly assess precisely where Bix stands in relation to his times and the music of those times. Bix was in all probability the better trumpet player and the one deserving survival. These things usually sort themselves out by some kind of ineffable law. But it is possible that circumstances conspired to relegate Hardy to an undeserved oblivion and that on intrinsic merit he is not less deserving of our contemporary attention.

With Bix himself the matter is complicated by the fact that we know very little about him as a jazz musician pure and simple. We know that he spent whole nights occupied in heated jam sessions with all sorts and kinds of colleagues, white and coloured, and it is almost certain that it was here that he played his best and most inspired music. He was frustrated by the environments in which he was obliged to do his daywork. But after hours he could and did play and for his private pleasure. If we could add what we do not know about Bix to what we do know, the problem of assessing him once for all would be considerably simplified. But that is all now beyond the realms of possibility. We have his records, which are authentic if incomplete evidence; and we have the testimony of his friends, which is valuable if not to be taken inevitably as the whole truth. The gaps we must fill in as best we may.

On the evidence of his records there was not one Bix but three at least. First, there is the extrovert Bix of the Wolverines—gay, carefree and vivacious. Then there is the Bix who worked with the big bands and who stepped forward when direction or inspiration compelled, to play a series of solos, sometimes lyrical and reflective, more usually forthright, and sometimes downright spiteful. Thirdly, there is the Bix of the small group sessions, mostly under his own name or that of Frankie Trumbauer. It is usually agreed that this latter is the real and enduring Bix. But that is not the whole story. Jazzmen, like any others, tend to get themselves type-cast and thereafter tucked neatly away in some pigeon-hole of the critical mind. Thus 'Cootie' Williams is invariably associated with the growl style he inherited from Bubber Miley, but which he did not create and which seldom showed him at his original and creative best. As a matter of fact, 'Cootie's' really creative work was done in a style that showed most clearly the influence of Armstrong. He played magnificently with the plunger mute; but if he hadn't been obliged to take over Miley's 'book' in the Ellington band he might have grown into one of the great stylists inspired, but not necessarily dominated, by Louis Armstrong. As it is, his mute was stuck like a small hat on his head, and there he sits in the portrait gallery of jazz, a fascinating but slightly dejected figure who provokes nostalgia for a sight and sound of his great predecessor and outstandingly original stylist, Bubber Miley.

I bring up the case of 'Cootie' Williams as an obvious case of mistaken identity because in another way Bix has also suffered some such misconception. Whenever his name is mentioned you will be sure to hear, quick as gunshot, the associated adjectives—lyrical, sweet-toned, etc. But Bix was more than a dreamer on the trumpet, just as Delius was more than the dreamer on the orchestra he is so often thought to be by those who must have a convenient label for everything under the sun. Lyrical Bix truly was—he was perhaps the most purely lyrical of all the early trumpet players, certainly all the early white trumpeters. But his teeth weren't drawn by his lyrical impulses. There are times when I hear delighted an improvised passage where this same Bix plays with such gusto and subjective ferocity that he seems literally to bite the notes off. Certainly his tone never deteriorated under pressure, as many have and do, and maybe that is why he acquired the reputation for playing without the essential energy and robust strength that is commonly supposed to be a principal characteristic of the type of music with which he identified himself. Did he lack the rawness, the rough edge, of the great Negro trumpet players of his day and age? Very well then. But what we have to ask ourselves is not whether Bix played like the famous Negro trumpet players (which is a foolish question anyway, because he was not a Negro trumpet player and had no intention of imitating anyone), but on the contrary, whether or not he revealed a fresh, personally expressive and subsequently valid conception of the jazz idiom considered not narrowly, and with hardened prejudice, but in the round. There are those who will tell you

that there is only one form of true jazz and that its gospel was written by Buddy Bolden or some such in the back ends of New Orleans. No one, I take it, denies the immense value of New Orleans jazz and its outstanding exponents. Equally, I take it that only those with the heaviest axes to grind now contend that no jazz worth the calling has ever come from sources other than New Orleans or in imitation, to a greater or lesser extent, of the New Orleans style. I have no intention of wasting my own or my readers' time in fruitless and stupid arguments of the Traditional *versus* Mainstream *versus* Modern type. I take it as proved and accepted that jazz may be played in many different styles without losing either basic character or legitimate birthright. I am simply, in fact, arguing in the present context that although the jazz played by Bix Beiderbecke had its roots firmly dug into the original soil it achieved a flowering of a new and original kind. The final value of that flowering has yet to be established.

It is, I think, reasonable to argue that although Bix played his trumpet professionally for around eight years, it is only in about three or four of his active career that he produced music of real consequence. It is probably even less than that, for at the end he was sick in mind and body and although the flame seems occasionally to have spurted into life the light it shed was sporadic and seldom intense. The Bix of the early days with the Wolverines was a gifted lad who played with more natural ability than his colleagues, no doubt; but it wasn't until later that the content of his music deepened and matured, that it became emotionally nourished from within, that significant content was added to natural ability.

If we place, for example, the Wolverines' recording of *Big Boy* beside the Whiteman band's *From Monday On*, in both of which Bix leads off with a solo improvisation on the melody, it is possible to see the one as a logical continuation of the other, pure and simple. But it is also hardly possible not to notice in the latter both a more complex structure and emotional overtones of a very different nature. Whereas in the first case Bix plays with a sort of happy abandon in the company of those who felt the same way, although they had not the same ability, in the second there is an unmistakable sense of struggle against a basically unsympathetic musical environment. We cannot blame Paul Whiteman for offering the sort of performances he did offer—it was simply the style of big band presentation he evolved and on which his contemporary fame was built. We can only regret that Bix should have found it necessary to earn his living in conditions under which his innate talent was to a considerable extent frustrated.

On the various small group-recording sessions in which he took part, and through which his best work is perpetuated, Bix is much more at home. But even here he had to contend with colleagues who were seldom his equals in musical capacity, who were too immersed in the dance-band idioms of the day and experienced difficulty in escaping from it. Bix may well have played on private nocturnal sessions with men who were his equals, but unlike Louis Armstrong at a similar period he did not record with them. His records live because of him alone, and because of Eddie Lang, although with a few exceptions Lang's most memorable work was done elsewhere. Bix had no Dodds and Ory to back superbly his own imaginative explorations into the living body of his music, and he found no Earl Hines to act as perfect foil and equal partner as his talents developed and expanded. Even Frankie Trumbauer, who was no mean musician and who exercised some influence on later saxophone players, notably Lester Young, proved in the end to be working in a technical and emotional *cul-de-sac*. When at the end of his life Bix made a few records with Hoagy Carmichael in the sort of company his gifts justified it was too late—he was sick in mind and enfeebled by the destroying life he had lived in the previous years. We are at liberty to speculate if we please on what Bix might have achieved had he lived longer and played regularly with such as Jack Teagarden, Benny Goodman, Bud Freeman, all of whom made significant and far-reaching contributions to jazz, as well as with some of the great Negro jazzmen with whom he had an instinctive sympathy. But it remains idle speculation, exciting to the fanciful imagination though it be. It could have saved Bix as man and musician; but it never had the proper opportunity.

Although it is true that, especially in jazz, expressive content is of considerably more importance than mere technique, we cannot hope to understand any man's work unless we first make some attempt to arrive at an objective assessment of the technical methods by means of which he achieved personal expression. We may apply the adjectives at our pleasure; but they will mean very little unless we define our terms of reference with some precision.

Let us take the matter of lyricism first. It is generally agreed that Bix was a predominantly lyrical player. But that does not in itself tell us very much about him. Jazz is an essentially lyrical form at bottom. Only by an abuse of language can we speak of 'epic' jazz. We may find in certain aspects of jazz certain broad affinities with the poetry of, say, Keats or Shelley; but we can nowhere find a similar affinity with Milton or Camoens. And although we may mark some resemblance, as that astute critic Charles Fox has done, between certain aspects of modern jazz, principally West Coast, and the minor poetry of the eighteenth century, there is nothing analogous in any form of jazz to the heroic couplet. Jazz, as I say, is fundamentally and, it may be asserted inevitably, a lyric art.

There is, of course, lyricism and lyricism. The lyrical is a general not a particular category in the wider sense. Probably the most lyrical trumpet player of today—perhaps the most purely lyrical since Bix himself—is Miles Davis. (I am naturally using the term lyrical in its narrower implications here.) But there is a world of difference between the pure, rounded, emotionally committed lyricism of Bix and the clouded tone and hazy chromatic outlines which Miles frequently exploits. It is a difference in kind not, necessarily, in quality, either way. I am indeed at a loss to understand how it can ever have come to be suggested that Bix Beiderbecke was in the smallest sense a progenitor of 'cool' jazz. I should have imagined it self-evident in a sane world that the opposite was nearer true. Whatever else may be said of Bix, that he played with personal warmth and depth of romantic emotion seems hardly to admit a counter-argument. It sticks out of every solo he chose to record. That he was at times emotionally reticent is not to the point. Reticence was for him another means of heightening emotional tensions. He had a remarkable gift for placing two phrases side by side, with a tendency to understatement individually, but expressing emotional power and urgency when placed together. Added to his unusual sensitivity to melodic line and accent its impact on the listener can be extremely profound. It is the secret that lies behind his characteristic reflective solos, of which *Singin' the Blues* is perhaps the outstanding example. When we have attended to and made due note of his exquisite phrases we are still only half-way to the heart of the matter if we do not at the same time understand the manner in which he habitually placed those phrases in juxtaposition. It is this at least as much as the beauty of phrase itself which gives his music its particular depth and richness of emotional content.

A leading element in Bix's style was his tone. And here is further evidence that he did not do anything that can be seen as a direct anticipation of the methods of the 'cool' tribe. A full, rounded tone of crystal clarity and absolute precision of intonation are not a characteristic of 'cool' jazz. Here, however, I beg leave to doubt whether we of today can be justly said to know just what it was in Bix's tone that excited his contemporaries. Remember that his records were all made years ago, before the days of a ubiquitous 'hi-fi'. I suspect that these records give us only the idea of Bix's tone, not the full tone itself. It is the same with the surviving records of the great opera singers of the day before yesterday. When we listen on our gramophones to Caruso and Tetrazzini and Tamango we can marvel anew at the perfection of vocal control, at the matchless shaping of melodic line and the superb covering of high notes; but can we in honesty say that we have more than an impression of the glorious sound, *qua* sound, that in physical presence so beguiled a former generation? To ask the question is to answer it. There is mechanical intervention which must dilute and diminish the impact experienced 'in the flesh' by our more fortunate ancestors. We know the quality all right; but not for us is the thrill of immediate and personal impact, the sheer physical delight in tone perfectly produced, the vibrations haunting the air and particles blending together in marvellous proportion.

Bix Beiderbecke was more fortunate than that, for he lived into the age of electrical recording. But inevitably something must be lost in the process. Only those who heard him at first hand can really know the ultimate secret of his tone in the fullness of its beauty. Hoagy Carmichael, who knew Bix for most of his active life and who played with him often, said that the notes 'weren't blown, they were hit, like a mallet hits a chime, and his tone had a richness that can come only from the heart'. At first sight those words may well sound like another example of the sort of thing that comes more from nostalgic recollection than from direct observation—as another aspect of the 'legend', in fact. But on closer scrutiny they prove to be extremely revealing and to place a sensitive finger on certain important qualities of Bix's style. To say that the notes were 'hit rather than blown', in the way a mallet hits a chime, is a remarkably apt description. If you listen to a typical Bix solo you will, I think, be struck at once not only by an unfailing accuracy of intonation, but even more by a sense of the notes being 'hit'. If you blow straight through a brass instrument you may produce true pitch and a clean tone with the sense of the air passing unimpeded *through* the coiled tubes. If, on the other hand, you so adjust your initial attack on the note that it appears to strike against the inactive air in the coils you can produce an effect as of a note rebounding from the metal. This is not easy to put into words but the result is perfectly evident to the ear. And it was precisely this 'bounce' or resilience in Bix's intonation which was most characteristic of his method. Of the other trumpet players who have made some use of this method I think most readily of Rex Stewart. Rex is frequently said to show Bix's influence in his lyrical open solos. His celebrated contribution to Duke Ellington's version of *Kissin' my Baby Goodnight* is usually held up as the outstanding example. I am not sure that I see the correspondence, at least not to any great extent. I fancy that a more pertinent example is Rex's equivalent solo on *Isn't Love the Strangest Thing?* because of the sharper outlines and more Bix-like placing of complementary phrases. But even here I am not entirely convinced. Rex's use of the half-valve effect and his tendency to cover his tone in these examples and their like is in some contrast to Bix's more forthright methods. It is true that some of the phrases are built much as a latter-day Bix might have built them; but I suspect a tendency once a man has a reputation for exploiting a certain style for anyone who follows even loosely in a similar vein to be saddled with an 'influence' that may well be nothing of the sort. Where I find Rex Stewart revealing himself as a true inheritor of Bix is in his most obviously 'hot' work, often with the mute. Bix did not exploit muted effects overmuch, never, so far as we know, the plunger; but there are instances where he thrusts a mute tight into the bell and punches out a solo of some fierceness and pugnacity. And it is here, when Rex mutes his cornet as tight as he can and drives his notes hard against it, that his intonation comes nearest to Bix. Also, in many of Rex's fiercest open solos (though not those which indulge in exuberant pyrotech-

Bix and 'Tram'

Melody Maker

nics), the resilience of his tone and intonation seem, let us say, in the direct line of Bix's original style.

I expect these remarks to cause some surprise in circles where Bix Beiderbecke is still thought of as no more than a *pretty* stylist with a charming but unforceful melodic gift. That, however, is where the great misconception may be said to begin. If we listen again to the many sturdily Dixieland records Bix made between about 1926 and 1928 we shall find frequent confirmation that he was in the habit of hitting his notes square and hard, that he built his phrases with strength as well as delicacy, that, in short, he had a robust and thrusting style as well as the reflective-lyrical

vein on which his reputation seems nowadays to rest. *Sorry* and *At the Jazzband Ball* are good examples of the former.

There is no doubt that Bix played usually in inferior company. The records he made with what he called his 'Gang' have much in them of crudeness. Those with Adrian Rollini on the bass saxophone and Don Murray on clarinet are generally the best, because Rollini had a superior sense to Min Leibrook of the difference between the melodic and the rhythmic functions of his instrument, and because Murray, while no memorable clarinettist, occasionally exploited those angular lines which recall the great Johnny Dodds and which fit admirably into this type of music. I am not going to defend the use of the bass saxophone as the bass instrument in jazz, no matter who blows down it, for I have always thought it tiresome and unsatisfactory in any capacity; but it was the thing of the day and best when in the hands of Rollini. A good trombonist eluded Bix all his days, and that was a serious gap. He played once or twice with Miff Mole; but he really needed Teagarden. I do not follow the argument that on the very few sessions where Bix and Teagarden do play together (with Hoagy Carmichael's studio groups) there is a noticeable lack of rapport. The point cannot seriously be sustained because at this time (1930) Teagarden was a young man with the world before him; a brilliant new star in the ascendant, his style not fully formed perhaps but with all the freshness of a finely confident beginning, while Bix was all but played out, his health gone, his spirit dimmed. Nor had they played together regularly. There is no discernible reason why Bix and Teagarden shouldn't have developed into admirable partners, the one a perfect foil for the other. Their mature styles were different but in many significant ways complementary. Eddie Lang, who must be accounted with Bix the most original and brilliantly gifted white jazz player of the period, played with Teagarden later on, and there is a fine understanding and sense of give and take

Melody Maker

Bix towards the end of his career

59

between them, and others. Bix in full health would quite obviously have made a notable addition to those later groupings.

A point that has struck me with increasing forcefulness is the resemblance between certain aspects of Bix's style with that of Sidney Bechet on the soprano saxophone. Whether Bix ever heard Bechet we do not know. But I cannot avoid the impression that in matters of phrasing and the construction of improvisations Bix and Bechet went to work on very similar principles. Of course, Bechet's wide, throbbing vibrato and quivering nervous energy seem on the surface very unlike Bix. On the other hand, Bechet articulates his saxophone in a manner more familiar to the trumpet, and, as I say, his building of musical phrase and sentence frequently calls Bix to mind, especially when they happen both to play the same tune. *Margie* may be taken as a convenient example. Superficially the resemblance is slight enough. But behind the obvious differences in method and technique it is not difficult to find certain marked similarities in the basic approach to jazz improvisation. Elsewhere too I have been often compelled to think of the one when listening to the other. Again, I do not postulate a direct influence, one way or the other. I suspect more some inner and unconscious correspondence due to a similarity of roots. It is by no means paradoxical that a white cornet player and a Negro saxophonist should show some correspondence of style and musical construction if we remember the relevant times and the fact that both were near to the mainsprings of jazz's growth to maturity. In the present context I am more concerned with noting a resemblance than in looking for some metaphysical significance in it.

Bix's style relied very little on the use of vibrato. He used it to give life and vitality to his melodic lines, naturally; but he never erected it into a principle. Less than most jazzmen, white or coloured, his particular style and tone production did not depend for emotional tension on a wide and expressive vibrato. None the less, I become increasingly convinced that this matter of vibrato is only incidental: it is seldom a major element in style. Even with Bechet it is more an added ingredient, an embellishment, than something organic. At times it appears to come near to mannerism, effective though it unquestionably is.

Another jazz player, a modern one this time, who makes frequent personal use of vibrato is Ruby Braff. Often enough Braff seems to be a player in the direct tradition of Louis Armstrong. I can think of records where it is perfectly feasible to mistake Braff for Armstrong. But I do not feel Armstrong's influence to be all-pervading. Braff is one of the most original of contemporary trumpet stylists. His basic style is compounded of many elements: he has taken what he wants from his colleagues, past and present, and evolved a style that is personal and creative. Superficially he seems not particularly related to Bix. But there are times when I am very conscious that the shade of Bix mingles with others in the making of an original modern conception of jazz trumpet playing. Consider the recording made by the Ruby Braff Quartet of *Louisiana*. At once the similarities and the differences become apparent. Braff frequently ends his musical phrases with a sharp burst of vibrato, amounting at times almost to a light trill. This Bix never did. Also Braff takes obvious pleasure in exploring the extreme ranges of his instrument—especially the lower ranges. But consider closely the building of phrases and the overall conception of the melodic line. I think it will not be denied that here, on a tune which Bix himself often played, Braff shows a marked similarity of style and feeling. He plays not so much like Bix (for that is most times mere imitation) but in the direct line of succession stemming from Bix. In many ways Braff reveals himself as one of the few modern trumpet players who have successfully combined the twin, and in many ways complementary, elements of Bix and Louis Armstrong into a style that is essentially original and personally expressive. Perhaps the link is via Rex Stewart. We have already engaged in some discussion of the Bixian elements in Rex Stewart's style. With Braff we find another legacy of Bix plus technical linkings recalling Stewart. Few men have made more creative use of the lowest register of the trumpet than Ruby Braff, unless it is Rex Stewart. As I say, we do not look for fructifying influence in simple imitation if only because imitation must in its nature be no more than a grafting on of alien externals. It is when we probe deeper and relate the original elements in different styles that we begin to discover really significant points of correspondence.

Bix made small use of the more extreme ranges of the trumpet or cornet. His solos were nearly always confined to the middle register. He used comparatively few notes. His compass was restricted because his melodic conceptions required no great extension of it beyond the middle range. Like certain composers—Arnold Bax, for example—Bix liked to confine his melodic invention within the scope of roughly an octave. This was simply his personal way of thinking and feeling in terms of music. It was in no sense because he was technically incapable of exceeding the range to which he generally confined himself. Because he was largely self-taught and could offer no written credentials it is often said that Bix was a poor technician—that he never achieved mastery of his instrument, and that in consequence he was not able fully to express his real musical thoughts. Such a charge is demonstrably false. The music he did play shows beyond question that he had all the technique he needed. If he didn't fulfil himself it was because he seldom found the right environment and was too often obliged to keep bad company, musically speaking. As a matter of fact, I am not at all convinced that Bix didn't fulfil his best abilities, as a trumpet player, in the years of his prime, brief though these were. He played as he felt and gave release to the music that was in him. If his colleagues didn't live up to his own standards he seems largely to have been oblivious to them—not because he compromised or deliberately played down to a lower level, but because he was entirely absorbed in his own playing and his subjective ideal. If he had played with men nearer his equal as musicians in the days of his maturity the recordings with which he is now and forever associated would undoubtedly sound a good deal better. But I am not convinced that Bix himself would have changed much. That he was unhappy and frustrated as a member of big commercial dance bands is another matter: that destroyed him as a man but not as a musician. Along with the weakness of character that brought him to an untimely end went a compensatory faculty for losing himself entirely while he was playing, of turning inward on himself with barely a consciousness of the world around and about him. It would be a nice point of psychology to inquire how far the two were inter-related.

To return to Bix's technique. One has only to listen to any representative selection of his best records to know that he had a fluency and a precision of instrumental technique entirely adequate to the music he wished to play. If he didn't indulge in pyrotechnics, that was because he didn't need to, because he was not by nature a flamboyant player

—certainly not because he hadn't or couldn't readily have acquired the necessary means. A technically feeble player can be spotted quickly enough. He is always trying what lies beyond him, over-reaching himself. He misses out because his thoughts go quicker than his fingers or his lip, if he be a trumpet player. But with Bix there simply isn't any sense of thought outstripping technique. We can put it at this—either Bix had all the technique he required, or he was a remarkably good musical actor—one almost too clever to be a bad technician. In any case I leave it to those who know what manner of man Bix was to decide for themselves where the truth lay.

By adhering to the cornet and modifying to his own ends its characteristic tones Bix evolved exactly the right sound for the musical and emotional statements he elected to make, much as certain modern trumpeters, including Miles Davis, have found in the darker, thicker tones of the flugelhorn the right medium for what they have to express. Bix, of course, never attempted the soaring virtuosity of Louis Armstrong. He adored Louis, but he wasn't intimidated. He knew that he must speak for himself, that he had his own music to make. Therefore he created the right sound and discovered the right technique for that purpose—for that and no other.

I have already touched briefly on the question of lyricism in jazz in general and in Bix in particular. I have called jazz an essentially lyric art, and Bix an essentially lyric player within the general framework. Obviously his lyricism was not the same as that of other jazzmen, especially coloured jazzmen. We have to keep constantly in mind that there are as many different types of lyric poetry as there are lyric poets. The same is true of music. Personal and autonomous creative impulses find their own means and adaptations within the over-riding lyrical forms. We can only understand the individual talent if we make some attempt to isolate its particular contribution while keeping the main picture always in view.

If we say that Bix was a lyric melodist we can only claim that it helps our appreciation of him if we first make some critical analysis of the sort of melody he played and the imaginative basis of his melodic construction.

The first requisite of a melodic improvisation is that it shall respect and not abuse the original theme. In this Bix was seldom at fault. All his most typical improvisations are imaginative extensions and explorations of the tune—never wilful impositions on it. Like Johnny Hodges Bix frequently begins from the basis of the common chord used thematically. The first phrase represents a preliminary statement springing from the root of the melody's structure. Thereafter phrase is placed against phrase in such a manner that the improvised melody supported by the fundamental harmony becomes a genuinely imaginative extension of the original, growing out of it as a spontaneously generated flowering. Bix had an exceptionally acute harmonic sense; he would, I fancy, have been not at all impressed or entertained by the endless wrangles between harmonic and melodic improvisation. His innate musicality told him quite clearly that the two go together hand-in-hand, that you cannot dissociate them arbitrarily without losing the living character of the basic theme. I say his 'innate' musicality because there is no evidence, either internal or external, to suggest that Bix ever worked out consciously the plan of an improvised chorus; he didn't harbour preconceived ideas about it or approach a tune with malice prepense. He played spontaneously; his particular talent both enabled and obliged him so to do.

I do not thereby condemn out of hand a more cerebral approach to improvisation—that in later stages of jazz's development became to some extent inevitable. In order to extend existing frontiers the deliberate taking of thought is frequently necessary. It is neither in itself a better nor a worse way of going to work: it all depends on what has to be done at a particular time and in a particular context.

Bix had a natural sensitivity to the shape and substance of a tune. He came to it creatively and treated it as something existing in its own right. Almost infallibly he alighted by natural insight on its significant features. And often these insights and musical perceptions are relatively simple and readily discernible. He was not by nature an ingenious man, one seeking odd and esoteric byways. He couldn't for the life of him have explored a tune as Thelonious Monk usually does, though I offer the opinion that he would have followed Monk's musical thought easily enough, as Jack Teagarden did and does, to the immense discomfiture of those who think that all 'traditionalists', carelessly so-called, constitute a species of musical primitives. Bix's musical faculty was anything but primitive: his mind was finely poised and tempered; indeed, it could be argued that

it was because his mind was precisely as it was that he suffered an artistic loneliness which as much as any single factor led him to an early death.

Straightforward examples of Bix's natural ability to discern the salient features of a melody may be found in his celebrated recordings, with Frankie Trumbauer, of *I'm comin'*, *Virginia* and *Way Down Yonder in New Orleans*. Notice how in the former he fixes upon the characteristic intervals in the melodic line, and how in the latter he makes equally imaginative use of the repeated notes. These are simple enough ingredients, no doubt, and easily detectable. Further and less obvious examples abound in his recorded work and may be studied at leisure on such of his records as remain in circulation. But then think of the needlessly involved methods of many of his successors—men often wealthy, famous and replete with recording contracts, who enjoy benefits Bix himself never knew. Can it really be maintained that such methods, often fraught with great complexity and the result of much heavy labour, really get us nearer to the heart of the matter than Bix by natural sensitivity and inborn talent did? Perhaps it may not unreasonably be said of Bix, in the words of Alexander Pope, that he gave new and significant meaning to 'what oft was thought but ne'er so well expressed'. Certainly he gave point to the distinction, noted by Blake, between simplicity and insipidity. Bix may have been many things, but insipid he assuredly wasn't. Like much genuinely creative art, major or minor, Bix's work frequently appears easy and straightforward—after the event. The impression is, of course, deceptive. We may point to its simplicity, its 'obviousness', even now. But who among us could have thought of it originally for ourselves?

Although Bix's style seems straightforward and uncomplicated his melodic construction has a clearly recognizable form of its own. He has left his fingerprints on it in every bar, not only in points of technique—tone production and articulation—but in its shape and accentuation. How often do we encounter some such figure as

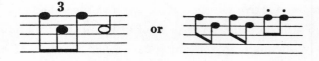

in a Bix solo; the interval, the rhythm, and the context

may vary, but the basic imprints remain. No doubt a more exhaustive study of his style broadly considered would reveal further and more subtly disguised personal touches, turning up with a regularity which marks them off as more than incidental; but for the time being these will serve to illustrate the point that his style was the natural and spontaneous creation of a readily identifiable musical talent. That these same figures tend to turn up in the section work of the bands in which he played bears further witness to the influence he exercised over the musical minds of his colleagues. It was not unknown for an arranger to note down the outline of one of Bix's improvisations and then score it for the complete brass section. Also as section leader of the Whiteman orchestra (also from time to time of Goldkette's) he moulded his colleagues' ideas to his own way of thinking. It must not be forgotten that in his great days Bix was valued almost as much as section leader as soloist. Not enough attention has been paid to this side of his work. We tend to think of him as a brilliant but intensely individualistic and frequently wayward soloist. But that isn't quite how his employers saw him. For them he was an invaluable inspiration to brass ensemble— a man who could lift his companions in brass out of rut and routine and leave his personal artistry and imprint on whole groups. It is for this reason that the Whiteman trumpets often sound like three Bixes playing in consort. Nowadays we might be tempted to think of it as an ingenious example of multi-taping; but when Bix lived and worked such pleasantries and refinements were still far away in the future.

Another neglected source of study or analysis in respect of Bix's style lies in the not unimportant matter of rhythmic accentuation. His sensitivity to accent was as remarkable as his sensitivity to melodic shape and line. We touch here on something of the first importance. However logical or sensitive the construction of a musical phrase may be, however clever its execution, and however original its shape, it will still come to nought if accent and emphasis are not so placed as to bring it subtly to life. All the great jazz soloists have possessed or do possess this inherent gift for accentuation: it is one of the principal means whereby they are able to give their improvisations life and meaning. As an object lesson, take almost any record of Duke Ellington and note how the texture comes constantly alive, all the time, not only in the solos but in the ensembles and accompanying figures, through a truly musical and imaginative placing of accent.

Bix had a naturally acute feeling for the shape and contour of phrases and his playing gained enormously from that sense; it became one of the hallmarks of his style. Play over again any Bix solo, long or short, fast or slow; play any of the old Paul Whiteman records where Bix is section leader, and note with what subtlety and imagination he places the accents, not obviously and aggressively, but with delicacy and a sure touch—an almost imperceptible increase of pressure here, a slight change of metre there, a holding back or emphasis of a note or group of notes so that every phrase and sentence has a distinction and shape of its own. There is nothing mechanical, nothing stylized— only the ineffable, inexplicable, and at bottom miraculous touch of art. I am not pleading a cause: I am simply relying on simple observation of the kind that can easily be verified by anyone who has a mind to do it for themselves.

The question of accentuation is particularly important for the jazz musician because of the regularity of the basic beat. It is one of the most potent means whereby jazz is rhythmically freed from the Ixion wheel of a remorseless $\frac{4}{4}$. The vitality, the individuality of jazz playing is achieved through what may be seen as a species of 'sprung rhythm', familiar enough in poetry but less so (or less readily recognized as such) in music. By opposing the strict basic beat with a free metre in the melodic line a form of rhythmic counterpoint is, or should be, established. This, of course, is by no means confined to jazz; but it has particular relevance there precisely because of the essential strictness of the basic metre. When the 'set' metre is not complemented by a freer, more pliable, one, both tend to become mechanical. The music, in short, does not 'swing'. The plodding beat and mechanical stress which is so infuriating and enervating in mediocre jazz is not always and inevitably the fault of the rhythm section alone. For a jazz performance really to swing it is essential that both the rhythm section proper and the front line soloists and ensemble players bring meaningful and imaginative accentuation and shapeliness of phrase to the making of the whole. It is precisely here that so much commercial dance music and stereotyped jazz falls flat on its face (or perhaps more accurately, sits back on its leaden heels)—a mechanical beat is emphasized and rendered lethal by a mechanical accent. Much of the music of the now discredited swing era came to grief in just this very way. Perhaps the most awesome example was the Casa Loma Orchestra. During the hard times some of Bix's friends tried to get him a job with the Casa Loma. But even he jibbed at that, unemployed and near to down-and-out though he was. It was also, this mechanical element, one of the things against which the pioneers of bebop revolted.

It is a fascinating study to mark mentally the metrical stresses in a Bix performance, solo or ensemble; to note how, despite the frequently unregenerate rhythm sections, Bix invariably injected meaning and purpose into what would otherwise have remained the merest dull routine stuff. Often the rhythm men defeated his best endeavours. Even so, he himself usually manages to keep his own playing alive and positive. Especially revealing are those records on which Eddie Lang appears also, for Lang had many of Bix's own qualities and their names ought really to be coupled together whenever the talk turns towards the creation of an original style in white jazz. With Bix in the front line and Eddie Lang in the rhythm section a deal of mediocrity could be, and often was, not only covered over, but actually touched with reflected glory.

When we say that Bix dignified and made great the records on which he played and that without him they would have sunk into a merciful oblivion long since, we mean, though we may not realize it at the time, that Bix's innate sense of rhythmic accent quite as much as his gift for melody lies at the heart of the matter.

I have tried in the foregoing pages to see Bix plain and to see him whole as a jazz musician. I have tried to analyse his style, without prejudice or preconceived enthusiasms or antagonisms. He was essentially a subjective artist, an introvert; and it is always difficult to bring such men under the microscope of objective assessment. They commit themselves in their art and so engage our emotions directly and often fatally if we are critics seeking objective criteria. But it has to be done for all that. We do no disservice to a man's memory by submitting his style to the test of reasoned critical and analytical first principles. Rather do we justify him and ourselves in the sight of posterity by the better understanding exactly what he was about.

3

It is frequently said in disparagement of Bix that compared with what Louis Armstrong was doing at the same time his own achievement was considerably less memorable. And that, of course, is very true. But of who else in jazz do we not have to say at least as much, with the possible exceptions of Johnny Hodges and Coleman Hawkins? And this remains true of any period in jazz history, certainly until we come down to Dizzy Gillespie and Charlie Parker. If we do not keep the whole picture in perspective we are likely to land ourselves in endless entanglements, whatever or whomever we may at the moment chance to be discussing.

Before we can begin to make direct comparisons, odious or otherwise, we have first to discover just what Bix and Louis were and were not trying to do contemporaneously. During the time of Bix's highest fame Louis was fronting his immortal Hot Five (both periods) and Hot Seven groups. For the purposes of comparative study it is perhaps easiest to direct attention first to a collection of Hot Five recordings made in 1926, issued by Fontana on a 10-inch L.P., which consists of predominantly popular material of the day. Although this may not be quite of the quality of some other records of the same time which are confined to more authentically 'jazz' themes, notably blues, it is useful in that it enables us to study Louis playing roughly the same sort of tunes that Bix himself was using and was for most of his working life obliged to use. We may then pass on to the supreme Armstrong/Hines Hot Five of 1928 to see just how far in those two or three years Armstrong had carried his art forward to new and greenly fresh pastures. Bix, in roughly the same time, actually a little longer, passed from the happy collegiate days of the Wolverines to his subsequent dependence on the big white dance bands of the period. And at once we see that although Bix's personal artistry developed and matured to a great extent during these years, the context of the music he played advanced very little, whereas both Louis' personal art and the music he conceived in the broader sense showed a remarkable progression, due entirely to his dominating influence. Beginning from the basis of a more or less pure New Orleans style with the Dodds/Ory Hot Five Louis swiftly advanced to a virtuoso conception of jazz trumpet playing in which the supporting band tended more and more to become a setting for his own triumphant virtuosity. When in the early nineteen-thirties Louis started playing in front of big bands—Carrol Dickerson's or Luis Russell's —this process became finally consolidated. In a short time, therefore, Louis had led jazz right out of one basic conception and into another, at least from his own personal point of view. Whether one is 'better' than the other is not germane to our present argument.

Bix Beiderbecke, of course, led no such development of the basic matter of jazz playing and conception, partly because of his own character as man and artist, and partly because of the musical context to which he was tied during his lifetime. To that extent, then, Bix's achievement was not in the larger sense anything like so extensive as Armstrong's. All the same, we have to be careful to get our values right: we have to ask, not so much whether Bix was doing the same as Louis Armstrong, as whether or not he was doing something on his own of intrinsic value. As I say, neither he nor anyone else seriously challenged Louis as a breaker of new ground or as a jazz player *per se*; but that doesn't necessarily mean that he was not doing something different and something valuable in another direction, of less lasting significance though in the end it may be seen to be.

What then was Bix doing in these years when Louis Armstrong, both as trumpet player and jazz musician broadly considered, was continually revealing new and potent horizons? To put it plainly, Bix was forging an authentically white style in jazz which had he lived might well have developed on complementary lines to Armstrong's development of an authentically Negro style. I do not suggest that Bix was consciously forming such a style, that he sat himself down and took deliberate thought

on the subject, any more than Louis was consciously and with deliberate forethought establishing a Negro jazz style, which was in any case largely unnecessary. It was simply that Bix was freely and spontaneously expressing himself as a white man through the medium of jazz as he felt and understood it, just as Louis was freely and spontaneously expressing himself as a Negro through the same medium. We get far from the heart of the matter if we see either as consciously motivated builders, as much metaphysical as musical.

The difference between Bix and Louis as jazzmen was as much due to racial background and inheritance as to purely musical capability. There is nothing in Bix analogous to the superbly baroque art of a Louis Armstrong or a Bessie Smith. But that was not, as we have seen, because Bix lacked the technique for a baroque-like virtuosity, but simply because he didn't feel and conceive his music that way. Because he possessed autonomous talent and was an original stylist, Bix didn't play second-hand Negro jazz but authentic white jazz. Had he lived longer he might have led the way to a decisive complementary white jazz that would have saved his successors from a deal of vain floundering. Even in death he might have done as much had his colleagues and those who followed him really understood what he was doing and why he did it, instead of merely adoring him from a distance and not really listening to his music.

It is perhaps easiest to understand the achievement of Bix, considered in the context of jazz as a whole, by looking at it in reverse, so to speak; by seeing first what he did not do before going on to discover precisely what he did do. I have already mentioned the criticism of Bix that he lacked the 'rawness' so characteristic of Negro jazz. Exactly. But why did he lack or eschew it? Because it is something that belonged and belongs particularly to the Negro consciousness and racial inheritance. This 'rawness' had its origins (when it was genuine and not merely contrived) in the years of suffering and social injustice that were for so long the inescapable lot of the American Negro. It was (and is) the direct outcome of certain ways of life, and certain deeply ingrained aspects of thought and feeling, imposed on a people by largely external circumstances. There was behind it, especially in the early days, a fierce spirit of protest.

However, that kind of rawness and protest were never an integral part of the white consciousness—certainly not in that particular form. Of course, white men can and do suffer just as much as Negroes; and equally do they take on the dignity of deep suffering. So much is obvious and self-evident. But that suffering and such protest as may accompany it (and let us never make the mistake in either case of equating the protest with self-pity) do not emanate from the same source, and do not therefore assume the same spiritual and psychological directions. It is a difference in kind, not in degree. Therefore, when the white jazzman tries to simulate the raw edge or 'dirty' tone of the great Negro musicians it can usually be detected without difficulty and recognized as phoney. That Bix never did, and never tried to, approximate either in tone or in spirit to, say, the almost grotesque lamenting and passionate protest of a Bubber Miley or a Joe Nanton is not only obvious, but entirely to his credit. It is simply not for *any* white man to speak of these things. They are not his property.

Bix did not play the blues—not the real and authentic blues, spiritually rather than technically considered—for the ample reason that the true idiom of the blues lies outside the white consciousness, and Bix, because his genius was autonomous and original and in no sense derivative, did not try to appropriate something that did not belong to him. Instead, he created a form, or style, of his own through which he was able to fulfil himself creatively and at first hand. He understood instinctively that for the white man the problem is not how to play the blues as such, but how to achieve a form of imaginative identification, a process of translation, as it might best be described, through which the universal elements that lie behind the particular in all art forms, especially folk-based art forms, can be used as a starting point for personal creativity. The distinction is a subtle one; but it is fundamental. It marks the difference between new-minted and counterfeit coinage. Because Bix understood that difference—whether consciously or unconsciously makes no matter—he offered white jazz a solution of its basic problems, even though few of his successors took due note of it.

Although Bix was destroyed by the life he led, it was perhaps his real tragedy, not that he died young, but that the promise he held out for the future of white jazz was never fulfilled. Bix was betrayed by his own comrades (or by those who should have been his comrades, even after his death)—stabbed in the back and rendered more than ever lonely. For these men who could and should have followed the bright lead he gave them lacked, when the time of reckoning came, both the heart and the brains to go back to the source of the problem. Although there are honourable exceptions (Teagarden most times, although he really found a different solution and contrived brilliantly to throw a sort of bridge across the gulf by playing in the blues style without losing identity as a white man, and Benny Goodman on many of the small group sessions) most of them fell back on blatant imitation or cerebral cleverness in juggling with techniques derived from European 'straight' music, not used as a fertilizing element but as a simple and not very ingenious hideout for a lack of the true creative passion. We are no nearer the ideal today, despite much cleverness and more striving, mostly blind. In some ways we are farther than ever from it. At least in the early 'thirties a few musicians tried to play a music that was both jazz and white. But generally speaking, the real problem was and is avoided with care and determination.

Nowadays there are white jazzmen around in profusion, many of them intelligent men, capable and trying to be honest. They sense, if they do not come to grips with, their dilemma; but they can't face the implications. Much of the time they simply flatter by imitation either Negro jazz or European straight music, frequently both. Their situation is at bottom far more tragic than the Negro's ever was, race injustice and all. Their music is without roots and without background; therefore they experience endless difficulty in finding themselves artistically. Abracadabra traditionalism, abracadabra modernism; abracadabra Bach, abracadabra Stravinsky or Bartók—but it won't work. The Muse cannot be deceived and offered counterfeit coin. The gold must be minted true, as Bix in his brief day minted it, or it will be taken and used in evidence.

We may take a concrete example, a fair and representative one, by comparing the music of Dave Brubeck with the music of John Lewis and the Modern Jazz Quartet. The M.J.Q. music has its roots in the mother earth of jazz, for all its delicacy, its delving into musical history and its coming up with ideas from other ages and other cultures. Precisely because it has its beginnings in its ends and its ends in its beginnings it is among the most imaginatively creative jazz ever produced outside that of Duke Ellington. I am, of course, speaking at the moment largely of composed jazz, loosely but not inaccurately so called. From a strong, a well-cultivated native soil a man may legitimately go out into the world and do some extensive and far-flung agriculture; but without those roots and the consciousness of that soil and its meaning he is condemned all the days of his life to a species of localized market gardening which may in itself be delightful and diverting, but which can never be more than restricted and essentially of minor importance. It seems to me that this is just what has happened in the case of Brubeck. His music is unquestionably charming and entertaining. But it is at bottom no more. It is strong in overtones but weak in fundamentals; to change the metaphor, probably for the better—it lacks roots. Brubeck is an accomplished musician and an intelligent man; but he remains on the surface of art and creativity. He has raided the classics for his ideas; but whereas Lewis's premises give him the right so to do, Brubeck's don't. He, Brubeck, lays himself open to the charge of petty larceny; Lewis has won the freedom of the city and what he appropriates is in effect the common property of freemen, but of them only.

Bix was not in that sort of position, although he knew his way about in fields other than his own immediate ones. The point is that he too kept his roots in a propitious soil and although he went about his business in another way, as he had to in the circumstances, he still minted a true currency. But his lead wasn't followed by those who could most have benefited from it. It is the sharpest irony that white jazz fell into the sort of mechanical mannerisms of the 'swing' band age that Bix himself had refused to entertain when he declined to remain a member of the Casa Loma orchestra, even though at the time he was in sore need of secure employment. It was a passing phase of course, the 'swing' of the big white bands; but if they had taken heed of the example and the dire fate of Bix Beiderbecke those who became embroiled in it might well have saved themselves much trouble and disapproval. They took the easy way out; and as usual it landed them with big bank balances but small artistic credit.

It was, so I believe, Bix's greatest achievement as a jazz musician that he showed the way for the evolution of a genuine complementary white style in jazz that could, had he lived or had his example been understood—had, that is, his adorers and his detractors alike listened to his music instead of lamenting or sneering at him in his cups—have developed side by side with Negro jazz—have developed in equality and with dignity. That it wasn't to be so is neither here nor there: what matters is that the potentialities were revealed, and revealed by the ill-fated trumpeter, Bix Beiderbecke. None other to this day has done as much, quite apart from the actual quality of his playing as soloist and section man. These are two distinct, though interrelated, aspects of Bix's position in the history of the music we call jazz.

I have in the course of these pages suggested that elements of Bix's style may be found in latter-day jazz players, Negro as well as white. I could, of course, instance more; but a comparative inquiry of this kind is only incidental to my purpose. The relationship or correspondence with Rex Stewart may on the face of it seem enigmatic in view of my observations on the essential 'whiteness' of the music Bix habitually made. But we need to tread with caution here. Rex Stewart is more representative of Negro ebullience than of Negro tragedy. His style is comprehensively Negroid, but less conscious of the bitter fruits than is Armstrong's or Miley's. He can play the blues superbly, although his basic style opens outwards more readily. In any case, it is in the manner of their playing rather than its content that Bix and Rex Stewart often appear to be working in similar directions.

An interesting side-light is thrown on Bix's style and its inner impulses by a device very characteristic of him—I refer to the sudden octave flare-up through the valves which Bix so often uses climactically. There is a touch of the half-valve technique here; but the interest really lies in the psychological genesis of this habit. It was neither protest nor ebullience, pure and simple, though it probably contained elements of both. It seems more to have been a sort of sudden release of pressure, always judged beautifully in the musical context and no doubt engendered in part by the emotional reticence (not, I repeat, inhibition) Bix used deliberately to exploit. The device itself is a commonplace of jazz trumpet playing: it is the precise way that Bix used it which gives insight into his musical mind and method.

At the end there are two basic questions we are obliged to ask—(a) was Bix Beiderbecke a significant jazz musician in view of the work he actually did; and (b) did he contrive to fulfil himself and his true abilities? On the available evidence the answer in the first case must, I think, be yes; and in the second case, yes and no. That Bix contributed an original and significant trumpet style to the general jazz æsthetic seems hardly in dispute, although agreement as to its value may not be unanimous. It is not necessary to claim that a man does something absolutely *better* than anyone else: if he does it freshly, creatively, and personally that is enough. I hope I have by this time argued with some conviction that Bix did play his instrument with freshness and originality and that his style remains at least one to be reckoned with. But I have said enough on that subject and must turn now to the second question asked above.

That Bix fulfilled himself as a trumpet player in the short time granted to him is fairly clear. His playing emerges as an intensely personal and private occupation, as well as a public entertainment. In this he resembles other great jazzmen as far removed in style and technique as Johnny Hodges, Bud Powell, and Milt Jackson. He played from the heart, from the inside: he was compelled to play as he did, not because he had worked it all out beforehand and thought it a clever thing to do, but quite simply because his innermost artistic impulses obliged him so to do. To this extent his music was a fulfilment of his life. But we cannot, so it seems to me, let it rest there. Much though he did to bring his talent to fulfilment, there is another sense in which he left a good deal undone that there was in him to do. It was not lack of technique that held him back, as we have already observed; it was something much deeper-seated inside him, more fundamental to his particular personality, and something he might never have overcome even if he had lived a full life's span.

I take with a grain of salt the familiar idea that Bix could only with difficulty read music and that he had small idea of music theory. I suspect, more on the evidence of his piano than his trumpet playing, that Bix knew pretty well what notes were about even though he often chose to keep that knowledge to himself. I fancy that in the musical circumstances in which he most times found himself he elected not to have more to do than he could reasonably help with the mastering of complicated written scores. He was not interested in the sort of 'symphonic jazz' frequently in favour with his employers and so didn't bother to come to grips with it. But the nature of his musical faculties suggests that had he taken the trouble before declining health and stamina made the task too formidable he might well have done both himself and his music much enduring good. His reluctance was a mistake; and in the end he knew it and suffered on its account. The tragedy is that by the time he realized what he needed to do his health defeated him and he couldn't make the effort. It wasn't that he lacked the taste for hard labour—indeed, he seems always to have been happiest and most at peace with himself when he was working. But he appears to have lacked the capacity for constant application. He was an indolent fellow, charming but wayward; he took decisions but was too easily side-tracked and regularly forgot what he had with such mightily good intentions decided on. And then, as I say, it was too late.

Bix was familiar with and deeply affected by the music of the contemporary masters of 'straight' music—with Debussy and Ravel and Stravinsky and some of the leading American composers such as Macdowell and Eastwood Lane. It was this side of his talent that he neglected and eventually allowed to run to seed. Had he not done so I believe he might well have turned to jazz composition and even have done for white jazz something of what Duke Ellington has done for Negro jazz. It is a large claim, I admit; but the ingredients were there—they only needed determined mixing. His few published piano pieces give hints of what might and could have been. In them Bix in many ways anticipates by a quarter of a century the modern infusion of fruitful influences from other musical fields into the living body of jazz which have opened up new potentialities, if they have also proved a snare and a delusion in unregenerate hands. Bix's native talents suggest unmistakably that had he persevered such music as he might have composed would have been truly fresh, original, and creative—as his trumpet playing most assuredly was.

There is, however, another point to be considered. Nothing we know about Bix leads us to believe that he was a born band leader, and the jazz composer has, generally speaking, to create both his music and the means for presenting it. Again the case of Duke Ellington springs inevitably to mind. Duke's orchestra is a direct and necessary extension of his musical personality. The same may be said, if to a slightly less extent, of the Modern Jazz Quartet, which has grown to strength and significance as a vehicle for the composing abilities of John Lewis. It seems that some such process is essential for the sure development of a jazz composer (as opposed to a jazz arranger). Even minor jazz composers, such as abound nowadays, have to face the problem, and may usually be found trying to do so with more or less successful results.

Could Bix have done the same? On the whole I doubt it. He was not a dominating personality. The records made by his own groups show small sense of leadership on his part—perhaps that is why they never contrived to make more than a negative impression and remain valuable only for Bix's contributions as soloist and ensemble player. It is the fashion among critics to expect every good jazz soloist to go about the place leading his own band. But not all men are made that way: some are born leaders, others are not. I suspect that Johnny Hodges is one who does not take naturally to band leadership. His own groups have produced some fine music; but he is essentially a quiet and undemonstrative man, often on the stand almost to the point of indifference, and he seems to do most justice to his unique artistry as a member of the Ellington orchestra. Bix, I think, was a similar case. He certainly had not Armstrong's capacity for dominating, musically speaking, the groups in which he played.

Bix simply wasn't cut out to lead so unruly and complex an affair as a modern jazz orchestra. For one thing he was too careless over detail ever to be an organizer, still less an employer of labour, willing or unwilling. On the occasions when he was charged with the arrangement of recording sessions he got into tangles. Jack Teagarden tells the story of how Bix telephoned him one day. Bix was in need of a trombonist for a record date: he wanted Teagarden, who was glad to oblige. Off went Bix, apparently happy. But he quickly forgot all about his previous exertions. He suddenly remembered that he needed a trombonist, whereupon he asked Tommy Dorsey to be present. But a while later in the day he was visited by inspiration a third time, and asked yet another trombone player to assist at the corporate effort, having let both the previous requests slip from his mind. If I remember aright, Teagarden says that

the problem of three trombonists present when only one was required was solved on the spot by giving each in turn a part in the subsequent proceedings. Internal evidence suggests that the sessions were the late ones by Hoagy Carmichael's Orchestra and that the third trombone man was Boyce Cullen. The story is certainly authentic—Teagarden tells it at first hand.

That sort of behaviour was entirely characteristic of Bix: he was like that—a rum sort of individual and something of an eccentric. He had sterling qualities and was beloved of his friends; but that didn't and couldn't in itself make him a natural leader of men and musicians. His cornet style was forceful enough. He has suffered from the one-eyed view of him that has arisen since his death and which represents him as a charming, reticent, and at bottom unassertive soloist—as a sort of white Arthur Whetsol, a gentle and melancholy player. But that is not the full Bix; it is at best only one side of him. He could also be strong, pungent, and robust—his style had guts. Even at the end, when his health was gone, he could suddenly flare up and play with much of the old fire. Among his last records were those made with Hoagy Carmichael's pick-up groups, and on one of these, the otherwise preposterous *Barnacle Bill, the Sailor*, Bix unleashes a splendid solo—fresh, vital, and propulsive, and about as 'cool' as a cat on a hot tin roof. Although the bright flame of his genius was burnt out, it could still be revived on occasion, if not in any state of permanence.

Bix, as we have seen, was a fine ensemble player and a richly imaginative soloist; but for the development of his full talents he needed better stimuli than he ever found during his active life. His association with Frankie Trumbauer was really a good deal less fruitful than on the surface it has come to seem. At the beginning Bix and 'Tram' complemented each other admirably. But later on divergences appeared which tended to leave Bix out in the cold. Trumbauer's later excursions carried his music a good way from jazz as Bix loved, understood, and wanted to play it. After Bix's death Trumbauer gradually faded out of jazz altogether. He lost direction and clarity of purpose, the simple directness and emotional expressiveness of true jazz, whether played by Bix, Armstrong, or Ellington. Thus Bix wanted for musical sympathy and support when he needed it most and where he most expected to find it. Even more is this true of the Whiteman band as a whole. Had he been able to find the right situation and the right circumstances he might never have succumbed to the temptations which destroyed him. If his destiny had led him to where he could have found associates playing music with which he could have absolutely identified himself, he might conceivably have found the moral and intellectual strength to prosper as man and musician. But that wasn't to be. The lead Bix gave to the music he loved and which he played with a natural and spontaneous ease was not followed by his contemporaries, any more than it was subsequently followed by those who came after him.

If we look for a last time at the musical scene of which Bix was a part, it is difficult to see just where he could have found the right and propitious conditions. The big white bands of the day offered him no real scope; and as he went on the opportunities became less and less. The social scene was changing and with it the popular music. Even if Bix had retained his health he would have experienced some difficulty in surviving the changes and maintaining his artistic integrity. Wanting that strength of character and continued health he found the going too hard and perished as a result.

Bix Beiderbecke
on Records

Bix's best records have had an erratic career in the British catalogues. During the nineteen-thirties a number remained available; those that weren't frequently fetched exalted prices among jazz collectors. When the fashion turned against white jazz in general interest not unnaturally declined. Then came the long-playing record and Bix, like other jazzmen of an older period, came back into circulation so that for a few years a large part of his best recorded work was in free circulation. However, the considerable reorganizations and changes of copyright that have since taken place in the British record industry have resulted in many of them coming into the deletions lists. Today the position is not very satisfactory. The two L.P.s still in the catalogues overlap to a considerable extent, and there are no examples currently available of his mature work with the Paul Whiteman orchestra during its contract with Victor, which from the jazz viewpoint was considerably more interesting than the subsequent American Columbia period. Therefore, I propose to divide this select discography into two parts—the first will contain a listing by titles and record numbers only of all the microgroove selections that are or have been released on the British market; and

secondly I shall break down those which remain available, giving full details of personnel and dates. At the end I shall give a short list of recordings by other jazzmen which have relevance to the arguments advanced in the text and which can be usefully employed as illustrations of various points of criticism and analysis. The symbol (D) following a record number indicates that the disc has been deleted from the British catalogues. But since copies may still be found in dealers' back stocks or on the shelves of second-hand record shops I have included them for reference. Also, it is possible that some of them may be re-issued at some time or other. This applies particularly to the valuable collection 'Salute to Bix', originally issued by H.M.V. This is no longer in the catalogues; but it, or something similar, could well find its way back into circulation on the R.C.A. label, which is now controlled in England by the Decca group. As much, unfortunately, cannot be said for the prospects of the two 10-inch L.P.s of the Wolverines once issued in the London 'Origins of Jazz' series but now deleted. Thus a big gap in our knowledge of Bix's playing exists and may not soon be filled.

BIX BEIDERBECKE ON MICROGROOVE

The following is a complete list of all long play items on which Bix Beiderbecke is featured at the time of going to press.

THE BIX BEIDERBECKE STORY, VOL. 1
BIX AND HIS GANG

Jazz Me Blues; Louisiana; Sorry; Thou Swell; Somebody Stole My Gal; Royal Garden Blues; At The Jazz Band Ball; Since My Best Gal Turned Me Down; Wa-Da-Da; Goose Pimples; Rhythm King   Columbia CL-844

THE BIX BEIDERBECKE STORY, VOL. 2
BIX AND TRAM

Singin' The Blues; Clarinet Marmalade; Way Down Yonder In New Orleans; Mississippi Mud; For No Reason At All In C; There'll Come A Time; I'm Comin' Virginia; Ostrich Walk; A Good Man Is Hard To Find; Wringin' And Twistin'; Crying All Day; Riverboat Shuffle
Columbia CL-845

THE BIX BEIDERBECKE STORY, VOL. 3
WHITEMAN DAYS

Margie; Take Your Tomorrow; Borneo; Bless You! Sister; Baby, Won't You Please Come Home; 'Taint So, Honey, 'Taint So; That's My Weakness Now; Sweet Sue; China Boy; Because My Baby Don't Mean Maybe Now; Oh, Miss Hannah   Columbia CL-846

THESAURUS OF CLASSICAL JAZZ

Three Blind Mice

Columbia C47-18

JAZZ PIANO ANTHOLOGY

In a Mist

Columbia KG 32355

Note: As a member of Paul Whiteman's Orchestra between 1928 and 1929, Beiderbecke may be heard on other recordings made by the orchestra during that period, including *Paul Whiteman Vol. 2*, RCA Victor LPV 570.

Following albums are no longer available:

BIX BEIDERBECKE AND THE WOLVERINES

Fidgety Feet; Jazz Me Blues; Oh, Baby; Copenhagen; Riverboat Shuffle; Susie; Royal Garden Blues; Tiger Rag; Sensation Rag; Lazy Daddy; Tia Juana; Big Boy   Riverside RLP 12-123

ON THE ROAD JAZZ

I'm Glad; Flock o'Blues (Sioux City Six); *Davenport Blues; Toddlin' Blues* (Bix and his Rhythm Jugglers) (other tracks by Wingy Manone and Charlie Pierce)
Riverside RLP 12-127

THE BIX BEIDERBECKE LEGEND

Jean Goldkette Orch.: *Clementine; I Didn't Know; Sunday;* Paul Whiteman Orch.: *Changes* (take 2); *Lonely Melody* (takes 3 and 1); *From Monday On; There Ain't No Sweet Man that's Worth the Salt of My Tears; San; Dardanella; You Took Advantage of Me;* Hoagy Carmichael Orch.: *I'll Be a Friend (with Pleasure)*   RCA Victor LPM2323

II

DATES AND PERSONNELS OF ALL AVAILABLE MICROGROOVE ISSUES

Instrument key: (*alt*) alto-saxophone; (*bj*) banjo; (*bs-sx*) bass saxophone; (*c-mel*) c-melody saxophone (*clt*) clarinet;

(cnt) cornet; (d) drums (g) guitar; (p) piano; (tbn) trombone; (ten) tenor saxophone; (tpt) trumpet; (tu) tuba; (vcl) vocal; (vln) violin.

FRANKIE TRUMBAUER AND HIS ORCHESTRA

Bix Beiderbecke (cnt); Bill Rank (tbn); Frank Trumbauer (c-mel); Doc Ryker (alt); Jimmy Dorsey (clt); Paul Mertz (p); Howdy Quicksell (bj); Chauncey Morehouse (d)   New York City, February 4, 1927

    Clarinet Marmalade
    Co CL-845

Izzy Riskin (p); Eddie Lang (g) replace Mertz and Quicksell   Same date

    Singin' The Blues
    Co CL-845

Don Murray (clt, sax) replaces Dorsey; probably Red Ingle (alt) replaces Ryker   New York City, May 9, 1927

    Ostrich Walk
    Co CL-845
    Riverboat Shuffle
    Co CL-845

Same personnel as last   New York City, May 13, 1927

    I'm Comin' Virginia
    Co CL-845
    Way Down Yonder In New Orleans
    Co CL-845

Bix Beiderbecke (cnt, p); Frank Trumbauer (c-mel); Eddie Lang (g)   Same date

    For No Reason At All In C
    Co CL-845

Same Trumbauer Orchestra personnel as May 13, 1927, except Doc Ryker (alt) returns; Adrian Rollini (bs-sx) added
            New York City, Aug. 25, 1927

    Three Blind Mice
    Co C47–18

Bix Beiderbecke (p)   New York City, Sept. 9, 1927
    In a Mist
    Co KG 32355

Bix Beiderbecke (cnt, p); Frankie Trumbauer (c-mel); Eddie Lang (g)   New York City, Sept. 17, 1927

            New York City, September 17, 1927
    Wringin' And Twistin'
    Co CL-845

BIX BEIDERBECKE AND HIS GANG

Bix Beiderbecke (cnt); Bill Rank (tbn); Don Murray (clt); Frank Signorelli (p); Adrian Rollini (bs-sx);

Chauncey Morehouse (d)   New York City, October 5, 1927
    At The Jazz Band Ball
    Co CL-844
    Royal Garden Blues
    Co CL-844
    Jazz Me Blues
    Co CL-844

            New York City, October 25, 1927
    Goose Pimples
    Co CL-844
    Sorry
    Co CL-844
    Since My Best Gal Turned Me Down
    Co CL-844

FRANKIE TRUMBAUER AND HIS ORCHESTRA

Bix Beiderbecke (cnt); Bill Rank (tbn); Don Murray, Pee Wee Russell (clt, sax); Frank Trumbauer (c-mel); Doc Ryker (alt); Joe Venuti (vln); Arthur Schutt (p); Eddie Lang (g); Adrian Rollini (bs-sx); Chauncey Morehouse (d)   New York City, October 25, 1927

    Cryin' All Day
    Co CL-845
    A Good Man Is Hard To Find
    Co CL-845

Bix Beiderbecke (cnt); Harry Goldfield (cnt); Bill Rank (tbn); Jimmy Dorsey (clt); Frank Trumbauer (c-mel); Harold Strickfadden (alt); Matty Malneck (vln); Lennie Hayton (p); Eddie Lang (g); Min Leibrook (bs-sx); George Marsh (d)   New York City, January 9, 1928

    There'll Come A Time
    Co CL-845

Bix Beiderbecke (cnt); Bill Rank (tbn); Frank Trumbauer (c-mel); Matty Malneck (vln); Carl Kress (g); Min Leibrook (bs-sx); Harold Macdonald (d); Bing Crosby and Frank Trumbauer (vcl)
            New York City, January 20, 1928

    Mississippi Mud
    Co CL-845

BIX BEIDERBECKE AND HIS GANG

Bix Beiderbecke (cnt); Bill Rank (tbn); Izzy Freidman (clt); Lennie Hayton or Tom Satterfield (p); Min Leibrook (bs-sx); George Marsh (d)
            New York City, April 17, 1928

    Somebody Stole My Gal
    Co CL-844
    Thou Swell
    Co CL-844

Harry Gale (d) replaces Marsh

New York City, July 7, 1928

Wa-Da-Da
Co CL-844

Roy Bargy (p); George Marsh (d) replace Hayton and Gale   New York City, September 21, 1928

Rhythm King
Co CL-844

Louisiana
Co CL-844

Note: The eleven titles by Paul Whiteman's Orchestra (Co CL-846) were made between May 1928 and May 1929. This was a large commercial dance orchestra and there is little point in listing full personnels, particularly as the only value of the records lies in the occasional Beiderbecke solos.

Miles Davis

BY MICHAEL JAMES

ACKNOWLEDGEMENTS

I am indebted to Messrs. Ira Gitler, Don Gold and Nat Hentoff for their kindness in providing me with information on Davis's career.

M.J.

Not many musicians could advance claims that their music had durably changed the course of jazz history. If we are to except the outstanding soloists such as Armstrong, Hawkins, Lester Young and Parker, it might well be said that influence has been more a matter of constant give-and-take than a division of musical practice into a large number of stylistic cliques, each with its acknowledged leader. Not that this never happens, however. Tristano is the obvious example of a man who was able to found an esoteric school within the broader sweep of his generation's style; and Eddie Condon, I suppose, has done something of the same, though in a less systematic way.

Miles Davis's most ardent admirer would hardly assert that his impact on jazz has been as great as that of the four soloists mentioned above. Yet he has contrived to secure for himself an imposing reputation, not with the breathtaking confidence of the giants, but with the purposefulness of the man who knows full well his direction and his object, though perhaps uncertain for a time of the ways and means of getting there. Today, at the comparatively young age of thirty-four, Miles Davis is an acknowledged leader of contemporary jazz thought, with a body of recorded work to his credit that corroborates the justice of this general view. And it does so not by its quality alone, for Davis has set down some dismal passages on record, but also by

the unerring sense of purpose it reveals, a single-mindedness untouched by fashion or the lure of monetary gain. Trumpeters as diverse as Art Farmer and Bill Hardman throw off occasional reflections of his style. Lesser performers on the same instrument dutifully produce carbons of his phrasing. The rebel of yesteryear, once confined to an economic wilderness of his own making, has somehow become the cynosure of the younger generation. The old, familiar, ironic tale, one might say, but with a new twist; Davis, arrived at last, is no pathetic shadow of his former self. The odds, in fact, are that he still has much to give.

The critic's task is not always a pleasant one. The musician who passes from inexperience to maturity, and then on to dreary repetition, is no figment of the novelist's imagination. He exists; and it is the writer's job to sift the good in his work from the bad, with understanding, certainly, but never with cowardice. Many jazzmen have found cause to complain of the unadventurousness of the audience; how it will demand the same tunes, the same arrangements, and sometimes the same solos. To stabilize one's playing in the interests of financial security must be an ever-present temptation to the successful musician, and stability, artificially induced, can have the worst effects. Only in recent years, I think, has Davis come up with records that conform to this stereotype, and their number is so very few that it would be absurd to suggest his talents have now run their course. 'What's all the fuss? I always play like that,' he sneered after an unusually warm reception at the 1955 Newport Jazz Festival. Commercial success or not, Davis has shunned concession: this particular event was the first time for years that he had been acclaimed by the jazz audience at large. It heralded an era of good money and steady work, yet made no difference to his basic attitude. By refusing to compromise, he has forged an intensely original style; and, more important, this style of his is obviously the perfect vehicle for what he has to say on his horn. The terms are far from mutually exclusive, I know, but there is a good case for claiming that the form of Davis's work has always been at the service of content: after all, this is only another way of saying that his expression has developed *from within*. From the first his borrowings were few and far between. Plagiarism, even in its mildest sense, is anathema to him. Here is the explanation of those nagging instrumental faults which have only recently been expunged from his work: no ready-made techniques would do. Such errors were perhaps the price of the very personal integrity that marked Davis off from the general run of musicians. At all events, they pale into insignificance beside the persuasiveness of the best of his recorded work.

Miles Dewey Davis was born on 25 May 1926, in Alton, Illinois. The following year his father, a fairly well-to-do dentist, moved his practice to East St. Louis, where Miles spent an uneventful childhood together with his elder sister Dorothy, and Vernon, a younger brother. His career got off to a slow and laborious start when his father gave him a trumpet for his thirteenth birthday. He had music lessons at school and also learned from an elementary chord book. In 1941 he began to work locally with Eddie Randolph's Blue Devils and subsequently got to know Clark Terry and Sonny Stitt; later he played with Adam Lambert in Springfield, Illinois. Judging from remarks he has passed in recent years, his budding interest in jazz was far from arousing general enthusiasm in the Davis household. It is generally acknowledged that his mother wished him to go on to study at Fisk University. 'She always used to look as if she'd hit me every time I played my horn,'[1] Davis said later. One is apt to forget that it is not the white American bourgeoisie alone which sometimes tends to look askance on jazz. Yet if his mother had misgivings about the vocation he had chosen, they were fortunately indecisive, and this in spite of the tardy progress he made. When Billy Eckstine's big band played St. Louis some time after its inception in the summer of 1944, the leader remained singularly unimpressed. 'He used to ask to sit in with the band,' Eckstine said. 'I'd let him so as not to hurt his feelings, because then Miles was awful. He sounded terrible, he couldn't play at all.'[2] By this time Davis had been studying the trumpet for upwards of five years, so it is readily apparent that the control he eventually gained over the instrument was hard-won indeed. One should remember, however, that he did receive an offer from Tiny Bradshaw, but his mother, insisting he finish his final year of high school, refused to let him go.

By now it must have been obvious to both his parents that his mind was firmly set on a musical career. In due course they yielded to his entreaties and he left for New York to enrol at the Juillard Institute. It is easy to tell where his immediate loyalties lay from the fact that he spent his first week in the city and the whole of his first month's allowance searching for Charlie Parker. Hitherto he had taken Roy Eldridge for a model, but both Parker and Gillespie had encouraged him, and his allegiance was very rapidly transferred to these two innovators of the day. Despite his immaturity there was something in the work of the youngster of nineteen that these comparative veterans must have

[1] *Esquire*, March 1959.
[2] *Melody Maker*, 4 September 1954.

78

felt was worth fostering. Thelonious Monk, too, took an interest in him. 'Monk has really helped me,' he told Nat Hentoff in a recent interview. 'When I came to New York he taught me chords and his tunes.'[1]

His first records show that his harmonic awareness was growing fast but also reveal lapses in technique, though these, strangely enough, are by no means so flagrant as on the later Parker quintet sides made for the Dial and Savoy companies. It might be as well to mention in passing that there is some doubt as to whether the November 1945 session under Parker's name was in fact the first on which Davis played. Jorgen Grunnet Jepsen, the Danish discographer, includes him among the personnel of a Herbie Fields group which made four titles for Savoy earlier in the year, though it had previously been thought that Snooky Young was the trumpeter on this date. Others have discounted this suggestion. The records are now unobtainable and until one or another of the musicians concerned enlightens us, the question must remain open. By a curious coincidence there has also been disagreement amongst collectors as to whether Gillespie rather than Davis played the trumpet solos on the November session for the same label. This matter was settled by pianist Sadik Hakim (formerly known as Argonne Thornton) who himself was present and shared the keyboard duties with Dizzy Gillespie. He confirmed[2] that Gillespie played trumpet only on *Ko Ko* and that Davis was responsible for all the other trumpet solos.

Generally speaking, his choice of notes shows that his harmonic thinking was certainly advanced for the time, but on *Billie's Bounce*, for example, his clumsy playing reveals his inexperience. Boldly asymmetrical, Parker's phrases nonetheless have a finished sheen to them. Without being anything like so adventurous, those Davis employs often seem to end in a very uncomfortable way; the pianist and drummer are left to fill in the gap as best they can. He also makes widespread use of two-note riffs throughout his choruses, a device which, like the repeated note motif J. J. Johnson was currently using, cleverly disguised his inability to fashion a more complex melodic line. Despite the fluent playing on all three versions of *Thriving From a Riff*, it is apparent that Davis lacked the instrumental virtuosity of men like Navarro or Shavers, nor is this at all surprising when one thinks how young he was.

All the more credit is due to him, then, for creating two excellent choruses on the fourth version of *Now's the Time*. In this one instance it is as though he had taken stock of his limitations yet had refused to be discouraged by them. His smooth yet broad tone goes hand in hand with the simple phrasing to evoke a highly distinctive emotional climate. Elsewhere on the session he occasionally echoes Gillespie, but here, despite his use of the high register, it is easy to discern the beginnings of an original style, much as his music was to change and develop in the years to come. One of the chief reasons for this is that the tempo, and the melodic shapes he favours in this case give greater latitude to his tone, which from the days of his apprenticeship onward has always been a vital part of his equipment. Davis has never been interested in a pronounced vibrato. His tutor had encouraged him to aim for a smooth, unruffled sound, and his admiration for Freddy Webster's playing set the seal on this aspect of his playing. Yet his eschewal of vibrato, novel as it was, did not mean that his improvisations lacked personality. On the contrary, he had already developed a tone whose character was remarkably affecting in the context of the other features of his work. Many of his contemporaries were to neglect tonal considerations in their desire to emulate Gillespie's achievements in harmonic and melodic fields. Davis, it is clear, fell into no such error, and in this respect his solo on the final version of *Now's the Time* seems decidedly prophetic.

Not only did Davis work with Parker during this, his first visit to New York, he also played with Coleman Hawkins and Eddie 'Lockjaw' Davis. Towards

---

[1] *Jazz Review*, December 1958.
[2] *Jazz Review*, February 1959.

the close of 1945 Gillespie and Parker left New York to travel to California where they were booked into Billy Berg's club in Hollywood. Davis returned to St. Louis and soon afterwards joined Benny Carter's band, which was also headed for the Pacific coast. He left the altoist after a few weeks, however, and for the greater part of the year was unemployed, working from time to time with Parker, who had stayed in California when Gillespie and the rest of the band returned to New York. It was during this period that he recorded for Ross Russell's newly formed Dial company. The material for the session, which took place on 28 March 1946, comprised four tunes. Despite the generally suitable context—the band included Parker, Lucky Thompson, and a sympathetic rhythm section, with Roy Porter's drumming outstanding—Davis's playing shows no great melodic advance and not one of his solos bears comparison with the aforementioned *Now's the Time*. Indeed, when one comes to relate this success to the body of his recorded work from 1946 to 1948, one is forced to conclude that it was something of a flash in the pan; or perhaps it would be more exact to suggest that after having experienced the musical ferment that was taking place in New York during 1945, he was led drastically to revise his basic thinking, to aim for more complicated melodic structures than he had previously envisaged. Doubtless the demands this widening of musical horizons imposed on him in terms of instrumental ability, made it impossible, temporarily at least, for him to produce quite as balanced a performance as that earlier solo.

The fourth take of *Ornithology* shows that he had already started to branch out along unfamiliar paths. His solo is by no means impressive, but its construction is less conventional than had previously been the case, since he forms his phrases without making them conform strictly to the usual sections of four or eight bars. His tone, too, had altered. On the earlier session it had been fairly broad; now it was smaller and more mellow, and though this change detracted from the power of his playing, it seems clear in retrospect that it was a necessary step along the road towards the very personal sound he was eventually to achieve. By this time he was restricting himself to the lower and middle registers of the trumpet. Could it be, perhaps, that he already felt a more aggressive approach to his instrument would make it all the harder for him to develop the tonal quality he desired?

In the summer of 1946 Davis joined Eckstine, taking over the solo book that had first been Gillespie's and later Fats Navarro's. We have the leader's word for it that by then he was a much-improved musician, and he stayed with the band until it broke up in the early part of 1947. Throughout this period Parker had been in hospital following his collapse at a record session for Ross Russell's Dial label. Soon after he recovered, he returned to New York and formed a quintet with Duke Jordan, Tommy Potter, Max Roach and Miles Davis. It was with this quintet that Davis was to spend the next eighteen months. The challenge was a formidable one for so young a musician and it is easy to believe that there were times when he felt inadequate to the task. His solo work on the records made for Dial and Savoy in 1947 and 1948 is characterized by many weaknesses, but looking back there can be no doubt that the experience he gained in Parker's band and the many lessons he learned were to have a crucial effect upon his subsequent career.

Whatever doubts may have been entertained at the time—for this was the period when Stan Kenton's orchestra was at the zenith of its popularity—it is now quite clear that throughout its existence, the Parker quintet's music embodied the most advanced trends in jazz development. The presence of the altoist himself, of course, was the chief reason for this. With his unprecedented departures in the fields of harmony, rhythm, and phrase distribution, he was opening up vistas that a younger generation of musicians were still to find absorbing long after his untimely death in 1955.

Next to the leader, Max Roach played the most important role. His resourceful imagination and vast technical powers, allied to an insistent swing, enabled him to function as a secondary voice to the horns and piano. Set out in series or isolated with telling succinctness in the form of punctuations, his cross-rhythms were an indispensable part of the quintet's aesthetic. Tommy Potter provided a sound foundation with his keen ear and large tone, whilst in Duke Jordan, as in Al Haig and John Lewis, who also played piano with the group at a later date, Parker had accompanists of rare sympathy and understanding. It is beyond doubt that Davis was the least proficient of the band's members; at the same time his devotion to the music and the growing emotional power of his playing partly atoned for his shortcomings on a technical level.

It should not be imagined, following upon the previous remarks, that the trumpeter's ability to play his instrument was in any way negligible. Whilst inferior to both Gillespie and Fats Navarro, in this respect he was no mere fumbler, as even the first recording session undertaken by the new quintet shows. Granted there are raw edges to the unison sound, but he negotiates the complex melodic line of *Donna Lee* to the listener's satisfaction. His solos on takes two to four of this tune are marred by split notes and faulty intonation, but his invention on the first version, somewhat more intricate melodically than on the sides made at the Dial date of the previous year, comes over fairly well. There are other signs of his having developed, too: the persuasive intimacy of his lower register tone on extended notes, which was eventually to become so characteristic a feature of his style, may be heard in embryo notably on the second take of *Chasing the Bird*. The above are significant aspects of his playing and foreshadow his later maturity, but the most convincing solo he set down on this occasion is to be heard in *Cheryl*. His three choruses on the complete version of this blues theme are not free from the faults already described, but their overall effect is, I think, a memorable one. The lyrical bent to his temperament was beginning to make itself felt and contrasts effectively with the dramatic starkness of Parker's playing.

Before going on to consider the principal ways in which Davis developed during the time he spent in Parker's quintet, it is well worth while investigating the August 1947 recording session, which was the first on which he appeared as leader. On this occasion Parker played tenor saxophone instead of his usual alto, John Lewis replaced Duke Jordan at the piano, and Nelson Boyd took over from Tommy Potter on bass. More important than these personnel changes, however, was the difference in nature of the thematic material used. If we are to judge from the body of its recorded work, Parker's group featured in its repertoire a very high proportion of blues, together with a number of slow ballads, such as *My Old Flame* and *Don't Blame Me*, and several original tunes based on the chord sequence of familiar melodies like *I Got Rhythm* or *Honeysuckle Rose*. The four sequences on which the musicians improvised at this session were therefore far from typical. *Sippin' at Bell's* is indeed a blues, but with altered changes, whilst the other three compositions are more sophisticated in character than those Parker generally preferred. He would imply all manner of passing chords in his solos, of course, but the themes he used were rarely so harmonically dense as the ones Davis chose for this session. Although the trumpeter performs with great care, he can hardly be said to excel himself. He makes very little use of rests and at the fast tempo of *Little Willie Leaps* his playing is altogether devoid of swing. Both versions of *Milestones* contain sober and intelligent trumpet improvisations, but there is no doubt that the prime interest of the session resides in the pointers it gives to his future activities. The relatively contrived material foreshadows the repertory of the orchestra he was to lead just over a year later at the Royal Roost.

It is hardly an exaggeration to say that when Davis rejoined Parker in early 1947, he had precious little individuality as a soloist; and that when he left the band some fifteen months or so later, he was fast emerging as a highly distinctive musician and an influence in his own right. Perhaps this is putting it a trifle too blandly, for he had never been a wholly derivative stylist, but few will contest that the experience he gained during this period was of capital importance. Disinterested he may have been by his continual inability, night after night, to measure up to the standards of the other men, but the intense competition and electrically-charged musical climate forced him into new and unconventional ways of thinking, taught him many lessons he could have learned nowhere save in the immediate context of Parker's band.

The most radical change in his playing over this period concerned the melodic line of his improvisations. Much earlier, Gillespie had recommended him to study piano, so that he would gain a better understanding of how to build up a solo from the underlying harmonic framework, and there is every reason to think he had profited from this advice. Yet until the closing months of 1947, as far as we are able to tell, there was scant variety in the time value of the notes he used, nor did he make very much use of rests to throw his phrases into any sort of relief. In many cases, especially at faster tempo, he would content himself with a drab procession of quavers. Now, with Parker's brilliant example constantly before him, he was not only expanding his limited vocabulary but also constructing his solos out of phrases of pleasingly diverse length. The E take of *Air Conditioning* and both versions of *Blue Bird* illustrate particularly well the extra interest this lent to his work. In musical surrounds where the asymmetrical melodic line was commonplace, he had every reason to cultivate the virtues of asymmetry.

A slow yet very significant improvement in tonal control, abetted by the growing use of inflexion, is also revealed by records made during the period under review. This development should not necessarily be ascribed to Parker's example, for such methods have a time-honoured place in jazz history, but we should remember that the altoist, true to his Kansas City origins, had always favoured a vocalized sound even if this did not take the form of a fierce vibrato, and it would probably be wrong to discount his influence altogether. When he first came to New York, Davis had been very enthusiastic about Freddy Webster's tone, and Sadik Hakim also tells us that he greatly admired Lester Young. Since then he had evidently aimed for a calm, unruffled sound, smooth in texture and free from vibrato. For much of the time, though, he had merely succeeded in eliciting from his trumpet a tone that was dull rather than forlorn, muddy rather than serene. By late 1947 the purpose underlying his rejection of the more traditional trumpet tone was finally becoming clear. At slow tempo, as, for example, in *Embraceable You*, he was obtaining an attractive glowing sound that was as expressive in its own way as the vibrant richness of Louis Armstrong's, or the singing clarity of Howard McGhee's.

It is perhaps a trifle misleading to say that there was yet another way in which his style began to mature in these two years, for the quality of resilience that began to mark his playing did not depend on such intangibles as attack and relaxation of delivery alone; it relied just as much upon the developments in phrase distribution and tone noted above. By speaking of it as though it were an altogether distinct facet, however, one at least emphasizes the new-found flexibility of his music. Although swing, as we understand the term from the playing of Harry Edison or Dizzy Gillespie, had never been nor was ever to be his forte, there is a definite pulsation about certain of his solos that derives both from an improved sense of timing and a continual slackening and tightening of the improvised line in relation to the beat. A similar style of phrasing was favoured by Lester Young in these years: listen to *Blues 'n' Bells* or *June Bug*, for example. By means of such a method the soloist introduces a greater variety of melodic shapes without forgoing the direct physical impact of a regular beat. Parker himself, of course, took the process a good deal further; his acute sense of time and magnificent technique enabled him to suggest two or even three *rhythms* within the compass of a single phrase.

It is no coincidence that the most successful recordings Davis made in 1947 and 1948 were those in which the personal flavour was most marked. Agreed, there are indications that he admired Navarro sufficiently to adapt some of his mannerisms for his own use, but primarily he was concerned with moulding a highly original mode of expression which would not call for the same kind of technical command that had hitherto been obligatory for the trumpet soloist in the new school. Other players, such as Kenny Dorham, Red Rodney and Doug Mettome, by patterning their style more or less on the established leaders, rapidly acquired fluency in the new idiom. Davis preferred to create his own language and his progress was in consequence a good deal slower. If plagiarism was repugnant to him, he had to pay the price for his aversion to it; hence the split notes, faulty intonation and scrambled phrases that mar much of his work in the first five years of his recorded career.

Because of the very nature of the brass instrument, it will often happen that a trumpeter plays badly on one recording session only to perform at a much higher level, say, a week or two later. Forthwith, it must be pointed out that this was definitely not the case with Davis during his tenure with the Parker quintet. Two main factors seemed to govern the standard of his solos: the tempo and the thematic material. At the very fast pace of *Bird Gets the Worm* or *Klaunstaunce* he was able, by dint of rapid fingering, to make his runs conform to the underlying beat, but this mechanical approach meant that the musical interest of his work was almost negligible. His phrases had scant melodic appeal, his note separation was exceedingly poor, there is not a vestige of swing, and the overall impression one receives is of an ill-controlled succession of sounds. What a difference we find when the pace is less demanding! It was unfortunate for the trumpeter, at least from the short-term standpoint, that

Parker was so partial to extremely fast tempi. Davis's passages on *How Deep Is the Ocean, All the Things You Are*, and indeed most of the ballads the group committed to record, are singularly attractive. In such leisurely conditions he obviously found it much easier to think clearly. The line he creates is full of inventive twists and turns and his tone has a beauty that is all its own, admirably suited to the clear-cut phrases. When these records were first released many people were quick to brand Davis an interesting but cold and detached player, lacking the communicative power of other jazz trumpeters. The fiction was to last for almost a decade, but today even his detractors, if pressed, will most of them agree that the emotional aura of these solos is a convincing and memorable one, though it may not appeal to them personally.

Not only the tempo affected his work on these records. Its quality also depended on the type of tune being interpreted. In fact it would not be a gross inaccuracy to say that the only performances to which he contributed praiseworthy solos apart from the ballads were the medium-paced blues. There are, agreed, the inevitable exceptions to this rule; on *Steeplechase*, for instance, he plays a nicely ordered chorus and also makes apt use of inflexion. For the most part, though, the twelve-bar form would seem to have been the only context in which he was really at his ease when the tempo was faster than thirty bars to the minute. *Air Conditioning, Bongo Bop* and the various takes of *Barbados* and *Perhaps* all have effective passages by him. It would be foolish to imply that these solos are faultless, but his conception is not distorted to the point of anonymity by the technical weaknesses, as is the case with his work on many of the other tunes recorded by the quintet. One is reminded of a drawing where the lines are imperfectly controlled, becoming almost indistinct in one or two places, but where the artist's vision comes over convincingly in spite of the flaws.

It is clear, then, that whilst a great many of his solos on the Parker quintet records of 1947 and

1948 are mediocre in the extreme, the experience he gained with the group was most valuable to him. He had begun to refine the texture of his work, at the same time intensifying its effect. In short, he was establishing his identity as a jazz soloist. He still had much to learn, of course, both in matters of construction and technique; but it is typical of his adventurous thinking that in the immediate future he was to turn his attention to other matters, concerning himself not only with the problems of improvisation, but more especially with those of composition and arrangement.

In the summer of 1948 Davis left the Parker quintet. Earlier the same year promoters Monte Kay and Ralph Watkins, in company with disc jockey Symphony Sid Torin, had opened a new club called the Royal Roost on Broadway. In June Dizzy Gillespie played there with his orchestra, sharing the stand with Thelonious Monk, and amongst the groups which followed them were those of Charlie Ventura, Tadd Dameron—and two units led by Miles Davis, the second of which was destined to have a far-reaching effect on small group writing. Appearing at the club for only two weeks, in September 1948, Davis's band comprised the unorthodox instrumentation of trumpet, trombone, French horn, tuba, alto and baritone saxophones, piano, bass and drums. The greater part of the book consisted of original tunes from the pens of George Wallington, Gerry Mulligan, John Lewis and the leader himself, whilst the arranging was handled primarily by Mulligan and Gil Evans. The band's booking lasted only a fortnight owing to lack of support, and according to Mulligan it played only one date in public, which took place at the Clique Club a year or so later. A recording ban was in force throughout 1948, but Davis subsequently managed to secure three recording sessions at which the group was recreated. Two of these were held in 1949, in January and April, and the third in March of the following year. The resulting records are of interest from a variety of standpoints, and in view of the praise which has been accorded them and the extent to which they have been identified with Davis's ideas by so many commentators, it is worth pausing for a moment to consider the events which led up to their creation.

It is beyond dispute that the Claude Thornhill Orchestra was the seed without which Davis's group would almost certainly never have come into being. Thornhill's was first and foremost a 'society' band, and except for the war years, when its leader was in the United States Navy, had been in existence since 1939. By 1947 its personnel included young musicians such as Red Rodney, Konitz and Mulligan. Gil Evans, who had been associated with Thornhill since the nineteen-thirties when both were writing for a bandleader called Skinnay Ennis in Stockton, California, was its principal arranger, whilst Mulligan, John Carisi and Gene Roland also contributed to the library. Because of his interest in the rhythmic and harmonic aspects of bop, Evans became friendly with Charlie Parker, sharing a room with him for some time, and it was probably through the altoist that Davis made his acquaintance. There is every reason for believing that Davis found the light textures of the Thornhill band's scores to his taste, for they echoed in an orchestral context the sound for which he himself was evidently striving; and their congeniality was doubtless enhanced in the case of *Anthropology*, *Donna Lee* and *Yardbird Suite*, three of Parker's tunes that Evans had arranged for the band. It should be remembered, however, that such pieces were not characteristic of the Thornhill repertoire, a fact that is borne out by Evans leaving the band in 1948 in protest at its leader's preoccupation with sheer sound as against linear and harmonic activity.

According to Gerry Mulligan, the idea of assembling a group which would make use of Gil Evans's arranging skill in a setting more akin to jazz than was the case in Thornhill's orchestra, did not stem from Miles Davis. Not until rehearsals were in progress did Davis assume the leading role; for some months beforehand Evans, Mulligan, John Lewis and John Carisi had been discussing the formation of the group, mapping out instrumentations and so on. It is clear, too, that the actual question of who was to play in the band was not settled by Davis alone. His original intention was that Sonny Stitt should play alto and John Simmons or Al McKibbon bass. He did not expect that Mulligan would take part other than as a writer. Once agreement was reached on the personnel, however, and the group started to rehearse, it was Davis who dictated the style of interpretation.

On the records the group made at the three sessions I have already mentioned, Davis gets more solo space than any other musician and his tone lends the scored passages a distinctive quality; but these two points cannot obscure the fact that these are essentially ensemble performances. Almost every one has some extraordinary feature. *Israel* contains contrapuntal passages; *Jeru* has an unconventional structure and makes use of different time signatures; *Moon Dreams* is a fascinating textural study. Most jazz writing dates rapidly; it is pleasant, therefore, to be able to say that at ten years' remove these performances remain as absorbing an experience as ever for the listener. The impression of serenity and restraint which marks them all is as convincing today as it was when the records were first issued.

Something of the same atmosphere is evident in the trumpet solos. The sense of emotional stress apparent in Davis's playing on many of the Parker

Photograph by Rex Warner and Derek Young

Miles Davis at the Midnight Concert given at the Concertgebouw, Amsterdam, on the night of 3 November 1956

Photograph by Rex Warner and Derek Young
Miles Davis during the Midnight Concert at the Concertgebouw, Amsterdam

quintet records has not vanished altogether, but for the most part it is hidden beneath a cloak of restraint. *Godchild*, which contains an excellent solo by the leader, serves to illustrate the principal changes. He ignores the eight-bar divisions, it is true, and in this way reveals his bop training; we have already seen that he had made considerable progress along these lines by the close of 1947. His tone, however, is considerably smoother, and he intersperses complex runs with sustained notes that are executed with a bare minimum of vibrato and attack. To judge from his playing on transcriptions

made of the Dameron group's programme at the Paris Jazz Fair which was held in May 1949, it seems likely that his style was in a state of flux in these years, for on the Dameron recordings he performs in a very different way, using a much broader tone and more aggressive phrasing. In the circumstances it is natural that his style would depend on the immediate musical surrounds, taking its colour from them. I do not wish the reader to infer from these remarks that his work on the Capitol sides is altogether devoid of character. On the contrary, it is noticeable that it has a warmer glow about it than have the ensemble passages or even the other solos; introspective his creations may be, but they have a communicative power that is largely absent from the contributions of Lee Konitz or Gerry Mulligan.

Apart from the chorus on *Godchild*, Davis is also heard to especially good advantage on *Jeru*, *Move*, *Venus de Milo* and *Rouge*, whilst on several of the other sides, such as *Rocker*, where his solo is interpolated in the ensemble, his playing is of interest. These sides certainly contain solos more elegantly formed than he had contrived at previous recording dates, but in some respects it was a pity that critics subsequently tended to use them as a yardstick to judge all his work, for from the standpoint of content they are by no means fully representative.

Although many musicians were enthusiastic about the original nine-piece group Davis led at the Royal Roost, public interest was not widespread enough to enable it to continue there and the trumpeter reverted to the orthodox small-group format. The recording ban ended on 15 December 1948, but its results were to plague the jazz world for many months to come. Very little instrumental music had been recorded during the time it was in force, for only the small independent labels, with the connivance of a handful of jazz musicians, had ventured to defy it. Singers, on the other hand, had made innumerable records, generally with the backing of musicians not subject to the union's decrees. As a result the public had lost any taste it may once have had for instrumentals. This was no catastrophe for the studio musicians, who were naturally very soon in demand again to accompany the vocalists, but on jazz, no matter of what kind, it had a disastrous effect. Many orchestras, such as Dizzy Gillespie's, were forced to disband by early 1950, and others were severely reduced in size. Jazz musicians who would make no concessions to the public at large found it harder than ever to obtain work, and of these Miles Davis was a typical example. January 1949 found him working at the Audubon, a small New York jazz-room, with Art Blakey and Sonny Rollins; and during the spring he played in a rehearsal band that Tadd Dameron had assembled, prior to travelling to Europe with the pianist, to appear, as previously stated, at the Paris Jazz Fair. He also spent two weeks in Chicago, but apart from these engagements, some record dates and the occasional gig, he was unemployed throughout the year.

For the five years from 1950 until 1955 Davis was something of a forgotten man as far as the jazz audience was concerned. These were the years of West Coast popularity, when many people imagined the focal point of interest had shifted from New York to Hollywood. Seizing avidly upon the possibilities inherent in the arrangements used by Davis's Royal Roost band, Shorty Rogers and other musicians who had worked in the Kenton orchestra, such as Shelly Manne and Bob Cooper, were quick to found a new school in which improvised passages were more often than not incidental to the scores. The rather stylized performances which resulted received far more notice in the trade Press than they deserved; and very many enthusiasts, preposterous as their attitude seems in retrospect, were pleased to regard the music played by Parker and his followers as old-fashioned, just as many of the Parker quintet's devotees had entertained nothing but contempt for the efforts of Louis Armstrong or Coleman Hawkins. Today it is clear that the path pursued by the Californian studio men was singularly ill-advised from the artistic standpoint, though several of them, Manne and Previn in particular, were to reap considerable financial reward by infusing popular tunes with a discreet jazz flavour. It is no coincidence, one may be sure, that the most compelling jazz to come out of the West Coast during the last decade has been made largely by Dexter Gordon, Rolf Ericson, Harold Land, Elmo Hope and Frank Butler, all excellent musicians who recognize the importance of self-expression and have shown no interest in experimentation for mere novelty's sake. Ornette Coleman, spectacular as his innovations were, may also be grouped with these men, for it is clear that his expansion of the jazz language was a natural growth and not the result of grafting foreign techniques on to an improvised music. The boast of bassist Howard Rumsey that the jazz clubs on the West Coast are 'on the same plane with the Bank of America or Safeway',[1] has a hollow ring to their ears, but for all the hardships they have encountered they can at least pride themselves on having kept their jazz free from the inroads of light music or the conservatoire.

If I have dwelt at some length on the shortcomings of the Hollywood musicians, it is only to illustrate how ill-founded was the neglect talents like Davis's underwent at the hands of the jazz audience. Davis himself, moreover, had to contend with personal as well as public misfortunes. Whilst featured in a concert tour with singer Billy Eckstine during 1950 he was arrested on a heroin charge; and although the case was subsequently dismissed, the adverse publicity made it more difficult for him to find employment. 'It is doubtful,' wrote Leonard Feather,[2] 'whether he worked more than six or seven weeks in 1951.' In 1952 he went out on the road again with a touring group entitled Jazz Inc., which was headed by Symphony Sid and included Milt Jackson and Zoot Sims, the latter being replaced eventually by Jimmy Heath. For the next three and a half years, however, his activities were restricted to recording sessions and occasional club dates. His health was far from satisfactory throughout this period and he is known to have returned once or twice to East St. Louis to convalesce on his father's farm. Some of his appearances in the recording studio were prompted mainly by the immediate financial advantage to be gained thereby. 'I didn't care then,'[3] he was later to say; but

[1] *Newsweek*, 29 February 1960.
[2] *Melody Maker*, 23 February 1952.
[3] *Esquire*, March 1959.

the music nevertheless remains and must be judged on its merits.

To speak of an art form is to presuppose the existence of evidence of some sort or another. It is in the very nature of jazz that its essence cannot be caught on paper, and if it were not for the gramophone record the appeal of the music, though initially just as strong, would be far less widespread. Recording techniques have given jazz a tradition which it would otherwise have enjoyed only by hearsay; the documentation they provide is invaluable if incomplete. For collector and critic alike, however, records have drawbacks other than the obvious ones. Prominent among these is the ease with which they allow the listener to imagine the music existing in a void, detached from the manifold forces, interior and exterior, which went into its making. Anyone who approaches Davis's records of the early nineteen-fifties in so idealistic a frame of mind is unlikely to get very much enjoyment out of them; for one thing, he will very probably fail to perceive their emotional power and, for another, the occasional technical lapses that troubled the trumpeter at this time will inevitably seem objectionable to him if he is in fact unaware of the cathartic strength which nine times out of ten transcends the faulty execution.

Records from these years show that Davis's instrumental command, far from growing steadily, was subject to the most surprising vicissitudes. On the Blue Note dates of 1952 and 1953, for example, he is in very good form, whilst the sides he recorded for the same company at a session held the year after reveal glaring weakness on his part. One can tell that he is thinking as inventively as ever on *Take-off*, *Lazy Susan* and the rest, but his execution is so dreadful that it is very hard indeed to appreciate the beauty of his ideas. Only *It Never Entered My Mind*, a ballad performed in mute, comes near to being a success, and this is a great pity, for the rhythm section, made up of Horace Silver, Percy Heath and Art Blakey, functions with all the swing and drive one could wish for. That Davis could play so badly a year and more after proving he could play so well, and then, only eight weeks later, come up with his splendid solo on *Walkin'* is ample evidence of the extent to which his proficiency depended on economics. The trumpeter himself has had very little to say about these matters; but Sonny Rollins has spoken of his own difficulties and the effect they may have had on his style. Since his remarks are of general as well as particular interest, it is worth transcribing them here. 'At that period, you see, between 1951 and 1953, I was out of work for much of the time and it may be that that affected my playing,' he told François Positif. 'Now that I'm working every evening, I know things are going much better. But I don't think you can build a theory up on that: I know some people who play every night and still can't manage to play properly! On the other hand, it's happened that after being away from my instrument for some time I've played extremely well the first night I took it up again, even better perhaps than if I'd gone on working every evening. But maybe that's because I'd got into a rut!'[1] Inconsistency, in fact, was the trumpeter's worst enemy at this stage of his career, and its effects were more obvious than might otherwise have been the case, since his imagination was constantly growing. Not only did this impose an extra strain on his control in terms of range, it also called for greater fluency and the ability to span intervals he had not previously attempted. His solo on the 1949 *Godchild* had been a particularly impressive one, and he was henceforth to develop the general conception it implied, enriching his work from almost every standpoint.

Before going on to consider in detail the more successful of the recording sessions he undertook from 1950 to 1955, it is well worth noting, I think, the context in which he chose to work. Even today he is linked in the minds of many listeners with stylists such as Stan Getz and Al Cohn, and around 1950 it was almost universally conceded that he had more in common with these men than with Charlie Parker or Bud Powell. This was owing, above all, to the character of his tone, which on the Capitol records in particular was light and clear, evoking images of detachment and calm. Most of the other aspects of his music, though, are not shared by the white tenor-men who took Lester Young's style of the nineteen-thirties for their inspiration. Davis's use of the pause—the audacity with which he ignored the convention that required the soloist to pattern his phrasing on the basic eight-bar divisions—indicates that his conception was inherently more complex than, say, Al Cohn's. Much the same is true of Lee Konitz, and it is also worth pointing out that both he and Davis would frequently attack a phrase with much more vehemence than was generally the case with Getz or Zoot Sims. 'When I play with either of them it sounds like one horn,'[1] Davis once remarked, alluding to Parker and Konitz; he at least was conscious of the mistake most people had made. It is hardly surprising, then, that he should have thrown in his lot with the younger players who had grown up to revere Parker and the style of improvisation for which he stood.

As early as January 1949, Davis had employed Sonny Rollins, who was then unknown outside New York City; and a glance at the discography will show that he was thereafter to choose his sidemen from the ranks of those who were closely associated with the bop movement. Some of these, Kenny Clarke, Art Blakey and Tommy Potter, for example, had played a prominent part in the early stages; others, such as Rollins, Jackie McLean, Gil Coggins and Philly Joe Jones, had clearly based their styles on the prime movers. On one session, it is true, Davis was partnered by Al Cohn and Zoot Sims, but this is a lone exception to the general rule. 'I think they just dropped that label on me,' he said later, when asked whether he thought there was any essential difference between bop and 'cool' modes of expression. In his insistence on a powerful and prolix drummer, his cultivation of a tone with personal inflexions, his use of phrases of

[1] *Jazz Hot*, April 1959.

[1] *Melody Maker*, 23 February 1952.

89

uneven length, in his whole conception of how a small group should function, Davis's style continued to evolve within the main stream of jazz development, which itself was none other than the amplification and extension of elements found in the work of the Parker quintet.

The small units with which Davis played and recorded from 1950 until 1955 represent a noteworthy link between the bop groups of the nineteen-forties and the so-called 'hard bop' of the following decade. It is a common misconception that the music of bands such as the Jazz Messengers or the many pick-up groups that have recorded for Blue Note and Prestige over the past five years is nothing more than a reiteration of the original bop style with the volume stepped up. Anyone who imagines this to be so has failed to comprehend the role of the drummer in these bands. Thanks to his exceptional imagination and unrivalled mastery of the alto saxophone, Parker was able to evoke exceptional rhythmic variety in his playing. No altoist to emerge since has enjoyed a comparable command of his instrument; but the rhythmic richness that was Parker's has not been lost. What has occurred in effect is a decentralization of his approach. Whereas Max Roach, in the original quintet, would weave a complementary pattern round the soloist's phrases, taking as much advantage as possible of the rests, Blakey, Art Taylor or Philly Joe Jones, a decade or so later, will not hesitate to lay a counter-rhythm right across the improvised line. If the soloist holds firm to his ideas. instead of allowing the drummer to dictate the shape of his phrases, a rhythmic tension is set up which, far from weakening the musical content, amplifies it. Parker would form his solos out of a number of apparently disparate elements; in much of contemporary jazz the same principle holds good, with the important provision that a similar goal is reached collectively, rather than by one man.

This practice, which has now become fairly widespread among the younger jazzmen, had its beginnings, so far as we can judge, in the late nineteen-forties. It would be wrong, of course, to draw a hard and fast distinction between the methods of Blakey, Philly Joe Jones and Art Taylor, say, on the one hand, and Max Roach and Kenny Clarke on the other. Roach in particular has shown himself to be remarkably adaptable. Whilst his playing on Parker's last quartet sessions, done in 1952 and 1953, is akin to his work of the preceding decade, he functions rather more prominently on the records made by the quintet he led with trumpeter Clifford Brown from 1954 until 1956, and this band was undoubtedly one of the most influential of the day in its anticipation of developments in the relationship between drummer and soloist within the small group. Also very important from this standpoint were the units led by Art Blakey from 1954 onwards. In fact, Blakey, more than anyone else, has been responsible for the revision of the drummer's role in the small group, and the records made by the various editions of his Jazz Messengers not only show the tremendous power and inventiveness of his playing, but stand as exceptionally clear illustrations of the trend with which we are concerned. It was no coincidence that he was present at the Miles Davis session of 5 October 1951, which was amongst the first to produce recorded examples of an ensemble style that asserted itself with increasing authority as the decade wore on.

It would be idle to pretend that Davis was the man chiefly responsible for this important development in small-group practice, for most of the credit must necessarily go to the drummers involved, and in any case the whole movement was very much a co-operative one. Nevertheless, there is no escaping the fact that he was amongst the few established figures who encouraged its growth. That McLean, Rollins, Philly Joe Jones and Coltrane were all protégés of his at one time or another is too seldom remembered, and it is ironic that the very musician who has so often been written off because of the alleged coldness of his playing should have fostered the careers of others who have been charged with purveying peevishness and hysteria.

None of the records Davis made in the early

months of 1951 bears comparison with the best of his work. Despite their faults, however, certain of his solos distil an emotional flavour more pronounced than had hitherto been the case. In *Blue Room*, for instance, he features a much broader tone than before. John Lewis's firm and sympathetic chording serves as ideal support, and despite obvious technical shortcomings on Davis's part, there is no mistaking the very personal air of sour nostalgia that pervades this performance. A half-chorus by Sonny Rollins sustains the mood perfectly, although it would appear that the record was made from two separate tapes. Neither the reunion under the Clef banner with Parker, nor the sides done with Lee Konitz for Prestige produced trumpet work of comparable impact, but brief solos on the Metronome All Stars' *Local 802 Blues* and *Early Spring*, the latter a charming score by Ralph Burns, are worthy of attention.

This period saw the introduction of the long-playing record on a commercial scale, and Prestige deserve every praise for having been amongst the first companies to use the new medium for jazz performances. Up to this time Davis, like most musicians, had been heard on record only in brief appearances of a chorus or so, and it had been difficult to gauge the true measure of his inventiveness, though the issue of different takes on the Dial label had shown him to be a genuine improviser. This impression was now to be confirmed by the seven titles recorded in the autumn of 1951 by a sextet featuring Davis, Rollins and Jackie McLean and a rhythm section comprising Walter Bishop, Tommy Potter and Art Blakey. All the performances are imperfect, but one would need to be peculiarly impassive to remain untouched by the deep emotional currents that flow through them, lending them a distinction that technical precision alone could never have conferred. Davis plays with great urgency throughout, and his contributions to *Bluing*, an extended twelve-bar, *My Old Flame* and *Paper Moon* are especially memorable. His soloing in the blues is very moving and speaks eloquently of his difficulties and disappointments. Following two

excellent introductory choruses by Walter Bishop he displays at some length the scope of his imagination, contrasting long phrases with short ones, splitting up the line in a most absorbing manner, often extending it across from one chorus to the next, and generally taking every advantage of Blakey's rolls and occasional double-timing without allowing them to restrict his inventiveness in any way. After resolute if immature solos from the two saxophonists he returns, evoking the same melancholic strength of purpose, and once again using his inflected tone to project his feelings in the best jazz traditions, though of course there is no contesting the very personal nature of his melodic ideas. The two standards have a warmer quality to them. *My Old Flame*, taken at slow tempo, shows how his tone had improved since 1947, when he recorded the same song with Parker. The second eight bars contain a beautiful paraphrase of the melody. Also of note are the intimate sound he obtains in the lower register and the way he sustains his notes without any loss of tonal quality. Beside contributing a delicate introduction, Walter Bishop plays very sensitive piano throughout the performance, and his chording in the last eight bars, together with apt support from Potter and Blakey, makes for an impression of completeness that is something of a rarity with ballad renditions of this kind. *Paper Moon* is a gay, medium-paced outing: Davis's choice of phrase, varied as it is, shows unusual continuity of thought, whilst his relaxed delivery and occasional use of the trill also call for favourable comment.

Apart from the insight these records provide into the development of the jazz group, a subject which I have already treated, they are also of interest for the light they throw on Davis's personality as expressed through his music. It is generally agreed that the emotional scope of his art is a narrow one. Compared with the broad sweep of feeling that Hawkins or Armstrong can command, his evocative power, though intense, is restricted in range. On the other hand, it seems to me mistaken to place undue emphasis on the circumscribed nature of

Photograph from Melody Maker *files*

An early photograph of Miles Davis

his gifts. Surely there is a significant difference between the harsh undertones of his work on *Bluing* and the coyness which marks out his soloing on *Paper Moon*? The question is a delicate one, and whilst acknowledging that each listener must answer it to his own satisfaction, personally I am inclined to believe that Davis's expression covers a wider area than is often claimed to be the case.

During 1952 he took part in only one recording session. All the members of the sextet he led on this occasion played well, with Oscar Pettiford and Kenny Clarke outstanding. It was probably owing in part to the rhythm section's aggressive swing that Davis's work took on a tougher character than had previously been the case on record. *Chance It, Donna*—Jackie McLean's *Dig* taken at medium tempo—and *Woody'n You* are all hard-driving performances that have the leader blowing with great confidence. His tone is broader and has more bite to it than before; and without losing their asymmetrical interest, his phrases carry extra impetus. This effect derives not only from his forceful delivery but also from his use of high-note passages. The arrangements, which in the case of the first and the last tunes named set the leader to improvise

Miles Davis—September 1960

Photograph by Marc Sharratt

over and against riffs played by the other two horns, make for additional tension, and the same emotional quality is predominant in the young McLean's characteristically jagged phrases. Yet beneath the sheer urgency of the music run strong undercurrents of sadness, an impression conveyed notably by the sourly-intoned melodies Davis elicits from the lower register of his instrument. It is from the interplay of these two extremes— exhilaration and a sense of bitter nostalgia—that his work draws much of its appeal, and nowhere is this more evident than in *Dear Old Stockholm* and the two slow-paced ballads, *Yesterdays* and *How*

Deep Is the Ocean. From the technical standpoint it is worth noting that Davis, though making one or two mistakes here and there, was in very good form on this occasion; the full sound he achieves when sustaining the high notes at the start of *Yesterdays* is especially impressive.

During the first half of 1953 Davis was in the studios rather more often, making records for both the Prestige and Blue Note companies. The problem of finding regular work, aggravated by his personal difficulties, continued to affect his playing. Poor intonation is a persistent weakness, as in both versions of *The Serpent's Tooth*, made at the

30 January session with Rollins and Parker, and on the records that emerged from the 19 May quartet date for Prestige; and there are times, too, when his work suffers from his inability to play high-note runs with any success. Occasionally, as on the session with Al Cohn and Zoot Sims, he solves the problem by restricting his invention, by and large, to the middle register; elsewhere he attempts to disguise his limitations by hitting an impressively high note and then allowing the phrase to cascade downwards, but the device does not always come off. Yet if his manifold difficulties, musical and otherwise, meant that his playing was often unpolished, even ragged at times, it seems in retrospect highly probable that they also made for a greater sense of urgency, as though he were searching in his music for an emotional outlet that the hard realities of his everyday existence denied him.

An article written by Stanley Goldstein and published in the August 1960 issue of *Playboy* throws a good deal of light on the problems Davis had to contend with at this stage of his career, and makes it easier to understand why much of the music he recorded conveys the authentic note of angry protest. Harder to comprehend, perhaps, is the gay lyricism which, in such performances as *The Serpent's Tooth* and *For Adults Only* blends with the sourer aspects of his work to produce that ambiguous emotional flavour which has always informed his best performances. Both versions of the former theme have exceptionally good trumpet passages and the two choruses he takes on the latter record are equally attractive. His execution is at fault on *Round About Midnight*, which was made on the same day as *The Serpent's Tooth*, but this rendition of Monk's celebrated tune should be mentioned for the depth of feeling both Charlie Parker and he infuse into their playing.

Two further sessions under Davis's name were held in 1953. The first of these, at which he led a group similar to that which had been featured on the Blue Note records of the previous year, was far more productive than the second, which has him backed by rhythm section only. Art Blakey's thunderous drumming must have been at once an inspiration and a challenge to the soloists, whilst the arrangements and repertoire were calculated to bring out the best in the leader by virtue of their suitability to the style of improvisation he favoured at that time. It is very interesting to compare the trumpet work in the original issues of *Tempus Fugit* and *Ray's Idea*. On the former record Davis employs long phrases that ride exuberantly over Blakey's persistent accents, whilst on the latter he breaks up the line, inserting his notes with telling precision around and between the beats yet cleverly retaining a sense of form that is the more striking for the fragmentary nature of the melodic material from which it derives. It has been suggested that the polyrhythmic nature of bop and its derivatives is alien to Davis's temperament, but the success of such performances as this cause one to doubt the truth of so sweeping an assertion. There is no denying that in recent years he has sometimes moved away, on his records at least, from the asymmetrical phrasing, underpinned by copious rhythmic support, which once characterized his work. One should none the less bear in mind that a soloist is not necessarily restricted to a single sector of musical endeavour; and whilst of late he has been content with a less effusive style, this does not of itself imply that his earlier efforts were misguided.

Several months spent in Detroit enabled Davis to get a firmer grip on his personal problems and his eventual success in overcoming his weaknesses finally led to economic stability, heralded by the acclaim he received at the 1955 Newport Jazz Festival. During most of 1954 his powers of execution seem to have been more reliable. At the two sessions held in March his technique is very poor and only occasionally answers the call of his imagination; but from April onwards any shortcomings there may be are far from flagrant and in any event never detract from the appeal of his playing. Looking back, it seems it was in this year that the evolution towards his present style began: he was starting to use a greater number of extended notes, his enunciation was more carefully defined than before, and there is more space in his solos. This is not so evident on *Walkin'* and *Blue 'n' Boogie*, commendable as these performances are, but comparison between *But Not For Me* and his Blue Note records of the previous year not only reveals the changes enumerated above but also suggests that by 1954 he was phrasing in a more relaxed and consequently less attacking way, placing his notes a trifle behind the bassist's statement of the metre. Rollins gives the impression of anticipating him in the theme statements, evidently because he phrases on the centre of the beat. Davis's tone was getting purer and altogether lacks the ringing hardness that had been so conspicuous a feature of *Enigma*, a ballad recorded the year before. The Christmas Eve session is more instructive than the others in this respect, for in terms of tonal beauty the trumpet solos it produced eclipse all Davis's earlier recordings. The original version of *Bag's Groove* contains two exceptionally brilliant solos by him. The first, which follows the theme statement, is notable above all for its inventiveness; with only a slight increase in volume he builds up to a climax by relying on the tensions engendered by his phrase distribution and seemingly inexhaustible flow of melodic ideas. After sets of choruses by Milt Jackson and Thelonious Monk, he contributes a further passage before the final ensembles bring the performance to a close. The pianist's style, spare and astringent, offers a piquant contrast to the trumpeter's lyrical delivery.

Although in 1954 Davis was by no means the popular figure he was soon to become—Chet Baker, who had come to general notice as a member of the Mulligan quartet, won the *Downbeat* Magazine Reader's Poll by a clear margin in that year— the records he made show that he was becoming a far more consistent player. He was still guilty of poor enunciation and tended to be out of tune at times, but his recorded work conforms to a very high standard when judged from a broader viewpoint than that of technical excellence alone. His improvisations on such records as *Walkin'*, *Doxy*, *Bag's Groove* or *The Man I Love*, to select the outstanding performances, are as absorbing in their own way as the most dazzling pyrotechnical flights of Fats Navarro or Dizzy Gillespie. Over the preceding years the greater part of his recorded work had fallen somewhat short of the standards these two musicians had set in the nineteen-forties. The original bent of his style, it is true, had never been in doubt since he had left the Parker quintet, and his influence had been a pervasive one amongst the younger generation of jazzmen. Shorty Rogers, Art Farmer, Clifford Brown and Conte Candoli, together with a host of lesser-known trumpeters, had been guided in one way or another by his example. His musical conception, in fact, had always been recognizably personal; but now he had expunged from it every detail which might be looked upon as derivative. In his spare melodic approach and concern for tonal values he had reached an important stage in his development. To speak of his playing at this time as mature would be misleading in view of the many transformations it has since undergone, but the evidence which remains to us suggests he was far more consistent stylistically throughout this year than he had ever been before.

By the late spring of 1955 Davis had evidently formed a fairly good idea of the kind of group he wished to work with regularly, because the band which recorded under his name on 7 June differed in only two respects from the quintet he was to lead from the autumn of the same year until the spring of 1957: Oscar Pettiford played bass and there was no saxophonist to partner the leader in the front line. The rhythm section attains a high standard but Davis himself is not at his best, although there are some attractive trumpet passages on *Green Haze*, a slow blues, and *A Gal in Calico*.

For much of the time he sounds dispirited. The familiar bugbear of faulty intonation partly explains this undesirable state of affairs, aggravated in one or two cases by a questionable choice of themes. *Night in Tunisia* will always be associated in the majority of enthusiasts' minds with the virtuoso displays of Dizzy Gillespie and Charlie Parker. This version is almost dull in comparison, and exposes Davis's relatively limited range; the break he improvises after the opening theme statement sounds especially unadventurous.

If the fruits of this session were, in the main, disappointing, they are nevertheless interesting for the ways in which they foreshadow his future development. The chief of these concerns the relationship between his phrasing and the basic metre. I have already remarked that throughout most of 1954 he appeared to have been playing just a trifle behind the beat; it would also be true to say that the time-lag, infinitesimal as it was, seemed altogether regular. Now, however, the link between phrases and beat has grown less strict, and there is greater rhythmic freedom in his improvising, but, inevitably, less swing. With a rhythm section as relaxed and as powerful as this one behind him, the last point is comparatively academic, for although Davis's playing, considered apart, can barely be said to swing at all, the listener is not aware of any such shortcoming in the work of the quartet as a whole. It might be mentioned in passing that the drive—or forward momentum—of his playing is not being impugned. I am talking purely of swing, a sensation which is not susceptible to even the most cursory verbal definition, but which will be readily understood by anyone acquainted with the music of the great jazzmen of the past four decades.

It was not with his quintet, nor indeed with this embryonic version of it, that Davis made his mark at Freebody Park in July, but with a motley group which had been thrown hastily together, as is so often the case on gala occasions. For the record, it comprised, in addition to Davis, Gerry Mulligan, Zoot Sims, Thelonious Monk, Percy Heath and Connie Kay. There seems little reason to believe that he excelled himself; it is far more likely that his unexpected acclamation by those present was merely yet another case of the jazz audience suddenly becoming aware of talent that had hitherto been concealed from it for lack of publicity.

Not until late October did Davis's new quintet make its first records, but in the interim he took part in two sessions, the first for Debut with a band which was obviously dominated by Charlie Mingus, although the trumpeter's name appears as leader on the label, and the second with a pick-up group for the Prestige company. The Debut album may be safely overlooked, for although Davis is his characteristic self from the tonal viewpoint, he sounds ill at ease and evinces little melodic inventiveness. It may be that he felt inhibited by the framework within which he was obliged to work, since the extended performances for Prestige find him in far more confident form. McLean is disappointing, but Davis, Milt Jackson and Ray Bryant all play brilliantly, aided by Percy Heath and Art Taylor. Subdued yet swinging, the rhythm section complements Davis to perfection on *Changes*, where his muted solos, the very epitome of tenderness, overshadow even Jackson's fleet choruses.

If one were to take these two recording dates as a guide to Davis's reaction to an arranged setting, it would appear that pre-set routines were inimical to his style; but as the Capitol records of 1949 and 1950 and those made for Blue Note in 1952 and 1953 had previously shown, this was not the case when he himself was able to dictate the form these routines were to assume. This important distinction was now to be stressed yet again by his new quintet, which worked regularly for some eighteen months with an unchanged personnel, and was thus able to develop ensemble techniques that were out of the question with a group assembled for a single record session or a short run of a week or so in this or that jazz room. These techniques concern not so much the relationship between the two wind instruments, though arranged passages, of course, there were, as the interplay between the solo horn and the various members of the rhythm section. I have already spoken of this subject in discussing Davis's records of the early nineteen-fifties, and have pointed out the important role played by the drummer, who was often responsible not only for implementing the beat but also for enriching the polyrhythmic content of the music as a whole. Continuous employment was now to give Davis the opportunity of amplifying this procedure in a number of intriguing ways, but before going on to examine actual instances, it will be instructive, I think, to consider the styles of the men he chose when assembling his band. A brief digression of this kind will help to explain the success of the major part of the quintet's recorded work and will also illuminate Davis's perceptiveness as a bandleader, an aspect of his talent which economics had hitherto obscured.

It was widely rumoured that he would have liked Sonny Rollins to join him, and there is little reason to doubt this, for he had frequently used him in the past when engagements had been forthcoming. Rollins, however, spent most of 1955 studying in Chicago, and presumably felt that the time was not ripe for him to accept Davis's offer; he eventually went with Max Roach instead, replacing Harold Land in the drummer's group. In his place the trumpeter chose John Coltrane, a Philadelphian who had been with Dizzy Gillespie's big band in the late nineteen-forties and had since appeared with Eddie Vinson and Johnny Hodges. Ever since his stay in the altoist's quintet Davis had preferred to work with saxophonists whose playing reflected Parker's ideas, perhaps because he felt that their multinoted flights made an interesting contrast with his own rather spare phrasing. Coltrane, who had also been influenced by Sonny Stitt and Dexter Gordon, fulfilled this condition in no uncertain way. At this time he was a relatively immature stylist, his harmonic researches leading him to employ a greater number of notes than he eventually found to be necessary, but whilst some of his solos with Davis in 1955 and 1956 were to sound rambling and incoherent, he made an exceptionally good foil for the leader, and his use of phrases of uneven length was in full accord with the asym-

metrical nature of the group's music.

On bass Davis chose Paul Chambers, a young Detroit musician who had quickly made himself a reputation in New York jazz circles through his work with George Wallington, with whose quintet he appeared at the Café Bohemia in September. His harmonic sense was nothing short of exceptional, his tone satisfyingly full, and—an important point where his work with Davis was concerned—he was able to create distinctive melodic lines; even when primarily concerned with stating the beat, the intervals he chose were always attractive to the ear. Philly Joe Jones, who was at the drums, had gained much of his experience in rhythm-and-blues bands. Possessed of enviable stamina and a driving swing, both doubtless acquired in this demanding field, he had also formulated by 1955 a style of accompaniment which was decidedly original, though deriving in part from Max Roach, with whom he had previously studied on an informal basis. Now that Davis's phrasing had grown freer of the beat, it was essential the qualities of drive and swing be abundantly present in his accompaniment, and it was because he recognized these so clearly in Jones's playing that his admiration for the drummer knew no bounds. 'Look,' he once said, 'I wouldn't care if he came up on the bandstand in his B.V.D.s and with one arm, just so long as he was there. He's got the fire I want. There's nothing more terrible than playing with a dull rhythm section. Jazz has got to have *that thing*.'[1] Just as vital in the context of this band was Jones's gift for elaborating the melodic line. He had at his command a rich variety of devices for doing this, and his exemplary volume control and uncanny anticipation enabled him to make the unexpected accent sound not only logical but inevitable. At times he would perform at a near contrapuntal level with the soloist, and in view of the prolix nature of his accompaniment it is clear that Davis made a wise selection in the quintet's pianist. Instead of complementing trumpet tenor or bass choruses with the filigree melodies of

[1] *Esquire* Magazine, March 1959.

97

an Al Haig, Red Garland restricted himself to spurring the soloist on with a series of hard, percussive chords. In this way he avoided obscuring the detail of the drummer's commentary yet still contrived to enrich the harmonic and rhythmic interest of any given performance. It seems likely that it was above all his skill in this sphere which recommended him to Davis, for his solo work, though showing great craftsmanship, is rarely so absorbing as one would wish. Immature and unfinished Coltrane's style certainly was at this time, but his contributions hold more interest than Garland's. On repeated hearings the piano solos tend to sound mechanical, partly because they are so often divided neatly into two halves, the first consisting of single-line improvisation over left-hand punctuations, the second made up of an unrelieved sequence of chordal patterns similar to those used by George Shearing or Erroll Garner. No one would contest his swing or sound musical knowledge, but a large proportion of his solos recorded with Davis lack the inventiveness of his playing, say, on *Traneing In*, which was recorded in August 1957.

During the year and a half or so of its existence, the quintet made records for both the Prestige and Columbia companies. Those issued by the former concern were done at three extended sessions held in November, May and October, the group playing a selection from its repertoire as though it were making a normal club appearance. A greater number of recording dates were held under the aegis of Columbia, but these brought forth fewer sides, which suggests that greater attention was paid to precise interpretation, the final choice for commercial release being made from several different versions of the same theme. Such methods very often entail a loss in spontaneity, and there is no doubt that the band sounds more subdued on its Columbia records. It would not do, however, to lay too heavy a stress on this difference, for it derives in part from the divergence in recording, the Prestige albums possessing far better definition than the others. Many Columbia issues from this period are similarly at fault; the rhythm sections are recorded most un-

satisfactorily, as with the albums by Art Blakey's Jazz Messengers. In practice, though, the principal split in the body of the quintet's recorded work was not between the records made for Prestige on the one hand and Columbia on the other, but between the ballad renditions and the medium or fast tempo pieces.

There Is No Greater Love, Bye Bye Blackbird and *All of You* typify a style of ballad playing which Davis has used widely in recent years, both with the band at present under discussion and its successors. The pattern is a fairly simple one: the melody is stated by trumpet in mute followed perhaps by a further passage of muted trumpet, Davis never straying far from the theme, before solos by Coltrane and Garland lead up to a final chorus, similar to the first. Performances of this kind made scant use of the group's artistic potential and when heard consecutively sound rather stylized, as though Davis and his band were going through a familiar routine. This is especially true of the leader's playing, for whilst he performs in a very individual way, utilizing his tonal resources to convey an emotional climate of acute melancholia, rarely does he appear to extend himself. In *Bye Bye Blackbird*, it is true, we find some interesting themal development, but for the most part he is content to stay very close to the melody as written, and one is led to wonder to what extent he was making concessions to the audience. In recent years Davis has frequently been accused of assuming a contemptuous attitude towards the customers of the jazz-rooms in which he works, and it is ironic in view of this that his music should be open to this charge. However that may be, comparison between *My Funny Valentine* and *You're My Everything*, ballad renditions which do not conform to the prevailing pattern, and the bulk of his recorded output in this vein lends support to the accusation.

There can be little doubt that the quintet's records at faster tempo were the more absorbing. At first its performances generally conformed to the normal modern small-group style, the soloists improvising freely over the rhythm section. *Ah-leu-*

cha, *How Am I to Know* and *Sposin'* are examples of this, with Davis contributing a splendid solo to the first. Two pieces from the group's initial session for Prestige, held in November 1955, more clearly illustrated its possibilities as a unit. *Just Squeeze Me* has Paul Chambers fashioning a second line beneath Davis's theme statement and also finds Red Garland tacit in places, but it is above all *The Theme* which features exhilarating interplay between the musicians. This performance begins with a fascinating duet between Chambers and Jones. Davis then enters, sustaining high notes to good effect, but the main melodic burden is carried by Garland who sets down some rollicking piano beneath the leader's austere line before the latter comes to the fore on the bridge. Solos follow from Davis, Coltrane and Garland, with Jones providing an exciting commentary on them all. Although the saxophonist is in poor voice, his phrases in double-time muddled and badly constructed, Chambers's strong musicianship holds this section together, and one is left with the agreeable impression that adventurous as the group's conception was, the understanding which existed between its members ensured that its music was always thoroughly integrated.

The unconventional character of *The Theme* foreshadowed the quintet's subsequent development. If records are any guide, it is safe to say that by late 1956 such renditions were an important part of its repertoire. *Oleo*, *Airegin* and *Tune Up* stand out as spectacular instances of the band's style and compare favourably with its more orthodox performances such as *Blues by Five* or *When Lights Are Low*. There is no profound schism between the one approach and the other, for all five of these records score with the listener by virtue of their polyrhythmic content; but on the first three an adept distribution of duties between the quintet's members steps up the interest already implicit in each single musician's work. In his soloing Davis maintains a high standard, using his improved technical powers to good advantage. *If I Were a Bell* has a characteristically intense contribution by him, whilst on *Airegin* he plays in an extremely aggressive

way, employing phrases that are as incisive as they are rhythmically free. Nor was he ready to forgo the felicities of inflexion: his improvisation on *When Lights Are Low* shows that he was continuing to use this most fecund device to strengthen the communicative power of his work. The confidence he exudes at fast and medium tempi suggests that he found ample inspiration in the polyrhythmic stylings of his group, and makes a strange contrast with his subdued contributions to the ballads, which, as I have already explained, are set in far simpler form, with the rhythm section restricting itself mainly to marking out the beat.

The strength of this band resided above all in the understanding which existed between its members, for at the time Coltrane was a relatively undeveloped soloist. In *'Round Midnight*, done in September 1956, he fashions a moving chorus, but on most of the quintet's records he falls a long way short of the standards he was eventually to set with *Traneing In* and *Good Bait*. It is not surprising, then, that Davis tended to be at his best when his group was working up to its full capacities *as a unit*.

Although this quintet had worked on a regular basis there had been times when it was inactive for one reason or another, as for instance when Davis came to Europe in late 1956; and in the spring of the following year it disbanded altogether. In the summer Davis formed a new band. Rollins was on tenor saxophone in place of John Coltrane and Art Taylor at the drums instead of Jones. Garland and Chambers, as before, completed the group. The same musicians, with the exception that Tommy Flanagan and not Garland played piano, had recorded together about a year before, and on that occasion the results had been more than encouraging; but by 1957 Rollins had developed further, and reliable authorities have it that he was dissatisfied with his position and yearned for a band of his own. In view of this it was to be expected that the new formation would not long stay together, and such indeed proved to be the case. The autumn found Davis once again signing on new men. Bobby Jaspar took over from Rollins, Flanagan joined on piano, and Philly Joe

Jones returned. Jaspar, featured on both flute and tenor, soon left, replaced in October by Julian 'Cannonball' Adderley, who joined the group during the course of a concert tour.

No records have been issued by any of these transitional groups, and indeed it is probable that none, in fact, were made, perhaps because of the frequent changes in personnel. Yet such hardly seems a satisfactory explanation when one considers that by 1957 Davis was a very popular figure with enthusiasts at large. His contract with a business corporation such as Columbia was now to consolidate his status with the jazz public, not only by way of small group recordings, but, more significantly, through a series of orchestral sessions held under the direction of Gil Evans, one of the arrangers who had been concerned in the mounting of the nine-piece group he had led at the Royal Roost in 1948.

The recording dates which produced the first of the albums on which Davis and Evans worked together in the late nineteen-fifties were held during May 1957. The record was eventually issued under the title of *Miles Ahead*. It consists of ten different pieces by various writers, including Ahmed Jamal, Dave Brubeck, and Johnny Carisi, assembled as a whole, with connecting notes or chords between one track and the next; although Evans himself contributed but a single composition—*Blues for Pablo* —he was responsible for all the arrangements, and his individual touch ensures that the collection offers an impressive degree of unity. The very nature of Evans's approach to the problems of arranging means that these pieces lack the rhythmic richness and vitality which abound in the Davis quintet's music, but in compensation they offer considerable harmonic appeal. The warmly lyrical tone Davis achieves on flügelhorn fits in perfectly with the orchestral textures; it is obvious on first hearing that it was a very wise decision which led him to forsake his usual instrument for this occasion, since the abrasive quality of his high-register trumpet work would probably have clashed uncomfortably with the voicings Evans devises. It is true that in the course of a second collaboration of this kind

when the material used comprised themes from George Gershwin's *Porgy and Bess*, Davis did indeed play trumpet on several tracks. However, the latter album often presents him as a soloist over and against a scored backdrop, rather than as a closely integrated voice in the general musical scheme, as is definitely the case with the *Miles Ahead* record. Comparison between *My Ship* and *Summertime*, each to some extent typical of its companion pieces, clarifies the difference between the two collections.

Since our immediate concern is with Davis's part in these undertakings, there is no point in going into their subtleties at any length, for it is Evans who must take the lion's share of the credit for the finished effect, in so far as he wrote all the arrangements and presided over the sessions at which the recordings were made. Nevertheless, if we are to judge by Davis's public pronouncements, he was very enthusiastic about co-operating with Evans in their production, and they show a facet of his musical personality which any comprehensive appraisal of his work must take into account. More convincing than most of his small-group ballad renditions, though cast in a similar emotional mould, they more often than not find him dealing in a wistful tenderness which has its own peculiar charm. The irony which creeps in with *It Ain't Necessarily So* is far from characteristic, and it is very noticeable that the sour and aggressive overtones of his medium and rapid tempo quintet or sextet performances are altogether absent. Here, it seems to me, is the reason why *Miles Ahead* and *Porgy and Bess* were accepted by the public at large, as distinct from the hard core of enthusiasts who had for some years previously bought most of the records issued under the trumpeter's name. It is no particularly original observation that the casual listener prefers not to be reminded of the dilemmas which face the artist in our society, and if the albums under discussion convey, first and foremost, an atmosphere of serenity and elegance, then this, we may be sure, is something of an asset from the commercial standpoint.

I trust nobody will infer from the above remarks that I wish to equate high sales figures with artistic poverty, for about such matters there can be no hard and fast rules, even under the present conditions of mass entertainment. Evans's collaborations with Davis, as I have already remarked, possess indisputable merits: his manipulation of the various instruments at his disposal bears witness not only to true originality on his part, but also to a remarkable flair for establishing a mood by sheer quality of sound alone. Here, I feel, we touch upon the essence of his achievement. The best of his records represent the phenomenon which in recent years has come to be known as 'mood music' at its highest level. He can present interesting individual textures of sound in a formal framework of some strength; but rarely can he evoke, even with a soloist of Davis's powers at his disposal, that exhilarating sense of emotional release which characterizes the trumpeter's finest small-group performances. Working in what is more or less a jazz context, using techniques that at times recall Duke Ellington, he has at his command only the faintest echo of Ellington's rhythmic understanding. Intent on harmonic and textural invention, he pays little attention to the cardinal quality of swing. It is no exaggeration, in fact, to say that he willingly sacrifices it at the altar of his first loves, a point that is borne out by the reticence of such excellent drummers as Art Taylor and Philly Joe Jones on the records made under his direction. With the issue of *Sketches of Spain*, which contains the results of these two men's most recent collaborations in the studio, it has become quite clear that Evans's strength is also his weakness, and that the same gift which allows him to express with such persuasive accuracy the allied feelings of sadness and nostalgia debars him from transcending these moods to arrive at a bold artistic statement. In these records we can discover the virtues of sensitivity and grace, but with one or two exceptions, the necessary backbone seems to be missing. Beautiful invertebrates, Evans's creations seldom lift their heads far above the ground.

Miles Davis had been something of a fixture at the Café Bohemia Club in Greenwich Village during 1957, except for a brief period when he underwent throat surgery; but at the close of the year he made a short trip to Paris in order to record the soundtrack for Louis Malle's *Ascenseur Pour l'Echafaud*. Inspired, it seems, by the simultaneous projection of the film on a screen in the recording studio, Davis provided an unfailingly apt commentary on the vicissitudes of the action. The collection is certainly superior to the album he made for Blue Note shortly after his return to New York. Though issued under Cannonball Adderley's name, this record is clearly dominated by his current employer, whose incisive choruses on *Somethin' Else*, the title piece, and *One For Daddy-o* make the altoist sound a discursive soloist in comparison.

In January 1958, John Coltrane rejoined Davis's group, having played with Thelonious Monk during the preceding summer. Adderley remained, so that Davis was now leading a sextet, and it was this band which recorded for Columbia some three months later. The atmosphere of cohesion that had been so striking an aspect of the group's work when Coltrane had previously partnered Davis is by no manner of means so striking, but some excellent solos are to be heard, and the rhythmic support is perfection itself. The trumpeter takes his best sequence of choruses in *Sid's Ahead*, a blues he had recorded in 1954 under the title of *Weirdo*, and a near relation to *Walkin'*. He performs with masterly precision, making every note tell, and generally using runs only to lead up to a sustained note. Adderley's task in having to follow a statement of such raw intensity is unenviable, and he fares no better than on the Blue Note session.

If no other evidence were at hand, this astonishing solo would be proof enough that Davis had learnt how to refine his style without weakening its substance; but with the departure of Red Garland, the band's character altered to some degree, with more emphasis being placed on a subdued mode of expression. 'Especially when he started to use Bill Evans, Miles changed his style from very hard to a softer approach. Bill was brilliant in other areas, but he couldn't make the real hard things come off,' Cannonball Adderley has said.[1] Evans spent eight months with Davis in 1958. His residence in the band coincided with two other important changes. The first has to do with a shift in the leader's musical sensibilities. During 1958 he seems to have been strongly attracted by the idea of basing his improvisations on a scale rather than a harmonic sequence. His phrasing grew sparer, the rests in his melodic line more prolonged. The second was Philly Joe Jones's leaving the group, and his eventual replacement by Jimmy Cobb, a steady drummer possessed of a crisp swing but lacking the immense verve, imagination and technical resources of his predecessor. All three of these factors—the advent of Evans and Cobb, together with the evolution in Davis's views—were clearly interdependent, and their influence is keenly felt in the music which may be heard on *Kind of Blue*, a collection containing performances recorded at two sessions held in March and April of 1959.

This album, the only one to be issued of Davis's small-group work since *Milestones*, which was done about twelve months previously, represents a new departure in his musical thinking. One of the pieces it contains, *Flamenco Sketches*, is cast in 6/8 time, whilst other selections find the leader and his men constructing their improvisations with a scale, rather than a given chord sequence, in mind. *All Blues*, for example, is a calm, reflective performance in which each soloist wends his way expertly through five different scales in turn. It says much for the maturity and group feeling of the musicians that none loses his grip on the direction of his solo, despite the wide melodic choice with which he is faced. Bill Evans is especially good here, doubtless because the style of interpretation is eminently well suited to his capabilities. It is significant that

on *Freddie Freeloader*, a more conventional mid-tempo blues, Davis saw fit to use Wynton Kelly at the keyboard. A less personal improviser, Kelly is a model accompanist for this type of number, and his presence explains in part why the track contains the leader's most cohesive solo of the album, a gripping, intense sequence which proves that Davis still finds ample inspiration in the more normal harmonic approach. *Flamenco Sketches*, *All Blues* and *So What* are interesting, often absorbing, but this performance, together with *Blue in Green*, a minute exploration of the inner recesses of melancholia, emerge as the highlights of the set. When one muses upon the very high standard the group attains both on this album and *Milestones*, it seems almost an impertinence on the part of those responsible that these two collations, supplemented by three rather less impressive renditions, should make up the entire catalogue of Davis's recordings with his regular group over the past three years. One hopes that other sessions have in fact been held in the Columbia studios and that in the fulness of time their fruits will be made available. Although the band has undergone one or two personnel changes over the past year or so, Adderley having left to form his own group in September 1959, and Coltrane having done likewise, with the same end in view, a few months later, the trumpeter has had no difficulty in maintaining a regular unit, thanks to a measure of popularity which must be unprecedented for a jazz musician over the past two decades. Currently he is leading a quintet which comprises Sonny Stitt on alto and tenor saxophones, and a rhythm section composed of Wynton Kelly, Paul Chambers and Jimmy Cobb. At the present writing the band is about to embark on a British tour. This event will give local enthusiasts a unique opportunity of evaluating Davis's present musical approach to their own satisfaction.

[1] *Jazz Review*, May 1960.

The same wave of acclaim that has brought economic security within Davis's grasp—he is reported to command fees in the region of $2,500 for one night's work and to possess $45,000-worth of stocks and shares—has inevitably been accompanied by the type of vulgar publicity usually reserved for popular entertainers such as Frank Sinatra or Johnny Ray. What is very curious is that so much that has been written about him turns upon his supposed antipathy to the people who pay to hear him. Perhaps because of the equivocal relationship that must always exist in an unintegrated society between a coloured performer and a predominantly white audience, Davis has made a point of refusing to acknowledge applause. Furthermore, very rarely will he announce the titles of the tunes his group plays, nor does he remain on stage whilst another musician is soloing. As a result, the trade Press is forever receiving letters from indignant customers who regard themselves as insulted by his behaviour. More surprisingly, many of the reports devoted to his club appearances by these same journals are concerned first and foremost with his bearing on and off the stand, often passing over the music proper with a brief phrase or two. Strangely enough, none of this publicity has proved to be as adverse as might have been supposed, and the anecdotes that abound regarding his hostility to employers and enthusiasts alike seem indirectly to have swollen his bank balance rather than depleted it. Although Davis maintains that he conducts himself with the best possible intentions and is anything but disdainful of the audience, one might be forgiven for supposing that he finds it extremely lucrative to perpetuate this image of himself as an arrogant outsider. However, the situation is not quite so simple as that. Since he was arrested and beaten up by police outside Birdland in August 1959, a violation of his rights as a citizen which would appear to have absolutely no justification, he is rumoured to have grown more irritable and short-tempered than ever, and many reports have it that his attitude is governed by a kind of reverse racial prejudice, though this, once again, he vehemently denies.

The degree to which attention has been focused upon Davis's stage presentation, or lack of it, reveals just how closely jazz is bound up with the mechanics of the popular music industry. Anecdotes about jazz musicians are still eagerly seized upon by record collectors, not so much for the extra light they throw on the music itself as for their entertainment value as novelties, in much the same way as countless people live out a surrogate existence by way of the daily newspaper gossip columns. In such a context it is hardly surprising that comment on Davis's recent *musical* activities has been at a premium.

It is to my mind undeniable that since Davis has achieved the kind of popularity enjoyed by such diverse musicians as Dave Brubeck, John Lewis and Gerry Mulligan, only a certain proportion of his records have been marked by the emotional intensity which characterized the whole of his output from 1950 to 1955. His technique, agreed, has grown a good deal surer. Though he still makes mistakes, generally in the higher register, they are far less frequent than in the past. Powers of execution, however, are only incidental to the point I am intent on making; if accuracy were a prerequisite of the successful jazz performance, neither the Armstrong Hot Five nor the Parker Quintet records could be regarded as milestones in the idiom's development, though this is what they very obviously are. Armstrong's occasional fluffs and Parker's recurrent squeaks are minor matters in the final analysis. Similarly, if Davis's 1951 recording of *My Old Flame* is compared with the version of *Stella By Starlight* done seven years later, it will be evident that the latter contains far fewer technical errors, if indeed any at all; but from the standpoint of melodic interest, rhythmic diversity, and—most vital of all—emotive power, the earlier selection is very clearly the better one.

Fortunately enough, the deterioration has been only partial and it is hard to see how anyone could unreservedly agree with the anonymous drummer who declared that 'a certain vitality isn't there any more. He lives a pretty lush life and his music gets kind of lush'.[1] Whilst he has latterly tended to deal in moods less aggressive than before, the best of his records in this vein, such as *Blue in Green* or *Summertime*, are every bit as convincing in their own way as *Airegin* or *Tune Up*, hard-driving performances done with his 1956 band. Whilst it seems probable that the comfortable existence he is now able to lead, in common with the more strictly musical factors already mentioned, has affected his choice of style, only at times, to judge at least from the records he has made, does he fall short of the artistic standards he established prior to emerging as a popular performer.

Only the very rash would care to predict what road Davis will take in the future, for at the present writing it is plainly impossible to know whether he will press on to an even sparer style of phrasing, or whether the influence of Sonny Stitt, currently working in his quintet, will cause him to lay more stress on rhythmic drive and melodic complexity. Yet wherever his alert musical spirit leads him, there is no gainsaying the fact that his talents have already had an enduring effect on jazz development as a whole. Attracted long before his twentieth birthday by the new form of jazz then being pioneered by his seniors, he matured within the bop idiom to develop a style of improvisation that was clearly his own, though based on the doctrines introduced to jazz by those who had originally inspired him. Over the past ten years he has worked to extend the range of his talents. The body of music he has produced during that time is extremely diverse, not only in feeling, but also in its formal character, yet this diversity in no way impugns the individual character of his work. His creative impulse has induced him to seek out new modes of expression whenever he felt they were needed, irrespective of prevailing fashions. It is most encouraging to reflect that his artistic growth may yet take unsuspected directions.

[1] *Playboy* Magazine, August 1960.

MILES DAVIS
RECOMMENDED RECORDS

Far from comprehensive, this listing has been chosen mainly to illustrate the text. Where a recording has been issued in more than one form, I have been guided by reproduction quality in my choice of catalogue number. Readers interested in Davis's formative years will wish to hear the five long playing records issued on Savoy, MG12000, MG12001, MG12009, MG12014 and MG12079, which contain the Parker quintet performances made between 1945 and 1948. It should be noted that Mr. Jorgen Grunnet Jepsen, the remarkable Danish discographer, has compiled a fully detailed listing of all the trumpeter's records. This work may be obtained from the publishers, Debut Records, Box 46, Brande, Denmark.

Key to Label Abbreviations:

Other label names are given in full. Asterisk indicates album no longer available.

Key to other Abbreviations:

(*alt*) alto saxophone	(*fl-h*) fluegel-horn
(*bar*) baritone saxophone	(*fr-h*) French horn
(*bs*) string bass	(*g*) guitar
(*bs-clt*) bass-clarinet	(*o*) oboe
(*bs-tbn*) bass trombone	(*p*) piano
(*bsn*) bassoon	(*perc*) percussion
(*clt*) clarinet	(*sop*) soprano saxophone
(*d*) drums	(*tbn*) trombone
(*dir*) director	(*ten*) tenor saxophone
(*e-g*) electric guitar	(*tpt*) trumpet
(*e-p*) electric piano	(*tu*) tuba
(*f*) flute	(*vcl*) vocal
(*f-bs*) fender bass	(*vib*) vibraphone

BN	Blue Note	Cap	Capitol	Co	Columbia
Prst	Prestige	Rou	Roulette	Svy	Savoy

CHARLIE PARKER'S RE BOPPERS:

Miles Davis (*tpt*); Charlie Parker (*alt*); Argonne Thornton (p) ; Dillon 'Curley' Russell (bs) ; Max Roach (d) .

New York City, November 26, 1945
Billie's Bounce
Now's the Time } Svy MG12079
Thriving from a Riff

CHARLIE PARKER QUINTET:

Miles Davis (tpt) ; Charlie Parker (alt) ; Duke Jordan
(p) ; Tommy Potter (bs) ; Max Roach (d) .

Bongo Bop
Bongo Bop (alternative master)   Rou RE 105
Dewey Square
Embraceable You   Rou RE 120
Dexterity   Dial LP905*
Prezology   Dial LP210*
Superman   Dial LP212*
Bird of Paradise
Bird of Paradise   Dial LP904*
   (alternative master)

MILES DAVIS AND HIS ORCHESTRA:

Miles Davis (tpt) ; Kai Winding (tpt) ; Junior Collins
(fr-h) ; Bill Barber (tu) ; Lee Konitz (alt) ; Gerry Mulligan
(bar) ; Al Haig (p) ; Joe Shulman (bs) ; Max Roach (d) .

New York City, January 21, 1949
Jeru
Move
Godchild } Cap M11026
Budo

Miles Davis (tpt) ; Jay Jay Johnson (tbn) ; Sanford Siegel-
stein (fr-h) ; Bill Barber (tu) ; Lee Konitz (alt) ; Gerry
Mulligan (bar) ; John Lewis (p) ; Nelson Boyd (bs) ;
Kenny Clarke (d) .

New York City, April 22, 1949
Venus de Milo
Rouge
Boplicity } Cap M11026
Israel

Gunther Schuller (fr-h) ; Al McKibbon (bs) replace
Siegelstein and Boyd. Kenny Hagood (vcl [1]) added.

New York City, March 13, 1950
Deception
Rocker
Moon Dreams } Cap M11026
Darn That Dream [1]

METRONOME ALL STAR BAND:

Miles Davis (tpt) ; Kai Winding (tbn) ; John LaPorta

(clt) ; Lee Konitz (alt) ; Stan Getz (ten) ; Serge Chaloff
(bar) ; Terry Gibbs (vib) ; George Shearing (p) ; Billy
Bauer (g) ; Eddie Safranski (bs) ; Max Roach (d) .

New York City, January 24, 1951
Early Spring
Local 802 Blues } Cap M11031

MILES DAVIS SEXTET:

Miles Davis (tpt) ; Jackie McLean (alt [1]) ; Sonny Rollins
(ten) ; Walter Bishop, Jr. (p) ; Tommy Potter (bs) ; Art
Blakey (d) .

New York City, October 5, 1951
Conception
Out of the Blue [1]
Denial [1]
Bluing [1] } Prst 7744
Dig [1]
My Old Flame
Paper Moon

Miles Davis (tpt) ; Jay Jay Johnson (tbn [1]) ; Jackie Mc-
Lean (alt [1]) ; Gil Coggins (p) ; Oscar Pettiford (bs) ; Kenny
Clarke (d) .

New York City, May 9, 1952
Dear Old Stockholm [1]
Chance It [1] } BN 81501
Donna [1]
Woody'n You [1] } BN 81502
Yesterdays
How Deep Is the Ocean } BN 81501

Note: Alternative masters of *Donna* and *Woody'n You* can
be heard on BN BLP1501.

Miles Davis (tpt) ; Charlie Parker, Sonny Rollins (ten) ;
Walter Bishop, Jr. (p) ; Percy Heath (bs) ; Philly Joe
Jones (d) .

New York City, January 30, 1953
Compulsion
The Serpent's Tooth
  (takes 1 and 2) } Prst 24022
'Round about Midnight

Miles Davis (tpt) ; Jay Jay Johnson (tbn) ; Jimmy Heath
(ten) ; Gil Coggins (p) ; Percy Heath (bs) ; Art Blakey
(d) .

New York City, April 20, 1953

Tempus Fugit
Enigma
Ray's Idea
Kelp
C.T.A. } BN 81501
I Waited for You [1] BN 81502

[1] Johnson and Heath out on this track.

Miles Davis (*tpt*); Jay Jay Johnson (*tbn*); Lucky Thompson (*ten*); Horace Silver (*p*); Percy Heath (*bs*); Kenny Clarke (*d*).

Hackensack, N. J., April 29, 1954
Blue 'n' Boogie
Walkin' } Prst 7608

MILES DAVIS QUINTET:

Miles Davis (*tpt*); Sonny Rollins (*ten*); Horace Silver (*p*); Percy Heath (*bs*); Kenny Clarke (*d*).

Hackensack, N. J., June 29, 1954
Airegin
Oleo
But Not for Me (2 takes)
Doxy } Prst 7847, 24012

MILES DAVIS ALL STARS:

Miles Davis (*tpt*); Milt Jackson (*vib*); Thelonious Monk (*p*); Percy Heath (*bs*); Kenny Clarke (*d*).

Hackensack, N. J., December 24, 1954
Bags' Groove (2 takes)
Bemsha Swing
Swing Spring
The Man I Love (2 takes) } Prst 7650, 24012

MILES DAVIS QUINTET:

Miles Davis (*tpt*); Jackie McLean (*alt* [1]); Milt Jackson (*vib*); Ray Bryant (*p*); Percy Heath (*bs*); Art Taylor (*d*).

Hackensack, N. J., August 5, 1955
Dr. Jackle [1]
Bitty Ditty
Minor March [1]
Changes } Prst LP7034*

Miles Davis (*tpt*); John Coltrane (*ten*); Red Garland (*p*); Paul Chambers (*bs*); Philly Joe Jones (*d*).

Hackensack, N. J., November 16, 1955

Stablemates
How Am I To Know
Just Squeeze Me
There Is No Greater Love [1]
Miles' Theme
S'posin' } Prst LP7014*

[1] Coltrane does not play on this number.

MILES DAVIS ALL STARS:

Miles Davis (*tpt*); Sonny Rollins (*ten*); Tommy Flanagan (*p*); Paul Chambers (*bs*); Art Taylor (*d*).

Hackensack, N. J., March 16, 1956
In Your Own Sweet Way
No Line
Vierd Blues } Prst 7847

MILES DAVIS QUINTET:

Miles Davis (*tpt*); John Coltrane (*ten*); Red Garland (*p*); Paul Chambers (*bs*); Philly Joe Jones (*d*).

Hackensack, N. J., May 11, 1956
In Your Own Sweet Way	Prst 24022
Trane's Blues	Prst 24034
It Could Happen to You	Prst 24001
Woody'n You	Prst 7373
It Never Entered My Mind	Prst 24034
Four	Prst 7822
The Theme (2 takes)	Prst 24034

Personnel as last.

Hackensack, N. J., October 26, 1956
If I Were A Bell Prst 24001
'Round Midnight Prst 24022
Half Nelson Prst 24034
You're My Everything
I Could Write A Book
Oleo
Airegin
Tune Up
When Lights Are Low } Prst 24001
Blues By Five
My Funny Valentine [1]

[1] Coltrane is not present on this track.

MILES DAVIS WITH ORCHESTRA UNDER THE DIRECTION OF GIL EVANS:

Miles Davis (*fl-h*); Bernie Glow, Ernie Royal, Louis Mucci, Taft Jordan, Johnny Carisi (*tpt*); Frank Rehak, Jimmy Cleveland, Joe Bennett (*tbn*); Tom Mitchell (*bs-tbn*); Willie Ruff, Tony Miranda, Jim Buffington (*fr-h*); Bill Barber (*tu*); Lee Konitz (*alt*); Danny Bank (*bs-clt*);

Romeo Penque, Sid Cooper, Edwin Caine (*f, clt*); Paul Chambers (*bs*); Art Taylor (*d*); Gil Evans (*dir*).

New York City, May 6, 1957
The Maids of Cadiz
The Duke
} Co CS8633

New York City, May 10, 1957
My Ship
Miles Ahead
} Co CS8633

New York City, May 23, 1957
New Rhumba
Blues for Pablo
Springsville
} Co CS8633

New York City, May 27, 1957
I Don't Wanna Be Kissed
The Meaning of the Blues
Lament
} Co CS8633

Note: The personnel given for these four sessions is a collective one. On one session Buffington replaces Miranda and Caine replaces Cooper.

MILES DAVIS QUINTET:

Miles Davis (*tpt*); Barney Wilen (*ten* [1]); Rene Urtreger (*p*); Pierre Michelot (*bs*); Kenny Clarke (*d*).

Paris, December 4, 1957
Générique
L'Assassinat de Carala
Sur l'Autoroute [1]
Julien Dans L'Ascenseur
Florence sur les Champs-Elysées [1]
Dîner au Môtel
Evasion de Julien [2]
Visite du Vigile [3]
Au Bar du Petit Bac [1]
Chez le Photographe du Môtel
} Co CL1268*

[2] Michelot only on this track; [3] Michelot and Clarke only on this track.

MILES DAVIS SEXTET:

Miles Davis (*tpt*); Julian Adderley (*alt*); John Coltrane (*ten*); Red Garland (*p*); Paul Chambers (*bs*); Philly Joe Jones (*d*).

New York City, April 2, 1958
Two Bass Hit
Straight, No Chaser
Milestones
} Co CS9428

New York City, April 3, 1958
Dr. Jekyll
Sid's Ahead
} Co CS9428

Miles Davis (*tpt*); Julian Adderley (*alt* [1]); John Coltrane (*ten*); Bill Evans [2], Wynton Kelly [3] (*p*); Paul Chambers (*bs*); Jimmy Cobb (*d*).

New York City, March 2, 1959
Freddie Freeloader [1,3]
So What [1,2]
Blues in Green [2]
} Co CS8163

New York City, April 22, 1959
Flamenco Sketches [1,2]
All Blues [1,2]
} Co CS8163

MILES DAVIS WITH ORCHESTRA UNDER THE DIRECTION OF GIL EVANS:

Miles Davis, Bernie Glow, Taft Jordan, Louis Mucci, Ernie Royal (*tpt*); Dick Hixon, Frank Rehak (*tbn*); Danny Banks (*bs-clt,f*); Albert Block, Eddie Caine (*f*); Harold Feldman (*o,bs-clt*); John Barrows, Jimmy Buffington, Earl Chapin (*fr-h*); James McAllister (*tu*); Janet Putman (*h*); Paul Chambers (*bs*); Jimmy Cobb, Elvin Jones (*d*); Gil Evans (*dir*).

New York City, Nov. 20, 1959
Concierto de Aranjuez   Co CS8271

Same as above except Jordan and Mucci (*tpt*) replaced by John Coles; Burrows and Chapin (*fr-h*) by Joe Singer and Tony Miranda; McAllister (*tu*) by Bill Barber; Romeo Penque (*o*), Jack Knitzer (*bsn*) and Elden Bailey (*perc*) added.

New York City, March 10 & 11, 1960
Pan Piper
Will o' the Wisp   Co CS8271
Saeta
Solea

MILES DAVIS AND HIS ORCHESTRA

Miles Davis (*tpt*); Herbie Hancock, Chick Corea, Josef Zawinul (*e-p*); Wayne Shorter (*ten*); Dave Holland (*bs*); John McLaughlin (*g*); Tony Williams (*d*).

New York City, Feb. 18, 1969
Shhh
Peaceful   Co CS9875
In a Silent Way
It's About that Time

MILES DAVIS AND HIS ORCHESTRA

Miles Davis (*tpt*); Wayne Shorter (*sop*); Larry White, Jack DeJohnette, Charles Alias (*d*); Benny Maupen (*bs-clt*); Chick Corea, Josef Zawinul [1], Larry Young [2] (*e-p*); Jim Riley (*perc*); Harvey Brooks (*f-bs*); Dave Holland (*bs*); John McLaughlin (*e-g*).

New York City, Aug. 19 & 21, 1969   *John McLaughlin*[2]
  Bitches Brew[1]   *Miles Runs the Voodoo Down*[2]
  Pharoah's Dance[2]
  Spanish Key[1, 2]   }   Co GP26
  Sanctuary[1]

Johnny Dodds

BY G. E. LAMBERT

I

HIS LIFE

In the years when New Orleans was the premier centre of jazz—that is from around 1900 to the closing of the Storyville red light district in 1918—it was a city flooded with music. Every possible occasion—picnics, advertising, trips on the Mississippi—was provided with music; every place of diversion—the bars, theatres, brothels and gambling joints—had its musicians. Parades by the various organizations had their brass bands, which also played for the unique New Orleans funerals, and dance orchestras of all types were to be heard within the city limits. In the Creole and Negro districts there was scarcely a family who did not boast of several part-time musicians, and there were hundreds of skilled local professionals playing in the various parade bands, jazz bands, society bands and riverboat orchestras. To judge from the material collected by later historians, the doings of the favourite musicians of the city were looked upon with the same interest which the mass of people today accord to sporting heroes and popular cinema or television personalities. There were trumpet players known for their vivacious playing and stamina on the long parades, and others who specialized in the dirges played on the way to and at the graveside; one trumpet player will be remembered for his volume and exuberance in the lower-class dance-halls, another for his unique ability and power of expression on the blues. A musician who was supreme in his field was known as a 'King' to his contemporaries; a fast, likeable young musician with what would today be called 'stage presence' would be nicknamed 'Kid'. But unlike the parallels which can be drawn with contemporary heroes of entertainment or of professional sport, these men were not remote figures to be seen only when performing, but neighbours with whom one would associate in everyday life. Music was an integral part of the lives of the city's inhabitants, and in the days before the standardizing influence of radio, gramophone and TV, the sounds of New Orleans music were peculiar to that city. Not many recordings of importance were made in New Orleans during the first boom in jazz recording in the 1920s, but the New Orleans musicians who moved north, particularly those who emigrated to Chicago, recorded prolifically.

On records, it is usually possible to recognize a New Orleans band, and almost always to pick out a New Orleans musician of the old school. Although there is an amazing richness of individual style among these men, they are always superb ensemble musicians. Making music together was a part of the New Orleans heritage when they were young, and the principal band styles of the city offered ample scope to the ensemble musician, without ever demanding that he gave up his musical identity. All the older New Orleans musicians remember the great days of jazz in the city, but they remember it in a rather amazed sort of way. When Henry Allen, the great New Orleans trumpet player, visited this country in 1959, I asked him about the old days. 'Well, we didn't *think* a great deal about it then, we were too busy just playing. But when I look back to my early days in New Orleans, well it just seems wonderful. It seems fantastic to have been a part of something like that, you know, but it didn't seem anything special to us kids at the time.'

Johnny Dodds was born on 12 April 1892, and his childhood environment was a musical one; his father and uncle were violinists, his sister played melodian, and in adolescence Johnny sang high tenor in the family vocal quartet. His instrumental skill was developed (as was the case with several other famous New Orleans musicians) on a toy flute. According to one story, the flute originally belonged to his brother Warren 'Baby' Dodds, four years Johnny's junior, who was shamed into parting with it when he realized his elder brother's natural flair for the instrument. When Johnny was in his late teens, his father bought him a clarinet, and the skill he had acquired on the toy flute was put to further use. He took occasional lessons from Lorenzo Tio, Senior, a member of a famous musical Creole family, who were noted for their skill in clarinet playing. Another musician who is said to have given instruction in clarinet playing to the young Dodds, is Charlie McCurdy or McCurtis, whose clarinet playing seems better remembered than the exact spelling of his surname. Indeed, regarding Dodds's own surname, we are informed by no less an authority than Samuel B. Charters, a historian who has made an extensive study of jazz in New Orleans, that before moving north in 1918, Dodds himself was known as Johnny Dot! Whether it is meant that this was the actual surname of Johnny's family, a corruption accepted through usage, or simply a nickname, it seems impossible to say.

As his clarinet playing approached mastery, the young Dodds started to accept semi-professional engagements, one of the first of these being with Frankie Dusen's Eagle Band. This was the group which was taken over by Dusen when the famed Buddy Bolden was committed to the asylum in 1907, and it is significant that Dodds's first musical engagement was one with a rough 'uptown' Negro blues-playing group. 'Downtown' the Creole orchestras with their more polite and much more academic approach to music-making held forth. Dodds himself was a Negro, of course, but by this time a good degree of mixing was standard in the New Orleans bands. For example, when Johnny took his first full time professional engagement, it was with Kid Ory's band; Ory is a Creole from La Place, a small town near New Orleans, who first brought his band into the city in 1913. Ory's natural showmanship soon made the band a success and gradually his hometown musicians were replaced by New Orleans men, many of them destined to become world famous names in jazz. King Oliver, Louis Armstrong, Mutt Carey, Wade Waley, Lawrence Duhé, Big Eye Louis Nelson, Kid Rena, Ed

Garland and Pops Foster all played at different times with the Ory band during this period, although some old-timers state that Oliver was the leader of the group during the height of his local fame. What appears to have happened was that while Ory retained the actual leadership he gave maximum publicity to the famous cornetist, who is said to have been nicknamed 'King' during his stay with the Ory band. According to a popular New Orleans story, it was the bassist Pops Foster who got Dodds his engagement with the Ory band, after hearing him practising clarinet as he passed the Dodds's house. This sounds rather fantastic, although Johnny's playing must have been really outstanding for him to have been offered a place in the famous Ory band as his first professional engagement. The circumstances in which Dodds left New Orleans are given differently in the various histories of this period. Certainly he travelled to Chicago with a Mac and Mac Minstrel Show around 1917 in the company of the trumpet player Mutt Carey, but there is some doubt as to whether he remained in Chicago or returned for a further period to New Orleans. A photograph used in several books concerned with New Orleans jazz, shows Dodds as a member of the Fate Marable band aboard the S.S. *Sidney Streckfus* along with his brother 'Baby', Louis Armstrong, Johnny St. Cyr and Pops Foster. The date usually given to this photo is 1918, which would seem to indicate that Dodds did return to the Crescent City after his first visit to Chicago. Certainly, Mutt Carey returned and told the locals that the Chicago weather was intolerably cold. Dodds apparently did not think so, for within a few months he returned to the north, spending most of his life in Chicago and never returning to New Orleans.

In 1920 Johnny replaced Jimmy Noone with the King Oliver band in Chicago and travelled to the West Coast with the group the following year. On their return to Chicago for a long engagment at the Lincoln Gardens, Oliver brought with him the nucleus of the famous band which was to have such a profound influence on jazz musicians and which made the first really important jazz recordings. By this time Johnny's younger brother had joined Oliver on drums and thereby hangs another of those curious tales which abound in the mythology which has grown out of the New Orleans jazzmen's reminiscences of their early days. This oft-told story is that when Baby Dodds was learning drums he used to sit in from time to time with the Ory band in New Orleans, whereupon the band filed off the stage one by one, invariably headed by brother Johnny, who had the lowest possible opinion of Baby's ability. Johnny is also reputed to have advised Oliver strongly against hiring his brother, while Kay Thompson (*Jazz Journal*, March 1951) quotes Baby as saying that Johnny walked off the bandstand in disgust when he joined the Oliver band, only to return and congratulate him on the improvement in his drumming. Yet against this we have the evidence of the photograph of the S.S. *Sidney Streckfus* band, containing both the Dodds brothers before either left New Orleans. Whatever the true facts are on this matter, they are probably lost for ever now that both the Dodds brothers are dead.

The King Oliver Creole Jazz Band must have been a fine band before Oliver sent to New Orleans for Louis Armstrong to join him as second cornetist, but with the arrival of Armstrong the group acquired a new and distinctive ensemble sound which placed it (in the opinions of those who heard the band in the flesh, and of later-day record collectors) among the very greatest in the entire history of jazz. The band's first recordings were made in 1923 for the Gennett Company, which had a reputation for poor recording even in those low-fi days. The Oliver recording sessions are also the subject of many stories of dubious authenticity. According to some authorities, the powerful sound of the Oliver brass (Joe himself and Louis Armstrong on cornets and Honoré Dutrey on trombone) knocked the needle clean off the cutter of the primitive recording machine, and they were all relegated forthwith to the back of the studio. It was impossible to record Bill Johnson's bass for this same reason and he is believed to have played banjo on some of the sessions. On the other hand Baby Dodds (on page 70 of *The Baby Dodds Story*) claims that Johnny, Louis and Honoré Dutrey were at the back of the studio with everybody else including Oliver close to the horn. As the recorded sound is very even in respect of the balance between the two cornets, this would make Oliver a very weak player indeed, especially as the two-cornet line is often lost behind the clarinet *obligato*! We must remember that Louis and Joe were the rage of Chicago at this time with their two-cornet

duets and breaks, which would hardly have been the case if Oliver had been so weak a player that his cornet, placed right up to the acoustic recording horn, could have been drowned out by a clarinettist operating from the back of the studio! In addition to the sessions for Gennett, the King Oliver Creole Jazz Band also recorded for Paramount and Okeh, the latter company providing them with the best recording quality to be found on any of their sides. On the stand at the Lincoln Gardens they were heard and admired by all the jazz musicians active in Chicago, which at that time was the centre of the jazz world. Pretty well everyone who heard the band speaks of it in words of the highest praise and claims that the recordings give a totally inadequate picture of the band's capabilities.

In 1924 several of the musicians left the Creole band—one of the reasons given is that some of the bandsmen suspected that Oliver was pocketing a larger share of the record royalties than he would admit—and Johnny Dodds was asked to take a band into Kelly's Stables, a cabaret on Chicago's South Side. Johnny took with him three other members of the Oliver band, Honoré Dutrey, Bill Johnson and Baby Dodds—adding Freddie Keppard on trumpet and Charlie Alexander on piano. Dutrey left as the management wanted a five-piece group and Baby Dodds soon followed after a disagreement with Burt Kelly, the owner, Baby claiming that this was because Kelly did not like his drumming. Zutty Singleton appears to have played with the band for a while around this time. Kelly's Stables was another of the favourite haunts of the Chicago jazz musicians, both white and coloured, and Baby Dodds recalls that many of the younger white musicians used to frequent the place and sit in with the band. It is said that Frank Teschmaker, whose playing is not notably Negroid on the few recordings he made, used to play in a style very similar to Johnny's when he sat in with the band.

Freddie Keppard was, according to many musicians, the finest cornet during the great years of New Orleans jazz, but by the time he came to record, his playing was on the decline. Kid Ory—who maintains that Keppard was foremost among jazz cornetists in New Orleans—says that he could not believe his ears when he heard Keppard in Chicago in the mid-'twenties, so different and inferior was the cornetist's style. Freddie was afraid that other musicians would steal his phrasing and, according to Ory, he used to play with a handkerchief over the valves so that his fingering could not be seen by other musicians. He was also a heavy drinker and it seems probable that his heavy consumption of whisky accounted for the decline in his playing; it should be noted that Keppard never had the reputation in the north that he had in his earlier New Orleans period. It was his drinking which caused him to be fired from his job with the Johnny Dodds group at Kelly's Stables, where he was replaced by Natty Dominique. During these years at Kelly's, Johnny Dodds made the famous recordings with Louis Armstrong and with Jelly Roll Morton, in addition to a number of lesser known titles with bands of his own, and with that strange group of musicians headed by the pianist Jimmy Blythe.

Johnny was a regular member of what could be called 'the washboard circuit', a group of men who appeared with small bands on countless Chicago recordings for the 'race' labels of the 1920s—a group including Dodds, Blythe, Keppard, Dominique, Roy Palmer, Stomp Evans, the Chicago clarinettist Jimmy O'Bryant, and the percussionist Jimmy Bertrand. The standard percussion instrument on these sessions, which were made as a rule by a four- or five-piece band, was usually the washboard, and the man responsible usually Jimmy Bertrand. Bertrand was very friendly with Jimmy Blythe, who organized most of the sessions. Baby Dodds occasionally played washboard, for example on the 1927 recordings by the Blythe 'Dixieland Thumpers' (Dominique, Blythe and the Dodds Brothers), and also on a couple of washboard sessions under Johnny's name. In April 1927 a session was recorded by Johnny Dodds and his Black Bottom Stompers, a group which included Louis Armstrong and Baby Dodds. This was the first of a series of band sessions under Johnny's name for Brunswick and Victor, which was continued for two years, during which time he also continued to record with Armstrong for Okeh, and with the various Blythe/Bertrand groups for the minor labels. A couple of months before the first of these band sessions, Dodds recorded two clarinet solos for Paramount which were therefore the first recordings to appear under his name.

Like almost all New Orleans reed players of note, Johnny Dodds was primarily a clarinettist, but during his stay at Kelly's Stables he had a brief flirtation with a saxophone. According to Baby Dodds the rest of the band did their utmost to dissuade Johnny from using this instrument, even going so far as to tell him repeatedly that he was playing badly, although they knew that he was in fact quite good on the instrument. Neither Baby nor Natty Dominique wanted a saxophone in the band and were prepared to go to any lengths to keep Johnny on clarinet. He did, as a matter of fact, record a couple of titles with the Louis Armstrong Hot Five on alto saxophone, *Come Back Sweet Papa* and *Don't Forget to Mess Around*, and a session with a Bertrand group, using the rarely heard sopranino sax, an instrument pitched above the soprano which has the highest range of any instrument in general use in the saxophone family. None of these recordings is of outstanding merit, although they certainly have a curiosity value.

After a couple of years Baby Dodds was back in the band at Kelly's Stables and stayed with the group until the closing of Kelly's in 1930. This year can be said to be the last in which Johnny Dodds had any reasonable degree of fame, or even of security, as a musician. By this time Chicago had ceased to be the jazz centre it had been in the middle 'twenties, and many of the famous jazz musicians had left the city. In the preceding year the New Orleans trumpet player Herb Morand had come to Chicago, and his first engagement was a recording session with the Dodds brothers and pianist Frank Melrose, the quartet calling themselves the Beale Street Washboard Band; it was, however, Johnny's last session for nine years, and his absence from the recording studios was symbolic of his lapse into obscurity. Moreover, the Depression was at hand, and the Negro audience for which the Dodds boys had played in Chicago were among the hardest hit by the slump and had little money to spend on music. However, Johnny Dodds was a conscientious leader and managed to keep his group playing during most of the Depression, although the money was often poor, and at one point Johnny and Baby were on the point of joining their elder brother Bill in his taxi business. Johnny kept the band occupied, and throughout the 'thirties they worked in various obscure night spots in Chicago. For a time the brothers had a trio with pianist Arthur Campbell, but generally the personnel, which altered surprisingly little, was built around a nucleus of Johnny, Baby and trumpeter Natty Dominique; sometimes Baby took other jobs, causing Johnny to call on a substitute drummer. During the early 'thirties, Ralph Tervalon and Stirling Todd were on piano, but in 1934 the latter was replaced by Little Brother Montgomery, who seems to have played fairly regularly in the band up to the time of Johnny's death in 1940. For a while Herb Waters played with the band on tenor sax, and Baby Dodds considers that he fitted in quite well, but on the whole the group remained a four-piece combo, with the occasional addition of a string bassist. For a good deal of the time they were playing for a white clientele and there was little demand for blues, which was unquestionably the music which Johnny loved and played the best. Popular tunes were learnt from stock arrangements and then given the band's distinctive treatment; sometimes students would call for numbers like *Anchors Aweigh*, while at one engagement at the K-Nine Club the group was called upon to play selections from *Faust* and an arrangement of Liszt's *Hungarian Rhapsody*! Baby recalls that Johnny was a very strict leader and insisted that the band should master the various types of music required by the clientele. For all that, the sound of the Dodds boys, Dominique and Little Brother rendering a selection from *Faust* must have been a pretty fantastic one!

When the swing era got under way in the late 'thirties, there was a slow awakening of interest in the earlier forms of jazz, but the full flood of this revival in New Orleans jazz came too late for Johnny Dodds, although his brother Baby was to play on many of the better New Orleans style recordings of the 1940s. In the later years of the preceding decade the change of wind must have become noticeable to the members of Johnny's little band. They were invited to jam sessions frequently, being honoured guests at the famous series run by the white New Orleans trumpet player, Paul Mares. At a benefit concert in 1937 for the pianist Joe Sullivan, who was seriously ill, the Johnny Dodds band appeared in what must have been one of the very first jazz concerts in Chicago. In 1938, at the instigation of Lil Armstrong, the Decca Company invited Johnny to New York for a recording session. This was Johnny's only visit to New York, but it could hardly be termed a successful one. With an insensitivity typical of the recording companies of those days, Decca used a number of musicians who played in a manner totally alien to

Dodds's New Orleans blues style, and although he contributes some good solos to the six titles recorded, his so-called 'Chicago Boys' do not even attempt to bridge the gap between their own concept of music-making and that of Dodds.

In 1939 Johnny played his last full engagment as a bandleader when he led a six-piece group at the Hotel Hayes, Chicago, with a band consisting of Lil Armstrong, Lonnie Johnson, and Sudie Raymond, in addition to the Dodds brothers and Natty Dominique. During this time Johnny had his first stroke, and when the engagement came to an end he opened with a quartet at the 9570 Club, again using Baby, Natty and Little Brother Montgomery. Baby Dodds claims that he held the contract for this job, and that at the request of the management had Johnny, who was still feeling the effects of his stroke, along to play week-ends. According to Walter C. Allen (see the list of Natty Dominique's engagements in *Hot Notes*, October 1947), the quartet opened at the 9570 in January 1940, but by February Johnny was too ill to play other than on Saturday nights. 'On the other nights Baby Dodds took over the leadership,' says Allen. In July of that year the Decca Company organized a couple of recording sessions at the Opera House in Chicago as part of the *New Orleans Jazz Album* they were making up as a response to the renewed interest in earlier jazz. Two sides each were cut by groups (virtually the same band in actual fact) under the direction of Jimmy Noone and Johnny Dodds. Johnny was concerned as he had just had all his teeth out, but despite imperfections in the music of the group as a whole, he played very well on what was to be the last of his many notable recording sessions. At this time, according to Baby, 'Johnny was pretty weak and he didn't walk too well. He wasn't crippled by his first stroke but he didn't walk too well.' On 8 August, Johnny had a second stroke at 10.30 in the morning; he never recovered consciousness and died shortly before noon.

The biography of Johnny Dodds is a tragic one, rising through his quick success in New Orleans, on to the triumphant years in Chicago with the Oliver band, and the many fine recordings he made while leading his own group at Kelly's Stables, only to fade suddenly into the twilight obscurity of the last ten years of his life. He was admired by all the musicians who heard him in the early days—

115

even Benny Goodman, a musician far removed in style and temperament, has said that he never heard anyone get a finer tone out of the clarinet than Johnny Dodds—while the majority of his 1920 recordings are numbered among the ageless classics of jazz. But in the following decade he was forgotten, only to die just as the interest in New Orleans jazz, of which he was one of the greatest masters, was reviving. Most of the New Orleans musicians who lived through the thin years of the 1930s saw at least some degree of recognition in the following decade. Johnny Dodds died just too soon for such recognition, and for the many fine recordings he would unquestionably have given us.

2

HIS RECORDINGS

Several bands contributed to the classic series of New Orleans style recordings which were made in Chicago during the 1920s, but the only one which was a regular unit outside the recording studios was the King Oliver Creole Jazz Band, which was playing its famous engagement at the Lincoln Gardens at the time of the recordings. These King Oliver discs were the first instrumental jazz recordings of real importance, and they remain among the very greatest of all jazz records. In 1923, when the Gennett, Okeh and Paramount companies recorded the band, Oliver's regular personnel was: King Oliver, Louis Armstrong (cornets), Honoré Dutrey (trombone), Johnny Dodds (clarinet), Lil Hardin (piano), Bill Johnson (bass) and Baby Dodds (drums). Later in the year Bud Scott (banjo) and Charlie Johnson (bass saxophone) were added. Owing to the primitive recording techniques the string bass was never used on records, Bill Johnson playing banjo on the earlier sessions; on some of the Okeh sides Johnny St. Cyr was used on banjo in place of Scott, although he did not play with the band outside the recording studios.

One of the main virtues of the Oliver records is the beautiful ensemble playing of the band. Their superiority to later bands, even such groups as Morton's Red Hot Peppers and the New Orleans Wanderers/Bootblacks unit, lies partly in the fact that they played together regularly; this band relied less on soloists than any of the others, and Oliver realized the potential of the New Orleans ensemble style more than any other leader. The New Orleans musicians were *natural* ensemble players, their whole environment having been that of collective music-making, in contrast to the emphasis on soloistic jazz in later decades. Even in such fine ensemble music as that of the Modern Jazz Quartet there is a certain feeling that the musicians are bending over to meet the other men half-way, a studied and self-conscious submission to the conception of the leader. In New Orleans jazz the musicians can be playing in a fully individual style, yet the ensemble will remain perfect. There was no apparent contradiction for the early New Orleans player between individuality and the needs of the group. The attitude of the musicians toward their fellow-bandsmen, and toward music in general, was such that a full blooded, expressive performance could be given by each man in the band without in any way impairing the balance of the ensemble or the shape of the overall conception. The mechanics of the New Orleans style had been developed under the influence of the magnificent spirit of the pioneer jazzmen and never fettered the creative fire of the individual musicians. In the past fifteen years we have had untold demonstrations of the fact that it was not merely the *mechanics* of the style which was responsible for this remarkable manner of music-making. It was, above all, the attitude of humanity and warmth held by the pioneer musicians which made New Orleans jazz the great music it was, and in many ways the King Oliver Creole Jazz Band epitomizes the music perfectly.

King Oliver was a strong leader who knew what sort of a band he wanted, was prepared to get the best men available to play in it, and then to see to it that they followed his conception of music-making. As a result the Oliver band was one of the most disciplined groups in jazz history. This may seem to contradict what was said in the last paragraph, but in fact this is not so. Initially Oliver selected men whom he knew would instinctively fall in with his ideas on music, and who would relish the discipline required to give a firm and secure basis to their own individual playing. This willingness to submit to Oliver's discipline is borne out by the fact that all the band's musicians who have discussed the matter recall their days with the Creole Jazz Band as among the happiest in their lives. Oliver had a bunch of young, temperamental jazzmen working with him, yet he held a firm grip on the band and gave each one of them an experience which is reflected in their playing in subsequent years and in the high esteem in which they hold their memories of the Oliver band.

The two-cornet lead, allied with Oliver's imagination as a band leader, gave the Creole band a variety of textures to work with, while in Armstrong and Johnny Dodds he had soloists of a stature equal to his own. Joe Oliver's musical outlook was never a merely decorative one. On some numbers—*Just Gone* is a good example of this—one steady texture is held throughout the performance; and the magnificent variety within this basic palette, along with the superb rhythmic buoyancy of the playing, is allowed to carry the performance to its balanced conclusion. On other numbers the contrast between Oliver's lead and that of Armstrong is stressed; some passages have the cornets playing in thirds, others feature Oliver's muted horn leading a four-part polyphony, while occasionally the ebullient Louis Armstrong is given the lead. Then there are those unique passages—for example the central ensemble choruses on the Okeh version of *Riverside Blues*—when both cornets play independent melodic lines within the ensemble polyphony.

To play a clarinet part in such a band called for a musician of remarkable ability, one who could adapt himself to the different textures with understanding and who could perform well on the various types of number used by Oliver's band—the stomps, rags, New Orleans marches, popular songs and blues. Johnny Dodds was a musician who not only fulfilled the role required of him, but did so with such a wealth of understanding, of strong and independent counter-melody, that his performances alone would be sufficient to raise the music to the stature of great jazz.

On the stomps and rags, Dodds's part is a tremendous stimulus to the other musicians, his counterpoint continually apt, the clarinet moving with ease round the lead in a continual line of singing melody. The rhythmic drive of the group is tremendously enhanced by Dodds's biting, stomping up-tempo manner, while the natural blues inflections of his playing keeps the music away from the shallow, novelty sound of a clarinettist like Larry Shields, Dodds's counterpart in the Original Dixieland Jazz Band.

Oliver's treatment of popular songs can be heard on such a recording as *Mandy Lee Blues*, in which the musicians break down the original melodic pattern into blues phrases; this practice is very common among jazz musicians, a classic example being Count Basie's opening piano solo on his 1937 recording of *Honeysuckle Rose*. Of course the Oliver band's achievement in adopting such songs for New Orleans band performance was thoroughly successful and Oliver's placing of breaks for different musicians on such numbers is comparable with Jelly Roll Morton's mastery of this device. On *Mandy Lee Blues*, Johnny Dodds plays the verse as written, yet simply by intonation transforms the melody from a trivial tune into quite a masterpiece of introspective music, his clarinet tone dark and brooding. By contrast Dodds's two breaks on this number demonstrate a mastery of a different kind, as the clarinet sings out momentarily in solo.

On a composition by Armstrong and Hardin, *Where Did You Stay Last Night?*, Oliver features a series of breaks, first by Dodds and then by the two cornets, which are unusual in that each uses the same break on every appearance. This has a unique effect, and the breaks played by Dodds are notable for the superb rhythmic timing and the crystal-like tone. The ensemble clarinet on this side is worthy of study, for here Dodds uses all registers of the instrument, enhancing each stage of the performance with perfectly fitting counterpoint.

The rags which were recorded by the Oliver band all have superb ensemble clarinet by Dodds, which give the lie to the assertion that he was simply a blues specialist. *Just Gone* and *Weatherbird Rag* both contain clarinet playing of a mobility and fluidity of execution which would be less remarkable in a musician of the Creole school, who were pre-eminent at this type of playing. On the latter title Dodds takes two breaks, the second of which is a perfect take-off of the rooty, white clarinet style which was prevalent at this time. This is an obvious piece of humour by Johnny, for throughout the remainder of the performance he plays in his usual highly musical manner. On *Snake Rag* and *Froggie Moore* the clarinet playing is of a forceful order rhythmically, as Dodds pierces the brass texture with his magnificent attack and his constantly creative counterpoint.

Another remarkable performance is that of Richard M. Jones's *Southern Stomps*, where the clarinet plays a highly 'orchestral' part against the rest of the group. Here Dodds abandons his usual mobile manner in favour of constant treble comments on the determined, rolling phrasing of the brass. This is a very unusual and rather under-rated performance by the band, which shows fully the effect of Oliver's strict discipline. Here, the fervent blues-playing of Dodds is welded perfectly into the unusual texture of the performance. The clarinet breaks are played with a superb tone and blues phrasing of the most moving kind.

By contrast, the Paramount *Mabel's Dream* (recorded at the same session as *Southern Stomps*) shows Dodds taking a less prominent role within the band. In all New Orleans performances the clarinet part is of considerable importance, and on *Mabel's Dream* Dodds's ensemble work is of his usual impeccable standard, constantly adding to the music, but never clashing with the playing of the rest of the band; the clarinet breaks, too, are taken in magnificent style, though they are of a 'functional' type after the manner of the breaks of *Where Did You Stay Last Night?* The primary role on *Mabel's Dream* is played by Oliver himself, and though he may have been past his prime when these recordings were made (and most of his contemporaries assure us that this was the case), such performances as this, on which he plays a fine open solo and then leads out the final ensemble in his plaintive muted style, are sufficient to indicate that here we were dealing with a jazz cornet player of the highest quality. On *Mabel's Dream* the clarinet is not 'featured' at all, yet it is significant to note

how much Dodds contributes to the music. The performance is at once a tribute to Dodds's superb musicianship and a reminder of how much scope for the creative musician there was in the genuine New Orleans ensemble style. How infinitely more rich is this music than the skimpy ensembles of the 'dixielanders' and the 'revivalists'!

Mention must be made too of the Oliver recording of *High Society*, or *High Society Rag* as he called it. This was the only occasion on which Johnny Dodds recorded this famous New Orleans march, with its traditional virtuoso clarinet solo. Dodds gives a satisfactory account, but it must be granted that he was not at his best on this type of performance and that his solo has been surpassed on recordings of *High Society* featuring clarinettists of lesser stature. It is not so much, as some writers have imagined, that Dodds was solely a blues musician, but rather that displays of so showman-like a nature were foreign to his personality. On the rags previously mentioned, Dodds gives the lie to the assertion that he was a mediocre musician when not playing blues, but it must be said that on such material he was invariably at his best, a blues clarinettist whose recordings have never been surpassed. Needless to say the Oliver blues performances feature Dodds at his very finest.

It would be impossible to pick out the best of Dodds's blues recordings with the Oliver band, for within this infinitely variable idiom each is a unique creation, each an incomparable masterpiece. Perhaps the Okeh recording of *Working Man Blues* is a good introduction, for here, in one of the Oliver band's finest performances, Dodds is at his greatest. The two themes are both excellent, and are played with great feeling and power by the band. Dodds's role here is a constantly changing one. At times he plays in the lower register, filling out the sound of the band and adding a surging rhythmic momentum; in other choruses his soaring descant is of such melodic strength that the clarinet part vies with the cornet lead in melodic interest. In his breaks on *Working Man Blues*, Dodds creates a series of melodic gems each perfectly dovetailed into the performance, each delivered with perfect timing and a glowing tone.

At the Gennett sessions which inaugurated the Oliver discography, three blues were recorded, all taken at a medium tempo. Of these *Chimes Blues* is the least interest-

Johnny Dodds about 1925

Franklin S. Driggs

ing, though Dodds can be heard to fine effect during the opening choruses, but the band's approach to the second theme offers little scope for creative playing by the clarinettist. *Dippermouth Blues* is a classic recording, and Dodds contributes fully to its success. The ensemble clarinet is constantly on hand with a superb second melody line to the cornets, while below Oliver's classic solo Dodds and Dutrey provide a sensitive foundation. It is worth listening closely to the accompaniment to this solo in order to realize how much musical depth there is in New Orleans jazz of the best quality. Dodds's own solo, which equals the Oliver in its constant melodic creation, is a superb two-chorus blues improvisation. On the Okeh recording of *Dippermouth Blues* Dodds plays virtually the same solo in each of his two choruses. This is generally a rather inferior performance to the Gennett (though still a very great one) and is taken at a faster tempo, thus sacrificing some of the superb relaxation and assurance of the earlier recording in favour of a stronger attack. An equally great performance is that of *Canal Street Blues*, a typical Oliver blues composition with its contrasting themes and stomping last chorus. Johnny Dodds plays a two-chorus solo here which must be con-

Louis Armstrong's Hot Five, about 1926. *Left to right*—Johnny St. Cyr,
Kid Ory, Louis Armstrong, Johnny Dodds and Lil Armstrong

sidered among his finest achievements, melodically simple but perfect in construction and in delivery. It is worth observing the difference here in the approach to the solo by Oliver's musicians on the Creole Jazz Band recordings and in their later discs made after they had left Oliver. This is noticeable even in so ensemble-conscious a musician as Johnny Dodds. On the New Orleans Wanderers/Bootblacks recordings for example, which certainly contain no virtuoso elements, the solos stand apart from the ensemble in quite a marked manner. But in the Oliver band a solo seems always a firmly rooted part of the total performance, in a way which is only equalled in the very best recordings of the Morton and Ellington bands, and a limited number of 'pure' New Orleans groups. Some jazz critics have used this phenomenon as a stick with which to beat later vir-

tuoso jazz, claiming that the latter was a decadent development. Without in any way wishing to depreciate the superb music of such soloists as Louis Armstrong, Coleman Hawkins or Charlie Parker, it does seem a remarkable tribute to the New Orleans idiom—and to Oliver's approach to it—that in the Creole Jazz Band recordings a musician such as Johnny Dodds, who, with all his fine qualities, had not the melodic inventiveness of these men, could produce solos equal in value to theirs.

Mention must also be made of the Oliver Okeh of *Sobbin' Blues*, which has fine Dodds in solo and ensemble, and a most delicate clarinet accompaniment to the peculiar swannee-whistle solo. This side illustrates as well as any, Dodds's contribution to the Oliver band, the constantly shifting emphasis of the clarinet part, the constantly

120

imaginative and creative outlook of Johnny as an ensemble musician. I do not think that any New Orleans band has been filled with musicians equally creative on every instrument. Indeed, the nature of the parts for banjo and bass, and to a large extent for piano and trombone, in the New Orleans ensemble structure, hardly allow for highly creative playing on every instrument. On piano and drums, for example, only Jelly Roll Morton and Baby Dodds have really exploited the possibilities of their instruments in New Orleans jazz. On the King Oliver Creole Jazz Band recordings the poor recording standards of 1923 prevent us from hearing the drums perfectly, while of the other instruments the piano playing is merely adequate, and the trombone work extremely variable. The banjo usually makes up for the rhythmic weakness of the piano playing, but most of the really creative playing comes from the two cornets and from Dodds's clarinet. In saying this we must remember that the performances are collective creations, and without Dutrey's adequacy the rest of the front line would have been quite unable to sustain their superb standard. On a recording on which Dutrey is really poor, the Okeh *Tears*, he pretty well ruins the whole performance, and only Armstrong's prophetic excursion into cornet virtuosity remains memorable. King Oliver must be given full credit as a bandleader for the remarkable discipline under which he held his men, but tribute must also be paid to the invaluable contributions of Armstrong, and more particularly of Johnny Dodds. The clarinettist was, indeed, one of the corner stones of the greatness of the Oliver group, and the value of his personal contribution should never be overlooked when we consider this most remarkable of all New Orleans bands.

A final word concerning the recordings of King Oliver's Creole Jazz Band must be addressed to those who are new to the music. In 1923, recording standards were low-fi in the extreme, and on the earliest of Oliver's recordings the quality is poor even for that date. At times it is all but impossible to pick out the two-cornet lead on first hearing some of the Gennett titles. A degree of imaginative listening is required here which would scarcely be justified if the music were not of so rewarding a quality. Most listeners find the sound of the Oliver records unbearably weak and 'tinny' and it is very easy for an uncritical listener to ascribe these qualities to the music itself. After all, in these times when 'progress' in art and entertainment is given such a high premium, it is all too easy to brush off recordings of nearly forty years ago as being quite outclassed in every way by more recent forms of music-making and of mechanical reproduction. In the case of minor jazz recordings of this period an argument can be sustained that they are of interest only to historians of jazz or specialists in the styles or musicians concerned. This is not so with the recordings of the King Oliver Creole Jazz Band, for they are a part, and a major part, of the jazz heritage, and those who will not take the trouble to pierce through the period recording to the music itself are missing jazz of a quality second to none. As the original masters of the Oliver recordings were destroyed long ago, present day re-issues have to be re-recorded from old pressings, some of them in none too healthy a state. As a result, not only is the music faint and rather flat in tonal quality, but it is also heard through a variable sieve of surface noise, even on the most carefully engineered microgroove re-issues. Among the devotees of the Oliver band there is a school of thought which considers that the only satisfactory way of listening to the music is to own the original issues, which have a tonal richness superior to any dubbed copies. This would be all very well if there were unlimited supplies of Oliver Gennetts, Okehs and Paramounts, but these are so rare that only those able and willing to spend very large sums of money on an Oliver collection are able to enjoy this pleasure. For the rest of us the re-issues will have to suffice. The best advice I can offer to a newcomer to these recordings is always to bear in mind that the weak twitterings heard on some of the Gennett sides were actually two very powerful cornet players, and always to remember the true tonal qualities of the instruments rather than the distorted versions heard on the discs. It also helps to play long sessions of such records, for it is surprising how the ear adjusts to the old recordings when not constantly reminded of more recent standards of quality. The Okeh sides are better recorded than the Gennetts, with the Paramounts somewhere in between, but as much of the band's finest music is to be heard on the Gennetts (e.g. *Canal Street Blues* and the finer of the two *Dippermouth Blues*) these also are essential listening. Most certainly the Olivers repay a hundredfold any attempt to overcome the technical disadvantages under which they were recorded.

Some two years after his final session with the Oliver band (a rather mediocre date for the Gennett label) Johnny Dodds recorded three titles with a group comprising four of the Oliver musicians—Louis and Lil Armstrong, Johnny St. Cyr and Dodds himself—plus the New Orleans trombonist, Kid Ory. The group was under the leadership of Louis Armstrong, and this proved to be simply the first of the famous series of recording sessions by Armstrong's Hot Five. The performances resulting from these sessions constitute a large slice of the Johnny Dodds discography, and they are, along with the Olivers, the most important recordings in which Dodds participated. In the standard of the music many of the Hot Fives equal the earlier Oliver discs, but the qualities they display are not those of the Oliver band, nor on the majority of the sides is Johnny Dodds heard at his best. The emphasis has moved from the ensemble basis of the Oliver discs, to a state where the ensemble is often less important than the solos. The value of these performances lies chiefly in the cornet playing of Louis Armstrong, who dominates every chorus in which he plays with his extraordinary virtuosity and unique creative genius. Even an ensemble which is mediocre by comparison with the Olivers—or with Morton's contemporary Victor recordings—is lifted into the realm of magnificent music by the sheer quality of the cornet lead. Armstrong's playing on these sides was revolutionary for the whole of jazz, and it is hardly surprising that the musicians with whom he recorded did not always seem completely at their ease. The blending of a clarinet part into the texture of an ensemble music such as Oliver's, with a well rehearsed and disciplined band, was a totally different proposition to fitting such a part to a lead cornet style which was far more complex musically than had been the solos in earlier days.

If we listen to the earliest Hot Fives, we notice two changes in the clarinet role in comparison with the Oliver recordings: it has diminished in importance and has become less melodic in ensemble style. Mention must be made of the recording quality of the sides, which is often extremely poor so far as Dodds's work is concerned. It would be easy to claim that Dodds's tone had deteriorated since the Oliver period, for if we listen to the whole of the initial Okeh series by the Hot Five—that is, from *My Heart* of December 1925 to *Irish Black Bottom*, recorded in

the following November—the obvious conclusion to be drawn is that Dodds had lost the purity of tone heard on the Olivers, and in general had become a rather untidy musician. The recording balance always finds the clarinet well in the background on these sides, which again enhances the view that Dodds had become a less potent force than of old. However, on the titles made during this period away from the Okeh studios (for example on the two sides recorded for Vocalion under the name of Lil's Hot Shots) we find that, although there has been a change in Dodds's style, the quality of his music is unimpaired and, above all, his tone is as fine as ever. One can therefore put down the weak tonal sound of the clarinet on the early Hot Fives to the work of the Okeh recording engineer. This is all the more marked as the cornet and trombone are adequately recorded.

Yes, I'm in the Barrel from the first Hot Five session is a fairly average example of their early recordings, without reaching the heights of some better known sides, but also avoiding the pitfalls of the vaudeville routines on others. Dodds turns in a reasonable solo, though the tone sounds poor, but it is in his ensemble playing that the most noticeable change is to be heard. The legato style of the King Oliver days has given way to a less flowing, altogether more 'bitty' melodic line. To some degree the clarinet has become an *accompanying* instrument, ceasing to carry out a role equal in importance to the lead cornet. Although this was a trend in ensemble jazz throughout the Chicago era, Dodds himself was rarely reticent in his conception of the clarinet's role. The reason for the unobtrusive clarinet on the early Hot Fives seems to be that although he was formulating the more forceful manner of the later Hot Five and Seven recordings at this time, he had not yet mastered this extension of his style. On *Gut Bucket Blues*, from the same session as *Yes, I'm in the Barrel*, Johnny sounds more assured, but even on the blues Armstrong's phrasing sometimes finds Dodds without a suitable antiphonal answer. Armstrong's playing is so magnificent that his work alone would make *Gut Bucket Blues* a classic of jazz, but the Chicago show business environment, reflected here in the preoccupation with novelty and with individual virtuosity, was obviously an unhealthy one.

On the next session Dodds played alto for the theme statement of *Come Back Sweet Papa*, and although the vibrato and phrasing are unmistakable, the experiment cannot be counted a success; the tone is as one would expect when played by a musician unused to the instrument, but it is doubtful if the alto saxophone would have suited Dodds's approach to music even had he persevered with it. Four days later the Hot Five recorded a session which produced several masterpieces, notably Armstrong's superb showpiece *Cornet Chop Suey* and the original version of Kid Ory's *Muskrat Ramble*. On the latter title, which has a stronger emphasis on the ensemble than many of these records, Dodds plays well both in solo and with the band, but again Armstrong easily dominates the music. To judge from these recordings Louis could carve any musician in sight at this time, and most of his New Orleans bandsmen seem to have regarded anything more than a purely mechanical approach to ensemble work largely as a forlorn hope. On *Georgia Grind* from this session Dodds plays some fine blues clarinet, but again Armstrong stands out during the ensembles.

The next Hot Five session was the one for Vocalion under the name of Lil's Hot Shots, and the difference in the recording quality is at once noticeable; Armstrong's tone is brighter and more vivid, and Dodds is heard to much better effect. Were it not that the later Okehs slip back into the old mould, one would have dated Dodds's solution of the problems posed by Armstrong's lead trumpet from this session. The first of the two titles is *Georgia Bo-Bo*, a medium tempo performance of *Royal Garden Blues*, with a superb vocal by Armstrong. At the very outset it is obvious that Dodds's clarinet has been far more strongly recorded than on the Okehs and that he is determined the clarinet shall play a true second part rather than a mere accompaniment. After the vocal Dodds takes a solo chorus of such magnificently intense blues-playing that one wonders what had happened to the clarinet on the earlier Hot Fives. In the two-chorus ensemble which follows Dodds's solo, and concludes the record, he provides a lashing counterpoint to Armstrong's lead, and with the strong support of Ory and St. Cyr the passage is probably the finest example of group playing in all the Armstrong Hot Five and Seven recordings. Of course, Armstrong's lead is simpler than on some of the other records, while Johnny Dodds is at his most forceful; the balance between the trumpet and clarinet is impressive here, and Armstrong's every phrase finds its

perfect counterpart in Dodds's imaginative clarinet. One cannot mention *Georgia Bo-Bo* without calling attention to the superb banjo playing of Johnny St. Cyr, who plays with an inspiring swing. This is all the more commendable when we remember that the other half of the two-piece rhythm section was a virtual passenger. On the second title from this session, a stomp entitled *Drop That Sack*, a mood of considerable exuberance is given full reign, and the ensembles are less closely knit. Armstrong and Dodds again have good solos, which stand out in contrast to Ory's somewhat pedestrian effort and the insipid piano chorus. The less melodic style of ensemble clarinet used here by Dodds was the more influential of his different styles— more than his manner with the Oliver band, for example, or the intense blues style of the Washboard Band titles. One can sense a certain opportunism in the clarinet playing as Dodds plays a harsh, attacking arpeggio style, whipping in a melodic phrase when there is some chance of it cutting through the richness and volume of the cornet lead. This is the pattern followed by Dodds on the subsequent Hot Seven recordings, but before these were made four further Okeh sessions were recorded by the Hot Five.

Surprisingly the style of the band went back to the manner of the previous releases by the Hot Five on this label, with Armstrong using a dryer, less brilliant tone and Dodds relegated to the background, with again a thin, 'gaspipe' tone, quite unlike that of the clarinet on the Vocalion session. *Lonesome Blues* from 23 June 1926, is a feature for Johnny's clarinet, but the recording does not help his tone and his playing is uninspired. Much happier is his playing on *Skit-Dat-De-Dat* from the next session, one of the very finest of all Hot Five recordings. This is a slow blues with liberal breaks for each member of the band; Louis uses scat-singing on some of these breaks in addition to playing trumpet of a most poignant beauty. Dodds plays a perfect ensemble part, while Kid Ory once more proves that for all his obvious limitations his seemingly intuitive understanding of the idiom makes him a peerless trombonist on this type of performance. It is notable that although Ory and sometimes Dodds play poorly on the less inspired selections for Okeh, on material such as *Skit-Dat-De-Dat* and *Muskrat Ramble* their contributions are generally excellent.

Ory was missing from the final Hot Five session of the

first series, a comparatively unimportant group of titles being made that day, including *You Made Me Love You* and a version of *Where the River Shannon Flows* under the title of *Irish Black Bottom*. The trombonist is thought to be John Thomas, and the falling off in rhythmic strength due to Ory's absence is noticeable. Armstrong plays superbly, of course, but the band work is of a mediocre quality compared with the best of the Hot Five recordings.

This session was made on 27 November 1926, and when Armstrong next assembled the group the following May he added tuba and drums to the rhythm section, the Hot Five thus being augmented to become the Hot Seven. There is a good deal of doubt as to who plays the trombone part on the first two sessions, and most certainly it does not sound like Ory, who was accepted for years as the trombonist on these recordings. It has been suggested that Johnny St. Cyr is also absent from the first session, but this seems rather improbable when we compare the guitar solo on *Willie the Weeper*, the first title recorded by the Hot Seven, with that on *Alligator Crawl* (on which St. Cyr is known to have played), for they are obviously by the same man, and are close in style to St. Cyr's guitar solos on some Jelly Roll Morton titles. The drumming on these dates is most untypical of Baby Dodds, the first two sessions in particular containing no sounds from the drummer other than cymbal playing of an unsubtle, though swinging nature. This is odd, as Baby plays in his most characteristic manner on a Jelly Roll Morton session only a month after the Hot Seven sessions, with the typical use of woodblocks and other accessories, along with a careful marking of breaks, flare ups and chorus endings. In his autobiography Baby recalls playing these Hot Seven sessions, but it is strange that his drumming should be so reticent, as the recording of the Hot Sevens is remarkably good in other respects for the period. Armstrong's tone is caught at its most brilliant and powerful, and Dodds can be heard to better effect than on the earlier series. The addition of Pete Briggs brought a greater fullness to the rhythm section and he is a remarkable performer on tuba, although the lugubrious quality which this instrument usually brings to a band is not altogether avoided.

The first Hot Seven session produced two numbers, *Willie the Weeper* and *Wild Man Blues*, both titles being dominated by Armstrong's superlative trumpet work. By this time any comparison with the Oliver band would be futile, for in Armstrong's playing we find a fullness and richness quite equal in musical substance to any ensemble jazz. Johnny Dodds's solo on *Willie the Weeper* is a very fine one, notable for the way in which he transforms the march-like melody into the purest of blues, but from Armstrong's entry after the guitar solo and through the final ensemble the music is swept along by the incomparable brilliance of the trumpet playing. In the opening ensemble Dodds can be heard playing well, but he is completely submerged by Louis's brilliant final outburst. This is not to suggest that Dodds's contribution was second rate, for it is certain that no jazz clarinettist could contribute a second part to trumpet playing so brilliant and self-contained as Armstrong provides here. The second Hot Seven title was a version of *Wild Man Blues*, reputed to have been Johnny's favourite theme. The record consists almost entirely of two extended solos, by Armstrong and Dodds, the former audacious in manner, with a golden tone and superb assurance, the latter in the lower register, the tone dark, the phrasing almost secretive when compared with Armstrong's. The very fact that Dodds could follow Louis without any sense of anti-climax reveals his very considerable stature as a soloist, for Louis here is at his very best. *Willie the Weeper* and *Wild Man Blues* are two recordings which rank among the finest ever made in the jazz idiom, but even they are slightly overshadowed by the two titles from the following session, *Alligator Crawl* and *Potato Head Blues*. On *Alligator Crawl* (issued on some labels as *Alligator Blues*), after an unaccompanied introduction from Armstrong, Johnny Dodds enters with one of his most intense solos, but again this is Louis's record, and the opening chorus apart, it is the trumpet which dominates the performance. *Potato Head Blues* contains some of the best playing of Armstrong's entire career and is considered by some authorities to be his finest achievement. Dodds is at his most forceful here, and provides a dancing counterpoint to Louis's trumpet in the opening chorus and then contributes a hard, forceful solo before St. Cyr's banjo introduces Armstrong's masterly final solo. Again the final ensemble is virtually a continuation of the trumpet solo. The later Hot Sevens are great jazz classics, but they do not quite equal the first four sides. The most notable items for Dodds's clarinet are *Weary Blues*, with a masterly low-

Johnny Dodds in King Oliver's Creole Jazz Band, 1921, in California. *Left to right*—Minor Hall, Honoré Dutrey, King Oliver, Lil Hardin, David Jones, Johnny Dodds, Jimmy Palao, Ed Garland

register solo, and *S.O.L. Blues*, with extended blues clarinet solo work by Dodds. On this latter title the closing ensemble is very good, with Armstrong and Dodds achieving a unity which is not exactly commonplace on these discs. *S.O.L. Blues* was never issued on Okeh and is actually a rejected version of a tune which was titled *Gully Low Blues* on its release, while *S.O.L. Blues* was only put out years later as part of an American Columbia re-issue project. *Gully Low* is a similar performance with more superb clarinet, different in detail to that on the first version. The other title recorded at the *Gully Low Blues* session was *That's When I'll Come Back to You*, with a diverting vocal duet by Lil and Louis Armstrong which receives a very fine backing from Dodds's clarinet. This was the last Hot Seven title to be recorded, and when the band assembled again the original Hot Five instrumentation and personnel were used.

The last Hot Seven session had taken place on 14 May 1927, and when the Hot Five reassembled in the September of that year the character of the band is seen to have changed again. The rhythmic approach (the absence of Pete Briggs no doubt being a contributary factor) is lighter than before, and Armstrong's playing seems to reflect this. The complexity of his lead work has increased yet again, and in all but a few instances the later Hot Five ensembles can be described as being by Armstrong *accompanied* by the other four members of the group. This effect, is enhanced by the recording balance which gives the clarinet less prominence than on the Hot Sevens. As a band performance the best of these recordings is *Ory's Creole Trombone*, a very fine number once the tiresome trombone breaks are through. Here Armstrong's playing sticks close to the melody with simple elaboration, and both Dodds and Ory contribute to the general excellence of the side. Dodds has a good solo on *Once in a While*, but generally speaking the pop-tune type numbers seem to have found Dodds content to turn in a routine performance, as on *The Last Time*. This was not always the case with him as can soon be realized if one compares the New Orleans Boot-blacks performance of this tune (re-titled *Mad Dog*) on which Dodds turns in a magnificent solo. The final recordings which featured Armstrong and Dodds together were cut by the Hot Five in December 1927, and on the first title, *Struttin' with Some Barbecue*, there is a good low-register clarinet solo. This is a rather interesting session in that it shows the Hot Five reflecting some of the habits of the white bands of the period, in the coda of *Struttin'* and in the diminuendo and crescendo effects in the final ensemble of *Got No Blues*. The last two sessions were augmented by Lonnie Johnson on guitar, and contain some fine work by him. *Once in a While* has already been mentioned, and Dodds also plays well on the blues *I'm Not Rough*; but most symbolic of the direction in which Louis Armstrong was travelling is the very last side he recorded with this New Orleans style band, *Savoy Blues*. In place of the old concept of ensemble blues this performance is largely a sequence of solos, with only the final chorus given over to band playing in the New Orleans manner, the previous two ensemble choruses being harmonized riffs. Even more astounding is the fact that on a blues performance so little is heard from Dodds. The fact is that in many ways the Hot Fives indicate why Dodds and many other New Orleans musicians were unable or unwilling to adapt their playing to the new solo-dominated concept of jazz, and gradually lapsed into obscurity. In making this observation I do not suggest that the newer manner produced inferior music—this is manifestly not so—nor that it was anything but an inevitable change in the social context of jazz of the 1920s. The Hot Fives and Sevens are among the finest jazz records extant, but on many of these almost the whole musical interest is to be found in Louis's trumpet work. When Armstrong next organized a recording band he used Jimmy Strong on clarinet and Fred Robinson on trombone, two musicians vastly inferior

King Oliver's Creole Jazz Band, 1924. *Left to right*—Baby Dodds, Honoré Dutrey, King Oliver, Louis Armstrong, Will Johnson, Johnny Dodds, Lil Hardin

Duncan Schiedt

126

to Dodds and Ory in jazzcraft, yet the musical results are hardly inferior to the later Hot Fives with the New Orleans musicians. One need only reflect how much difference such changes would have made to the Oliver recordings, or the more traditional of the Armstrong-Dodds-Ory numbers, such as *Skit-Dat-De-Dat* or *Georgia Bo-Bo*, to realize how the altering pattern of popular jazz styles was putting the virtues of a Johnny Dodds at a discount. Although he continued to record regularly with other bands for another two years (as indeed he had throughout the Hot Five/Seven period) such sides were well off the mainstream of jazz development and were aimed, I think, at a dwindling section of the Negro record-buying public. By 1930 New Orleans style jazz was not a commercial proposition, nor was it to be so for another fifteen years. By the time New Orleans style sessions were commonplace again, Johnny Dodds was not around to participate.

A recording session which should be considered along with the Hot Fives and Sevens is the first of the two under Johnny's own name for Brunswick, in which he used Louis Armstrong on trumpet. The remainder of the band has always been doubtful, but it seems to consist of Louis, the Dodds brothers, Barney Bigard (on tenor sax) and Earl Hines, along with unknown trombone and banjo. On one occasion the French critic Hugues Panassié vehemently denied that the trumpet to be heard on two titles from this session—*Weary Blues* and *New Orleans Stomp*—was by Armstrong. Certainly the trumpet playing is below Louis's usual standard, but even the greatest of musicians occasionally have their off moments. Louis plays pleasantly on *Melancholy Blues*, and approaches his real form on *Wild Man Blues* with a solo of great restraint, in marked contrast to the Hot Seven recording of this number. As on that version Dodds follows with a long clarinet improvisation, and here his more limpid tone and legato phrasing contribute to a solo which is the equal to that on the Hot Seven version, though quite different in character. Despite the personnel (which looks good enough on paper) this was a somewhat stodgy session, with only *Wild Man Blues* of really classic stature, although Johnny's clarinet is consistently good on all titles.

This session by 'Johnny Dodds and his Black Bottom Stompers' was recorded in April 1927, and the following October this band title was used for another four items for the Brunswick label, this time featuring an instrumentation identical to that of the King Oliver Creole Jazz Band. Unfortunately, the band was somewhat stiff, particularly the brass team, and the clarinet provides the most memorable moments. Constantly adding to the ensembles, Dodds here is on superb form, whether driving the band along in the exciting *Come On and Stomp, Stomp, Stomp*, or adding his inimitable blues countermelodies to *Joe Turner Blues*. The former title has a fine Dodds contribution with the hard pure tone of the *Potato Head Blues* solo, while *After You've Gone* by contrast, features a delicate subdued clarinet, with the soft tone of the Black Bottom Stompers version of *Wild Man Blues*.

In 1926, the year of the early Hot Five sides, Johnny Dodds recorded two sessions with similarly constituted bands which, without Armstrong's eruptive (and often disruptive) genius, were typical examples of New Orleans band playing of the period. On Paramount he appears in the only important recordings made by the famous New Orleans trumpeter Freddie Keppard. This is one of the items on which the identity of the clarinet has been argued for some years, some collectors being of the opinion that a somewhat obscure Chicago musician by the name of Jimmy O'Bryant was responsible. Similar doubts have been expressed as to which of these two clarinettists play on certain titles by Jimmy Blythe and Lovie Austin. O'Bryant recorded frequently with Blythe at this time and seems to have been a popular musician among the Negro audiences of the Chicago South Side. Like some other northern musicians he was influenced by Johnny Dodds, but his approach is altogether less intense than that of the New Orleans man and he seems quite happy in using novelty effects for the amusement of his audience. What seems to have happened is that on some of the informal Blythe sessions, Dodds returned the compliment by using some of O'Bryant's mannerisms. This is a subject which has been insufficiently explored by specialists of this period, but any extended consideration of the matter here would be out of place. On the Freddie Keppard titles the clarinet is unmistakably that of Dodds in the phrasing, the tonal variations and the rhythmic attack. Only two titles were recorded, *Stockyard Strut* being good average New Orleans jazz of the looser variety, with forceful trumpet from Keppard and a busy counterpoint from the rather thinly recorded clarinet. The blues *Salty Dog* is a masterpiece, with really 'lowdown' blues playing from both Dodds and Keppard, and a full ensemble part from the little known trombonist Eddie Vinson or Vincent. Keppard reveals a perfect mastery of blues trumpet style and is far better here than on any of his other recordings, while Johnny Dodds, as always, excels in this idiom, the interplay between trumpet and clarinet being typical of New Orleans jazz at its finest.

Slightly earlier in the year, Dodds's clarinet was the prominent voice on two Columbia sessions organized, apparently, by Lil Armstrong. The variable standards of recording at this time can be seen when we consider that the Keppard Paramounts were made three months *after* these Columbia New Orleans Wanderers and Bootblacks sides, though to judge from the recording one would place them a good few *years* earlier. The band on the Wanderers/Bootblacks sides consists of the Armstrong Hot Five line-up with George Mitchell replacing Louis, and Jimmy Walker added on alto sax. The first title, *Perdido Street Blues*, was actually cut without Walker, and despite three choruses of mediocre solos by piano, banjo and trombone, it is a classic performance, with Dodds's clarinet featured in several solo passages against stop-time figures for the rest of the band. He utilizes all registers of the clarinet, and his bold melodic conception combines with his expressive tone and superb timing to produce one of the greatest jazz solos on record. *Too Tight*, though not a blues in form, contains long passages of Dodds in similar style though mainly in the high register. I can think of only a handful of Bessie Smith's finest recordings and some of Sydney Bechet's blues which are comparable in their simple yet direct majesty with Johnny Dodds's work on *Too Tight*. For all the considerable advances in melodic and harmonic thought among jazz soloists, few of them have been able to create a music so eloquent and moving as does Johnny Dodds here. If human values of expression are to be considered paramount, as I believe they should, then Dodds's playing on such records places him among the greatest of jazz soloists. The final ensemble on *Perdido Street Blues* is a masterpiece of New Orleans band playing, with each voice perfectly balanced within the texture yet adding its own distinctive contribution to the total sound. The cornetist on these titles, George Mitchell, was not a New Orleans musician, but he assimilated perfectly not only the style but also the spirit of the Crescent City men. He was not a very creative musician, nor a very forceful one, but on these titles, and on the famous Morton sessions of the same year, he made a contribution the value of which is not always obvious behind the modest simplicity of his style. Whereas a Louis Armstrong will constantly parade his genius before our astounded ears, the virtues of a musician like George Mitchell are not so obvious. At all times the part played by the cornet on these records is in perfect accord with the total concept of the band, and Mitchell's solos, simple enough it is true, always have the incomparable virtue of absolute fidelity to their context. The alto saxophone of Jimmy Walker, who is a pleasant though not outstanding player with a style similar to some of the Kansas City reed players on the earliest Benny Moten records, imposes certain problems in the ensemble. In considering the use of the saxophone in such music as this, it should always be remembered that the musicians were never so puritanically minded about this instrument as certain latter-day critics —it is illuminating here to note that *every single side* recorded by a band in New Orleans in the 1920s featured this instrument! None the less, it should be realized that the better New Orleans style ensembles are those without any saxophone, and a noticeable result of the addition of this instrument on the Wanderers/Bootblacks sides is that in the ensembles Dodds is forced to remain in the higher register. Walker appears to have had a good deal more ensemble sense than, say, Stomp Evans, and the band playing on such titles as *Gatemouth* reaches a quite classic perfection. Dodds is at his best here, his clarinet never failing to add to the beauty and variety of this exuberant music. There are fine solos too—Dodds has an outstanding chorus on *Mad Dog*, but like all great New Orleans jazz it is the total effect of the group, rather than the outstanding virtuosity of any one member, which gives these records their true greatness. To this Johnny Dodds contributes in a way which is at once fully individual, yet perfectly judged as a part of the overall performances.

The following year Johnny recorded a couple of sessions with Jelly Roll Morton, the only occasions on which these two masters of New Orleans jazz recorded together. Jelly's recordings are, with the Olivers and Armstrongs, the greatest of the New Orleans sessions made in Chicago in the 1920s. On his finest titles the clarinet was played by Omer Simeon, an extremely fine musician who is said to have been Morton's favourite on the instrument. The two Morton sessions with Johnny Dodds featured a band much inferior to the Red Hot Peppers of the previous year. George Mitchell was retained, but the trombone playing of George Bryant cannot be compared with that of Kid Ory, who was at his very best on the Morton 1926 sides. But much the worst feature of the band was the addition of Stomp Evans on alto sax. Evans was a musician who recorded frequently in Chicago in the 1920s—so frequently that at one time discographers seemed to think that all recorded saxophone playing emanating from the Chicago of this decade was by him. As a result he was blamed for some poor playing for which he was not responsible, but it is doubtful if any of this was worse than his contribution to these Morton sessions. Evans's playing combines all the rooty effects of the popular saxophone styles of the 1920s to a remarkable degree, and a break by him is liable to start with rhythmic incoherence and end with cackling slap-tongue effects. Jelly Roll's arrangements on these 1927 records are elaborately fussy, with breaks and flares occurring with such regularity that the telling effect these devices had on the earlier Peppers sessions is quite lost here by their over-use. About the only musician to benefit from these arrangements is Baby Dodds, and his drumming can be heard to very good effect here. Brother Johnny is in particularly fluent form, although he sticks mainly to the lower register, probably on Morton's instructions. The best titles are *Wild Man Blues*, *Jungle Blues* and *The Pearls*, although all suffer from an overdose of Evans's alto. *Wild Man Blues* has good Dodds, although the device of including alto-sax breaks during the clarinet solo is not one of Morton's happier ideas; indeed, the whole performance sounds over contrived when compared with the classic simplicity of the Armstrong-Dodds versions, or indeed with Jelly's own *Smoke House Blues*, his finest blues recording. *The Pearls* is one of Morton's most important compositions, and the record is of great interest because it is the only band version of the piece, but it is doubtful if the performance itself adds anything to the composition. At the second of these two Morton sessions a couple of trio numbers were recorded with just Jelly and the Dodds brothers, and on these Johnny again plays exclusively in the lower register, as Morton wanted the clarinet to play a second part to

the piano. These two titles—*Wolverine Blues* and *Mr. Jelly Lord*—are not quite so fine as the trio titles Jelly made with Omer Simeon or Barney Bigard, and one feels that Dodds, though he plays well, is not altogether in sympathy with Morton's ideas.

Johnny Dodds also recorded, at various times in his career, a number of trio titles under his own name, in addition to one session for Paramount with just piano accompaniment. He rarely is found at his best in such surroundings, appearing to have preferred at least one other front-line instrument in a band. On the session with Tiny Parham for Paramount he sounds peculiarly uncertain, and sticks to the melody of *Loveless Love* throughout the performance. The best of these Johnny Dodds Trio recordings are the 1929 sides he made with Lil Armstrong and Bill Johnson for Victor, although Lil's piano work is hardly substantial as a second solo voice, and Dodds is thrown into a prominence which is hardly ideal for such a group-conscious musician.

On one trio session we hear Dodds in unusual but apparently congenial surroundings; this is a session with the blues singer and guitarist Blind Blake and that unusual character Jimmy Bertrand. The latter was known best for his washboard playing but was not adverse to turning his talents to such unusual instruments as the xylophone and, as on this occasion, the swannee whistle! The session was actually under Blind Blake's name, and on one title the other two musicians accompany his singing of *C. C. Pill Blues*, but another title, *Hot Potatoes*, is purely instrumental apart from Blake scat-singing an odd chorus. Blake was fond of guitar rags and skiffle numbers, and certainly there is hardly a recording in the latter category which equals *Hot Potatoes* in sheer good spirits and natural exuberance. Bertrand doubles on woodblocks and swannee whistle, and although his playing is of little worth in itself he fits perfectly in this excellent atmosphere. Johnny Dodds is superb; his constantly weaving clarinet and easy, yet inspiring phrasing, gives the record a rare musical distinction.

A very high proportion of Johnny Dodds's recordings were done with washboard bands, and there is some fine clarinet playing on many otherwise mediocre sides by such musicians as Jimmy Blythe and Jimmy Bertrand. Pianist Blythe recorded hundreds of titles with washboard bands under his direction and most of the casual recordings by

129

small groups of the time contain Blythe or some of his associates. Johnny was apparently friendly with this musician and appears on a good proportion of the Blythe output. The merits and the character of the music produced by these bands is somewhat difficult to define. The general sound of the Blythe/Bertrand groups is easy to recognize—but its defining feature is not so much the presence of a washboard player as a sort of general musical disorganization, a sloppiness of approach which is only occasionally relieved by the sort of good-humoured playing which is found on the Blind Blake *Hot Potatoes*. Blythe and Bertrand were a somewhat pedestrian rhythm team, and the groups almost always featured a poor trumpet player—usually Natty Dominique. Keppard is present on some titles, but does not play well. Typical of the recordings of this group of musicians are the titles cut under the band name of the 'Dixieland Thumpers'. Dominique's lead is abominable here and the rhythm section heavy handed; the only really interesting moments are during Dodds's clarinet solos. Dominique's limitations are woefully evident on *Weary Way Blues* where he commences out of tune and finishes off key. Even in the carefree days when almost anyone who could blow a note could record for the race lists, such excruciating sounds were rare.

Much better are the Blythe/Dodds sides recorded for Okeh under the name of the Chicago Footwarmers, although again Dominique's playing leaves much to be desired and only the clarinet is constantly worthy of attention. On an unusual Bertrand date for Vocalion in April 1927 Louis Armstrong is on trumpet, and with Bertrand, Blythe and Johnny Dodds making up the quartet they produce some lightly swinging jazz of excellent quality. Two of these titles, *I'm Goin' Huntin'* and *If You Want to be My Sugar Papa*, were re-issued some years ago on English Vocalion, and are well worth obtaining.

Among the best of all the Johnny Dodds washboard recordings are the two titles cut in July 1929 by the Beale Street Washboard Band, consisting of Herb Morand on trumpet, the white pianist Frank Melrose and the Dodds brothers. Morand sounds rather nervous, for this was not only his first recording session but also his first engagement of any kind outside New Orleans, and the trumpet is hardly comparable with his easy, mellow playing on the better Harlem Hamfats sides. For all the stiffness and jerky phrasing, however, the trumpet playing here is a considerable advance on that of Natty Dominique on the Blythe records. As on the slightly earlier recordings for Victor by his own Washboard Band, Johnny Dodds here seems to play in a fashion closer to his King Oliver style than the sharper, more forceful manner of the Hot Seven recordings. The balance between Morand's trumpet and Dodds's clarinet is excellent as the lead changes from one to the other. In particular the clarinet throughout both *Piggly Wiggly* and *Forty and Tight* maintains a quite miraculous flow of magnificently melodic music.

The Victor sides by the Johnny Dodds Washboard Band fall into a different category than the records we have just been discussing. The characteristic sound of all these titles is the thin trumpet lead with loose *obligato* by the clarinet and a heavy beat from piano and washboard. On the Dodds Victors, however, we have a much fuller band sound and also a less casual approach to the music. The band assembled by Dodds in the Victor studios on 6 July 1928 was virtually his regular band of the time with Baby Dodds switching to washboard. Natty Dominique, Honoré Dutrey and Bill Johnson play trumpet, trombone and bass respectively, but the pianist has never been established for certain, Lil Armstrong and Jimmy Blythe being the players usually nominated for this chair. The four titles cut by this group were all blues, two of them fast, *Blue Washboard Stomp* and *Bull Fiddle Blues*, and two slow, *Bucktown Stomp* and *Weary City*. Dominique is at his best here, and although he was far from being an ideal player in many respects, he certainly has the virtue of a very acute awareness of the function of the trumpet in such a group as this. His tone has an unpleasantly thin and rather nasal quality, while his phrasing is often jerky in a manner which belies his considerable reputation as a blues player. Yet his solos on the slow blues here have a certain nostalgic quality which fits well with the general mood of the performances, and it must be granted that for all his limitations Dominique fits better into the pattern of this band than would such a musician as Louis Armstrong or Henry Allen. Dutrey and the pianist are adequate, the former filling out the ensembles well without having the rhythmic strength of the best New Orleans trombonists. The records flow over a superb foundation provided by the bass of Bill Johnson whose playing here constantly informs the whole band with a loose, swinging, supple beat. Baby Dodds plays well, although naturally enough the full force of his remarkable musicianship can hardly be heard when he is performing on washboard—an instrument for which he had little affection.

The sound of the Johnny Dodds Washboard Band is a very distinctive one, with a certain rawness of texture which is quite unmistakable. Dodds's own playing on these sides —particularly on *Weary City* and *Bucktown Stomp*—is among his finest on record, a contribution of almost virtuoso style yet welded firmly to the playing of the other musicians in the band. There is little of the angular, hard phrasing of the Armstrong Hot Sevens here, and the clarinet is much closer to that on the Oliver recordings, with a pure yet vibrant tone, limpid yet forceful phrasing. The agile runs through the various registers of the instrument are in a way reminiscent of such representatives of the Creole school of New Orleans clarinet playing as Jimmy Noone, Albert Nicholas or Barney Bigard. The instrumental and rhythmic style is different, and appears to be largely Dodds's own personal concept rather than any established way of playing among New Orleans clarinettists. Johnny Dodds's tone was beautifully rounded and full in all registers of his instrument, and nowhere can this be heard to better effect than on the Washboard Band sides. Moreover the numbers recorded by the band were all in Johnny's favourite form, the blues, and his playing on these sides has rarely been equalled and never surpassed by a clarinettist of any school of jazz.

The same band—with Baby Dodds reverting to drums— later recorded a further six titles for Victor under the name of Johnny Dodds's Hot Six, and they contain some fine clarinet work without achieving the classic quality of the Washboard Band sides. The band sounds fuller with Baby reverting to drums, but the material was, on the whole, less suitable than that of the washboard recordings. On all these Victor sessions the freedom of style and the general relaxation of Dodds's own playing is very noticeable when compared with the majority of his recordings of the mid-'twenties, and it is no doubt due in part to the fact that he was recording with a regular band for the first time since he left Oliver. What superlative music may have resulted had Dodds lived to play in the days of the New Orleans revival can only be conjectured, although it must be stressed that

his approach to music, with its strong accent on the blues, is unlikely to have made as great an impact on later audiences as that of Kid Ory. Certainly Dodds's music had little in common with the superficial sort of Dixieland playing which constitutes a large part of the revivalist output. In fact Johnny Dodds did make one session in 1940, with most of his regular band, as a result of the increased interest in New Orleans jazz. But two and a half years before this in January 1938 he made a visit to New York to front a group at a session which Lil Armstrong had arranged for him with the Decca people.

The band assembled for him was probably the most incongruous jazz unit which could have been selected at this time to play with a New Orleans musician, consisting for the most part of a group of musicians from John Kirby's little combo, who were used by Decca as a sort of 'house band' to record with a considerable variety of artists. John Kirby's group featured a light, sophisticated sort of jazz which was pleasant enough in its way, though superficial and rather slick. The shallow style of the Kirby musicians was a direct contrast to the forthright, expressive manner of a Johnny Dodds. From the Kirby band the session featured trumpeter Charlie Shavers, drummer O'Neill Spencer and Kirby himself on bass, along with Dodds, Lil Armstrong and Teddy Bunn. The latter was an acoustic guitarist and a good if sophisticated blues-player whose solos are acceptable in themselves without really being in sympathy with the clarinet. The themes were, for the most part, numbers associated with Dodds's earlier recordings, and a comparison of the 1938 version of *Wild Man Blues* with the three interpretations from the 1920s shows up the limitations of this band in a glaring manner. Even worse is *29th and Dearborn*, an alternative title to Richard M. Jones's *Riverside Blues* which Dodds had recorded twice with the Oliver band. This piece, so excellent a platform for a band performance, is treated as just another 12-bar blues, although Dodds plays the two themes in his opening solo. This title was available for a long time on Brunswick 78 r.p.m., backed by a number called *Blues Galore* which featured the mediocre blues singing of the drummer O'Neill Spencer. On the whole, Johnny Dodds plays very well during his lengthy solos on this session, although at times his playing sounds a shade hesitant and certainly lacks the rhythmic force of almost any of his other recordings. This is probably due to the rhythm section, a good one of its kind but not of a type to which Johnny was accustomed, nor with which he was likely to feel relaxed. By far the greatest mistake on the session was the use of Charlie Shavers on trumpet. Shavers is an erratic, sometimes brilliant trumpeter in the jam session or big band styles of the 1930s and early 1940s, but he was a poor choice for such performances as these. It is odd that so incongruous a musician should have recorded with three of the great New Orleans clarinettists around this time, for his outlook was particularly insensitive to the requirements of group improvisation. One need only compare the playing of Rex Stewart and Sidney de Paris with Bechet to Shavers's work on his sessions with Bechet, Dodds or Noone, to realize that it was not so much a matter of style, but of temperament, which prevented Shavers from fitting in with such groups. On the opening chorus of *Stackalee Blues*, Shavers plays a sober, simple lead, but for the rest his playing is erratic, over busy, unmelodic and completely without concern for what anyone else in the group may be playing. All the ensembles are a jumble, but the last two choruses of *Blues Galore* are particularly notable for the utter chaos which prevails. This session (unfortunately titled as by Johnny Dodds and his Chicago Boys) should have remained an object lesson to record supervisors on how not to organize a jazz session. Unfortunately the mixing of stylistic elements here has often been emulated, almost always with similarly dire results.

It cannot be claimed that the two titles Johnny Dodds recorded at his last session (as a contribution to the Decca 'New Orleans Jazz' album) are a complete success, but they are certainly records of a different kind from those of the New York session. A band of New Orleans musicians resident in Chicago was assembled, and the presence of such men as Preston Jackson, John Lindsay, Lonnie Johnson and the Dodds brothers promised music of a high quality. Unfortunately two very poor arrangements were contributed by Richard M. Jones, who played piano on that date, and what little may have been extracted from these by a good trumpet lead was completely lost on Natty Dominique, whose playing is unpleasant in the extreme. There is a very strained atmosphere about both *Red Onion Blues* and *Gravier Street Blues*, and though Johnny Dodds plays well, one cannot help but notice that the band plays below its potential. For all that, there is a certain harshness and bitterness about the emotional climate which seems a direct expression of feeling rather than simply the reflection of an obviously unhappy session. Johnny Dodds, one Boyd Senter-like yelp apart, plays wonderfully, and his mastery of the blues is as notable as ever. The sides recorded by Jimmy Noone with virtually the same band are much smoother (Dominique improves for one thing), but they do not have the emotional impact of these two unusual Dodds titles. Altogether Johnny Dodds's last recording session is one of the most paradoxical in jazz and the individual listener must decide for himself whether these two titles are simply examples of musical crudity or whether they narrowly miss, in their elemental rawness, a greatness which is rare even in blues recordings.

The recorded output of Johnny Dodds covers a wide range of musical forms within the jazz idiom, from the closely knit work of the King Oliver Creole Band, through the earliest examples of jazz virtuosity in the Armstrong Hot Fives to the loose and sometimes crude music of the washboard and jug bands. On almost every title he recorded, Johnny Dodds adds considerably to the music, whether as an ensemble musician with Oliver or as the only soloist on the Armstrongs whose work is comparable with that of Louis himself. Yet to some writers and collectors he is simply an historical figure, a worthy pioneer but hardly a jazzman of major stature. With the vast changes which have come over jazz in the three decades since Dodds's finest recordings were made, his music cannot always be easily approached by listeners accustomed to later values. In the remaining pages of this book some attempt must be made to assess Johnny Dodds's contribution to jazz, and to examine his music in relation to the jazz scene as a whole. To newcomers to jazz whose taste is inclined toward what are loosely referred to as traditional styles, Johnny's playing will have an obvious appeal. But it is this writer's view that we are dealing here with an artist whose value transcends that of a particular style and whose contribution to jazz is of a value far above the narrow limits of stylistic fads. As a creative artist and as a musician with a dedicated approach to his art, Dodds can in many ways be an example and an inspiration to those who follow him as 'name' musicians in jazz, even though their music may be many moves from his so far as details of style are concerned.

3

HIS CONTRIBUTION TO JAZZ

In a discussion of the contribution of the blues idiom to jazz in his book *Jazz: Its Evolution and Essence*, André Hodier, a noted French critic, makes the following observation: '... on the other hand, some very fine players of the blues, like Johnny Dodds, may be mediocre jazzmen, as we have seen.' Hodier is a brilliant musical analyst and in the book from which I have just quoted he makes a valued contribution to jazz literature in his analytical studies. Unfortunately, Hodier's understanding of the background of jazz and of the work of the early New Orleans groups is lacking to a truly astounding degree, while his appreciation of vocal blues—so essential to a true understanding of jazz —is non-existent. Hodier's intelligent and lucid book expresses ideas which, in the hands of other writers, often remain semi-articulate. It is for this reason that I have chosen to discuss his attitude here, for it provides a classic example of a totally unsuitable approach to such musicians as Johnny Dodds. It is also (although this is incidental to our purpose here) an approach which makes the realization of the essence of jazz, after which Hodier so earnestly strives, quite unattainable.

One of the most scathing dismissals in *Jazz: Its Evolution and Essence* is of a clarinettist 'to whom even Johnny Dodds could have shown a thing or two about getting the notes in the right place rhythmically'. Hodier is much concerned about what he considers to be the rhythmic deficiencies of early jazz, and finds it hard to conceive that anyone could accept such jazz recordings as a satisfying aesthetic experience after 'fifteen years of perfected rhythm'. It is certainly true that until the lessons of Count Basie's original rhythm section had been absorbed by the 'middle period' jazzmen their work was sometimes shaky in this respect. But what eludes Hodier is the fact that the New Orleans concept of swing was quite different from that of the post-Basie musicians, and that, contrary to the opinion of many writers, the King Oliver group was rhythmically one of the most accomplished in the entire history of jazz. Almost any of the breaks by Oliver or by Dodds on these records are as perfected rhythmically as anything in later jazz, but the emphasis and the style were different, and unless we realize this we cannot help but fall into the error of constantly undervaluing the work of the New Orleans musicians. They were not simply pioneers whose place in jazz history was to pave the way for Louis Armstrong and his successors, but men with a fully developed and valid way of playing. It is true that an approach to this sort of jazz can be made neither with the techniques of the European academy, nor if one wishes to find in jazz a pleasant appendage to European culture.

Hodier's writing on Johnny Dodds, who is the only important New Orleans musician discussed in the book apart from Louis, is insensitive in the extreme. To start with he selects for analysis a number of the early Okeh Hot Fives, because 'they were all issued in France during the same month'! This remarkable method of selection (even from Armstrong's own playing, these are not among the better titles by the band) allows Hodier to pinpoint a number of sides on which Armstrong easily outplays his sidemen, and on which Johnny Dodds sounds altogether uncomfortable. Presumably such titles as *Skit-Dat-De-Dat* or the later Hot Sevens, on which Dodds makes a major contribution to the music (and on which Louis plays better too) were released in France in different months! By selecting these sides on which Dodds is under-recorded and uncertain, Hodier is able to prove that even so noted a pioneer musician as he is little more than an historical figure, vastly overrated by the majority of jazz writers as a musician. Dodds is criticized for not playing his harmony part exactly along with Armstrong on one record—he doesn't, of course, because New Orleans clarinettists hardly ever did phrase exactly with the trumpet. They used a technique which lent a greater rhythmic and melodic variety to ensemble jazz by playing *almost* the same melody as the lead but not quite. With Louis Armstrong this does not come off, but Hodier's taste must be questioned here if he imagines that Dodds's part would have sounded better if he had phrased along with Armstrong's lead. For all the excellence of his use of this manner of playing with Oliver, Dodds soon abandoned it when recording with Louis, but we must remember that his playing on these early Hot Fives is in part an attempt to solve the problem of fitting a clarinet part to Armstrong's lead. Of course, this criticism of Hodier's is a part of his general thesis that early jazzmen in general, and Johnny Dodds in particular, were incapable of precise rhythmic placing, of 'getting the notes in the right place'. It is true that Dodds and Ory make rhythmic mistakes on these records, but on countless others their playing is superbly balanced rhythmically—one only needs to listen to Ory's recordings with Morton to realize that he was not quite the blundering fool his detractors would have us believe. Could a man so deficient in rhythmic qualities have made quite the difference that Ory does to the Hot Fives and Sevens on which he is present, compared with the rest?

So far as Johnny Dodds is concerned, any such criticism shows an almost incredible ignorance of the qualities of his recorded output as a whole. For one gem among many, take Dodds's unaccompanied introduction to the Hot Five recording of *The Last Time*; the rhythmic placing here is quite perfect, and swings in a most excellent manner. Could the great, long melodic lines of *Perdido Street Blues*, *Too Tight* or *Georgia Bo-Bo* have been maintained if the clarinettist had constantly fumbled rhythmically? Without rhythmic placing and swing of a high order the clarinet part in the final two choruses of *Georgia Bo-Bo* would have been swept aside by Armstrong's trumpet in no uncertain manner. It can honestly be argued that on only a small number of the Hot Fives and Sevens does Dodds provide a clarinet part which adds an interest equal to that of Armstrong's lead. This is true enough, but it is a greater achievement than that of any of the other clarinettists Louis has recorded with in collective ensembles, a list which includes such great names as Sidney Bechet, Barney Bigard and Edmond Hall. The fact is that this 'mediocre jazzman' remains the only player who could even occasionally match Armstrong in ensemble jazz, and one of the very few who could create solos of a calibre not to be completely outshone by Louis's supreme genius.

To some younger listeners the tone of the early jazz musicians is a deterrent to the appreciation of their music. To those grounded on the near academic tone of Goodman and his contemporaries, let alone symphonic clarinet players, the work of such musicians as Dodds and Bechet (particularly when the latter played clarinet) sounds unbearably crude, and, in the case of recordings from the 1920s, quite unmoving. When heard under tolerable recording conditions, Dodds's tone is a magnificent one for jazz, full, rounded and thoroughly personal. The roughness of much early jazz and blues-playing is inexplicable by academic standards, but to the understanding ear it is one of the music's greatest virtues. For allied to the expressive use of varied timbre and rough tone is an emotional honesty which is the greatest strength of this music. Among instrumental performers, none used these devices in a more eloquent and unsentimental manner than Johnny Dodds. Generally speaking, the New Orleans jazzmen were divided into two groups, the 'downtown' Creoles with their background of French academic practice, and the rough untutored 'uptown' Negroes. Many of these musical distinctions had worn thin by the time the musicians from the Crescent City came to record in Chicago, but some of the difference is still noticeable, particularly among the clarinettists, on which instrument the Creoles had a long and distinguished tradition. The Creole manner of playing is perhaps best known to present day listeners from the work of Albert Nicholas and, in a modified form, Barney Bigard, although the greatest exponent of this school on records was Jimmy Noone. The pure tone of these players was matched by a superbly fluent style of phrasing, and the 'hot' qualities of their playing comes more from the rhythmic placing and melodic style rather from the tone itself. The Johnny Dodds manner is in many ways different from theirs, although it is not the complete antithesis that some critics have maintained. For example, Dodds's superb *arpeggio* work on many of the Olivers, or the fluidity of his line on the Beale Street Washboard Band sides, is quite close to the *legato* Creole manner. On the other hand Dodds's tone is harder, the *vibrato* more pronounced and more Negroid and his attack far more forceful. The tone and *vibrato*, moreover, are part of the expressiveness of the style in a more personal sense than is the case with Noone or Bigard. Sometimes Dodds will insert a deliberately sour note into his melodic line and the effect of this device is often most moving. Johnny Dodds rarely featured 'growl' devices, his use of tonal variety being a very subtle one within the context of a standard timbre. His use of *vibrato* similarly is carefully judged and never excessive; the Johnny Dodds *vibrato* is one of the most personal sounds in jazz, and is an immediately recognizable one. On some records (e.g. the opening chorus of the Hot Seven's *Alligator Crawl* or the New Orleans Wanderers' *Perdido Street Blues*) the *vibrato* gives the music a remarkable intensity of expression without ever sounding a superficially imposed ornament.

To move from the quiet introspective musing of the clarinet solo on the Black Bottom Stompers' *Wild Man Blues* to the fierce, attacking entry of the solo clarinet in *Come on and Stomp, Stomp, Stomp*, is to cover a considerable range of mood, and any suggestion that Dodds was a limited artist can soon be dispelled by considering the very varied emotional range in his recordings. His tone was a pliable and expressive one, and he exhibited certain individual characteristics in each of the various registers of the clarinet. In the higher register the clarinet tone is crystal clear and hard enough to cut through the texture of the brass instruments, as in the Oliver band, or the complex weave of the four-part polyphony of the Wanderers/ Bootblacks recordings; on slow blues in the higher register he played usually in the 'singing' manner of the *Perdido Street Blues* solo, on fast titles in the attacking style of *Come on and Stomp . . .* or *Potato Head Blues*. In the middle register his tone was less brilliant (unlike Noone for example, whose tone was equally clear in any register) and his solo style more likely to be of the fluid, flowing variety as on many choruses on the Beale Street Washboard Band or Oliver sides. In the low register his tone became darker still, the blues inflexions which were never absent from his playing giving to some of his solos in this register a most unusual emotional quality when allied to his unusual timbre. A good instance of this is on the Oliver *Mandy Lee Blues* where Dodds plays the melody of the verse pretty well as written, yet transforms the piece into a remarkably original evocation of mood. At other times he would play low register solos with a powerful rhythmic attack as on

both the Black Bottom Stompers and the Hot Seven versions of *Weary Blues*.

Johnny Dodds was a fairly influential musician during the Chicago period, while since the New Orleans revival there have been many imitators of his style, although several of the musicians who started their careers with revivalist bands as Dodds imitators have changed over to following the path of Sidney Bechet, or the style of the Noone/ Nicholas school. In the early days of the revival in England both Wally Fawkes and Ian Christie were Dodds men, although one would hardly think so when listening to their present-day work. Of the British revivalists Sandy Brown, on occasion a very fine blues player, has learned much from Johnny Dodds's records without ever, except perhaps at the very outset of his career, being simply an imitator. In recent years other influences have affected his playing too, and much of the directness of the early Sandy Brown band has given way to a more sophisticated approach. None the less, Brown remains one of the most interesting of European jazz musicians, and it will be worth noting how much of the basic Dodds idiom remains in his playing as his style moves away from a pseudo-New Orleans context. Of American revivalists two of the clarinettists who recorded with the Lu Watters band were influenced by Dodds, but their playing was inept to a remarkable degree. Perhaps the clarinettist to come nearest in sound to Dodds among his revivalist followers was the French musician Claude Luter, who before becoming a mediocre Bechet imitator used to lead a very crude but enthusiastic bunch of musicians in an imitation of the King Oliver band. So rudimentary was most of the playing by this band that the one service which they might have rendered to jazz— in giving an aural approximation of the actual Oliver sound, which we know only from accoustic recording— was quite ruined by the abominable tone of the cornets and trombone, not to mention the lugubrious rhythm section. Luter himself was not a very accomplished musician, but his Dodds imitations were occasionally quite life-like, as in his solo on his band's recording of *Sweet Lovin' Man*. Like the majority of revivalist bands the group had no creative artistic policy and the Oliver imitations soon gave way to a more anonymous, though no less derivative, style.

The musicians whom Dodds influenced during his Chicago days were a group who would never have entertained the idea of a mere imitation, but a number of clarinettists from the 1920s show traces of the Dodds manner in their playing, and he seems to have been as influential as any reed player during the Chicago period. The case of Jimmy O'Bryant has already been mentioned, but Dodds's influence with coloured musicians seems to have been slight during the Chicago period, partly because of the trend towards big band playing, in which Dodds's clarinet style would have been an anachronism. In New Orleans he was a famous and no doubt much imitated musician, but we lack the evidence to chronicle the details of this period. Among the white Chicagoans Dodds was a prime influence, although some of the results were peculiar in the extreme. The clarinettist Frank Teschmaker was a great admirer of Johnny's and often used to sit in with the band at Kelly's Stables. Tesch was an unusual musician who was influenced by many diverse kinds of music, but he died too young to get the elements of his highly personal style into perspective. His violent attack was no doubt in part an adaptation of the Dodds *Potato Head Blues* style, while his melodic manner was often a weird juxtaposition of Dodds's phrasing and melodic ideas derived from the white cornetist Bix Beiderbecke. The clarinettist who succeeded Teschmaker as the leading representative of the Chicago school on this instrument, Pee-Wee Russell, is a musician whose work is characterized by various distortions of tone. But Russell, like Rod Cless and other members of the later Chicago school, seems to have built his style, particularly in an ensemble sense, mainly on that of Dodds. Unfortunately the aspect of Johnny Dodds's playing which the Chicagoans utilized was the least valuable of his several ensemble styles, namely that of the Hot Five and Seven performances and of the informal Washboard Band sides.

The development of more complex solo styles in jazz and the lessening opportunity for disciplined band work, ensured that many of the most valuable aspects of Johnny Dodds's playing would go unused by his successors. Like the work of Sidney Bechet and Duke Ellington, Dodds's individual manner of playing was such that it proved a difficult style for other creative jazzmen to assimilate, compared with the music of such influential figures as Louis Armstrong or Count Basie.

There were many admirable aspects of Johnny Dodds's playing and his approach to music. He was a diligent performer and his contribution to any band he played with was invariably a notable one. He was a perfect *band* player, never forcing his role on our attention above the dictates of the group. Many of the ensembles he played with were rough by present-day technical standards, but they have an expressive power which overcomes any crudities. Above all the *spirit* of the bands with which Johnny played comes over on his records with an ageless vitality and warmth.

As an individual musician Dodds was also a 'rough' player. I do not mean by this that he made a lot of mistakes, but rather that his whole style and concept of music-making was different from that of musicians who aim to produce a smooth, unruffled sound. Johnny Dodds was an expressive musician who played music in a wholehearted way; his generation never thought of themselves as 'artists', but they put everything into their playing. On a blues Johnny Dodds will play with a roughness of tone, of attack, which is a moving aesthetic experience because of the complete honesty of his work—the whole man is in this music, not just a cultivated part of the man called 'artist'. It is perhaps best to let Johnny's brother, Baby Dodds, have the last word, for in this quotation from his autobiography, *The Baby Dodds Story*, he expresses perfectly the spirit of the music of Johnny Dodds and his generation of New Orleans jazzmen. The roughness of their music may offend the ears of those concerned with the more sophisticated styles of later jazz, but the qualities of which Baby Dodds speaks here are more fundamental than questions of musical complexity or an over-cultivated 'good taste'. 'The musicians of those days were remarkable men. When the leader of an orchestra would hire a man, there was no jealousy in the gang. Everybody took him in as a brother, and he was treated accordingly. If a fellow came to work with anything, even a sandwich or an orange, the new man would be offered a piece of it. That's the way they were. They believed in harmony. That's how they played music, in harmony. And that's the way the fellows were, those old-timers.'

JOHNNY DODDS
RECOMMENDED RECORDS

The following listing includes most of Johnny Dodds' finest recordings, along with a small number of items below his best which serve to give a rounded picture of his career and his music. No attempt has been made to give the full contents of any LP cited, nor the backings of old 78's, as the constantly shifting pattern of the re-issue of old jazz material would soon render such data obsolete.

It is regretted that the current unavailability of many of Dodds' most important records has resulted in the necessity to include quite a few items that are not at present in the catalogue. These are marked with a star.

Key to Instrumental Abbreviations:

(alt)	alto saxophone		(p)	piano
(bj)	banjo		(tbn)	trombone
(bs)	string bass		(ten)	tenor saxophone
(bs-sx)	bass saxophone		(tpt)	trumpet
(clt)	clarinet		(tu)	tuba
(cnt)	cornet		(vcl)	vocal
(d)	drums		(wbd)	washboard
(g)	guitar			

Abbreviation	Label	Prefix	Type
RCA	RCA Victor	LPM	LP(12")

KING OLIVER AND HIS CREOLE JAZZ BAND:

Joe "King" Oliver, Louis Armstrong (cnt); Honoré Dutrey (tbn); Johnny Dodds (clt); Lil Hardin (p); Bud Scott or Mill Johnson (bj); Warren "Baby" Dodds (d).

Richmond, Indiana, March 31, 1923
Just Gone
Canal Street Blues ⎫
Mandy Lee Blues ⎬ Riv RLP12–122*
Chimes Blues ⎭

As above, with Johnson definite on *bj.*

Richmond, Indiana, April 6, 1923
Weather Bird Rag
Dippermouth Blues ⎫
Froggie Moore ⎬ Riv RLP12–122*
Snake Rag ⎭

Bud Scott (*bj*) replaces Johnson.

Chicago, June 22, 1923
Snake Rag
Sweet Lovin' Man ⎫
High Society ⎬ Epic LN3208*
Sobbin' Blues [1] ⎭

[1] Slide whistle solo by Baby Dodds on this number.

Chicago, June 23, 1923
Dippermouth Blues   Epic LN3208*

Charlie Johnson (*bs-sx*) added; Johnny St. Cyr (*bj*) replaces Scott.

Chicago, October, 1923
I Ain't Gonna Tell Nobody ⎫
Room Rent Blues ⎬ Epic LN3208*
Sweet Baby Doll
Working Man Blues ⎫
Mabel's Dream ⎬ Epic LN3208*

St. Cyr out.

Chicago, November, 1923
Mabel's Dream ⎫
Southern Stomp ⎬ Riv RLP12–122*
Riverside Blues ⎭

Note: Louis Armstrong and pianist Lil Hardin were married in 1924, and the latter subsequently used the name Lil Armstrong on all engagements.

LOUIS ARMSTRONG HOT FIVE:

Louis Armstrong (cnt, vcl [1]); Kid Ory (tbn); Johnny

Dodds (*clt*); Lil Armstrong (*p, vcl* [2]); Johnny St. Cyr (*bj*).

Chicago, November 12, 1925
Gut Bucket Blues [3]   Co CL851

   [3] Verbal introductions to solos by Armstrong and Ory.

NEW ORLEANS WANDERERS:

George Mitchell (*cnt*); Kid Ory (*tbn*); Johnny Dodds (*clt*); Jimmy Walker (*alt*); Lil Armstrong (*p*); Johnny St. Cyr (*bj*).

Chicago, July 13, 1926
Perdido Street Blues [1]
Gatemouth
Too Tight   } Epic LN3207*
Papa Dip
   [1] Walker does not play on this number.

NEW ORLEANS BOOTBLACKS:

Same personnel.

Chicago, July 14, 1926
Mixed Salad
I Can't Say
Flat Foot   } Epic LN3207*
Mad Dog

LOUIS ARMSTRONG HOT FIVE:

Previous Hot Five personnel.

Chicago, November 16, 1926
Skid-Dat-De-Dat   Co CL851

JOHNNY DODDS' BLACK BOTTOM STOMPERS:

Louis Armstrong (*cnt*); unknown *tbn* (possibly Honoré Dutrey); Johnny Dodds (*clt*); Barney Bigard (*ten*); Earl Hines (*p*); Bud Scott (*bj*); Baby Dodds (*d*).

Chicago, April 22, 1927
Wild Man Blues   De DL8398*

LOUIS ARMSTRONG HOT SEVEN:

Louis Armstrong (*tpt, vcl* [1]); unknown *tbn* (possibly John Thomas); Johnny Dodds (*clt*); Lil Armstrong (*p, vcl* [2]); Johnny St. Cyr (*bj, g*); Pete Briggs (*tu*); Baby Dodds (*d*).

Chicago, May 7, 1927
Willie The Weeper
Wild Man Blues   } Co CL852

Honoré Dutrey definitely on *tbn*.

Chicago, May 10, 1927
Alligator Crawl Blues
Potato Head Blues   } Co CL852

Kid Ory (*tbn*) replaces Dutrey.

Chicago, May 11, 1927
Melancholy Blues
Weary Blues   } Co CL852

Chicago, May 13, 1927
Keyhole Blues
S.O.L. Blues [1]   } Co CL852

Chicago, May 14, 1927
Gully Low Blues [1]
That's When I'll Come Back To You [1,2]   } Co CL852

JELLY ROLL MORTON'S RED HOT PEPPERS:

George Mitchell (*cnt*); George Bryant (*tbn*); Johnny Dodds (*clt*); Stomp Evans (*alt*); Jelly Roll Morton (*p*); Johnny St. Cyr (*bj, g*); Quinn Wilson (*tu*); Baby Dodds (*d*).

Chicago, June 4, 1927
Wild Man Blues   RCA LPV 524
Jungle Blues   RCA LPM1649*

JELLY ROLL MORTON TRIO:

Johnny Dodds (*clt*); Jelly Roll Morton (*p*); Baby Dodds (*d*).

Chicago, June 10, 1927
Wolverine Blues
Mr. Jelly Lord   } RCA LPV 546

LOUIS ARMSTRONG HOT FIVE

Louis Armstrong (*tpt, vcl*); Kid Ory (*tbn*); Johnny Dodds (*clt*); Lil Armstrong (*p*); Johnny St. Cyr (*bj*); Lonnie Johnson (*g*).

Chicago, December 10, 1927
I'm Not Rough   Co CL851

JOHNNY DODDS' TRIO:

Johnny Dodds (*clt*); Lil Armstrong (*p*); Bill Johnson (*bs*).

Chicago, July 5, 1928
   Blue Clarinet Stomp
   Blue Piano Stomp } RCA LPV 558

JOHNNY DODDS' WASHBOARD BAND:

Natty Dominique (*tpt*); Honore Dutrey (*tbn*); Johnny Dodds (*clt*); Jimmy Blythe or Lil Armstrong (*p*); Bill Johnson (*bs*); Baby Dodds (*wbd*).

Chicago, July 6, 1928
   Bucktown Stomp
   Weary City
   Blue Washboard Stomp
   Bull Fiddle Blues } RCA LPV 558

JOHNNY DODDS' HOT SIX:

Same personnel, except Lil Armstrong is definitely on piano and Baby Dodds switches to drums.

Chicago, February 7, 1929
   Goober Dance
   Too Tight } RCA LPV 558

JOHNNY DODDS AND HIS ORCHESTRA:

Natty Dominique (*tpt*); Preston Jackson (*tbn*); Johnny Dodds (*clt*); Richard M. Jones (*p*); Lonnie Johnson (*g*); John Lindsay (*bs*); Baby Dodds (*d*).

Chicago, June 5, 1940
   Red Onion Blues
   Gravier Street Blues } De DL8283*

Duke Ellington

BY G. E. LAMBERT

ACKNOWLEDGEMENTS

The sources for the biographical data presented in this book are too various to list, but I would like to acknowledge in particular, *Duke Ellington* by Barry Ulanov (Musicians Press, London, 1947) and *Duke Ellington: His Life and Music*, edited by Peter Gammond (Phoenix House, London, 1958), which were the principal sources used.

I would also like to thank the many friends who assisted in various ways towards the completion of this book. In particular, Miss Anne Bradbury and Mr. Percy Buckley for checking the MS.; Miss Bradbury and Miss B. Kenyon for assistance with the typing; and the following local collectors for the loan of records to fill out my own Ellington collection: Alan Buckley, Percy Buckley, Alec Greenhalgh and Tony Whale.

G.E.L.

I. A BIOGRAPHICAL SKETCH

Edward Kennedy Ellington was born on April 29th, 1899, in Washington, D.C. His family seem to have been fairly well-to-do, by Negro standards in the American capital, his father being a butler who, at the time of his son's birth, occasionally served at White House functions. Later James Edward Ellington became a blueprint maker for the U.S. Navy, and from all reports he was an easy, relaxed individual. Edward Kennedy was brought up an only child, his sister not being born until he reached the age of sixteen, and the happy atmosphere of his home life during childhood can be gauged from the fact that to the son, as well as to visiting relatives, James Edward was known as 'Uncle Ed'. 'Uncle Ed sure provided for his family,' Duke has said, 'we didn't want for anything.' His mother, Daisy Kennedy, seems to have been a perfect foil for the more easygoing James Edward; a woman of strict principle and, we are told, prim manner. In the Washington of this period, when racial segregation laid very great stress on a Negro family, Ellington's childhood environment must have been unusually happy to have provided the basis of temperament for the relaxed, urbane, master of all situations which he became in later years. Perhaps the index of his childhood is to be found in that strong sense of loyalty which he felt for those close to him and which he demanded in turn from his musicians and his friends.

His hobbies as a child followed the usual pattern for a young American of this era—baseball, football and the movies. He once recalled that his first musical memory was of his mother playing *The Rosary* when he was four years old, but though he started to take piano lessons from a lady by the improbable sounding name of Klingscale (other versions of this name have been reported as Mrs. Klinkscale and Mrs. Chinkscale), he derived little satisfaction from the piano at that tender age. Although he played at a church concert given by Mrs. Klingscale, he had little enthusiasm for music and avoided practice whenever possible. Unlike those other members of what have been termed 'jazz nobility', 'King' Oliver, who was so styled by his admirers in New Orleans and 'Count' Basie, named by a radio announcer, Edward Kennedy Ellington had his title bestowed upon him many years before he played jazz. The name, so utterly correct in its definition of the princely manner of the man, was given by a boyhood friend and neighbour at the rather early age of eight!

Duke Ellington spent some three years at what was one of the leading high schools for Negroes in Washington at that time. During the first of the three years or so that he was at the Armstrong High School, Duke's greatest interest seems to have been in drawing, at which he showed very great promise. He also took regular music lessons at the school, later supplemented by private lessons from a Henry Grant of the Dunbar High School, who was also the teacher of both Otto Hardwicke and Arthur Whetsol.

About this time Ellington won a poster contest sponsored by the National Association for the Advancement of Coloured People, and just prior to his leaving the Armstrong High School in June, 1917, he was offered a scholarship to the Pratt Institute of Applied Arts. This he turned down, presumably on account of his increasing pre-occupation with music, for by this time Duke had come into contact with the house rent parties which were so common a feature of Negro city life during this period. Each large American city had, in those pre-mass entertainment days, its own favourite party piano players. Chicago's Jimmy Yancey and Cripple Clarence Lofton became known in later years through their recordings, whilst many of the New York rent party pianists became international figures through their later fame in the worlds of jazz and popular entertainment—for example Count Basie, Fats Waller and, of course, *the* pianist of New York in the 'teens and 'twenties—James P. Johnson. Although he was impressed by the local heroes of ragtime piano—men like Clarence Bowser, Louis Thomas, Louis Brown, Lester Dishman and Doc Perry—the prime influence on the young Ellington was without doubt the great James P. Johnson. He used to describe how he obtained a piano roll of Johnson's famous *Carolina Shout*, and played it on the pianola very slowly so that he could follow the fingering and study the intricacies of James P.'s style. Duke also paid tribute to Doc Perry as the man who taught him to 'read notes, not just spell them out'.

When James P. Johnson came to Washington, so one legend goes, Duke played in a carving contest against him and, with the strong local support in the audience, succeeded in 'carving' the master. Duke has denied this in recent years, and it seems indeed a rather unlikely story, although there is no doubt that around this time Ellington did play at some party and made quite an impression with James P. While still at Armstrong High, Duke took an after-school job at the Poodle Dog Café as a 'soda jerker', and he named his first composition, *The Soda Fountain Rag*. As soon as opportunity presented itself, Duke played this at a local café: he played it straight, as a blues, as a foxtrot, as a waltz and finally as a fast tempo stomp. 'They never knew it was the same piece,' recalled Duke, many years later. 'I was established . . . I had a repertoire.' Subsequently Duke played several jobs as solo pianist and with local bands, the latter along with two other young musicians who were later to find fame as members of his orchestra—Otto Hardwicke and Arthur Whetsol.

In 1918 Duke married Edna Thompson, a girl he had been friendly with at school and who had helped him with his piano studies; the following year their son, Mercer, was born. At first he worked gigs in the evenings and painted posters during the day in order that his family would be well provided for, but he found that he was more and more able to use his musical ability as a means of income. He had been playing for some time with a group of young musicians and had noticed that the better-known local band leaders had large advertisements in the phone book. Duke bought one just as big as theirs, and before long he and his musicians were handling all the engagements they had time for. During this period a drummer from New York, Sonny Greer, was playing at the Howard Theatre in Washington, and when the Ellington musicians heard him they were impressed by his abilities, and soon persuaded this somewhat colourful character to join them. This was in 1919; Sonny Greer left Duke Ellington's orchestra in 1950!

In 1922 five of this group of young Washington musicians left for New York—Ellington, Hardwicke, Whetsol, Greer and banjoist Elmer Snowden, the pretext being a telegram from Wilbur Sweatman asking Greer to join his band. The job with Sweatman did not last long however, and, although the young musicians hung around New York for some time, work and food were both in short supply. It was during this period that Ellington heard the pianist Willie

'The Lion' Smith, who probably influenced his own keyboard style more than any other single musician during his formative years. Duke also had many opportunities to hear the playing of James P. Johnson and his brilliant young pupil Fats Waller while in New York, and it was Waller who persuaded them to try New York again when they had returned to Washington after three months of scuffling. After playing various odd engagements in New York they were able to land a regular job at a place called the Hollywood Club, later re-named the Kentucky Club. It is doubtful if this group had much to offer in the way of jazz, the line up in the spring of 1923 being Arthur Whetsol, trumpet; Otto Hardwicke, alto; Duke Ellington, piano; Elmer Snowden (the nominal leader of the band at this time), banjo; and Sonny Greer, drums. The band spent the next four and a half years at the Kentucky Club, and it was here that Sonny Greer won considerable fame as the man who tipped off the waiters as to which of the customers were to be provided with drinks during those days of prohibition. Most of the customers were acceptable, as the Club was mainly a place for theatre and show-business people, but if anyone looked suspicious the waiter would see Sonny, behind his typically extravagant drum kit, shake his head and for that individual prohibition would be in force even within the Kentucky Club!

After some disagreement with the other members of the band, Elmer Snowden left and was replaced by Fred Guy on banjo, while the leadership of the group passed over to Duke Ellington. Another personnel change which had a greater impact was the addition of Charlie Irvis on trombone. Whetsol and Hardwicke, who recorded prolifically with Ellington in later years, were both 'sweet' rather than 'hot' musicians, and it was Irvis who first added a distinct jazz voice to Ellington's band. He was a rougher player than the Washingtonians; his style partly inspired by the New Orleans trombonists and partly made up of an individual manner of playing with a mute—a sort of embryonic form of the style later perfected by Irvis' successor, trombonist Joe Nanton, and by Bubber Miley, a trumpet player who joined Ellington whilst he was still at the Kentucky Club. The reason that Miley joined Ellington was that, despite the protests of his fellow bandsmen, Arthur Whetsol was going back to Washington to complete his medical studies, and Duke needed a replacement. Bubber Miley was to play with Ellington for six years, and he was without doubt the most influential musician who ever played with the band in his effect on Ellington's music. Miley played muted in almost all his solos, and along with his manipulation of the rubber plunger he would combine growls and blue inflexions, at times seeming to make the trumpet talk. His style has often been described as 'wa-wa' or 'growl', and he was a very great influence on many younger musicians who adopted this manner of muted playing. Yet Miley's melodic line was also unique and he must be given credit for his part in the creation of several of the finest works associated with Duke Ellington. *East St. Louis Toodle-oo*, *Black and Tan Fantasy* and *Creole Love Call* all bear Miley's name as part-composer, and it is probable that Ellington would have taken a good deal longer in arriving at his own maturity as a musician had it not been for the cathartic effect Miley had on the band, and upon its leader's creations. For Miley, like all good jazzmen, was basically a blues musician, and it was the influence of this infinitely pliable material, more than Bubber's exotic growl, which revolutionized the young Ellington's outlook on music. 'Our band changed its character when Bubber came in,' says Duke. 'He used to growl all night long, playing gutbucket on his horn. That was when we decided to forget all about the sweet music.'[1]

Charlie Irvis left the band in late 1926 and was replaced by Joe 'Tricky Sam' Nanton, whose trombone style was a reflection (on his lower pitched instrument) of Bubber Miley's trumpet. Around this time the band augmented its rhythm section to a quartet by the addition of Bass Edwards on tuba. Three further additions brought the band to the strength we know from its earliest recordings as a complete unit—an additional trumpet player to take the open solos and provide the lead in Louis Metcalf; a tenor saxophonist who was also an able clarinettist in Rudy Jackson; and a second alto, Harry Carney, who had the unusual distinction for that day of doubling on baritone saxophone. The first two did not stay with the band for very long, but Harry Carney's baritone still graced the Ellington bandstand until his death in 1974—forty-eight years after he first joined the band! Throughout the history of the Ellington Orchestra Carney added to the texture of Ellington's scores a deep, rich sound which, it seems, only he could draw from the baritone. He was of course the leading soloist on his instrument and one of the most distinguished and accomplished musicians in jazz. This personnel—Miley and Metcalf on trumpets, Nanton on trombone, Hardwicke, Jackson and Carney on reeds, and the rhythm section of Ellington, Guy, Edwards and Greer—was probably the one heard by the impresario, Irving Mills, when he made his historic entry into the Kentucky Club one evening in 1926.

According to Ellington the band were playing *St. Louis Blues* when Mills walked in and, after the number was over, Mills asked Duke what it was. Mills said that it sounded nothing like *St. Louis Blues*—'so maybe that gave him ideas,' says Duke. Mills' version is rather different; the number which attracted his attention was *Black and Tan Fantasy*. 'When I learned that it was Duke's composition, I immediately recognized that I had encountered a great creative artist and the first American composer to catch in his music the true jazz spirit.'[2]

II

Irving Mills was not a musician (despite the large number of Ellington compositions bearing the credit 'Ellington–Mills'), but he was an important figure in the life of Duke Ellington. In having the business and publicity worries handled by Mills, Duke was able to devote the maximum amount of time to composition and the band's musical development. Whatever one's personal opinions of the entertainment business may be, there can be little doubt that the emergence of Irving Mills to take up the business side of the Ellington orchestra was an unqualified blessing, in the social context of the 1920s. Mills, a prodigiously energetic individual, was a song publisher, band manager, publicity agent and, in later years, record company executive. Ellington was served by Mills in all these capacities. Together they formed a company known as Ellington, Inc., and Mills set into motion the means of making Ellington an internationally known figure. First of all Mills arranged a number of recordings for labels better known than the somewhat obscure ones on which the Ellington musicians had thus far appeared. It was through Mills that the band landed the long engagement at the Cotton Club in late 1927, after a theatre owner in Philadelphia had been persuaded to release the band from a contract to enable them to appear on the opening night. The means of 'persuasion' employed was to send a local gangster to the manager in question with the simple proposition, 'Be big, or you'll be dead.' He was 'big', and the band opened on time. For the next few years they were a permanent feature at the Cotton Club, with the exception of a few months in the summer of 1930, when the band went to Hollywood to take part in the Amos an' Andy film, *Check and Double Check*. Significant changes were made in the band during this period, the first being the replacement of tuba player, Bass Edwards with the New Orleans string-bass player, Wellman Braud, just before the band moved in to the Cotton Club. Another New Orleans man in clarinettist Barney Bigard, who had experience with both Jelly-Roll Morton and King Oliver, added his very distinctive voice to the band in January of 1928. In March of that year Arthur Whetsol returned to make the trumpet section up to three pieces, and eight months later Freddy Jenkins replaced Louis Metcalf, adding an individual style and an extremely colourful personality to the band.

The most important personnel change occurred when Otto Hardwicke left in June of that same year. He was replaced by Johnny Hodges, already a distinctive soloist on alto and soprano saxes, and a musician who was, in a few years' time, to become the greatest soloist on his instrument that music has ever known. A remarkably even musician in his constant inspiration and in the unvarying quality of his work, Johnny Hodges, who died in 1970, was one of the few artists in any field who *never* perform badly.

The environment at the Cotton Club was hardly one in which the music critics (who were in a few short years to compare Ellington with Delius, Debussy and Stravinsky) would have expected to find a budding genius. For much of the time the band were either playing accompaniments to popular singers of the day, such as Adelaide Hall, Ethel Waters and the Mills Brothers (who were just becoming well known as the first of the vocal quartets), or playing background music to dancing routines. Much of the music played at the Cotton Club was not Ellington material at all, yet during this period he recorded many of the masterpieces which were to bring him acclaim from so many diverse sources. He also recorded many of the popular tunes of the

[1] Nat Hentoff and Nat Shapiro (Editors), *Hear Me Talkin' to Ya*, p. 209 (Peter Davies, 1955).

[2] Ibid. p. 211.

day, some of which were only average by the not particularly elevated standards in this field. Many of these records, however, proved to be gems of orchestral jazz; the section playing, the solos and the scoring showed that Duke could more than hold his own with other large jazz groups, even without the unique compositions which are naturally associated with him.

In February, 1929, Bubber Miley left the band, and Ellington replaced him with Charles Melvin Williams, a young trumpet player from Mobile, Alabama—better known amongst jazz devotees as 'Cootie'. Cootie Williams had made quite an impression on the New York jazz scene during brief periods with the orchestras of Chick Webb and Fletcher Henderson, although his reputation had come solely from his open playing. Ellington hired Williams as a replacement for Bubber Miley however, and, with some assistance from Tricky Sam Nanton, Cootie mastered the growl style of his predecessor, and it was this style with which he became associated in later years. He is also an authoritative player on the open trumpet, with much of the majesty of Louis Armstrong's best work, and is certainly one of the finest of jazz trumpet players who ever lived. The story of Bubber Miley's life after leaving Ellington is brief and tragic. He played for a while in the bands of Noble Sissle and Zutty Singleton, and later formed a group of his own under the sponsorship of Irving Mills to play in the review *Harlem Scandals*. Although he had been warned that he was tuberculous some time before, in early February, 1932, he had to give up playing because of his condition, and he died on May 20th of the same year. It is said that not one musician attended the funeral of this remarkable jazzman; the only tribute to his contribution to music at Bubber Miley's funeral was a very large wreath of flowers from Duke Ellington.

During their stay at the Cotton Club the playing of the Ellington band was often referred to as 'jungle style'. This was because, although situated in Harlem, the Cotton Club was in actual fact a club for the whites who came uptown to hear and see 'primitive' music and entertainment. The Cotton Club's jungle décor catered for this very taste, and as Ellington's more 'exotic' compositions (i.e. those including 'growl' brass features) were used to back the dances during the 'jungle' sequences, it was not surprising that, with the aid of astute publicity, Ellington's band was soon associated with 'jungle music'. Ellington's titles reflect this tendency for from this period come such titles as *Jungle Jamboree*, *Jungle Blues*, *Jungle Nights in Harlem* and *Echoes of the Jungle*; titles which owe more to the publicity office of Irving Mills than the compositions of Duke Ellington to which they are appended. It is essential to the newcomer to Duke Ellington's music to understand this, for the growl style perfected by Miley and Nanton is a perfectly legitimate development of the 'vocalization' of instrumental tone and inflexion which is so primary a characteristic of American Negro music. It is in fact a part of the blues tradition in jazz, and most emphatically neither a borrowing from nor an impression of African Negro musical idioms. It is rather odd that some commentators have considered the use of 'growl' style by Ellington to be an exotic superficiality, whilst in fact it is one of the most traditional elements in his style. The Ellington band used various pseudonyms when recording for different companies in the 'twenties and

'thirties, and it is a rather ironic commentary on the environment of the band to recall that the first serious attempt at extended composition in jazz, *Creole Rhapsody*, which Duke recorded in 1931, was issued as by 'The Jungle Band'!

In 1930, Ellington finally split with his wife, Edna Thompson, and he was married a second time, to Mildred Dixon, a dancer at the Cotton Club. During this time Duke's parents and his son Mercer lived with him in New York, and the Ellington home was a happy, if somewhat hectic place. In 1929, a few months after Cootie Williams had joined the band, Duke added a second trombonist in Juan Tizol, a musician from Puerto Rico who specialized on the valve trombone. Rarely featured in jazz solos, Tizol was to become a distinctive voice with the Ellington ensemble through his collaboration with Duke in such compositions as *Perdido, Caravan, Congo Brava*, etc.; numbers which employ (with the exception of the first named) exotic Latin-American rhythms and scoring. In 1932 the trombone section was brought up to the then unheard-of strength of three by the addition of a musician from the West Coast, Lawrence Brown. Brown was already known to jazz collectors through his recordings with Louis Armstrong, and his addition to the Ellington ranks was the cause of the first of those unfavourable uproars created periodically by the critics when a new jazz musician has joined the orchestra. Such influential writers as John Hammond in America and Spike Hughes in England condemned the addition of Brown; it was not that he was considered a poor musician, but it was felt that his personality was too 'sophisticated', his style too 'virtuoso', for the 'essentially direct and simple music' of Ellington. 'It is not that his individuality is too strong,' wrote Hughes, 'just misplaced.' Similar outcries have been made about Rex Stewart (1934), Jimmy Hamilton (1943) and Clark Terry (1951) when they joined the band, and however justified the critics appeared before the results of such changes were heard on record, Ellington always proved conclusively that he knew better who would fit into his band than the most perceptive of critics. It is only just to point out, however, that not all commentators have considered that Ellington's output has been uniform in quality through the years. Spike Hughes, for example, considers that from about this period Ellington's music started to decline in quality and that generally his work in the middle and late 'thirties suffered from over-sophistication and too great a concern with harmony. A further addition to the band at this time was vocalist Ivie Anderson, who was the first regular singer that Duke carried with the band. Vocalists have never been Ellington's strongest suit, but on many recordings Ivie Anderson's singing blends well with the band's performances and she is probably the finest singer that he has ever had.

Despite the great commercial success of the band in America and the appreciation of his immense talents as a composer, both in his own country and in Europe, Duke Ellington had, by 1932, become dissatisfied with his mode of living. With the continual commercialism of the Cotton Club, and of other such engagements, the 'high life' which he had led for the past few years began to pall. His friends noticed a new moodiness, a certain cynicism in the manner of this previously happy individual. In his brilliant study of Ellington's personality, *The Hot Bach*, Richard O. Boyer quotes Duke's recollections of this period: 'I'd bring something I thought was good to the music publishers and they'd ask, "Can an eight-year-old child sing it?" I'd bring something new to them and they'd say, "This ain't what we're looking for. We want something like Gazookus wrote last week." I'd see guys writing little pop numbers that were going over big. I didn't see why I should try to do something good. I thought I'd stop writing. . . . If something bad was plugged it would go over better than something good that wasn't. I felt it was all a racket. I was on the point of giving up.'[1] Whether the reputation that Ellington's records had made for him amongst music lovers in Europe was the deciding factor, or whether the travel and change of environment were the things desired most by Ellington, we do not know, but a European trip was decided upon. In the summer of 1933 (despite Ellington's fear of icebergs) the band set sail for England, the first stage of a European tour.

III

In England, Ellington's reputation rested solely on his records, and the audience for these included not only the lovers of the latest dance music craze, but also a growing band of jazz record collectors and a number of figures of some eminence in the world of European concert music. Such writers on jazz as Leonard Hibbs and Spike Hughes stressed continually the importance of Ellington's music, and the distinguished composer Constant Lambert was a great admirer of his work. In America the composer Percy Grainger had compared Ellington with Bach and Delius, and much was made of this comparison in England. The names of Debussy and Ravel were also bandied about somewhat freely in connexion with Duke's compositions at this time. Of course there was a huge press barrage of publicity of a less esoteric nature promoted by Irving Mills and the British band-leader Jack Hylton, who was organizing the band's European trip. They played variety theatres in various large cities in Britain and also two concerts in London sponsored by the *Melody Maker*, the first of which provoked a bitter controversy. Designed to show Ellington as a composer, the first half consisted of such music as *Echoes of the Jungle*, *Blue Tune*, *Creole Rhapsody* and *Black and Tan Fantasy*. The audience reaction to the muted work of Cootie Williams and Tricky Sam Nanton was that of people hearing a clever piece of instrumental trickery, or some weird novelty, rather than a colourful, integrated part of Ellington's tonal palate. Sensing that the audience were not (when they laughed at Tricky Sam's solos) taking the attitude that he and his critical followers had hoped, Duke changed the programme for the second half and included Lawrence Brown's *Trees*, Freddie Jenkins singing and dancing *Some of These Days*, and such popular material as *Minnie the Moocher* and *Tiger Rag*. The serious devotees of Ellington's music were horrified; Duke had 'debased himself'; he had commercialized his art! The most angry voice was that of Spike Hughes, and in the programme of

the second concert, which was held three weeks later, the audience were advised by Hughes how to conduct themselves in a concert hall. 'Don't laugh at Nanton,' said Hughes. 'Don't applaud during numbers.' He was promptly dubbed 'the hot dictator', and his part in these events has been constantly maligned by almost all writers who have discussed Ellington's 1933 tour. However strongly one may disagree with the opinions Hughes later expressed about the decline of Ellington's music, there is no denying that if Duke was able to create music worthy of the time and attention of a concert audience, then Spike Hughes was completely right. Ellington did indeed offer music of such quality, the playing of Williams and Nanton being an integral part of this music, and no person in his right mind can consider that to have someone laughing at every muted solo was a desirable state of affairs. Hughes' methods were drastic, but well justified. The attention paid to Ellington's music throughout the European tour must have been pleasing to Duke, yet the last thing that Irving Mills wanted was for Ellington to be considered 'highbrow'. Respect for his music, yes; but Ellington's popularity could be seriously affected by too much of this sort of thing. Nothing sells less well amongst the general public than that which is labelled 'highbrow', and much of the criticism of Hughes' approach came from within the Ellington camp. But this European tour was a good thing for Ellington, as is shown by his statement, 'The main thing I got in Europe was *spirit*; it lifted me out of a bad groove. That kind of thing gives you courage to go on. If they think I'm *that* important, then maybe I have kinda said something; maybe our music does mean something.'[1]

Although in 1932 he was given the annual award by the New York Schools of Music for his *Creole Rhapsody*, the activities of Ellington's band were still largely confined to appearances at the larger night clubs and at dances. In the autumn of 1933 they made their first tour of the South and in 1934 he took part in a number of films—*Murder at the Vanities*, *Belle of the '90s* (with Mae West) and *Symphony in Black*. This was the year in which Constant Lambert's study of twentieth-century music, *Music Ho!*, was published, during the course of which he made the now famous statement that there is 'nothing in Ravel so dexterous in treatment as the varied solos in the middle of the ebullient *Hot and Bothered* and nothing in Stravinsky more dynamic than the final section'.[2] During the time this book was published Ellington was engaged in playing dances for Jim Crow audiences in America's Southern States, and leading his band in brief snatches of third-rate films!

In Christmas week 1934 a new and important voice was added to the trumpet section, that of Rex Stewart, who replaced the ailing Freddy Jenkins. A veteran jazzman, Stewart had played for several years with the famous Fletcher Henderson Orchestra, in addition to spells with McKinney's Cotton Pickers and Luis Russell, Rex, who died in 1967, was a musician who was constantly underestimated by

[1] Richard O. Boyer, *The Hot Bach*, reprinted in *Duke Ellington*, p. 56, edited by Peter Gammond (Phoenix House, 1958).

[1] Barry Ulanov, *Duke Ellington*, p. 151 (Musicians Press, 1947).
[2] Constant Lambert, *Music Ho!*, p. 156 (Faber & Faber, 1934, and Penguin Books, 1948).

the critics, both in his achievements and his influence. Roy Eldridge has stated that Rex was one of the musicians who influenced his playing, whilst traces of the Stewart manner can be found in such diverse musicians as Taft Jordan and Clark Terry. As a voice in the Ellington Orchestra, Stewart's work was invaluable in its versatility, for he commanded virtually *every* style of jazz trumpet, including a masterly adaptation of the Bubber Miley growl style, and a manner which he devised himself of playing with the valves of the instrument half depressed. The partnership of Cootie Williams and Rex Stewart in the Duke Ellington brass section from 1935 to 1940 was one of the greatest in jazz history. In the late fifties both men suffered an undue neglect, yet an album they made together in that period shows they were still amongst the very finest of jazz trumpet players.[1]

1935 saw the dawning of the so-called 'swing era' which began with the success of Benny Goodman's first big band. Duke Ellington's name was so established that at first he was not considered to play the same type of music as the newly established bands of Goodman, Bob Crosby, Tommy Dorsey and Jimmy Lunceford. In addition to this factor it must be observed that the white bands throughout the 'swing' period had the best publicity and the best jobs, at the expense of the coloured orchestras who were almost invariably superior in musical content. But the astute publicity chief of the Irving Mills organization, Ned Williams, went to work to assure the public that Duke Ellington led a 'swing' orchestra, and soon the band was accepted by the public as such. In late 1935 bassist Wellman Braud left the orchestra, and it was a sign of the band's success that Ellington could afford for a few years to experiment with two bass players, Hayes Alvis and Billy Taylor. Both men worked with Ellington until 1938, but early in that year Alvis departed and Taylor remained with the band until the advent of Jimmy Blanton in October, 1939.

Ellington had been told in 1933 that his mother was a sick woman but she refused to go into hospital when advised to do so. Finally she entered Providence Hospital, Detroit, a cancer sanatorium and research centre, early in 1935. Duke arranged his bookings so he could be near at hand and he was with her continuously during the last three days of her life. She died on May 27th, 1935, and her death was a great shock to Ellington—'I have no ambition left,' he told his friends. 'The bottom's out of everything.' It was in the months immediately after his mother's death that Ellington wrote *Reminiscing in Tempo*, by far the most ambitious composition in the jazz idiom at this date, running for some twelve minutes and covering four sides of the then standard 10-inch 78 r.p.m. records. Critical reaction was hostile; in America, John Hammond headed his review of the work 'The Tragedy of Duke Ellington'. In England ('I wrote it just for them,' said Duke) Spike Hughes described it as a 'long rambling monstrosity', and Edgar Jackson said frankly that he did not understand the work. Leonard Hibbs also found it dull and meaningless at first, but 'at the same time, I had too high an opinion of Duke to think

he would willingly perpetuate anything like the pointless joke that this appeared to be . . .' So Hibbs listened to the work several times, finally coming to the conclusion that it was a significant and worthy piece of Ellingtonia. Would that other critics in the turbulent world of jazz might show such admirable modesty![1]

In 1937 and 1938 Ellington was again associated with the Cotton Club, although he took time off to visit Hollywood and make another film, *The Hit Parade*. One of the numbers played in this film was *I've Got To Be A Rug Cutter*, a typical title of the day, with a hastily improvised vocal trio of Harry Carney, Rex Stewart and Hayes Alvis! Whilst on the West Coast the band played a concert at the University of California, which was the first of a series of concerts at various colleges and universities. But 1937 brought further tragedy for Duke in his family life, for in early November of that year his father died. Once again he was thrown into the depths of depression and for a long time he did little or no composing. In this same year Arthur Whetsol, who had been a friend and associate of Ellington's right from the early days in Washington, left the band. After some shuffling around in the trumpet section Wallace Jones took over the first trumpet chair; although a lead man of great efficiency Jones was no soloist, and Whetsol's delicate trumpet style was a considerable loss to the orchestra. In 1938 Ellington wrote another concert work, *The Blue Belles of Harlem*, on a commission from Paul Whiteman for a work for his orchestra. Although this was performed some years afterwards by the Ellington Orchestra at a Carnegie Hall Concert, it has unfortunately never been recorded.

In the spring of 1939 Duke was married to Bea Ellis, shortly after his divorce from his second wife, Mildred. Another long-standing partnership was broken when Ellington split with Irving Mills, signing a new contract with the William Morris agency, and in March of this year Ellington sailed for Europe, this time having to miss out England owing to union restrictions. On the eve of the Second World War the Ellington band covered France, Belgium, Holland, Denmark and Sweden in a thirty-four-day concert tour. The tour was a success in every way, and, to add to the frustration of English jazz enthusiasts who were unable to hear the band, the musicians called at London on their way back to the U.S.

IV

Before leaving for Europe the band had recorded a song called *Something to Live For*, an Ellington composition with lyrics by a young lyric-writer and musician, Billy Strayhorn. Legend has it that Strayhorn was hired by Duke purely as a lyric writer and that, whilst the band was away in Europe, the young man became fascinated by the Ellington scores which he studied with great interest and enthusiasm. In actual fact Strayhorn had done some scoring for

---

[1] *The Big Challenge*, American Jazztone J1268, 1957 (not available in England).

[1] For further details of the critical reaction to *Reminiscing in Tempo* see Charles Fox in *Duke Ellington*, pp. 89–90, edited by Peter Gammond (Phoenix House, 1958), and Barry Ulanov, *Duke Ellington*, pp. 164–6 (Musicians Press, 1947).

small band dates by the Johnny Hodges contingent before the band's departure. We may deduce from this that Duke already had his mind on the idea of letting this highly talented young musician do some of the scoring for the full orchestra. Billy Strayhorn's compositions became a regular feature of the band's repertoire. Apart from such well-known numbers as *Take The 'A' Train*, *Midriff* and *Day Dream*, he is joint composer of several of the longer concert works, such as *The Perfume Suite* and *Such Sweet Thunder*. Like Ellington himself, he has always paid great attention to the musical character of the men in the band, and it is often impossible to tell whether a number is an Ellington original or a Strayhorn composition, so closely has the younger man assimilated the Ellington manner. Yet no other musician in jazz has ever been able to achieve anything sounding remotely like the 'Ellington effect', as Strayhorn himself terms it! It was Strayhorn who coined the well known and very perceptive saying: 'Ellington plays the piano, but his real instrument is his band.'

Later in 1939 two other important additions were made to the Ellington band when Duke increased his sax section to five pieces with the addition of the Kansas City tenor player Ben Webster, and bassist Billy Taylor was replaced by Jimmy Blanton. From being the least important member of the reed section, the tenor saxophone had developed under the influence of that great musician, Coleman Hawkins, to a position where it challenged the trumpet as the most important solo instrument in jazz. Every large band, except Ellington's, had by this time at least one tenor saxophone soloist of distinction, and the Count Basie Band had two, in Lester Young and Herchel Evans, whose contrasting styles were an outstanding feature of the Basie group of this time. The only tenor with Duke was clarinettist Barney Bigard, who rarely played the instrument solo, and then in a rhapsodic manner. In Ben Webster Ellington not only selected a musician who is amongst the finest of jazz soloists, but he added a fifth voice to his reed section, which meant further harmonic scope for his writing. Duke discovered another remarkable musician in Jimmy Blanton, who was only eighteen when he joined Ellington in December, 1939. His tragic death from tuberculosis in January, 1942, gave him less than two years in the public eye, yet he is unquestionably the most famous bass player in jazz. He not only revolutionized jazz bass playing, but he set a standard which has never been equalled by any of the fine musicians who have been influenced by him. Blanton raised the string bass to the standard of a solo instrument, the richness of his melodic line on such records as *Jack the Bear* and *Sepia Panorama* being truly breathtaking, whilst the range of inflexion he achieved on pizzicato bass is equally fantastic. The addition of Webster and Blanton commenced what was perhaps the greatest period Ellington has ever had as a bandleader, his fifteen-piece orchestra containing a magnificent array of varied solo talent. 1940 was one of his peak years as a composer, and amongst the timeless masterpieces recorded during this year are *Jack the Bear*, *Ko-Ko*, *Concerto for Cootie*, *Cotton Tail*, *Never No Lament*, *Dusk*, *Bojangles*, *A Portrait of Bert Williams*, *Blue Goose*, *Harlem Air Shaft*, *Sepia Panorama*,

In a Mellotone, *Warm Valley* and *Across the Track Blues*. The personnel of the Duke Ellington Orchestra at this time makes extraordinary reading, for in its solo strength alone (which after all is only one facet of the music of this orchestra) it has never been equalled by any ensemble in jazz. The trumpets were Wallace Jones, Cootie Williams and Rex Stewart, the latter having by this time switched to cornet; on trombones Joe Nanton, Lawrence Brown and Juan Tizol, the latter on valve trombone; the reeds were Otto Hardwicke (alto sax), Johnny Hodges (alto and soprano saxes), Barney Bigard (clarinet and tenor sax), Ben Webster (tenor sax) and Harry Carney (baritone sax and bass clarinet); Ellington himself of course was on piano, and his work at this period as a band pianist reached a new standard, whilst the rhythm section was completed by Fred Guy (guitar), Jimmy Blanton (bass) and Sonny Greer (drums). An all-star band indeed!

Although in the years which followed Ellington always led a band of remarkable quality, the 1940 band does represent one of the high-water marks of his career. The first member of this group to leave was Cootie Williams, who had been with Ellington for over eleven years. He was replaced by Ray Nance in December, 1940. Loud were the cries of horror from the band's admirers when the news was heard. Both amongst the fans and fellow musicians there were mutterings foretelling the doom of the Ellington band. Raymond Scott, leader of a light music aggregation somewhere on the boundaries of jazz, wrote a dirge called *When Cootie Left the Duke* and this sums up very well prevailing opinions of the time. Since Ellington continued to be the foremost figure in jazz until his death, this seems absurd, yet Cootie Williams had been a leading figure in the ensemble ever since he replaced Bubber Miley in 1929, and his commanding trumpet was to many listeners both the most distinctive solo voice in the band and a formidable link with the orchestra's glorious past. (After fronting his own band, Cootie returned to the Ellington Orchestra in 1962.) Within the Ellington organization things were not quite so gloomy, as the talented Ray Nance had joined the orchestra and the flow of great music was carried on without a pause. Williams' section mate, Rex Stewart, was an equally adept practitioner of the growl style, although perhaps not so well known as Cootie. As Nance was also a fine soloist on trumpet, in addition to being a proficient violinist and amusing vocalist, the loss was not so great as had been feared. In September, 1941, Jimmy Blanton's terrible illness compelled him to leave the band and his immediate replacement was Jimmy Bryant, who stayed only a few months before being succeeded by Junior Raglin. The following year another mainstay of the band departed in the person of Barney Bigard, and for a year the clarinet chair was filled by Chauncey Haughton, a soloist of little distinction, until he in turn was replaced by Jimmy Hamilton in 1943. The trumpet section was increased to four with the addition of Harold Baker, a distinguished lead man and lyrical soloist.

In January, 1943, a 'Duke Ellington Week' was held to celebrate the twentieth anniversary of Ellington's début in New York and it concluded with a concert by the band in Carnegie Hall, the first of what was to become an annual series. The centrepiece of this concert was a new extended composition by Ellington, *Black, Brown and Beige*, which ran for forty-five minutes. The critical reaction to this work was mixed, and, owing to a recording ban being in force at this time, it was never recorded in its entirety. A suite from *Black, Brown and Beige* was recorded in 1944 and two of the movements from this suite—*Work Song* and *Come Sunday*—have received extended treatment on L.P. The complete programme played by Ellington at this first Carnegie Hall concert makes interesting reading today. It was as follows:

Black and Tan Fantasy
Rockin' in Rhythm
Moon Mist
Jumpin' Punkins
A Portrait of Bert Williams
Bojangles
Black Beauty (announced as *A Portrait of Florence Mills*)
Black, Brown and Beige
Ko-Ko
Dirge (a Strayhorn composition, not recorded)
Stomp (actually Strayhorn's *Johnny Come Lately*)
Are You Sticking (featuring Chauncey Haughton)
Bakiff (featuring Juan Tizol and Ray Nance)
Jack the Bear (featuring Junior Raglin)
Blue Belles of Harlem (featuring Ellington on piano)
Day Dream (featuring Johnny Hodges)
Rose of the Rio Grande (featuring Lawrence Brown)
Boy Meets Horn (featuring Rex Stewart)
Don't Get Around Much any More (a popular adaptation of *Never No Lament* which was something of a 'hit')
Goin' Up
Mood Indigo

The penultimate number was featured briefly in *Cabin in the Sky* in which the band had appeared in 1942. A more significant all-coloured enterprise, the show *Jump for Joy* featured an Ellington score and the Ellington orchestra for three months in 1941, with spots for the band's soloists, such as Rex's *Concerto for Klinkers*, an unrecorded successor to *Boy Meets Horn*. Ellington has dabbled from time to time in writing music for shows, for one of which, *Man With Four Sides*, he also wrote the book.

The personnel changes which were becoming ever more frequent continued in 1943, the most significant of these being the departure of Ben Webster, who was replaced by Al Sears, a capable but less distinguished tenor sax soloist. The trumpet section was in a state of considerable turmoil; Rex Stewart leaving for a short period and being replaced by Taft Jordan; Wallace Jones leaving and the lead trumpet chair being taken over by Shelton Hemphill. A little-known trumpet player by the name of Dizzy Gillespie played for a few weeks with the band in November of this same year. The success of the first Carnegie Hall appearance had been so great that the band was booked again in this famous hall for a second Ellington concert in December, 1943: *Black, Brown and Beige* was given again, but this time in the shortened form we know from records. It is said that the general hostility of the critics persuaded Ellington to adopt this course, and the same reason is given for the quick withdrawal from the band's repertoire of the new work performed at the December, 1943, concert—*New World A-Comin'*.

V

Due to a dispute between the American Federation of Musicians and the recording companies there had been no Ellington recordings (apart from the forces' 'V-Discs') from July, 1942 until December, 1944. It was in this latter month that *Black, Brown and Beige* was recorded, and by this time further changes had taken place. Cat Anderson had replaced Harold Baker, and Claude Jones had come in on trombone for Juan Tizol. Rex Stewart returned to the band, thus increasing the trumpets to five, whilst in the reeds, Otto Hardwicke, one of the oldest members of the orchestra, was replaced by Russell Procope, a veteran of the Chick Webb, Fletcher Henderson and Teddy Hill bands. In 1946 a fourth trombone was added in the person of Wilbur de Paris, and Oscar Pettiford replaced Junior Raglin on bass. This rapid changing of personnel, a common enough feature with other large bands, was in marked contrast to the stability of the Ellington orchestra up to about 1941. In spite of this the band's character was not impaired and the recordings from this period contain many outstanding works. A new venture for Ellington was the employment of an academic soprano in the person of Kay Davis. At first she was used in wordless accompaniment to other singers in such numbers as *I Ain't Got Nothin' But the Blues* and *Solitude*, but soon Ellington was to score a number of special compositions built round Kay's voice, such as *Transblucency* and *On a Turquoise Cloud*. In 1946 Tricky Sam Nanton died, and the Ellington Orchestra lost another distinctive voice. In August, 1947, Tyree Glenn replaced Wilbur de Paris in the trombone section; apart from being a fine soloist on open trombone and a proficient vibraphone player, Tyree took over the 'wa-wa' solos with the band in an individual variant of the style established by Nanton.

The annual appearances at Carnegie Hall continued and the orchestra were playing an increasing number of concerts throughout the U.S.A. It was a productive period in Ellington's concert writing, *The Deep South Suite* being premièred at Carnegie Hall in November, 1946, and the *Liberian Suite*, which was commissioned by the government of the small West African republic, in December of the following year. In 1948 another recording ban kept the band out of the studios for a few months and during this time Al Sears departed and Ben Webster returned for a brief stay. In the summer of this year Ellington made a short tour of England, but owing to the ban imposed by the Musicians' Union he was unable to bring his band. Therefore he disbanded for a few months and toured with only Ray Nance and Kay Davis, of his own musicians, accompanied by a British rhythm section consisting of Malcolm Mitchell (guitar), Jack Fallon (bass) and Tony Crombie (drums). They were classified as variety artists rather than musicians, and the reaction amongst jazz enthusiasts was bitter indeed when it was realized that but for such restric-

Duke Ellington during his early years as a bandleader

tions they would have been listening to the full Ellington Orchestra, rather than just the augmented trio as part of a variety bill or concert package.

The course of the Ellington orchestra during 1949 and 1950 is hard to plot, the changes within the band being so numerous. It is impossible to list these in detail in a book of this size, but the situation can be summarized briefly. Fred Guy left and was not replaced, Ellington having subsequently kept his rhythm section down to three pieces. Ben Webster had not stayed long and the matter of a tenor soloist was not settled until Paul Gonsalves, who had previously played with Count Basie, joined in late 1950. The trumpets wavered between four and five pieces, sometimes the band having to carry two lead men owing to Al Killian's

lip trouble. Quentin Jackson came to the trombone section in place of Claude Jones, but Tyree Glenn ceased to be a regular member of the band. For the European tour of 1950 (with the full band this time, but omitting England from the itinerary owing to the union ban) Ellington was without Tyree Glenn and he brought *two* drummers with him, Greer and Butch Ballard. The tenor sax chair was vacant so he signed up ex-Basie tenor man Don Byas, who was resident in Europe, for the duration of the tour. Oscar Pettiford had left and been replaced by Wendell Marshall, cousin of the late Jimmy Blanton into whose old chair he now moved. This was a bad period for big bands and both Count Basie and Woody Herman, Duke's keenest rivals since the mid-forties, had been forced to disband their

151

The Duke Ellington Orchestra in the 1930s
Front row: Wellman Braud (bass), Duke Ellington (piano). *Second row*: Otto Hardwicke, Harry Carney, Johnny Hodges, Barney Bigard (saxes), Fred Guy (guitar). *Third row*: Joe Nanton, Juan Tizol, Lawrence Brown (trombones), Cootie Williams, Arthur Whetsol, Freddy Jenkins (trumpets). *Rear*: Sonny Greer (drums)

groups. In February, 1950, he was presented with an award from the magazine *Downbeat*, in addition to which he was presented with a parchment scroll commemorating the fact that his was the only leading band from the magazine's 1949 poll still in existence!

On January 21st, 1951, Ellington gave a concert at the Metropolitan Opera House, New York, in aid of the National Association for the Advancement of Coloured People. The centrepiece of the programme was Ellington's new *Harlem Suite*, his first large-scale composition for some years. As long playing records were now a prominent feature of the record industry it was to be expected that the *Harlem Suite* would fare better than such predecessors as *New World A-Comin'* and *The Deep South Suite* which had

not been recorded. But before the expected recording session took place the Ellington orchestra underwent the greatest upheaval of its entire career, three key men in Johnny Hodges, Lawrence Brown and Sonny Greer giving in their notice. During the constant shuffling of the previous few years these men, along with Ray Nance and Harry Carney, had comprised a nucleus of long-serving sidemen. Hodges had been with Duke since 1928; Brown since 1932; whilst Greer was the last survivor of Duke's Washington days, a musician who had been associated with him for over thirty years. From the time Lawrence Brown joined the band in 1932, the cry had periodically been raised that Ellington was finished, but now even the most devoted of the band's followers were perturbed.

Greer's drumming had latterly been very uneven (hence the second drummer on the European trip the preceding year), but Brown was a long-established solo voice in the orchestra and Hodges was by far the finest soloist on whom Ellington could call. Hasty replacements were made, only one being of a permanent nature in trombonist Britt Woodman who came in for Brown; but even here the situation was still critical as no permanent replacement had been found for Tyree Glenn, who had played only occasionally with the band during the previous year. Help came a month after the departure of the three key men, from a rather unexpected source. When he left the Ellington orchestra in 1944, Juan Tizol joined the Harry James orchestra, and in March, 1951, Ellington not only persuaded Tizol to rejoin the band but also to bring over two jazzmen of note from the James band, in the persons of Willie Smith and Louis Bellson. Altoist Willie Smith had been for some years a mainstay of the Jimmie Lunceford band and, although prone to a certain vulgarity in long solos, he is one of the finest leaders of the saxophone section in jazz. Drummer Louis Bellson may not have Greer's flair for coloration, but he is a drummer of considerable drive, whilst Tizol, though no jazz soloist, made a welcome return to the band both for his impeccable section playing and for his distinctive way of playing the Latin-American numbers he had written for the band. Although, from the point of view of solo jazz or new compositions, this was not one of Ellington's greatest periods, there is no doubt that a new spirit was alive in the band at this time. Cat Anderson had returned to the band, and with his talents as a high note specialist, Ray Nance's incredible singing and dancing, and the skilled drum solos of Louis Bellson, Ellington's band was a popular concert attraction wherever they played, containing as it did three certain show-stoppers.

VI

In May, 1951, the band played a concert held in aid of the Damon Runyon Cancer Fund in New York, and for the second half they combined with the NBC Symphony Orchestra in performances of Ellington's *New World A-comin'* and *Harlem Suite* in arrangements by Luther Henderson. This last work was recorded under the title *A Tone Parallel to Harlem* in December of that year, by which time the trumpet section was undergoing further changes, but by early 1952 it had settled to a regular four-man team of Ray Nance, Cat Anderson, Clark Terry and Willie Cook, which was to remain unchanged until late in 1957. The other sections continued to undergo changes, however, Willie Smith leaving in June, 1952, to be replaced by Hilton Jefferson, who stayed only six months. He in turn gave way to Rick Henderson, a young musician with a considerable Charlie Parker influence in his style. Back in the 1940s bassist Oscar Pettiford had tried to persuade Ellington to employ several of the bop stylists, but it was not until Clark Terry entered the band in 1951 that Ellington employed any 'modern' soloists. Unlike so many of the stereotyped modern jazzmen, Clark Terry is too individual a musician to be passed off with any period tag. A soloist of unusual distinction, his tone is too warm, his style too

witty to be classified with the zombie music of the cool musicians. In January of 1953 Louis Bellson was replaced by Butch Ballard, the drummer who had travelled to Europe as Sonny Greer's deputy in 1950. At this time Ellington was recording for the Capitol label, and in June, 1953, he recorded an album of piano solos—a very unusual departure for him. The constant changes of personnel were unquestionably having an effect on the band's music, and jazz 'standards', arranged by men outside the Ellington organization, were a prominent feature of the book around this time. An album consisting of such material, along with three new recordings of old Ellington numbers, were collected from a number of sessions in 1953 and 1954 and issued under the title *Ellington '55*. By this time Tizol was out and Ballard had given way to Dave Black on drums. Despite the personnel changes and the outside material, jazz critics were agreed that *Ellington '55* was one of the oustanding big band L.P.s for years. It is interesting to note that at a concert at Pasadena in March, 1953, Duke played his old 1937 composition *Diminuendo and Crescendo in Blue*, with a five-minute tenor solo for Paul Gonsalves sandwiched in between the two movements—the same arrangement which was to provoke a near riot at the Newport Jazz Festival more than three years later.

The situation as far as Ellington's recordings were concerned was far from healthy around this time, such hit parade material as *Bunny Hop Mambo* and *Twelfth Street Rag Mambo* being recorded by the band. Ellington had complained earlier to Leonard Feather that no one cared who was in the band any more and that the only reason he had the highest payroll in the world was that he liked to listen to the band himself. Although a new Ellington composition, *Night Creature*, was played by the band and The Symphony of the Air at a Carnegie Hall concert in March, 1955, the situation seems, on the whole, to have worsened. In the summer of that year the band worked for several months in the *Aquacade* show at Flushing Meadows, Long Island, and Ellington not only allowed the band to be augmented by a second pianist, a string section and two girl harpists, but several of his musicians were unable to play in the show owing to union troubles—Willie Cook, Britt Woodman, Rick Henderson, Paul Gonsalves and Dave Black missing this lengthy engagement. Once again the cry went up that the band was finished, but within a year Ellington was to lead one of the very finest bands of his entire career—thus did Duke confound the critics at every turn!

In early 1955 Jimmy Woode replaced Wendell Marshall on bass, and a new drummer, Sam Woodyard, teamed with him to provide a well integrated rhythm section, but the most important change of all was the return of the great Johnny Hodges in place of Rick Henderson. With John Sanders filling the trombone chair vacated by Juan Tizol, Ellington had once more assembled a band of the highest potential; it was the first time for many years that his orchestra could be compared, in the number and variety of soloists, with his bands up to the middle 'forties. An Ellington renaissance was due and for those who had followed the orchestra's fortunes through the years this was announced by a new L.P. recorded in February, 1956: *Historically Speaking, the Duke*. Covering in chronological order thirty years of Ellington compositions, the band's performance on this L.P. confirmed that Ellington had once more a suitably talented group of musicians to interpret his work. The opening number of this L.P. was the thirty-year-old score of *East St. Louis Toodle-oo*, a remarkable instance of the permanent value of Ellington's writing. As Paul Rossiter remarked in reviewing the record in *Jazz Monthly*, '. . . what other leader would dare use a thirty-year-old score today?' At the 1956 Newport Jazz Festival the band scored a tremendous success, provoking a near riot with the performance of the nineteen-year-old *Diminuendo and Crescendo in Blue*, with a long tenor solo for Paul Gonsalves generating an exciting atmosphere. In the same year the band played at the Shakespearian Festival at Stratford, Ontario, and Ellington was so pleased with the reception he and the band received at this event that he planned to write a Shakespearian suite in appreciation. In this year he also wrote and narrated a TV production for the orchestra, several solo singers and a full choir—the highly controversial work, *A Drum is a Woman*, a parallel to the history of jazz, which was conceived in a characteristically satirical vein.

The following year saw the first performance of his Shakespearian suite, *Such Sweet Thunder*, dedicated to the Shakespearian Festival, and which proved to be one of his finest concert works. Late in 1957, Harold Baker returned to the trumpet section, replacing Willie Cook, and, after scoring a further success at the Newport Festival of 1958, the band set sail for its fourth European tour. By this time the British Musicians' Union had agreed to let in American bands on an exchange basis and, to the delight of British jazz lovers, the Ellington band played its first concert in this country since 1933 when they opened the tour at the Royal Festival Hall on Sunday, October 5th, 1958. Again there were strong criticisms of the band's performances, but this time on the basis of too many solo features, as opposed to band interpretations of Ellington compositions. While it is true that there were several points at which the performances on this tour could be criticized when compared with the recorded output of the band, there could be little doubt that here was the greatest jazz orchestra of the day—as it had been for over thirty long years. Every musician in the band proved his solo capabilities, and the ensemble playing through the great variety of scores Ellington presented at each concert was perfect. The personnel of the touring Duke Ellington Orchestra is given below:

Ray Nance—Trumpet, violin, vocal.
Cat Anderson—Trumpet.
Harold Baker—Trumpet.
Clark Terry—Trumpet.
Britt Woodman—Trombone.
Quentin Jackson—Trombone.
John Sanders—Trombone.
Russell Procope—Alto, clarinet.
Johnny Hodges—Alto.
Jimmy Hamilton—Tenor, clarinet.
Paul Gonsalves—Tenor.
Harry Carney—Baritone, bass clarinet.
Jimmy Woode—Bass.
Sam Woodyard—Drums.

The vocalist on the 1958 tour of England was Ozzie Bailey (who is to be heard on the *Drum is a Woman* L.P.), and Billy Strayhorn also travelled with the band. When not delivering his witty announcements or directing the orchestra, Duke Ellington sat at the piano and demonstrated his great skill as a band pianist, and as a band *leader* in the truest sense of the term.

For the next thirteen years, the Duke Ellington Orchestra was seen and heard throughout the world, including the Near East, the Far East, Africa, South America, and the Soviet Union. In 1963, he wrote a pageant of black history, *My People*, and in 1970, a ballet, *The River*, for Alvin Ailey and the American Ballet Theatre. Throughout the sixties, however, he turned increasingly to performing 'sacred concerts' in churches and cathedrals throughout the world, with his most prestigious engagements being at Coventry Cathedral in 1966 (where he performed his jazz suite, *In the Beginning God*) and Westminster Abbey in 1973.

Throughout his career, Ellington received many honors. To commemorate his 70th birthday in 1969, he was given a birthday party at the White House and President Nixon awarded him the Presidential Medal of Freedom. Four years later, he was elected to France's Legion of Honor. He was even honored with his likeness on postage stamps issued by two African countries, Chad and Togo. One award he did not receive was the Pulitzer Prize. This was because in 1965 the Pulitzer Advisory Board rejected the unanimous recommendation of its music jury that Ellington be given the coveted prize. The 66-year-old Duke shrugged off his disappointment with the remark, 'Fate is being kind to me. Fate doesn't want me to be famous too young.'

Ellington continued to give concerts when he was in his 75th year. Failing health, however, made him turn over the leadership to his son, Mercer, a gifted composer, arranger and trumpeter. In March 1974, Duke was hospitalized in New York for lung cancer. He died May 24 of complications caused by pneumonia.

VII

To have survived almost fifty years as a big name in American show business; to have directed, during the whole of this period, a jazz orchestra of matchless skill; to have composed hundreds of pieces from popular songs like *Solitude* or *I'm Beginning to See the Light*, to full-scale concert works such as the *Harlem Suite* or *Such Sweet Thunder*, in addition to such comparatively minor achievements as being one of the very finest band pianists in jazz and the writer of several scores for musicals; to have done all this and still remain a relaxed and unruffled individual, Duke Ellington was indeed a remarkable man. Unlike most other bandleaders Duke was easy on discipline. His manager once tried to persuade him to take a stronger line on the matter of advances on the musicians' salaries, and Duke replied, 'I won't let these goddam musicians upset me! Why should I knock myself out in an argument about fifteen dollars when in the same time I can probably write a fifteen-hundred dollar song?'[1] He retained a perfect calm through the most difficult situations—one of his musicians once claimed that 'his pulse is so low he can't get excited, his heart beats slower than an ordinary man's'.[2] Duke himself said, 'You see, I don't worry any more. Everybody thinks these great circles under my eyes are the result of worry. No, no! My bags are the accumulation of virtue and a few hearty laughs. I don't worry.'[3] His calm was reflected in his easy manner and his composure, the loose discipline reaped its reward in the way his musicians were always themselves. Never in the most complex Ellington scores does one hear a mere 'trumpet solo' or 'alto solo'—the part was written not for the instrument, but for the man; for Clark Terry or Cootie Williams, for Barney Bigard or Jimmy Hamilton. Such creative participation by the bandsmen could hardly be *demanded* of them, or enforced by discipline. Tales of the Ellington musicians turning up late for dates are legion (at the 1956 Newport Jazz Festival four of the band were absent during the opening set), but the Duke knew that a rigid, uniform discipline would produce rigid and uniform musicianship, and that was the last thing he required from his band. The musicians respected him for this, as is shown from Ben Webster's statement: 'Duke is a great guy to work for. He understands musicians better than any leader. He's quick to judge a man's ability accurately, and he can write a piece or concerto for him that will fit the individual man.'[4] Ellington was a man who believed strongly in the integrity of the individual, his output throughout the years always bearing the imprint of his own strong personality. When asked a few years ago if he would consider using strings with his band, as certain other jazz leaders had done, he replied, 'Strings? positively no! What on earth would I want with strings? What can anybody do with strings that hasn't been done wonderfully for hundreds of years? No, we always want to play Ellington music—that's an accepted thing in itself.'[5]

Duke Ellington was an American Negro, and the sometimes bitter and humiliating treatment handed out to him by the apostles of 'white supremacy' could never have been a helpful factor during his long career. But this very career was a triumphant acclamation of the rights of his people, amongst whom he was a highly respected figure. He held the respect not only of fellow jazz musicians but of men distinguished in the world of European concert music. His use of Shakespearean characters as well as Negro work-songs as subjects for his works show the all-embracing versatility of his mind and art. Duke Ellington, drawing at all times on the great musical traditions of his people, raised his music to a universal level, and the genius which he brought to his work was of such magnitude that he became one of the great artists of the twentieth century, the quality of whose prodigious output would be difficult to match in any field of artistic creation.

[1] Richard O. Boyer, *The Hot Bach*, p. 25, reprinted in *Duke Ellington*, edited by Peter Gammond (Phoenix House, 1958).
[2] Ibid., p. 35.
[3] Barry Ulanov, *Duke Ellington*, p. 270 (Musicians Press, 1947).
[4] Quoted by Stanley Dance in *Duke Ellington*, p. 18, edited by Peter Gammond (Phoenix House, 1958).

[5] Quoted by Alun Morgan from an interview with Leonard Feather in *Downbeat*. See *Duke Ellington*, p. 114, edited by Peter Gammond (Phoenix House, 1958).

2. THE MUSIC

The major figures in jazz have, with very few exceptions, achieved their eminence through the medium of the solo, the ensemble usually being a background before which the soloist creates the essential drama or comedy of the work. The serene, almost mystical poise of Louis Armstrong's greatest work, the profuse, richly creative playing of Coleman Hawkins, and the agonized contours of the incredibly inventive Charlie Parker, all belong to this standard medium of jazz expression. Many of the finest big bands in jazz have been dance orchestras with talented arrangers and soloists who have raised their music above a purely functional level, such bands as those of Chick Webb and Jimmy Lunceford being the best examples of this type. The orchestra of Count Basie from the 1950s onward is another example, but in its earlier years the Basie band had a somewhat different pattern. Working with simple arrangements this ensemble was able to carry over into the big band a fire and spontaneity more usually associated with small groups, whilst throwing the main emphasis on such great soloists as Lester Young, Herchel Evans, Buck Clayton, Dicky Wells and Harry Edison.

These then are the principal vehicles for expression in jazz: the soloist, working either with a small group of sympathetic musicians or within the framework of a large orchestra, and the arranger, who usually provides in his scores ample room for individual solos from the members of the band. In a band of the Webb–Lunceford type the arrangement is primarily the vehicle of the band's ensemble ability, in a musical rather than a purely technical sense. Even the best of jazz arrangements, such as those by Sy Oliver for the Lunceford band or those by Neil Hefti for the current Basie orchestra, have a low value as compositions, requiring the interpretation of a great ensemble to give them validity. On the other hand the creations of the great soloists of jazz have far more compositional unity than the arrangers' scores: compare Armstrong's *Potato Head Blues* solos or the alto work in *Parker's Mood* with the best arranged jazz, and the difference in terms of musical substance and structure becomes obvious.

The achievements of Duke Ellington are different from those of other jazz musicians not only in quality, but are of an entirely different order. His orchestra contained in its ranks a large number of soloists of the highest calibre—even in his best years Basie could not surpass Ellington in this respect— and the context for their work provided by the ensemble was clearly superior to that of any other band in jazz; but the unique quality of Ellington's output lies in his compositions, which are the only jazz scores which in terms of subtlety and structure can be considered important artistic creations in themselves. The constant emphasis which is placed upon his compositional achievements should not cloud the listener's understanding of the distinction between composition in the academic sense and the means Ellington uses. The European composer writes for a particular instrument or group of instruments and knows, from the standardization of instrumental techniques within the European tradition, that pretty well the same sound will result from the playing of his scores by any one of a hundred symphony orchestras. The conductor's interpretation and the very slight variants in instrumental techniques between musicians of different nationalities are of course variable factors, but they are small indeed when compared with the highly individual approach of the jazz musician to his instrument. The latter is of course in most cases a creative artist himself, and will interpret his part within the framework of his own style. The likelihood of successful composition becoming a frequent achievement in jazz is therefore remote, for the standardization of instrumental usage that this would entail would rob the music of many of its most valuable characteristics. Duke Ellington's genius was many-sided, and his unique qualities as a bandleader enabled him to create in his orchestra a medium for his compositions, without in any way impairing the individuality of the jazzmen within the band. In *Jack the Bear* (1940), Ellington built a work entirely around his soloists, a composition which is typical of its creator while remaining a suitable vehicle for the soloists. This is true of all Ellington's best work, but *Jack the Bear* is a particularly good example as the ensemble is only heard briefly in other than an accompanying role. His understanding of the musical character of the bandsmen made it possible for Ellington to use his musicians in this way. It is interesting to follow on records the introduction of each new voice into the Ellington band, and the increasingly important parts each new soloist was given as Duke grew to know his style.

II

Although Duke Ellington made a few records in 1925 and 1926 (some with his regular band), the first really distinctive recordings are those from 1927, a year which saw the recording of three pieces still performed by the Ellington orchestra today—*East St. Louis Toodle-oo*, *Black and Tan Fantasy* and *Creole Love Call*. The first two are clearly achievements of the Duke Ellington–Bubber Miley partnership, the style of the trumpeter setting the mood whilst the manner in which the material is organized is obviously Ellington's contribution. *East St. Louis Toodle-oo* opens with what sounds like a slowed-down fugue subject in minims played by the saxophone section, which becomes the accompaniment to Miley's solo. The piece is cast in the conventional thirty-two bar song form, and the exposition of the main theme is played by Miley in the first eight bars of his solo. The melodic line is characteristic of Miley, with

its stuttering, vocalized, repeated notes and unexpected stresses. The second eight bars is a variant hinting both rhythmically and melodically at the change of atmosphere to be found in the release or middle eight, which bursts out in a totally different mood of exuberance expressed both by the solo trumpet and in the changed accompaniment. The brooding atmosphere created by the heavy tread of the saxophone melody is replaced by a slight echo of the trumpet line on Nanton's trombone, the rhythm section also seeming lighter when freed from the lugubrious measure of the saxophones. The final section of this chorus returns to the original theme and mood, the following choruses featuring solos based on a contrasting theme which is stated by the brass section after the solo variations. Neither the rather obviously jaunty tune nor the ordinary sounding solos have the substance to be other than a mere contrast to the opening chorus, and it is only when Miley recapitulates the opening theme in the final eight bars that the record again achieves a distinctive sound—what goes on in between being typical big band jazz of the period. In the Victor–H.M.V. version of *East St. Louis Toodle-oo* (by far the best) Nanton's solo has considerable vigour but little melodic distinction, the other solos by Hardwicke and Jackson adding little to the work as a whole.

The best solution to the problems set by his orchestra at this time is found in *Black and Tan Fantasy*, which achieves a remarkable unity with apparently diverse elements. The work opens with a blues theme in the minor played by Miley and Nanton over a marching beat from the rhythm section; this twelve-bar theme is followed by a sixteen-bar melody played in a voluptuous manner by Otto Hardwicke on alto sax. The music pauses for a moment after this episode, then we return to the twelve-bar blues form for a two-chorus solo by Miley, commencing with a long held high C. Ellington's ragtime-flavoured piano takes a chorus, followed by Nanton on muted trombone who re-establishes the rather sombre mood of Miley's contribution. Finally Bubber returns with a chorus which raises the pulse of the music to an almost exultant note, only to lead to the famous coda, which is a quotation from Chopin's Funeral March. The two finest early versions of *Black and Tan Fantasy* are the Brunswick of April 7th, 1927 and the Victor–H.M.V. of October 26th, 1927, the former having an altogether more dignified, more sombre sound when compared with the October version, in which at times the exuberance of the performance seems about to destroy the mood of the piece. Miley's two-chorus solo, one of his finest creations, is varied only in detail on these two recordings, the Brunswick having a most suitable accompaniment from the tuba of Bass Edwards. A third version, made for Okeh and released in England on Parlophone, has Jabbo Smith replacing Bubber Miley, and although it contains some very good solo work it lacks the unity of the other recordings; perhaps Smith's solos lack the astringency to offset Hardwicke's sugary reading of the second theme.

Creole Love Call is somewhat different from either of the two works so far discussed. It is a variant of King Oliver's *Camp Meeting Blues*, which Ellington presumably learned from his clarinettist, Rudy Jackson, who played with Oliver before joining him; the number had therefore no direct association with Miley. The arrangement recorded at the same session as the Victor–H.M.V. *Black and Tan Fantasy* made use of the voice of Adelaide Hall in an 'instrumental' way. The opening theme is stated by her strange wordless singing set against three clarinets, Ellington's fine selection of tone colours here being typical. In sharp contrast Miley's muted trumpet takes the next chorus in a beautifully constructed solo, remarkable in its absolute perfection, which is followed by Rudy Jackson who plays the long melody of the second theme with a suitably violin-like tone. The following two choruses consist of simple ensemble arrangements with the reed section playing against the brass, first on saxophones and then on clarinets; finally Adelaide Hall returns again with a vocal chorus, which concludes the work. Little of musical interest occurs after the first three choruses, but these are so perfect, both in themselves and in their contrast with each other, that even today they remain among the classics of recorded jazz. Bubber Miley demonstrates how much the creative jazz musician can say in twelve bars, in a solo which is a perfect miniature of musical architecture and a study in the use of inflexion and variation of timbre to extend the emotional range and increase the musical tension.

It can hardly be said that any of Ellington's other recordings from 1927 bear comparison with the three already discussed, although *Birmingham Breakdown* and *Washington Wobble* are interesting exhibits in the light they throw on the evolution of the big band. The following year saw a considerable widening of Ellington's scope as a composer and an increase in the solo potential of the orchestra. Nanton and Carney were becoming more important figures within the band, Barney Bigard and Johnny Hodges came in, and Arthur Whetsol brought his distinctive trumpet back to the Ellington ensemble. It was Whetsol's trumpet which took the theme statement of the pastoral *Black Beauty*, perhaps the first notable Ellington work in which Miley does not play solo; Whetsol even indulges in a little growl trumpet on the Brunswick version of this! *Misty Morning*, another successful composition which does not make use of Miley's trumpet, provides in its second chorus the first example in jazz of a section playing a scored, solo-like variant on the theme, an idea considered novel enough twenty years later when it was adopted by the modernists. One of the most interesting of the fast tempo sides of this period is *Hot and Bothered*, an altered version of *Tiger Rag*, wherein the brilliant scoring for the orchestra takes second place to the vivid and colourful use of the soloists in the middle section. The most notable title from 1928 is *The Mooche*, which shows an increasing subtlety in Ellington's use of colour and harmony. The best of the three versions of this number is probably the Brunswick with its magnificent solo sequence, Johnny Hodges taking a very fine chorus, although the Okeh–Parlophone–Columbia with Lonnie Johnson on guitar is different in detail and perhaps even more evocative in mood. The Victor–H.M.V. has Whetsol doing the growl trumpet passages and is rather spoilt by Greer's irritating use of temple blocks. *The Blues with a Feeling* was cut at the same session as *Misty Morning*, when Wellman Braud appears to have been obsessed with the potentialities of the bowed bass in the jazz rhythm

section. It is one of the band's finest blues creations, with superb solo work from Nanton, Hodges (on soprano sax) and Miley. Some of Miley's finest playing is found on lesser sides from this period, notably *Jubilee Stomp* (Victor–H.M.V. version) and *Bandana Babies*; the former containing a superb trumpet solo with a brilliantly taken break. On *Yellow Dog Blues*, Miley plays the rather unmelodic verse, and without straying very far from the theme as written, creates a solo of unusual power and individuality.

Bubber Miley left the band in February, 1929, but before this they visited the studios for another two sessions. The first of these was for Brunswick, and after a rather poor version of *Doin' the Voom Voom*, the band recorded a two-part *Tiger Rag* which is largely given over to the soloists. In addition to a good Miley solo, Freddy Jenkins and Barney Bigard take excellent choruses, Bigard's first solo being one of the finest clarinet solos on record. The second session produced a much finer version of *Doin' the Voom Voom*, which is notable for the colourful scoring of the themes and a vibrant duet between Harry Carney and Tricky Sam Nanton. *High Life* contains further excellent Jenkins and Bigard, both in much the same vein as in *Tiger Rag*, whilst the slow *Saturday Night Function* has solos by Bigard, who was playing superbly at this time, and Nanton, whose blues playing very rarely receives its due from the critics.

The measure of the loss suffered by Ellington when Bubber Miley left the band can be judged from *Flaming Youth*, one of the last sides they recorded together. The performance is notable for its extreme exuberance (although the number is taken at a medium tempo) and the vigour of the first chorus (Miley's) is never quite recaptured by the succeeding soloists, Hodges and Nanton. The driving, vigorous trumpet with its unexpected turns of phrase and savage attack sets a mood which the remaining musicians are unable to sustain; indeed whenever Miley takes the first chorus in one of the band's recorded performances the contributions which follow (no matter how excellent in themselves) always have a faint air of anti-climax. The emotional climate of the compositions which Ellington created along with Miley is unique, and apparently conveys contradictory moods to different listeners; to some they embody a 'tearful silliness' while to others they are sinister works comparable with the macabre writings of Edgar Allan Poe.

Miley's own genius has been overshadowed by that of Ellington, for in regarding his work retrospectively in the light of his influence on Ellington we are perhaps too prone to ignore the originality of his playing. Yet he is a jazzman of outstanding achievement and it is doubtful whether any other soloist in jazz has created so individual a style with apparently so little influence from other musicians. The Duke Ellington Orchestra has featured other great soloists, men who can justly be compared with Bubber Miley in achievement, but never again was one single soloist in the band to exert such an influence on its style.

III

When Cootie Williams came in to the Ellington band as replacement for Bubber Miley he was not a growl specialist.

Ellington's superior taste shows itself here in that he hired a first-class replacement, rather than a second-class musician who played in the Miley style, although much of the book was made up of scores demanding a Miley-style growl trumpet soloist. Cootie's open playing was an immediate asset to the band's solo strength, the trumpet section already including the exuberant Freddy Jenkins, whose solo in *High Life* was an oustanding contribution, remarkable for its range and phrasing compared with the playing of the majority of jazz trumpet players in 1929. The section was completed by Arthur Whetsol, hardly a 'hot' musician, but a player whose sweet tone and lyrical style had already found a place in Ellington's compositions with his contributions to *Black Beauty* and *Misty Morning*. The brass was rounded off by the trombone of Joe 'Tricky Sam' Nanton, never an outstanding open player, but a fine soloist with the plunger or wa-wa mute. The reeds were led by Johnny Hodges, whose beautifully constructed solos on alto and soprano saxes had at this time an astringent, direct quality which was, in later years, to be replaced by a warmer, more sensuous approach. Barney Bigard, one of the great clarinettists of the New Orleans Creole school, played tenor sax in the section, though rarely soloing on this instrument. On clarinet his tone is most beautiful and expressive, and possesses in the low register a rich, deep sonority which is quite unique. Bigard is an exceptionally agile player, able to move from the low to the high register within a single phrase without the slightest suggestion of incongruity,

Melody Maker

Duke in a thoughtful mood during the recording of
Such Sweet Thunder

while the fluidity of his counterpoint when playing against the full band is equally remarkable. In his ensemble playing on many Ellington records Bigard demonstrates the possibilities of the New Orleans clarinet style within a big band, and his playing can be said to be the most successful use of the clarinet in a big-band context. Harry Carney doubled alto and baritone during this period, his work on the latter instrument giving the reed section much of its distinctive quality. For many years Carney was the only major jazz soloist on baritone sax, his rich tone and agile phrasing being beyond the scope of his contemporaries. His warm, good-humoured voice is an integral part of many of Ellington's happiest scores, while in the more sombre pieces Carney's dark sonority is invaluable.

On banjo was Fred Guy (who was shortly to switch to guitar) a reliable but not outstanding musician. Another New Orleans jazzman, Wellman Braud, was featured on bass, a musician whose contribution to the Ellington orchestra has often been underrated. He did not, of course, possess the melodic style of Jimmy Blanton and his successors, but that yardstick is historically inadmissible when considering a bassist of this era. Braud is capable of swinging the whole band single-handed, even on bowed bass, and his distinctive off-beat slap gives a pleasantly buoyant sound to many Ellington records of the 'thirties. Sonny Greer's drumming may lack the drive of other jazz percussionists, but his subtle and colourful use of cymbals and other accessories added light and shade to the Ellington

rhythm section and contributed also to Ellington's range of sounds.

The leader's piano solos on records from this period are oddly paradoxical. Sometimes he will contribute unusual, rather incongruous choruses, which seem to be searching ahead of the band toward styles later to be consolidated in his writing, while in other choruses he will be content to turn out an average solo in a near-ragtime style. There can be little doubt that his imagination was very much concentrated on the band, and the increasing complexity of his scores can be seen by comparing *The Mooche* from late 1928 with any of the recordings from the early part of the year. From this year onwards the deployment of his forces becomes increasingly orchestral, the contrasts of tone colour become more subtle, the harmony takes on more and more what Strayhorn has called 'the Ellington effect'.

Amongst the best records from the period immediately after Miley's departure are *Paducah*, an arrangement of a Don Redman number, and *Cotton Club Stomp*. *Hot Feet*, a popular show tune, receives a really colourful arrangement with a chase chorus by Cootie Williams' scat singing and the growl trumpet of Freddy Jenkins. The latter played the growl solos for a time after Miley left, and he can be heard in this role in *Harlemania* and *Jungle Nights in Harlem*. Cootie was featured on open trumpet on many numbers, including a striking contribution to the mournfully lyrical contingent record of *Saratoga Swing* and a vigorous solo on the driving *Double Check Stomp* (H.M.V. version). Similar

Melody Maker

A 1958 photograph of Duke Ellington during one of his concert appearances

159

in mood to *Saratoga Swing* but less successful in its ensemble choruses is *Sloppy Joe*, with wordless vocal by Greer; the solo sequence however is notable for one of Bigard's best-recorded solos, preceded by a dreamy, introspective piano chorus by Ellington. A second version of *Saturday Night Function*, released as by 'Sonny Greer and his Memphis Men', has more superb Bigard, the latter playing his famous riff from *Harlem Flat Blues* to much greater effect here than on the 'original'.

Tricky Sam Nanton's work on these records is outstanding, ranging from the poignant blues solos on both versions of *Saturday Night Function* to the tightly-muted ebullient solo on *Hot Feet*. On the latter the sound seems to be forced out of the bell of the trombone *in spite* of the heavy muting, yet the solo rides with a happy buoyancy over the propulsive rhythm of Braud's bass. It is unjust to consider Nanton a mere stylistic shadow of Miley, for the personalities of the two musicians are quite different and are perfectly reflected in their manner of playing. Nanton is really a much more intimate musician than Miley, his work having a remarkable directness; a musician who, for all his clever manipulation of mutes, never suggested mere gimmickry. Although Ellington often used Nanton's wa-wa playing with a perfect aptness, this facet of the trombonist's work had been unduly stressed, obscuring the fact that much of his best work is in such solos as those on *Saturday Night Function*, when the graduations of tone via the manipulation of the mute are slight but telling. The constant alterations of timbre by skilfully judged growls and slurs give the music a remarkable variety despite the melodic limitations of Nanton's art.

Nine months after Cootie Williams joined the band came the first of a series of wonderful growl solos, on *Ring Dem Bells*, which also features fine work by Bigard, Hodges, Carney and Nanton, and concludes with a sort of jazz stretto by the band with Bigard playing against the brass. Cootie's growl style is easily recognizable, there being a certain dryness—one might almost say aridity—about his tone and attack, which sounds far less natural than does Miley's muted playing. The melodic line becomes more concentrated than is the case in Williams' open playing and there is a pronounced tendency to attack certain notes repeatedly, as if shaking the very essence out of a phrase. Indeed the tightness of Cootie's muted work contrasts strangely with his loose open playing, for when the long lyrical phrases associated with his open style put in an occasional appearance, they are delivered with a deep sombre tone, and a pronounced growl. The ascending phrase half-way through his second chorus on *Ring Dem Bells* is a good example of this.

The most popular, and indeed perhaps the most significant, of Ellington's records of 1930 was a slow blues scored for trumpet, trombone, clarinet and rhythm which was called at first *Dreamy Blues*, but later re-named *Mood Indigo*. The two brass instruments are tightly muted and the whole performance is quiet and dreamy in mood, soft and delicate in colour, Whetsol's lead setting the tone of the theme statement. Bigard's rich low-register clarinet plays a second theme in a loose, relaxed manner, followed by Whetsol's sweet-toned trumpet for a further chorus; four bars of unaccompanied piano and a recapitulation of the first chorus and the record is over, but for all its simplicity *Mood Indigo* remains one of the highlights of jazz composition. A mood is created and its essence distilled within the brief space of a three-minute record, with only three wind instruments accompanied by a rhythm section; yet within the limitations thus imposed Ellington achieves an undoubted masterpiece. The Brunswick version of *Mood Indigo* is the best, with the Okeh–Parlophone a close second: the H.M.V. recorded two months later with the full band fails to capture the intimate mood of these two versions, and seems less perfect formally owing to an ensemble variant being played before Bigard's solo, which here lacks the slight shift of emphasis which made it so important a part of the original structure. The number has been recorded several times in later years by the band (an L.P. version from 1950 runs for fifteen minutes) but on none of these is there any attempt to capture the perfection in miniature of the original recording. Equally perfect in its balanced form, although totally different in mood, is *Rockin' in Rhythm*, a number which Ellington used to accompany dancers at the Cotton Club. The sequence of the themes, the quasi-oriental section featuring Bigard's clarinet and the gruff trombone solo of Tricky Sam are masterly, with a truly classical balance of both instrumental colour and thematic material. Three versions of this piece were recorded within three months—the Okeh–Parlophone of November 8th, 1930, the Brunswick of January 14th, 1931 and the Victor–H.M.V. of two days later. These three versions are worthy of study, for they show the amount of variation worked out by the band on the original framework. The clarinet solo is a set piece hardly varied through the three versions, but the trombone solo, although similar in mood and melodic construction, gives us a remarkable lesson of what is essential in Nanton's art as we run through the three recordings. Some slight variation of timbre or rhythmic accent gives each solo a freshness which is remarkable when we consider the supposedly limited means the trombonist employs. The fact is that it was by such subtle 'vocalization' of the melodic line that jazz was able to evolve from the folk-song of the American Negro as a fully-developed form of musical expression. In this respect the art of Tricky Sam is far more rewarding and instructive than that of many so-called 'traditional' musicians, that is if we study such choruses as these rather than 'atmospheric' wa-wa solos as in *Chloe* or in the *Work Song* from *Black, Brown and Beige*. In the ensemble parts of *Rockin' in Rhythm* too we find variations not only of tempo or phrasing but of the actual material. In the first two versions there is an open solo by Cootie Williams which is replaced on the third by a riff section for muted brass and the saxophone section. There are of course several Ellington numbers which were recorded two or three times during this period and all are worth noting for the instructional value of the creative approach of the orchestra to the material. Happily, *Rockin' in Rhythm* has been issued in all three versions in this country and the quality is even throughout.

Duke Ellington's music was becoming increasingly complex in texture and harmony, increasingly resourceful in style, its creator achieving a greater mastery over his material. It was almost inevitable that he would sooner or later break out of the limitations of the three-minute dance record and expand the form of his music as well as its harmonic content. The first Ellington composition of this type was *Creole Rhapsody*, a short enough work by today's standards in its six-minute running time, but revolutionary in 1931. The work differs only slightly from many of Ellington's better short pieces of the period, these differences being in a somewhat freer use of the ensemble as a source of thematic variation and in the more complex formal pattern. Much use is made of the soloists and this is remarkably successful considering the nature of the piece, the only blemish being Freddy Jenkins' disastrous *rallentando* just before the final in-tempo section. *Creole Rhapsody*[1] is the first piece of American Negro music which adopted the attitude of European art-music as a non-functional, non-popular creation intended for attentive listening. Obviously enough there had been, prior to this date, much jazz of very considerable artistic value, but it had been conceived as dance music in the main, and marketed as a popular commodity. The musical success of *Creole Rhapsody* is therefore more remarkable when we consider its pioneering nature. Hardly amongst the finest of Ellington's music, it remains still a stimulating record to hear and a piece giving considerable insight into Ellington's musical character.

Two further important Ellington records were made in 1931, *The Mystery Song* with its *pianissimo* theme statement by muted brass, and the magnificent blues, *Echoes of the Jungle*. If some deliberate alliance with the so-called jungle atmosphere of the Cotton Club Shows can be detected in *Jungle Nights in Harlem*, recorded the preceding year, in the case of *Echoes of the Jungle* it seems certain that the title was bestowed on the work after its completion, for it is a blues typical of the Ellington band's work in this form. Sidney Finkelstein has pointed out that the folk-song character of many of Ellington's blues is of a sweeter type than those of the Mississippi blues singers or the Louisiana jazzmen, suggesting that they have their origin in the mountain ballads which have been the source of other jazz standards such as *Careless Love Blues* or *How Long Blues*. Like the latter, *Echoes of the Jungle* is based on an eight-bar theme which is stated by the muted brass at the outset, with an *obbligato* by Johnny Hodges. Finkelstein[2] also points out how Ellington has preserved the 'antiphonal, two-voiced character of the blues'; a typical example of the unique way he has adapted this traditional material is in his use of Hodges on this record, the alto adding a sinuous *obbligato* to complement the music at various points throughout the performance. The major soloist here is Cootie Williams who plays a long solo of thirty-two bars, the first half open, the second muted and in his growl style. The contrast between the singing, lyrical

open style and the fierce savagery of his growl manner is very apparent here. After a brief bridge passage by Hodges we arrive at one of those peculiar passages in Ellington's music which seem to be derived less from jazz than from the lower reaches of programme music. The passage in question is a repeated phrase on low-registered clarinet with 'ghostly' *tremolo* effects from Guy's banjo, sounding for all the world like the incidental music to some third-rate horror film of the period. The remarkable thing about the passage, which incidentally Duke had used in *Blues of the Vagabond* two years before, is that it fits perfectly within the context and becomes an integral part of the piece. This section is followed by a wa-wa riff on the trumpets (from *Harlem Flat Blues*) and a brief solo by Nanton, with Hodges cementing the parts together. The final chorus has the brass again singing the melody, this time against an *obbligato* from the clarinet choir. Vic Bellerby has rightly said that this is one of the finest big-band blues in jazz; indeed it ranks with the finest blues creations in any medium, one of the very best of all Ellington's recordings.

The year 1932 saw yet another Ellington masterpiece, the superb *Lazy Rhapsody* or *Swannee River Rhapsody*, a fragile, soft-toned piece, played with beautiful delicacy by the orchestra, the pastel tones of the muted brass blending with Bigard's clarinet and Braud's softly slapped bass. It seemed inevitable in the 'twenties and 'thirties that when the Ellington orchestra recorded for Victor it should have a less subtle, more extrovert character than in its Brunswick recordings; two popular 'standards' from this year illustrate this well— *Rose Room* for Brunswick by a band obviously the same as that on *Lazy Rhapsody* and featuring Bigard in similar vein, and the clamorous *Bugle Call Rag* which was made in the Victor studios. A study in shifting accents and varied rhythms, this latter arrangement looks forward some years to the so-called 'swing' era; the word 'swing' featured in its true meaning as a verb in one of the band's biggest popular successes, *It Don't Mean a Thing If It Ain't Got That Swing*, with a period vocal by Ivie Anderson and excellent solo work from Joe Nanton and Johnny Hodges. The year 1932 saw the first of the many re-recordings Ellington has made through the years of numbers from an earlier period, the custom being inaugurated by *Creole Love Call* in a four-minute 'concert arrangement'. This is a superb version of the tune with fine solo work from Cootie Williams and Barney Bigard, the heavy arrangement giving a totally different view of the work than the lightly scored 1927 version.

The addition of Lawrence Brown in 1932 had not only given Ellington a new (and controversial) solo voice but had also raised his trombone section to three pieces. In the *Slippery Horn* of February, 1933, we find him exploiting the possibilities of the trombone trio in a slowed-down variant of *Tiger Rag*. The whole brass section is featured in the beautifully melodic *Drop Me Off at Harlem*, the constantly changing patterns of brass writing, adding colour to the repetition of the distinctive melody. *Bundle of Blues* recorded a few months later, just before the European tour of that year, is a further contribution in the band's constant output of blues recordings, this time with solos by Cootie, Lawrence Brown, Bigard and Hodges. The best of the four

---

[1] The Brunswick-Vogue Coral version of this work, which is the one discussed here, is vastly superior to the later H.M.V.

[2] See Sidney Finkelstein, *Jazz: A People's Music*, Chapter 6 (Citadel Press, New York, 1948).

161

sides the band cut in London is *Harlem Speaks*, but a finer version of this was made in August when the band had returned to America. On the debit side it must be said that parts of this number are ruined by clumsy playing from Brown, a musician whose occasional slips of intonation and errors of taste stand out oddly from his general air of elegance. The other solos on *Harlem Speaks* are excellent, Williams and Hodges being outstanding. Two further examples of Ellington arrangements of other people's material stand out in this year's output: *Dear Old Southland* and *In the Shade of the Old Apple Tree*, the latter a delightfully whimsical version featuring a humorous *obbligato* by Freddy Jenkins to the theme statement, in addition to excellent solos by Nanton and Hodges. Critics had for some years been making comparisons between Ellington's harmony and that of such European impressionists as Debussy, Ravel and Delius; it is said that when Ellington was first told of his similarity to Delius he had never heard a bar of that composer's music. There can be little doubt however that by 1933 he was well acquainted with European concert music and was adding to his harmonic palette techniques from this music. One of the most successful of his 1933 recordings is a work which shows such influence clearly, although it must be stressed that there is no question of outright imitation, the techniques being thoroughly adapted to Ellington's own musical language. The number in question is the oddly titled *Rude Interlude* (so named, it is said, from Mrs. Constant Lambert's renaming of *Mood Indigo* as *Rude Indigo*) which opens with the hints of melody being almost lost in a thick curtain of nebulous harmony, accompanied by irregular piano punctuations. Brief contributions by Cootie's angry growl trumpet and Louis Bacon's wordless voice add to the oppressive mood, which is only slightly lightened in the more melodic final chorus scored for the brass and reeds. Another sort of impressionism is found in *Daybreak Express*, a successor to the previous year's *Lightnin'*, a composition which had also expressed Duke's love of trains, and the escape they symbolize to the travelling bandleader.

The year 1934 saw the recording of *Solitude*, one of Ellington's popular songs, but more important than this is the magnificent *Saddest Tale*, a piece of masterly tone painting with a brief lyric chanted by Duke after the striking introduction. In a more vigorous mood is *Stompy Jones*, one of the band's most driving performances, while the blues receive a lighter though still colourful variant in *Blue Feeling*. Both these numbers have superb open trumpet solos by Cootie Williams, and indeed his playing on an otherwise mediocre side, *Troubled Waters*, lifts this movie tune to considerable heights. The versatility of Ellington's art can be judged from his work around this time. From such high-class popular tunes as *Sophisticated Lady* or *Solitude* he would turn to tone painting of a mood of utter despair, as in *Saddest Tale*; from the blues of *Blue Feeling* or the uninhibited joy of *Stompy Jones* to the delicate pastoral tones of *Delta Serenade*, with a theme statement by the soft voices of Bigard's clarinet and Whetsol's trumpet.

IV

The band was strengthened in 1935 by the addition of Rex Stewart, already a veteran of many of the finest jazz orchestras of the preceding years; he had in fact sat in the same section as Cootie Williams in the Fletcher Henderson band at a time when Bubber Miley was still with Duke. A versatile musician, his playing runs from a fierce, biting manner to a lyrical style, passing through a comprehensive mastery of muted techniques and the expression of his highly individual sense of humour. As has already been noted, the trombones were augmented to three by the addition of Lawrence Brown, who joined veteran Tricky Sam Nanton and the Puerto Rican valve-trombonist Juan Tizol. The reeds had been increased to four with the return during 1932 of Otto Hardwicke, who like Tizol is rarely to be heard in solo. The rhythm section still consisted of Ellington, Guy, Braud and Greer, although Braud was replaced by Billy Taylor during the course of the year, and for some time during the years 1935 to 1938 Ellington was to experiment with the use of two string basses. Rex soon made his presence felt in the band with characteristic passages in *Margie* and *Show Boat Shuffle*, the latter being another successful piece of tone painting. The most arresting Ellington creation of this period was, however, *Reminiscing in Tempo*, a new concert work running for some fifteen minutes.

Whether jazz loses its identity whenever it is deliberately written for the concert stage is an argument which has fascinated jazz lovers for years, and there is certainly something to be said for the view which regards with great suspicion each new move toward European musical orthodoxy. The difference between the concert music evolved by modern jazz musicians in the past decade or so and Duke's extended works is that, whereas the former have almost invariably lost the character of the jazz idiom in the process, Ellington has always retained the warm, flexible manner of jazz phrasing in his writing. *Such Sweet Thunder* is a long way from the blues of a Big Bill Broonzy or a Bessie Smith, but without the tradition they have come to symbolize it could not exist; it has the same roots and speaks the same language. In some ways *Reminiscing in Tempo* is Ellington's nearest approach to European music, yet it remains a work very obviously the creation of the writer of *Lazy Rhapsody* or *Drop Me Off at Harlem*. The principal theme of the work is announced by the trumpet of Arthur Whetsol, after he and Duke have provided a brief introduction. The theme is announced over an *arpeggio* figure on the saxes, and most of the material is worked from this theme and its accompaniment. The most interesting part of the work is on the third side, where the clarinets are used in the harsh, brittle manner of such twentieth-century composers as Stravinsky or Milhaud, rather than in the warm, lyrical manner more often associated with Ellington. The bleak, swirling, restless despair of this side is to some extent resolved by the conclusion of the work, which fortunately foregoes any 'triumphant' rhetorical ending and returns to the rather passive mood of the opening. The form of the work is loose, in a 'reminiscing' vein as the title indicates, but freedom from the restrictions of the usual simple song forms of jazz composition was obviously welcome to Duke. Although it is not one of his greatest creations from an aesthetic standpoint, *Reminiscing in Tempo* remains one of Ellington's most interesting and revealing creations.

The following year, 1936, saw the first of Ellington's 'concertos' which do not, as the title may suggest to the un-wary, attempt any fusion of jazz with the European con-certo forms, but are rather compositions designed to present one of the band's major soloists in a featured role. The or-chestra does not contend with the soloist or indeed take a major role as is the case in the European form, but rather provides an important background for what are above all portrayals of the musical character of the musicians for whom Duke designed the works. The first two of these were originally titled *Cootie's Concerto* and *Barney's Con-certo*, but later re-named *Echoes of Harlem* and *Clarinet Lament*. The former has a hushed, brooding quality as Cootie plays muted over a jerky rhythm on piano and bass, and the later section, when he plays open trumpet, is in a similar mood, with a remarkably dark tone from the lower register of the solo trumpet. *Clarinet Lament* is more of a virtuoso performance, with Bigard playing in every register of his instrument. Outstanding even on so fine a perform-ance as this, are the breaks—perfect examples of how to make the most of two bars of music. Shortly afterwards *Trumpet in Spades* (*Rex's Concerto*) and *Yearning for Love* (*Lawrence's Concerto*) were recorded, but they are much inferior to the first pair, the Stewart contribution being a rather dull study in trumpet pyrotechnics, the trombonist's piece echoing all too well the sentimental aspect of Brown's playing; both are indeed rather dull compositions. More acceptable than either was *Kissin' My Baby Good Night*, a non-Ellington popular tune of the time with a characteristic vocal by Ivie Anderson and some very good solo work, in particular a beautifully relaxed, lyrical contribution from Rex Stewart. A particularly noteworthy session was that of July 29th, 1936, which produced *Exposition Swing*, an un-inhibited stomp; *In a Jam*, with a wonderful duet between Hodges and Williams in one of Ellington's most exuberant records; and *Blackout* (also known as *Uptown Downbeat*), a blues of a rather sinister character, with a sinuous Bigard solo, a snarling contribution from the muted trumpet of Cootie Williams and Hodges' soloing on soprano sax.

From late 1936 until March, 1940, the records of the Ell-ington band were made for companies which did not, at the time, have an outlet in this country and English en-thusiasts were denied knowledge of the band's develop-ment. In later years a fair number of the sides from this period have been released here and it has been possible to some extent to put Duke's output during this time in per-spective. It was in fact a time of transition, in which Ell-ington continued the line of development first sensed in such works as the two concertos and *Blackout*, a consolidat-ing of the harmonic advances of the early 'thirties and the blending of such elements with the blues tradition. The year 1937 saw the recording of *Diminuendo and Crescendo in Blue*, a work covering two sides of a standard 78 r.p.m. record which, like the *Black and Tan Fantasy* of the follow-ing year, has sometimes been issued on separate discs. The situation with these two works on English records is a typical example of the sort of bungling which record com-panies are allowed to get away with in their jazz releases. *Crescendo in Blue* was available for a time in the late-1940s on 78, but the original version of *Diminuendo* has never been issued here! During the same period, Part Two of *Black and Tan Fantasy* was put out with an unrelated coupling, while Part One has recently been issued on an L.P. which omits the second part! *Diminuendo and Cres-cendo* can be heard in a 1956 version from the Newport Jazz Festival, but the second half was recorded during a near-riot provoked by a tenor sax solo between the two move-ments and is thus partly inaudible! From 1938 also came the original recording of the most delightful of all Elling-ton's popular songs, *I Let a Song Go Out of My Heart*, in a superb instrumental rendering which makes the later ver-sions with vocal choruses seem almost sacrilegious. Rex was given a more suitable concerto in this year in the de-lightful *Boy Meets Horn*, a whimsical study in freak trumpet techniques. Duke paid tribute to Willie 'The Lion' Smith, a pianist who influenced him in his early days, in the sprightly, bouncing *Portrait of the Lion*, which contains delightful solos by Hodges and Stewart. At the same March, 1939 session which produced this side came *Something To Live For*, one of the first fruits of the Ellington–Strayhorn part-nership and a record which is often cited as Ellington's own favourite of all his own recordings. Those who are not familiar with the rather odd taste exhibited by many lead-ing jazz musicians should be warned that this is a rather dreary pop number sung by Jean Eldridge and, in the English pressings at least, so badly recorded that any in-terest in what goes on behind the commonplace lyrics is largely unrewarded. Many interesting sides remain little known to the English collector from this period, these in-cluding a new recording of *Doin' the Voom Voom* and a new variant on *Bugle Call Rag* under the name of *The Sergeant was Shy*. Of the sides available here, and not so far men-tioned, *Tootin' Through the Roof* is perhaps the most in-teresting, as it contains a masterly duet between Cootie Williams and Rex Stewart.

With the recording of a session by Rex Stewart and his Fifty-Second Street Stompers in 1936 a new series of con-tingent records was inaugurated, and in the following three years alone over one hundred sides were cut by small groups from the band under the leadership of Stewart, Williams, Bigard and Hodges. There is some superb music on these contingent records, the musicians enjoying the less formal surroundings of a small group, as compared with the discipline of the full band, and some of the finest work of all the major Ellington soloists of the period can be found in these miniatures of Ellingtonia. Mention must be made of *The Jeep is Jumpin'* by the Hodges group and *Barney Goin' Easy* by Bigard's, the latter containing magnificent playing by the leader in the lower register of the clarinet.

V

In late 1939 Jimmy Blanton joined the band on bass and Ben Webster came in on tenor sax on a permanent basis, having played with the band on odd recording dates in 1935 and 1936 (he solos on *Truckin'* and *Exposition Swing* from these years). Stimulating as these two highly creative musicians must have been to Duke, their influence alone cannot account for the remarkably high quality of the band's output in 1940, a year in which merely good Ellington records are rare, the norm being excellent. Ellington's approach to his music reached maturity in this year, his attitude to jazz composition becoming more settled. The

163

experiments of the mid-thirties, which had in some cases moved away from the blues in the direction of European concert music, now reaped their full reward. The tendency towards the gathering-in of his various styles into one central manner had become noticeable from about 1936 onward, and in 1940 the blending was complete. To say this is not in any way to disparage his earlier work, for as early as 1930 Ellington had a greater mastery of the jazz orchestra than any other musician before or since. But the Ellington of *Mood Indigo* speaks with a different voice from the Ellington of *Rockin' in Rhythm*, and the same could be said of *Sophisticated Lady* and *Blue Ramble* or, to a lesser extent, of *Reminiscing in Tempo* and *Blackout*. This cannot be said of his 1940 works, a year which saw an even greater mastery of his self-created idiom, a greater synthesis of his style. Even without Duke his 1940 orchestra would be the perfect jazz group of its size, the superb ensemble work being allied to a matchless combination of great soloists—Williams, Stewart, Nanton, Brown, Bigard, Hodges, Webster, Carney and Blanton. To these impressive ingredients for jazz performance Duke added his own unique scores, and it is hardly surprising that masterpieces resulted. What is amazing is their profusion, for virtually every master cut by the orchestra in this year is a perfected gem.

When *Jack the Bear* was released in England the reaction was one of profound shock—Ellington, it was claimed, had deserted his own music to front a 'swing' band. This attitude is largely explained by the fact that no recordings by the band later than 1936 had been heard by those of the jazz public who did not import American records. This hostility, however, has gradually given way to an acceptance, realized at once by the more perceptive critics, that here indeed Duke had brought the traditions he created in the 'twenties and 'thirties to a new stage of development.

It would be impossible in a book of this size to detail every highlight of this year, and a rapid survey will have to suffice. *Jack the Bear* (the Harlem character who 'ain't nowhere') is a bouncing medium tempo number with Blanton, Bigard and Nanton outstanding; the harmonic mastery of the composer is carried a stage further in the savage *Ko-Ko*, supposedly an excerpt from an unfinished opera; *Morning Glory* features Rex in lyrical vein; *Conga Brava* is a jump number based on the opening Latin-American theme played by Tizol; *Concerto for Cootie*, perhaps the best of all such works by Ellington, has wonderful solo work by Williams, both in his growl style and his majestic open manner; *Me and You* features Cootie, Ivie Anderson, a duet by Hodges and Brown, and some remarkable drumming by Greer; *Cotton Tail* is a powerhouse number featuring Ben Webster and brilliant scoring for the sections; *Never No Lament* (later to be popularized as *Don't Get Around Much Any More*) has fine Hodges and Williams; the tone poem *Dusk* is rich in orchestral colour, and has a sympathetic solo by Rex; *Bojangles*, a portrait of tap-dancer Bill 'Bojangles' Robinson, is one of Duke's happiest scores; *A Portrait of Bert Williams* is a sketch of the old Harlem comedian, being entrusted in the main to the solo voices of Stewart, Bigard and Nanton; *Blue Goose* is a constantly shifting kaleidoscope of orchestral tone and solo styles;

Harlem Air Shaft is a fast, busy portrayal of Harlem, featuring a solo by Rex Stewart which is surely the most vehement on record; *Sepia Panorama* is noticeable for its formal structure and for the fine work of Jimmy Blanton, both in solo and in duet with the piano; *In a Mellotone* is a straightforward swinger, Cootie and Hodges being the soloists; *Across the Track Blues* is a magnificent performance in the form Duke never forgets, the principal soloist being Bigard; the latter again demonstrates his unrivalled skill at taking breaks in *The Sidewalks of New York*, an arrangement of a non-Ellington number, which also features one of Nanton's best latter-day solos.

Even on the numbers on which he does not solo Jimmy Blanton's bass playing is an outstanding feature—note the importance of the string-bass work in *Concerto for Cootie* as an instance of this. Ben Webster, the other newcomer, shows his presence not only in his excellent solos but by the improvement of the saxophone section as compared with its work in the previous year. Yet the greatness of these 1940 recordings lies mainly in the brilliance of the scores, excellent though the solo and ensemble work is. Every passage seems to be perfect in its scoring, in its balance and in its formal structure, the solos receiving beautifully apt backgrounds while an inexhaustible sequence of melody informs each record. This was truly a peak year for Duke Ellington.

VI

The first side the band cut in 1941 was destined to become one of their best-selling records and to replace *East St. Louis Toodle-oo* as their signature tune. This was Billy Strayhorn's *Take the 'A' Train*, a medium-fast jump number featuring the excellent trumpet playing of newcomer Ray Nance. Three numbers by Duke's son, Mercer Ellington, were also recorded at this session: *Jumpin' Punkins*, featuring the good-natured voice of Carney's baritone and excellent drumming by Greer, the latter fitting perfectly into the arrangement; *John Hardy's Wife*, with further bouncing Carney, one of Rex's best growl solos and passages for Ellington's piano and Brown's trombone; *Blue Serge* is by contrast a moody, heavy-textured tone poem, featuring Nanton's plaintive trombone half engulfed in brooding saxophone harmonies and Webster's tenor seeming to struggle against the oppressive, heavy atmosphere. The themes of these recordings may be by Mercer Ellington, but the scoring bears the imprint of Duke's unique methods. The scores contributed by Strayhorn (*After All*) and Tizol (*Bakiff*) are comparatively lightweight, but make pleasant enough listening. The best of the popular numbers from this year are *Just A-Settin' and A-Rockin'* with casual tenor from Webster, and *I Got It Bad and That Ain't Good*, sung by Ivie Anderson. This last title featured Johnny Hodges who for the first time employed the exaggerated *glissandi* and slurs which were to become associated with his playing from this period onwards. The concise phrasing of his early solos gave way to a sinuous, smoother manner, which has been used to good effect on ballads and in Ellington's concertos for Hodges. Some commentators have criticized this manner as sentimental and vulgar, but this is far from being the case, for the tone, though rich and sensuous, retains its masculine strength, the phrasing being disciplined by a strongly musical mind. On the session after this Hodges is featured in a typically airy fast tempo in *Jump for Joy*, the title number of Ellington's musical of 1941, which is badly sung by Herb Jeffries.

Although they had switched to the Victor label in early 1940, the policy of recording contingents from the band was continued during the following two years, although not at quite the pace set earlier for Variety and Vocalion. These contingent sides from 1940 and 1941 are perhaps the best of the whole series, those by the Hodges group being of a superb quality. The oustanding titles include *Squaty Roo* with magnificent Hodges and a driving beat from Blanton, and *Things Ain't What They Used To Be*, a blues featuring incredibly melodic solo work from Hodges and a thoughtful contribution from Ray Nance. Some of Rex Stewart's best blues playing is to be heard on the small band sides under his name, notably in *Mobile Bay* and *Poor Bubber*, while the driving *Subtle Slough* has Rex's growl trumpet playing against low-pitched riffs by the rest of the group, the whole being powered by Blanton's tremendous swing.

In mid-1942 the American Federation of Musicians banned all its members from the recording studios owing to a deadlock between them and the record companies on the matter of recording fees. Before this, however, the Ellington band, now without the great Jimmy Blanton, were able to record some dozen titles, including *Perdido* and *C-Jam Blues*, both of which have since become jazz standards. Despite the large number of recordings by both Ellington groups and other bands in the succeeding years, the original version of *Perdido*, taken at an easy medium tempo, remains the best. Two tone poems were recorded at this time: *Moon Mist* featuring Nance on violin and *What Am I Here For*, with solo contributions from Nanton, Stewart and Webster. Probably the best of the band's 1942 records is a swinging up-tempo twelve-bar blues, *Mainstem*, which once more proves the strength of this tradition, and contains choruses by each of the leading soloists with the exception of Carney.

VII

The A.F.M. ban was in operation until December, 1944, and apart from air-shots and V-Discs we have no record of the band's work during this period. Shortly after the resumption of its recording activities for Victor the band recorded a four-movement selection from *Black, Brown and Beige*. The suite opens with *Work Song*, a movement continually whipped into tempo by the menacing drum rhythm; Carney and Nanton are featured here. *Come Sunday* is, by contrast, quiet and restful, introduced by Ray Nance's violin and featuring a long, melodic solo by Johnny Hodges over a hushed background. The third movement is *The Blues*, more a painting of a mood than an exploration of the traditional blues form. Joya Sherrill sings the lyrics over stop chords and odd wisps of melody from the band, who later present a twelve-bar theme which leads back to the vocal section, after a coarse-textured solo from Al Sears. The last movement consists of three dances, a fiery *West*

Indian Dance and a bouncing *Emancipation Celebration* (the last superbly scored and, incidentally, looking back to the *Dallas Doings* of 1933) being contrasted with the placid smoothness of the final *Sugar Hill Penthouse*. The following year the band recorded the Ellington–Strayhorn *Perfume Suite*, a less important score than *Black, Brown and Beige*, which has to contend with a disastrous opening vocal from Al Hibbler. The four movements portray the character that a woman may take on under the influence of various perfumes, the most successful being the two middle movements: *Balcony Serenade* with its excellent saxophone scoring, and *Dancers in Love*, a satirical miniature played as a piano solo with only string-bass accompaniment. Another concert work from 1945, *New World A-Comin'* was recorded for V-Disc, but is unavailable on commercial labels. Duke Ellington and Billy Strayhorn obviously had their minds very much on the concert stage at this time, a fact which can be seen from the heavily arranged versions of older Ellington numbers recorded in 1945. The band was carrying no fewer than three girl singers during this year, and they can all be heard on *It Don't Mean a Thing* and *Solitude*. Al Hibbler is fourth vocalist on the latter, which has a Hodges solo accompanied by the three girls singing wordless harmonies! The extravagance of these arrangements is seen in *In a Sentimental Mood* (with Hardwicke's last recorded solo with the band) and *Caravan*, the last being the most swinging version of Tizol's famous number. These re-makes are capped by a sombre new version of *Black and Tan Fantasy*, with Carney taking the second theme and Nanton all the growl work. In 1946 the band made an album of standard blues themes arranged by Ellington, including good performances of *Memphis Blues*, *Beale Street Blues* and *Royal Garden Blues*; but the finest records from Ellington's last Victor sessions are *Rockabye River* and *Transblucency*. The former is a Johnny Hodges feature, whilst *Transblucency (A Blue Fog That You Can Almost See Through)*, is an adaptation of the *Blue Light* of 1938 to the wordless singing of the concert-trained Kay Davis.

In the last few months of 1946 the band recorded a number of sides for the Musicraft Company, which leave a lot to be desired, as the recording itself was very badly engineered. Of the concert music the outstanding item is *Happy Go Lucky Local*, a portrait of a wheezy old train which had formed the fourth movement of Ellington's *Deep South Suite*, another concert work only recorded in its entirety for V-Disc. Outstanding among the shorter pieces are two superb feature numbers for Johnny Hodges, *Magenta Haze* and *Sultry Sunset*. Jeff Aldam has dismissed these two works as 'expertly contrived *schmalz*', and it is for some reason fashionable to regard them as unworthy creations. In fact they are delightful miniatures, in which the almost classical beauty of Hodges' melodic line keeps the music well clear of any undue sentimentality. A further 'concerto', this time for clarinettist Jimmy Hamilton, is *Flippant Flurry*, where the general air of nonchalance of Ellington's composition fits perfectly with the cool, academic style of the clarinettist. *Concerto for Four Jazz Horns* (Taft Jordan, Brown, Hamilton and Carney) and *Trumpet No End* feature several soloists playing against the full band, the latter

165

having solos by four trumpeters on the chord sequence of *Blue Skies*, concluding with a truly stratospheric contribution from Cat Anderson. The most amusing of Ray Nance's vocal numbers, *Tulip or Turnip*, was recorded at this time with Ray also playing distinctive trumpet over a superbly scored and swinging band.

Ellington started recording for Columbia in August, 1947, and the change of company certainly meant improved recording on this occasion, although the band were called upon to turn out a high percentage of popular material of dubious merit. The works of true Ellingtonian character which were recorded in this year were of an exceptionally high quality. Two numbers with important solos by Tyree Glenn on trombone are amongst the best of these: *Sultry Serenade* and the blues *Hy'a Sue*, the latter containing one of Johnny Hodges' finest choruses. In Ellington's impressionistic vein we were given *Lady of the Lavender Mist* and *On a Turquoise Cloud*, the latter featuring Kay Davis, while the band demonstrates its power and solo strength in *Three Cent Stomp*, a number with superb scoring for the sax section. Unusual in that they both feature Ellington's piano as the principal solo voice are *The Clothed Woman* and *New York City Blues*. Both are in Ellington's impressionist manner and are somewhat removed from the jazz idiom, the second piece being a study in nostalgia rather than a blues in the jazz sense of the term.

The Liberian Suite was recorded complete for Columbia just before the premiere at Carnegie Hall, but this is one of Ellington's most uneven works. The opening movement is entitled *I Like the Sunrise*, and features a vocal by Al Hibbler which starts the work off very badly, despite the melodic excellence of the theme. The remainder of the suite is divided into five dances, and although there is much music of a high quality the work has little unity and is very uneven in quality. Some of the weakest pages are those towards the end of the final *Dance No. 5* when Tyree Glenn plays some very mediocre passages in a poor imitation of the Tricky Sam Nanton manner. It would appear that it is the scoring which is at fault as Glenn plays well enough in the wa-wa style on other records. The best of the dances is probably the first, which shows that a musician of Ellington's calibre can write excellent music round a tenor solo, by Al Sears, which at times descends into the vulgarity of the rhythm-and-blues style.

Another recording ban kept the band out of the studios for the whole of 1948, and the state of the big-band business probably accounts for the poor material which makes up much of the output for 1949. This year did, however, include an outstanding version of *Creole Love Call*, featuring Kay Davis, which has never been issued in England. In December of 1950 the band recorded four extended scores for Columbia, with which the latter were to inaugurate the jazz section of their L.P. catalogue. One of the pieces recorded was a concert work of some twelve minutes' duration, entitled *The Tattooed Bride*. This work describes the honeymoon of an athletic character who spends the first three days playing such strenuous games that by evening he is utterly exhausted and falls asleep at once. On the fourth night he makes the rather alarming discovery that

his bride is tattooed, a fact signalled by the long-held clarinet note during the slow section. The construction of this composition is as ingenious as its programme, the material being worked from the simple theme presented in the opening piano solo. The principal soloist is Jimmy Hamilton, and in a sense the work is a concerto for him, but the most arresting feature of the performance is the playing of the trumpet section, which is in magnificent form. The other three numbers on this L.P. are extended versions of Ellington's standards, the finest being a fifteen-minute *Mood Indigo* with a magnificent Johnny Hodges solo and a passage for the band in 3/4 time, while Harold Baker contributes a gem of a solo to *Sophisticated Lady*, another superb arrangement. The difference between the popular songs of other composers and those by Duke is noticeable when we consider the amount of music Ellington has made over the years from such numbers as *Sophisticated Lady*. The arrangements on this L.P. have been criticized as being too episodic, which is true enough; why certain critics object to this is difficult to understand, for Duke gets more into an 'episode' than most jazz arrangers can manage in several compositions!

The first records by the band in which Smith, Tizol and Bellson replaced Hodges, Brown and Greer are a mixed bag. The finest are *Fancy Dan*, a whimsical piece built around the soloists (this despite the loss of two of Duke's principal solo voices) and *V.I.P.'s Boogie*, featuring Carney and Hamilton. *Jam with Sam* is an exciting jump number which gets rather out of hand towards the end, while *Monologue* features Duke narrating the slight, whimsical story of *Pretty and the Wolf* over a background of three clarinets. The weakest of all is the Louis Bellson arrangement, *The Hawk Talks*, which had the band running through a powerhouse number of a type more usually associated with Woody Herman's band than Duke's. Whatever his limitations as an arranger, however, Bellson was an inspiration to the band in this difficult period with his excellent drumming; his work sparks several of the contingent sides made around this period, including one of Cat Anderson's Latin-American scores *She*, and *Cat Walk*, a blues featuring Anderson in one of his rare growl solos.

Despite the changes in personnel the band recorded *A Tone Parallel to Harlem* in the December of 1951, a seventeen-minute piece which is perhaps Ellington's masterpiece so far as concert music is concerned. Without any break in continuity or any suggestion of the stringing together of brief episodes, the mastery of Ellington's grasp in this work gives the lie to those who consider him to be a mere miniaturist. There are, of course, episodes of a contrasting nature, but the thematic unity of *Harlem* is such that the impression is one of economy rather than the somewhat lavish spreading out which characterizes such pieces as the *Liberian Suite*. *A Tone Parallel to Harlem* opens with a two-note motive on muted trumpet which forms the germ of the first theme of the work, which goes through several variations, mostly of a dance-like character, before the second theme, a 'spiritual' melody, is introduced on solo trombone. Notice in the development of this theme the excellence of Duke's scoring for the individual voices of Russell Procope's clarinet (in contrast to the way he writes for Jimmy Hamilton earlier) and Harold Baker's singing trumpet. The work concludes with a mighty climax built out of the two main motives, the tremendous *power* of the band being harnessed in a magnificent surge of sound.

VIII

Although the band had a record in the best-selling lists in Louis Bellson's extended drum solo, *Skin Deep*, 1952 was one of Ellington's least productive years, only re-makes of *The Mooche* of 1928 and *Perdido* of 1942 being of the standard we have come to expect from his recordings. The following year, amid a heavy crash of publicity, Ellington signed for Capitol records, declaring himself well pleased with their policy. Unfortunately things did not turn out as expected, and the band produced during the next few years a flood of popular trash which joins much of the Cotton Club material recorded in the 'thirties as the low-water mark in Ellington's output. *Bunny Hop Mambo* and *Twelfth Street Rag Mambo* vie with the abominable *Blue Moon*, which features Jimmy Grissom, surely the poorest of all the mediocre male vocalists Ellington has carried through the years. Ellington's *Satin Doll* and *Ultra Deluxe* are, along with Strayhorn's *Boo-Dah*, among the best of the singles by the band from 1953, but more interesting than these is the intimate set of piano solos by Duke with bass and drums. For the band, however, the best of the records from the Capitol period is the L.P. *Ellington '55*, a selection of numbers from various sessions in late 1953 and early 1954. Much of the material is of a non-Ellington origin, but three Ducal compositions were re-recorded: *Black and Tan Fantasy* (1927) and *Rockin' in Rhythm* (1930) being new arrangements of old material. The second number receives a wild, abandoned performance, the band playing with tremendous attack and enthusiasm. The third Ellington piece was a new recording of the 1946 *Happy Go Lucky Local* from the *Deep South Suite*. In the intervening years the old engine has become even more rickety, and protests vigorously at the slightly faster ride she makes here. The brakes are even more rusty, Cat Anderson's trumpet shrieking its protest as the train draws to a halt. Musical portraits of trains are fairly frequent in twentieth century music, in such folk-songs as *Rock Island Line* or jazz numbers like *Honky Tonk Train Blues* on the one hand, and Honneger's *Pacific 231* or Villa Lobos' *Little Train of the Caipira* on the other. But on none of these do we find the affection, humour and warmth of this composition of Ellington's, which can justly be said to be the finest of all such portrayals. The thin trickle of worthwhile recordings in 1954 and 1955 caused one of the periodic cries that Ellington was finished, which was shattered to silence with the appearance of a magnificent new L.P. for the Bethlehem label, *Historically Speaking the Duke*. This was devoted entirely to Ellington originals and featured a band revitalized by the return of Johnny Hodges, and the presence of an excellent new rhythm section. *East St. Louis Toodle-oo* and *Creole Love Call* are the opening tracks, and each of these thirty-year-old compositions is given a superb performance.

Ray Nance is featured on the former playing growl trumpet, a role he fills on several numbers in this album. *Stompy Jones* is given over to the soloists, the original score being played behind their contributions. The two trumpets take the honours here, Nance with a warm, softly phrased chorus and Cat Anderson in an exciting high register solo which climaxes the piece. Johnny Hodges is heard on *Creole Love Call*, *The Jeep is Jumpin'* and *In a Mellotone*, his solo on the last-named being outstanding. The solo strength of the band is shown in the fact that neither Clark Terry nor Paul Gonsalves are given a single-bar solo on the whole L.P. The ensemble plays with a great understanding of the rather varied series of compositions they are called upon to interpret and indeed the record is above all a triumph for the band as a unit and for Ellington himself. A second L.P. from the same February sessions, *Duke Ellington Presents*, is less successful, although *I Can't Get Started*, *My Funny Valentine*, *Day Dream* and *Blues* are excellent tracks with good Clark Terry on the last title.

After these two L.P.s for Bethlehem the band returned to Columbia, the first important L.P.s on this label being those from the 1956 Newport Jazz Festival. The long *Diminuendo and Crescendo in Blue*, with the riot-provoking 'interlude' by Paul Gonsalves, is a very exciting performance, but the last half is spoilt by the noise of the audience. It is a significant item in any Ellington discography, however, for the great success of this performance once again pointed out to the general public Ellington's pre-eminence in the jazz world. It also stressed the importance of other factors too long neglected by the currently fashionable modernists, for, as Albert McCarthy pointed out in his *Jazz Monthly* review, 'It is a triumph of a great swinging band and the twelve-bar blues . . . it is also a reminder of what jazz was like before the cool boys ripped out its heart.' In addition to this the Newport recordings include showcases for Harry Carney on *Sophisticated Lady* and Johnny Hodges on *I Got It Bad*, and two more fine blues performances in *Blues to be There* (from the *Newport Festival Suite*) and *Jeep's Blues*. This last is the finest of the Newport recordings, featuring magnificent playing by Johnny Hodges. Johnny was the leader in a superb contingent session for Norman Granz's Clef label recorded four months after the Newport Festival, a series of performances equal to the best of the small group sides from the 'thirties and 'forties. This L.P. opens with a six-minute *Meet Mr. Rabbit*, with Hodges playing some superb blues choruses, and includes a wonderfully relaxed *Take the 'A' Train* and a chamber music version of *Black and Tan Fantasy*. Hodges proves himself once more to be the finest alto player in the history of jazz, while Clark Terry and Jimmy Hamilton are also at their very best. Despite the presence of Strayhorn on piano, the Ellington atmosphere of these recordings is a very large factor in their complete success.

The next L.P. by the band is one on which they are joined by an assortment of vocalists (including a choir!) and extra percussionists, in a performance of the Ellington–Strayhorn television production, *A Drum is a Woman*. Narrated by Duke, this is a very loose extravaganza on the history of jazz, which has met with a good deal of hostility from critics who have insisted on taking it very seriously indeed. Taken as an intelligent piece of entertainment it is quite acceptable, indeed very enjoyable, and it seems rather absurd to compare this with the *Harlem Suite* or *Such Sweet Thunder*. Ellington was quite obviously attempting something totally different. In between the racy narration and the vocal numbers there are a number of items on which the band play with characteristic excellence, Clark Terry being particularly good in the *Hey, Buddy Bolden* section. Commenting on this L.P. in *Jazz Monthly* Edward Towler suggested that if this is a criterion for Ellington's work in progress, then, of the many qualities which have made him a major figure in twentieth century art, only the originality of his music will remain. It was not a criterion however, for the next Ellington recording was the Shakespearian suite *Such Sweet Thunder*, which ranks with *A Tone Parallel to Harlem* as his finest concert music. The suite is in twelve movements and, with the exception of the rather dull *Sonnet for Sister Kate* and the out of character finale *Circle of Fourths*, all are excellent. Much of the music is written in a mildly satirical vein, for example in the jazz waltz *Lady Mac* who had, according to Duke, 'a little ragtime in her soul', and in *Madness in Great Ones*, a sketch of Hamlet who was, as Duke says, trying to convince people that he was crazy, but 'in those days crazy didn't mean the same thing it means now'. This movement features Cat Anderson playing one of the most remarkable passages in all Ellington's music, where Duke uses the extreme high register playing of which Anderson is the master to most unusual effect. The Romeo and Juliet movement features Johnny Hodges, and, like Hamilton's *Sonnet for Caesar*, is in a more serious mood. The wittiest of all these character sketches is *Up and Down*, where Clark Terry is cast as Puck and dances happily through a movement which makes striking use of Nance's violin in the orchestration. With this superb suite Ellington, Strayhorn and the band have once more demonstrated their unique abilities, once more shown their pre-eminence in the world of jazz. In a television interview when he was in this country someone asked Duke why, at the age of 59, he still travelled around with his band, rather than living a quieter life, which he could so easily do from his considerable income from royalties on his songs and records. He explained that he is, above all, a writer, comparing his position with that of the many composers who are lucky to hear one performance in a year of their works, while he has his orchestra on hand to play his music whenever he wishes. Duke Ellington is, as he remarked in an earlier interview, in the band business today mainly out of 'artistic interest', and he stresses that 'we stay in it fifty-two weeks a year'. Duke knows that in his band he has what is one of the finest musical ensembles in the world. If this seems a rather sweeping statement, let the reader visualize any other group which could interpret a complex score like *Such Sweet Thunder* and then split into smaller units which could *create* such magnificent music as is heard on the 1956 Johnny Hodges contingent L.P.

The next album after *Such Sweet Thunder* was one of popular standards (only three out of eight titles are Ellington numbers) which, although pleasant enough, does not show off the band to its best advantage. The welcome return of Harold Baker is signalled here by two excellent solos, on *Mood Indigo* and *Willow Weep for Me*. More interesting is the new version of *Black, Brown and Beige*, despite the total failure of the second side, which has gospel singer Mahalia Jackson singing *Come Sunday*, a most unsuitable blending of talents, not in any way assisted by maudlin lyrics. The first three sections, however, contain much of interest, the first two being new scorings of the *Work Song* and *Come Sunday* movements, the last a rather odd blending of the two themes.

In 1958, the Ellington band recorded half of a four-disc set for Verve entitled *Ella Fitzgerald Sings the Duke Ellington Song Book*. The banal lyrics which were tagged on to Ellington's themes by a host of hack lyric writers detract, to some extent, from the pleasure the Ellington enthusiast will derive from these L.P.s, and equally out of place is the 'baby talk' scat singing indulged in by Miss Fitzgerald on many numbers. No lover of *Concerto for Cootie* is likely to enjoy its popular variant, *Do Nothing 'til You Hear From Me*, with its inane lyrics, while the listener is even more infuriated when a superb arrangement of *Rockin' in Rhythm* is played by the band with Ella scatting away in the foreground. The music of Duke Ellington is of a quality which can hardly be enhanced by the addition of a popular singer, even the best (and Ella is without doubt the best), and the L.P.s are interesting only when we are allowed to hear the band which plays very well indeed. The most rewarding music in these albums is to be found in the nonvocal *A Portrait of Ella Fitzgerald* which, despite Duke's verbal introductions, seems to have little connection with its subject, and turns out to be one of Duke's 'lightweight' concert works after the pattern of the *Newport Festival Suite*. A four-disc set of *Duke Ellington Plays the Duke Ellington Song Book* would have been a superior proposition musically, although perhaps not so great a commercial success.

IX

Today, under the direction of Ellington's son, Mercer, the Duke Ellington Orchestra is still the finest jazz ensemble in the world, a band unrivalled in its solo strength and ensemble ability. Despite the claims made by lovers of New Orleans jazz on behalf of the bands of King Oliver and Jelly-Roll Morton, the finest ensemble playing in jazz is to be found on the records of the Duke Ellington Orchestra. It is beyond dispute that the finest big-band scores in jazz are those of Duke Ellington and Billy Strayhorn, the extended compositions no less than the generally accepted shorter pieces being works of characteristic quality. The Duke Ellington Orchestra has without doubt created a greater bulk of jazz masterpieces than any group in the whole history of the music. These achievements are generally recognized, but it is not so widely appreciated that Duke Ellington was the most truly progressive figure in jazz. Other so-called 'progressive' musicians have been only too willing to sacrifice the basic blues style of the music, in order to utilize the impressive harmonic and formal resources of the European tradition. Ellington for his part always remained within the jazz idiom in his concert works (with the exception of a few odd piano pieces) because his language was always that of the blues tradition, his harmonic and formal advances being made within this framework.

If such musicians as Miles Davis or Jimmy Giuffre continue to be regarded as the *avant-garde* of jazz, then the music will move closer to the European academic tradition, and the distinctive qualities of jazz will be lost. Much of the music which has followed the bop revolution in jazz has been emotionally sterile, many of the so-called progressive devices having reduced the music to the level of polite tea-dance music, more fitted to the Palm Court than either the concert stage or a Negro dance-hall. No art-form remains static, and a return to the music of the Harlem or the Kansas City of the 1930s is as unlikely as a return to the environment and music of New Orleans in the early years of this century. Younger jazz musicians will naturally evolve a different musical language from that of earlier generations, and no critic worthy of the name would object to this process. What the critic must point out is that as *jazz Saddest Tale* is more progressive than *Boplicity*, *A Portrait of Bert Williams* more progressive than *Django*, and *Such Sweet Thunder* more progressive than *Miles Ahead*.

Duke Ellington's pre-eminence in jazz is not only because of the very high aesthetic standard of his output, not simply due to his remarkable abilities as pianist, composer and bandleader, but also to the fact that he extended the boundaries of jazz more than any other musician, without abandoning the true essence of the music.

SELECTED DISCOGRAPHY

The records listed in the selected discography are intended to give the listener a rounded picture of Duke Ellington's music. The selection has been made with two objects in mind—to give a balanced and representative listing and to cite only music of outstanding quality. Such a basis is bound to reflect the compiler's taste; the author believes that the following selection would, although it is a purely personal choice, meet with the approval of the majority of Ellington specialists. It must be pointed out that the omission of any title is not intended in any way to be a commentary on its quality; the limitation of space has caused many excellent Ellington records to be passed over.

LP records originally available on Brunswick are now on Decca; those on Camden and "X" are on Victor; those on Musicraft are on Prestige; those on Okeh are on Columbia.

As the discography is not a complete listing of Ellington's recorded output it has been decided to omit matrix numbers; for this reason and for reasons of space, only American catalogue numbers are given. Records that are no longer in the catalogue are marked with an asterisk.

Acknowledgment is due to *Jazz Directory*, Volume Three (compiled by Dave Carey and Albert J. McCarthy) and the Record Guide in *Duke Ellington* (edited by Peter Gammond), which were the principal sources in the compilation of this discography. The layout is based on that of *Jazz Directory*, which, in the author's view, is both the most logical way of listing jazz records and the one which has received the most universal approval.

Key to Instrumental Abbreviations: acc = accompanied by; alt = alto saxophone; bar = baritone saxophone; bj = banjo; bs = string bass; bs-sx = bass saxophone; clt = clarinet; cnt = cornet; d = drums; fl-h = flugelhorn; fr-h = French horn; g = guitar; p = pianoforte; sop = soprano saxophone; tbn = trombone; ten = tenor saxophone; tpt = trumpet; tu = tuba; vln = violin; v-tbn = valve trombone.

NOTES.

(1) Harry Carney has used the bass clarinet from the middle 'thirties onwards, in addition to the more usual B♭ instrument.

(2) From aural evidence it would appear unlikely that Johnny Hodges played soprano saxophone after 1943.

(3) Juan Tizol plays valve-trombone on all records on which he is present, while John Sanders switched to this instrument shortly after joining the band.

(4) Rex Stewart plays cornet on all records on which he appears.

KEY TO LABEL ABBREVIATIONS

Beth	Bethlehem
Cap	Capitol
Co	Columbia
Prst	Prestige
Vic	Victor
Vrv	Verve

DUKE ELLINGTON AND HIS ORCHESTRA:
Bubber Miley, Louis Metcalfe (*tpt*); Joe 'Tricky Sam' Nanton (*tbn*); Otto Hardwicke (*alt, bs-sx, clt*); Rudy Jackson (*clt, ten*); Harry Carney (*bar, alt, clt*); Duke Ellington (*p*); Fred Guy (*bj*); 'Bass' Edwards (*tu*); Sonny Greer (*d*).
New York City, April 7, 1927
Black and Tan Fantasy
De 79224E

Wellman Braud (*bs*) replaces Edwards.
New York City, October 26, 1927
Creole Love Call[1] Vic LPV 568
Black and Tan Fantasy
Vic LPV 568
[1] vocal by Adelaide Hall on this track.

New York City, December 19, 1927
East St. Louis Toodle-oo
Vic LPV 568

Arthur Whetsol (*tpt*) added; Barney Bigard (*clt, ten*) replaces Jackson.
New York City, March 26, 1928
Black Beauty Vic LPV 568
Jubilee Stomp Vic LPV 568

Johnny Hodges (*alt, sop*) replaces Hardwicke.
New York City, Jun 5, 1928
Yellow Dog Blues   De 79224E

Lonnie Johnson (*g*) added.
New York City, October 1, 1928
The Mooche [1]   Co C3L27
Hot and Bothered [1]   Co C3L27
   [1] vocal by Baby Cox on this track.

Johnson out.   New York City, October 17, 1928
The Mooche   De 79241E

Johnson returns; Freddy Jenkins (*tpt*) replaces Metcalfe.
New York City, November 20, 1928
Blues with a Feeling
Co C3L27
Misty Mornin'   Co C3L39

Johnson out.   New York City, January 16, 1929
Flaming Youth   Vic LPV 568
Saturday Night Function
Vic 741028
High Life   Vic 741028
Doin' the Voom-Voom
Vic 741028

Arthur Whetsol, Cootie Williams, Freddy Jenkins (*tpt*); Joe Nanton (*tbn*); Johnny Hodges (*alt, sop*); Barney Bigard (*clt, ten*); Harry Carney (*bar, alt, clt*); Duke Ellington (*p*); Fred Guy (*bj*); Wellman Braud (*bs*); Sonny Greer (*d*).   New York City, March 7, 1929
Hot Feet [1]   Vic 741029
   [1] vocal by Cootie Williams.

Cootie Williams (*tpt*); Barney Bigard (*clt*); Johnny Hodges (*alt*); same *p*; *bj*; *bs*; *d*.
New York City, May 3, 1929
Saratoga Swing   Vic 741029

Arthur Whetsol (*tpt*); Joe Nanton (*tbn*); Barney Bigard (*clt*); Johnny Hodges (*alt*); same *bs*; *d* as last.
New York City, May 28, 1929
Saturday Night Function
Vic 741028
Note: The above was issued as by "Sonny Greer and his Memphis Men."

Personnel as for March 7, 1929 except Juan Tizol (*v-tbn*) added.   New York City, April 11, 1930
Double Check Stomp
Vic 741039

Charlie Barnet (*chimes*) added.
Hollywood, August 20, 1930
Ring Dem Bells [1]   Vic VPM 6042
   [1] vocal by Cootie Williams.

Arthur Whetsol (*tpt*); Joe Nanton (*tbn*); Barney Bigard (*clt*); same *p*; *bj*; *bs*; *d*.
New York City, October 17, 1930
Mood Indigo   De 79247E

Previous full band personnel, but without Charlie Barnet.
New York City, November 8, 1930
Rockin' in Rhythm
Co C3L27

New York City, January 14, 1931

Rockin' in Rhythm
De 79247E

New York City, January 16, 1931
Rockin' in Rhythm
Vic 741068

New York City, January 20, 1931
Creole Rhapsody, Parts 1 and 2
De 79247E

New York City, June 16, 1931
Echoes of the Jungle
Vic LPV 506

Lawrence Brown (*tbn*) replaces Tizol; Guy doubles on *g*.
New York City, February 2, 1932
Lazy Rhapsody (Swanee River Rhapsody) [1]
Co C3L27
   [1] vocal by Cootie Williams.

New York City, February 11, 1932
Creole Love Call   Co C3L39
Rose Room   Co C3L39

Juan Tizol (*v-tbn*); Otto Hardwicke (*alt, bs-sx, clt*) added.
New York City, February 17, 1933
Drop Me Off at Harlem
Co C3L27

New York City, May 16, 1933
Bundle of Blues (Dragon's Blues)
Co C3L27

New York City, August 15, 1933
Harlem Speaks   Co C3L27
In the Shade of the Old Apple Tree
Co C3L39

Louis Bacon (*tpt, vcl*) added.
Chicago, September 26, 1933
Rude Interlude   Vic LPV 506

Tizol out.   Chicago, January 9, 1934
Stompy Jones   Vic LPV 506

Chicago, January 10, 1934
Blue Feeling   Vic LPV 506

Tizol returns; Bacon leaves.
New York City, September 12, 1934
Saddest Tale [1]   Co C3L27
   [1] talking by Duke Ellington.

Arthur Whetsol, Cootie Williams (*tpt*); Rex Stewart (*cnt*); Joe Nanton, Lawrence Brown (*tbn*); Juan Tizol (*v-tbn*); Otto Hardwicke (*alt, bs-sx, clt*); Johnny Hodges (*alt, sop*); Barney Bigard (*clt, ten*); Harry Carney (*bar, alt, clt*); Duke Ellington (*p*); Fred Guy (*g*); Wellman Braud (*bs*); Sonny Greer (*d*).
Chicago, September 12, 1935
Reminiscing in Tempo, Parts 1–4
Co C3L39

Hardwicke and Braud out.
New York City, February 28, 1936
Clarinet Lament (Barney's Concerto)
Co C3L27
Echoes of Harlem (Cootie's Concerto)
Co C3L27

Hardwicke returns; Ben Webster (*ten*) added; Hayes Alvis (*bs*) replaces Braud.

New York City, July 29, 1936

In a Jam Co C3L27
Blackout (*Uptown Downbeat*)
Co C3L39

Webster out; Wallace Jones (*tpt*); Freddy Jenkins (*chimes*) replace Whetsol.

New York City, March 5, 1937

New East St. Louis Toodle-oo
Co CSP JCL558

Tizol and Jenkins out; Harold Baker (*tpt*) added.

New York City, January 13, 1938

New Black and Tan Fantasy
Co CSP JCL558

Tizol returns. New York City, March 3, 1938
I Let a Song Go Out of My Heart
Co C3L27

Baker and Alvis out. New York City, March 21, 1939
Portrait of the Lion
Co C3L27

DUKE ELLINGTON AND HIS ORCHESTRA:
Wallace Jones, Cootie Williams (*tpt*); Rex Stewart (*cnt*); Joe Nanton, Lawrence Brown (*tbn*); Juan Tizol (*v-tbn*); Otto Hardwicke (*alt, bs-sx, clt*); Johnny Hodges (*alt, sop*); Barney Bigard (*clt, ten*); Ben Webster (*ten*); Harry Carney (*bar, clt, alt*); Duke Ellington (*p*); Fred Guy (*g*); Jimmy Blanton (*bs*); Sonny Greer (*d*).

Chicago, March 6, 1940

Jack the Bear Vic LPM 1715
Ko-Ko Vic LPM 1715

Chicago, March 15, 1940

Concerto for Cootie
Vic VPM 6042

Hollywood, May 4, 1940

Cotton Tail Vic VPM 6042
Never No Lament Vic VPM 6042

Chicago, May 28, 1940

Dusk Vic LPV 517
Bojangles Vic LPM 6009*
A Portrait of Bert Williams
Vic LPM 1364*

New York City, July 22, 1940

Harlem Air Shaft Vic LPM–1715

New York City, July 24, 1940

Sepia Panorama Vic LPM–1364*

Chicago, September 5, 1940

In a Mellotone Vic LPM–1364*

Chicago, October 28, 1940

Across the Track Blues
Vic LPM 1715

JOHNNY HODGES AND HIS ORCHESTRA:
Cootie Williams (*tpt*); Lawrence Brown (*tbn*); Johnny Hodges (*alt*); Harry Carney (*bar*); Duke Ellington (*p*);

Jimmy Blanton (*bs*); Sonny Greer (*d*).

Chicago, November 2, 1940

Day Dream Vic LPV 533

REX STEWART AND HIS ORCHESTRA:
As for last Hodges group except Rex Stewart (*cnt*); Ben Webster (*ten*) replace Williams and Hodges.

Chicago, November 2, 1940

Mobile Bay Vic LPV 533

DUKE ELLINGTON AND HIS ORCHESTRA:
As previous full band personnel except Ray Nance (*tpt, vln*) replaces Williams. Chicago, December 28, 1940
Sidewalks of New York
Vic LPV 517

Hollywood, February 15, 1941

John Hardy's Wife Vic LPV 517
Blue Serge Vic LPM 1364*

Hollywood, June 26, 1941

I Got It Bad and That Ain't Good [1]
Vic VPM 6042
[1] vocal by Ivie Anderson.

REX STEWART AND HIS ORCHESTRA:
As for Stewart session of November 2, 1940.

Hollywood, July 3, 1941

Subtle Slough Vic LPV 533

JOHNNY HODGES AND HIS ORCHESTRA:
As for Hodges session of November 2, 1940 except Ray Nance (*tpt*) replaces Williams. Hollywood, July 3, 1941
Squaty Roo Vic. LPV 533
Things Ain't What They Used to Be
Vic. LPV 533

DUKE ELLINGTON AND HIS ORCHESTRA:
Previous full band personnel except Junior Raglin (*bs*) replaces Blanton. Chicago, January 21, 1942
Perdido Vic VPM 6042

Hollywood, June 26, 1942

Mainstem Vic LPM 1364*

Shelton Hemphill, Taft Jordan, William 'Cat' Anderson (*tpt*); Ray Nance (*tpt, vln*); Joe Nanton, Lawrence Brown, Claude Jones (*tbn*); Otto Hardwicke (*alt, bs-sx, clt*); Johnny Hodges (*alt, sop*); Jimmy Hamilton (*clt, ten*); Al Sears (*ten*); Harry Carney (*bar, alt, clt*); Duke Ellington (*p*); Fred Guy (*g*); Junior Raglin (*bs*); Sonny Greer or Hillard Brown (*d*).

New York City, December 11, 1944

BLACK, BROWN AND BEIGE SUITE
Part 1 *Work Song* Vic LPM 1715
Part 2 *Come Sunday*
Vic LPM 1715

New York City, December 12, 1944

Part 3 *The Blues* Vic LPM 1715
Part 4 *Three Dances*
Vic LPM 1715

[1] vocal by Joya Sherrill.

Rex Stewart (*cnt*) added; Greer on *d*.

New York City, May 11, 1945
Caravan   Vic LPV 541
Black and Tan Fantasy
          Vic LPM 6009*

Shelton Hemphill, Francis Williams, Taft Jordan, Harold Baker, Cat Anderson (*tpt*); Ray Nance (*tpt, vln*); Joe Nanton, Claude Jones, Lawrence Brown, Wilbur De Paris (*tbn*); Russell Procope (*alt, clt*); Johnny Hodges (*alt, sop*); Jimmy Hamilton (*clt, ten*); Al Sears (*ten*); Harry Carney (*bar, alt, clt*); Duke Ellington (*p*); Fred Guy (*g*); Oscar Pettiford (*bs*); Sonny Greer (*d*).

Hollywood, July 9, 1946
Rockabye River   Vic LPM 6009*

Anderson and Nanton out.

New York City, October 23, 1946
Magenta Haze   Prst 24029

Anderson returns.   New York City, November 25, 1946
Sultry Sunset   Prst 24029
Happy-Go-Lucky Local, Parts 1 and 2
          Prst 24029

Anderson out.   New York City, December 11, 1946
Tulip or Turnip [1]   Prst 24029
     [1] vocal by Ray Nance.

Wilbur Bascomb (*tpt*); Tyree Glenn (*tbn*) replace Jordan and De Paris.   New York City, August 14, 1947
Hy'a Sue   Co G32564E
Lady of the Lavender Mist
          Co G32564E

Baker out.   New York City, October 6, 1947
Sultry Serenade (How Could You Do a Thing Like That to Me)
          Co G32564E

Harold Baker (*tpt*); Wilbur De Paris (*tbn*) added.
          New York City, November 10, 1947
Three Cent Stomp Co G32564E

Lawrence Brown, Tyree Glenn (*tbn*); Jimmy Hamilton (*clt*); Johnny Hodges (*alt*); Al Sears (*ten*); Harry Carney (*bar, clt*); Duke Ellington (*p*); Oscar Pettiford, Junior Raglin (*bs*); Sonny Greer (*d*).
          New York City, December 22, 1947
On a Turquoise Cloud [1]
          Co G32564E

Harold Baker, Al Killian (*tpt*); Jimmy Hamilton (*clt*); Johnny Hodges (*alt*); Harry Carney (*bar*); same *p*; 2 *bs*; *d*.   New York City, December 30, 1947
New York City Blues
          Co G32564E

Harold Baker, Cat Anderson, Nelson Williams, Andrew 'Fats' Ford (*tpt*); Ray Nance (*tpt, vln*); Lawrence Brown, Quentin Jackson, Tyree Glenn (*tbn*); Russell Procope (*alt, clt*); Johnny Hodges (*alt, sop*); Jimmy Hamilton (*clt, ten*); Paul Gonsalves (*ten*); Harry Carney (*bar, clt*); Mercer Ellington (*fr-h*); Duke Ellington, Billy Strayhorn (*p*); Wendell Marshall (*bs*); Sonny Greer (*d*).
          New York City, December 18, 1950

     [1] vocal by Kay Davis.

Mood Indigo [1]   Co CSP JCL825
Sophisticated Lady [1]
          Co CSP JCL825
     [1] vocal by Yvonne Lanauze.

New York City, December 19, 1950
The Tattooed Bride
          Co CSP JCL825
Solitude   Co CSP JCL825

DUKE ELLINGTON AND HIS ORCHESTRA:
As last personnel above plus Harold Baker, Nelson Williams, Fats Ford (*tpt*); Ray Nance (*tpt, vln*); Quentin Jackson, Britt Woodman (*tbn*); Russell Procope (*alt, clt*); Jimmy Hamilton (*clt, ten*); Harry Carney (*bar, clt*).
          New York City, May 10, 1951
Fancy Dan   Co J20

Monologue [1]   Co J20
     [1] Ellington (narrator) acc Hamilton, Procope, Carney (*clt*) only.

Clark Terry, Willie Cook, Dick Vance (*tpt*) replace Anderson, Ford and Nance.   New York City, December 7, 1951
A Tone Parallel to Harlem
          Co J6

Cat Anderson, Clark Terry, Willie Cook (*tpt*); Ray Nance (*tpt, vln*); Quentin Jackson, Britt Woodman (*tbn*); Juan Tizol (*v-tbn*); Russell Procope (*alt, clt*); Hilton Jefferson (*alt*); Jimmy Hamilton (*clt, ten*); Paul Gonsalves (*ten*); Harry Carney (*bar, clt*); Duke Ellington (*p*); Wendell Marshall (*bs*) Louis Bellson (*d*).
          New York City, July 1, 1952
The Mooche   Co CSP JCL830

Tizol out; Rick Henderson (*alt*); Dave Black (*d*) replace Jefferson and Bellson.   Chicago, December 29, 1953
Black and Tan Fantasy
          Cap DT1602

George Jean (*tbn*) added.   Chicago, January 17, 1954

Rockin' in Rhythm
          Cap DT1602

John Sanders (*v-tbn*); Johnny Hodges (*alt*); Jimmy Woode (*bs*); Sam Woodyard (*d*) replace Jean, Henderson, Marshall and Black.   Chicago, February 7 and 8, 1956
East St. Louis Toodle-oo
          Beth BCP–60*
Creole Love Call   Beth BCP–60*
Stompy Jones   Beth BCP–60*
In a Mellotone   Beth BCP–60*

Newport, R. I., July 7, 1956
Diminuendo and Crescendo in Blue
          Co CS8648
Jeep's Blues   Co CS8648

New York City, August 7, 1956
SUCH SWEET THUNDER (Figures in parenthesis indicate the order of the movements.)
Half the Fun (11) Co CSP JCL1033
Sonnet for Caesar (2)
          Co CSP JCL1033

JOHNNY HODGES AND THE ELLINGTON ALL STARS:
Clark Terry (*tpt*); Ray Nance (*tpt, vln*); Quentin Jackson
(*tbn*); Jimmy Hamilton (*clt*); Johnny Hodges (*alt*);
Harry Carney (*bar*); Billy Strayhorn (*p*); Jimmy Woode
(*bs*); Sam Woodyard (*d*). New York City, October 1956
 Meet Mr. Rabbit Vrv MGV–8203*
 Duke's in Bed Vrv MGV–8203*
 Black and Tan Fantasy
 Vrv MGV–8203*
 Take the 'A' Train
 Vrv MGV–8203*

DUKE ELLINGTON AND HIS ORCHESTRA:
Previous full band personnel. New York City, April 15, 1957
 SUCH SWEET THUNDER
 Sonnet in Search of a Moor (5)
 Co CSP JCL1033
 Sonnet for Sister Kate (8)
 Co CSP JCL1033
 New York City, April 24, 1957
 Such Sweet Thunder (1)
 Co CSP JCL1033
 Lady Mac (4) Co CSP JCL1033
 Up and Down (7) Co CSP JCL1033
 New York City, May 3, 1957
 Sonnet to Hank Cinq (3)
 Co CSP JCL1033
 The Telecasters (6)
 Co CSP JCL1033
 The Star-Crossed Lovers (9)
 Co CSP JCL1033

 Madness in Great Ones (10) Co CSP JCL1033
 Circle of Fourths (12) Co CSP JCL1033
Cootie Williams, Cat Anderson, Mercer Ellington, Herbie Jones
(*tpt*); Lawrence Brown, Buster Cooper, Quentin Jackson,
Charles Connors (*tbn*); Johnny Hodges, Russell Procope (*alt*);
Jimmy Hamilton (*ten*); Harry Carney (*bar*); Duke Ellington
(*p*); John Lamb (*bs*); Louis Bellson (*d*).

 New York City, Dec. 26, 1965
CONCERT OF SACRED MUSIC Vic LSP 3582*
In the Beginning God
 Vocal by Brock Peters; Herman McCoy Choir
Tell Me It's the Truth[1]
Come Sunday[1]
The Lord's Prayer[1]
 [1] Vocal by Esther Marrow
Come Sunday
Will You Be There?
Ain't but the One
 Vocal by Jimmy McPhail
New World a-Comin'
 piano only, by Duke Ellington
David Danced Before the Lord with All His Might
 Tap dancing by Benny Briggs
Jackson (*tbn*) out; Paul Gonsalves (*ten*) added; Rufus Jones
(*d*) replaces Bellson.

 New York City, 1967
 Far East Suite Vic LSP 3782*
Clark Terry (*fl-h*) added; Aaron Bell (*bs*) replaces Lamb;
Steve Little (*d*) replaces Jones.

 New York City, Aug. 28, 1967
 Boo-Dah Vic LSP 3906*
 Blood Count Vic LSP 3906*
 Rock Skippin' at the Blue Note Vic LSP 3906*
Duke Ellington (*p*).

 New York City, Aug. 30, 1967
 Lotus Blossom Vic LSP 3906*
Previous full band personnel. Terry (*fl-h*) out.

 New York City, Sept. 1, 1967
 Snibor Vic LSP 3906*
Jeff Castleman (*bs*) and Sam Woodyard (*d*) replace Bell and
Little.
 New York City, Nov. 16, 1967
 Charpoy Vic LSP 3906*
 The Intimacy of the Blues Vic LSP 3906*
 Day Dream Vic LSP 3906*

BIBLIOGRAPHY

Carey, Dave and McCarthy, Albert J., *Jazz Directory*,
 Volume Three (E.F.G.), The Delphic Press, Fording-
 bridge and Cassell & Co. Ltd., London, 1951.

Dance, Stanley, *The World of Duke Ellington*, Scribner, New
 York, 1972.

Ellington, Duke, *Music Is My Mistress*, Doubleday, New York,
 1973.

Finkelstein, Sidney, *Jazz: A People's Music*, The Citadel
 Press, New York, 1948. See Chapter 6, 'The Experimental Laboratory and the New Jazz'.

Gammond, Peter (Editor), *Duke Ellington: His Life and
 Music*, Phoenix House, London, 1958.

Hentoff, Nat and Shapiro, Nat (Editors), *Hear Me Talkin'
 To Ya*, Peter Davies, London, 1955. See Chapter 13,
 'Ellington plays the piano, but his real instrument is his
 band', and other references.

Hentoff, Nat and Shapiro, Nat (Editors), *The Jazz Makers*,
 Peter Davies, London, 1958. See Chapter 13, 'Duke
 Ellington' by Leonard Feather.

Hodier, Andre, *Jazz: Its Evolution and Essence*, Secker and
 Warburg, London, 1956. See Chapter 6, 'A Masterpiece:
 Concerto for Cootie'.

Ulanov, Barry, *Duke Ellington*, Musicians Press, London,
 1947.

Dizzy Gillespie

BY MICHAEL JAMES

ACKNOWLEDGEMENTS

Mr. Leonard Feather's *Inside Bebop* has been a most useful source of information to me in regard to Gillespie's early career. I am also indebted to Monsieur Charles Delaunay for the details he kindly afforded me concerning the European tour made by the Gillespie Orchestra in the early months of 1948.

The success of Dizzy Gillespie's appearance at the Paris Jazz Fair in March 1952 was an interesting commentary upon his musical evolution over the preceding fifteen years. He had made his first visit to the French capital in 1937 as a sideman with the Teddy Hill band; at that time his talent as a soloist, as yet undeveloped, was overshadowed by the playing of Shad Collins and Bill Dillard, the more experienced members of Hill's trumpet section. It is significant that Gillespie appeared on none of the recording sessions in which his fellow musicians took part during the band's European tour. Eleven years later, he came to Paris once more: in the interim he had emerged as one of the more important architects of the bop evolution; his recordings had already made his reputation with American enthusiasts. On this occasion a series of hastily staged concerts were successful in compensating for the disastrous Swedish tour his orchestra had just undertaken. During the next four years, the diffusion of modern jazz, both by way of the gramophone record and concerts by American and European musicians, had its inevitable effect upon public receptivity, with the result that his appearance at the 1952 Paris Jazz Fair was a triumphant one from both monetary and musical standpoints.

Although it is apparent in retrospect that his individuality as a soloist was established as early as 1945, and that the part he played in adapting the innovations of the new school to the requirements of the big band were largely complete by the end of 1947, it was not until this late date that he found a wide measure of acceptance. Even then it is dubious whether this achievement was wholly the result of his musicianship: it is noteworthy that his success was gained as a virtuoso performer, rather than as leader, composer, or arranger. It is a sobering thought that despite the amplitude of his accomplishment, nearly as generous in its own way as Parker's was in his, a talent for comedy was a considerable feature of many Gillespie performances at this time. This fact no more reflects upon the trumpeter's playing than Armstrong's traditionally outsize sense of humour does on his; but it is instructive to see how large a part of the repertoire was given over to musical clownery in the form of bebop vocals and instrumental extravagance—clownery which now and again seems rather forced—when Gillespie brought his own band to Europe again the following year. Just as artistic progress, in the sense of an inevitable improvement in quality, is a mistaken notion, any reference to amelioration of public taste must always be heavily qualified. Although, in 1952, he was a well-paid performer with an international reputation, his position *vis-à-vis* the public had, in some ways, changed only slightly since 1937, when he sat, a young and inexperienced musician, in the trumpet section of Teddy Hill's band.

Born on October 21st, 1917, the son of a bricklayer, in Cheraw, South Carolina, John Birks Gillespie—for those were the Christian names, so long neglected for the colourful pseudonym of Dizzy, which have only recently found an amazing resuscitation—had an early, wide, but strictly unacademic introduction to music. His father led a local band, and the musicians' instruments were kept in the house; the youngest Gillespie—for he was the last of nine children—must have found great pleasure in attempting to get an approximation of the right sounds out of them. It was some two years after his father's death, while he was attending the Robert Small school, that he began to have the advantages of some sort of tuition; his first instrument was the trombone. Not until some months later did he obtain a trumpet, and this, like the trombone, was borrowed. On the strength of his progress he managed to get a scholarship to the Laurinburg Institute, which was a kind of Negro industrial school in the neighbouring state of North Carolina. In his book *Inside Bebop*, Leonard Feather mentions, in the course of an authoritative description of his childhood and early career, how, despite a mediocre reading ability, he had sufficient instrumental competence to play conventional swing arrangements in a band composed of other young musicians.

In 1935 he followed his family north to Philadelphia, and not long afterwards found work in a local group alongside Charlie Shavers; it was about this time that he is reputed to have first heard Roy Eldridge over the wireless, and to have been sufficiently impressed by his playing to take him as an exemplar. His admiration, as it happened, was to prove particularly helpful, for when he found himself in New York with no certain prospects of employment, having left Philadelphia and the Fairfax band to take a job with Lucky Millinder which eventually did not materialize, Teddy Hill took him on because he wanted a musician whose conception was similar to Eldridge's. Frankie Newton, as a matter of fact, had originally replaced Eldridge in the Hill band, but Gillespie secured the second trumpet chair mainly because of the style he had chosen. He was not very popular with the other musicians, owing to his eccentric and sometimes facetious behaviour at rehearsals and his general reluctance to submit to the mildest form of discipline on the stand, but his ability seems to have gained him the respect of the leader, and when the band left for a European tour, he stayed in spite of the threats made by some sidemen that they would leave if he were taken along. The somewhat less charitable suggestion has, however, been made that Hill's keeping him on was prompted above all by his talents as a nurse to the bandleader's young daughter.

Before the trip, in March, 1937, Gillespie played his first recorded solos with the band: *King Porter Stomp* and *Blue Rhythm Fantasy* have greater historical significance than anything else, for they show how conscientiously he had patterned his playing on his model, Roy Eldridge. There is not the same intensity to the younger man's work, but it would be impossible to overlook the likeness. He figures on these two sides as a musician of unconventional promise even at this early date: and one prophetic feature, remarkable, maybe, in retrospect only, is that he seems to have difficulty in fitting the phrases he chooses into the rhythmic substructure. It is of incidental interest to note that the last eight bars of the first chorus of *Blue Rhythm Fantasy* use a melody similar to that of Monk's *Well You Needn't*. The first alto player in the Hill band, Howard Johnson, is reported to have transcribed a number of Eldridge solos to help Gillespie in his self-appointed task; at the age of twenty he was still quite under the spell of his master, a situation which reveals itself to be of no small importance when the relatively rapid development of Parker, Bud Powell and Fats Navarro is considered. Like Thelonious Monk—to judge from the 1941 transcriptions, where the pianist features a style reminiscent of Teddy Wilson's—Gillespie not only had a thorough grounding in the swing idiom, but, in contrast to Charlie Parker, when the three years' age difference is considered, was also slow at first to evolve from the style. The altoist's early recorded solos, as on the McShann band's *Swingmatism* and *Hootie Blues*, made before his twenty-first birthday, testify to a very personal manner. At the same age Gillespie's work still showed the considerable influence of Roy Eldridge. Perhaps it is only a question of a score of months or so, and perhaps it would be wrong to overstress the point, but his steadier growth towards an individual mode of expression points to the differences in temperament between the two men which were to be caught in sharper focus in the course of their subsequent recordings and careers. For all his antics on and off the stand, Gillespie's approach was the less intuitive of the two.

After the band returned to the U.S.A., Gillespie left, having decided to become a member of the New York local of the American Federation of Musicians. This necessitated a period of relative musical inactivity, but, once admitted, he rejoined Hill. It was about this time, on May 9th, 1938, to be precise, that his marriage to Lorraine Willis took place.

In September, 1939, he played on a small group recording with several of the contemporary jazz stars, including Hampton, Carter, Hawkins, and Webster. Though his improvisation on the main eights of the first chorus of *Hot Mallets* is rather overshadowed by the elegance of Carter's playing of the release, his is a thoroughly creditable contribution which, in the abundance of notes, an abundance which steers well clear of verbosity, points to his eventual flowering as a highly individual soloist. Late in 1939 he joined Cab Calloway. During the two years he spent with the band he was featured on several recordings, including *Hard Times*, *Bye Bye Blues*, and *Cupid's Nightmare*. These, unfortunately, are unavailable in this country, and at the present writing difficult to acquire elsewhere. This is a great pity as they are very important from the historical standpoint. More readily obtainable, though not issued locally, are the sides taped by a young collector, Jerry Newman, at late night Harlem jam sessions, held at such places as Minton's and Monroe's Uptown House. Both the statements of contemporary observers and the slight recorded evidence point to these after-hours sessions as the breeding ground of the harmonic and rhythmic developments taking place at the time. Before a preponderantly esoteric audience composed mainly of other musicians and cognoscenti, men like Clarke, Monk, Christian and Clyde Hart enjoyed a freedom to experiment which the paying public would never grant. On two versions of *Stardust*, dating from 1941, Gillespie reveals an unforced lyricism, and though his performance is not rich enough in contrasts to compare with his later work, the two performances are pleasant enough without being particularly moving. The same remarks apply to *Kerouac*, taken at mid-tempo, with three sections of trumpet choruses separated by two piano solos by Ken Kersey. Gillespie plays with poise and imagination in a driving style, which, though certainly more restrained, carries echoes of the Eldridge manner. The melodic invention is sustained fairly well throughout this lengthy performance, but its content is neither intense nor versatile enough to continuously engage the listener's emotions. Years later, in a July, 1956, issue of *Downbeat*, Gillespie, subjected to a blindfold test, remarked upon the waywardness of the immature musical mind. 'He must be a very young boy,' he said, speaking of the guitarist Thornel Schwartz, 'because I know when I was younger, I would start playing something and right in the middle of a phrase I'd think of something else that might sound better.' These transcriptions suggest that by the middle of 1941 he had already passed through this stage, for his execution gives no signs of hesitancy. For all the experimental nature of his style—his adventurous harmonic conception was regularly earning him jibes from his current

employer—he seems to have gone forward in a very methodical way, with his ideas never outpacing his technique.

His sojourn in the Calloway band came to a violent end in the autumn of 1941. Wrongly accused—or so Milt Hinton claims—of throwing spitballs onstage, he was incensed enough to draw a knife on Calloway, who was nicked badly in the ensuing fracas. His next job was with Ella Fitzgerald. Lasting only a short while, it was followed by employment in Benny Carter's sextet. At the turn of the year, he temporarily left Carter to tour briefly with Charlie Barnet, and then, soon after the Carter group was disbanded, he joined Les Hite's orchestra. During his stay with the band, he was featured on *Jersey Bounce*, a recording testifying to his continuing evolution. It is rumoured that when Hite wanted to get rid of Gillespie, he hesitated to give him notice outright, being apprehensive of a possible recurrence of the Calloway incident; accordingly, he took the least line of resistance, disbanded altogether, and then signed up the same musicians with the sole exception of Gillespie. If true, this story suggests in no uncertain way that his impact in professional circles was not dependent on musical prowess alone.

His stay in the Millinder band was short-lived, but two twelve-bar choruses on *Little John Special*, extrovert, well-organized, and exciting, emphasize the rapid strides he was making: the last four bars are exceptionally impressive for his technical mastery.

Disgruntled, perhaps, by the paucity of work available, Gillespie returned to Philadelphia to work with a local trio. His next band job was with Hines, and lasted until September, 1943. The Hines band of the day was in many ways a nucleus of young jazz talent, including as it did Parker, Benny Harris, and Oscar Pettiford. Billy Eckstine was working with the band, and his popularity ensured its success with the audiences. Sarah Vaughan, recently discovered by Eckstine, was an additional attraction, and these two vocalists not only guaranteed the band's solvency, but also shared the enthusiasm felt by most of the sidemen for the new forms. The story that describes how Gillespie persuaded Oscar Pettiford to carry his bass through a snowstorm, so that they could play in a private jam session together, typifies this enthusiasm. Milt Hinton, too, has told how, when he and Dizzy were together in the Calloway

179

band, they would experiment together in the interval between shows. Anecdotes such as these do more than demonstrate the eager integrity of the men concerned; they underline the hard work and constant practice vital to the creation of the music which was to follow.

With Eckstine strongly featured, the group was making good money, but when offers for his services began to be made by other leaders, Hines's booking agency decided to have the singer make a solo career: the result was that Hines transformed his complete orchestra in an effort to compensate for this loss, adding a female string section to make a total of about thirty pieces. It is hardly surprising that Gillespie left the band soon afterwards. His three-week-long sojourn in the Ellington band, which he joined in October, 1943, was not, however, a successful one. On reflection, it is difficult to imagine a less likely combination. The typical Ellingtonian performance offered no scope to a revolutionary such as the trumpeter in many ways was at this time. The large groups he had previously been featured with had not shared his ideas to any vast extent, but the solo space he commanded had enabled him to put his own aims into practice, even though they might have been mistrusted by the majority of his colleagues. It was in this way that he had managed to go his own original way since his first important job with Teddy Hill. Calloway, like many of Gillespie's employers, may have found his explorations distasteful, but the concept of all these bands, less decidedly orchestral than Ellington's, did not inhibit the trumpeter's expression to anything like the same degree. Furthermore, the experience he gained from 1937 to 1943 was a very definite asset to his future development. Quite apart from the wide general knowledge he had gained in this way, he must also have acquired a sense of confidence, trust in the emotional power music can have over the audience. There is no gainsaying the fact that he had met with widespread opposition in his efforts to attain an original mode of expression: but at the same time, he had seen again and again that musician and listener can share the same artistic experience, and that this experience can be fertilized anew by their common participation.

It is natural that the debt Gillespie owes to the music of his immediate forerunners has been largely neglected. That emphasis should have been placed upon the respects in which his style differed from previous trumpet styles should be no cause for surprise when one thinks of the contrasts in tone, rhythmic approach, and harmonic bases involved. Nevertheless, the debt is no imaginary one. There are grounds for assuming that the strained, nervous quality found in the work of many of the younger modernists is the upshot of a mistrust of the efficacy of their playing. In a recent interview Donald Byrd spoke of the tremendous confidence exhibited by Fats Navarro, who, it will be recalled, worked for some considerable time in the early 'forties with the bands of Snookum Russell and Andy Kirk. A plethora of recording sessions, for all the financial benefits involved, will not necessarily provide the artistic incentive required for the creation of music representative of a man's talent, and it is to Byrd's credit that he has been ready to recognize this. At the same time he has unwittingly emphasized, some fifteen years or so later, the beneficial influence the big bands of an earlier period had upon the young musicians of the time, an influence which transcended all question of style, and one by which Gillespie, like so many of his contemporaries, profited to a significant degree.

It is readily apparent that though he gained a great deal from his apprenticeship in the big bands Gillespie could scarcely have continued to evolve in such an environment. The few recordings extant from this period of his career show that his rhythmic approach called even more vehemently than his harmonic ideas for a new and more suitable setting. This could be more easily found with the small group of up to six musicians than with a larger aggregation, where a more rigid routine is invariably called for to ensure cohesiveness. The opportunity arrived not long after he left Hines; the dearth of competent musicians, caused by the war, had meant a greater availability of work for those who had not been affected, and this resulted indirectly in Gillespie and Oscar Pettiford being asked to form a unit to play at the Onyx, a 52nd Street club. Comprising Don Byas, George Wallington, and Max Roach, in addition to the co-leaders, the group was the first to offer a regular outlet in downtown New York to the ideas which had been crystallizing since the beginning of the decade in the various big bands and the different Harlem after-hours rendezvous.

The group as such did not record, but there is consolation in that Coleman Hawkins, who had much sympathy for the innovations of the pioneers, used all the members of the quintet, George Wallington excepted, to form the nucleus of a band assembled purely for the studio. One peculiarity of this group was that although it contained a three-strong trumpet section no trombonists were used; the explanation is the very simple one that it was exceedingly difficult to obtain the services of trombonists proficient enough to interpret the intricate passages the scores would doubtless have presented. *Bu-Dee-Daht*, composed by Bud Johnson, who played baritone on the date, was one of the three performances—*Woody'n You* and *Disorder at the Border* were the others—which were not given over to Hawkins alone. On *Bu-Dee-Daht* Gillespie takes eight solo bars in confident manner and also plays over the ensemble towards the end of the performance. His tone is full and rounded, his execution above criticism. An outstanding feature of both this side and *Yesterdays* is the superb work of Hawkins himself, who, if quality is any guide, was eminently satisfied with this setting. His forceful interpretation of the Kern ballad must have been a tremendous inspiration to the younger musicians present.

When Don Byas left the quintet, he was replaced by Bud Johnson. The experimental nature of the group's music is shown by the fact that Johnson and Pettiford reputedly suggested that the trumpeter should write out some of his improvisations so that they might be played in unison by the two wind instruments: it is accordingly to be assumed that previous to this solo sequences had been the absolute rule. This was of relatively small importance—and, furthermore, even desirable when the need to develop the relationship between solo voice and accompaniment is borne in mind—but the time was imminent when the dictates of a big band, composed in the main by the members of the embryonic modern school, would enforce a more developed form of organization. In retrospect, it is strange that within months of the first modernist small group being formed, a big band should have been assembled with roughly the same musical objectives in view, but this, thanks to the vicissitudes of public taste and the persuasive powers of Billy Eckstine, was what actually happened.

The vocalist, who had been alternating with Gillespie's group at the Onyx, using John Malachi on piano and the Gillespie rhythm, had not been particularly successful since leaving Hines, and booker Billy Shaw, to whom he was introduced by John Hammond, suggested that he front a band. After some discussion, it was decided that the policy should be a frankly modernist one, and Eckstine therefore set out to assemble a group made up of men favourably disposed toward the new style. The trumpet section was to be led by Gillespie, who was also, to many people's amazement, appointed musical director of the orchestra. It should, however, be remembered that although his name had long since become a byword for foolery of every description, the dizziness of his character, or at least the front he presented, did not apply to his musical activities. He had been writing arrangements since his stint with Calloway, and also had a number of compositions to his credit. It is interesting to note that Eckstine, who presumably has no axe to grind on this matter, has gone out of his way to state that Gillespie deserves much of the credit for the transcription and organization of the melodic fragments which occurred in the spontaneous extemporization of his colleagues. Though this may very well be so, his début in his new position of responsibility was highly inauspicious. After three weeks' rehearsal, the orchestra was scheduled to make its first public appearance in Wilmington, Delaware; but he fell asleep on the train and travelled on to Washington while the band played its opening date without him.

It was not until the turn of the year that he left Eckstine to form a small group and many of the records the band made reflect his ideas and superb section work, though few feature him in solo passages of any length. *Opus X*, recorded on December 5th, 1944, has eight bars from him in free, attacking style, and also contains a fluent alto contribution by John Jackson, Bird's erstwhile partner with McShann. It is reported that after the initial mishaps—for the first week there was no regular drummer, as Shadow Wilson had been conscripted—Gillespie worked hard, doing his best to fill any vacancies that occurred in the line-up. Touring with Eckstine's band in such a prominent capacity must have made him known to many enthusiasts, and the reputation he acquired in this way may well have been a definite asset to the big-band ventures he was to mount in the years to come.

Back in New York City with a small group that included Parker, he was quick to profit from the interest which had grown in the new style, now popularly known as *bebop*, from the supposed resemblance of this neologism to the characteristic phrasing. On February 9th, 1945, he cut two sides with a group including Dexter Gordon and Shelly Manne; the first, *Groovin' High*, was rejected, but *Blue 'n Boogie* found its way on to the market. After piano and tenor contributions, Gillespie begins his solo with a scream—this was a favourite device of his at the time: it occurs again in *Shaw 'Nuff*—and then composes himself to play four choruses of intricate but relaxed music, of which the second is particularly remarkable. During the spring of 1945, he appeared on numerous sessions, including some where one might hardly have expected to find him. *Evil Gal Blues*, recorded on April 14th, and featuring blues singer Albinia Jones backed by Don Byas's Swing Seven, has one chorus of his trumpet work, broad-toned yet incisive; he also played on a session held about the same time on which the band, nominally led by Clyde Hart, played a subsidiary role to the vocal talents of Trummy Young and Rubberlegs Williams. One of the most valuable sides is *Sorta Kinda*, which contains, in addition to some good tenor accompaniment by Don Byas, a chorus chase shared by Gillespie and Charlie Parker. *Seventh Avenue*, also recorded at this date, has sixteen bars of typically poised trumpet. Gillespie also played on two recording sessions featuring Sarah Vaughan: on *Mean to Me*, from the second of these, held on May 25th, he takes an excellent eight bars. The jubilant mood of his playing here is similar to that of his work on *Interlude*, a record from another Vaughan session. On the instrumental sides of the same period, on which he is generously featured, his work is not so overtly emotional, though its spryness, evident even in the most involved passages, shows how strangely his musical disposition differed from Parker's.

Apart from the date for the Manor company on which Gillespie, Byas, and Trummy Young had the support of a rhythm section made up of Clyde Hart, Oscar Pettiford and Shelly Manne, and which produced four excellent performances, including a remarkable *Good Bait*, there are three more important sessions from the first half of 1945 which prove that Gillespie was already a musician possessed of a cohesive and original style. The same qualities of instrumental confidence mark the playing of Parker, who was present on all three occasions. The records made for Guild on February 29th confirm that the excellence of his work on the solitary side to be issued from the first session for the same company was no fortunate coincidence, but an accurate reflection of his contemporary attainments. Each performance has particularly engaging features over and above the very high musical level. *Groovin' High*, based on the chords of *Whispering*, has a superb coda from the trumpeter; *Dizzy Atmosphere* offers a splendid unison variation of the basic riff theme; and *All the things you are* is notable for the consistency of the nostalgic mood evoked, though one senses that Gillespie, in his last eight solo bars, finds it an exacting task to impose the necessary restraint upon his natural exuberance. On the second of these sessions, which took place on May 11th, featuring the same two hornmen, his playing is very similar in mood and style. *Salt Peanuts*, whose characteristic phrase is to be found on the Millinder record of *Little John Special* already mentioned, contains a suitably nonsensical lyric sung by Dizzy; while the other three tunes emphasize his versatility. On *Lover Man* he fills in admirably behind Sarah Vaughan's vocal and also plays in mute the release following the initial chorus, prolonging the languorous mood by the use of sustained notes executed with a minimum of vibrato. *Shaw 'Nuff*, a dedication to his agent, and *Hot House* have exciting trumpet passages, particularly the former, in which his multi-noted phrases have the irresistible attraction of the clown's acrobatic bonhomie. The virtuosity he displayed at this time was always directed to a logical end; criticism has frequently been made that his deployment of extravagant devices served no significant purpose, but at this stage of his career the great majority of his solos are very well conceived: their homogeneity brings out the brashness of his character in a way which does no injury whatsoever to the musical fabric. Content, means and construction find suitable reconciliation throughout his recorded work of the time. Nor was the context of stylistically similar musicians a prerequisite of this unity; the third purely instrumental session on which both he and Bird appeared featured a band composed in the main by musicians whose reputations had already been made. On performances such as *Congo Blues*, *Hallelujah* and *Get Happy* Gillespie plays coherent, exciting and intricate solos with an enviably precise blend of relaxation and attack. Rather than being unnerved by their musical surrounds, Parker and he seem inspired to produce their finest form: the fast riff they play together at the end of *Congo Blues* characterizes the confidence they exhibit on every side. There can be little doubt that they were resolved to outshine the other musicians present, and even less that for the most part they succeeded in doing so. The assurance of Teddy Wilson and Flip Phillips is always impressive, but Red Norvo—the nominal leader—is often overshadowed. All the same, it is well to remember that the general superiority of the younger men here rests not on the complexity of their playing alone, but, more specifically, on the enthusiasm and emotional power they display.

The summer of 1945 saw the formation of Gillespie's first big band. His appearances with his unit at the Three Deuces and Spotlite clubs had been most successful and it was now thought opportune to assemble a large group for touring purposes. Walter Fuller wrote the arrangements for this band, which included at the outset musicians who were later to achieve their own solo reputations, among them Kinney Dorham and Charlie Rouse. The package comprised comedians and a vocalist, which should have helped towards its financial stability, but the itinerary was ill-chosen. The conditions under which the orchestra was forced to work and travel in the southern states entailed frequent changes of personnel as the sidemen left to return to the north; moreover—and this should surely have been foreseen by the agents concerned—the audiences were unimpressed by the repertoire. Gillespie was obliged to play the style of music demanded, which meant that he was unable to feature Fuller's scores. In New York, where the jazz audience had had time to become accustomed to the melodies, harmonies, and rhythms of the new style, the music of Gillespie's orchestra would have been understood; elsewhere in the U.S.A., especially in the south, a band was primarily expected to cater for the dancers. The orchestra was ill suited, temperamentally and musically, to play the functional role expected of it. The direct form of communication supplied by the Negro bands of the 'thirties, such as those led by Lunceford, Basie, McShann, and so on, had little place in the aesthetic of the new jazz generation. Until the American audiences at large had been persuaded, with the help of palliatives such as comic hats and scat vocals, to accept the new style on grounds other than the traditional ones, the formation of a large orchestra of this kind was a precarious venture. Reports would indicate that even today, almost fifteen years later, the situation is hardly any better in this respect. Bop, as a novelty, has been dead since 1950, and the Negro audience which supported the jazzmen of the 'twenties and 'thirties now finds its entertainment in the sphere of rhythm and blues and spirituals.

Back in New York in the closing months of 1945, he took part in a session for the Savoy company held on November 26th under Parker's name and featuring the trumpet playing of Miles Davis. The precise extent of Gillespie's participation is in doubt. There is general agreement that he is present on both takes of *Ko Ko,* and few would question that Miles Davis is the trumpet soloist on *Billie's Bounce* and *Now's the Time;* the tune about which there is considerable dissension is *Thrivin' from a Riff,* destined to be recorded again by Gillespie three months later under the title of *Anthropology.* There are certainly similarities of phrasing between the trumpet passages on all three takes of this theme and those on *Now's the Time* and *Billie's Bounce,* but in view of slight tonal differences and the more consistently assured execution and construction, it would seem likely that Gillespie had replaced Davis by the time these three performances of *Thrivin' from a Riff* were recorded. The melodic similarity is none the less surprising, and suggests that if Gillespie was in fact the featured trumpeter, his intention was to hoodwink prospective buyers of the record into believing that they were listening to Miles Davis. From what we know of Gillespie's sense of humour, this seems in no way out of the question.

It was most unfortunate for all involved that Gillespie's next booking after the failure of his large group should be just as unsuccessful. Whatever the merits of the music produced there today, America's West Coast in late 1945 was virgin territory as far as bop was concerned. Appearing at Billy Berg's club in Hollywood, Gillespie's group encountered an uninterested and even hostile audience. The sides Gillespie and Parker made with a group led by Slim Gaillard soon after their arrival in California make interesting comparison with those cut by the same musicians in the following year. Parker was at this time subject to the periodic illnesses, induced by his addiction to drugs and alcohol and aggravated by dismal living conditions and public obliquity, which were eventually to lead to his collapse and subsequent confinement to the Camarillo Hospital, so it is not to be wondered at if his 1946 recordings reveal him as a sick and embittered person. On the other hand, Gillespie, through all the difficulties of his years of experimentation, had never sounded so dispirited as on the February 7th, 1946, date made for Ross Russell's Dial company. Both takes of *Dynamo,* for instance, have typically brash contributions from him, occasionally too brash for comfort, as his note separation is far from exemplary; even more to the point is his unusual tone, which takes on, even at this tempo, a pleading quality reminiscent at times of Fats Navarro's later recordings. These characteristics, though less marked, are also found in his work on the Jazz at the Philharmonic transcriptions dating from January 29th. The double-tempo passage found toward the end of *The Man I Love* is especially similar to his playing on the Dial session. In terms of content, his work on these two occasions must rank with his least typical. Yet while it is not up to the same level as that of the previous year, the music gives valuable insight into the problems facing the new school; the frustrations evoked here were to make their unhappy mark on countless records by other modernists, though they were seldom again to find comparable expression in the trumpeter's own playing.

For those who doubt the validity of this comparison between December, 1945, and February, 1946, sessions, there can be no better answer than to point to the four sides recorded for Victor immediately upon the band's return east. These records have trumpet solos of such attack, precision of execution, and logic, that they belong with the finest jazz recorded on the instrument. The setbacks of the Hollywood expedition, the lack of public interest, the interdiction on the issue of the Kern compositions recorded with strings, and the clash with Slim Gaillard, whose group was the alternating one at Berg's, find no reflection here. The clipped, joyous intricacy of Gillespie's chorus on *Anthropology*, with its long phrase extending into the release, is typical in form and spirit of his work elsewhere on the session. *Ol' Man Rebop* has twenty-four bars of less complicated though quite as typical trumpet improvisation. *Night in Tunisia* and *52nd Street Theme* show most clearly of all his phenomenal control in the high register. Objection has been taken to J. C. Heard's presence in the rhythm section, and theoretically this is justified, since his drumming, excellent as it is, has few of the characteristics of the new school; but though he makes little attempt to accompany and underline the soloist's lines, in the manner of a Kenny Clarke or a Max Roach, his work, flexible and swinging, provides a sure basis for the trumpeter's melodies, and seems in no way to hinder the latter's invention. Gillespie ensures a plenitude of melodic interest by contrasting straightforward details, such as the slightly adapted quotation found at the start of his solo on *Anthropology*, with the

most complex runs, dependent on the harmonic extensions he had helped to introduce over the preceding five years. From this standpoint, it is instructive to compare his work on *52nd Street Theme* with the guitar solo by Bill de Arango which precedes it. Gillespie's playing here represents in a variety of respects the zenith of his development. It is not implied that his subsequent work is inevitably less valuable by virtue of this, though few of his recording sessions have found him in such consistently fine form. Since the mid-forties he has widened the scope of his playing in several ways, notably in his greater use of tonal effects. None the less, all the principal characteristics of his formed style are already present, in a thoroughly integrated manner.

A further recording session, held some three months later, marked Gillespie's début under contract to the Musicraft company, and, a more cogent point, featured a rather more uniform personnel. With Sonny Stitt on alto and Kenny Clarke on drums, the unit made four excellent sides. Perhaps their most striking feature was the playing of the young altoist, who seemed not in the least overawed by his musical environment. The only apparent evolution in Gillespie's approach is his slightly more lyrical manner, induced by a return to the comparatively broader tone he had used on most of his recording sessions of the previous year.

Soon afterwards, Gillespie once again formed a big band. On this occasion he was to find the good fortune which had eluded him a year before. In the interim, modern jazz had gained a wider following; its adherents were no longer to be found in New York alone. The diffusion of the new style by way of records, the touring band of Billy Eckstine, and, the point must not be missed, the lengthy if financially disastrous travels of Gillespie himself had created a situation considerably more favourable to a second orchestral venture. On commercial and musical planes the trumpeter had at last arrived: just as he had played his part over the years in nurturing a public willing to accept the new jazz, so had he managed to weld the embryonic features of a personal style into a thoroughly satisfying mode of original expression. His obvious desire to reorganize a big band, therefore, seems a trifle surprising. Yet, the monetary angle aside, this was the wisest course; for all his splendid technical and inventive powers, his work lacked the tremendous emotional appeal of Parker's work; without this impetus his style might quickly have degenerated, in the confines of the small group, into a collection of polished mannerisms. With the large orchestra, he was to continue his experimentation, not within purely personal boundaries, but governed by the framework of the band as a whole: and by so doing he was to ensure the continuing vitality of his solo playing.

The first two sides the orchestra recorded—*Our Delight* and *Good Dues Blues*—both show that Gillespie, unlike the majority of improvising musicians, finds it easy to relax with a big band behind him. On the former side, there is bite to his high register work, but simultaneously the slight extra tonal contrast in middle and lower registers is abetted by a wider use of rests than had formerly been the case in his solo construction: both features ensure greater light and shade in his playing. Similarly, his solo on the vocal side is aggressive, yet, at the same time, speaks of a control not restricted to his instrument alone. The second session, which took place on July 9th, 1946, a month or so later, confirms

Melody Maker

The trumpeter, young and debonair, in reflective mood

185

Melody Maker. Photograph by 'Popsie'

Gillespie's imagination goes hand in hand with his involvement
in the music

these remarks: Gillespie was possessed of a temperament self-contained enough to allow him to play, at one moment, phrases of sufficient volume and trenchancy to be audible above the band's riffing, and, at the next, notes of the most delicate timbre. It is this contrast, source of a consistent air of the unexpected, which plays the major part in engaging and holding the listener's attention. It is not suggested that so important an element had been altogether absent from his earlier recordings; but on these first records with a big band, it was made more effective by the increased use of

silences. The point is borne out by the solo trumpet on *He Beeped when he Shoulda Bopped*, though this performance is rendered memorable, in quite accidental manner, by the incongruous enunciation of the singer, Alice Roberts. At times her voice seems to take on, in its quest for the ultimate in sophistication, an eerie, almost Roedean-like quality, strangely at variance with the brashness of the ensemble.

The band recorded only once more in 1946, at a session held in mid-November, when two sides, *Emanon* and

I Waited for You, were made. It was not until the late August of 1947 that it was again to enter the studio, and by then some significant changes had occurred, both in the general style and the leader's soloing. On the whole, the conception favoured on its first eight records had been a far from revolutionary one: the problems facing the arrangers arose principally from the need to find a suitable setting, adapted from the intimate, small-group bop style, in which the soloist would be able to give his imagination full play without endangering the cohesion of the performance. The result was that while melodic and harmonic resources of the modern school were exploited up to a point, its developments in the rhythmic sphere were mostly ignored. The resulting sound was not so very different from that produced by the Basie band of the early 'forties. Section was deployed against section rather than a more involved musical texture being devised; and though it would be untrue to claim that subtlety was altogether non-existent, the band's appeal stemmed in the main from its blatant force and seemingly inexhaustible power. This can be attributed only to the temperaments of the sidemen; such is their power of instant involvement that one is persuaded to believe they would have been incapable of a more restrained or modulated performance. This suggestion finds a measure of support from the recording of *Things to Come*, the Fuller score which aroused much interest at the time. The orchestra, though quite uninhibited by the technical demands made upon it, sounds far less effective here than in the more open ensemble style of *Ray's Idea*. This stricture points to the wisdom of the more traditional approach. The compromise effected was, all things considered, the best solution.

Throughout 1946 and 1947 the band steadily increased its popularity, often drawing large crowds at venues where it had previously enjoyed no success. The widespread publicity which surrounded it, distasteful as it often was, must have been a great commercial asset to the group, but its influence upon jazz as a whole was regrettable. In much the same way as Benny Goodman had been fêted in the 'thirties, the Kenton, Herman, and Gillespie orchestras were hailed in some influential quarters as the newest and thus the only important exponents of American jazz. Furthermore, in the case of the last of these groups, the sartorial eccentricities favoured by the musicians were soon confused in the public mind with the music itself. The most flagrant absurdities about *bebop* were perpetrated in the press and on the radio. The upshot was that when the fever died down, Gillespie and his band were not the only losers. A large proportion of the public which had supported his appearances had been attracted by the ephemeral lure of the incidental trappings rather than by the quality of the music itself.

Until 1949, however, it seemed that the melting away of the dancers, whose support had been a *sine qua non* of the survival of previous bands, presented no insoluble problem. In 1946 and 1947 the orchestra found regular employment; moreover, the consistently high musical level seems to have been maintained, as is shown by the August 22nd session of the latter year, when the first recordings for the Victor company were made. All four sides show that a greater polish had been acquired without any detriment to the swing and explosive power conspicuous on the 1946 records. It is interesting to compare *Stay On It* with the previously recorded *Our Delight*, both compositions being by Tad Dameron. Not only does the band achieve a better internal balance in its interpretation of the former score, but the arrangement itself is more compact. Another point is that John Lewis's *Two Bass Hit*, which he was later to expand into the composition known as *La Ronde*, makes more play with rhythmic possibilities than most of the previous sides. The bop vocals on *Oo-Pop-a-Da*, which contains a scat chase between the leader and Kenny Hagood, represent one of the strongest elements in the group's commercial appeal, but it would be foolish to take exception to the record on this account. Gillespie's singing is more than acceptable as an expression of his personality, while his soloing here, as on all the sides made, is superb. Deriving, as it were, the maximum of inspiration from his musical surrounds, he gives vent to what can only be described as a spirit of ferocious optimism in such a balanced and tasteful way that the accusations of exhibitionism which have been levelled against him seem worse than misleading.

The eight sides produced by two further recording dates which took place in the last fortnight of 1947 evince much the same characteristics as those discussed above. *Cool Breeze* and *Ool-Ya-Koo*, like *Oo-Pop-a-Da*, explain in part the popular appeal without concealing the very real jazz qualities; *Good Bait*, though containing some stilted trombone work, illustrates the leader's great melodic gifts in a short though highly effective solo. Yet perhaps the most memorable aspect of these eight performances, taken as a whole, is the drumming of Chano Pozo, the Cuban virtuoso who was to die, knifed in a brawl, the following year. His remarkable playing on *Algo Bueno* behind Gillespie, not to mention his own features such as *Manteca*, and *Cubana Be*, with its companion piece *Cubana Bop*, proves how valuable an addition he was to the band. It was not merely that such versatile rhythmic support provided extra colour: his super-abundant energy appeared to inspire the musicians to blow with the maximum of attack. The employment of a Cuban drummer, especially of so talented an artist as he, had supplied the third dimension—the intricate rhythmic interest—lacked by the orchestra of the previous year. Owing to this, and also, in part, to the more closely knit arrangements, the twelve performances recorded in the latter half of 1947 remain as the best examples of the group's studio work.

Shortly after the last of these three sessions, the orchestra left the U.S.A. for a tour of the Scandinavian countries. After several appearances the Swedish promoter is reported to have absconded, leaving the sidemen and Gillespie himself in a highly delicate financial position. In a despairing gesture, the musicians embarked on a ship bound for Antwerp, where upon their arrival the Hot Club de Belgique managed to organize some concerts. From here they travelled on to Paris to fulfil a hastily arranged engagement at the Salle Pleyel. Though a Customs dispute meant that the curtain rose over an hour late, the band made a profound impression on a packed auditorium, and its success, together with the ensuing publicity, made possible the arrangement of several more dates, including appearances at a cinema and two night clubs, in addition to two further concerts at the Salle Pleyel. At the first of these, held on February 22nd, the programme was recorded for eventual issue on the Swing label. The transcriptions, despite their shortcomings, make it possible to glean some idea of the band's immense power, and thus explain the unusual impression made on the Parisian audiences. One especially thrilling moment occurs towards the close of *Round About Midnight*, when the leader carves out a memorable line high above the ensemble. Chano Pozo's magnificent conga work is another unforgettable feature of the concert, while the saxophone solos are of considerable merit. Besides Paris, the orchestra also gave concerts in Marseilles and Lyons: the success of these, as of most of the others, enabled the band's agent, Billy Shaw, to facilitate its return to the States.

The most remarkable aspect of the French tour was that success had been achieved despite the flimsiest preparation. It is true that the widespread publicity which followed the band's début brought this welcome situation about, but much of the credit must go, in the first place, to the musicians themselves, who, despite fatigue and frustrations, scored brilliantly with their initial audience. Another point worth mentioning is the enviable receptivity of the musical public, all the more surprising when one considers that Parker or Gillespie discs had a severely limited circulation in France at the time.

Back in the States, response remained as favourable as before the tour. The album made in August at the Pasadena Auditorium, Los Angeles, by promoter Gene Norman contains a programme of great interest both from solo and group standpoints. The band functions as a single force: its cohesion is such that it becomes impossible to think of it as a collection of individual musicians. No detailing of the actual musical substance in the form of melodies and rhythms could ever convey the contagious enthusiasm displayed. Gillespie's tone is trenchant as never before, the excitement he generates irresistible. No one could doubt the utter involvement of the audience, nor the spur this must have represented for leader and sidemen alike. It is very probable, though, that the confidence familiarity with the routines had given the musicians had removed any remaining vestiges of technical uncertainty. Moreover, Gillespie's knowledge of the stock arrangements had in no way stultified his talent, as might have been feared, but, on the contrary, had afforded his invention more scope. In *Stay On It* his solo line is beautifully integrated with the patterns punched out by brass and reeds. The eight performances transcribed remain as the finest testament to the group led by the trumpeter between 1946 and 1950: the changes of personnel never seemed, until 1949 at least, to affect adversely the tremendous spirit which informs all its recorded playing, and which was never more evident than upon this occasion.

The ensuing months saw a slow but certain decline in the standard of the band's work. *Lover Come Back to Me*, from a date held in the last few days of 1948, has its moments, but the overall effect is a rather mannered one, with the sudden tempo changes too contrived for reasonable continuity. *Swedish Suite* and *Katy*, from dates held the following spring, show that the conception was becoming increasingly sophisticated. The Fuller composition, including a spirited trumpet solo, was not very far below the level of the best previous performances, but the imagination displayed in the writing cannot quite atone for an undeniable loss of interpretative fire. *Katy* is less impressive: the stylized manner in which the piano echoes the trumpet phrases, not to mention the glutinous trombone passage, are representative weaknesses. Yet if the last of the Victor sides are largely inferior, those made for the Capitol company at the end of the year, and, at a second session, in January 1950, are simply not to be compared with the main body of the group's recordings. *You Stole My Wife*, a trite vocal in whose lyric the enthusiast may care to look for a deeper meaning, has a fair trumpet solo but is otherwise no more remarkable than any other commercial performance of the day; as for *Say When*, the lack of imagination in the writing and the listlessness of the section playing must be heard to be believed. It is truly a saddening experience to listen to records such as these when one is aware of the potential of the orchestra, which, though numerous replacements had been made, was still composed of gifted musicians. The day after the second of these sessions, Gillespie was featured in the Metronome All-Stars recording; it is perhaps significant that his contribution is not as arresting as might have been expected. His efforts to disguise his musical origins, with the end of the economically favourable period when his orchestra had flourished, had been unsuccessful. The Capitol sides show that it could not emulate the slickness, vital to public approval, of its rivals in the field; worse still, the attempt to move away from an outright jazz conception had meant that the music played was of negligible value. The romance was over; Gillespie was finally forced to disband.

The dissolution of the orchestra was no unique contemporary event: Basie, Charlie Barnet, and Woody Herman were other leaders who had found themselves obliged to do likewise. The repercussions of the situation, too, were not wholly regrettable. Gillespie's appearances on record over the past four years had been almost completely restricted to those with his own band. Apart from one or two rare transcriptions, all his work of the period falls into this category. The surrounds of the small group were now to give fuller exposure to his soloing, and also to make him rely, to a greater degree, upon the resources of his trumpet work, in terms of tone, volume, and range, to arrest and hold the attention of the audience.

In the summer of 1950, Norman Granz, that much-criticized paternalist of American record and concert fields, brought about a musical reunion of Charlie Parker and Dizzy Gillespie at a studio session. Thelonious Monk was the pianist on the date, Curly Russell the bassist, and Buddy Rich—not the ideal choice, despite his unquestioned drive and swing—was on drums. The two hornmen had made only the briefest of appearances together on record since the 1945 Guild sides, and those mainly in the form of Metronome All-Star dates, where the policy of giving everyone solo space had usually meant, in the confines of the three-minute record, a thoroughly incomplete display of the musical talent available. It must be admitted that Gillespie's work on the date is not notable for its consistency. On several of the numbers his note separation is not of the same standard found in his playing with the big band. This is most evident, as might be foreseen, at faster tempo, as in take three of *Leapfrog*. For the previous four years he had been accustomed to using very high notes to soar above the ensemble: the difficulties of adapting himself to a small band conception, with the advisability of a more balanced employment of phrases throughout the range of the instrument, are hinted at by the unattractive blurred effect given by his middle register execution on the third version of *An Oscar for Treadwell*. In compensation for the shortcomings, one can point to the pleasing use of emphasis in the second eight bars of his chorus on take three of *Relaxin' with Lee*; the development of his solo towards a more austere style in take four of *Mohawk*; and the inventive agility of his playing on the fourth take of *Leapfrog*, considerably better than its predecessor in this connexion. On a good half of the performances the duel between Bird and himself—no one could doubt the rivalry that finds expression here—ends in a draw, with his constructive and technical powers standing him in good stead; but on the blues, and on *Melancholy Baby*, too, where Parker plays superbly, the altoist's tremendous projective force tends to make him sound ornate, perhaps even evasive. That the value of a jazz soloist's work is not to be adjudged on the grounds of his rhythmic, melodic, tonal, or harmonic capacities alone, nor even upon a consideration of all these four, unless it turn upon the meanings of their various relations, is abundantly illustrated by these performances.

A session for Prestige, including some of the musicians—Milt Jackson and Percy Heath were two—who regularly composed the small band he led in 1950 and 1951, took place on September 16th. None of these records is at all outstanding. From the overall viewpoint, however, there might well be grounds for considering them superior to those made with Johnny Richards' orchestra six weeks or so later; certainly the music, whatever the level of the separate contributions, is more integrated than on these later sides with their string accompaniments, a novel enough idea, but tedious for the want of any real imagination. Gillespie's lines are unfailingly melodic and beautifully played: unlike his other work of the period which offers some support for his contention that a bicycle accident that took place in 1949 had restricted his range. At their best, the records offer a curious attraction. Such is the case with *Swing Low Sweet Chariot*, which boasts a vocal and bongo drumming, in addition to strings and a delightful trumpet passage.

In 1951 Gillespie founded his own record firm in an alleged attempt to escape the impositions made upon him in the course of his work for other companies. Dee Gee Records—such was the title—was principally a means of selling the recordings made by his own band, but sides were also issued by the Milt Jackson quartet. At the first session, held in Detroit on March 1st, some excellent music was played. *Tin Tin Daeo*, credited jointly to Walter Fuller and the late Chano Pozo, offers some restrained trumpet in a highly suitable setting, while *Birks Works*, a blues, has for its initial eight bars the theme later recorded by Barney Kessel and called *Salute to Charlie Christian*. Beginning in sombre reflective vein, the leader quotes at the start of his second chorus without breaking the mood; the smooth yet muffled tone he gets here was said to have been obtained by the use of a beret pierced with holes as a mute.

It is hard to visualize, within the bounds of the same idiom, a distinction as pronounced as that which exists between these two performances and *The Champ*, recorded only a month and a half later. This up-tempo blues riff has solos from Gillespie, Milt Jackson, and Jay Jay Johnson, as well as a final set of choruses by Bud Johnson which call to mind the wilder moments of Illinois Jacquet. The rhythm section is brilliant throughout, but the synthetic flavour of the closing tenor choruses tends to disguise the quality of the preceding solos. Other recordings made by Gillespie in the same year would suggest that a deliberately frantic atmosphere was engineered on this occasion in order to give a commercial fillip to Dee Gee Records. That Dizzy was eager that his company should stay solvent is indicated by the profusion of vocals on the sides made in 1951. Jo Carroll is featured on most of these, including *I'm in a Mess*, which, besides a pleasant enough vocal, has eight bars of ensemble reminiscent of the leader's 1945 group, and a solo of equal length conspicuous for the exact sense of time and unusually mellow tone. The trumpet playing on *They Can't Take that away from Me* and *Oo-Shoo-Be-Doo-Be* shares these advantages, as it does on *The Bluest Blues*, taken at a slightly slower pace than its Salle Pleyel sequel. On this last tune, the construction of Gillespie's solo is less complex than normal. Though delightfully humorous in the main, all these performances have their shortcomings: one would wish for longer contributions from the leader, while Bill Graham's baritone work, though spirited and swinging, speaks of a paucity of imagination.

Viewed in perspective, these recordings figure as evidence of Gillespie's varying reactions to the problems caused by the disbandment of his orchestra. The policy he currently favoured was evidently intended to guarantee bookings for his group while at the same time allowing as much scope as possible to strictly musical qualities. It would have been foolish to expect him to return to the closely integrated style which had preceded his big-band venture; quite apart from the altered economic circumstances, his own playing had evolved between 1946 and 1950 towards a virtuoso presentation. With the sudden disappearance of its setting, his solo work had to be adapted to meet the needs of the changed environment. The ensuing evolution was to bear full fruit in the Paris recordings of 1952 and 1953, but the 1950 and 1951 sides are important for the insight they afford into the solutions he devised in a situation which was hardly of his own choosing.

During his visit to the French capital, Gillespie undertook a very strenuous recording programme, as if to compensate for the sporadic activity of the previous two years. Some sides were even made with the string section of the Paris Opera but, despite his consistently tasteful playing, these are no more successful than the 1950 Hollywood performances. Any integration between soloist and accompanying group is strictly coincidental: the music leaps to sudden life each time the trumpet sails joyfully in, only to relapse into the stilted jargon of light music with the conclusion of the improvised passage. The records made with small groups of various personnels and sizes are far better, for on them the leader's temperament is given full rein, so that his expression is hedged in only by the conventional time limit, which is scarcely a restriction in the case of much of the material used. Most compelling of all are the ballads, of which a surprisingly large number were recorded. They show how his soloing had evolved since the demise of his big band in 1950 into a less constantly intense style. His playing is characterized by a wide range of tonal effects, superb control of volume and vibrato, and a strikingly imaginative use of melody. The first two sessions held on March 25th and 27th for the Blue Star and French Vogue companies respectively produced fine trumpet work from the leader, with sympathetic backing from the tenor saxophonist Don Byas, who has been resident in France for some years now. *Hurry Home* and *I Cover the Waterfront* are two of the highlights here, with Gillespie using a quotation from *Undecided* in his rendering of the second tune. Some small group sides were also cut on the same day as the recordings made with the operatic strings, and these too are well worthy of notice, including as they do a version of *Sleepy Time Down South*, interpreted by Gillespie with sensitivity and humour. These two qualities mark nearly all his 1952 sides from the Paris studios. The very personal blend of feeling, though, incurred no awkwardness of expression: despite the high proportion of slow-paced tunes, there is never any trace of monotony. *Everything Happens to Me*, from the April 11th session, is characteristic enough to underline the chief reasons for this. The tentative feel about his playing at the very start takes on an air of hard decision with the increase in volume towards the end of the first eight bars; but this atmosphere

soon disappears, as the tone becomes softer again. Towards the close of the second eight the overt romanticism is abandoned as he suddenly indulges in one of the typical fast runs reminiscent of his up-tempo flights. The contrasts in light and shade which mark the first sixteen bars, with their variations in tone, power and melodic approach, are shown even more markedly in the last half of the performance: the release is played in a way that seems decidedly grotesque when analysed, though the tonal beauty tends to reconcile the disparate elements of the other features of his expression; in the last eight bars, he falls back into a more conventional interpretation. This return to the melody serves as an agreeable interlude between the half-valve effects obtained at the beginning of the middle section, followed as they are by a playful quotation from the introduction to *Shaw 'Nuff*, and the brash yet apt coda set powerfully against the harmonies provided by the accompanying horns. *Everything Happens to Me*, like the majority of the ballads he recorded at this time, demonstrates his skill in weaving together the most unlikely of details to form a convincing whole; the lyrical mode ensures the efficacy of the emotional content, without making the constant, almost obtrusive demand upon the listener's sensibility which is so prominent a feature of the styles of many of the younger Negro musicians active today. At its most forceful, there is a relaxation about all these sides which brings to mind the work of such men as Hawkins, Willie Smith, and Jonah Jones. Gillespie's vocabulary is a different one, but the spirit of his work has more in common with theirs than it has with the relentless attack of a Bill Hardman or the studied understatement of a Tony Fruscella, for all the harmonic similarities.

It is tempting to equate this musical sophistication with the business acumen which has often been attributed to him. The powers of organization evident in his improvisation have also been useful in his financial dealings: he has the reputation of being one of the most astute of jazzmen. An instance of his impatience with some of the absurd decrees of hall managements and suchlike was given during his two Dutch concerts held before his arrival in Paris. Feeling that the order not to play less than a fixed number of minutes was a ridiculous one, he more than once made the tacit

Gillespie singing with the Count Basie Orchestra

protest of bringing the set to a premature end in the middle of a number. While such conduct must have been annoying to the audience, it is understandable and perhaps even commendable when the problem is seen as a whole. As long as the jazzman continues to be forced to earn his living in the atmosphere of exploitation characteristic of the world of commercial entertainment, such manœuvres, trifling as they may be, can deserve no honest reproof.

Gillespie returned to New York towards the end of April, but did not record again until three months later. The sides, cut with his regular group for issue on his own label, and featuring the type of comedy material associated with the band, are certainly of no outstanding interest. All have vocals by Jo Carroll, who is on occasion joined in the same role by the leader. Better than these, though still not approaching his finest work, are the sides made at Birdland for the M.G.M. concern on November 21st of the same year. Of the tunes on which he plays, *How High the Moon* is the most impressive: probably because it was the most suitable to his approach. The choice of *Muskrat Ramble* was induced by the gimmick underlying the session; the modern-styled group was to play the same tunes as the band which in-

Gillespie soloing on the instrument he designed himself and has used since 1954 *Robert Parent*

cluded Jimmy McPartland, Edmond Hall, and Vic Dickenson. The upshot, of course, was that only a proportion of the repertoire was suited to each unit. After a rather strained and self-conscious announcement by Gillespie referring to the 'Battle of Jazz', Max Roach's cymbal sets the tempo, and after a short introductory figure by Ronnie Ball, the English pianist who had only recently emigrated to the States, Gillespie plays in mute a moody rephrasing of the song against a countermelody supplied by Don Elliott on mellophone and Ray Abrams on tenor. After a thrusting solo from the latter, he returns playing open in a far less restrained way, building up the tension with a repetitive figure at the start of his second chorus and maintaining it well until the inevitable introduction of *Ornithology*, the Benny Harris tune modelled on the same chord sequence, brings the performance to a close. *Battle of the Blues* is of a much lower standard. It contains some amusing if negligible riffing, Gillespie beginning his solo with a playful tag from the *Marseillaise* and demonstrating his exceptional range

and power in the final chase choruses. Typical of his technical accuracy is the descending phrase which rounds off this musical burlesque.

Neither of these American 1952 sessions contains trumpet playing of a standard equal to that found on the Parisian dates of the same year. The recorded evidence is meagre, but all the same it suggests that his work had suffered some slight decline; mediocrity is by far too strong a word to describe his performances of the time, but their very average quality when set against his previous production cannot be overlooked. Gillespie has made no secret of his liking for the big band: perhaps these records reflect his dissatisfaction with the economic strictures which made it impossible to form a group larger than his current touring unit; it may be significant that between his two trips to Europe he appeared on only two recording dates: a surprising number in view of his stature. Upon his arrival in Sweden on January 31st, 1953, he was reported to have talked of re-forming a large orchestra, asserting that they were not yet popular enough to allow him to go ahead with his plans.

On his previous year's European tour, when, incidentally, his projected concerts in Stockholm had been cancelled owing to previous commitments, he had worked as a single, appearing with pick-up groups. In Holland he had been accompanied by drummer Wally Bishop's quartet, which included Sandy Mosse and Rob Pronk; for his French concerts he had been supported by a mixed Franco–American contingent; at recording sessions he had employed, among others, Lena Horne's accompanying trio: Arnold Ross, Joe Benjamin, and Billy Clark. On this occasion, however, he had brought his own band, which comprised vocalist Jo Carroll, baritonist Bill Graham, and a rhythm section composed of Wade Legge, Lou Hackney and Al Jones. It is of interest to note that in more than one interview held at the time he spoke of the importance of the beat to jazz and of the risks entailed by a more overtly European approach, with less emphasis upon rhythmic qualities. Since his own style had been only remotely touched by the fashionable trends of the previous two years as exemplified by the whole school of white tenormen, represented by such musicians as Herbie Steward or Stan Getz, it is reasonable to suppose that he was referring to jazz as a whole rather than to his own mode of expression. Not a few of his published statements point to his appreciation of the importance of the beat to good jazz and his own improvisation, even in the most bizarre surrounds, such as the sides cut with strings, demonstrates his adherence to a pronouncedly rhythmic manner. If there are criticisms to be made of the group he brought to Europe, a lack of drive is not one of them. Well received in Stockholm, the band continued its tour, appearing at Helsinki and Copenhagen. The transcription of the concert held at the Salle Pleyel in Paris on February 9th gives an excellent idea of the type of music he was featuring at the time, and throws into relief both its strong and weak points.

There is no contesting the fact that much of the band's production was poor by any musical standards. The rhythmic pulse was never absent, perhaps, but much of the improvisation was obviously inspired by commercial factors. 'I'm not interested any more in going down in history,' Gillespie was reported to have said when he arrived in Hanover during the same tour. 'I want to eat.' This attitude, understandable in view of the precarious economic position of the jazzman, found expression in bop vocal routines such as *Oo-Shoo-Be-Doo-Be*. None the less, there are inevitably passages of value, such as Gillespie's reconciliation of the grotesque and the sublime on *Intermission*; and a few of the sides contain trumpet playing of real sensitivity and charm. *They Can't Take that Away from Me* is the outstanding example here. Of especial appeal is the forceful figure with which Gillespie increases the tempo, changing the mood of the performance from subdued nostalgia to a more extrovert expression of feeling. The work of piano and baritone players is an asset to him here, but humour gets the upper hand in the end, and he finishes with a military-styled quotation as if to forewarn the audience of the coming battery of fierce if undisciplined sound.

After leaving Paris, the band continued its extensive tour, appearing at principal towns and cities in France, Italy and Switzerland. On February 22nd, however, Gillespie was once more in the French capital. He took advantage of his return to take part in two more recording sessions. The first, for the French Vogue company, was held during the afternoon with a group of slightly different composition from his regular one. For some reason or other Bill Graham failed to make an appearance, so the services of Nat Peck, a trombonist resident in Paris, were secured to fill his place. Despite the hurried preparation, with rapid sketching out of trombone parts, this album proved to be in many ways more attractive than the concert transcription of a fortnight or so earlier. Ballads preponderate, as on the dates held a year before, but all in all the results give an accurate portrayal of the band's musical capabilities. *This is the Way* and *Moon Nocturne* each have the trumpeter fashioning a very striking solo with apparent indolence; such obvious gifts for lyrical expression tend to be taken for granted: it should not be forgotten that few jazzmen can treat a song in so personal a way at the same time attaining a compositional level superior to that of the tune as written. Many achieve an individual and convincing projection by virtually rejecting the melody, using the harmonic sequence as a foundation on which to build their own characteristic line; frequently, though, the resulting solo lacks dimension and strength because it is deficient in continuity. This is rarely Gillespie's method: at this session his work has logic and cohesion, both on the slower and faster tunes; and, as distinct from many of the concert renditions, his playing on such a side as *Oo-Bla-Dee*, the entertaining bop novelty piece devised by Mary Lou Williams, never sinks into incongruous exhibitionism.

The same is true of the album made with brass, woodwind and strings, similar in concept to the corresponding session of the previous year. Though the score evokes once again the laboured nostalgia of so much popular light music, the solo trumpet passages rank with the finest technical feats in jazz. The main weakness, as usual, is that the soloist's emotional projection is convincing, while the atmosphere engineered by the arranger is not; yet if the listener can manage to overlook this fundamental failing, he will be impressed by the power, accuracy and good taste of Gillespie's playing. A memorable effect is obtained by his treatment of the first middle-eight in *Stormy Weather*: his use of stop time, together with his earthy tone, is an excellent antidote to the viscous sentimentality of the ensemble, and in more than one respect brings to mind the virtuoso playing of Louis Armstrong. The resemblance is stressed by most of the sides with strings from this session. Like Armstrong, he can be both terse and expansive, rhapsodic and mean in his suggestion of moods; and like him his style is never rendered suspect by affectation.

Gillespie's invention on the two tracks cut with rhythm support alone—*The Way You Look Tonight* and *Undecided* —bears, on the contrary, little similarity to his forerunner's style. He plays tightly muted, and, as befits the muffled yet sometimes trenchant tone he obtains, devises long and involved phrases. The swing is never lost, but the directness and instantaneous appeal of his playing on the other tracks is absent. Except for an inconclusive ending to *Undecided* both are cohesive performances: and this despite the whimsical insertion of a number of quotations in his two solos on *The Way You Look Tonight*. Even the outrageous snippet from *Charmaine* distils its sly humour without damaging the construction. Neither side is immediately striking; neither offers, for example, the breathtaking accuracy and power of the magnificent descending phrase, evidence of his tonal control throughout the range of the instrument, found in the third chorus of *Fine and Dandy*. Yet their qualities, though less obvious, are still very real, and they also stress how wide is the gamut of his emotive power. As far as suggestions of mood are concerned, he has constantly shown a greater degree of sophistication than the mass of his contemporaries. Personal setbacks and difficulties which find a faithful echo in the stylistic vicissitudes of Parker, Miles Davis, and a host of other jazzmen, are seldom reflected in his work. Rather than by personal factors Gillespie, in his later years, has been primarily affected by the immediate *musical* environment.

Among the recordings which lend especial support to this generalization—for it would be foolish to dogmatize on such a question—are those made of the concert at the Massey Hall, Toronto, which took place on May 15th, 1953, and featured five of the foremost jazzmen of the past two decades. Often the bringing together of highly personal talents has the paradoxical effect of making for anonymous music, as if the reconciliation of separate musical temperaments necessarily entails the sacrifice of a degree of individual expression; it may be said without hesitation that such was certainly not the case in this instance. Parker, Gillespie, Powell, Mingus and Roach work admirably together, and although some of the ensemble passages point to a strict minimum of rehearsal, the overall impression gained is one of unity. Without conceding the essence of his work, Gillespie makes a generous contribution to the music at large. The eccentricities are still present, but not so as to disrupt the general atmosphere of cohesion. The attack of his playing, more marked here than on many of his post-1950 sessions, does much to make this possible. Though Bud Powell's impetuous flow of ideas overshadows the less consistently aggressive contributions of the hornmen, so well does he play that this remark should not be construed as a serious criticism. There is no denying, however, that on *Perdido* Gillespie's solo is a poor one: he indulges in too much trickery, and though this found an uproarious welcome with the audience at the time, his obsession with half-valve effects does not wear well on repeated hearings. On this side he is cut badly by Powell, whose involved yet strongly rhythmic style makes no concessions to the fancies of the crowd. Elsewhere Gillespie plays well, sometimes brilliantly: *Night in Tunisia* finds him constructing a solo of logic, imagination, and undeniable emotional quality. Employing a rather more caustic tone than usual, he increases the tension cleverly at the end of first and second choruses and successfully maintains the momentum of the solo. The prolific number of descending runs, in strict accord with the other stylistic features, never weakens the attack, but rather lends extra strength as if, with each downward sweep of the melodic line, he were penetrating closer to the heart of the mood. On *Wee* the welter of notes, though not conspicuous for the precise separation of his earlier work, is beautifully controlled, while the searing effect obtained at this rapid tempo reminds one of Eldridge's insistent ferocity. The effective yet relatively simple phrase with which he prolongs the mood of Bird's solo, stresses once again his power of objective appraisal; while his work on this tune is once more impressive, with skilfully integrated quotations from *Laura* and Bizet's *Carmen*. All in all, his playing at the concert, or that part of it which remains to us on record, is notable for the simultaneous projection of two theoretically opposed emotions: a blend of exasperation and caprice seems on the face of it an impossible combination, but Gillespie reconciles them here, and the resulting amalgam is surely the central characteristic of his work.

The Massey Hall transcriptions were the last important

records made by Gillespie before his signing with Norman Granz. Two sides which appeared on the Showcase label were recorded in June, 1953, with a quintet including Sahib Shihab. Henceforth, the trumpeter's recording activities were to be confined to this one company. His appearances with the Jazz at the Philharmonic unit and on the numerous jam session recordings have fortunately had no adverse effect upon his playing. While more delicate artistic temperaments have either wilted or overreached themselves in the electric climate of the Granz organization, Gillespie has been only favourably affected. Numerous criticisms have been made of Granz's predilection for the musically absurd, and it is true that many are justified; but it is also true that he has brought a decent standard of living within the reach of many musicians who for all their unquestioned abundance of talent would otherwise have been hard put to it to scrape an existence from the novelty-ridden atmosphere of American jazz circles.

The first session on which Gillespie played after signing with Granz was a studio jam session date held on September 2nd, 1953. On this occasion the usual formidable array of talent was assembled, and, as at the Massey Hall concert, the presence of so many prominent jazzmen must surely have acted as a spur upon the trumpeter. Quite apart from the fact that this, his first recording under a new banner, had him playing alongside many musicians of greater experience, the presence of Roy Eldridge, his erstwhile idol, must have been an additional incentive to him to produce his best form. *Just You Just Me* contains an excellent Gillespie solo. Feeling his way in the first chorus, he unveils his power at the start of the second, producing a brutal, almost snarling effect, attenuated by some typical fast runs in the second eight. The third and final chorus finds him in more consistently attacking mood, as the tension mounts again, abetted by a relative economy of melodic construction. An amusing moment occurs in the last eight bars, as he doffs his cap to Eldridge, the next soloist, with a riff characteristic of the older man's style. In passing, it is worth remarking that though Eldridge's sense of dynamics is not as logical, his playing carries even greater urgency and excitement.

He too, it seems, must have felt the significance of the occasion.

Gillespie's performance on this tune is perhaps a trifle superior to his other contributions to the session, but he is guided all the time by the extrovert nature of the proceedings. The importance of the prevailing mood and the influence it has over each musician was further underlined by his next recording date, held in December, 1953: partnered by Stan Getz and supported by a rhythm section made up of Oscar Peterson, Herb Ellis, Ray Brown and Max Roach, he projects a more subtle expression, mixing extravagance with a quality verging on shyness. It is interesting to compare the agility of his work on *It Don't Mean a Thing* with his pert rendering of the melody of *Exactly Like You*; similarly, while restraint is abandoned from time to time, he plays many passages whose tastefulness is unquestionable: an example is his backing to Getz towards the close of *Talk of the Town*.

Sophistication is very definitely the keynote of his work here, though the poise he displays is not inimical to emotional projection. Enjoying the ability to transmit a wide range of moods, he emerges from the session in a more favourable light than his front-line partner. While he is able to match Getz's calm reflective style, the tenorman cannot rival his fiery playing at rapid tempo. This is shown quite blatantly by *Impromptu* and *It Don't Mean a Thing*: both tracks expose the shortcomings of Getz's current style and stress the amplitude of Gillespie's talent. In 1953 at least, the highly competitive atmosphere of a studio session of this type was very definitely not the ideal setting for Getz's tenor; neither, though, did the emphasis on technical prowess, an inevitable upshot of this collision of musical temperaments, appear to have an exclusively beneficial influence on the trumpeter's expression. Comparison with the sides made with the much larger group two months earlier points to the chief weakness: when he embarks upon the impressive pyrotechnics, which are in normal circumstances an important but contributory element in his style, he does not always fit them satisfactorily into the pattern of his solo. Complexity becomes an end in itself and gaiety degenerates into exhibitionism. It seems possible that the temptation to eclipse the acknowledged virtuosity of his single front-line partner by a sheer instrumental display proved too strong. The criticism is only of occasional pertinency, for, as I have pointed out, there are trumpet passages of true elegance and power.

Nevertheless, the intermittent inconsistency of melodic construction and lack of directness are both thrown into relief by the less immediately striking but far more characteristic sides cut with Hank Mobley and rhythm section in the summer of the next year. For a second date, held shortly afterwards, Jimmy Cleveland was added on trombone. The conception on these is at once bolder and more relaxed. Gillespie's musicianship is just as sound, but somewhat less conscious. As a result, the music gains in impact. Buster Harding's highly functional writing is exceptionally well suited to the styles of the participants. Mobley and, to a lesser extent, Cleveland, concern themselves with the creation of a particularly solid swing: cast in a subsidiary role, they none the less do much to ensure the success of each performance. Among the highlights are the leader's straightforward blowing over background figures of distinctly Ellingtonian flavour at the start of *Blue Mood*; his unashamedly rhythmic contributions to *Sugar Hips*; and, for those with a taste for the baroque in jazz, the vocal on *Money Honey*. The words themselves are a welcome antidote to the usual unbelievably trite concoctions of the commercial lyricist; but their overt cynicism is tempered by Gillespie's singing. He brings to them a sly humour which makes them perhaps more convincing and certainly more memorable than they would otherwise be. The repetition of the catchphrase, in tones of burlesque, is made more effective by its sudden replacement in the final verse by one stark monosyllable, as if to hammer home the gist of the song. Not that the trenchancy of the side can be explained away by diction alone: as with Armstrong's version of *Mack the Knife*, this song owes its effect to the timing and delivery of the singer. Both have the most unsavoury of subject matter; their treatment, different as it is from all normal treatments, bulges with a good humour that will not be denied. In so far as the spirit of the performance is concerned, *Money Honey* is typical of Gillespie's playing on both sessions: witty and incisive, sober and rumbustious, it steers well clear of diffidence on the one hand and pretentiousness on the other.

From the recording viewpoint, 1954 was an exceptionally good year for Gillespie. Apart from the two dates already mentioned, he figures on a studio jam session, a Jazz at the Philharmonic transcription, and, of rather more interest, an album with Roy Eldridge and rhythm section, a big-band collation, and a set of Afro-styled pieces with large and small groups, orchestrated by Chico O'Farrill. Gillespie has been attacked on numerous occasions over the past five years for alleged poverty of taste, wildness of execution, and sterility of ideas; not one of these records substantiates such extravagant charges. It would be arrant prejudice to go to the other extreme and assert that he has none of these weaknesses; but to make such criticisms without recognizing the accompanying merits indicates just as flagrant a bias. The listener who looks in Gillespie's work for the careful precision and balance offered by the Modern Jazz Quartet or the Chico Hamilton group is bound to be disappointed. Yet to criticize him on this score alone is tantamount to attacking Armstrong because of Jelly Roll Morton or Eldridge because of Ellington. It is far from being my intention to suggest that in jazz composition and improvisation are two diametrically opposed values. Each has its own attractions, and while discretion must always be used similar criteria may be applied to both. On the other hand, the wildest of

Gillespie's eccentricities are part and parcel of the freedom of his expression. It is for each listener to determine for himself where the boundary line between passion and exhibitionism lies and to make his judgements accordingly, but it is only fair to point out that with many jazzmen, including Gillespie, the failings are inseparable from the virtues. To assess his musical worth by using the identical standards one would apply to the work of Duke Ellington or John Lewis is short-sightedness and nothing more.

The sides recorded with Eldridge in November, 1954, underline many of the points made above. On *I Found a New Baby*, there are several occasions when Gillespie lets loose a blatant scream, often at the beginning of an eight-bar section, only to make sense of this erratic detail with a cleverly wrought descending phrase. Admittedly, there are other times when this is not done, but on the whole a sense of musical proportion is maintained. One of the most absorbing aspects of this session is the stylistic comparison it affords between the two men: Gillespie is the more generously endowed from the technical standpoint, and enjoys, for instance, a facility in the top register which his former exemplar cannot rival. Yet, on the whole, the most memorable passages are contributed by Eldridge. The reason for this, I feel, is the immense force of expression crammed into his playing of the terse, stabbing phrases which abound in his improvisation. Beside them the most complex flights of his partner seem almost otiose. 'We was a great disappointment to Norman,' Gillespie was reported to have said to the musicologist Ernest Borneman a year or so later. 'We'd *never* fight. We was *friends*.' Listening to the recordings, it is hard not to feel that this declaration of non-aggression after the fact was a trifle contrived. All the same, Gillespie plays very well, and while the framework is a very sketchy one, consisting of unison passages at the beginning and end of each performance, sometimes relieved by a very functional counterpoint, the improvised choruses hold much interest.

The sides with big-band and Afro rhythm show a facet of the trumpeter's musical character which the small group, even with the incentive provided by Eldridge's presence, rarely brings to light: an intensity of expression comparable to that possessed by such jazzmen as Charlie Parker or Sidney Bechet. Throughout his career Gillespie has appeared to draw power from the accompaniment of a large group, especially when the rhythmic underlining is complex in character; in the last decade, when his youthful exuberance has become rather diffuse, the comparison between his recorded work with groups large and small is even more striking. The powerful coda at the end of O'Farrill's Suite shows the naked force he can get into his music in these circumstances. At the same time his peculiarly objective talent ensures that he is also capable of the most restrained interpretations. There are one or two passages in the Suite which show this, but *Con Alma*, one of the tunes recorded with flute and Afro rhythm only, embodies a very different mood from the other performances, owing mainly to the trumpeter's subdued, almost doleful playing. In some ways, the small-group tracks from the album are superior to the Suite itself: the wealth of detail in the writing becomes burdensome on repeated hearing. Gillespie's playing of the *Night in Tunisia* theme over the riff supplied by Gilberto Valdes' flute gains in contrast because of its relative simplicity.

As the years have passed more and more stress has been laid upon Gillespie as the virtuoso musician, and his recordings have faithfully mirrored the trend in his everyday musical activities. The tendency has been apparent ever since the mid-forties, for he was very much the star of his own big band. Since the dissolution of this orchestra he has led small units of varying composition, but hardly because he preferred to do so: the situation has been dictated by economic pressure. Though it was not until 1956 that he managed to assemble a new orchestra and keep it together for a reasonable period of time, his first years spent under contract to Granz did at least mean that the spotlight was turned upon his solo ability in no uncertain way.

Nineteen fifty-five found him recording with just as great a variety of groups as the previous year, but the most important session was that held in May; partnered by Sonny Stitt on alto and supported by the Modern Jazz Quartet rhythm section, augmented by the guitar of Skeeter Best, and with Charlie Persip in the place of Connie Kay, he gives out with some very forceful playing. One of the chief reasons for the aggression of much of his work on this date was in all probability the presence of Stitt. On *Mean to Me* his alternately soaring and trenchant improvisation outshines Gillespie's, but elsewhere it has a more desirable effect, though the rivalry leads now and again, particularly in

198

Dizzy Meets Sonny, to technical displays of only incidental value. *How Deep is the Ocean* is a tasteful though maybe inconclusive ballad; *Blues for Bird* contains the best trumpet work in the album. Cut two months after Parker's death, this musical tribute has inspired work from everyone, with Gillespie making wide use of half-valve effects in a way at once logical and moving, as he creates a solo rich in light and shade, yet still of a powerful intensity.

From a Jazz at the Philharmonic concert held later in the year featuring the musicians then composing the Granz touring unit, *The Modern Set*, which has Lester Young and Gillespie playing together, is something of a disappointment in view of the stature of these two musicians. They succeed in generating a high degree of excitement, but tend in the process to lose sight of other values. This performance is among their least impressive work, and like several similar productions, reveals the dangers of a virtuoso-type musical presentation. If the musicians are not inspired—and the most demanding of listeners hardly expects a constant stream of musical brilliance—there are no compensations. The sparser the fabric, the stronger each separate thread must necessarily be.

On the evidence of this isolated recording, or even on that of all the records he made about the same time, it would be imprudent to assert that Gillespie's frustration in not having a big band at his disposal was making itself felt in his work. Nevertheless it is very likely that a man with his powers of musical organization felt too restricted without having the control of a group of musicians, however generous the scope afforded to his solo ability. The chance finally presented itself early in 1956, when the U.S. State Department commissioned him to form an orchestra with a view to touring the Middle East. The morals of this venture are clearly questionable when the racial problem within the U.S.A. itself is considered in relation to the obvious purpose behind the tour, but it is hard to blame Gillespie for accepting the offer. The records made by the band do not compare with those made by the orchestra he led in the second half of the 'forties in so far as verve, attack, and originality of ideas are concerned; yet the section playing, though not quite so fierce, is superior by academic standards. Because of the success of the enterprise another tour was arranged for the band soon after its return. This second itinerary included most of the South American countries. On his return to the

States in the late summer, Gillespie joined the Granz touring unit once more, but towards the end of the year the interest provoked by his overseas activities had the effect of allowing him to re-form the band, though with several notable changes in personnel. The following July, it appeared at the Newport Jazz Festival, and its recorded performances, taken together with the 1956 and 1957 studio sides, reveal accurately enough its faults, its virtues, and the difficulties it faced.

The studio session of May, 1956, produced results of infinitely more interest than the vast majority of the Newport sides. *Tour de Force* and *I Can't Get Started*, of dissimilar mood and pace, both stress once again Gillespie's versatility and mastery of dynamics. In contrast to these tunes, *Stella by Starlight*, an arrangement by Melba Liston, reveals the fine section work. In so far as Gillespie's solo playing is concerned, the main difference from the earlier band is that there is considerably less vehemence to his expression. His work on these tracks is of a more consistent quality than that found on most of his Granz releases, but while the general average is high, one could hardly single out any of his solos as being exceptional by his own standards. In marked contrast, the Newport performances of the following year are almost valueless. *I Remember Clifford* has some beautifully lyrical trumpet, but with the exception of Mary Lou Williams' *Zodiac Suite*, all the other tracks veer dangerously close to outright rhythm and blues, with the result that the potential value of the band as a band is never realized. The studio sides from the same year, despite their commercial leanings—*Autumn Leaves* and *Over the Rainbow* are two apposite instances—are preferable to the interminable tenor solo on *School Days*, with its multitude of honks and squeals. Gillespie was eventually forced to disband at the start of 1958. During the first part of this year he toured widely with the Jazz at the Philharmonic group, coming to Europe in the early spring, and again in July, not this time with Granz, but as a solo artist, to play at the Knokke and Cannes festivals. To judge from the records his orchestra made during the previous year, the economic pressures were already building up. It is a depressing thought that his band should have had to resort to sentimental ballads or the improbable gymnastics of rhythm and blues in its struggle to survive. The brutal fact is that no big band can continue in business without making concessions of some sort to its audience. Count Basie's orchestra is perhaps the sole exception, but it is unlikely that it would have lasted so long had it not been for the selling power of Joe Williams' vocals.

Throughout the span of his big band's existence, Gillespie's recording activities were not limited to sessions with his own aggregation. Still under contract to Granz, he has figured during the last three years in the usual small-group studio dates, and, as might be expected, his playing has varied from poor to very good. The normal strictures in regard to Granz's policy cannot be applied in the case of Gillespie: it is impossible to forecast the quality of his work on the basis of the stylistic surroundings. One may hazard a guess at the style, but the standard is unforeseeable. He will play very badly indeed when one least expects it: on, for example, *Lover come back to Me*, from the September, 1956, session with Stitt and Getz, where his improvisation is disjointed and lackadaisical in the extreme; while, on the other hand, the tracks with Stuff Smith, on the face of things the least likely of partners, are generally good and in one case at least superb: on *Purple Sounds*, he plays with tremendous conviction; one has the impression that each note he chooses is the only possible one in the given situation. Such intensity is rare indeed. It is certainly attained nowhere in his choruses on the *Sittin' In* date with Getz, Hawkins, and Paul Gonsalves held on June 26th, 1957. Of the two ballads he contributes to this album, *On the Alamo* is the most pleasing, showing the instrumental control which is still indubitably his: the manipulation of tone is a durable and almost astonishing exception to the generally uncompromising approach of the trumpeters to emerge in the last decade. On the up-tempo tunes—*Dizzy Atmosphere* and *The Way You Look Tonight*—his conception is verbose, imposing, but unremarkable by his own standards; at times exhilarating, such agility continually verges upon the gratuitous. The performances of the past two years show little deviation from the general pattern of his post-1950 recordings.

It is not to be wondered at that Gillespie should have settled down, the period of experimentation once over, into inevitable maturity. His inspiration, to be sure, has not run so consistently high in this decade, but, as if to compensate for this weakening in intensity, his expression has taken on a wide scope, unparalleled among the jazzmen of his generation. The range of moods evoked by his playing is a very broad one, broad enough to provoke comparison with the immense warmth of Armstrong's playing. Latest reports from the U.S.A. indicate that Gillespie's present small group is not finding it especially easy to get bookings; yet his recent recordings, in spite of the obvious variation of quality, emphasize just how fallible is the theory which likens jazz to a piece of machinery, and decrees that when a newer and more intricate musical mechanism comes along, it must at all costs usurp the longer-established model. Gillespie's best recordings of the present decade, some of which I have mentioned, are great indeed, and there are few other jazzmen who could emulate either their compulsion or their design. In any case, it is hard to see the nature of his style, its complexity or otherwise, as an explanation of the slackening of public interest. His construction is just as *advanced* as any of the young arrivals, his execution considerably more assured than most.

A more likely answer is that he has been unable to achieve a thoroughly secure economic position because of the fadism which pervades a young audience. The situation finds a reflection in many other fields: the tendency to prefer something novel, irrespective of worth, pandered to and encouraged by the mechanism of advertising, is a strong and unhealthy contemporary trait which is not restricted to music, but finds almost universal expression. The blame is to be laid upon this general pattern of behaviour, rather than any particular aspect of his style. It is significant how many trumpet players have paid homage to his instrumental powers. Thad Jones and Miles Davis are but two who have stressed his superiority. The reverence felt for his prowess compares with the awe in which the late Art Tatum's piano artistry is held.

At the same time, there can have been few jazzmen of similar standing who have recorded so much mediocre music. Gillespie's taste has often been very dubious indeed, so dubious, in fact, that one automatically wonders whether the erratic and sometimes frankly exhibitionistic playing is not perhaps essential to the production of the occasional gems which crystallize out of the least likely surrounds in a way that hinges upon the miraculous. The 1957 Newport Festival collection shows how this can happen without apparent reason. On almost every track the trumpet work is wildly flamboyant, as though he were out to provoke a spurious emotional response, attained by sheer excitement rather than by any deeper exposure of thought or feeling. And yet, suddenly, in the midst of these acrobatics, he finds it possible to create such a performance as *I Remember Clifford*, whose beauty lingers in the mind long after the impact of the rest of the album has passed. The recurrence of such moments as this are frequent enough in his recorded work to point to a close link between extravagance and a convincing emotional expression. It is as if the one cannot be achieved without the other. This connexion once granted, it is difficult to apply the traditional criterion of *good taste* to his playing. This clearly seems paradoxical when it is considered how advanced is his control over his instrument in terms of range, tone, and so on. In theory it would appear highly improbable that a brilliant technician could be guilty of unintentionally loose or eccentric playing, but much of Gillespie's production disproves this.

Gillespie will without doubt go down in the history manuals as a brilliant innovator and technician, one of the musicians who helped to expand the jazz vocabulary. Gifted with a remarkable ear, and endowed with the instrumental competence to translate his conceptions into sound, his contributions to the music's evolution and the influence he had upon contemporaries and younger men alike are attested by countless records. His innovations have long since been widely recognized and discussed, but despite their unquestionable importance, it is very necessary to bear in mind that his talent was not restricted to innovation alone: if he helped transform a tradition, he was careful not to lose sight of the major values it already held. The objection might be made that tonal beauty was sacrificed to speed of execution, and this seems true enough of one stage of his career; in recent times, however, he has returned to a more traditional style in this respect. In any case, it is dangerous in the extreme to single out a particular facet such as this for critical examination, without reference to his playing as a whole. There is, at all events, one capital aspect of his work which is above reproach: its consistent swing.

Similarly, his persistent recognition of this especial virtue is inseparable from the general outlook which makes comparison with such men as Armstrong, Hawkins, and Eldridge natural and inevitable. The spiritual climate of much of the jazz played in the last two decades has been far from joyful: and like his contemporaries, Gillespie, too, has dealt widely in the musical equivalents of the more sombre moods. This concern with the gloomier side of life, with sorrow and separation, is an integral part of experience, and it is to be expected that jazz, as a living art, should mirror it in its own characteristic way. It is understandable, too, that these past few years should have seen an aggravation of such tendencies. In the aesthetic of many of the younger jazzmen, optimism is conspicuous only by its absence, and humour, where it exists, is invariably of a sardonic brand; but Gillespie, it seems, has never felt the need to set such bounds to his music. Laconic, morose at times, its general direction is none the less emphatically centrifugal. Just as its designs and motifs range from the elemental to the complex, the spirit of his work draws strength from its unusual emotional freedom, impatient of limits of any kind, jubilant in its variety.

SELECTED DISCOGRAPHY OF DIZZY GILLESPIE

It should be stressed that this listing is purely of an arbitrary nature and has been chosen as a complement to the foregoing text. Records that are no longer in the catalogue are marked with an asterisk.

LIONEL HAMPTON AND HIS ALL STARS:

Dizzy Gillespie (*tpt*); Benny Carter (*alt*); Coleman Hawkins, Ben Webster, Leon 'Chu' Berry (*ten*); Lionel Hampton (*vib*); Clyde Hart (*p*); Charlie Christian (*g*); Milt

Hinton (*bs*); Cozy Cole (*d*).

New York City, September 11, 1939
41408 *Hot Mallets*   Cam CAL–517*

COLEMAN HAWKINS AND HIS ORCHESTRA:

Dizzy Gillespie, Vic Coulsen, Ed Vanderver (*tpt*); Leo Parker, Leonard Lowry (*alt*); Coleman Hawkins, Don Byas, Ray Abrams (*ten*); Budd Johnson (*bar*); Clyde Hart (*p*); Oscar Pettiford (*bs*); Max Roach (*d*).

New York City, February 16, 1944
R1001 *Bu-Dee-Daht*
R1002 *Yesterdays*   } Apo LP101 *

BILLY ECKSTINE AND HIS ALL STAR BAND:

Dizzy Gillespie, Freddy Webster, Shorty McConnell, Al Killian (*tpt*); Trummy Young, Claude Jones, Howard Scott (*tbn*); Billy Eckstine (*v-tbn, vcl*); Budd Johnson, Jimmy Powell (*alt*); Wardell Gray, Thomas Crump (*ten*); Rudy Rutherford (*bar*); Clyde Hart (*p*); Connie Wainwright (*g*); Oscar Pettiford (*bs*); Shadow Wilson (*d*).

New York City, April 13, 1944
107 *I Got a Date with Rhythm*   DeL 3206 *
109 *Good Jelly Blues*   DeL 3000 *

Dizzy Gillespie, Gail Brockman, Shorty McConnell, Fats Navarro (*tpt*); Jerry Valentine, Chippy Outcalt, Taswell Baird, Howard Scott (*tbn*); John Jackson, Bill Frazier (*alt*); Dexter Gordon, Gene Ammons (*ten*); Leo Parker (*bar*); John Malachi (*p*); Connie Wainwright (*g*); Tommy Potter (*bs*); Art Blakey (*d*); Billy Eckstine (*vcl*).

New York City, December 5, 1944
120–3 *Blowing the Blues Away*   DeL 3001 *
121–2 *Opus X*   DeL 3002 *

DIZZY GILLESPIE AND HIS SEXTET:

Dizzy Gillespie (*tpt*); Dexter Gordon (*ten*); Frank Paparelli (*p*); Chuck Wayne (*g*); Murray Shipinsky (*bs*); Shelly Manne (*d*).

New York City, February 9, 1945
555 *Blue 'n Boogie*   Prst 24030

Dizzy Gillespie (*tpt*); Charlie Parker (*alt*); Clyde Hart (*p*); Remo Palmieri (*g*); Slam Stewart (*bs*); Cozy Cole (*d*).

New York City, February 29, 1945
554 *Groovin' High*
556 *Dizzy Atmosphere*   } Prst 24030
557 *All the Things You Are*

ALBINIA JONES ACC. DON BYAS' SWING SEVEN:

Albinia Jones (*vcl*) acc. Dizzy Gillespie (*tpt*); Don Byas (*ten*); Gene Sedric (*alt*); Sammy Price (*p*); Leonard Ware (*g*); Oscar Smith (*bs*); Harold West (*d*).

New York City, April 14, 1945
NSC49 *Evil Gal Blues*   EmA MG36017*

DIZZY GILLESPIE AND HIS ALL STAR QUINTET:

Dizzy Gillespie (*tpt*); Charlie Parker (*alt*); Al Haig (*p*); Curly Russell (*bs*); Sid Catlett (*d*); Sarah Vaughan (*vcl* [1]).

New York City, May 11, 1945
566 *Shaw 'Nuff*
567 *Lover Man* [1]   } Prst 24030
568 *Hot House*

RED NORVO AND HIS SELECTED SEXTET:

Dizzy Gillespie (*tpt*); Charlie Parker (*alt*); Flip Phillips (*ten*); Red Norvo (*vib*); Teddy Wilson (*p*); Slam Stewart (*bs*); J. C. Heard (*d*).

New York City, June 5, 1945
T10C *Bird Blues*   Dial LP903 *

CHARLIE PARKER QUINTET:

Dizzy Gillespie (*tpt, p*); Charlie Parker (*alt*); Argonne Thornton (*p* [1]); Curly Russell (*bs*); Max Roach (*d*).

New York City, November 26, 1945
S5852–1 *Thrivin' from a Riff* [1]
S5852–2 *Thrivin' from a Riff* [1]
S5852–3 *Thrivin' from a Riff* [1]   } Svy MG12079
S5853–1 *Ko Ko*
S5853–2 *Ko Ko*

SLIM GAILLARD AND HIS ORCHESTRA:

Dizzy Gillespie (*tpt*); Charlie Parker (*alt*); Jack McVea (*ten*); Slim Gaillard (*vib, g, vcl*); Dodo Marmarosa (*p*); Bam Brown (*bs*); Zutty Singleton (*d*).

Los Angeles, December, 1945
38 *Dizzy Boogie*
39 *Flat Foot Floogie*
40 *Poppity Pop*   } Svy MG12014
41 *Slim's Jam*

JAZZ AT THE PHILHARMONIC:

Dizzy Gillespie (*tpt*); Lester Young, Charlie Ventura

(ten); Willie Smith (alt); Mel Powell (p); Billy Hadnott (bs); Lee Young (d).

Los Angeles, January 29, 1946

411–12	Crazy Rhythm	} Vrv MG2*
413–14	Sweet Georgia Brown [1]	
	The Man I Love	Vrv MG5*

[1] Al Killian (tpt); Charlie Parker (alt) added on this track.

DIZZY GILLESPIE'S JAZZ MEN:

Dizzy Gillespie (tpt); Lucky Thompson (ten); Al Haig (p); Milt Jackson (vib); Ray Brown (bs); Stan Levey (d).

Hollywood, February 7, 1946

D1001	Confirmation	
D1002	Diggin' for Diz	
D1003A	Dynamo A	} Dial LP212 *
D1003B	Dynamo B	
D1005	Round About Midnight	Dial 1003 *

DIZZY GILLESPIE SEXTET:

Dizzy Gillespie (tpt); Don Byas (ten); Milt Jackson (vib); Al Haig (p); Bill de Arango (g); Ray Brown (bs); J. C. Heard (d).

New York City, February 22, 1946

D6–VB–1682	52nd Street Theme	Vic LPV 530
D6–VB–1683	Night in Tunisia	
D6–VB–1684	Ol' Man Rebop	Vic 40-0130*
D6–VB–1685	Anthropology [1]	Vic LPV 530

[1] Byas out on this track.

DIZZY GILLESPIE SEXTET:

Dizzy Gillespie (tpt); Sonny Stitt (alt); Milt Jackson (vib); Al Haig (p); Ray Brown (bs); Kenny Clarke (d).

New York City, May 15, 1946

5498	Oop Bop Sh'Bam	} Svy MG12020
5500	That's Earl Brother	

DIZZY GILLESPIE AND HIS ORCHESTRA:

Dizzy Gillespie, Dave Burns, Raymond Orr, Talib Daawood, John Lynch (tpt); Alton Moore, Leon Comegeys, Gordon Thomas (tbn); Howard Johnson, Lucky Warren, Ray Abrams, John Brown, Saul Moore (reeds); Milt Jackson (p); Ray Brown (bs); Kenny Clarke (d); Alice Roberts (vcl [1]).

New York City, June 10, 1946

5550	Our Delight	Svy MG12020
5551	Good Dues Blues [1]	Prst 24030

James Moody (ten) replaces Abrams; John Lewis (p) added; Jackson switches to vib [2].

New York City, July 9, 1946

5609	One Bass Hit: part 2	
5610	Ray's Idea	} Svy MG12020
5611	Things to Come [2]	
5612	He Beeped When He Shoulda Bopped [1]	Prst 24030

Dizzy Gillespie (tpt, vcl [1]); Elmon Wright, Ray Orr, Matthew McKay (tpt); Ted Kelly, Bill Shepherd (tbn); John Brown, Howard Johnson (alt); James Moody, Joe Gayles (ten); Cecil Payne (bar); John Lewis (p); Al McKibbon (bs); Kenny Clarke (d); Chano Pozo (conga d); Kenny Hagood (vcl [2]).

New York City, August 22, 1947

D7–VB–1542	Ow!	} Vic LPV519
D7–VB–1543	Oo-Pop-a-Da [1, 2]	Vic 20-2480*
D7–VB–1544	Two Bass Hit	Vic 20-2603*
D7–VB–1545	Stay On It	Vic LPV519

Dave Burns (tpt) added; Lamar Wright, Benny Bailey (tpt); George Nicholas (ten) replace Orr, McKay and Moody.

New York City, December 22, 1947

D7–VB–2932	Algo Bueno	Vic 20–3186 *
D7–VB–2933	Cool Breeze [1, 2]	Vic 20–3033 *
D7–VB–2934	Cubana Be	} Vic LJM1009 *
D7–VB–2935	Cubana Bop	

New York City, December 30, 1947

D7–VB–3090	Manteca	Vic 20–3033 *
D7–VB–3092	Good Bait	Vic LJM1009 *
D7–VB–3093	Ool-Ya-Koo [1, 2]	Vic LPV530
D7–VB–3094	Minor Walk	Vic 20–3186 *

Dizzy Gillespie (tpt, vcl [1]); Elmon Wright, Willie Cook, Dave Burns (tpt); Jesse Tarrant, Bill Shepherd (tbn); John Brown (alt); Ernie Henry (alt, vcl [2]); James Moody, Joe Gayles (ten); Cecil Payne (bar); James Forman (p); Nelson Boyd (bs); Teddy Stewart (d); Chano Pozo (conga d).

Pasadena, California, August 1948

Emanon	
Good Bait	
Manteca	
Ool-Ya-Koo [1, 2]	
Stay On It	} Cres 23
One Bass Hit	
'Round About Midnight	
I Can't Get Started	

Sam Hurt (*tbn*) added; Andy Duryea (*tbn*); Budd Johnson (*ten*); Al McKibbon (*bs*); Joe Harris (*conga d*) replace Shepherd, Moody, Boyd and Pozo; Luis Martinez (*conga d*) added.

New York City, December 29, 1948
D8–VB–4150   *Lover Come Back to Me*
Vic LPV530

Dizzy Gillespie, Willie Cook, Benny Harris, Elmon Wright (*tpt*); Jesse Tarrant, Andy Duryea, Sam Hurt (*tbn*); John Brown, Ernie Henry (*alt*); Yusef Lateef, Joe Gayles (*ten*); Al Gibson (*bar*); James Forman (*p*); Al McKibbon (*bs*); Teddy Stewart (*d*); V. D. V. Guerra (*conga d*).

Chicago, April 14, 1949
D9–VB–471   *Swedish Suite*   Vic LJM1009 *
Guerra out.
New York City, May 6, 1949
D9–VB–1010   *Katy*   Vic LJM1009 *

Dizzy Gillespie (*tpt, vcl* [1]); Don Slaughter, Elmon Wright, Willie Cook (*tpt*); Sam Hurt, Matthew Gee, Hanifan Mageed (*tbn*); Jimmy Heath, John Coltrane (*alt*); Jesse Powell, Paul Gonsalves (*ten*); Al Gibson (*bar*); Adrian Acea (*p*); John Collins (*g*); Al McKibbon (*bs*); Charlie Wright (*d*).

New York City, November 21, 1949
4316   *Say When*
4318   *You Stole My Wife* [1]   } Cap M11059

METRONOME ALL STARS:

Dizzy Gillespie (*tpt*); Kai Winding (*tbn*); Buddy De Franco (*clt*); Lee Konitz (*alt*); Stan Getz (*ten*); Serge Chaloff (*bar*); Lennie Tristano (*p*); Billy Bauer (*g*); Eddie Safranski (*bs*); Max Roach (*d*).

New York City, January 10, 1950
CO42629   *Double Date*   Har HL7044*

DIZ AND BIRD:

Dizzy Gillespie (*tpt*); Charlie Parker (*alt*); Thelonious Monk (*p*); Curly Russell (*bs*); Buddy Rich (*d*).

New York City, June 6, 1950
410–4   *Bloomdido*
411–3   *An Oscar for Treadwell*
411–4   *An Oscar for Treadwell*   } Vrv 6–8006
412–3   *Mohawk*
412–4   *Mohawk*   Vrv 6–8002
413–2   *My Melancholy Baby*
414–3   *Leapfrog*
414–4   *Leapfrog*   } Vrv 6–8006
415–2   *Relaxin' with Lee*
415–3   *Relaxin' with Lee*

DIZZY GILLESPIE WITH JOHNNY RICHARDS' ORCHESTRA:

Dizzy Gillespie (*tpt, vcl* [1]); Phil Shuken (*alt, f*); Haskell Issenhuth (*f*); Harry Steinfeld (*oboe*); Shirley Thompson (*bsn*); Henry Coker, Dick Kenny, Hal Smith (*tbn*); John Graas (*fr-h*); Mischa Russell, Henry Hill, Jack Shulman, Felix Slatkin, Walter Edelstein, Victor Arno, Harry Bluestone, Sidney Brokow, John Quadre (*vln*); Eleanor Slatkin, Cy Bernard ('*cello*); Barbara Whitney (*harp*); Paul Smith (*p*); Jack Cascales (*bs*); Charles Wright (*d*); Carlos Vidal (*bo*); Johnny Richards (*arr, dir*).

Hollywood, October 31, 1950
385   *Swing Low Sweet Chariot* [1]   Svy MG12110

Hollywood, November 1, 1950
392   *Interlude in C*   Svy MG12110

DIZZY GILLESPIE SEXTET:

Dizzy Gillespie (*tpt*); John Coltrane (*ten*); Milt Jackson (*vib*); Kenny Burrell (*g*); Percy Heath (*bs*); Kansas Fields (*d*).

Detroit, March 1, 1951
4015   *Tin Tin Daeo*
4020   *Birks Works*   } Svy MG12047

Dizzy Gillespie (*tpt*); Jay Jay Johnson (*tbn*); Budd Johnson (*ten*); Milt Jackson (*vib*); Percy Heath (*bs*); Art Blakey (*d*).

New York City, April 16, 1951
3638   *The Champ*   Svy MG12047

DIZZY GILLESPIE AND HIS ORCHESTRA:

Dizzy Gillespie (*tpt, vcl* [1]); Don Byas (*ten*); Art Simmons (*p*); Joe Benjamin (*bs*); Bill Clark (*d*).

Paris, March 25, 1952
14777   *Cognac Blues*   Atl LP1257*
14779   *Sabla-Y-Blu* [1]   Atl LP138 *

Arnold Ross (*p*) replaces Simmons; Umberto Canto (*conga d*) added on 4211.

Paris, March 27, 1952
4210   *Hurry Home*
4211   *Afro Paris*   } BN BLP5017 *
4213   *I Cover the Waterfront*   Rst 591 *

DIZZY GILLESPIE AND HIS OPERATIC STRINGS:

Dizzy Gillespie (*tpt*); Arnold Ross (*p*); Joe Benjamin (*bs*); Bill Clark (*d*); Strings of the Orchestra of the Paris Opera.

Paris, April 5, 1952
14790 *Night and Day*
14793 *I Waited for You* } Clef MGC–136 *

DIZZY GILLESPIE QUINTET:

Personnel as for March 25.

Paris, April 5, 1952
15173 *Sleepy Time Down South*
15175 *One More Blues* } Atl LP1257*

DIZZY GILLESPIE ORCHESTRA:

Dizzy Gillespie (*tpt, vcl* [1]); Bill Tamper (*tbn*); Hubert Fol (*alt*); Don Byas (*ten*); Raymond Fol (*p*); Pierre Michelot (*bs*); Pierre Lemarchand (*d*).

Paris, April 11, 1952
4224 *C.C.C. Blues* [1]   BN 1617 *
4226 *Somebody Loves Me*
4227 *She's Funny That Way*
4228 *Wrap Your Troubles in Dreams*   } BN BLP5017 *
4229 *Sweet Lorraine*
4230 *Everything Happens to Me*
4231 *I Don't Know Why*   Rst 591 *

THE COOL STARS:

Dizzy Gillespie, Jimmy McPartland [1], Dick Cary [1] (*tpt*); Don Elliott (*mell, tpt* [1]); Ray Abrams (*ten*); Ronnie Ball (*p*); Al McKibbon (*bs*); Max Roach (*d*).

Birdland Club, New York City, November 21, 1952
52–S–510 *Battle of the Blues* [1]
52–S–512 *How High the Moon* } MGM E194 *

DIZZY GILLESPIE AND HIS ORCHESTRA:

Dizzy Gillespie (*tpt, vcl* [1], *conga d* [4]); Bill Graham (*bar, vcl* [3]); Wade Legge (*p*); Lou Hackney (*bs*); Al Jones (*d*); Joe Carroll (*vcl* [2]).

Salle Pleyel, Paris, February 9, 1953
The Champ [1, 2]
They Can't Take That Away From Me
Good Bait   } Cres 9006
On the Sunny Side of the Street [3]
Swing Low Sweet Cadillac [3, 4]
Oo-Shoo-Be-Doo-Be [1, 2]

Nat Peck (*tbn*) replaces Bill Graham.

Paris, February 22, 1953

4459 *Always*
4460 *Mon Homme*
4461 *I Got Rhythm* [2]
4462 *Fais Gaffe*
4463 *Moon Nocturne*   } Cres 9006
4464 *This Is the Way*
4465 *S'Wonderful*
4466 *In the Land of Oo-Bla-Dee* [2]

Peck out.

THE QUINTET OF THE YEAR:

Dizzy Gillespie (*tpt, vcl* [1]); Charlie Parker (*alt*); Bud Powell (*p*); Charlie Mingus (*bs*); Max Roach (*d*).

Massey Hall, Toronto, May 15, 1953
Perdido
All the Things You Are
Salt Peanuts [1]
Hot House   } Fant 86003
Wee
Night in Tunisia

JAM SESSION:

Dizzy Gillespie, Roy Eldridge (*tpt*); Johnny Hodges (*alt*); Ben Webster, Illinois Jacquet, Flip Phillips (*ten*); Lionel Hampton (*vib*); Oscar Peterson (*p*); Ray Brown (*bs*); Buddy Rich (*d*).

September 2, 1953
Blue Lou
Just You Just Me } Vrv MGV-8062*

GILLESPIE–GETZ SEXTET:

Dizzy Gillespie (*tpt*); Stan Getz (*ten*); Oscar Peterson (*p*); Herb Ellis (*g*); Ray Brown (*bs*); Max Roach (*d*).

Los Angeles, Cal., Dec. 9, 1953
1366 *It Don't Mean a Thing*
1367 *I Let a Song Go Out of My Heart*
1368 *Exactly Like You*
1369 *Talk of the Town*   } Vrv MGV–8141*
1370 *Impromptu*
1371 *Girl of My Dreams*
1372 *Siboney*

DIZ AFRO:

Dizzy Gillespie, Quincy Jones, Ernie Royal, James Nottingham (*tpt*); George Matthews, Jay Jay Johnson, Leon

Comegeys (*tbn*); Hilton Jefferson, George Dorsey (*alt*); Lucky Thompson, Hank Mobley (*ten*); Danny Bank (*bar*); Wade Legge (*p*); Ray Concepcion (*Afro p*); Lou Hackney (*bs*); Robert Rodriguez (*Afro bs*); Charlie Persip (*d*); Jose Manguel, Ray Santamarie, Ubaldo Nieto, Candido Camero (*African percussion*).

New York, N. Y., May 24, 1954

1711	*Manteca Theme*	
1713	*Jungla*	Vrv MGV-8191*
1712	*Contraste*	
1714	*Rhumba Finale*	

DIZZY GILLESPIE QUINTET:

Dizzy Gillespie (*tpt, vcl* [1]); Hank Mobley (*ten*); Wade Legge (*p*); Lou Hackney (*bs*); Charlie Persip (*d*).

New York, N. Y., May 25, 1954

1717	*Hey Pete* [1]	
1719	*Money Honey* [1]	Vrv MGV-8117*
1716	*Sugar Hips*	

DIZZY GILLESPIE AND LATIN-AMERICAN RHYTHM

Dizzy Gillespie (*tpt*); Gilberto Valdes (*f*); Al Hernandez (*p*); Robert Rodriguez (*bs*); Ubaldo Nieto, Candido Camero, Jose Manguel, Rafael Mirando (*African percussion*).

June 3, 1954

1739	*Caravan*	
1740	*Con Alma*	Vrv MGV-8191*
1738	*Night in Tunisia*	

DIZZY GILLESPIE SEXTET:

As last plus Jimmy Cleveland (*tbn*).

New York, N. Y., June 1954

1756	*Blue Mood*	
1757	*Rails*	Vrv MGV-8117
1758	*The Devil and the Fish*	
1759	*Rhumbola*	

ROY AND DIZ:

Roy Eldridge, Dizzy Gillespie (*tpt*); Oscar Peterson (*p*); Herb Ellis (*g*); Ray Brown (*bs*); Louis Bellson (*d*).

New York, N. Y., Oct. 29, 1954

2018	*Trumpet Blues*	Vrv MGV-8110*
2022	*I Found a New Baby*	Vrv MGV-8109*
2024	*I Can't Get Started*	
2023	*Pretty Eyed Baby*	Vrv MGV-8110*
2017	*Algo Bueno*	

MODERN JAZZ SEXTET:

Dizzy Gillespie (*tpt*); Sonny Stitt (*alt*); John Lewis (*p*); Skeeter Best (*g*); Percy Heath (*bs*); Charlie Persip (*d*).

June, 1955

Tour de Force	
Dizzy Meets Sonny	
Mean to Me	Vrv MGV-8166*
Blues for Bird	
How Deep Is the Ocean [1]	

[1] Stitt and Best not present on this track.

JAZZ AT THE PHILHARMONIC:

Dizzy Gillespie (*tpt*); Lester Young (*ten*); Oscar Peterson (*p*); Herb Ellis (*g*); Ray Brown (*bs*); Buddy Rich (*d*).

Opera House, Chicago, October 2, 1955

The Modern Set	JATP Vol. 18*

DIZZY GILLESPIE AND HIS ORCHESTRA:

Dizzy Gillespie, Joe Gordon, Ermet Perry, Carl Warwick, **Quincey Jones** (*tpt*); Melba Liston, Frank Rehak, **Rod Levitt** (*tbn*); Jim Powell, Phil Woods (*alt*); **Billy Mitchell**, Ernie Wilkins (*ten*); Marty Flax (*bar*); Walter Davis, Jr. (*p*); Nelson Boyd (*bs*); Charlie Persip (*d*).

May, 1956

Dizzy's Business	*Night in Tunisia*	
Jessica's Day	*Stella by Starlight*	
Tour de Force	*The Champ*	Vrv MGV-8174*
I Can't Get Started	*My Reverie*	
Doodlin'	*Dizzy's Blues*	

FOR MUSICIANS ONLY:

Dizzy Gillespie (*tpt*); Sonny Stitt (*alt*); Stan Getz (*ten*); John Lewis (*p*); Herb Ellis (*g*); Ray Brown (*bs*); Stan Levey (*d*).

Los Angeles, Oct. 16, 1956

4029	*Be Bop*	
4030	*Wee*	Vrv MGV-8198*
4031	*Dark Eyes*	
4032	*Lover Come Back to Me*	

Dizzy Gillespie and his Orchestra:

Dizzy Gillespie (*tpt, vcl* [1]); Lee Morgan, Ermet Perry, Carl Warwick, Al Barrymore (*tpt*); Melba Liston, Al Grey, Ray Conner (*tbn*); Jim Powell, Ernie Henry (*alt*); Billy Mitchell, Benny Golson (*ten*); Pee Wee Moore (*bar*); Wynton Kelly (*p*); Paul West (*bs*); Charlie Persip (*d*).

Newport, R. I., July 6, 1957

Dizzy's Blues	
Cool Breeze	
Doodlin'	
School Days [1]	Vrv 6–8830
I Remember Clifford	
Manteca	

Instrument Key:

(*alt*)	alto saxophone	(*g*)	guitar
(*bar*)	baritone saxophone	(*mell*)	mellophone
(*bo*)	bongo(s)	(*p*)	piano
(*bs*)	string bass	(*tbn*)	trombone
(*bsn*)	bassoon	(*ten*)	tenor saxophone
(*clt*)	clarinet	(*tpt*)	trumpet
(*d*)	drums	(*vib*)	vibraharp
(*f*)	flute	(*vln*)	violin
(*fr-h*)	French horn	(*v-tbn*)	valve trombone

(*alt*)	alto saxophone	(*g*)	guitar
(*bar*)	baritone saxophone	(*mell*)	mellophone
(*bo*)	bongo(s)	(*p*)	piano
(*bs*)	string bass	(*tbn*)	trombone
(*bsn*)	bassoon	(*ten*)	tenor saxophone
(*clt*)	clarinet	(*tpt*)	trumpet
(*d*)	drums	(*vib*)	vibraharp
(*f*)	flute	(*vln*)	violin
(*fr-h*)	French horn	(*v-tbn*)	valve trombone

Other Abbreviations:

(*arr*) arranger, arranged by
(*dir*) director, directed by
(*vcl*) vocalist, vocal

Key to Label Abbreviations:

Apo	Apollo	Har	Harmony
Atl	Atlantic	JATP	Jazz at the
BN	Blue Note		Philharmonic
Cam	Camden	Nor	Norgren
Cap	Capitol	Prst	Prestige
Cres	Crescendo	Rst	Roost
DeL	DeLuxe	Svy	Savoy
EmA	EmArcy	Vic	Victor
Ev	Everest	Vrv	Verve
Fant	Fantasy		

Jelly Roll Morton

BY MARTIN WILLIAMS

ACKNOWLEDGEMENTS

My own introduction to Jelly Roll Morton's music comes chiefly from Morton himself, from Eugene Williams in his *Jazz Information* magazine and his note to the Brunswick reissue album of Morton solos, from an essay Hugues Panassié wrote for Williams's magazine in about 1940, from the essay by William Russell which is quoted herein, and from Alan Lomax's book, *Mr. Jelly Roll.*

In parts of this book I have used (with some paraphrasing) sections of the notes which I was privileged to write for the Riverside records issue of the Morton Library of Congress recordings (Riverside 9001–9012). I have also made use of an essay on Morton which I originally wrote for the *Evergreen Review*, No. 12. I wish to thank Riverside Records and the Grove Press, respectively, for allowing me to draw on this material here.

M.W.

INTRODUCTION

To begin with, a series of quotations from not-so-imaginary interviews:

'He was a very good piano man when he came through New York around 1911. Everybody thought so and they listened to him. But by the time he started making those records, he had lost his touch and was out of date.'

'He didn't hit his stride until the 'twenties, when he made those band records called the Red Hot Peppers. Then he really made some music. There are things on those records that everybody has picked up since. And *some* things nobody has been able to get with yet.'

'He had a talent for bragging and that's about all. I've heard amateurs play better piano.'

'That man lived music. Nothing else *really* mattered to him.'

'He was a pool shark, using his music to cover up for what he really did.'

'What? *Musician?* Well, I know he played some piano, but as far as I am concerned he was a pimp, pool shark, and general hustler after easy money.'

'He was a genius, if jazz has ever had a genius. He was the first great composer in jazz.'

'Composer? Piano player? Well, I don't know about that. When I knew him on the riverboats he said he was a singer.'

'He was a fine band pianist, a great composer, and an excellent leader. If he'd had any business sense at all he would have been a wealthy man, too, because his music was also popular.'

'No, I don't think he ever played professionally in New Orleans. Used to hang around some of the piano players, because he had a girl who he was— you know—sort of loaning out. But he never played nothing. I understood he played a little guitar and I've heard he tried the trombone for a while. But no piano.'

'Sure. He played very good piano back in New Orleans. Wrote some fine pieces, too. Remember the blues they called *New Orleans Joys* on the record? That was his, and it goes 'way back.'

'Brag? He sure did brag, but he could back up everything he said. Pimp? Well, he sold fake patent medicines, phoney hair straighteners, shot pool, did comedy on stage, too. But he was a musician really. He couldn't get away from it. He always talked like he wanted to be rich and was going to be. But most of all he wanted to be a musician. And he was.'

His life would be difficult for us to trace in detail, especially from the time he left New Orleans until he began to succeed in the Middle West in the mid-'twenties. His music—the part of his life that matters to most of us? Well, we don't know what James P. Johnson heard in New York in 1911. All we know is what was published beginning in 1915, and what was recorded, beginning in 1923 and ending in 1940. That is all of it that exists, and all we have to judge him by.

Jelly Roll Morton was obviously an exasperating and enchanting man—and some of that personal side of him exists, too, on the recording he made for the Library of Congress through the intervention of Alan Lomax. There he is on these recordings, one moment sounding like an inflated 'has-been' of fairly small-time show business, the next emerging as an intellectual, a perceptive theorist about jazz the like of which has not come from the ranks of its players before or since. And braggart and liar—often just the kind of hyperbolic liar who does not really expect to be believed.

Of all the things that make us know that jazz is something we should call 'art' and not just acknowledge as a remarkably expressive folk culture, is the fact that its best works survive the moment. In doing that they defy all, for not only are they *intended* for the moment (as is all folk culture), but being jazz they are often made up, improvised, for the spur of the moment. But a lot of jazz does survive as 'work', with larger emotional meaning and artistic form.

To hear if it does, of course, we must be willing to forget what is merely stylish and what is merely nostalgic. Probably no man in jazz was ever more the victim of both stylishness and nostalgia, than Jelly Roll Morton. Because of the innovations of Armstrong, he was already going out of style before his major work was recorded; and because of an infatuated possessiveness with which some have written about jazz, he had begun to seem a colourful old character before many people had tried to appraise his music seriously or to write down his biography.

A kind of bumbling nostalgia still hovers around his reputation. The series of recordings he did for the Library of Congress is available, but in the editing of that material, a piece he begins in the first volume is finished ten L.P.s later! Another current American L.P. casts this composer and orchestral disciplinarian in the role of narrator of the glorious old days of the Storyville whorehouse entertainer—a role he filled superbly during the recital. Another draws on his first great recordings, a series of compositional piano solos which in 1923–24 announced his talents; it includes several poor pieces and omits major pieces like *London Blues* (*Shoe Shiner's Drag*), *The Pearls* and *Frog-i-more Rag*. And a fourth collection, available in both the U.S. and Britain, drawn from the brilliant series of orchestral recordings on which his reputation really depends, presents his masterpiece *Dead Man Blues* in a composite tape including parts of a rejected run-through version on which some of the musicians made mistakes.

I have implied that some commentators have made him a character. The temptations were strong, perhaps irresistible. For surely this puzzlingly complex man, this diamond-toothed dandy, this braggart, this audacious liar, this direct speaker of the truth, this ostentatious egotist, this great musician and theorist, could be his own enemy.

BIOGRAPHY

I

NEW ORLEANS

The city of New Orleans seemed almost to have a part in everything Ferdinand 'Jelly Roll' Morton talked about and played during his life. Actually, he was born in Gulfport, which happens to be just across the border in Mississippi, but he belonged to New Orleans. And sometimes, to hear him tell it, it seemed almost as if it belonged to him, for a while anyway.

Morton told Alan Lomax of his parentage this way, '. . . As I can understand, my folks were in the city of New Orleans long before the Louisiana Purchase, and all my folks came directly from the shores of France, that is across the world in the other world, and they landed in the new world years ago. . . .

'My grandmother bore sons named Henri, Gus, Neville and Nelusco—all French names; and she bore the daughters Louise, Viola, and Margaret—that was the three daughters. Louise, the oldest daughter, so fair she could always pass, married F. P. La Menthe, also an early settler and considered one of the outstanding contractors and demolishers in the entire South. Louise happened to be my mother, Ferd (Jelly Roll) Morton.

'Of course, I guess you wonder how the name Morton came in, by it being an English name. Well, I'll tell you. I changed it for business reasons when I started travelling. I didn't want to be called Frenchy.'[1]

However, Lomax's own research yielded a rather different story. Morton was the name of a man who did portering and who married young Ferdinand's mother after the apparently irresponsible Mr. La Menthe had left.

When Lomax later asked Morton to sing an old song about a man named Robert Charles, Morton refused. Most men from New Orleans, coloured, Creole, Negro, even white, would have refused. The berserk homicidal behaviour of Robert Charles set off a series of riots in New Orleans, riots that Jelly Roll Morton remembered. Those riots are usually said to have signalled the final step in the gradual installation of formal segregation in New Orleans. The history of cast, class, and colour line in that city is complex. As Dr. Edmond Souchon has described the situation that existed in his youth, a time when Morton was still in the city, (in the *Record Changer*, for February 1953), 'Jelly Roll's attitude was in no small measure due to his complete rebellion against the strict Jim Crow laws of the South, but he also presented a very interesting subject for investigation by a psychoanalyst. Jelly Roll was the victim of his particular "cult" or "social group", if you will; for in New Orleans the self-imposed colour line between the light and the dark Negro is much more marked than is the Jim Crow line between white and coloured.'

There were three classes in New Orleans, then. And, as 'the prejudice' came, these Creoles of Colour, proud families, often landowners, small

---

[1] From *Mister Jelly Roll* by Alan Lomax.

businessmen, often educated abroad, were hit hard. Marshall Stearns gives the background: 'The Black Code of 1724 made provision for the manumission, or freeing, of slaves. Children shared the status of their mother. When a white aristocrat died . . . his will frequently provided that his part-African mistress and slave should be freed. His children by the same woman were automatically free. A class known as Creoles of Colour grew up with French and Spanish as well as African blood in their veins.'[1]

There is no doubt that in his own attitudes, Morton was often a victim of the snobbery of this class. His attitudes were defensively complicated by the fact that his family was not a particularly prosperous one in the Creole community and the fact that he perhaps was not really sure (so it seems) of his own parentage.

One gets the impression that Morton's grandmother had the strongest influence on him as a child. And one also gets the impression that at a rather young age Ferdinand was running off and rather freely associating with men on the fringes of the Storyville district—and not only musicians, but also the gamblers, pool sharks and pimps, and he was hearing all the talk that went inevitably with their way of life about 'big money'.

He began to study guitar at seven and piano at ten. He sang and he listened.

Whether he admitted it to himself or not, he had in effect rejected the *bourgeois* Creole world (no matter how often it clung to the face he showed), before that world rejected him. Morton gave his account of it in *Mister Jelly Roll*. 'My grandmother gave me that Frenchman look and said to me in French, "Your mother is gone and can't help her little girls now. She left Amede and Mimi to their old grandmother to raise as good girls. A musician is nothing but a bum and a scalawag. I don't want you around your sisters. I reckon you better move."

[1] From *The Story of Jazz* by Marshall Stearns.

'My grandmother said all this and she walked up the path to the white columns of the front porch, went inside, and shut the door.' That way of life rejected him, and he it, but some of its attitudes and its pride remained a part of him—perhaps because of the very nature of that rejection—to be reflected often enough in the proud face he turned towards the world.

Morton led us to believe it was his music that led his grandmother to turn him out. Was it? Or was it other activities in Storyville in which he may have also been involved? Both and all, probably. What did Morton think—that he was about to enter into the life of a musician, or a musician with certain sidelines, or a man with certain musical sidelines? Perhaps it doesn't matter, really. Before his grandmother had shut the door on him, Morton had cast his lot with a music that had captured him. And he was true to it even as he wandered, gambled, pimped, pursued the diamonds and the Cadillacs. Whatever else he pursued, the music always seemed to triumph and lead him on. Hearing that music, we so often feel that it says much more about the man and his real feelings than his public masks, his pride, and his bragging can ever tell us.

Jelly Roll Morton said he found work and a high income playing piano in the 'houses' in Storyville. But is that where jazz was born: in the houses of the 'district'? In an interview with Countess Willie Piazza, 'The First Lady of Storyville' (in the *Record Changer*, for February 1951), Kay C. Thompson quoted, 'Where jazz came from I can't rightly say, but . . . I was the first one in New Orleans to employ a jazz pianist in the red-light district. . . . In those days jazz was associated principally with dance-halls and cabarets. . . . Jazz didn't start in sporting houses . . . it was what most of our customers wanted to hear.'

Jazz was, first of all, the music of the Negro community. And in New Orleans it was achieving a unique instrumental development. The pianists followed that development. They apparently did not originate it, but because of the musical knowledge they were likely to have, and because of the nature of their instruments, they made important contributions.

And there was music everywhere for them to absorb.

'One of my pleasantest memories as a kid growing up in New Orleans was how a bunch of us kids, playing, would suddenly hear sounds. It was like a phenomenon, like the Aurora Borealis—maybe. The sounds of men playing would be so clear, but we wouldn't be sure where they were coming from. So we'd start trotting, start running—"It's this way!" "It's this way!"—And, sometimes, after running for a while, you'd find you'd be nowhere near that music. But that music could come on you any time like that. The city was full of the sounds of music. . . .'[1]

When Morton says he had played drums and trombones in parades, no one who has heard his left hand will be much surprised.

No matter how often one hears about it, one is repeatedly struck by accounts of the remarkable cross-section of life which operated so freely in the Storyville district. People from every class, every race, every economic group and from all over the world came there. Did Morton work there as a pianist and have the kind of celebrity that Tony Jackson, Albert Carrol, Albert Wilson, 'the game kid', and the rest? It has lately been contended that he didn't have their success, and even that he didn't work as a pianist in New Orleans at all—that he

was exaggerating about all that as he exaggerated about many things. He surely worked *out of* New Orleans into nearby towns and cities, taking its music with him. And I think in a larger context, whether or not Morton was, as he implied, a piano king in more expensive Storyville houses, becomes, in one context, almost a matter of detail.

I have said that I think that when one hears his music, his pride, snobbery, and delusions will fall away. They do even in music that is not really his. On the recordings for the Library of Congress, Morton re-created a scene he called the 'Georgia Skin Game', a card game with a bunch of sharp characters Morton admired for their skill and for the quasi-romantic life they led, but a life which his grandmother, and the Coloured Creole *in him*, would surely have disapproved of. As he told the story, the card gave climaxes in a song sung to the cards by one of the players. Here Morton's artistic talent and memories came forth, and almost made Jelly Roll into a different being.

The song is like a work song, the slap of the cards is the stroke of the labourer's hammer. Its melody also suggests the spiritual, *Motherless Child*. The loving passion with which Morton sings its beautifully haunting 'blue' notes shows how deeply he felt about this music, about this kind of simpler 'folk' music, however he might act or whatever he might say on another day and to a certain man. And the dramatic vividness with which he re-creates that scene is not only evidence of a talent but of a passionate apprehension and wondering admiration of the human beings involved. If his art can help us to see thus, as his deeper self could see them, he will have served all men well.

[1] Danny Barker in *Hear Me Talkin' To Ya*, edited by Nat Shapiro and Nat Hentoff.

2

GULF COAST, WEST COAST, THE RIVER, LAKE MICHIGAN

There is a passage in *Life on the Mississippi* in which Mark Twain remarks on the number of Negroes who travelled: it was as if they had decided to make up for all the years when they and their forebears could not travel.

Morton travelled. He travelled the way we think of an itinerant blues singer as travelling. In *Mister Jelly Roll*, Alan Lomax writes: 'After 1904 he was constantly on the prod, using New Orleans only as a base of operations and nurturing ambitions mortal strange. . . .'

And soon, his base of operations was no longer New Orleans, but apparently wherever he happened to be. 'I went to Memphis about 1908. At that time I was very shy about playing the piano any place.' Then, James P. Johnson remembers Ferdinand, by now 'Jelly Roll' Morton, in New York in 1911. Lomax quoted Johnson, 'First time I saw Jelly was in 1911. He came through New York playing that *Jelly Roll Blues* of his. He was, well, he was what you might call pimping at the time, had that diamond in his tooth and a couple of dogs [prostitutes] along. That diamond helped him in his business, you know—it made some of these gals think he was a big shot. Of course, Jelly Roll wasn't a piano player like some of us down here. We bordered more on the classical theory of music.' Reb Spikes knew him in Tulsa in 1912 and said Morton wanted to be a comedian. In the same year he also worked in St. Louis. During 1913 to 1915 he was in and out of Chicago, where Will Rossiter published his original *Jelly Roll Blues*. In 1917, Morton left Chicago for Los Angeles (his second trip) and for five years it was his base. William Russell has written of these years, 'During his second California visit (1917–22), he was associated with the Spikes Bros. Publishing Co. in Los Angeles. . . . He had as always a variety of interests. He worked at first in various Central Avenue resorts—the Cadillac Café, the Newport Bar, and the upstairs Penny Dance Hall at 9th Street. There was also the band with Buddy Petit and Frankie Dusen down at Baron Long's in Watts, and later a six-piece band at Leek's Lake and Wayside Park (where he entertained King Oliver as guest star one night in April 1922). The period was one of Jelly's happiest and most prosperous. He could have his big car, his diamonds, and could keep his music just as a sideline for special kicks while he made his real money from the Pacific Coast "Line". As one friend put it, "You don't think Jelly got all those diamonds he wore on his garters with the $35 a week he made in music." But whether Jelly was really "one of the higher ups", as he claimed, or just a procurer is immaterial, for Jelly's real interest undeniably was always music. On the Gulf Coast they'd called him a pool shark and gambler, with music as a "decoy". But the important point is that to his dying day Jelly loved music. . . .

'So up and down the Coast from Vancouver, Canada, to Tampico, Mexico, Jelly went, always carrying with him, among the other commodities of "good time", the *new music* of New Orleans. In San Diego, at the U.S. Grant Hotel . . . someone told Jelly the hotel paid their white musicians $75 a week, he pulled his band out without notice. In San Francisco Jelly even participated in the final days of the notorious Barbary Coast and played for a while at the Jupiter on Columbus Avenue at Pacific.'

A musician who worked with him then remembered a white hotel owner who requested a waltz. Morton replied loudly, '*Waltz?* Man, these people want to *dance?* And you talking about waltz. This is the *Roll* you're talking to. I know what these people want!' Again, it was Morton's identity, of course. Was he Negro—Coloured Creole? Not white, exactly, but . . . He was *the Roll*! He had nothing against waltzes, really, and he even had some jazz waltzes he used.

For every story of the pianist or the band leader in these years, there is a story of the hustler, the card shark, the pool shark, singer or comedian, patent medicine pedlar, and the rest. But I suspect that music more and more impressed itself on him as his undeniable calling during the California years, and the composing there seems to have been prolific.

He is reported in Kentucky and in St. Louis (working in Fate Marable's riverboat group) in 1923, but that year he had shifted his sights back to Chicago and (as anyone with a nodding acquaintance with the history of jazz will know) with good reason, for the music was in demand there.

3

SUCCESS AND FAME

'Morton,' wrote Whitney Balliet, 'gave the American dream an awful pummelling before it finally cut him down.'

The period when he seemed to be winning, and only with his music, began in 1923 when he was working in and out of Chicago—'out of' chiefly because he did not often function as a musician, or anything else, in Chicago because, it is said, he would not cater to the hoods who ran most of the places where he could find work in that city in the 'twenties. The 'out of' included St. Louis, which in the length of time he spent there, was important. But the really important events of the early 'twenties for Morton did take place in Chicago. He formed an alliance with the Melrose Brothers music company, out of Walter Melrose and Marty Bloom's music shop. They published his pieces, published 'stock' arrangements, and helped get him recording dates— at first as a soloist, then with the New Orleans Rhythm Kings and with groups of his own. Finally, beginning in September 1926, with the Victor company, as leader of the 'Red Hot Peppers' for a series of recordings that carried him to a kind of national fame, and many of which have been available to record buyers almost ever since.

They were beautifully recorded. They were beautifully conceived, led, orchestrated, rehearsed, and played. They are still among the great artistic successes in jazz recording. And they sold very well.

Johnny St. Cyr, who played banjo on all but four of the Chicago titles described Morton's approach, 'Jelly was a very, very agreeable man to cut a record with,' largely because he would let his men take breaks and choruses as and where they felt they best could: '. . . he'd leave it to your own judgement . . . and he was always open for suggestions.'

In 1945, Omer Simeon, clarinettist on most of Morton's most successful recordings, told in more detail about the sessions in Art Hodes's *Jazz Record* magazine. 'We used to go to his home for rehearsals and the first time I was there, he handed me a piece called *Mamamita*, which had a pretty hard clarinet part. I guess he was testing me out. . . .

'Walter Melrose brought all the music down from his music store. Morton was working for Melrose then and the pieces we played were mostly stock arrangements Jelly had made up and published by Melrose. Jelly marked out parts we liked and he always had his manuscripts there and his pencils and he was always writing and changing little parts. . . . Jelly left our solos up to us but the backgrounds, harmony and licks were all in his arrangements. He

217

was easy to work for and he always explained everything he wanted. . . .

'We would have a couple of rehearsals at Jelly's house before the date and Melrose would pay us $5.00 a man. That's the only time I ever got paid for a rehearsal. . . . Technicians set the stage for the date—Jelly had to take orders there for a change. . . .

'Melrose spared no expense for a record date—anything Jelly Roll wanted he got. Melrose worshipped him like a king. Jelly was great for effects, as on *Sidewalk Blues* and *Steamboat Stomp* and later on like the opening on *Kansas City Stomp*. . . . For the second date he got Darnell Howard and Barney Bigard in for the trio effect he wanted on two of the sides. I played all the clarinet part and Howard and Bigard just sat there and held their clarinets except for the few strains Jelly wanted them to play. . . .

'He was fussy on introductions and endings and he always wanted the ensemble his way but he never interfered with the solo work. He'd tell us where he wanted the solo or break but the rest was up to us. . . . I remember on *Dr. Jazz*, the long note I played wasn't in the stock arrangement. Jelly liked it and had Melrose put it in the orchestration. . . .'

Baby Dodds, drummer on three of the Chicago sessions has spoken of the way Morton worked, 'John and I also made records with Jelly Roll Morton's Red Hot Peppers. On all the jobs with Jelly Roll it was he who picked the men for the session. He went around himself and got the men he wanted to record with him. We weren't a regular band. . . . But when Jelly Roll gave us a ring we met for rehearsal and we all knew what was expected of us. Of course we all knew each other from New Orleans but those record sessions were the only times we all got together to play music. But there was a fine spirit in that group and I enjoyed working with Jelly Roll immensely. . . .

'At rehearsal Jelly Roll Morton used to work on each and every number until it satisfied him. Everybody had to do just what Jelly wanted him to do.

During rehearsal he would say, "Now that's just the way I want it on the recording," and he meant just that. We used his original numbers and he always explained what it was all about and played a synopsis of it on the piano. . . . You did what Jelly Roll wanted you to do, no more and no less. And his own playing was remarkable and kept us in good spirits. He wasn't fussy, but he was positive. He knew what he wanted and he would get the men he knew could produce it. But Jelly wasn't a man to get angry. I never saw him upset and he didn't raise his voice at any time. . . .

'Although Jelly used to work out all the different parts himself, he often gave us something extra to do, some little novelty or something. When we made the *Jungle Blues* he wanted a gong effect and I think I used a large cymbal and a mallet to produce the effect he wanted. . . . And the records we made with Jelly were made under the best of recording conditions. They were recorded in the Chicago Victor studio on Oak Street near Michigan Avenue, and the acoustics there were very good. It was one of the best studios I ever worked in.'[1]

Chicago in the early 'twenties—there were King Oliver, Jimmy Noone, the Dodds Brothers, the New Orleans Rhythm Kings, a young Louis Armstrong. But, as I say, not much Morton, outside of the Melrose shop and the Victor studios. He toured the Middle West to considerable success, however.

In 1928, Morton decided to go where so many jazzmen were going, to the place that was becoming the centre of jazz and has more or less remained so since: New York. Armstrong, Oliver, the young 'Chicagoans' (Eddie Condon & Co.) went or had gone.

Artistic success continued, on records at least. But not personal or monetary success. Guitarist Danny Barker wrote in the *Jazz Review*, 'Jelly Roll spent most of the afternoons and evenings at the

[1] From *The Baby Dodds Story*, as told to Larry Gara.

218

Jelly Roll Morton at the keyboard in the 1920s

Duncan P. Schiedt

Rhythm Club and everytime I saw him he was lecturing to the musicians about organizing. Most of the name and star musicians paid him no attention because he was always preaching, in loud terms, that none of the famous New York bands had a beat. He would continuously warn me: "Don't be simple and ignorant like these fools in the big country towns." I would always listen seriously because most of the things he said made plenty of sense to me.

'Jelly was constantly preaching that if he could get a band to rehearse his music and listen to him he could keep a band working. He would get one-nighters out of town and would have to beg musicians to work with him.'

Wilbur de Paris told Orin Keepnews, 'He was nothing special: Henderson and McKinney were *the* bands, and Jelly was just another leader making gigs.'[1]

Still, Morton had the diamonds in his tooth and

[1] From *Jelly Roll Morton* by Orin Keepnews in *The Jazz Makers*, edited Nat Shapiro and Nat Hentoff.

his garters, the two big cars, Lincolns, Cadillacs, etc., and could flash the bank roll and the thousand-dollar bill.

Omer Simeon described his continuing pride and bearing in New York, '. . . He could back up anything he said. Every one liked to hear him talk and argue . . . in New York, when swing was becoming popular, Chick Webb used to kid him—told him he

As I say, the good records continued at first. The most successful were the earliest and still used the older conception of three horns, piano and rhythm. They were made with a band he had at the Rose Danceland in the spring of 1928: with Ward Pinkett's trumpet, 'Geechy' Fields on trombone, Lee Blair on banjo, and the Benford brothers, Bill and Tom, on tuba and drums. It was one of the few

didn't know anything about jazz and asked him about New Orleans. That would start him off about being the pioneer of jazz. He was always talking about New Orleans; about Buddy Bolden, Frankie Dusen, Buddy Petit, Tony Jackson—he could take off their mannerisms on a job and he was always a comedian. It was hard to keep up with him—he could talk twenty-four hours in a row.'

times Morton recorded with his regular band; only Omer Simeon was brought in from another group, the Louis Russell band at The Nest.

Two years later, the Victor contract was up. And the great Depression was on. Morton was sure that his failures were due to a conspiracy of booking agents, music publishers, tune and idea thieves, a conspiring A.S.C.A.P. (which never elected this composer of at least three enduring national 'hit' pieces to membership!), and a West Indian who put a voodoo spell on him.[1]

He still had music and he wanted to play, one feels sure. Despite a kazoo here, a bit of vaudeville banter there, or the artistic error of a schmaltzy *Someday Sweetheart* (with violins, and apparently not even intended to be a jazz performance), I think that, during the whole course of his recording career, Morton's musical integrity is constant and admirable. One suspects a gradual realization that he was a part of a movement that was terribly important, that had spread widely, and whatever else he was in it for, he was in it to contribute (though he may not have put it that way), to keep things on the track, to try out things that might work within it, to show what would work. In his arguments with Chick Webb and his musicians, whatever we hear of con-

ceit and perhaps of jealousy, we hear also a devotion to the principles of jazz that he stood for and a rejection of tendencies he did not believe in. His theories of jazz (often misunderstood, I think) are not a mere effort to portray himself as important, but also an attempt to explain practice and to defend the integrity of a music against public misunderstanding, against exploitation, and against tendencies within it which to him were wrong ones.

Morton knew, or came to know, that jazz was a music with an identity and heritage that was unknown or badly misunderstood. At the same time, he did not want it to be esoteric or cultish. At times one feels he believed he could communicate his music to *anyone*. Perhaps he was right at that, but the point is that the communication was to be made in his terms, not theirs, and the music was to say what it said, not what they wanted to hear. Whatever his delusions about wealth or boasts about his position, there is an integrity to his craft and art which came back to him in his most adverse moments. Even at those times in his wanderings and in his myriad of enterprises when Morton seemed almost to be fighting his destiny the music would take hold.

[1] Vodun, Hoodoo, Voodoo—it has echoes in several directions. The original slaves brought to New Orleans were Dahomeans, and Vodun was their worship. According to Marshall Stearns's book, *The Story of Jazz*, West African influences survived for years in *laissez-faire* New Orleans and gradually blended with European music in 'private vodun ceremonies and public performances in Congo Square'. Vodun is a powerful and continuing fact and New Orleans is its centre in the United States. Morton himself was a Catholic. However, he described his aunt as a hoodoo witch who, during his childhood, had used Vodun to cure him of an illness. In New York at this time, Morton burned his clothing and 'spent thousands of dollars trying to get this spell taken off of me'.

4

A 'FAILURE' FOR POSTERITY

By 1937, Morton was in Washington, D.C., not in very good health, running a small club for its owner (a woman) which was known by a different name almost from month to month; The Blue Moon Inn, The Music Box, The Jungle Inn. Business was very poor. But a kind of adulation began to develop. Record collectors, jazz scholars, real Morton fans (like Roy J. Carew, from New Orleans, who subsequently published all of Morton's later pieces and

still keeps them in print) began to come by to see him and talk about jazz. Finally, through their kind of persuasion, folklorist Alan Lomax recorded Morton on an inexpensive portable disc recorder and a fine Steinway, for the archives of the Library of Congress.

Such events, and his appearance on a Ripley 'Believe It or Not' radio programme (refuting Ripley's claim that W. C. Handy was 'the originator of jazz and blues') encouraged him to try New York again. There were a few jobs, some 'all star' records for Victor (the music and conception were more slanted towards a vague re-creation of New Orleans for the public than towards Jelly Roll Morton, jazz orchestrator); other recordings—some of them of rather commercially intended Morton songs (*We Are Elks, Good Old New York*); and there was the very charming and musically successful 'New Orleans Memories' album of Morton playing and singing. But they say that the sign of the times was that he was more often at the pool table than the piano. One occasion when he did take over at the piano (a possibly true story goes) was when he jumped up out of the audience as a big swing band was playing Fletcher Henderson's version of Mor- ton's *King Porter Stomp*, read the leader off, sat down at the piano and demonstrated how it *should* be played.

In 1940, he went to southern California. His god- mother was dying and his godfather was blind, but perhaps that was just an excuse. He chained his two big cars together and went. He was soon rehearsing a big band—but only two days of a week. The other five, he might have to spend in bed with 'heart trouble and asthma'. 'Will write soon. Still sick,' he sent his Mabel in New York in April 1941, hurriedly written across an application for a postal money order.

On 10 July 1941, Jelly Roll Morton died in Los Angeles. His pallbearers were Kid Ory and the members of Ory's band.

THE MUSIC

I

AN INTRODUCTION

Morton said that a good jazz pianist should try to imitate a band—and almost all of them have tried to imitate bands or horns. Therefore almost every- thing in his orchestral style comes from his piano. But, as we shall see, he did some decidedly pianistic things as a soloist that he knew had to be changed when he orchestrated his pieces. The left hand is his trombone and rhythm section, the right his trumpets and reeds—true enough. But the roots of his style include other things. The first of these is ragtime, and its European analogues and sources—marches, polkas, etc. The second is the blues.

Ragtime was a separate movement in American music. It is not a kind of crude, pre-jazz, although it made important contributions to jazz. In several respects, it is more polished and formal than jazz has ever intended to be. It may derive some of its themes and a few of its devices from Negro folk songs, spirituals, etc., but it has a close relationship to the Western tradition. It is primarily melodic: its rhythms are fairly bright and constant and one kind of syncopation frequently dominates it.

Ragtime compositions (and the pieces *are* com- positions in the strictest sense) were made of several equally important, related themes. The simplest structure was (to give each separate theme-melody a letter), A B C D; very frequent was A B A C D (as in the most famous, Scott Joplin's *Maple Leaf Rag*); cyclical and rondo forms were also used. Although ragtime performances may have involved some improvisation (undoubtedly there was much embellishment) and there are some published rags with written variations, it does not seem essential to this music.

At the turn of the century, ragtime had become *the* dominant popular music in America. Of course, it was simplified, commercialized, and even exploited. In more authentic circles, it gradually became a kind of showman's piano for rather meaningless displays of technique. It soon attracted inferior composers and performers, and with some important exceptions, had largely spent itself *as a movement* by about 1910.

Morton once claimed to have 'invented' jazz. Whether he did or not, his music shows a crucial transition. Most of his important pieces are built like rags of several themes, usually on three, plus a chorus or two of written variation on the third (thereby most important) theme. He used more than one kind of syncopation and more rhythmic freedom and variety, polyrhythms, more variety in harmony, 'blue dissonances', polyphony between the hands, but, more important, a Morton piece *depends* on that pre-set (or pre-sketched) variation in the score and, as he played it, on improvisation in performance as well.

Morton's music combined the formal and melodic approach of ragtime—and the dances and songs (music of European origin) that he heard around him—with the rhythms, melodic devices, polyphonies in Negro blues, work songs, spirituals, etc., and produced something new. Like all folk music, these blues and spirituals used improvisation. But Morton made variation a crucial part of his music, and his sensibility in making variations was outstanding enough to carry such a burden.

Morton was, in several ways, a modernist in his day. That is why he might ridicule ragtime players. He was a part of a movement which saved this 'Afro-American' music from a degeneration at the hands of pseudo and second-rate rag men and continued its development. He obviously respected the *best* ragtime men, however. And that is also why he frequently scorned blues pianists, 'one-tune piano players'. His work was more sophisticated, formal, knowledgeable, resourceful, varied—more *musical* than theirs.

It is interesting to speculate on what banal 'rhythm-making' jazz might have become if it did not have the formal, melodic conception of ragtime in its background. At the same time, one shudders to think what might have happened if the deep passion, the freedom, the poetry and rhythmic variety of Negro folk music and blues had not replenished it, as it were, 'from below'.

When Morton was asked by Alan Lomax for his theory of jazz, he gave, of course, not a theory but some basic things about it which were important to him. Some were obviously directed at your old Aunt Sallie who thinks jazz has to be loud, fast and disorganized.

Morton said that he worked out his style at medium tempos—almost all jazz styles have originally been worked out that way. (Hear the recordings made at Minton's in the early 'forties, hear Armstrong's 'ballads' in the 'thirties.) His first point was the famous 'always keep the melody going some way'. He acknowledged that melodic variation is his way, but this remark is really a part of his insistence on continuous, proper, and interesting harmonization.

His next remarks were on riffs. Much has been made of his insistence that they are for background, but Morton himself did not always use them that way: several of his tunes have riff melodies, and the very one he used in the bass here is the last strain of his band recording of *Georgia Swing*. At any rate, one could hardly question the effectiveness of riffs behind a soloist.

223

His third point, that a pianist should imitate an orchestra, at least has historical confirmation; almost every piano style in jazz (from Hines through Garner, Morton through Powell) has been derived from the imitation of a band or a horn style.

As Morton put it, 'breaks' are 'one of the most effective things you can do in jazz'. In a sense they are the culmination of the syncopation and the rhythmic resources in jazz (unless 'stop time' carries things a step further). Charlie Parker's famous break in *A Night In Tunisia* became a fable immediately after his record of it was released, but today breaks are often poorly made and usually at the beginning of choruses, where they are possibly least effective. Certainly Morton's subtle sense of time and suspense in making them is the bane of his 'revivalist' followers.

Complete with pretentious arpeggios made on the Library of Congress piano, came the just assertion that jazz can be soft, sweet, and slow. To this day, many a jazz band wisely tests its ability to swing by trying to do so at a pianissimo whisper. And the problem of swinging at slow tempos is one which has plagued many jazzmen in all periods.

Morton's remark that ragtime players would keep increasing their tempos because a perfect tempo hadn't been picked for that style has puzzled many and will continue to. Jazz players can increase their tempos, too (Morton may himself), and a blues pianist like Will Ezell does it in a way that makes it seem quite intentional. The device is standard in many musics, including West African, of course. As we have seen, Morton said that he hit on his own style because he couldn't make fast tempos at first, and then discovered that he could incorporate rhythmic variety, embellishments, and variations of many kinds at such speeds. Certainly if a player uses a simple ragtime, 'octive' bass, he may well tend to speed up, and if he is building in his performance by rhythmic-melodic variation, he will not need the 'false' climax of merely increasing his speed.

What Jelly Roll Morton called 'the Spanish tinge' in jazz—or in his jazz—and the influence of what is called 'Latin' music on his music and on New Orleans jazz, is both more general and more deep than the fact he wrote many jazz-tango pieces will account for.

'New Orleans was inhabited with maybe every race on the face of the globe. And, of course, we had Spanish people, plenty of them. . . .' Morton said. Spanish music was a part of the city's musical heritage and life. The tango and what was sometimes called the 'Mexican serenade' was also a continuing part of the popular music of the day. Unfortunately many of the discussions of the constant flirting of jazz and Latin rhythms quickly become a matter of listing tunes: several of Morton's; *St. Louis Blues*; Armstrong's *Peanut Vendor*; *Monteca*; *Barbados*; *Un Poco Loco*; *Señor Blues*, etc., etc. (They might also mention the 'samba' qualities in some ragtime, Scott Joplin's tango rag *Solace*, and some others.)

According to recent opinions of musicologists, the habañera was of Hispanic origin, not African as once thought. It came from Cuba as such. In the poorer sections of Buenos Aires about 1900, the habañera was combined with the milonga to make the tango, became a popular dance, and spread. It is not supposed to have been syncopated there before 1905, but I have the feeling that it was syncopated in New Orleans before that.

But what is the relationship of early jazz to the tango? Is it only a matter of a man like Morton having written tangos of a special kind? Is it a matter of using tango themes as a part of certain compositions? Is it a matter of occasional rhythmic effects? There are several records by King Oliver's Creole Jazz Band whereon Lil Armstrong will spontaneously break into tango rhythm behind the polyphony of the horns. She may be quickly joined by Bill Johnson and Honoré Dutrey, or she may continue alone, playing against everyone else's beat. The effect of this is exciting and the possibilities for rhythmic variety are obvious. Morton will frequently do much the same: often in his band records we hear him suddenly inject tango rhythms against the prevailing beat, with a kind of sublime intuition about just when to do it and how long to keep it up. We also hear this sort of thing in his solo piano, of course. One can sometimes hear it, too, in Baby Dodds's drum solos and accompaniments. Some 'modern' drummers (and other instrumentalists) similarly found a source of rhythmic variety in Latin patterns. (One might even say that modern drummers *re*-discovered their polyrhythmic and melodic role, one which swing drummers largely neglected.)

Thus we can perform jazz tangos, we can use tango themes and interludes, we can use tango rhythms for, as Morton put it, a 'seasoning'. But it goes further than that, I think. Just as Dizzy Gillespie's trumpet phrasing frequently shows his keen ear for trumpeters in rumba bands, certain of Bunk Johnson's or Louis Armstrong's phrases come from the melodic-rhythmic manner of the tango.

Duncan P. Schiedt

A publicity still for the Red Hot Peppers

225

It may even be that both of the latter were encouraged to play so markedly behind the beat not only by their apprenticeships as second trumpeters but also by the delayed pulse of tango phrasing. The same kind of thing shows up constantly in Morton's playing and composing. For example, the 'trio' strain of one of his most successful pieces, *The Wolverine Blues*. The placement of the notes there

chief musical points he talked about is his use of 'blue' harmonies in the piece and the effect of the juxtaposition of the two rhythms.

Morton made two other piano versions of *Mama 'Nita* (sometimes called *Mamamita*), but the improvisation on the Library of Congress version can make the others sound rather pallid. The piece has three themes; actually the second is a rather dull

Duncan P. Schiedt

Jelly Roll Morton with the Red Hot Peppers, the band which he founded in 1922

corresponds to the placement of the heavy beats in a tango. The result automatically plays one rhythm against another.

In his demonstration on *La Paloma* on the Library of Congress records, Morton went at the problem the other way around. He did not show tango effects in a jazz piece, or play a jazz tango, but remade a well-known tango into jazz. One of the

interlude which becomes interesting when he alters it, and the third is almost a variant of the first. Morton performed on them in cyclical form. One point that immediately strikes one is the wonderful alliance he made between the tango bass and his characteristic use of trombone-like polyphonic bass lines; these two elements usually become one in his work.

226

Morton's *New Orleans Blues* (or *New Orleans Joys*) is a piece quite celebrated in certain quarters for the masterful way he drops behind the beat. It is a twelve-bar blues-tango and, the way he has organized it, two themes emerge. In performance he would play them: A, A, B (introduced by the bass figure); B, B, B (the bass figure has risen to treble; this is the 'behind the beat' chorus, by the way); A, A (the last two choruses drop the tango effect and, as Morton put it, 'stomp').

But as you see, I have already begun to discuss Morton's piano style in specific performances. I would like to do more of it, and again I will put some emphasis on the Library of Congress recordings.

2

THE PIANO SOLOS, EARLY AND LATE

In several respects *Hyena Stomp* (although not a major piece as a composition) gives one a good idea of the kind of music Morton created, particularly as he recorded the piece as a piano solo in 1938. *Hyena Stomp* is uncharacteristic of Morton in that it has only one theme and that is a very simple one—but the simplicity is a help. Morton recorded it twice: there is also an orchestral version from 1927, and a comparison of the two gives a further insight into Morton's conception.

The theme, as I say, is simple—the basic strain is stated in the first two measures. That statement is harmonically modulated through a chorus of sixteen bars which serves as an introduction. There follows the second sixteen-bar chorus in which the melody is again stated in bare form. In these first two statements the harmony (full for its time and beautifully appropriate) is necessarily made clear, and there are occasional hints of the kind of rhythmic variation that is to come. There follows a series of six melodic variations and embellishments. Each is based on a musical idea which he works out, each is related to what precedes and what follows, either as contrast or complement, and each is a part of the total pattern of the whole performance.

There is one aspect of Morton's approach which the band recording of *Hyena Stomp* brings out, the variations are instrumentally and orchestrally conceived; as we have seen, Morton believed that the basis of jazz piano style was in its imitation of an orchestra.

The first variation (the third chorus in performance) is primarily rhythmic—an appropriate contrast to the careful harmonic emphasis of the dual theme statements. He simplifies the melody and harmony drastically, preparing to rebuild it. It is a kind of 'barrelhouse' variation in which a swinging rhythmic momentum is first introduced. It is another passage for the whole band, with the work of the rhythm section, the trombone, and the accents of the horns above them. The next chorus is an elaborate lyric transformation of the theme, lightly dancing after the heavier motion of what preceded it. Obviously Morton had the clarinet's lower register in mind. This chorus is melodically the most complex. From this point on, as we gradually return to and build on the rhythmic momentum set up in the first variation, we hear an increasing melodic simplification and dynamic building. The third variation is an excellent stroke. It still refers to the melody, of course, but also transforms (by simplification) the previous variation. It is the clarinet in the upper register. It thus forms a kind of two-chorus unit with the preceding variation. The next chorus is a contrast, but one which has been subtly prepared for. It is a variation made in the bass; Morton's left hand imitates the polyphonic line of a trombone (a rather complicated one for the time) under his treble. And in the preceding chorus there had been much activity in his left hand, readying our ears for this one. In the fifth variation, we are reminded of trumpet figures, and these gradually build into an ensemble variation in the sixth. Morton leads into and makes his climax, the dynamics and the sonority continue to build excitement, the rhythm swings freely and simply. This chorus shows that special quality of excitement completely articulated, never frenzied, of which Morton was a master, and the performance justly ends with a restored calm.

There is a lot of music made from that simple theme, made in ways so widespread in all kinds of music that one is tempted to believe that Morton is in touch with something implicit in the nature of music itself. But if you hear this apparently simple piece again, I think that you will see Morton even more deeply involved with possibilities in the material he chose and in his form than we have seen already.

The chorus unit is sixteen measures (the structure of the march and of ragtime). But, as we have seen, Morton has used variations which have a close continuity across two choruses, in variations 2 and 3 (the two 'clarinet' choruses) and in variations 6 and 8 (the 'brass' choruses). At the same time, each chorus by its nature may readily fall into two eight-bar units. These in turn may fall into units of four bars each. Then there is the fact that we began with: that the basic melodic content can be stated in two bars. Morton takes some interesting advantages of these things during the piece. For example, the final

chorus (variation 6) consists of a continuous eight-bar line, followed by two four-bar units. And there is the contrast in the two 'clarinet' variations. The first of these is based on a parallel repetition of two-bar units, the second begins with an improvisation which makes contrasting two-bar units. Thus Morton makes a strikingly effective use of what some might see as, necessarily, a melodic limitation inherent in a two-bar phrase, and makes it one of the basic structural conceptions and chief virtues of his playing. He builds variations in a continuity within sixteen-bar choruses, he combines some of these into double choruses, and within this, he works out smaller structures of two, four, and eight bars which contribute by contrast, parallel, and echo to the total development and form.

Morton's command of the materials and devices which he used was that of an artist. Still, jazz was for him a performer's music and he could improvise and could project emotion spontaneously and immediately. However, I believe that once one grasps the fact that ordered and frequently subtle melodic variation is essential to his music, its excitement and its beauty and its uniqueness will possess him even more strongly and lastingly.

For *Kansas City Stomps*, a brief account of the form of the solo on the 1938 version will suffice for the point at hand. It is a unique performance of that piece—or any similar multithematic Morton composition—since it completes the implicit rondo and does it in unique improvisational form. As published, *Kansas City Stomps* consists of an introduction (a 'tune up' motif) and three themes, thus: A (E flat), A (an exact repeat), C (A flat), C' (a melodic variation). Both A and B are sixteen-bar themes (out of ragtime and marches) and C is an unusual twelve-bar melody with stop-time at bars one and two, seven and eight—making two six-bar units possible. The performance at hand goes this way: Introduction, A, A' (a variation), B, B' (a variation), A'' (another variation), C, C' (a variation), introduction (as a modulation), A''' (a third variation). Thus a rondo, with each return to each theme a variation on that theme. I have the strong feeling that if anyone even attempted such an 'extended form' today, phrases like 'daring experimenter' and 'searching innovator' would be thick in the air.

Jungle Blues is a deliberately archaic, harmonically 'primitive' blues. Morton played it for Lomax as a part of his criticism of Duke Ellington, something about Ellington playing 'jungle music' and his having made that kind of music before him. (Morton's criticism of Ellington seems to miss the point as much as Ellington's often quoted attack on Morton.) It may sound like a kind of improvisation on blues chords, but it is not; the basic sequence and development were compositionally pre-set. I think one of its nicest effects is the way Morton will keep one kind of rhythm going to the brink of monotony and then shift his treble to a counter-rhythm—the kind of relieving contrast wherein Morton's instincts seldom failed him. We will say more of the piece when discussing Morton's Red Hot Pepper recordings.

Between 17 July 1923 and 20 April 1926, Morton recorded piano solo versions of over twenty compositions, all but one or two of them his own. Inevitably, several of them are inferior, but the records include *King Porter Stomp, New Orleans Joys (Blues), Grandpa's Spells, Kansas City Stomps, Wolverine Blues, The Pearls, London Blues* (later called *Shoe Shiner's Drag*), *Mamamita, Froggie Moore* (or *Frog-i-More Rag*), *Shreveport Stomp, (Original) Jelly Roll Blues, Big Foot Ham, Stratford Hunch* (later called *Chicago Breakdown*), and an unissued *Milenberg Joys.* Jazzmen have been proclaimed 'major figures' on the basis of far less achievement than these solos represent.

In 1944 William Russell wrote an analytical review, for the magazine the *Needle,* of Morton's rediscovered *Frog-i-More Rag* solo. It is an excellent introduction to Morton's style. 'Jelly Roll had a more formal musical training and background than many New Orleans musicians. . . . At times the close-knit design [of his compositions] is marked by an economy of means that amounts to understatement. . . . Jelly took great pride in his "improvisations" [on a theme]. . . .

'Jelly's performance is a revelation of rhythmic variety by means of such devices as shifted accents, slight delays, and anticipations. Of course, to some . . . this is only a bad performance by a pianist unable to keep correct time, of a piece any third-grade conservatory pupil could play right off at sight. Curiously, as raggy as Jelly's performance . . . is, it is nevertheless in perfect *time*; the regular pulse can be felt throughout with no loss at all in momentum. . . . The melodic invention of this finale is as notable as its immense rhythmic vitality. . . . Jelly's rhythmic impetus and melodic embellishment give the effect of a fantastic and frenzied variation. Actually each bar is directly related to its counterpart in the first simple statement and all of Jelly's most characteristic and fanciful "figurations" are fused with the basic idea as though they belonged there originally. . . . With Jelly Roll, no matter how exuberant rhythmically or varied melodically . . . there is never any doubt of their musical logic and that every note grows out of the original motive.'

In some respects these early solos of 1923–6 may impress us differently than the later recordings I have used as a basis for some of this discussion of Morton's piano and style. There is a rhythmic vigour and optimism in Morton's 1923 work that the later versions do not have. And in several of them there is a decided rhythmic affinity to ragtime which Morton's music was otherwise breaking away from.

Comparisons among various versions of the same piece are always instructive and herewith invited. And even during the 'twenties Morton recorded several of the pieces several times, either in alternate 'takes' or at later sessions. With these remarks as an introduction, I shall now leave the pleasures of further comparisons largely to the reader. But I will append remarks on two more of the pieces. *Mamamita* (or *Mama 'Nita*, or 'Mama Anita') is seldom mentioned among Morton's best pieces, but it is a very good composition. In the version done for Paramount it is played with some ingenious polyrhythms in its tango section and one really striking chorus of melodic variation. (Originally issued on the other side of *Mamamita*, however, was the pseudo-blues *35th Street*, a dull song whose rhythmic monotony is relieved only by a couple of Morton's bass cliches.)

Then there is the structural sophistication of *London Blues* (later *Shoe Shiner's Drag*) which was still intriguing jazzmen in the later 'thirties, and remains an implicit challenge to jazz composition even now. It is a twelve-bar blues in form (and in spirit) but it is ingeniously harmonized in part. The fourth section (as given by Louis Gottlieb in *Jazz: A Quarterly of American Music*, $1) has this chord sequence:

$$B\flat \mid F7 \quad C\sharp dim \mid B\flat \mid B\flat 7 \mid E\flat \quad E\flat min6 \mid$$
$$B\flat \quad Fmin6 \mid G7 \mid C7 \mid F7 \mid B\flat \quad E\flat \quad B\flat$$

3

PROLOGUE TO THE RED HOT PEPPERS

If Jelly Roll Morton had never made the Red Hot Pepper records for Victor records, his reputation would probably have to rest on the early published scores and the early piano solos made for Gennet, Paramount, Rialto, etc. Before he made the Victor series, Morton did make some orchestral records and some of them are so bad that they must have seemed to show that his talent had already spent itself on that handful of compositional piano solos. But in retrospect we can notice that in them he attempted everything that he later brought off so brilliantly, even the 'big band' effects of the later Victors. We also hear that most of the virtues of unity, cohesion, and individual skill of the players of the Victor sessions are not to be heard in these earlier recording groups.

There are, however, two successes and they are apparently Morton's first recordings: *Muddy Waters Blues* and *Big Fat Ham*.[1] The group that played

them had a rare unity and swing and performed with confidence and verve. The firm, Keppard-like trumpet leads with authority (could it *really* be Natty Dominique? I doubt it), and Jasper Taylor's fine (if over-recorded) drumming shows both a splendid comprehension of Morton's rhythmic conception and very infectious good spirits. *Big Fat Ham* (later *Big Foot Ham* and *Ham and Eggs*) is a very good composition, and Morton's swinging orchestration outlines his later work. He uses unison, harmony and polyphony in a constantly shifting yet finally unified texture surpassed only by some of the Victors. And the clarinet and particularly the trumpet solos on *Water* might instruct even the dullest head about the blues. Finally there is—besides the trumpet (or cornet), Roy Palmer's trombone, Wilson Townes's clarinet, Morton's piano, and Taylor's woodblocks (no bass or guitar apparently)—an alto saxophone, possibly Arville Harris. I do not want to get into a discussion of the appropriateness of the saxophone to the New Orleans style, particularly since the earliest photographs

[1] For details of these sessions, the reader is recommended, herewith and subsequently, to the Jelly Roll Morton discography compiled by Jorgen Grumet Jepsen, published by Deput Records, Bande, Denmark.

and accounts and recordings of the musicians frequently include them (and include guitars and string basses too). Suffice it to say that saxophones do seem to tangle with the collective improvisational balance on several records. This one does not, and perhaps the reason is not a matter of group style, but because the player here has good timing and swings well. At any rate, using a four-man front line is a problem Morton will take up again, and with some success.

The other important side among the early band recordings is the Gennet version of *Mr. Jelly Lord* (1926). There is some good piano (as there is on nearly every recorded version of this piece) but most important there is a large brass section and a three-man reed section that plays with respectable discipline and swing—and if you know histories of jazz, you know it isn't supposed to have happened quite that early.

Morton is clearly musical director of the four (possibly five) pieces he recorded in 1923 with the New Orleans Rhythm Kings; some of the pieces are and almost all of the ideas of orchestration and effect are his. He helped that group, otherwise sometimes a stiff one, to easy tempos that encouraged them to swing better. And on that NORK version of *London Blues*, Morton ably alternated passages in harmony, counterpoint, solo, and breaks, all along the lines he was later to perfect. The Okeh version of *London Blues* (and *Someday Sweetheart*), from the same year, is done almost entirely in polyphony and solo, however. It would have been a successful record if it were not for the stiff, unswinging clarinet of Horace Eubanks.

The four pieces recorded for the Autograph label in 1924 are interesting chiefly for *Fish Tail Blues* as an early sketch for *Sidewalk Blues*. It was a poor band; here a schmaltzy alto trips over the polyphony and often forces the clarinet into a purely harmonic part, and the playing has constant rhythmic and melodic disunity.

To deal with any more of these early orchestral recordings would be to repeat the same story, or a similar one. And yet, as I say, on them Morton tried everything that he later brought off. And some essentials of his approach to jazz can be heard in them, at least in retrospect and with the benefit of having heard his later and better recordings.

One of the cliches about Morton's orchestral style is that its essence is 'New Orleans polyphony'.[1] But, as we have seen, Morton's earliest orchestral records include unison and harmonized passages, and solos. Morton's earliest Victors use polyphony but, in a sense, use it sparingly. They use unison, harmony, and solo frequently and pronouncedly. At the same time they have a melodic, harmonic, and tonal sophistication which by comparison can make King Oliver's fine early records seem no more than the work of a highly skilful blues band—and that impression endures despite the fact that sooner or later Oliver's band used all the same devices that Morton did, but with far less orchestral skill and point.

If Morton's boast, 'Listen, man, whatever you blow on that horn, you're blowing Jelly Roll,' is taken to mean 'I *originated* everything in jazz and everybody got it from me,' it is obviously not a little absurd (and the ghosts of Scott Joplin, James Scott, and the rest might throw the words back in his face). But one can say that Morton raised or reflected many possibilities for jazz (obviously borrowing some, undoubtedly arriving at others for himself) and solved many of them well. One might say that in several respects, he cuts across years of development in jazz.

I think that this is the best point at which to append a note on two subjects which will plague anyone trying to deal with Morton's music, the questions of plagiarism and of collaboration. The first thing to remember, I think, is that these questions may be raised about the work of *any* major jazzman and about anyone who deals with folk

[1] I have used and am using the term 'polyphony' throughout this account in the way that it is usually used in jazz writing when the New Orleans style is discussed. Actually 'heterophony' might be a better term to borrow from the terminology of Western music for the style.

material. It seems undeniable that Morton once did, in 1929, deliberately and overtly plagiarize three pieces to retaliate against former business associates. But, for example, in contrast, when he recomposed Santo Pecora's *She's Crying For Me* excellently into *Georgia Swing*, he left Pecora's name on the piece, and Charles Luke is fully credited with *Smokehouse Blues*.

On the question of collaboration: it has sometimes been hinted that Morton could hardly read and write music and that he got a collaborator to do all the work of harmonization and orchestration once Morton had presented him with a 'lead sheet' of the melody lines of his pieces. It is quite true that the names of Tiny Parham, Elmer Schoebel and others appear on the Melrose 'stock' orchestrations of his pieces. Some of these orchestrations date from a time after the pieces were recorded for Victor, and are labelled transcriptions of the recordings; others date from before the Victors. However, the real point is that both in the piano style and in the orchestrations—done in Chicago and later in New York—there is one developing musical sensibility to be heard. Morton may have needed technical help; he admitted freely that he did on some matters at some points in his career. But the musical conception, and its careful refinement and evolution, was his own.

4

DUETS, TRIOS, QUARTETS

It used to be said that Morton 'invented' the jazz trio of clarinet, piano, and drums, and that others 'exploited' his idea (the 'others' chiefly being Benny Goodman, of course). Unless one hung out at Pete Lala's place or Dago Tony's in Storyville, or in many other such places in many other cities where such trios might have played, such a claim is on shaky historical grounds. But he did apparently record such units first.

There are only two really successful trio sessions, I think, the *Wolverine Blues* one with Johnny and Baby Dodds, and *Shreveport Stomp* with Omer Simeon and Tommy Benford. The four 1929 trios with Barney Bigard use inferior material and I would say that Bigard's virtues as a clarinettist were ones Ellington helped him develop later.

The 1924 Paramount small group performance of *Mr. Jelly Lord* exists in two 'takes', with quite different piano work. Piano, sax, and a kazoo make a pretty dreadful record on the face of it, but Morton himself was really playing that day and did some ingenious and effective things.

The Autograph duet of *Wolverine Blues* from 1925 with Volly de Faut might be called merely an early effort in the direction of the Victor clarinet trios if it were not for de Faut. One might want him to swing more or question his intonation, but he did some good improvising on a comparatively difficult part. On *My Gal*, the duet becomes a trio when a kazoo enters. Oliver's having Louis Armstrong play slide whistle seems bad enough to us today, but such raucousness in Morton's careful music is harder to take.

The two recorded duets with King Oliver are largely Morton's. On *King Porter Stomp* Oliver plays it almost straight, but despite a brief faltering of cornet and breath techniques here and there, it comes down to a *tour de force* of very expressively played lines, played with fine momentum and swing —and with some splendid and unique ideas about brass-and-mute interpretations of that piece. The other duet from that date, *Tom Cat Blues* (a splicing of themes better known as *Whining Boy* and *Nobody Knows the Way I Feel This Morning*) has some improvising by Oliver with a very good break and variation at the end—in a style, by the way, which, through Armstrong's use of it, told everybody which direction to take for at least twenty years.

The 1927 trio on *Wolverine Blues* with the Dodds brothers seems even better now that we have two 'takes' of it for comparison. It begins as a Morton piano solo, settles into a good swing as Johnny and Baby Dodds enter on the trio section. The clarinet does not play the theme but an arpeggio variation on the chords, and the drummer is almost exemplary in his varied textures. Johnny Dodds's variation on the recently released alternate 'take' is quite different and perhaps even better.

On *Shreveport Stomp*, Omer Simeon plays melody fairly straight but with fine flow and a sense of its singing yet military quality, and with the kind of emotional control that made him so good at Mor-

ton's music. Notice that in one of its interludes there is a long, continuous melody, unbroken by bar lines —a problem few dared to take up again until Lester Young and Charlie Parker. (Writer Dick Hadlock once found the 'introduction' theme to *Shreveport* in Rudy Weidoff's *Saxophobia*, by the way. Morton probably got it from there, perhaps even consciously so.)

Perhaps the real masterpiece of the small group recordings, however, is *Mournful Serenade* (1928), Morton's re-working of King Oliver's *Chimes Blues* for a quartet: Omer Simeon's clarinet; Geechy Fields's trombone; his own piano; and Tommy Benford's drums. The themes have a very different character at Morton's slow tempo and in the passionate interpretation of the horns, sometimes over Morton's almost jocular counterstatements on piano. The handling of the instruments makes *Mournful Serenade* almost a Red Hot Peppers score; it is at least a fine introduction to Morton's scoring—and to the interpretations he could coax from his players, individually and collectively.

5

THE RED HOT PEPPERS

Jelly Roll Morton's audacity was musical enough and his musicianship comprehensive enough to produce an orchestral record like *Black Bottom Stomp* for three horns and rhythm on which, in less than three minutes' playing time, three themes, variations on some of them, a variety of rhythmic and orchestral effect including variations between a 2/4 and a 4/4 rhythm, stop-time harmony, polyphony, call-and-response riff patterns, solo against rhythm —all these things and others happen. Furthermore, in that record Morton had the brilliance to try

something that is still against everyone's thinking: he makes his strongest climaxes not by increasing volume or instrumental mass but by holding back Johnny Lindsay's string bass and Baby Dodds's bass drums until key emotional moments and rhythmic-melodic peaks.

In the course of *Black Bottom Stomp*, to be a bit more detailed, we hear an introduction (we later realize it was borrowed from the second theme) stated in a 'call and response pattern'. The first theme (actually almost a series of chords) is given in harmony, then in solo 'call' by the trumpet and in variational 'response' by the clarinet and trombone, then back to harmony. The second, B, theme then comes in polyphonically with pronounced swing, Lindsay in strong, and includes breaks as well. The clarinet delivers a variation, in effect almost a new theme. Then the piano. Then trumpet against intermittent 'Charleston' rhythms, banjo against string bass (but with a break). Trumpet, clarinet, trumpet with very light rhythm. Then a heavy 'stomp' chorus, with audible bass, bass drum, and with trombone breaks.

It all sounds impossibly cluttered and perhaps pretentious, of course, but it is neither. *Black Bottom Stomp* flows from beginning to end, inevitably and apparently simply, like fate. As I have said, commentators have usually lumped Morton orchestrations of this kind, with the ruggedly integrated improvising of King Oliver's band and the easy blues playing of Johnny Dodds's little pick-up groups, all together as something called 'New Orleans style'.

Morton's best records, however, are among the few that we have that prove that jazz can go beyond the excellence of the improviser, even than the improviser in the ideal setting, for they integrate collective improvisation, pre-arranged sketch, solo, and group textures into a total form and effect greater than the sum of its parts. Besides his records, a few others show how far jazz can go in fulfilling such larger tasks—from recent years, *Israel* and *Boplicity*, some of the Modern Jazz Quartet's performances, some of Thelonious Monk's; from earlier years, many of Ellington's recordings. And that is about all.

The smallness of that formal heritage alone would make Morton's work important; the uniqueness of his work makes it invaluable.

One of the things that holds a *Black Bottom Stomp* together, for all its array of effects, is an ingenious and developing relationship in both quality and kind among its three melodies. Another is the patterns of musical and rhythmic echo Morton used in the orchestration: polyphony, fragmented and split melodic lines, and stop time, will all fade and recur at key moments in ways that give a sense of order to the liveliness of the whole.

Above I have referred to a masterpiece, *Dead Man Blues*.[1] It would be one if only because it managed to juxtapose a sober seriousness and a glinting sprightliness with complete and deceptive success. It is a beautifully planned orchestration. After a snatch of the Chopin funeral march, the first theme is stated in a lightly dancing polyphonic chorus. That chorus will be beautifully echoed at the end of the recording by the fact that the third appearance of the third theme is also played polyphonically. In themselves, these two choruses would make an exceptional performance: they sing and dance with a beauty of individual lines, an integration of those lines, and a lightness of rhythms and touch (quite unlike most 'dixieland') that I believe brings that early jazz style to the highest development it had.

The second 'theme' is actually a series of blues variations. First Omer Simeon's lovely clarinet chorus after which Morton's trumpeter George Mitchell shapes two exceptional blues choruses. Not only does each one of Mitchell's phrases develop beautifully out of its predecessor but his second chorus is both a beautiful foil to his first and an ingenious rhythmic and melodic preparation for what follows it, in the third part. This trio section following begins with the simplest moment of the record, a kind of interlude and fresh thematic start from which to rebuild in reverse the kind of thing that has preceded. Morton first has a trio of clarinets playing the straightforward riff-like melody for one chorus. Then, as they repeat it, Kid Ory's trombone

[1] I will again give warning that the version of *Dead Man Blues* current on twelve-inch L.P. is a strange composite editing of several 'takes' including parts of an inferior one that had technical errors, was originally rejected, and should probably have remained so.

enters to sing a blues counter-melody beneath them. Then, as if encouraged by Ory's quiet hint, the polyphonic horns of Mitchell and Simeon re-enter for the three-part chorus that concludes *Dead Man Blues* on an echo of its beginning.

Mitchell and Simeon were excellent musicians for Morton to have chosen. Simeon's forte was an exceptional capacity to make splendid, responsive counter-lines in ensemble. Mitchell's secret sense of swinging time perfectly carried out the transition Morton was making between the clipped 2/4 of an earlier day and the impending 4/4 of the swing style. He also responded excellently to Morton's expressed or implied syncopated tango rhythms that were so intimately a part of that transition. But most important, Mitchell's style probably carried complexity as far as it could then go and still allow for an integrated ensemble lead voice from the trumpet in polyphonic improvising. A little more of the virtuoso soloist and the ensemble collapses, as Armstrong's work of those years was making increasingly evident.

Another of the best of this series, *Grandpa's Spells*, clarifies how crucially orchestral and instrumental these pieces were. Most of them are, of course, re-workings of the earlier piano solos, and the piano solos are in conception to begin with often pianistic: the pieces are not 'songs' or 'tunes' harmonized and played on a piano; although, as we have seen, the piano's point of departure is clearly the imitation of an orchestra, they are also transmuted in terms of its resources. In re-composing them for orchestra, Morton did not simply try to score this pianistic conception back to its orchestral source. If we compare the piano version of *Grandpa's Spells* to the orchestral record, we see that in the latter Morton used one of the themes only in variation. He did it, obviously, because the original version was formed too closely in terms of the piano keyboard.

Grandpa's Spells is probably the masterpiece of

all Morton's fast stomps. It is a shade better conceived than its rivals, *Kansas City Stomps* and *Black Bottom Stomp*, if not quite so well executed, and its melodies are better on the whole. Again, the plan is ingenious but to break it down would tell only part of the story. There is the variety of polyphony, harmony, solo, rhythms, stop-time breaks, ingenious use of rhythm instruments—including a conversation between the group and string bass, something not supposed to have been brought off until Ellington's *KoKo*. And, still again, the point is that all the richness is never merely complicated, is indeed so apparently simple and easy.

However, for all the problems it raises in a sense, it may be easier to sustain a piece for three minutes if one is using several themes, especially if variation-on-theme is mandatory. If he runs out of ideas for one melody, he can just turn to the next, it would seem. Would it not be more difficult, in some ways, if one worked with only one theme and had to sustain it for the length of a record? Swing and bop musicians did that, of course, but they did not invent it. Morton's *Jungle Blues* even makes the task more difficult by its deliberately archaic quality. In it he took a very primitive blues bass line (two notes for a full twelve bars to begin with) and an almost naïve riff for a theme. These are shaped into three variant melodies, a variety of rhythmic effects, and pushed to the brink of monotony before Morton ends the whole at just the moment-too-soon. Similarly, *Doctor Jazz* is a jazz-man's version of a one-theme pop tune, performed, by the way, with fine swing and movement. The orchestral version of *Hyena Stomp* might have been a memorably developed set of instrumental variations on riff-theme but Morton chose to introduce the hyena of the title in person throughout the piece. (Perhaps it represents a realistic approach to one's audience, and it *is* funny, but it is only apt to annoy us today.)

Morton had the audacity to put so much into one

235

piece and the comprehensive brilliance to make such a conception work, but, of course, he was not creating in a vacuum. For there was, before 1920, a firm and quite sophisticated tradition in jazz which he had absorbed and was extending. An *Original Jelly Roll Blues* does not come about with only a few 'country blues' shouters and jug bands in its heritage. For all we can say about the importance of French and Spanish folk song, Baptist hymn, spiritual, and even John Philip Sousa to New Orleans jazz, it is clear that the crucial contributors to Morton's music were, as I have said, ragtime and the blues.

But no such account will explain how he could break the slow and passionate movement of *Smokehouse Blues* for double-timing, then for quadruple timing, and not destroy its beauty but rather enhance it. To deal with that, I think we need a word like *artist*.

Having stated such an orchestral conception on some twenty-odd recorded sides by June 1928—having experimented with the clarinet trios, with quartets, and with adding an extra voice to the polyphony (the alto sax that all but works on *The Pearls* and *Beale Street Blues*)—Morton did not merely rest and repeat himself. He met the challenges that both the north-east and south-west were laying down: larger bands with more harmonized section writing, and smaller bands where the emphasis was on solo variations with opening and closing theme-statements. The later Morton records are always said to be not so good as the earlier Victors, but I think that, for example, a *New Orleans Bump* succeeds in being just the kind of big band piece Duke Ellington and Don Redman were working on. And *Burning the Iceberg* rather successfully expands the older conceptions of harmony, polyphony, and solo—now assigning it to a larger group of three brass, four reeds, and rhythm. And *Blue Blood Blues* depends for its success largely on its soloists and players—Ward Pinkett's trumpet, Albert Nicholas's clarinet, Geechy Fields's trombone, and Morton's piano—in a way that few other small group records do until the late 'thirties.

One can find a lot of reasons for calling this man with the clown's nickname still important in the jazzman's heritage. In him jazz produced one of its best composers, best leaders, best masters of form, one of its few theorists. More important, in Morton jazz produced one of its first real artists.

JELLY ROLL MORTON
SELECTED LONG PLAYING RECORDS

Brunswick and Riverside albums are no longer available. Other album titles are as follows:

Atlantic 2-308.   The Commodore Years
RCA Victor LPV 508. Stomps and Joys
RCA Victor LPV 524. Hot Jazz, Pop Jazz, Hokum and Hilarity
RCA Victor LPV 546. Mr. Jelly Lord
RCA Victor LPV 559. I Thought I Heard Buddy Bolden Say
RCA Victor LPM1659. King of New Orleans Jazz

Key to Instrumental Abbreviations

alt=alto saxophone   p=piano

bj=banjo
bs=string bass
clt=clarinet
cnt=cornet
d=drums
g=guitar

sop=soprano saxophone
tbn=trombone
ten=tenor saxophone
tpt=trumpet
tu=tuba
vcl=vocalist

Key to Record Label Abbreviations

Atl   Atlantic   RCA   RCA Victor
Br   Brunswick   Riv   Riverside

JELLY ROLL MORTON'S STOMP KINGS:
unknown (*cnt*); Roy Palmer (*tbn*); Wilson Townes

(clt); probably Arville Harris (alt); Jelly Roll Morton (p); Jasper Taylor (woodblocks)

Chicago, June 1923

| 1434 | *Big Fat Ham* | Riv RLP12-128 |
| 1435-2 | *Muddy Water Blues* | Riv RLP12-128 |

JELLY ROLL MORTON (p)

Richmond, Indiana, July 17, 1923

| 11537a | *King Porter Stomp* | Riv RLP12-111 |
| 11538a | *New Orleans Joys* | Riv RLP12-111 |

Richmond, Indiana, July 18, 1923

11544	*Grandpa's Spells*	Riv RLP12-111
11545a	*Kansas City Stomps*	Riv RLP12-111
11546	*Wolverine Blues*	Riv RLP12-111

JELLY ROLL MORTON'S STEAMBOAT FOUR:
unknown (alt); unknown (kazoo); Jelly Roll Morton (p); possibly unknown (bj)

Chicago, April 1924

| 8065-2 | *Mr. Jelly Roll* | Riv RLP12-128 |

JELLY ROLL MORTON (p)

Chicago, April 1924

| 8071 | *Mamamita* | Riv RLP12-128 |
| 8072 | *35th Street Blues* | Riv RLP12-128 |

Richmond, Indiana, June 9, 1924

11908	*Shreveport Stomp*	Riv RLP12-111
11911	*Jelly Roll Blues*	Riv RLP12-111
11912	*Big Foot Ham*	Riv RLP12-111
11913	*Bucktown Blues*	Riv RLP12-111
11914	*Tom Cat Blues*	Riv RLP12-111
11915	*Stratford Hunch*	Riv RLP12-111
11917	*Perfect Rag*	Riv RLP12-111

JELLY ROLL MORTON'S KINGS OF JAZZ:
Lee Collins (cnt); Roy Palmer (tbn); "Balls" Ball (clt); Alex Poole (alt); Jelly Roll Morton (p)

Chicago, September 1924

635	*Fish Tail Blues*	Riv RLP12-128
636	*High Society*	Riv RLP12-128
637	*Weary Blues*	Riv RLP12-128
638	*Tiger Rag*	Riv RLP12-128

Note: Some reviewers have claimed that there is a second trumpet present on the above titles, suggesting it is Natty Dominique.

KING OLIVER (cnt) acc Jelly Roll Morton (p)

Chicago, November 1924

| 685 | *King Porter* | Riv RLP12-130 |
| 687 | *Tom Cat Blues* | Riv RLP12-130 |

Note: The two titles above appear on an LP devoted to King Oliver and none of the other tracks feature Morton.

JELLY ROLL MORTON'S JAZZ TRIO:
Volly De Faut (clt); Jelly Roll Morton (p); unknown kazoo-1

Chicago, May 1925

| 791 | *My Gal*-1 | Riv RLP12-128 |
| 792 | *Wolverine Blues* | Riv RLP12-128 |

JELLY ROLL MORTON'S INCOMPARABLES:
Ray Bowling, S. Jones, possibly Punch Miller (tpt); unknown (tbn); unknown (clt); unknown (alt); unknown (ten); Jelly Roll Morton (p); unknown (bj); unknown (tu); Clay Jefferson (d)

Richmond, Indiana, February 16, 1926

| 12467 | *Mr. Jelly Lord* | Riv RLP12-128 |

JELLY ROLL MORTON (p)

Chicago, April 20, 1926

E2863	*The Pearls*	Br BL54015
E2866	*Sweetheart O'Mine*	Br BL54015
E2867	*Fat Meat And Greens*	Br BL54015
E2869	*King Porter Stomp*	Br BL54015

JELLY ROLL MORTON'S RED HOT PEPPERS:
George Mitchell (cnt); Edward "Kid" Ory (tbn); Omer Simeon (clt); Jelly Roll Morton (p); Johnny St. Cyr (bj); John Lindsay (bs); Andrew Hilarie (d)

Chicago, September 15, 1926

BVE36239-2 *Black Bottom Stomp*

RCA LPM1649

BVE36240-2 *Smoke House Blues*

RCA LPM1649

BVE36241-3 *The Chant* RCA LPM1649

Darnell Howard, Barney Bigard (clt); Marty Bloom (claxton) added

Chicago, September 21, 1926

BVE36283-3 *Sidewalk Blues*-1 RCA LPM1649
BVE36284-3 *Dead Man Blues*-1 RCA LPM1649
BVE36285-1 *Steamboat Stomp*-1, 2

RCA LPM1649

-1 Spoken introduction on this title by Morton and St. Cyr; -2 Howard and Bloom not present on this title

George Mitchell (cnt); Edward "Kid" Ory (tbn); Omer Simeon (clt); Jelly Roll Morton (p); Johnny St. Cyr (bj); John Lindsay (bs); Andrew Hilaire (d)

Chicago, December 16, 1926
BVE37254-3 *Someday Sweetheart*-1

RCA LPV546

BVE37255-1 *Grandpa's Spells* RCA LPM1649
BVE37256-2 *Original Jelly Roll Blues*

RCA LPM1649

BVE37257-3 *Doctor Jazz*-2 RCA LPM1649
BVE37258-2 *Cannon Ball Blues* RCA LPM1649
-1 Two unknown violins — one probably Darnell Howard—added on this title; -2 vocal on this title by Jelly Roll Morton
George Mitchell (cnt); George Bryant or Gerald Reeves (tbn); Johnny Dodds (clt); Stump Evans (alt); Jelly Roll Morton (p); Bud Scott (bj); Quinn Wilson (tu); Warren "Baby" Dodds (d); Lew Le Mar (vcl-1)

Chicago, June 4, 1927
BVE38627-2 *Hyena Stomp*-1 RCA LPV524
BVE38628-2 *Billy Goat Stomp*-1

RCA LPV524

BVE38630-3 *Jungle Blues* RCA LPM1649
Possibly Norman Mason (alt); Johnny St. Cyr (bj) replace Evans and Scott; Bryant is definite on trombone.

Chicago, June 10, 1927
BVE38661-1 *Beale Street Blues* RCA LPM1649
BVE38662-2 *The Pearls* RCA LPM1649

JELLY ROLL MORTON'S TRIO:
Johnny Dodds (clt); Jelly Roll Morton (p); Warren "Baby" Dodds (d)

Chicago, June 10, 1927
BVE38663-1 *Wolverine Blues*

RCA LPV546

BVE38664-1 *Mr. Jelly Lord* RCA LPV546

JELLY ROLL MORTON'S RED HOT PEPPERS:
Ward Pinkett (tpt); Geechy Fields (tbn); Omer Simeon (clt); Jelly Roll Morton (p); Lee Blair (bj); Bill Benford (tu); Tommy Benford (d)

New York City, June 11, 1928
BVE45619-2 *Georgia Swing* RCA LPM1649
BVE45620-3 *Kansas City Stomps* RCA LPM1649
BVE45621-2 *Shoe Shiner's Rag* RCA LPM1649
BVE45622-2 *Boogaboo* RCA LPV508

JELLY ROLL MORTON'S TRIO:
Omer Simeon (clt); Jelly Roll Morton (p); Tommy

Benford (d)
New York City, June 11, 1928
BVE45623-1 *Shreveport Stomp*

RCA LPV508

JELLY ROLL MORTON'S QUARTET:
As last with Geechy Fields (tbn.) added
New York City, June 11, 1928
BVE45624-1 *Mournful Serenade*

RCA LPV508

JELLY ROLL MORTON'S RED HOT PEPPERS:
Edwin Swayzee, Eddie Anderson (tpt); Bill Cato (tbn); Russell Procope (alt, clt); Joe Garland (ten); Paul Barnes (sop); Jelly Roll Morton (p); Lee Blair (bj); Bass Moore (bs); Manzie Johnson (d)
New York City, December 6, 1928
BVE48434-1 *Red Hot Pepper Stomp*

RCA LPV546

BVE48435-3 *Deep Creek* RCA LPV546

JELLY ROLL MORTON (p)
Camden, New Jersey, July 8, 1929
BVE49448-2 *Pep* RCA LPV543
BVE49449-2 *Seattle Hunch* RCA LPV508
BVE49450-1 *Fat Frances* RCA LPV543

JELLY ROLL MORTON'S RED HOT PEPPERS:
Ward Pinkett, Bubber Miley (tpt); Wilbur De Paris (tbn); Russell Procope (alt, clt); Jelly Roll Morton (p); unknown (bj); Bernard Addison (g); Billy Taylor (tu); Tommy Benford (d)
New York City, March 20, 1930
BVE59644 *Ponchatrain Blues*

RCA LPV508

JELLY ROLL MORTON (p)
Washington, D.C., May-June 1938

King Porter Stomp	Riv RLP12-132
New Orleans Blues	Riv RLP12-132
The Pearls	Riv RLP12-132
Fickle Fay Creep	Riv RLP12-132
Hyena Stomp	Riv RLP12-132
Pep	Riv RLP12-132
Jungle Blues	Riv RLP12-132
The Crave	Riv RLP12-132
Kansas City Stomps	Riv RLP12-132
Mama Nita	Riv RLP12-132
Creepy Feeling	Riv RLP12-132

Spanish Swat Riv RLP12-132

Note: The above is a selection from the Library of Congress Recordings mentioned in the text. A full set, from which these items have been selected, was available on Riverside RLP9001-RLP9012 respectively (twelve LPs in all).

JELLY ROLL MORTON (p, vcl-1)
New York City, December 14, 1939

| R2561 | *Original Rags* | Atl 308 |
| R2562 | *The Crave* | Atl 308 |

R2564	*Mister Joe*	Atl 308
R2565	*King Porter Stomp*	Atl 308
R2566	*Winin' Boy Blues*-1	Atl 308

New York City, December 16, 1939

R2570	*Buddy Bolden's Blues*-1	Atl 308
R2571	*The Naked Dance*	Atl 308
R2572	*Don't You Leave Me Here*-1	
		Atl 308
R2573	*Mamie's Blues*-1	Atl 308

New York City, December 18, 1939

| R2579 | *Michigan Water Blues*-1 | Atl 308 |

King Oliver

BY MARTIN WILLIAMS

ACKNOWLEDGEMENTS

Anyone who writes about King Oliver—or, for that matter, anyone who listens to the recordings he has left us—should make constant use of the monograph of Walter C. Allen and Brian Rust, *King Joe Oliver*. I am not only indebted to that valuable piece of scholarship but to Mr. Allen personally for making his collection of Oliver records available to me.

One of the earliest accounts of Joe Oliver was the reminiscences of trombonist Preston Jackson which appeared in *Hot News* when Oliver was still alive but living in obscurity. Frederick Ramsey Jr.'s biographical chapter on him in *Jazzmen* (1939) was one of the earliest pieces of real scholarship in jazz, and it preserved much information before it was too late.

Finally, I wish especially to thank the musicians mentioned in the text whose comments on Oliver's style and repertoire outside recording studios have been so valuable.

BIOGRAPHY

I

INTRODUCTION

To a number of the followers of jazz in the United States, Great Britain, and France, Joseph 'King' Oliver has become as much a kind of culture hero as he is a source of aesthetic respect. But unlike John Henry's or Stack O'Lee's, Oliver's is not the kind of story from which an epic is made—although Oliver the 'King' of New Orleans moving in to conquer Chicago's south side, delighting a public and amazing musicians might promise an epic of a sort. The details are not worked out nor the emotions refined; Oliver's story is potentially tragedy, and it is in an attempt at tragedy that it has often been told.

The story was not taken up by folk balladeers or the singers on the 'race' lists as were other epics and tragedies of jazz, but by the writers and documentarians of jazz, specifically in its first history, *Jazzmen*. The pathetic presence of Joseph Oliver somehow almost pervades that book and at least it served to objectify the special nostalgic, somewhat defensive, often sentimental attitudes that characterized the approaches of so many of the Continental and American writers on jazz of the period. An even more sugary version of that mythic figure was made the focal point and a central character of Hollywood's first attempt at the 'movie about the epic of jazz', *Syncopation*, obviously inspired by *Jazzmen.*

Oliver's was, then, the medieval tragedy of success fallen on to bitter days by fate. But 'fate' in this story was not so unknown a force as it had been to Boccaccio. Fate was public caprice, American 'commercialism', and the boorishness of popular taste. Thus Oliver could be praised by these writers because he 'set Chicago on its ear' and had the public flocking in the early twenties, and then he could be revered because an insensitive and unaesthetic public had abandoned him. And it even refused to respond to him when, some would say, he tried to sell out to that public and the controllers of its taste, and formed 'big bands'.

The Oliver myth fits neatly with the others in jazz of the time, like the rather Keats-ian interpretation of Bix Beiderbecke's life that was already prevalent in the thirties and which captured the tenor of those times so well for a certain segment of bohemia. Jazz, like left-wing politics and 'the common man' was a *cause*, a special kind of emotional (not really either aesthetic or political) outlet and here the ageing Oliver could supplement the artist-cut-off-in-his-youth-by-the-crass-world story of Bix.

Both men in these stories were too perfect and too put upon to be real tragic heroes and what we got was a crude and sentimental story of the fallen hero in which the 'public' appeared as both the discoverer of artistic talent and the enemy of artistic integrity. Both myths survive today, chiefly in certain more 'conservative' areas of jazz 'criticism'—areas where the Oliver character could be, and has been, supplanted as the hero of the story by Tommy Ladnier, by Joe Smith, by 'Hot Lips' Page, and currently even by Cootie Williams and Roy Eldridge. The myth repeats and repeats, the name changes. But in all such accounts the realities of the individual, his responsibilities to his talent, and the facts of the world in which

he functions are either ignored or too sentimentally presented to be tragic, and such proto-myths must die as symptoms of a time which commented without perception in terms which the realities of a living music cannot sustain.

But Oliver's is indeed a pathetic story. His letters, from his last years, published in *Jazzmen*, are among the most moving documents which have been preserved from the past in jazz, and the nobility in adversity which they show could not come from that kind of show-biz delusion which was the source of Jelly Roll Morton's bravura.

I receive your card, you don't know how much I appreciate your thinking about the old man . . . Thank God I only need one thing and that is clothes. I am not making enough money to buy clothes as I can't play any more.

* * *

Soon as the weather can fit my clothes I known I can do better in New York.

* * *

We are still having nice weather here. The Lord is sure good to me here without an overcoat.

* * *

My heart don't bother me just a little at times. But my breath is still short, and I'm not at all fat . . . Don't think I will ever raise enough money to buy a ticket to New York. I am not one to give up quick. If I was I don't know where I would be today. I always feel like I've got a chance. I still feel I'm going to snap out of the rut I've been in for several years. What makes me feel optimistic at times. Looks like very time one door close on me another door opens . . . I am going to try and save myself a ticket to New York.

* * *

I open the pool rooms at 9 a.m. and close at 12 midnite. If the money was only a quarter

244

as much as the hours I'd be all set. But at that I can thank God for what I am getting.

And one can only report the awesome fortitude represented by the entries from Paul Barnes's 1934–35 notebooks which are published in full in the Allen-Rust monograph. ('W' and 'N' mean white or Negro audiences, the figures give each man's wages in dollars and cents, and (c) means the engagement was cancelled.) Some examples:

1934

May 9–Williamson, W. Va.	N	1.50
May 10–Norton, Va.		(c)
May 11–Bristol, Tenn./Va.	W	0.50
August 2–Fulton, Ky.	N	0.00
August 4–Clarksville, Tenn.	W	1.00
August 12–Danville, Ky.	N	0.75
August 13–Crab Orchard, Ky.	W	0.75
October 28–Greenville, S.C.	N	0.15
October 31–Danville, Va.	N	(c)
November 21–Huntington, W. Va.	W	0.00

or the 'Merry Christmas' of:

December 18–Ashland, Ky.	W	2.71
December 24–Charleston, W. Va.	N	0.00
December 25–Ashland, Ky.	W	5.00
December 26–Welch, W. Va.	W	4.00
December 27–Williamson, W. Va.	N	4.00

And what the table does not show: cars and buses broken down, fires which burned instruments, crooked promoters cheating the band, constant problems with personnel, competing groups using Oliver's name, and all the rest of it.

And there are things that one can only repeat as rumours, rumours which persist even today, like the one which has two of Louis Armstrong's sidemen in a Southern city while on tour seeing an old man on a street corner, selling what are called 'snow balls' (crushed ice with flavoured syrup) recognizing him as the one-time 'King' Joseph Oliver and being too overcome to speak to him.

2

NEW ORLEANS

Joseph Oliver was born in New Orleans[1] in 1885 in a house on Dryades Street in the 'district'. His family moved several times, largely within the 'Garden district' of the city, between that time and the day in 1900 when Oliver's mother died in a house at Nashville and Coliseum Avenue. It was then that Joe Oliver's older sister, Victoria Davis, who had nursed him as a baby, began to look after his welfare—and it was to her that his last letters were addressed in 1938.

According to Bunk Johnson, Oliver was first introduced to music about 1899 by a Mr. Kenehen who formed a brass band among the children in

[1] The main source for subsequent biographies of Oliver has been Frederic Ramsey Jr.'s chapter in *Jazzmen*. However, Samuel B. Charter's reference volume, *Jazz New Orleans 1885–1957*, gives a rather different account of Oliver's early life. Mr. Charter's facts in several of his entries have been questioned by several researchers. Joseph Oliver, according to Charter's account, was born on the Saulsburg Plantation, located fifteen miles from Donaldsonville, Louisiana, where his mother worked as a cook. He came to New Orleans as a boy, where he got a job as 'yard boy' with a family named Levy. He lived with the Levys but spent his week-ends with an aunt in Mandeville. His first instrument was the trombone, but he played it so loud that his teacher changed him to cornet. He was in the Melrose Brass Band by 1907.

his uptown New Orleans neighbourhood with Oliver playing on a cornet. (Buddy Bolden, whom most New Orleans musicians credit with having started it all in jazz, was playing and improvising, mostly for dancers, and to great public acclaim, as early as 1894.) This youthful band even toured a bit locally and once got to Baton Rouge, and it was from that trip that Oliver returned with a deep scar over his left eye (an earlier accident, it is said by some, had left that eye blind since infancy).

The details of Oliver's musical career in New Orleans once he was older and skilled enough to get jobs in the regular brass dance bands of the city have been variously reported. Indeed, like many men in the city, he probably played in several groups at the same time, for these men were not necessarily 'professional' musicians; most of them held day jobs and played for parades, funerals, and dances as a natural part of a community life. Oliver worked as a butler.

Perhaps more important than the names of the bands with which Oliver played are the names of some of the men with whom he played in them, for they may give us some indication of what kinds of music these groups made and what they stood for. Thus, the Melrose Brass Band featured trombonist Horne Dutrey, as also did the Magnolia Band, the Eagle Band (which was certainly celebrated in the city) had Frank Dusen (only a legend to most of us). Then, in and out of the Magnolia Band, all reportedly while Oliver was in it, were George 'Pops' Foster, bass; Lorenzo Tio Sr., clarinet; George Baquet, clarinet; Johnny St. Cyr, banjo and guitar.

Besides such community engagements with the brass bands (which also, of course, would play at evening dances at the many lodges and clubs in the Negro community), there were other kinds of jobs. For example, there was a job in the Storyville district at the Abadie Cabaret (at Marais and Bienville Streets) with a quartet led by pianist-composer Richard M. Jones which included Louis Nelson Delisle on clarinet, and Delisle was undoubtedly Jimmy Noone's major inspiration. It was during this engagement that Oliver's reputation rose, for down the street at Pete Lala's café played the powerful Freddy Keppard, one of the first 'Kings' of New Orleans trumpeters after Bolden, and many thought Oliver was out-playing him.

Keppard was also the leader of the Olympia Brass Band, but probably most significant was his tour with the Original Creole orchestra beginning in 1911, which took the jazz music of New Orleans from Coney Island, New York, to Los Angeles, California. When he left, A. J. Piron took over the Olympia Band and he used Joseph Oliver on cornet. The group at Pete Lala's then included Sidney Bechet, and, at various times, Zue Robinson on trombone, Lorenzo Tio Jr. (teacher of so many including Barney Bigard and Omer Simeon) on clarinet. Meanwhile, Piron's dance group was playing 'society' jobs and featured the leader's violin. One might conjecture that Oliver's formal knowledge of music grew as he worked for Piron. Oliver also toured at this time through Louisiana, not entirely successfully, and Clarence Williams was a 'comedian' with the troup.

Williams was later manager of Lala's in 1914, when the band, which included clarinettist Johnny Dodds and bassist Ed Garland, was led by Kid Ory. Ory replaced his trumpeter with Oliver and began to bill him in advertising as 'King', a title which public acclaim alone apparently had earlier awarded to Bolden and Keppard. There were, of course, many changes of personnel in this group (clarinettists Sidney Bechet, Jimmy Noone, and Albert Nicholas were all in and out of it, for example), and it was during this time that the touring and the closing of the Storyville 'district' (10 November 1917) all led New Orleans musicians north to Chicago and west to Los Angeles.

Early in 1918, bassist Bill Johnson (who had

lured Keppard on the tour) sent first for cornetist Buddy Petit and, when he would not come, for Joe Oliver to play an engagement at the Royal Gardens Café in Chicago; Oliver left New Orleans.

3

THE MUSIC OF NEW ORLEANS

It is very difficult for us to reconstruct the music that Oliver heard and absorbed in New Orleans or what its players' intentions were; difficult in the sense that there were all sorts of popular music played in that city, from the more or less formal French and American folk songs and dances of the Creoles of Color to the most elementary kind of country blues singing and playing of the Negroes who had migrated to the city from nearby plantations; and some of the very same men may have participated in and played all of it.

Besides the excellent players it nurtured, and its style, perhaps the most essential thing that the New Orleans music which came to be called 'jazz' offered has been described by clarinettist Garvin Bushell in an article by Nat Hentoff (*The Jazz Review*, January 1959) as 'feeling' and what is now called 'soul'. Bushell is admittedly speaking of what he had heard mostly in the 'twenties, but he does not credit New Orleans so much with a style (except that the men used four beats instead of two), or with making variations (which was featured in some performances of ragtime), or with improvisation (which is, of course, in any blues singing or playing—or in any folk music anywhere). But Bushell does say that in the face of musical and social trends among some Negroes, which constantly led them away from everything supposedly 'negroid' and into some strange but still understandable snobberies, the New Orleans musicians preserved and spread a

transformed, instrumental version of the passionate soul of the blues, and they played it unashamedly.

In New Orleans the music fulfilled the functional role which any such music would in any community: it was for dances, parades, and atmosphere in bars, and in all of these it expressed the feelings of its audience. It is possible, of course, for such communal music to express what its audiences would like to think it felt, but one would not need verbal confirmation to know that New Orleans jazz was too honest an art for that. We have often been invited to see this 'jazz' that evolved—the best exposition of this is probably in Alan Lomax's *Mister Jelly Roll*—as a result of the coming together of the more or less formal 'Downtown' musics of the proud 'Creoles of Color' and the 'Uptown' blues and church musics (largely vocal) of the 'black' Negroes, some of them the ex-slaves who had migrated to New Orleans. The 'Creoles of Color' were the offspring of French (and Spanish) Colonials and of their Negro slaves who were sometimes freed and given property and land, and even educated abroad. After the Civil War, and as social discrimination and segregation gradually encroached upon New Orleans, their pride tumbled (at least on the surface) and they became a part of the larger Negro community, and New Orleans instrumental 'jazz' music resulted. Probably the best idea available to us today of what this combination of formal

247

musical knowledge and European dance rhythms, and the spirit and rhythms of the blues may have sounded like in early days can be heard on some of A. J. Piron's recordings made for Columbia. Those that he made for Victor show only what dullness *might* have resulted with less of the 'soul' of the blues.

There is, in the recorded work of Bunk Johnson (both in his own playing and in his re-creations of Buddy Bolden's style), of Freddy Keppard, of Jimmy Noone, of Jelly Roll Morton, a remarkable common characteristic of style which is undeniable, particularly since some New Orleans players—Louis Armstrong, Johnny Dodds and Sidney Bechet, for example—do not often show it. The approach of Morton and Keppard to variation, according to their records, was formal, chorus by chorus, and developmental in larger patterns. Each variation is based on a single, frequently simple idea, which is thematic in point of departure, continued throughout each chorus, and related both to the preceding and following chorus-variation, and (if the player were capable) to a total pattern. Armstrong's variations, Bechet's, and Dodds's blues are freer, less formal in conception, and in the style perhaps of younger men. In a sense Oliver's playing on records represents, as we shall see, both approaches. And, I think they both reflect something which can only be a conjecture: however much improvisation and variation were practised elsewhere in Negro-American musics, in New Orleans they had been a *cornerstone* of style for a long time, a basic attribute which musicians worked hard to develop in their playing.

4

CHICAGO, CALIFORNIA, AND NEW YORK

Actually, two jobs awaited Oliver when he arrived in Chicago. He played at the Royal Gardens with Bill Johnson's group, along with Jimmy Noone (who had left New Orleans with him) and drummer Paul Barbarin, and he doubled for a while in Lawrence Duke's group at the Dreamland Café, along with Roy Palmer on trombone, Sidney Bechet on clarinet, Lil Hardin on piano, Wellman Braud on bass, and Minor Hall on drums. Lil Hardin described her joining that group:[1] 'King Oliver and Johnny Dodds came over together that night, and so he said to me he came to work at the Royal Gardens. And he said he'd be very glad if I could come over and work with him. So, I told him I had to give two weeks' notice. And it was a thrill to me to think that the great King wanted me to come and play with him.'

By January 1920 Oliver was leading a band of his own at the Dreamland, and again doubling in a State Street cabaret and gangster hang-out from one to six in the morning. In this group were Johnny Dodds, Horne Dutrey (trombone), Lil Hardin, Ed Garland and Minor Hall.

In 1921 Oliver got a letter from the manager of the Pergola Dance Pavilion in San Francisco.

[1] All of my quotations from Lil Hardin Armstrong come from her recent autobiographical record, *Satchmo and Me*, Riverside RLP 12-120 (USA). I do not think that the fact that she differs here from the biographical detail I am giving need detain us. Johnny Dodds might easily have replaced Noone or Bechet in either of the groups Oliver was working with in Chicago at first.

The man had heard Kid Ory's band and wanted him. Ory had another contract and told him about Oliver. (It was this Ory Band, by the way, which made the first jazz recordings by a Negro group and give us the earliest idea of New Orleans jazz that we have.)

With various changes of personnel (including one which got Johnny Dodds's brother Warren 'Baby' into it) the Oliver band played in Los Angeles, where Oliver also played with a large one led by Jelly Roll Morton which featured three trumpets and a three-man reed section. Oliver later returned to Oakland and soon back to Chicago, despite an assurance of continued success in the Bay Area.

About the band, Lil Hardin says 'Johnny was sober where Baby Dodds was kind of wild—he was kind of the playboy of the orchestra. King Oliver was sober too . . . He smoked cigars, but he didn't drink. None of them drank hardly. And Dutrey, he was a very business sort of a fellow. He was always buying property or something.'

Back in Chicago, the billing at the Lincoln Gardens (the Royal Gardens re-named) was 'King Oliver's Creole Jazz Band' and the personnel included Horne Dutrey (trombone), Johnny Dodds (clarinet), Bertha Gonsoulin, later Lil Hardin (piano), Bill Johnson (bass), Baby Dodds (drums). In the summer of 1922, a young cornetist named Louis Armstrong received a telegram in New Orleans from King Oliver, who had encouraged him years before, to come to Chicago and join his band on second cornet—a role Oliver had played in New Orleans with Manuel Perez, and Bunk Johnson had played with Buddy Bolden. It was this band which had the most astonishing local popularity that Oliver had ever seen, had musicians listening in awe, had many travelling from elsewhere to hear, and which was, in sessions for Gennett, Okeh, Paramount, and Columbia, to begin the first regular recordings of jazz music. Much has been written about this group, from the contemporary write-ups of the *Chicago Defender*, the reminiscent accounts of its popularity and power by Preston Jackson, and the accounts by George Wettling of how he and other drummers would come nightly to study Baby Dodds. But Louis Armstrong did not 'make' this band. Again, these are the words of Garvin Bushell to Nat Hentoff (*The Jazz Review*, February 1959):

'We went on the road with Mamie Smith in 1921. When we got to Chicago, Bubber Miley and I went to hearing Oliver at the Dreamland every night. It was the first time I'd heard New Orleans Jazz to any advantage and I studied them every night for the entire week we were in town. I was very much impressed with their blues and their sound. The trumpets and clarinets in the East had a better 'legitimate' quality, but *their* sound touched you more. It was less cultivated but more impressive of how the people felt. Bubber and I sat there with our mouths open.

'We talked with the Dodds brothers. They felt very highly about what they were playing as though they knew they were doing something new that nobody else could do. I'd say they did regard themselves as artists in the sense we use the term today . . .

'Before I went to Dreamland every night, I'd heard a New Orleans band that played a lot where a carnival was taking place. It was the Thomas New Orleans Jug Band, and it was more primitive than Oliver's . . . It had the same beat as Oliver's—what we called in Ohio the "shimmy" beat. They played mostly blues and they played four beat, as did Oliver . . . After we'd heard Oliver and Dodds, they were our criterion.'

Here is Lil Hardin's account of the attention they were getting at the Lincoln Gardens. 'While we were playing at the Royal Gardens, a bunch of white musicians, ten, twelve, fifteen, sometimes twenty would come, and they would row up right in front of the bandstand to listen . . . Louis and Joe said they were some of Paul Whiteman's band that Bix was in the bunch . . . They used to talk to Louis and King Oliver and Johnny . . . Several of them would sit in occasionally. But they would listen so intently . . .

'King Oliver . . . said to me one night that Louis could play better than he could. He said, "But as long as I got him with me, he won't be able to get ahead of me. I'll still be king".'

By the spring of 1923, this band had, with some personnel changes, a chance to tour and to record. Lil Hardin has described their first of several sessions.

'Then we got the record date . . . At the first session—we were recording in a great big horn then, you know the style then. And the band was around the horn. And Louis was there, right there, as he always was, right next to Joe. It didn't work out. You couldn't hear Joe's playing. So they moved Louis 'way over in the corner, away from the band. Louis was standing over there looking so lonesome. He . . . thought it was bad for him to have to be away from the band. He was looking so sad. And I'd look at him and smile—you know. That's the only way they could get the balance. Louis was, well he was at least twelve or fifteen feet from us on the whole session.'

Then there were tours the next year on the Orpheum Theatre circuit through Ohio, Wisconsin, Michigan, even Pennsylvania, but now with Zue Robinson, then John Lindsey in for Dutrey, Buster Bailey, then Albert Nicholas and Rudy Jackson on reeds; Charlie Jackson on bass sax, Bud Scott on banjo and 'Snags' Jones on drums as replacements in the group. Lil Hardin explained it, 'Johnny Dodds found out that Joe had been collecting $95 for each member of the band, while he had been paying us $75. So naturally he had been making $20 a week a piece off of· us for I don't know how long. So Johnny Dodds and Baby Dodds, they threatened to beat Joe up. So Joe brought his pistol every night to work in his trumpet case in case anything happened. Everybody gave in the notice except Louis. Louis always was so crazy about Joe, you know he was his idol, so he wouldn't quit. If Louis didn't quit, so naturally I wouldn't quit. So Louis and I stayed with Joe. Now that is why you don't find Dutrey, Johnny Dodds, and Baby Dodds on this Eastern tour with us. He had to replace everybody except Louis and myself.'

In the summer of 1924, Louis Armstrong left Oliver, first to play with Ollie Powers at the Dreamland for three months and then to New York in September to join Fletcher Henderson. Oliver had returned to the Lincoln Gardens in June 1924.

It is often said that the next Oliver bands to record, known on records as the 'Dixie Syncopators' or 'Savannah Syncopators' were, in their use of a reed section and written arrangements, an effort at commercialism. On the other hand, reed sections, *with saxophones*, had been in New Orleans groups (and not just the 'legitimate' Downtown ones), in the riverboat bands, in the Morton bands previously mentioned (and on his earliest band records), in many Chicago groups, in the 1919 group Oliver had led at a Liberty Bond Drive, and in the group Oliver had just taken on tour in 1924. It seems very likely that in that earlier group on the 1924 tour and in the one Oliver now took into the Lincoln Gardens (which at first had Buster Bailey on clarinet and alto saxophone, Rudy Jackson on tenor saxophone and Charlie Jackson on bass saxophone) some basis for his future styles (however much these styles may have owed to conventional dance bands of the time and his own past) was laid. However much polyphony was employed and continued to be, more conventional, solo and section work must have been used before the Syncopators. Indeed, it had been all along Oliver's bands; there are such harmonized passages as those on the Creole Jazz Band's version of *Chatanooga Stomp*, for example. But to call these changes evolutionary and inevitable is not to call them improvements, of course.

Oliver and Creole Jazz Band 1921—California
Left to right: Minor Hall, Honore Dutrey, Oliver, Lil Hardin, David Jones, Johnny Dodds, Jimmy Palao, Ed Garland

Business was not good, the personnel changed, the band tried to get outside jobs, and in September 1924, Oliver left the group in charge of Bob Shoffner, his second cornet, to go to New York to try to get a recording contract. He failed and on his return the Gardens was open only three days a week.

By late December, a redecorated Lincoln Gardens and a re-vamped Oliver band, but with the same basic instrumentation, was ready to open. In it were Lee Collins, Paul Barbarin, and, fresh from New Orleans, Nicholas and Barney Bigard on reeds, and Luis Russell. But this group never played. On the day it was to open, the Gardens caught fire.

Oliver, with a band and no place to use it, took

Oliver's Dixie Syncopators 1925—Chicago
Geo. Filhe, Bert Cobb, Bud Scott, Paul Barbarin, Darnell Howard, Oliver, Albert Nicholas, Bob Schoffner,
Barney Bigard, Luis Russell

Duncan Schiedt

251

Duncan Schiedt

Chicago 1923
Baby Dodds, Honore Dutrey, Oliver, Armstrong, Bill Johnson,
Johnny Dodds, Lil Hardin

a chair as the 'World's Greatest Jazz Cornetist' with Dave Payton's Symphonic Syncopators at the Plantation Café. There he apparently kept his music book stubbornly closed, played his parts by ear, and very soon had arranged an engagement there at the Plantation for his own group— perhaps his real objective in the first place. That

job lasted for two years, and saw such men as Tommy Ladnier and Kid Ory in a changing personnel.

In March 1926, Oliver got a contract to record regularly for the Vocalion 'race' series. The labels read 'electrically recorded', and 'King Oliver and his Dixie Syncopators'. There were some decided

King Oliver's Creole Jazz Band 1924
Chas Jackson, Clifford 'Snags' Jones, Buster Bailey, King Oliver,
Zue Robertson, Louis Armstrong, Rudy Jackson, Lil Armstrong
Duncan Schiedt

'hits' between 1926 and 1928 in this series: *Snag It, Sugarfoot Stomp* (the earlier *Dippermouth Blues* retitled), *Someday Sweetheart, Deadman Blues, West End Blues*, and on such records as these, and not earlier ones, Oliver's national *public* reputation and popularity was largely made, of course.

In March 1927, the Plantation was closed, possibly by the police, and just as it was scheduled to re-open, a fire destroyed it. Oliver took to the road, playing at college dances and brief engagements in Milwaukee, Detroit, and St. Louis.

The band was stranded in St. Louis, but by May 1927, headlines in the *Chicago Defender* announced the band's arrival in New York with 'King Oliver made good at Savoy'.

In 1927, as in every year until the late forties, the Savoy Ballroom was a testing ground for any Negro orchestra. Oliver was there for two weeks and was hardly a failure, although such an engagement probably does not warrant so blatant a claim as the *Defender*'s, 'King Oliver takes New York by storm'. The men had arrived by the cheapest and slowest trains, just in time to go directly on to the bandstand, still tired and dirty from a long trip.

One night engagements in the New York City/New Jersey area followed, and then came what turned out to be opportunity knocking. A new night club, to be called The Cotton Club, was to open and Oliver's band was offered the job of providing the house band for dancing, floor shows, and, as it turned out, a radio wire which would spread the music across the United States. Oliver, again proud and stubborn, decided his name and his orchestra were worth more money than the Club was offering and refused the offer; the job went to a young man from Washington D.C. named 'Duke' Ellington, who stayed for three years.

Oliver played briefly in some major cities in the east (Philadelphia, Washington, Baltimore), but soon his men had drifted away except for a nucleus of three or four musicians.

For three years, Oliver had no band or, as one musician put it, the only band, office, or engagements he had were in his hat. He did keep his recording dates up for Vocalion–Brunswick, to be sure, but by the end of 1928 was using Luis Russell's band, or Elmer Snowden's as his own for recordings, or simply picking up the best men he could find. At the same time, Oliver was recording on his own with various Clarence Williams groups.

In late 1928, Oliver had, through the efforts of agent Harrison Smith, a new recording contract (and $1,000 advance) and one that most leaders would have envied him for. It was with Victor, a large and powerful company then as now. But Jimmy O'Keefe at Vocalion–Brunswick had largely let Oliver have his own way with his own records; Victor, he soon learned, was not so liberal towards him. Another characteristic of the Victor series is that, although there are many trumpet solos by Oliver, there are also many by other trumpeters and that a great deal of the work in assembling and organizing the bands, and much of the composing and arranging was done by Oliver's nephew trumpeter Dave Nelson.

The Victor contract kept him going, but Oliver did get a few jobs in the New York area, and there was a tour into the Mid-west in 1930. On it Oliver refused to play his Victor repertoire, the group was stranded in Kansas City, and Oliver was taken ill in Wichita for three months. But he had still refused jobs in Chicago and New Orleans because he did not like the terms offered. (Louis Armstrong and Earl Hines accepted two of those jobs.)

By the end of 1930, Oliver was in New York, the Victor contract was up, the band had broken up, and Dave Nelson left with many arrangements which he had made but had not been paid for.

5

SEVEN YEARS 'ON THE ROAD'

But the next year Oliver had a new band, composed of younger men, and went off on a tour of the South and South-west. One might say that Oliver spent the rest of his life making this tour. In the beginning it was a comparatively good tour, but soon salaries were being cut and musicians were leaving.

Joseph Oliver had apparently been one of those who were 'born an old man'. As some men do, he conducted himself as though he were at least middle-aged nearly all his life. Pianist Don Kirkpatrick has spoken of how he sat almost sullenly in front of his band when it opened at the Savoy, with soft slippers on his feet, speaking shortly and gruffly to his men, and stood only for his own solos. But by now he was prematurely ageing in more than conduct. He had pyorrhœa, his gums bled, and his teeth were coming out— and if that story about Oliver's keeping a bucket of sugar water for the band to drink from at the Lincoln Gardens is true, little wonder that they did. Therefore, he could play less and less. And he had heart trouble and frequent colds.

It was during this period, this seven-year 'tour' of the South and South-west, confounded by the Depression, that the letters and the log book we have quoted above were written. Personnel changed, cars and buses broke down, engagements were broken, jobs were played without pay, and fires destroyed equipment. But always Oliver managed to keep up a front: a public one that meant keeping uniforms neat and clean and a private one that he would 'get back to New York' or 'a new door would open soon'. But the realities of life included the night the bus broke down in the West Virginia mountains and, to keep warm, the men had to burn the tyres. And the fleeting encouragement of a radio wire at one engagement. (The band could play it over but their singer, Rudy McDonald, couldn't use it; such are the strange ways of Jim Crow.)

By 1935, Oliver could no longer play, but the touring, such as it was, continued. In 1936, his headquarters were in Savannah. He had not enough clothes, he was ill. Again, there was still some touring, but in his last year, he ran a fruit stand and later worked fifteen hours a day as janitor in a pool hall.

On Friday, 8 April 1938, Joseph 'King' Oliver died of cerebral hæmorrhage. His sister spent her rent money to have his body brought to New York. On 12th April Louis Armstrong, Clarence Williams and a loyal group of musician friends saw him buried at Woodlawn Cemetery, the Bronx, New York. There was no headstone on his grave.

I

THE CREOLE JAZZ BAND

King Oliver's is indeed a pathetic story and the medieval writer was not wrong in holding that such tales of the caprice of fortune have their meaning for us all. One could probably find many biographies that are about as pathetic and exemplary as Oliver's, although one might find few men with his fortitude and dignity. But the Oliver that exists for most of us exists through recordings. We are interested in his music; that is what makes us interested in his biography and not the other way round. And we are interested in his music, not so much as an historical or social 'document', not only as precedent for what followed it, but first because some of it survives today as valid and meaningful musical art. And it is a music whose emotional content would not brook for a moment the nostalgia or the sentimentality with which Oliver's story is sometimes told.

In the recorded history of jazz (all forty odd years of it!) there are certain groups of celebrated recordings: the Hot Fives–Sevens of Louis Armstrong, the early Jelly Roll Morton Red Hot Peppers, the Ellington's of 1938–40, the Basie records of 1936–39, the seven 1945 Gillespie–Parker records, the twelve Miles Davis Capitols, for examples. And one of the first—the King Oliver Creole Jazz Band records for Gennett, Paramount, Okeh, and Columbia. These are celebrated, first, for the reason that I have said that the band was celebrated: with a certain degree of musical sophistication they preserve and extend the strong and unique emotional content of Negro folk music. A music, then, which had instrumental and ensemble skill (often of a unique sort to be sure) and deeply expressive content. But there are details which are important: the integration of parts and individuals in its dense, often polyphonic, textures; the sureness and control in choice of tempos; the ease and firmness with which the group could project excitement. These men knew that one does not artistically imitate or re-create an emotion simply by feeling it himself.

I am going to quote at some length from a recent critique by Larry Gushee (in *The Jazz Review* for November 1958) of a group of these recordings because it seems to me an excellent account not only of what many have felt about them but of what they mean to one perceptive listener as well.

'There have been blessed few bands that have ever played together like Joe Oliver's . . . If a band can be said to have a clearly recognizable and highly original sound, it must consist of something more than the arithmetic sum of a certain number of individual styles. I suspect that the *sine qua non* is discipline; which chiefly finds expression as consistency and limitation. . . . Begin with a group of musicians out of the common run, who are guided by some dominant principle or personality and the resultant sound will be truly unique, pleasing to the ears because it is musical, to the soul because it is integral. . . . And so these recordings, in their way, are a norm and object lesson of what a jazz band needs to be great. . . .

'Whether the tempos, so often felicitous, were Joe Oliver's independent choice, or determined by prevailing dance style, I cannot know . . . (But) the tempos . . . never exceeded the players' technical limitations . . . I am sure that this accounts for much of the superb swing of the Creole band.

'But even more important is the manner in which the separate beats of the measure are accented . . . a truly flat four-four. . . .

'The truly phenomenal rhythmic momentum generated by Oliver is just as much dependent on *continuity* of rhythmic pulse—only reinforced by uniformity of accentuation in the rhythm section and relaxed playing. . . . One never feels that, with a little less control, a break or an entire chorus would fall into musical *bizarrerie*. Oliver's swing is exciting after a different fashion: it is predictable, positive, and consistent. Only rarely is the total *manqué*, as in *Froggie Moore*, where the stop-and-go character of the tune makes consistency more difficult. . . .

'Its consistency is . . . largely the result of Oliver's personal conception of a band sound. How much he moulded the musicians to fit the ideal pattern of his own imagination or how much he chose them with the knowledge that they would fit in . . . is something we can't determine. . . . We have no record of how Louis sounded before he came to Chicago—we know he is full of the spirit of King Joe although their ideas of instrumental tone were divergent. Johnny Dodds's rare gift [is] of phrasing, his ability to use his clarinet to bridge the gap between trumpet phrases . . . and to place the final note of his phrase on the beginning of a trumpet phrase. . . .

'The impression of consistence is made all the stronger by the refusal of the musicians to permit themselves too much freedom. In successive choruses of a tune Oliver's side-men often play the same part . . . with only slight variation—notice trombonist Horne Dutrey in *Froggie Moore*, especially; Dodds in the same tune and in *Snake Rag* . . . Dutrey . . . often plays a pretty strict harmony part, but . . . his mannerisms, his agility and grace, are strictly his own. . . .

'A riff produces somewhat the same kind of excitement as does Oliver's "consistency" stemming ultimately from the irritation born of sameness and expectation of change unfulfilled . . . the excitement of riffs, however, is bought too cheap . . . most effective in the physical presence of a band. The Creole Band's way is less obvious, more complex, and, in the long run makes a *record* that remains satisfying year after year.

'. . . The Creole Jazz Band . . . sets the standard (possibly, who knows, only because of an historical accident) for all kinds of jazz that do not base their excellence on individual expressiveness, but on form and *shape* achieved through control and balance.

'. . . I love this band and its myth, the perfection it stands for and almost is, its affirmation and integrity, the sombre stride of *Riverside Blues*, the steady roll of *Southern Stomps*, the rock of *Canal Street Blues*, the headlong spirit of *Weather Bird Rag*. . . .

This band . . . was one of the very best that jazz has ever known.'

It was indeed a band of integrated self-subordinated discipline. But it was that, not in the sense that Morton, or Ellington, or John Lewis, have made groups of fine players produce a music of disciplined *form*. Oliver's was a band of *players*, first of all, but players who happened to be able to play together superbly (the several changes of personnel on records in 1923 did not affect this much either, notice); Oliver's was still 'a blowing group' as the expression now goes. That is why it is hard to single out this or that performance as especially good. To be sure, one record is better than another, one of three versions of *Mabel's Dream* may be better than the others, but we could pick out no single masterpiece that seems to fulfil most of what this band intended or had to offer, as we can say of Morton's *Dead Man Blues* or *Kansas City Stomps*, or of Ellington's *Ko-Ko* or *Concerto For Cootie*. This band achieved its best simply by playing *together*—simply by being and doing.

Nevertheless, one can delight in details: the marvellous interplay of Oliver and Armstrong (marvellous the first and the fiftieth time) on the Paramount *Riverside Blues;* following Dodds throughout *Canal Street;* noticing the way Lil Armstrong and the rhythm instruments, sometimes led by Dutrey, will momentarily use syncopated tango rhythms with a wonderful secret knowledge about just when to start it and when to stop it for perfect effect—hear *Weather Bird Rag* and *Mandy Lee Blues*, or what happens behind Oliver's really splendid final choruses on *Alligator Hop.*

But, despite the fact that it was basically a sublimely co-operative blowing group, there are effects of arrangement and sequence that show it could go beyond that towards form in another sense. Performances on records are undoubtedly not like those done in person and the cutting down of pieces for record length is often very well done,

especially on multi-thematic compositions. Take *Froggie Moore:* the pacing of themes, the placement of Armstrong's solo, however much it owes to composer Morton's own scheme, seem perfectly balanced for the length of the performance. Or take the detail of handling of the trio on *Chatanooga Stomp:* the theme statement comes suddenly in harmony between a muted Oliver and Jimmy Noone. They play gradually with less perfect unity deliberately (or at least in effect) in order to prepare for the following polyphonic variation, one that seems so excitingly wild but, under the surface, is perfectly controlled and sure—and at this fast tempo. And the way the variation is introduced: by the cornet (it's Armstrong—or is it Oliver?) breaking through at the last note of the theme-statement filling in the 'empty' bars, announcing to the whole band that it is time to improvise together for thirty-two bars—beginning HERE. He hits the note on the first chord of the second trio chorus, already joined, it seems, by the other cornet who could not wait to begin the interplay.

It is unfortunate and unfair for both men that in most accounts of New Orleans jazz that the 1926–28 records of Morton's Red Hot Peppers and those of Oliver's Creole Band are lumped together as exponents of 'New Orleans style'. Morton's conception was different in basic respects: more formal, sophisticated, learned. Beside Morton's masterful integrations of solo, harmonized ensembles, polyphonic interludes (in two, three, or four parts), and concepts of total form, Oliver's, despite the arranged effects, was the music of a fine blues band which played some jazz-style marches as well. Morton's music has the form of a director–leader–composer where in each part is a function of a compositionally conceived whole; Oliver's the form of improvisers working together wherein each man is a function of a group of fine players.

There are other differences: Morton's rhythmic conception is older than Oliver's, closer to ragtime (he handled it perfectly and with swing), at the same time that his compositional and formal ideas were advanced beyond anyone else's in jazz that we know of.

But to make such distinctions is not necessarily to give them relative value. Oliver's way (and his band's way) was his own way, the one that led him to produce music. An art needs all approaches. An art even needs approaches which fail, of course, but neither Morton nor Oliver did that.

Some idea of what a marvellous experience this band must have been and a wonderful way for us to get 'inside' its music (and also to help our ears with the limitations of 1923 recording) comes from the fact that the group did some of the same pieces more than once on records. If we carefully hear and compare the Gennett and Okeh versions of *Snake Rag*, of *Dippermouth Blues*, of *Workingman Blues*, or the Paramount and Okeh versions of *Riverside Blues*, the quality and size of this music begins to take shape for us. Perhaps the most fruitful of all the comparisons we can make is among the three versions we are lucky enough to have of *Mabel's Dream*. Because of their likenesses and differences they clarify for us so many of the things that the group could do. Because of Oliver's part in them, they expand our ideas of his abilities.

Two of them were made successively for Paramount records and both happily got released.[1] The other was recorded the same month for Okeh.

Basically *Mabel's Dream* is a multi-thematic rag-like (or march-like) jazz performance, i.e. a rag played as if it were a blues. The second theme (the first amounts only to an introduction) is based on an intriguing little descending phrase intermittently completed by *ad lib* 'breaks' supplied in performance by clarinet and trombone. One

can well imagine the origin of such a phrase in a ragtime piece, but the clipped *rhythms* of ragtime are not in this performance. The three recordings treat this section in more or less the same way, even to the melodies in breaks themselves—except that in the Okeh version the orchestral texture is denser, perhaps because the tempo is faster. The interesting part for our purposes comes with the closing theme.

Basically the two Paramount versions take the same approach, a remarkably 'classic' approach, one like Morton's. There are three choruses of the trio and they make a developing set of related variations.

Let us say that the lead cornet here is Oliver throughout the three; that is the consensus of opinion and, as we shall see, the music on the Okeh version all but confirms it. The theme has melody closely tied to its harmony: it is impossible to hum it without the simple underlying chords springing into one's head—and such themes lend themselves easily and readily to the kinds of variations jazzmen made in the twenties—think of the popularity of *Wolverine Blues*, say, and the drastic melodic departure Johnny Dodds is able to make from the third strain on Morton's trio record of it; or think of the last strain of *Froggie Moore*. Here, the entrance of this selection is appropriately a theme-statement by the cornet lead. Departures from a strict statement of the melodic line are there (and if we don't catch them at first a comparison of the two versions will bring them out), but they are simple. The second chorus is a variation in melody and rhythm, or rather melody-rhythm, since it is as clear an indication of the relationship of these two in jazz as one could ask for. Oliver wants to *swing* this theme now and to do it he has both to reorganize its metres and recast its melodic line. The simplest device Oliver uses to do this is to accentuate the rhythm by note-doublings here and there. But the first Paramount version (master #1622–1) shows

---

[1] A reliable rumour has it that unreleased alternate 'takes' of Oliver Paramounts exist in 'master' records and will some day be issued. A less reliable rumour says the same is true of some of the Gennetts.

that Oliver has also partly reduced the theme to a bare minimum of notes which suggest its outline, has taken the 'open' places in the melody (places where there are sustained notes or no notes) and filled these in with original, very blues-like, melodic fragments. One could see this as a distillation of the melody plus an obbligato, both played by the same man. But it is far more fruitful, because of what follows, to see Oliver building a new melodic line out of a bare outline of the old. Naturally, along with the greater rhythmic emphasis and the transformed melody, the feeling in the passage is changing, but this is as if to prepare for the next variation. One could only call it a melodic-emotional variation. Such a coinage is not so naïve as it may sound. Oliver has now transformed the initial theme into an original *blues* melody, and to deliver this final and most drastic departure he uses his wa-wa mute; he has re-composed a rather naïvely optimistic military strut into a plaintive yet dignified blues. And if one looks even more closely, some other details of the way Oliver has broken up and redistributed the original melody can fascinate. The simple structure of the theme is delivered in spurts of two bars, the basic melodic motif covers three bars plus a rest of one bar. In building a new theme out of this Oliver ties units together and puts his bar lines and rests at very different places. The often delivered dictum that early jazzmen were victims of brief, mechanical phrasing ignores the wonderful ingenuity which they always showed within their idiom—and, of course, that kind of mastery of one's idioms and *use* of its conventions is the source of art, never the conventions themselves.

In the second Paramount version of *Mabel's Dream*, Oliver uses basically the same pattern on this trio section. The theme is first stated with a few blues-like interpolations which prepare us for what is to come. In the second chorus he swings the melody more, simplifies it and departs from it further. In the third he builds a new

melody. The really ingenious thing here is not so much that this third chorus (or 'second variation', if you will) is different from the one Oliver had improvised a few minutes before. (It *is* different and, I am inclined to think, superior.) But it is also the almost inevitable result of what Oliver had been building all along in this version. If one now re-plays this whole section and compares it to the first, one gets some idea of how comprehensive a musical mind Oliver could show. In the first take, everything from the slight changes and little interpolations in the theme-statement and the improvised changes in the first variation seem to prepare almost inevitably for just the kind of melody Oliver built up in the last chorus. In the second take, Oliver ends up with a very different final melody preparing for it beforehand just as logically, with different sorts of embellishments and departures which lead to it. He was 'thinking' three choruses then, making them a continuous developing unit, and, apparently within a few minutes, making two very different things of the same basic material and following the same general plan.

Jelly Roll Morton did use the same generally 'classic' plan of variation 'in sets' but comparing Oliver's first two versions of *Mabel's Dream* shows a growing looseness and freedom—at least in rhythm—compared to Morton. Morton undoubtedly went far (and it can be quite far as a comparison of his records of several of his pieces will show); Oliver also went far in his way. And the point perhaps is that neither tried to go so far that he did not retain his own sense of order and form.

Once we have begun to absorb these two takes of *Mabel's Dream*, the Okeh comes as a surprise. The tempo is faster, and the group's sure handling of this different tempo makes the same composition into something different. To put it simply, what had been a march transformed into a plaintive blues now becomes a faster march transformed into a sprightly and thickly polyphonic dance or 'stomp'. The first and second strains, which are rather stodgy on the Paramounts, here take on more life and Baby Dodds's liveliness almost makes up for brother Johnny's mechanical runs. Early in the record Armstrong announces what he is up to by flashing through with easy replies to the group.

The trio strain is handled as an improvised polyphonic interplay between the two cornets, with Oliver in the lead, which gradually increases in complexity and density until, at exactly the right moment and in precisely the right way, Johnny Dodds enters his upper register in the last chorus and makes it a three-part interplay. The almost immaculate timing and pace involved in these three choruses, the subtle discipline involved in the most spontaneous event, and the

firm artistic sureness with which the most exciting pitch is handled and then topped can make so many of the ensemble passages in recorded 'dixieland' seem the strained and noisy naïveté of amateurs. (Would that we had an alternative 'take' of *this* version!)

We may hear and enjoy a lot of things about this group without any such exercise as the foregoing, but such comparative listening does help us to hear more and to understand more, and once having done it, we can never never go back, I think; we can never again hear this band without a better hearing and broader and deeper delight in its art. Then, we not only enter into the different versions of *Riverside Blues* but we are unlikely ever to be able to play *Canal Street Blues* without discovering something new in it.

2

AN INTERIM NOTE ON OLIVER'S PLAYING

One can discuss many of the merits of the Creole Band without discussing its members very much. Indeed, one almost has to because, as we say, its virtues are the virtues of a whole greater than a sum of parts. But, one cannot discuss Oliver's subsequent bands and career, nor his effect on others, without discussing Oliver's own playing. And immediately one encounters an obstacle: Louis Armstrong.

Armstrong's long-standing insistence that Oliver was his stylistic inspiration was strongly reasserted in interviews after the death of Bunk Johnson. It was recently strongly confirmed by Lil Hardin Armstrong, but she also added that

although Louis did play like Oliver while with him (and, according to Oliver's own admission, better), that when Louis left him he played like no one had ever heard before.

Therefore, when Oliver's brilliant accompaniment to 'Sippie' Wallace on *Morning Dove Blues* seems technically a slightly simpler version of the one Louis Armstrong gave Bessie Smith on *St. Louis Blues* a few months earlier, we might reasonably speak of influence, but when very Armstrong-like ideas show up on *Jet Black Blues* (with 'Blind Willie Dunn') or when the cornet breaks through with such fire on *Deep Henderson* in the way Louis did with Erskine Tate or Perry Bradford, we cannot really be sure of who influenced whom. Nor can we be sure when, as Maitland Edey points out (*The Jazz Review*, August 1959), Armstrong sounds like Oliver on the first chorus of Trixie Smith's *Railroad Blues*. We should remember, surely, how many people marvelled at Bunk Johnson's choruses on *When The Saints Go Marching In*; so like Louis, they said. Indeed, they were right because, as Bunk privately admitted, he had taken a lot of what he played from Louis's record of the tune. The basic ideas in Oliver's *Willie The Weeper* (April 1927) variation are the same as those in Armstrong's (May 1927). Master and pupil? Perhaps, but what had Oliver perhaps heard Armstrong do with that piece in Chicago before April 1927? We cannot be sure.

Inevitably, when one discusses Oliver with musicians one of the first points they will make is that Oliver was 'a master of mutes' (that's the phrase that is usually used). Trombonist Preston Jackson, in that first story on Oliver in *Hot News* put it more tellingly: 'Later on, about 1914, I should say, Joe began to improve a lot. He used to practise very hard. I remember he once told me that it took him ten years to get a tone on his instrument. He used a half-cocked mute, and how he could make it talk!' His 'wa-wa's', his piercing cries, were not the crude or haphazard attempts of a musical semi-literate to play (and to imitate the human voice) expressively by bastard and essentially non-musical means. They were the careful and deliberate personal techniques of a sensitive and innovative player-artist. 'The almost unbearable anguish of King Oliver's horn' (as John Martin called it) was something he worked long and carefully to be able to project.

Another and perhaps more crucial point Jackson made immediately followed: 'He played the variation style too; running chords I mean. His ear was wonderful—that helped a lot,' and trumpeter Louis Metcalfe has said that Oliver first made him aware of chord structures and of playing on them!

Here, I think we have something crucial, for the *way* in which Oliver 'ran the chords' is important. He could have known chords or learned them well enough from many Creole-trained musicians in New Orleans. But in the blues and rag-like themes which he recorded, he did not use an arpeggio style as Jimmy Noone so often did; in none did he simply 'open up' chords by playing the notes in them as they passed. Oliver, as Dodds often did, or even Lester Young did, used the intervals to *write* new or variant themes while improvising. His imagination was melodic-rhythmic in short—as is Armstrong's. This may perhaps seem a bold technical statement to be making of a man who has left few records but simple blues of eight, twelve, and sixteen bars and rag-march themes of sixteen or double-sixteen bar sequences, and whose harmonic sense was hardly complex. But on his level, Oliver might have stood for a lot of other things; Noone[1] did stand for one other and that one could have been a defeating one for many players to adopt. Oliver did stand for *melody* in improvising. Since he stood for honest emotion as well, he stood for music and not technique. And since he stood for a special integrated rhythmic content too, he stood for jazz.

Standing for jazz he stood, in part, for himself and, as we shall see, that means that his music always had a dimension of dignity and of pride.

Perhaps it is that which makes our discussion of his techniques worth while.

[1] Of course, Noone's beautiful blues choruses on Ollie Powers's *Play That Thing* is one of several exceptions to my characterization of his work here. And as his records with Oliver (*Chatanooga Stomp, New Orleans Stomp, London Blues,* and *Camp Meeting Blues*) show, his knowledge of harmony and his Creole-based dance rhythms could make him a uniquely effective ensemble player.

3

THE DIXIE SYNCOPATORS

The first thing that strikes one about the records by The Dixie Syncopators is the unevenness.

A man who had been so sure of his conception and had led a band so sure in its execution, now seemed unsure, and results vary widely. The second thing one realizes is that on these and subsequent records, we learn what kind of player and soloist Oliver was and what his solos have to tell us.

The general intention of the Syncopators is obvious enough: the Creole band's style much modified in part by borrowing a small saxophone section from the conventional American dance (or even parade) band.[1]

Now at the same time, Fletcher Henderson was working on a similar problem: how to transform a conventional dance band into a jazz band. But Henderson worked from the other direction; although on some early records he directly imitates Oliver's Creole band, Henderson's real career begins when he takes a dance band and tries to make a jazz band out of it. Oliver, who had a jazz band, wanted to keep it that, while he borrowed a section from a conventional dance band.

Curiously, both men failed in similar ways. Henderson stuck it out—luckily he could—until he had it finally licked about 1934. Oliver continued to fail in certain respects and he again changed his approach gradually in the late twenties. But for both, there were several individual and exemplary successes.

(To continue, for the record, on the formulation of 'big' bands, unlike Henderson's conversion of a dance group into a jazz group, Ellington began at a different point. For it was not until he had a 'show' or 'pit' band to convert into a jazz orchestra that Ellington began to find his way. Benny Moten, profiting by both the work of New Orleans men (Oliver, Morton) and by Henderson, made a jazz band from a dance band which was made, in turn, out of a brass band. Count Basie was *not* the heir to Moten's conception, however, Jimmy Lunceford was. Basie, guided by Walter Page's Blue Devils and profiting greatly from a simplication of Henderson's work, built up a big jazz band from the small south-western jump-blues group.)

There are some moments in the earlier Creole Jazz Band records which we must simply bear with —they are the dated things like the chime effects on *Chimes Blues*, the silly slide whistle on *Sobbin' Blues*, but they are not failures. The Dixie Syncopators' records are full of strange failures: rhythmic heaviness and unsureness in percussion and horns, poor ensemble playing (poorly intoned and poorly unified), passages which do not swing at all between passages which do, players who suddenly trip over themselves and lose their way rhythmically; solos which swing for four bars, then don't swing for six, then do for two, and solo styles which flounder badly.

Certainly jazz *was* in the midst of a rhythmic change with Armstrong now in the lead, and many men did not know which way to turn to, old or new rhythms. And just as certainly other bands with

---

[1] A comparison among several versions of *Dippermouth Blues–Sugarfoot Stomp* helps clarify this relationship (see below). A comparison of the versions of *Sobbin' Blues* by the Creole Band and the Syncopators, however, does not —although it may be said to clarify the superiority of the former group in personnel and conception.

intentions like Oliver's were having similar problems with reeds and with unity. But there seems to be more involved than that. At any rate, there seems to be *much* more involved when one hears the successes in this series. How could there *be* such success, we repeatedly ask ourselves, when, in general, this group sometimes seemed to have so little firmness of guiding principle or end—or even awareness of means.

Some kind of answer may come when we realize that several of the more successful recordings by the band (or bands, actually, since there were many personnel changes) were arranged by alto saxophonist Billy Paige, who was briefly in the group and recorded with it between 11 March and 26 May 1926. Paige arranged both *Too Bad* and *Snag It*. In them and in the other recordings which work, the rhythmic momentum (if not rhythmic style) of the Creole Band is maintained, the sax section is *used* but not (as in the failures) as if it were the centre and virtue of things. There is a minimum of cluttering 'effects' and the players seem to know where they are going from the start of a number.

Several of the records are well worth discussing in some detail and in order. *Too Bad* is a good arrangement and performance. Its fast tempo is controlled and it is used: the tempo does not use the players. The brief theme (by Billy Meyers and Elmer Schoebel) saves itself from a harrowing harmonic monotony by its rhythmic variety; the marvellous Charleston syncopations at its beginnings are, like soliloquys or chorus lines which tap-dance, as irresistible as they are 'old-fashioned'. Even Barney Bigard's slap tongue sax fits the airy generosity of the piece and performance. The firm pride with which Oliver's horn re-enters at the end gives the performance an emotional balance and depth which shows the sound intuitions of an artist at work and reveals just what kind of artist Oliver was. Not a first-rate record, *Too Bad* does almost set a standard for handling tempos in this new style, and it does make possible a later *Wa Wa Wa.*

Snag It (the first or 'vocal' version) is a success for similar reasons. It has little waste and a firm purpose. It also has variety. It is all very well to say that the 'breaks' chorus in this record was 'influential' if one doesn't mean only that it shows up in the mid 'forties in a Lionel Hampton pseudo-boogie woogie record. Perhaps the real point of this performance again is Oliver. His playing has a passion and a dignity which saves what might otherwise have been a mere series of effects; notice, for example, how he completes both the break and 'call and response' (riff) choruses in the last few bars of each by gradually converting their basically tricky raw materials into what are really lovely blues melodies. Again, it is a double level on which they are working—of surface 'style' and deeper feeling—that makes the good Syncopators' recordings good, and, again, it is largely Oliver's emotional power and his skill at using it which gives one of those levels its existence. The later version of *Snag It* (the one without the vocal chorus and sometimes issued as *Snag It #2*) is hardly up to this one, and it fails chiefly because Oliver does not play well on it.

Perhaps *Deep Henderson* reveals something of the crisis in the orchestra. Luis Russell has a piano chorus on it: rhythmically it is like pseudo-ragtime, emotionally it is shallow, melodically it is, like several of the arrangements Russell did for the group, a series of tricks used to no real end even as tricks.[1] Oliver's strong horn pierces through it marvellously and so like the Armstrong of 1923-26.

Jackass Blues is a fine case in point of Oliver's abilities. His solo is very simple and made of a few very simple things, yet it is a work of art. Basically, what he does is take several of his *Dippermouth Blues* (*Sugarfoot Stomp*) phrases and piece them together in different order. That order is compositional, it is in this case not a re-statement or para-

[1] I do not intend these remarks as an estimate either of Russell's talent or subsequent career, only of his performance here.

263

phrase of the theme but the creation of a new one, and it is a melodic and emotional whole—a new essence. Is some of it (perhaps a lot of it) simply a use of 'traditional' blues melodies as are many blues solos of the period? Does that matter? As it is and where it is on this recording, the solo is the statement of an artist. In a slightly different form or from another man it might indeed have been a cliché.

Sugarfoot was recorded about a month later. A comparison between it, Oliver's two earlier versions of *Dippermouth*, and Henderson's early *Sugarfoot* records is the best basis I could have for my earlier arguments about the conception of this band and that of the 'Creole' group and Henderson's. This Syncopators' recording has several fine things about it, and some not so fine but interesting things as well. Among the latter is the way Albert Nicholas begins with his version of Johnny Dodds's choruses and then immediately converts himself into his real idol, Jimmy Noone. Both fine and interesting is Kid Ory's way of making a 'bass' instrument (for such it is in earlier polyphonic styles) into a solo horn by using blues ideas several trumpeters (including Armstrong—hear *Gut Bucket Blues*) were playing at the time. Towards the end, Ory 'calls' the group to riff pattern 'responses' and the figures Ory plays are in the basic pattern for almost all trombone section writing in orchestral jazz until the 'forties. Oliver on this record is weak, shaky in ideas and execution and sounding as though he is 'faking' notes by forcing breath and embrochure. When Oliver is weak like this, and he became so increasingly but with recoveries, there is a pathos in his playing that draws us to him, but we had better be clear that this is *not* an aesthetic response, but a personal one. We are only pulling for the man; we do not respond to what the artist can reveal.

So many of the successful things on the earlier records that work seem to prepare for *Wa Wa Wa*; indeed, it all but perfects what *Too Bad* conceived. And Oliver's own role in it begins where *Deep Henderson* leaves him and fulfils what that record

implies. It is probably the best record the Syncopators made—a fact which is all the more striking when one remembers how decidedly unique and nearly sublime Oliver himself can be on slow blues for *Wa Wa Wa* is a fast stomp. Walter Allen has remarked on the variety of muted and wa-wa playing here. The momentum of Oliver's rhythm throughout is given the most telling kind of confirmation in the way that Nicholas loses swing in his break but Oliver and Bob Schoffner do not at all. Certainly there are clichés here, even clichés of awkwardness like the sax section work and there is a clarinet trio. But nothing *en route* could stand in the way of the purposeful power of *Wa Wa Wa*— a kind of savage energy sublimated and transmuted by conscious craft into a fearless joy of living. (Could the man who made this record have made the corny *Farewell Blues* a year later? He did.)

Again, one cannot be sure about the influence of such playing on Armstrong, but one should say that each man made something rather different out of the general approach. But one is more than tempted to declare that such rhythmic drive as Oliver shows here had its repercussions everywhere. Of such a thing as the striking, behind-the-beat coda on *Tack Annie*, so like Armstrong's style, and also the one Bunk Johnson showed in the 'forties, one cannot say, except that it is there.

Someday Sweetheart and *Dead Man Blues* were public successes, Oliver's best-sellers. (They were coupled on opposite sides of the same release and of course Morton gave it out that *Dead Man* caused the sales.) The former was arranged by Luis Russell and is, in performance at least, a combination of *schmaltz* and the kind of honesty that gives *schmaltz* the lie. Again, Russell's rhythmic conception is raggy: Oliver could carry such rhythms (understood them as well as his own newer ones) without sounding corny and superficial but Bert Cobb's statement of the theme on tuba (for all its *outré* sound today) seems shallow. Oliver plays the verse of the piece with the rhythmic ease at shifting accents and making delays of a near-innovator, an ease that no one else here was up to, not even Johnny Dodds. Dodds does 'save' the performance, however, by a beautifully honest (though hardly humourless) response to Barney Bigard. Bigard's theme statement is corn and not in the modish sense—he is not so much old fashioned as he is false in emotion and affected in manner. Dodd's clarinet manages both honesty and *bravura* at once, in a way that only he (and perhaps Verdi) knew about, in his re-statement of the theme. The melody itself is ideally suited for such an irony, for if one does not take a jazzman's advantage of the way its rhythmic accents fall (as Dodds does), its melodic contours *could* lead him into the worst kind of turn-of-the-century music-hall sentimentality.

Jelly Roll Morton's Victor record of the same piece (complete with violins that are both heavy and lush) is just that kind of mawkishness. But with his own *Dead Man's Blues*, Morton made one of his three or four orchestral masterpieces, and one which could have shown both Oliver and Henderson most of what there is to know about how to get reed sections to play with unity and swing. But Oliver's record was the hit. It doesn't survive; it is fast enough to be downright coy, whereas Morton managed sadness, optimisim, wit, and depth all in one three-minute complex unit of both device and feeling. Oliver leaves us with only a fairly academic appreciation of Bob Schoffner's behind-the-beat solo.

One can only feel of *Willie The Weeper* that its effort at variety in arrangement is simply affected and misguided (Morton was often more complex in fact, far less so in effect) and only draws attention to itself and that there are poor solos. If Oliver was not imitating the outline of the solo Armstrong was to record a few days later, then Oliver must have been imitating himself, and not very well.

By the time one gets to blues *Speakeasy* and *Aunt Hager's*, things are clearly running out for the Dixie Syncopators. The personnel has changed over and over, the conception of the scores is floundering and confused, and the emotional dimension that almost any Oliver solo might give almost any record is not present, for Oliver does not solo. One cannot be sure what these arrangements intend: the earlier Syncopators idea of a modified New Orleans group, the idea of a small ensemble playing scored themes and effects around a string of solos (like the Clarence Williams records of the time), or of a big 'pre-swing' band conception that was beginning to emerge in Harlem and that Oliver was soon to flirt with. Only a reed riff on *Speakeasy* survives. Ed Anderson is the trumpet soloist on both. One can only say that he does very well at elaborating a style like Oliver's, one that the most advanced younger men had already abandoned for another style (i.e. Armstrong's) which Oliver's had already inspired.

But before those two records were made there are a succession of three other more or less slow blues, *Black Snake Blues*, *Tin Roof Blues*, and *West End Blues*, and they show the band's range of failure and success.

Black Snake uses Omer Simeon (he took up soprano saxophone just for the arrangement) to advantage, but hardly to the near-brilliance that Morton did—it is quite possible that Simeon was always a better ensemble improviser than soloist. Ory manages again to be both witty and deeply serious. Oliver's opening is sure and the slightest technical shakiness of his final chorus is fully overcome by his dignity and force. *Black Snake* is one Luis Russell arrangement for the Syncopators that does manage variety without clutter, but it is variety of a rather pointless sort, a variety of several good effects within a score, but with such little attention to over-all pattern. If the total effect of such writing is good, it is almost an accident.

I do not know why Frederick Ramsey Jr. insisted in *Jazzmen* that *Tin Roof Blues* was taken from Oliver's *Jazzin' Babies Blues*. It was not, although George Brunis did use a fairly commonplace bass-tuba theme that is on the *Jazzin' Babies* record as the basis of his solo. At any rate, Oliver's 1928 *Tin Roof* is hardly distinguished except for Oliver's very lovely solo at the end of it.

One cannot say, however, that the original Oliver record of *West End* is undistinguished or even careless: it is simply bad. It is incongruously bad; one hardly knows how it was intended or how to take it. Oliver obviously made it up with care of two distinguished blues themes, the second of them harmonically lovely and quite provocative for an improviser. Oliver opens the record with a rhythmic archaic chorus for some reason. When we then hear Ernest Elliot's confused burlesque of a clarinet solo (it is made up of blues clichés and Ted Lewis-like whinneys), we hardly know what to think. And when Oliver's ending is so beautiful, so proud, and so honest, the listener's confusion is confounded.

I have hinted at, spoken of, and even pointed to certain obvious rhythmic crises in the Syncopators' records on which I shall now try to take a stand. There is far too much of the kind of rhythmic momentum cum suspense which we call 'swing' in, say Jelly Roll Morton's records, for me to take the position that swing must be based on an even 'four' time sense, but clearly there is a rhythmic difference between, say, Morton and Armstrong (or for that matter, between Morton and Bessie Smith). Oliver could *swing* in a rhythmic mode based either on a modified 2/4 rather like Morton's, or a mode based on an even 4/4 like Armstrong's—indeed he may have adopted the latter from certain kinds of 'low' blues playing and passed it on to Armstrong. I believe he did. Oliver swings for example in both parts of *Tin Roof*, in all of *Wa Wa Wa*, or *Too Bad*. Nicholas uses the more ragtimy 2/4 rhythmic conception on *Wa Wa Wa* but there does not swing.

Morton did not *always* swing; neither did Oliver, but the question is not merely that of an underlying 2/4 or 4/4 time sense. Furthermore, a man may keep perfect *time* and not swing (example: Charlie Shavers) and he may swing beautifully and have imperfect time (example: Jo Jones).

One further point about the Syncopators deserves attention. There is an assumption in many circles that jazz has gradually achieved a rhythmic lightness over its fifty years. As a generalization it is valid enough, I suppose, but in detail it is hardly true. The Creole Jazz Band, despite a preponderance of rhythm instruments and an overlapping of their functions (one example bass, trombone, and piano bass-line) had a rhythmic lightness, sureness, spring, and ease, that one does not often hear either in the rhythm section or in the horns of the Syncopators. And the rhythmic lightness that Morton achieved on certain Red Hot Pepper records has all the aspects of a controlled miracle. But the Syncopators, like so many early medium and large groups which used arrangements, had a usually heavy and sluggish rhythm section which affected most of the horns. That it seldom affected Oliver himself is a sign of the size of Oliver's talent in jazz. But one other aspect of that rhythm is even more striking. Its lack of flow is so much more evident where it shouldn't have been by all reasonable expectations: on slow and medium blues, and it is less evident where it might have given trouble: on fast numbers. *Too Bad* and *Wa Wa Wa* can dance with such relatively rhythmic movement and dash, yet slow blues like *Black Snake*, say, in a tempo which gives even the untutored 'folk' musician no rhythmic trouble at all, often have a dull, heavy and unmoving pulse thumping away in them.

266

4

KING OLIVER 'AND HIS ORCHESTRA'

It is often said of Oliver's 1929–30 Victor recordings that in effect many of them were made by the Victor bosses rather than Joe Oliver. This is undoubtedly true of such things as *Everybody Does It In Hawaii* with Roy Schmeck's guitar, but the majority of the numbers on them were written by Oliver and/or Dave Nelson, and by Paul Barbarin or Luis Russell, and were scored by Nelson.

Perhaps the first thing that one notices is the polish of the groups. The reeds play better, with more unity and better intonation, the rhythm sections are usually firmer and more integrated with the groups, the full ensembles are more unified. But, except for those times when Oliver had the nucleus of a working group (which would include trombonist Jimmy Archey), these records were made by groups assembled for the dates or working bands of other leaders borrowed in part or whole by Oliver for records. Obviously, these men were musicians with standards of professionalism, but one must admit that the soloist sometimes does not meet the standards of feeling which some of Oliver's earlier side-men, for all their bungling, had set. And there are many of the same problems with swing in the solos, except that now the soloists will have their own rhythms set and maintained and those rhythms will either swing or not swing. There is little tripping or faltering within choruses as with some of the Syncopators' soloists.

Perhaps more important than any of this is a change in conception that soon becomes evident. It is hard to say how much pressures from the Victor company to get records which would sell well influenced things—or how much Oliver might have been affected in some ways by the same desires—but one can say that on the whole these records have more devices of scoring and approach which are dated than his others. The Syncopators' failures may be failures of execution not of score. The same sort of dated scoring mars some of Jelly Roll Morton's records of the period, but that would not be said of his earlier records nor of most of Oliver's. Henderson and Ellington might have failed in these same years, but most of the time their conception seems to have been on the right track. Oliver's often was not. For example it is difficult to understand what a *mélange* of devices like *I Can't Stop Loving You* intends, unless Oliver was convinced (or had been convinced) that for popularity one should do what others did and not what one did best. At any rate, it was several years before Don Redman and Jimmy Lunceford, in their different ways, perfected the kind of thing that *I Want You Just Myself* attempts, and to do it each of them had to bring about considerable transmutation into jazz of the 'dance band' devices he employed.

Even more important is further evidence already

hinted at above, that Oliver was gradually changing his basic approach. He usually kept his instrumentation the same: two or three brass, two or three reeds, and rhythm. But less and less did his approach sound like a modified New Orleans ensemble with reeds for clarinet; more and more did it sound like a cut-down version of the New York 'big band' of the period.[1] And as we have said, it was a band in which the worst elements of style of the 'hotel' dance band of the time were used directly without their being really transformed or assimilated into the jazz idiom.

Also, one must remark on Oliver's own playing and especially since the Victor contract began with three record dates on which Oliver did not play at all—and on the first of which Louis Metcalf did an imitation of Louis Armstrong's innovative recording of Oliver's earlier composition *West End Blues*. In 1929 and 1930, King Oliver might follow a recording on which he did not play with one on which he played very well, and follow that with one on which he falters technically and seems to be forcing himself badly. That is about the best that one can make of the difficult tangle of Oliver's cornet and trumpet solos in these years.[2] He could follow dates with no solos or simple, quiet ones by taking those really bravura solos on *Too Late* and *New Orleans Shout* for himself. But it is that kind of pride that he was made of.

Sweet Like This is one of the most celebrated of the Victor series and it deserves to be. It has no startling improvisation and it has a bit of rather bad writing and playing for the reeds (behind the first trumpet solo), but has two charming themes and it seems to know what it intends to say without the waste motion of many of these records. The themes themselves again show that art is a matter of how one handles one's conventions no matter what those conventions are. For the themes are again the blues, one twelve- and one sixteen-bar blues, and Nelson and Oliver have fashioned two themes of touching, almost nostalgic, lyricism on these cliché patterns, and themes which also complement each other excellently. (I believe, incidentally, that it is Oliver who plays the first solo on open trumpet—the theme statement—and Nelson who plays the simple muted variation—although Allen, Rust, and Hughes Panassie have it the other way around.)

Too Late, the next side from the same date, is also a good one and an even better arrangement in the reed-work. Actually, it again returns to the sixteen-bar blues for still another use, for its thirty-two-bar theme is the kind made of what amounts to splicing two sixteen-bar sequences together. Its ending, with probably Oliver playing solo in his fast stomp style over excitingly executed riffs figures, is one of the best things in the Victor series.

The other record from this date is what is surely one of Oliver's loveliest later pieces, *What Do You Want Me To Do*, and it has Oliver's lovely obbligato to a theme-statement by tuba, but it is another of those arrangements in which the effort of the times to use the whining 'sweet' 'hotel-band' saxophone style[1] in a jazz setting does not work as jazz. The truth may be, as I say, that in 1929 nobody really knew what to do with three reeds in a jazz band—or that those who did, did not always do what was best. Certainly, Oliver was alone neither in the attempt nor in the failure, but unlike the others, Oliver had a style before 1925 that was maturely

---

[1] One might object that the musicians available could play no other style, except that most of them have before or since.

[2] Almost any musician will say of Oliver that, until he finally had to stop playing the cornet, he would play less and less frequently, but that when he did solo, he could play well. Lester Young, who may have been with him as late as 1933, has said so, and Keg Purnell says his lip was still good in 1935. On the other hand, his lip may *sound* very bad on some of the 1929 records and sound excellent a few days later on another record date. Any horn player has bad days, of course, but Oliver seems to have had extremes. (The switch from cornet to trumpet came about 1930.)

[1] The style may well be at least in part an effort at an 'adaptation' by 'hotel bands' of the jazz clarinet style of the 'teens and early 'twenties—but, then, so is Ted Lewis's clarinet style. We can hear it put to quite different use in what Lester Young made of Frankie Trumbauer.

a jazz style—but one, alas, out of fashion. Henderson, Redmond, and Ellington were working to transform such things into the language of jazz. Oliver, at forty-four, his major work (whether he knew it or not) probably already done, was stuck with them and (again, whether he knew it or not) with the times.

But not always, because for every *You're Just My Type* there are very successful records like Luis Russell's composition *Call of the Freaks*, Metcalfe's *Trumpets Prayer, Stingaree Blues* (with Oliver's memorable solo), *Mule Face Blues, Boogie Woogie*,[1] or *Nelson Stomp*. In composition, in scoring, and in performance these records take the best road available, the one that everyone would be on in about six years, and take it decisively and well. They are exceptional performances. And some like *Shake It and Break It* could even catch at least a bit of the joyous side of the stomps of an earlier time.

For some of the others, one can only hear and report; report that after the magnificent swing of the opening of *Olga*, it is abandoned for another kind of rhythm, a *mélange* of effects and mostly stodgy solos; or report that on *Rhythm Club Stomp*,[1] Charlie Holmes's clarinet solo (as usual) and the fine closing ensemble generate more swing than anything else which happens; or report that one *Frankie and Johnny* could (despite the burden of Roy Schmeck and an harmonica) create and sustain a good, almost barrel-house beat, while the stodgy one made fifteen days later has little to offer but Holmes again and Oliver's lead in the last chorus.

Oliver's Victor recordings are usually either dismissed or spoken of as the flounderings of an almost helpless 'old man'. But of about thirty-eight titles, at least ten are very successful recordings for their whole length and several others have fine moments. For some of the failures Oliver must ultimately take the blame, but when we remember that most of the records were made by 'pick up' bands, that for some of them he had 'commercial' gimmicks forced on him, that jazz was in a state of rhythmic and stylistic flux, and, above all, that Oliver was working with a comparatively new conception of orchestral jazz with which even his younger colleagues were having daily trouble and failure, ten such very good records made in 1929–1930 would represent real achievement for anyone.

[1] An unusual piece for Oliver, by the way, since it is in the thirty-two bar AABA, Tin Pan Alley form with B as a 'bridge' or 'release'. The piece has nothing to do with the kind of percussive blues piano which shares its name.

[1] A tune by the way which perhaps should have got Oliver and Nelson royalties from *Old Man Mose* in the thirties.

5

JOE OLIVER, ACCOMPANIST AND SIDE-MAN

The Victor recordings represent Oliver's last recorded work chronologically except for a brief return to Brunswick for three dates, the third a pseudonymous one. Meanwhile, Oliver had worked as a blues accompanist and as a side-man on recordings since 1924. Many of these enlighten us about Oliver's style. On some of them he played very good solos, and two of them I think are, in some ways, among his best recorded work.

Oliver as an accompanist again presents us with

contradictions like those we have often come across in this survey of his records: he will do something brilliantly on one occasion and seem hardly able to do the same thing more than competently on another; or, he will take one approach successfully on one occasion but take an entirely different one on another.

On the four Sarah Martin records that have been reissued, *Death Sting Me Blues*, *Mistreatin' Man Blues*, *Mean, Tight Mama*, and the *double entendre* 'patter' song *Kitchen Man*, Oliver does not play simple 'replies' at the ends of her lines as would many others at the time. He often enters behind and under the singer's lines to begin his phrases, *completing* them as 'responses' at the ends of her lines. The effect, of course, is different: that of a continuous interplay and, finally, of an integrated balance between voice and instrument into an entity. But Oliver's playing here, largely muted and usually wa-wa, is often a matter of almost cautious plaintive sounds. Only occasionally does a phrase have a fuller melodic content and line, but those that do are lovely. That is also the approach Oliver took on his first accompaniments, to the vaudeville team of Butterbeans and Susie on *Construction Gang* and *Kiss Me Sweet*. Besides an introduction and an interlude of rather simple variation-on-theme by Oliver, there is some very full and here more melodic playing behind the singers.

Oliver's masterpiece of blues accompaniment, and one which can stand comparison with the best work of Armstrong or Joe Smith, is surely the *Morning Dove Blues* with Sippie Wallace. In the first place, Sippie Wallace was, unlike Sarah Martin, a real blues singer with an expressive, even commanding voice. The blues itself is a very good one, even if the rest of it is not quite up to the poetry of its first stanza:

> Early in the morning, I rise like
> a mourning dove.
> Early in the morning, I rise like
> a mourning dove.
> Moaning and singing about the man
> I love.

The performance builds excellently. Oliver uses all approaches as part of a developing structure. He plays an introduction and, at first, replies and fills at the ends of the singer's lines. Each time, he comes up with a real musical idea, an appropriate one, and it is always expressively played. Gradually as the interplay between the two increases, Oliver's melodies will not only respond to her previous line but lead her beautifully into her next. Then, again gradually, he begins to accompany her lines beginning his phrases behind her, playing them in response to her, completing them by calling for her next line. In this single performance, Oliver has worked out the very delicate artistic problem of how a singer and accompaniment can balance and mutually contribute to a performance without competing with each other. And he has done it without the effect of an exercise, but of a finished work of art. If there is anything that challenges the unique pace and evolving tension one hears on *Morning Dove*, it might be the way Sippie Wallace raises her voice in the final stanza of *Every Dog Has His Day*, a kind of paradoxical triumph-and-pain in one, as Oliver continues behind.

All of these recordings show, I think, how the vocal–instrumental blues was dealing with the very difficult problem of balancing poetry, singer, and instrument. There is always a clash among the three in any coming together they may have: the opera librettist knows he cannot make his lines too good or they draw too much attention to themselves as poetry. And the operatic composer knows he has got to balance his singers and his instrument so that one does not overshadow the others. And the so-called 'country blues' singer knows that he had best keep his guitar simple and appropriately functional for he is primarily a poet. If that kind of balancing of the arts of poetry–song–instruments has ever been better handled in jazz it is surely only on the best of the Joe Smith and Louis Armstrong accompaniments. The interplay of Lester Young and Billie Holiday in the mid 'thirties might sometimes surpass it in some ways, but there is no question of any 'poetry' in *A Sailboat In The Moonlight* (*And You*), so the problem has changed. And today for a Mahalia Jackson, the problem is even simpler. She is primarily a singer and both the verses *and* the accompaniment take second place to her voice and delivery. The most advanced blues artists of the 'twenties—writers, singers, instrumentalists—obviously solved a subtle artistic problem for themselves that few have even dealt with since—and which perhaps only German *lieder* solved before it. And George Thomas's *Morning Dove Blues* as performed by Sippie Wallace and Joseph Oliver is a classic, and almost self-explicating, example of what they achieved.

I do not think that many of Oliver's recordings with Clarence Williams's sometimes stodgy groups are successful—that is, that many of his solos on those records are the best Oliver. I do not say this of *all* his solos on them, and even the poorest of them give us some idea of how he played and all such ideas are valuable.

Oliver has one at the end of *Bimbo* (*I'm Gonna Take My Bimbo Back to Bamboo Isle*) in which he has some delightful rhythmic and metric displacements. To put this performance beside the two versions of *Speakeasy Blues*, the one by Oliver's Syncopators with Oliver's solo and the one by Clarence Williams's Orchestra with a solo by Ed Anderson is instructive. Anderson plays the theme on *Speakeasy* with a great deal more freedom with the rhythm and metre than Oliver does but the origin of what Anderson does can clearly be seen, I think, in such things as Oliver's solo on *Bimbo*.

Also there may be a more plaintive feeling in Oliver's playing of *What You Want Me To Do* with Williams's 'Novelty Four', than there is on his own Victor record of that piece, but there is nothing on the Williams version to match the agility of Oliver's obbligato to Clinton Walker's tuba on his own.

However, there is one record with Oliver as a side-man which, I think, is in some ways among his best. It is the curious *Jet Black Blues* by 'Blind Willie Dunn and his Gin Bottle Four', apparently with Oliver[1], Eddie Lang and Lonnie Johnson, with, perhaps, Hoagy Carmichael.

Oliver, as usual, presents us here with a contradiction. The playing, withal, does show straining and some faltering in technique. The record opens with Lonnie Johnson playing, with his usual feeling, a simple eight-bar blues theme rather like the classic one, *How Long*, as Eddie Lang answers him. Then with Lang in the lead, Johnson plays rhythm and there is that strangely appropriate pitched 'bell' sound entering behind. Now begins Oliver's part of the record: in effect four choruses, in two groups of two, each built on a variation of the theme that Johnson and Lang had introduced. Basically, Oliver's variant theme is made of eight notes, some of them at effective (albeit simple) intervals from those in the Johnson–Lang theme. In each of his first two choruses Oliver ties these notes together with interweaving runs. The runs themselves are virtually the same in each of the choruses; the interesting thing is that they make a climax, getting gradually more complex as each chorus proceeds. After a rather stilted piano solo and a 'scat' vocal chorus which just misses banality and which he quietly accompanies, Oliver re-enters for his second pair of choruses. He begins with a direct three-note reference to his previous solo and then proceeds to build these two choruses as a variation of those earlier two. The germ idea before had been an ascending phrase; here it is a descending one. Here the higher notes give it both tension and, gradually, an optimism missing before. His fourth and last chorus *swings* the melody of his third; the optimism becomes almost a joy which dances now with the doublets and triplets and, as a climax, an Armstrong-like

---

[1] Oliver's presence on this record has been doubted. I am convinced that it is he, but even if it were not, the playing represents much of what he stood for, I think.

eighth note skipping around with the time and the rhythm at its end.

He said something almost like this I think: 'This is my music, the music I stand for. I am proud of it; I give it to you.'

So brief an account as this does not need a summary, I think. But Oliver's story does call for some kind of a conclusion: It is quite reasonable to contend that without Joseph Oliver, the feeling and form of his music and the techniques he found to express them, jazz could not have happened as we know it. But perhaps without the pride, the dignity, the fortitude, the hope, and finally the joy he gave it, it might not have continued as jazz at all.

DISCOGRAPHY
KING OLIVER ON MICROGROOVE

THE DIXIE SYNCOPATORS
Decca 79246. *Snag It; Deep Henderson; Jackass Blues; Sugar Foot Stomp; Wa Wa Wa; Doctor Jazz; Show Boat Shuffle; Every Tub; Willie the Weeper; Black Snake Blues; Farewell Blues; West End Blues; Lazy Mama; Speakeasy Blues; Aunt Hagar's Blues; I'm Watchin' the Clock.*

KING OLIVER AND HIS ORCHESTRA
RCA Victor LPV 529. *Too Late; Sweet Like This; What You Want Me to Do; I'm Lonesome, Sweetheart; New Orleans Shout; Frankie and Johnny; Edna; St. James Infirmary; Rhythm Club Stomp; Olga; Mule Face Blues; Struggle Buggy; Don't You Think I Love You?; Shake It and Break It; Nelson Stomp; Stingaree Blues.*

Following albums no longer available:

THE CREOLE JAZZ BAND
Riverside RLP12-122 contains *Chimes Blues, Just Gone, Canal Street Blues, Mandy Lee Blues, Weather Bird Rag, Dipper Mouth Blues, Froggie Moore, Snake Rag, Mabel's Dream, Southern Stomps, Riverside Blues* (Gennett).

Riverside RLP12-101 includes *Alligator Hop, Krooked Blues, I'm Going Away To Wear You Off My Mind* (Gennett).

Epic LN-3208 contains *Snake Rag, Mabel's Dream, Room Rent Blues, Dippermouth Blues, I Ain't Gonna Tell Nobody, Working Man Blues, High Society, Sweet Baby Doll, Sobbin' Blues, My Sweet Lovin' Man* (Okeh), *London Cafe Blues, Camp Meeting Blues* (Columbia).

MISCELLANEOUS RECORDINGS
Riverside RLP12-130 contains *King Porter Stomp, Tom Cat Blues* (duets with Jelly Roll Morton), *Mistreatin' Man Blues, Mean Tight Mama, Death Sting Me, Hole In The Wall, Kitchen Man, Don't Turn Your Back On Me* (accompaniments to blues singer Sara Martin as member of Clarence Williams Group), *Squeeze Me, Long Deep And Wide, New Down Home Rag* (with Clarence Williams Group—no solos).

Charlie Parker

BY MAX HARRISON

THE EARLY STEPS

A beginning in Kansas City—The McShann band—
The first New York period—The Hines band—
The Eckstine band

No city was richer in jazz than Kansas City in the nineteen-twenties and 'thirties. Mary Lou Williams called it 'a heavenly city' and if the stories can be believed of the marathon jam sessions and the clubs that were always open it was almost a musicians' town. In the Negro quarter, on 12th and 18th Streets, there were fifty or more cabarets and the great drummer Jo Jones said you could hear music twenty-four hours a day there. Andy Kirk, Harlan Leonard, Jay McShann, Bennie Moten, and, after him, Count Basie, all had fine bands, as did other leaders of lesser reputation such as Milton Larkins. Some clubs had small groups led by musicians like the boogie pianist Pete Johnson, himself one of a line of Kansas City blues pianists. There were so many good musicians that it was impossible for all of them to win fame, and some like Herman Walder, the brilliant tenor saxophonist with Moten, had little reputation beyond the immediate vicinity. Similarly not all the bands could survive and Walter Page's Blue Devils, a forerunner of Basie's group and described by some musicians as the greatest they ever heard, had to break up. A full list of the musicians associated with Kansas City would be almost tedious, but among the greatest were Lester Young, Ben Webster, Harry Edison, Dick Wilson, Mary Lou Williams, Hershal Evans, 'Hot Lips' Page, and Joe Turner. Few of these were actually born there but all came to musical maturity in Kansas City and their gifts were strengthened by participation in its musical tradition.

Such was the vitality of that tradition that besides producing several great bands and a host of distinguished soloists it contained some of the seeds of a new development in jazz that, while rooted in the past, were considerably different from anything that had gone before. Modern jazz was the creation of a number of musicians who at first worked independently and only came together later, but several of its elements derived from Kansas City. Thus Kenny Clarke, the founder of modern drumming, developed his ideas from Jo Jones's work with Basie and modern pianists adopted Basie's approach to accompanying soloists. But most important of all, Charlie Parker, the master of modern jazz, was born there.

In his relatively brief span of thirty-four years this Charlie Parker was to change jazz to an extent that only one man, Louis Armstrong, had changed it before. Parker's approach to jazz was unusual by normal standards but perhaps typical of the man he was to become. The year of his birth—1920—would seem nicely calculated to allow his formative years to coincide with the richest period of jazz activity in the city yet, despite the remarkable quantity of music-making that went on, the young Parker heard none of the great bands. Many jazz musicians spend their youth listening to and learning from the outstanding players of the day: thus Louis Armstrong in New Orleans and the Austin High School group in Chicago in the 'twenties. Parker played the baritone horn in his school band, but heard neither Basie at the Reno nor Kirk at the Pla-mor—or if he did they made no impression on him. Instead he listened to the radio and at the age of fifteen his favourite programme was that of the crooner Rudy Vallée who also played the alto saxophone, and it was he who inspired Parker to take up the instrument. Despite this he never apparently intended to play Vallée's type of music; once he had decided on an instrument his ambitions were directed towards jazz.

Jazz has had its share of adolescent prodigies but, despite his enormous technical facility in later years, Parker was not one of these. After twelve months' study he was not very proficient but, like so many jazz musicians, he began playing professionally as soon as possible. His first job appears to have been with the pianist and singer Lawrence '88' Keyes. One cannot say whether Keyes detected latent promise in Parker's efforts or if his chief recommendation was his cheapness as an employee. The band as a whole was a young one but Parker was its weakest member. He was rarely allowed to sit in at the countless jam sessions around town and when he was the results were sometimes humiliating. In later years he recalled when he 'tried jamming for the first time. It was at the High Hat at Twenty-second and Vine in Kansas City. I knew a little of *Lazy River* and *Honeysuckle Rose* and played what I could. It wasn't hard to hear the changes because the numbers were easy. I was doing all right until I tried doing double tempo on *Body and Soul*. Everybody fell out laughing.' Another time members of Keyes's band were sitting in with Basie. Jo Jones waited until Parker began his first solo then took his cymbal off its stand and threw it the complete length of the dance floor. It landed with a deafening crash and, as the performance came to an abrupt halt, Parker put his saxophone into its case and left without a word. However necessary Jones may have felt it to give vent to his feelings this was a harsh and stupid gesture to a young and obviously inexperienced musician.

An artist sometimes owes more to his adversaries than his friends and these unpleasant events gave Parker a stern determination to improve. After several months with Keyes he left and joined a band led by George E. Lee. Each year Lee took his group to a summer resort in the mountains for two or three months. Parker's stay with him coincided with one of these visits and he must have spent all his spare time at the resort in study for when he returned to Kansas City he had improved enormously. Aside from weaknesses as an instrumentalist Parker had not fully understood the chord changes upon which jazz improvisation must be built. He was helped in this respect by the guitarist Efferge Ware and with his new-found technical accomplishment and theoretical knowledge became a far more confident musician. The next we hear of him is that he was one of a number of players who habitually went to Kansas City's Paseo Park and held all-night open air jam sessions!

Parker was then, and for some time to come, quite happy, and appeared settled in a moderately successful career as a side-man in Mid-Western bands. Yet already he had acquired the narcotics addiction that was to cloud his whole life, giving him countless hours of agony and leading to his premature death. There has been an unfortunate tendency, especially among the 'purist' advocates of New Orleans jazz, almost to gloat over the gin-mills, brothels and disreputable halls in which early jazz found a home, almost as if they were essential to the music instead of accidental. The atmosphere of such places had no permanent relationship to the music and such effect as they had on it was inimical. In Kansas City coloured musicians found employment in similar places for no others were open to them and it is doubtful if much can be said in favour of the city's cabarets except that they provided work for musicians and entertainers. Parker was introduced into this sordid world at an immature age and became acquainted with 'hard' drugs very soon. He said, 'I began dissipating as early as 1932, when I was only twelve years old; three years later a *friend*[1] of the family introduced me to heroin. I woke up one morning very soon after that, feeling terribly sick and not knowing why. The panic was on.' At fifteen it must have been easy to tempt him to try a new experience 'just for a thrill' and by the early nineteen-forties he was spending most of his money to satisfy the destructive craving.

His first musical influence was the playing of Buster Smith, a Texas musician sixteen years his senior, who had worked with Walter Page's Blue Devils and later settled in Kansas City. Parker said, 'I used to quit every job to go with Buster' and he worked with him at Lucille's Paradise in 1937. Smith played the clarinet as well as the alto and his group also included Emile Williams, piano, Mack Washington, drums, and a guitarist. He was also with the twelve-piece band Smith organized later the same year.

On leaving Smith he joined Jay McShann, probably early in 1938. This pianist had a band at Martin's Club, one of the best locations in the city and in it were Orville Minor, trumpet, William Scott, tenor, Gene Ramey, bass, and Gus Johnson, drums. Parker left after a few months and rode a goods train to Chicago. It was here, at the age of eighteen, that he made his first strong impression on others and gave some hint of his potentialities. Upon arrival

[1] Author's italics.

276

he apparently went to a breakfast dance at the 65 Club where the band was led by King Kolax, trumpet, with Goon Gardner, alto, John Simmons, bass, and Kansas Fields, drums. The singer Billy Eckstine was also present and recalled Parker—'the raggedest guy you'd want to see'—asking to sit in. Eckstine goes on, 'This cat gets up there, and I'm telling you he blew the bell off that thing! He blew so much until he upset everybody in the joint and Goon took him home, gave him some clothes, and got him a few jobs.'[1]

Parker remained in Chicago for some time and then returned to Kansas City. There he spent a period in Harlan Leonard's band but decided he would like to work with McShann again. By this time McShann had a big band and Parker became deputy leader in his absence. McShann later spoke of the inspiration Parker was to the band. In an interview with Frank Driggs he said, 'He was very serious about his music. He'd keep a note-book and took down the time when the guys used to make rehearsals and when they were late, etc. He'd really get tight if they didn't take their music seriously. I used to work on him by telling him the brass section and the rhythm were in terrific shape and they'd blow his reed section right out of the hall. This made him work to keep them in top form and it would also make the rest of the band work.'[2] Gene Ramey, the group's bassist, confirmed this and said, 'The McShann band was the only one I've ever known that seemed to spend all its spare time jamming or rehearsing. We used to jam on trains and buses, and as soon as we got into a town we'd try to find somebody's house where we could hold a session. All this was inspired by Parker because the new ideas he was bringing to the band made everybody anxious to play.'[3] Clearly by the age of nineteen Parker was an exceptionally promising musician and had come very far since he was ridiculed at jam sessions. Ramey also provides our first glimpse of his personal qualities: 'He was one of the reasons it was such a happy-go-lucky band. He used to say, "If you come on a band tense you're going to play tense. If you come a little bit foolish,

act just a little bit foolish and let yourself go. Better ideas will come." '

Parker again left the band temporarily in 1939, this time to visit New York. At a jam session there he made an important discovery relating to his subsequent development. He said later, 'I remember one night I was jamming in a chili house on Seventh Avenue between 139th and 140th. It was December 1939. Now I'd been getting bored with the stereotyped changes that were being used all the time and I kept thinking there's bound to be something else. I could hear it sometimes but I couldn't play it. Well, that night I found that by using the higher intervals of a chord as a melody line and backing them with appropriately related changes I could play the thing I'd been hearing. I came alive.'[1] The full significance of this will be made clear when Parker's mature style is discussed but it is worth noting here in view of the objections to modern jazz as an artificial idiom that he was not concocting a style of forced originality but simply trying to perform something he could already hear in his head.

His exact movements at this time are uncertain but during this stay in New York he played in the trumpeter George Treadwell's band at Clark Monroe's Uptown House on 38th Street. Monroe's opened at about four in the morning when the other clubs closed, so many musicians went there. Soon they were talking about Parker because he sounded, they thought, like Lester Young on alto. He always denied this, saying, 'I was crazy about Lester. He played so clean and beautiful. But I wasn't influenced by him. Our ideas ran along different.' Among those who listened to him at Monroe's in 1940 were three musicians who were to be of utmost importance in the music with which he was later identified: Kenny Clarke, Thelonious Monk and Dizzy Gillespie. According to Clarke they went to hear him 'for no other reason except that he sounded like Lester. That is, until we found he had something of his own to offer. He used to play things we'd never heard before—rhythmically and harmonically. It aroused Dizzy's interest because he was working along the same lines, and Monk was of the same opinion as Dizzy.'[2] It is odd in view of the affinity between them that Parker had no

[1] *Melody Maker*, 14 August 1954.

[2] *Jazz Monthly*, March 1958.

[3] *Melody Maker*, 28 May 1955.

[1] *Hear Me Talkin' to Ya*, Peter Davies Ltd.

[2] *Hear Me Talkin' to Ya*.

personal contact with these men. But soon he was up and away again, back to Kansas City and Jay McShann's band.

They were now managed by Consolidated Artists in Kansas City and spent much of their time touring, often travelling considerable distances. McShann said it was on one of these journeys that Parker acquired his nickname of 'Yardbird', or 'Bird'. 'We were on the road in Texas in two cars and he was in our car when we ran over a chicken. Bird put his hands on his head and yelled for us to stop the car. He said we had to go back and pick up that "yardbird". This is what he called chickens then. He got out of the car and carefully wrapped up the bird and took it with him to the hotel where we were staying and made the chef fry it for us that night. He was very insistent that we eat that "yardbird" for dinner.'[1] It was comparatively near home, at Wichita, Kansas, that Parker took part in his first recording session. The band broadcast from the local radio station and one of the executives was so enthusiastic over their work he persuaded them to make some records. Six sides were cut by a contingent from the band consisting of Buddy Anderson and Orville Minor, trumpets, Joe Taswell, trombone, Parker and Bob Mabane, saxes, and the rhythm section. The compositions included *I Found a New Baby* and similar pieces. Of course, these were only made for the station's use and copies were never distributed. It is safe to assume they included solos by Parker but these first recordings must be presumed lost. Shortly after this, in April 1941, they made some more records in Dallas, Texas. They were auditioned by an executive of Decca Records and played him some twenty items from their repertoire, including a Parker composition later known as *Yardbird Suite*. However the executive was only interested in blues material and they eventually recorded *Hootie Blues, Dexter Blues, Confessin' the Blues* and one non-blues item, *Swingmatism*. Parker's pre-eminence in the band is confirmed by his soloing on three of these. His contributions to *Dexter Blues* and *Swingmatism*, although cleanly executed, are of little interest and give no indication of what so excited Eckstine and the other musicians in Chicago three years before. The solo on his own composition, *Hootie Blues*, is a different matter and, wise with the knowledge of his later work, it is possible

[1] *Jazz Monthly*, March 1958.

to detect faint hints of his subsequent development. His tone is a little harder than was usual with the saxophone, having in this instance a suggestion of the clarinet sound. He already swings in a way slightly different from the rest of the band and his phrasing is a little more involved. Although the growth of his creative power determined that he should soon leave the band his work still fitted into it because it was firmly rooted in the Kansas City blues style. The band did not in any case think these records were representative of their real capabilities and were surprised when *Confessin' the Blues*, with Walter Brown's singing, became a big success. Perhaps if they had been allowed to record the non-blues items they preferred Parker's solos would have accorded more perfectly with their settings.

Despite the incipient divergence between Parker's and the band's style his work had considerable personal significance for his companions. Gene Ramey remembered, 'Everything had a musical association for him. He'd hear dogs barking, for instance, and he would say it was a conversation—and if he was blowing his horn he would have something to play that would portray that thought to us. When we were riding in the car between jobs we might pass down a country lane and see the trees and some leaves, and he'd have some sound for that. And maybe some girl would walk past on the dance floor while he was playing, and something she might have would give him an idea for something to play on his solo. As soon as he would do that, we were all so close, we'd all understand just what he meant. He might be looking another way but as soon as he played that little phrase everybody would look up and get the message.'[1]

In 1942 the McShann band went to New York and played at the Savoy Ballroom. They also made some more records in the July of that year. They were *Get Me on Your Mind, Lonely Boy Blues, The Jumpin' Blues* and *Sepian Bounce*, with Parker solos on the last three. The debated Lester Young influence is clear enough in the *Sepian Bounce* solo, both in tone and phrasing. Of greater significance is his solo on *The Jumpin' Blues*. According to Gene Ramey this piece was a pure 'head' arrangement, devised by Parker, and despite the portents of the earlier *Hootie Blues* the alto solo it contains is the first

[1] *Melody Maker* 28 May, 1955.

to convey anything of the real Parker. Its first four bars reappeared several years later as part of the modern jazz composition *Ornithology*.

Although such things meant little to Parker it was while he was at the Savoy with McShann that he gained his first critical recognition. Barry Ulanov wrote, 'The jazz set forth by the Parker alto is superb. Parker's tone tends to rubberiness . . . his continuous search for wild ideas, and the consistency with which he finds them, compensates for weaknesses that could easily be overcome.'[1] Four months later Bob Locke said he used 'a minimum of notes in a fluid style with a somewhat thin tone but a wealth of ideas'.[2] This now seems rather fulsome praise if the solos he had up to then recorded were typical, but it is possible he was able to do more within the looser framework of extended performances at the Savoy.

Parker's prospects looked bright at this time and coming to New York seemed to be an important step forward. Indeed so it was, in the light of his growth as a creative musician if not in terms of a conventionally successful career. The drug addiction acquired in his youth had begun to assert itself and the enthusiastic side-man who once inspired the whole band had changed. According to McShann, 'We'd never be able to find him half the time, and he began getting undependable with the band, too. For instance on *Vine Street Boogie*, which featured just myself and the rhythm section, one time Bird comes rushing out on stage without his shoes on and starts soloing right in the middle of a chorus. The audience burst out laughing and he couldn't finish what he had started.'[3]

Despite these aberrations Parker was developing his ideas steadily and even within the McShann band—now typed by its records as a straight blues group—he was experimenting much as was Gillespie in Cab Calloway's orchestra. Gene Ramey said in some pieces like *Cherokee* he was using chords unrelated to any in the numbers' basic harmonizations and that he would try to explain what he was doing to the rest of the band. Gradually the elements of his style were coming into being.

During the latter part of his service with McShann

Parker at last had some direct contact with the other primal modernists. Gillespie sat in at the Savoy very often and Parker again played after hours at Monroe's Uptown House. When McShann left New York later in 1942 Parker went with him as far as Detroit then, because he realized he no longer belonged, he left the band that had been his musical home for five years and turned back. He recalled, 'At Monroe's I heard sessions with a pianist named Allen Tinney; I'd listen to trumpet men like Lips Page, Roy Eldridge, Dizzy and Charlie Shavers outblowing each other all night long. And Don Byas was there, playing everything there was to be played. I heard a trumpet man named Vic Coulsen playing things I'd never heard. That was the kind of music that made me quit McShann.'

In New York he began to sit in at Minton's along with Monk, Clarke and others. (It has never been established that he and Gillespie played together there although by now they were obviously acquainted.) The precise rôle played by the after-hours jam sessions at Minton's and Monroe's in the development of modern jazz has often been disputed. Some habitués have asserted that no special musical experiments were conducted at all. The bassist Oscar Pettiford said, 'All I know is the guys used to come in and jam. I never saw anything experimental about it. Monk . . . didn't seem at all strange to me.'[1] In Monk's view, 'Those years at Minton's and the other places uptown was that we were just fellows working, and all the musicians would come by and jam.'[2] Yet in Kenny Clarke's view, 'Things began at Minton's in terms of modern jazz in the latter part of 1940. We often talked in the afternoons. That's how we came to write different chord progressions and the like. Monk, Joe Guy, Dizzy and I would work them out. We often did it on the job, too. Even during the course of the night at Minton's.'[3]

It is extremely unlikely these men went along to sessions with the preconceived idea of making something new. Valid creation is rarely the result of a conscious desire for originality. Modern jazz was probably as much an accident as previous developments in the music. The combination of a large number of favourable circumstances resulted in its initial appearance and the creation of the modern

---

[1] *Metronome*, March 1942.
[2] *Down Beat*, 1 July 1942.
[3] *Jazz Monthly*, March 1958.

[1] *Down Beat*, 21 March 1957.
[2] Ibid., 25 July 1956.
[3] *Hear Me Talkin' to Ya*.

form was the result of several like-minded musicians happening to come together in New York in the early nineteen-forties. We have already seen that when Monk, Gillespie and Clarke heard Parker in 1940 they recognized a kindred spirit, the first, perhaps, they had encountered. Later when Parker was experimenting in the McShann band Cab Calloway was telling Gillespie to 'Stop playing that Chinese music in my band.' Clarke was sacked from the Teddy Hill band because of his experiments with a new approach to drumming and the first musician to understand and encourage him was Roy Eldridge—who was so great an influence on Gillespie. Tadd Dameron, the outstanding modernist composer and arranger, began developing a new harmonic style about 1938. He had some contact with Parker the following year and when Gillespie heard him at a jam session in 1941 he greeted Dameron with, 'I've been looking all over for a guy like you.' Again, a musician who heard Charlie Christian playing in Bismarck, North Dakota, during 1938 said his guitar solos were very modern, and rhythmically some of his ideas sounded like bop even then. This is not the place to mention all the factors that contributed to modern jazz, but enough has been said already to indicate what happened. The key musicians each produced certain ideas independently and when they came together in New York they discovered their affinities and stimulated each other to further effort. Over a period of several years this produced a synthesis of new elements based on old that became known as modern jazz, or bop. No attempts at contrived originality or artificial procedures were involved.

Despite this the new music had a reception more hostile than that accorded to any other fresh development in jazz, before or since. It was commonly held to have no connection with real jazz at all and to be a derivative of contemporary European straight music. Gillespie light-heartedly put that theory in its place: 'All the time them cats would walk up to us and say, "What do you think about Hindemith, Mr. Gillespie? What about Schoenberg? How about Stravinsky?" Man, the only Stravinsky I knew ran a delicatessen up in Harlem, and Schoenberg I always thought was some sort of big-time financier. I didn't know *nothin'* in them days.'[1] There is a parallel here to the occasions

[1] *Melody Maker*, 2 July 1955.

in the 'thirties when Ellington was compared to Delius, and he had never heard of the English composer. Jazz travels in a different direction to straight music but it does sometimes cross the same territory. No, the new music was simply the way Gillespie and his friends felt jazz.

Parker's rôle in the changes that were gradually coming about is not easy to define, for despite his appearances at Minton's from 1942 he was never so consciously involved in the movement as were Christian, Gillespie or Clarke. In his earlier twenties he became a supremely fluent soloist who incorporated the innovations produced by the others because they accorded with his own new ideas. The complexity of Monk's harmonic ideas fitted in with the procedures he was developing in his solos and the blues basis of Christian's work fitted in with his Kansas City background. Parker belonged with these men even if he was less aware of what was happening than they. On this point Kenny Clarke said, 'I don't think he was aware of the changes in jazz he was bringing about. Dizzy was more aware of what was happening and his own part in it.'[1] Yet at times Parker's imagination and facility guided the others for Billy Eckstine declared, 'The whole school used to listen to what Bird would play; he was so spontaneous that things which ran out of his mind—which he didn't think were anything—were classics.'[2]

The Minton sessions were clearly the centre of his interests at this time but he was earning his living playing very different music. He had a variety of engagements but spent the longest period—about nine months—with Noble Sissle, one of the most commercial of Negro orchestras. He did not get on very well with Sissle and only had one feature number in the book. Parker also played clarinet with this group.

He was originally approached to join the Earl Hines band in 1942, partly at the suggestion of Scoops Carey and Benny Harris. Harris especially was associated with the modernists and spent a lot of time at Minton's. Hines was at that time organizing a new band assisted by Bud Johnson and Billy Eckstine and was persuaded to listen to Parker at Minton's. However it was not until 1943 when

[1] *Hear Me Talkin' to Ya.*
[2] *Melody Maker*, 4 September 1954.

Johnson left and Parker found himself unemployed that he joined, remaining for about a year. No alto chair was vacant by this time so Hines bought him a tenor and he took Johnson's place. Besides Benny Harris the trumpet section also included Dizzy Gillespie and this was the first time they worked regularly together. The band spent three weeks rehearsing at the Nola Studios in New York and each evening the modernist côterie went to Minton's. Parker continued playing tenor on these occasions, no doubt in an attempt to become accustomed to it. One evening Ben Webster, one of the greatest tenor players, walked in and, never having heard Parker before, asked, 'What the hell is that up there? Is that cat crazy?' He walked over and snatched the instrument from Parker's hands and said, 'That horn ain't supposed to sound that fast!' Yet later he told everyone, 'I heard a guy—I swear he's gonna make everybody crazy on tenor.' Despite this Parker was not very happy with the instrument. 'Man, this thing is too big,' he used to say. Although he twice used it on recording sessions in later years, producing reasonably characteristic improvisations with it, he never adjusted his thinking to the instrument's particular qualities.

The presence of several modernists in the band made it something of a nursery for new ideas and certainly the regular contact between Parker and Gillespie was fruitful later. Some time afterwards Hines said they played the same type of music while in his band as when they became famous a few years later. This is probably a slight exaggeration for, as we shall see, the records Parker made in 1944 show his style was not then fully formed. Hines also spoke of their exceptional keenness and remembered their carrying books of technical exercises round with them and practising in any spare moments. It is unfortunate that the American Federation of Musicians placed a ban on all recording starting from August 1942, that prevented any of this band's work being preserved. Had any records been made they would not as a whole have reflected the influence of the bop movement but would have been in the usual mode of big band swing associated with Hines. Yet Parker, Gillespie, Harris and the trombonist Benny Green might well have been given occasional solos and we might have expected to hear Sarah Vaughan, who was sharing the vocals with Billy Eckstine. It is a definite gap in our knowledge that we do not know how far their ideas had developed at that time.

Parker's behaviour in the Hines band was even more erratic than during his latter days with McShann, and he was now clearly on the way to the complete breakdown that was to come three years later. He missed almost as many performances as he attended and would spend much of his time asleep in odd corners. The other members of the band's modernist côterie remonstrated with him continually as they felt he was letting down them and the music for which they all stood as well as himself. Eventually he was shamed into doing something, and when the band was at the Paramount Theatre, Detroit, he said, 'I ain't gonna miss no more. I'm going to stay in the theatre all night to make sure I'm here.' The following day he failed to appear and the band played its whole show without him. Just as they were leaving noises were heard from under the band stand and Parker emerged from beneath. He had crawled there earlier in the day and slept through the entire evening. He often went to sleep on the stand while the band was playing, too. As he wore dark glasses all the time, it was impossible to see whether his eyes were open or shut and he possessed the enviable gift of being able to sleep while remaining upright. He would sit erect with his instrument held to his mouth and Hines was often not sure whether he was playing or not. Sometimes he would even be asleep during pieces in which he had a solo. Scoops Carey, the saxophone section leader, sat next to him and would nudge him, saying, 'Hey Bird, wake up, you're on', and Parker used to jump up and run over to the microphone for his solo. Another habit was removing his shoes on the band stand and on at least one occasion he stepped out to solo in his stockinged feet!

Such incidents seem amusing until it is remembered that Parker was not simply a man with a wayward and eccentric disposition. His drug addiction resulted in his having an increasingly uncertain contact with reality and we shall later see how this affected his attitude towards his own music. At this stage he was finding it impossible to adapt himself to duties for which his gifts should have made him ideally suited. What is remarkable about

Parker is that while this dislocation impaired his integration on a social level it had almost no effect on his musical development.

Despite Parker's aberrations the Hines band did extremely well. This was very largely due to Billy Eckstine's singing for he had an extensive following. He left in 1944 because another tour of the Southern states was contemplated. Almost every big band found it necessary to go South in order to secure enough engagements to keep working steadily. Although it was the most lucrative area for Negro bands the musicians naturally found these tours unpleasant because the colour bar was much stronger. By this time Eckstine had been with Hines five years and felt he was safe to work on his own. When he left, nine others, including Parker, Gillespie, Bennie Harris and Shadow Wilson quit the band as well. Eckstine soon received attractive offers from both Duke Ellington and Count Basie and this convinced his agent of his possibilities as a solo act. Soon it was decided to assemble a band under Eckstine's leadership. While there had been a definite modernist côterie in the Hines group, Eckstine's was the first big band formed under the influence of the new music. Eckstine probably felt that by now modern jazz stood a chance in the open market and tried to engage as many as possible of the men who had left Hines with him. Parker, who on leaving had worked briefly with Andy Kirk and Cootie Williams, had gone to Chicago but returned to New York to join, once more able to play the alto. Gillespie was appointed Musical Director. Also included were Gail Brockman and Shorty McConnell, trumpets, Benny Green and Gerry Valentine, trombones, Lucky Thompson and Gene Ammons, tenors, and the rhythm section had John Malacchi at the piano, Tommy Potter, bass, and Connie Wainwright, guitar. Sarah Vaughan had by now left Hines too and shared the vocals with the leader.

As with the Hines band, Eckstine's singing was undoubtedly this group's biggest selling point and although the nineteen-forties was not a good time for big bands they enjoyed considerable success. Much credit for the band's impact was due to the arrangements of Tadd Dameron and Jerry Valentine. Even though it was not fully defined in 1944, bop was essentially a small group idiom and while the band's music was forthright and exciting its scores were a compromise between the technical devices of the new jazz and established big band arranging practice of the previous decade. (In this connexion it is interesting to note that Eckstine's *Opus X* is based on the same riff as the Lunceford band's *Lunceford Special*.) However, the influence of the recent developments upon the scores meant that they provided more fitting contexts for the solos of Parker, Gillespie and the rest than they would have had on any of their previous engagements. Further, their itinerary took them to many parts of the country and they gained considerable insight into the varying degrees to which new ideas were acceptable. According to Parker himself the new music always met with a favourable reaction in New York, whereas in the Middle West coloured audiences liked it while whites did not. In the South-West nobody liked it and in the deep South they would have nothing but simple blues.

Despite the necessary stylistic compromise, the band's records have a fine air of exuberance and enthusiasm characteristic of a vital new movement. This feeling is imparted particularly by Gillespie's trumpet section in some of the scores. Instances are the upward glissando by the whole section after the solos on *Blowing the Blues Away*, the trills following the vocal on *I Got a Date with Rhythm* and the incisive interjections behind the *Good Jelly Blues* vocal. Gillespie's solo trumpet rides strongly over the ensemble in *Opus X* and this piece also includes a fluent alto solo by John Jackson, perhaps the first of Parker's disciples, who had been with him in McShann's band.

Parker never recorded with Eckstine but in September 1944, shortly after he joined the band, he was included in a session led by Tiny Grimes on the Savoy label. Also taking part were the pianist Clyde Hart, a significant transitional figure in the growth of the modern idiom, Jimmy Butts, bass, and Doc West, drums, another musician who had been with Parker in his McShann days. This is a 'jump' band producing deftly executed swing music. The themes are attractive, Hart's work is of great interest, but Grime's guitar solos are a little too neatly patterned and tidy to convey much. It is obvious that during the two years since *The Jumpin' Blues* and *Lonely Boy Blues* he has made enormous advances and become an exceptionally fluent and articulate soloist. His tone does not yet have quite the personal quality of his later playing but is already full and confident. At this stage the phrasing is still largely based on conventional melodic patterns but already exhibits his characteristic mobility, attack and freedom of accentuation. *Romance without Finance is a Nuisance* and *I'll Always Love You Just the Same* have vocals by Grimes and fine alto solos. Several versions have been issued of *Tiny's Tempo* and Parker's own composition *Red Cross*, and these enable us to compare the differences between the solos on succeeding performances. On the three takes of the former and two of the latter he improvises solos that are quite fresh, in each case containing many ideas. These alternative versions demonstrate how vivid was his imagination and how fluent his inventive faculty at the age of twenty-four.

Photograph from Melody Maker files

Charlie Parker

Parker was always at his best with small groups, because of the freedom they afforded. Here he is with Thelonious Monk (piano), Charlie Mingus (bass), and Roy Haynes (drums)

Photograph by Robert Parent

YEARS OF ACHIEVEMENT

The emergence of modern jazz—A visit to California—
A series of great recordings—A visit to Europe—
The Clef records

After leaving Eckstine he played with various groups in New York on 52nd Street, including one led by Ben Webster, and then with Gillespie at the Three Deuces. This was not the first modern small group on the Street because Gillespie had led a unit at the Onyx with Max Roach and George Wallington in 1944. Early in 1945 Oscar Pettiford had a group at the Spotlite that included Benny Harris and Clyde Hart. The new ideas were also spread by the considerable amount of sitting in that went on between musicians in the many 52nd Street clubs and the time was ripe for Parker and Gillespie to appear together in a small band of their own.

Too much writing on modern jazz has given the impression that the music was created solely at the sessions at Minton's and Monroe's—before them there was nothing and afterwards the idiom was fully formed. The importance of these sessions in bringing the key figures together has already been noted but the forging of a new style of solo and ensemble playing and the creation of a virtually new repertoire naturally took several years. Some hint of the lengthy nurture of modern jazz was given by the presence of Parker's *Yardbird Suite* in McShann's books as early as 1941 even though it was not recorded until 1946. By 1945 the process was complete and this Parker/Gillespie group was the first to create music that, although rooted in the past, was in an independent and homogeneous idiom that reflected all their ideas.

One reason many listeners found it difficult to accept bop was that it presented innovations on several musical levels at once. The fresh harmonic complexity brought about a richer melodic language employing a greater range of intervals. Rhythmic accentuation was more varied than in any swing music and in this one respect bop recalled the complexity of the best improvised New Orleans ensembles. It was also necessary for listeners to absorb the new repertoire. Many new compositions had been written and such standards as were retained were usually drastically adapted—often with a new melody and more elaborate harmonization. In addition the rôles of some of the instruments had been modified. The drummer now maintained a steady rhythmic pulse with the top cymbal instead of with the bass drum and the string bass was now the spearhead of the rhythmic attack. The rest of the percussion was used to punctuate and under-score the solo lines in so detailed a way that the drummer was actually taking part in a duet improvisation with the horn soloist. A harmonic and rhythmic commentary on this was given by the pianist, who played fill-ins in a style derived from Count Basie and quite different from the regular backing employed by men like Teddy Wilson or Fats Waller when they accompanied a soloist. It is probable that the angularity of the melodic style was the biggest stumbling block for most listeners however.

There was a considerable increase in the amount of recording activity in 1945 as a result of which the younger jazz musicians were able to make more records than might otherwise have been the case. Gillespie had a contract with the new Guild company and in February and May he and Parker led two sessions that produced definitive examples of the new music. The first date employed Clyde Hart, piano, Remo Palmieri, guitar, Slam Stewart, bass, and Cozy Cole, drums, and the significant titles were *Groovin' High* and *Dizzy Atmosphere*. The later session had Al Haig and Curly Russell from their regular group, with Sidney Catlett on drums, and produced *Salt Peanuts, Shaw 'Nuff, Hot House*—a fine Tadd Dameron piece—and *Lover Man*, which featured beautiful singing by

Sarah Vaughan. Almost all the solos were of striking brilliance and facility and both they and the compositions employed illustrated the new concepts with clarity and precision.

Although the alto solos are the most valuable feature of these recordings Parker's work during 1945 was notice-ably inconsistent as far as we may judge from recordings. His contributions to the above titles represent a small but distinct advance on his work with Tiny Grimes the previous year but on several other sessions he was variable. This general unevenness is quite easily explained. While the basic musical idiom known as bop was clearly estab-lished by the early months of 1945, Parker's solo style—in effect a highly personal variant of this—was not wholly defined until the end of the year. When he recorded with Grimes he was a promising but still conventional soloist, but during the following year he was moving towards a new mode of utterance. All his records made that year are thus of interest to students of his work, for in them may be traced, in a fragmentary way, his final steps towards mature expression. The best solos of Parker's mature years are the finest expression of modern jazz and it is to be expected that when on the verge of perfecting the style in which they were to be created he should betray uncertainty and moments of indecision. Thus his solo on Red Norvo's *Slam Slam Blues* is a memorable example of his blues playing while *Twentieth Century Blues*, recorded with 'Sir' Charles Thompson three months later, displays a curiously elementary conception and little except the warm, full instrumental tone marks the music as his. *Takin' Off* and *The Street Beat*, both from the latter session, are improvements, and Norvo's *Hallelujah* contains Parker's most representative solo thus far. (While discussing his miscellaneous 1945 recordings it may be mentioned that there is a good alto solo on Sarah Vaughan's *Mean to Me* and a fine obbligato to Rubber Legs Williams's singing in *Four F Blues*.) This final transitional period came to an end with Parker's Savoy recordings of November 1945, the first recordings to be made under his own name. In this, the first session to preserve modern jazz of indis-putable greatness, Parker achieved full expression of his musical personality. *Billie's Bounce, Warming up a Riff, Now's the Time, Meandering, Thriving from a Riff*, and

285

Ko-Ko are the first mature fruits of ten years of playing and thinking.

One of the most revealing parts of a jazz musician's equipment is his instrumental sound and it is noteworthy that each of the great ones has an absolutely unmistakable tone that remains unique no matter how much it is imitated. Parker's sound here and on most of his subsequent records is large, richly expressive, and quite unforgettable. At the same time it exemplifies a completely different conception of alto tone from those of his great predecessors Willie Smith, Benny Carter or Johnny Hodges, being hard, strident, sometimes even harsh. His melodic lines contain the greatest variety of intervals not simply because of the more complex nature of the themes employed but because in improvising on a given sequence of chords he would imply many other passing chords not actually stated by his accompanists. Rhythmically his playing showed unprecedented freedom. The accents would fall on or between the beats in a number of different ways and sometimes, with an opposition of on- and off-beat accents he would create the effect of two simultaneous rhythmic patterns. Irregular phrase-lengths, a common feature of most bop improvisation, are very marked in Parker's work and he had a singular faculty for imparting shape, balance and proportion to solos composed of phrases of very diverse length and character. All these qualities had appeared singly in his earlier recordings but at this session they were impressively integrated. Thus the intensity of his tone was precisely suited to his forceful melodic ideas and the variable phrase structures and accentuations were clearly an entirely natural, indeed unconscious part of his musical thinking. Basic to all these characteristics were the blues as the root of his whole style. One of the most significant things Parker did in his music was to reaffirm the importance of blues to modern, as to all vital phases of jazz.

Parker did not only define his style at this session, he also outlined the whole of his subsequent work. There are some artists whose work evolves continually from one stage to another and such a case in jazz is Louis Armstrong. Others find the essence of their style early and their work then expands from a given centre without further startling, or even unexpected, changes. Parker belonged to the second category and while he was to create greater solos

than these, his style was never modified in any essential respect.

All the compositions recorded on this occasion were by Parker and were similar to those used on most of his subsequent small group sessions. Based on the twelve-bar blues or thirty-two-bar standard frameworks, they usually had rather involved melodic lines and were stated by the horns in unison at the beginning of the performance and exactly repeated at the close. There were not infrequent exceptions to this, as in *Meandering*, which is an improvisation on the chords of *Embraceable You* and has no theme, or *Thriving from a Riff*, in which, on the version originally released, the theme only appeared at the end. Another identifying feature of this, as of so many of Parker's best sessions, was Max Roach's drumming. Of all the musicians who recorded with Parker Roach was the one who understood his aims best and whenever they played together his drumming complemented the altoist's invention with something very like perfection.

By the time these records were on the market Parker and Gillespie were famous. 1945 was not only the year in which modern jazz properly defined itself but also the year the jazz public became aware of the movement that had been so long under way. Perhaps they became aware a little too late and paid too much attention to the cultist aspects of the movement—the bop berets, bop glasses and goatee beards—rather than to what had gone into the music. The joint engagement at the Three Deuces proved to be the turning point. Their salaries were substantially increased after the first week and in May and June they appeared in concerts at New York Town Hall. Bop meant something quite definite in New York by the end of 1945, even if it was essentially a minority movement, and younger musicians began to imitate the originals.

Experience the previous year with Eckstine's band had proved that their music was by no means acceptable in every part of the country, but their success in New York no doubt led them to be optimistic of the future. At the end of the year, together with Al Haig, Milt Jackson, vibraphone, Ray Brown, bass, and Stan Levey, drums, they travelled out to Billy Berg's club in Hollywood. The audiences were quite unprepared for a new kind of jazz and the engagement was a failure in every respect. Afterwards Gillespie said, 'They were so hostile out there, they thought we were just playing ugly on purpose. They were really *very* square. Man, they used to stare at us so tough!' Relations with Slim Gaillard's group, who were sharing the engagement, became strained, even leading to an exchange of blows. Before this, however, Parker and Gillespie, together with the pianist Dodo Marmarosa, recorded with Gaillard for a small local company. As a whole the tracks produced are typical of the novelty material associated with Gaillard but Parker plays well on *Poppity Pop* and Gillespie blows with power and enterprise on the inconsequential *Slim's Jam*. As the situation deteriorated they felt themselves to be in enemy country, spoke in whispers on the band stand, and rented a basement room in which they could play unheard after hours.

Much the most difficult aspect of their plight was Parker's fast failing health for by now the effects of ten years' drug addiction were becoming very plain in his behaviour. His appearances at the club were so irregular that Gillespie was forced to hire the tenor saxophonist Lucky Thompson as a permanent deputy. It is singularly fortunate that despite their difficulties and the hostile reaction of most of the audiences one man at least, Ross Russell, the proprietor of a local record shop, divined the value of their music and recorded them for what became the Dial Record Company. The first session took place in February 1946, and Parker was only able to participate in one performance, a muddled version of *Diggin' Diz*.[1] Several successful titles were completed by the rest of the group. Shortly after this Gillespie returned thankfully to New York, taking most of the group with him. Parker stayed behind, perhaps because he was too ill to travel with the others.

His condition must have improved after this for the following month a session was recorded under his own leadership that included the few modernists to be found on the West Coast at that time. Among them was the trumpeter Miles Davis, who had played on two of Parker's Savoy titles of the previous year as well as working with him in New York. Davis was temperamentally a member of the 'cool' school of jazz that followed bop and he was to play a prominent part in its development. The essentially lyrical quality of his ideas made them unsuitable to a

bop context and his presence on so many of Parker's recordings is regrettable.

At this session Parker harked back to his McShann days and selected *Yardbird Suite*, which we have noted was written as early as 1941, and *Ornithology*, the theme hinted in the alto solo on *The Jumpin' Blues*. The music produced was not quite up to the standard of the Savoys and there is a definite element of tension in Parker's work. Despite this, on all four titles—the above and Gillespie's *A Night in Tunisia* and a characteristic Parker theme called *Moose the Mooche*—he played solos of vivid expressiveness. His tone is generally a little smoother and more confined than before and some of his phrases have unusual delicacy of structure. He does not blow as strongly as on the Gaillard session. Dodo Marmarosa provides well calculated keyboard backing on each title and *Moose the Mooche* is notable for Roy Porter's forceful but sympathetic drumming. *A Night in Tunisia* contains a four-bar break that is an astonishing outburst of virtuosity at the end of which Parker falls nonchalantly onto the first beat of the next bar. One musician compared the preceding ensemble riffs to a jet engine warming up and the break itself to the machine sweeping up into space. The simile is a little exaggerated but this passage does serve to illustrate the perfect rhythmic sense Parker shared with all great musicians.

What was to be his last recording session for some time took place the following July. It was designed to feature him with the trumpeter Howard McGhee, a leading modernist often rated second only to Gillespie, and a rhythm section consisting of Jimmy Bunn, piano, Bob Kesterton, bass, and Roy Porter again at the drums. The records produced on this occasion give us an unpleasantly accurate impression of Parker's pitiful condition at this time. Although his muscles were subject to uncontrollable twitches and jerks he somehow managed to get through four titles. On *Be-Bop* and *Max is Making Wax* he is virtually carried through the ensemble unisons by McGhee, while in the solo choruses he is supported by Bunn's strong if not over-subtle chording. His playing in these fast-tempo pieces is barely coherent and on *The Gypsy* he is scarcely better. Most revealing is *Lover Man*. His tone has an awful, lifeless quality and the hesitant, groping phrases convey an impression of the remnants of his

[1] Issued in Great Britain as *Bongo Beep*.

287

technique instinctively communicating the confusion of his mind in musical terms. It is an illuminating comment on the uninformed writing on modern jazz of that time that this title was soon widely praised as one of Parker's best recordings! After the four tracks had been cut he collapsed. The subsequent report in the September 1946 issue of *Metronome* read, 'The man who is credited by many as having created be-bop, Charlie Parker, will not blow his alto sax for probably a long time to come. The famous musician suffered a complete mental collapse on a recent Dial recording session in Hollywood, climaxing a succession of weird symptoms by blowing his top in an hotel lobby. He was rushed to Carmarillo, a mental institution, where he has been reported progressing favourably. Charlie Parker is not expected to blow again for at least six months.'

It appeared as if the effects of Parker's drug addiction had finally overwhelmed not only his musical faculties but the balance of his mind as well, and many of his friends were none too optimistic of his rehabilitation. He later admitted he needed a quart of whisky to get through the *Lover Man* session but this and his final collapse were only the climax of tensions that had been building steadily throughout the previous years. Parker was not at all an anti-social being in himself but, as his conduct with the McShann and Hines bands and at Berg's club had made increasingly plain, his contact with reality, and especially with other people, had become tenuous. In his own words, 'I don't know how I made it through those years. I became bitter, hard, cold. I was always in a panic—couldn't buy clothes or a good place to live. Finally I didn't have any place to stay, until someone put me up in a converted garage. The mental strain was becoming worse all the time.'

By the time Parker went to Carmarillo he was—within the jazz world—a national figure and, because of the recordings, his reputation had even begun to spread to other countries. Already several alto saxophonists, notably Sonny Stitt in the East and Sonny Criss in the West, had come forward with styles that were firmly rooted in his work. Before long his influence, the darting mobile lines, the aggressive tone, the complex melodic structures, showed on other instruments. By 1946 all musicians were aware of the modern jazz movement and its individual

participants, but it became clear that Parker's was the greatest individual influence and no one else could be regarded as the key figure during his lifetime. By around 1950 he had become a legend and, because of his unique prestige, his numerous followers adopted a less selective attitude to his work than was necessary and copied his poorer records as diligently as his best. Parker quarrelled seriously with Ross Russell because the latter issued the results of the July 1946 session. His indignation was justified and he was distressed to find younger altoists learning, of all things, the *Lover Man* solo. Russell made amends both before and after the event by arranging for him to go into Carmarillo and helping him when he came out, but Parker felt that those records, besides showing him in a singularly unflattering light, held him up as a bad and misleading example to others.

More distress was caused by the suggestion made in some quarters that he was, at any rate indirectly, responsible for the rather widespread use of hard drugs among musicians. It is natural that an artist of Parker's extraordinary qualities should inspire others to attempt like achievements, but to suggest that his disciples had a similar desire to embrace the failings that finally led to his downfall, or that he was in effect responsible for the weaknesses of others, is both ridiculous and irresponsible. The more so since Parker's own words on the subject, with their tragic overtones of personal experience, leave no room for any illusions: 'Any musician who says he is playing better either on tea, the needle, or when he is juiced, is a plain, straight liar. When I get too much to drink I can't even finger well, let alone play decent ideas. And, in the days when I was on the stuff, I may have *thought* I was playing better, but listening to some of the records now, I know I wasn't. Some of these smart kids who think you have to be completely knocked out to be a good hornman are just plain crazy. It isn't true. I know, believe me. That way you can miss the most important years of your life, the years of possible creation.'

Parker stayed in Carmarillo for six months. When he came out he was an apparently balanced and healthy individual once more. He was happier, perhaps, than he had been since the far-off years in Kansas City. He must surely have wanted to leave the West Coast as soon as possible but was still due to make some more records for the Dial company as his contract with them had not yet expired. Soon after leaving hospital he presented himself at the studios while a session was in progress featuring the vocalist Earl Coleman and the Erroll Garner Trio. Although he had not played for several months he decided to sit in, accompanying Coleman and in quartet performances with Garner, and the routines for each number were quickly revised. While Garner may be described as a modern musician he was hardly touched at all by the bop influence and the combination of him and Parker would not seem a very appropriate one. In the event, although the piano chording behind the alto is a little too emphatic in places, the partnership worked well and aided by the fine playing of Red Callender and Doc West they created two memorable pieces in *Cool Blues*[1] and *Bird's Nest*. Parker's tone is warm and large again, his phrases full and ample, and the feeling of constriction that marked his playing in the months before his illness is altogether absent. On the titles with Coleman—*Dark Shadows* and *This is Always*—he is heard in the rather unusual rôle of accompanist. He fills in between the vocalist's phrases, complementing his line with aptness and imagination, and *Dark Shadows* includes a good alto solo.

Parker went to work with a band led by Howard McGhee and returned to the Dial studios a week later to lead a septet. The personnel was a particularly strong one and this was in some respects Parker's most completely satisfactory session thus far. Certainly the four titles recorded—*Relaxin' at Carmarillo*, *Cheers*, *Carvin' the Bird* and *Stupendous*—are more cohesive as musical wholes, with almost no weak points, than most of his earlier studio work. It is also easy to feel that this was one of his happiest sessions for, while retaining all the usual tonal and melodic qualities of his style, there is a dancing, airy lightness about his solos that must surely be a reflexion of his frame of mind and soon communicated itself to others. Don Lamond's drumming has an infectious vitality and Wardell Gray's blues-inflected tenor playing proved to be an admirable foil to Parker's ideas. Dodo Marmarosa, still the only pianist on the West Coast really suited to Parker, again took part.

Soon after this Parker returned to New York and

formed a quintet with Miles Davis, Duke Jordan at the piano, Tommy Potter, bass, and Max Roach. He employed this instrumentation on nearly all his most successful recordings and it seemed to provide the appropriate stimulus for his finest work. In this it is also revealing to compare him with his great predecessors. Whereas the sensuous, rhapsodic sound of Johnny Hodges's alto was heard to best advantage as part of the variegated tonal palette of the Ellington orchestra and the force and exuberance of Willie Smith's playing was most suited to the virtuoso Lunceford ensemble, so the emotional starkness of Parker's most typical work was best displayed against the spare, though by no means simple accompaniment of a bop rhythm section. The unit found a resident engagement at the Royal Roost, a fried chicken restaurant on Broadway that specialized in featuring modern groups. Parker certainly proved the truth of his remarks about drug addiction for 1947 was his most richly creative period. If the selective discography is consulted it will be noted he made far more outstanding records this year than any other. It is clear that the psychological complications that brought about his personal difficulties also dammed up a considerable part of his creative potential. When most of his personal difficulties were removed music flooded from him as never before. In this year he worked for both Dial and Savoy, always recording with Miles Davis and Max Roach. Jordan, Bud Powell or John Lewis were at the keyboard and he employed either Potter or Nelson Boyd on bass. With them he created a group of recordings that is one of the finest flowers of all jazz music. A few inferior performances may be found here but the level in general maintained can fairly be described as phenomenal. This corpus of music can only be compared with Ellington's 1940 recordings or, more significantly, with Armstrong's Hot Sevens of 1927. Despite this overall high quality certain of these records are especially noteworthy as illustrating particular aspects of Parker's work.

Blue Bird, *Cheryl* and *Buzzy* contain blues playing of outstanding power and conviction and it is in performances like these that Parker reaffirmed the roots of his art and its participation in the central tradition of jazz. However complex the harmonic implications of his melodic line, he never leaves the 'climate' of the blues. *Cheryl* is also notable for one of Bud Powell's best solos in small group record-

---

[1] Alternative versions of this title were issued as *Hot Blues* and *Blowtop Blues*.

Photograph from Melody Maker files

Parker and Dizzy Gillespie

ing. While Powell is a musician whose brilliance could almost match Parker's he was not so sensitive an accompanist as Jordan, Lewis or Al Haig. Parker valued apt keyboard support highly, and although both Lewis and Jordan showed remarkable understanding of his musical thought processes there is little doubt Haig was the most perceptive pianist ever to record with him.

If anything, the character of his phrases is less varied in blues than elsewhere, but on slow ballads the opposite is true. The three versions of *Embraceable You* are probably his greatest achievement in this sphere and on these and several similar pieces like *My Old Flame, Don't Blame Me* and *How Deep is the Ocean?* his imagination is at its richest. The phrases, now probing and incisive, now smooth and almost off-hand, follow one another with what seems to be absolute inevitability and form structures of rare and elaborate beauty. The sharp contrast of succeeding phrases is always one of the essential devices of Parker's method and is very clearly demonstrated in *Quasimodo*, while on *Dexterity* the tension created by double tempo passages is immediately relieved by calmer, more simple phrases. It is this kind of thing that results in the exceptional feeling

Photograph by Popsie, from Melody Maker files

Charlie Parker

of balance and control which even the most adventurous Parker solos have. Another instance of what might be termed virtuosity of melodic construction is *Klactoveedsedstene*, in which the alto solo begins with disjointed little fragments that are made to form part of a coherent design. Listeners approaching Parker for the first time may well find his complexity disconcerting but despite this his melodic idiom is essentially a natural one. And rarely do his elaborate means involve any diffuseness; his style is both concentrated and concise.

Other fine recordings are *Chasing the Bird*, with a contrapuntal theme statement in place of the normal unisons, *Donna Lee*, an outstanding improvisation on the chords of *Indiana*, and *Charlie's Wig*, which includes an excellent muted trombone solo by J. J. Johnson. It need hardly be remarked that Parker, like most great jazz improvisers,

291

could express himself equally well on good and poor themes. Whether he is soloing on a carefully worked-out composition like *Ko-Ko* or *Hot House*, or on a trite, mechanical melody such as *Constellation* it makes little difference. Far from providing the sustenance for his improvisations, the themes often seem to be little more than a framework. In a few cases this tendency is carried to its logical conclusion and in records such as *Bird's Nest, Klaunstance* and *Bird Gets the Worm* no theme is stated. These and several similar particularly fast pieces, seem to form something of a special category in Parker's output and are especially characteristic. Ultra-fast tempos were very often employed by bop musicians and only a few of them, usually Gillespie, Navarro, Bud Powell, J. J. Johnson and a few others, were able to remain themselves in them. Parker, however, was always particularly happy in such circumstances and his ideas would flow with absolute readiness and his technique was always able to communicate them with perfect ease and relaxation. This relaxation or absence of apparent effort is another basic characteristic of his work, and applies equally to torrential performances like the above and to slow ballads and blues.

The period in which these records were made was probably the happiest in Parker's life. Living in a small but pleasant apartment on the lower East side of Manhattan he came nearer to leading a normal existence than at any other time in his adult life. Yet although he was free of drug addiction the Carmarillo cure had not resulted in his complete adjustment to reality and, finding himself still unable to cope with many of life's complexities, he found it necessary to seek oblivion from time to time. He started drinking heavily in an attempt to stay away from drugs and began to deviate in other ways too, becoming unreliable in fulfilling his engagements and sometimes arriving an hour, or a whole day late. The relationship with his bookers also began to assume its former chaotic nature and one friend said managers left him like a succession of horses shot from under a cavalryman. Parker liked appreciative audiences as much as any artist but he fancied himself as a business expert and had, at times, a kind of cunning that made him very difficult to get on with. Among many stories illustrating this is one concerning a particularly successful session played to a capacity house. After a time Parker left the stand and his place was taken by a group he had engaged and who played the tritest kind of pseudo jazz. The audience began to protest and the promoter remonstrated with Parker. 'You fool,' he replied. 'You just don't understand business. The place is full and these guys are so bad some of the people will start to leave and we'll be able to let others in. We need a turnover.' On other occasions, as if to prove to himself that he was free and could be bought by no man, he would leave the club at which he was supposed to be playing and sit in somewhere else just for a few drinks. The drinking became very serious and eventually he had to go into hospital with a violent ulcer attack. He was told that if he resumed drinking again it would be fatal.

Many great recordings were still to be made, but Parker's output in 1948 was understandably smaller than the previous year. He was now free of the contract with Dial but made two fine sessions for Savoy. There were magnificent improvisations on *Steeplechase* and *Merry-go-round* and the already mentioned *Constellation* was another fine example of his up-tempo mode. *Ah-leu-cha* had the same kind of contrapuntal theme chorus as the earlier *Chasing the Bird* and in view of the satisfactory results obtained in both cases one wonders why Parker did not use this kind of material more often. Perhaps, because thematic material was unimportant to him, it was too much trouble. *Barbados* was an interesting blues in which the theme is played over a Latin-American rhythm but the outstanding recorded achievement of the year was the unforgettable *Parker's Mood*, one of the greatest instrumental blues performances in all jazz. Outwardly the year was comparatively uneventful, despite the personal upsets. His group continued playing at the Royal Roost and when this closed they moved to a larger establishment called Bop City. Al Haig took over from Duke Jordan and towards the end of the year Miles Davis left and was replaced by Kinny Dorham. Dorham was not at that time a very consistent player but his work was patterned on the ideas of Dizzy Gillespie and he was a more suitable foil to Parker.

It was also in 1948 that Parker recorded with the Machito orchestra in performances of what was known as 'Afro-Cuban jazz', or 'Cubop'. As early as 1945 he had sat in with Machito along with Gillespie, Al McKibbon and other modernists. He always enjoyed the experience, saying, 'That Afro-Cuban rhythm is real gone! I like to play with those drummers—man, it's so relaxed.' The jazz musician is always interested in new rhythms so this reaction is not unexpected but the extensive association between the modernists and several bands like Machito's did not enlarge the scope of jazz permanently to any appreciable extent but there is no doubt that musicians on both sides found the exchange stimulating. The small group obviously offered the best chance of real integration of the two musics and the matter will be discussed in more detail when we come to Parker's recordings in which bongos and conga drum were added to his usual quintet instrumentation. Of the recordings made with Machito *Okiedoke* is the most nearly successful. The alto solos contain the expected good ideas but continuity is lacking because Parker has to fit in his ideas with the obtruding, alien patterns of the arrangement. Similar remarks apply to *No Noise* and *Mango Mangue*.

Although his health remained unsteady Parker continued to work regularly with his group into 1949 and in the spring made his first visit to Europe to play at the Paris Jazz Fair. The concerts featured both traditional and modern jazz and he shared top star billing with the veteran Sidney Bechet. His work was widely appreciated in Europe—perhaps more positively than at home—and his records had led to his recognition by students of modern jazz as the idiom's outstanding exponent. Parker's concerts entirely confirmed this view and in the eyes of the musicians and enthusiasts who flocked to hear him from several neighbouring countries he not merely sustained but enhanced his reputation. Whereas the other significant modern group at the Fair—a quintet led by Tadd Dameron and including Kenny Clarke and Miles Davis—still seemed very advanced to many ears Parker had no difficulty in communicating, and even those opposed to the new ideas were able to recognize his work as modern jazz at its best.

While Europeans were prepared for the unique quality of his playing little was known at that time of Parker's personality and his demeanour before audiences surprised many. A short, thick-set man, he would hug his alto to his stomach, sink his head on the mouthpiece and fix the listeners with an unseeing stare. He ended each number by turning his back on the audience and stamping out the beat for the next. At some concerts he briefly acknowledged applause but always jumped in on it to start the next piece. Although European audiences were surprised by this independence of audience reaction it was typical of the boppers. Usually their attitude during performances was one of complete concentration on the music, seemingly unaware of the presence of an audience. In its way this was understandable. They were refusing to conform to the normal stereotype of the Negro entertainer and their platform manner—more like that of straight musicians than jazzmen—derived from a wish to be judged on the basis of musical merit alone. This offended and puzzled older jazz musicians who had been brought up in a tradition of more overt showmanship. Friction between musicians of the old and new schools had been growing throughout the 'forties and by the end of the decade had assumed considerable bitterness. Critical support of each school had been singularly unrestrained in their abuse of the opposing faction and the dispute was of such violence that the jazz world became divided into two mutually exclusive camps.

This did the music and musicians considerable harm, and performers whose work did not fit into either the traditional or modern patterns were forgotten. Both accepted factions were subjected to rigid doctrinaire 'criticism' that was more concerned with theories of 'true'—and therefore not to be changed—jazz or of 'progress' than with musical values. Musicians on both sides were generally more restrained than their supporters but many features of bop, although based on earlier practices, were undeniably confusing to men unaccustomed to them. Some remarks by the very gifted drummer Dave Tough typify the reactions of many of the older musicians: 'As we walked in these cats snatched up their horns and blew. One would stop all of a sudden and another would start for no reason at all. We could never tell when a chorus was supposed to begin or end. Then they quit all at once and walked off the stand. It scared us.' This referred to Gillespie's 1944 group on 52nd Street, and speaking of Max Roach's drumming Tough said he could never tell in advance where Roach's punctuations would fall but when they came they invariably sounded right. Such things were naturally perplexing to men who had not helped develop the new practices, who were in effect outsiders, and a number of them, egged on by their supporters, spoke disparagingly of bop. Among them was Louis Armstrong, who thereby broke a life-long rule never to speak ill of any musician.

Before the differences between the new and old styles were understood swing and bop musicians often recorded together. The alliance was always an uneasy one and if these mixed personnels helped to throw the qualities of the new music into strong relief and thus lead to its proper appreciation, the overall musical results of such sessions were almost never satisfactory. As far as the jazz public at the end of the nineteen-forties was concerned the modern form had an audience in every country to which its recordings had penetrated, but that audience was still small, and despite the success of Gillespie's 1946–48 big band it remained a minority movement within the world of jazz.

All this imposed a degree of isolation upon the modernists that did not unduly affect most of them but was particularly unfortunate for Parker. During the happy post-Carmarillo days of 1947 he had shown, and continued to show spasmodically, great warmth in his dealings with other people, but as he fell into his former chaotic way of life his contacts with reality once more became uncertain. A classic instance of this occurred during his 1949 stay in Paris when a British journalist tried to interview him. The meeting was entirely unproductive for Parker would not enter into coherent discussion but insisted on reading aloud extracts from Omar Khayyám! In isolation such behaviour seemed unaccountable, but by this time he was determined, at least for long stretches at a time, to keep almost everyone at arm's length. Finding it apparently impossible to adjust to life, he was convinced the world was an evil place and, feeling it was beyond his capabilities to have meaningful contact with others, he would usually take the easy way out when difficulties arose. It was largely because of this that conversations with him one day tended to have little relation to conversations on another and he would go along with whatever opinions were expressed by others, not because he had no views of his own but because he did not find it worth the effort, and rarely sufficiently rewarding, to establish contact and have a real exchange of views. He often expressed an interest in contemporary straight composers and this was confirmed when during a 'blind-fold test' he recognized a Stravinsky composition. On another occasion he said that as far as straight music was concerned he 'First heard Stravinsky's *Firebird* suite. In the vernacular of the streets, I flipped. I guess Bartók has become my favourite. I dig all the moderns. And also the classical men—Bach, Beethoven, etc.' Yet on another occasion he asserted Sammy Kaye's *On a Slow Boat to China* was his favourite record. This seems to parallel Louis Armstrong's admiration for Guy Lombardo's

band, and once he even expressed great liking for Roy Rogers: 'I was hung up in hospital once, feeling beat. So were we all. And who should come into the ward to entertain us but Roy Rogers in that funny Western suit, playing and tapping that foot. It was the wildest.'

It is hard to account for a knowledge of Stravinsky and an admiration for Roy Rogers, even in so variable a man as Parker, but this leads us to one of the few things on which he was consistent. This almost aggressive broad-mindedness was part of his reaction against the criticisms levelled at modern jazz. He appeared particularly to resent writers' attempts at pigeon-holing and rigid classification. It was really all one, he insisted, being different aspects of the same thing. He once said, 'You can't classify music in words—jazz, swing, Dixieland etc., it's just forms of music; people have different conceptions and different ways of presenting things. Personally, *I* like to call it music.'[1] Without altogether agreeing with this it is possible to sympathize with Parker's reaction to the tendency of so much jazz writing to concern itself with classification and name-calling rather than with musical content, and his refusal to be used as a tool in the futile arguments that split the jazz world. This was perhaps one case when his lack of real contact with others was actually an advantage.

After the Paris trip Parker returned to New York. Bop City had closed, but he was soon at work, still with the same group, at a new club called Birdland. He had already been recording for the Clef Record Co. for some time and continued to do so for the rest of his life. It has since been asserted that he used to do just as he wished at all his sessions but this seems very unlikely and would certainly be against that company's usual policy. We have seen that for his many Savoy and Dial sessions he chose the quintet instrumentation that clearly suited him best, but for Clef he recorded with some very diverse and unsuitable accompaniments. In other cases a really excellent personnel was assembled—and then spoilt by the inclusion of one musician whose style was altogether out of keeping with the rest. An instance of this was one of the sessions Parker recorded just before his visit to Paris. To his usual group was added Tommy Turk, a trombonist with a style of facile vulgarity that had no connexion whatsoever with modern jazz. Both *Visa* and *Cardboard* contain good alto solos, but

[1] *Metronome*, August 1948.

Turk's presence leads to a certain stiffness in the ensemble choruses that communicates itself to the leader's playing. This is the more noticeable when these titles are compared with those produced at the next session, which took place only a few days before they left for Europe and did not include Turk. *Passport* is a distinctly jaunty performance and *Segment* is one of the finest of all Parker's Clef records. The Haig/Potter/Roach team was possibly the greatest modern rhythm section and it is doubtful if they ever played better in a recording studio than on this title. Their combination of drive, lift and sensitivity to the soloist's ideas makes *Segment* a model for all modern pianists, bassists and drummers.

It was also in 1949 that Parker began recording with string orchestras. At first he embraced this decidedly incongruous idea with enthusiasm. This is a little hard to understand, but he probably felt that the experiment was worth trying and many prominent jazz musicians were to follow his lead. But perhaps his motives were more complex. Although he never seemed altogether aware of the fact, he had now achieved a more widespread recognition and had won a considerable number of popularity polls, first in *Esquire*, then in *Down Beat*, *Metronome* and a number of publications in other countries. Despite this, certain of his acquaintances believed he had a deep-seated and not altogether conscious sense of rivalry with Dizzy Gillespie, particularly in view of the success of the latter's big band and the greater amount of publicity he had been accorded. The strings idea was almost unprecedented and he may well have felt it could bring him a like degree of acceptance. He did not realize he possessed powers Gillespie could never claim and he was in any case incapable of the compromises his erstwhile partner had made. (There is something of a parallel here to the case of Jelly Roll Morton. When the post-New Orleans small band jazz of the 'twenties went out of favour Morton, unlike Armstrong, was unable to adapt himself to the new conditions and lapsed into obscurity.) As it was, the combination of Parker and strings had almost no success musically. This was not because there is any inherent incompatibility between the strident sound of Parker's alto and the string orchestra —the string scoring of Bartók and Stravinsky has shown how harsh and unrelating a sound they can produce—but because the arrangements written for him were all dominated by light music conceptions. No jazz arranger has the necessary knowledge of advanced string writing to produce appropriate scores.

Parker recorded with strings four times altogether—in November 1949, July and September 1950, and January 1952—but on each occasion the astringency of his tone revealed the insipid triviality of the accompaniment rather brutally. Instead of playing original compositions of his own he employed standard ballads and although in a few instances like *Just Friends* and *If I Should Ever Lose You* he cuts loose, he is generally restrained and stays close to the original melody. Each theme is rephrased in his characteristic manner but the variations are far more purely decorative than usual. Despite compromises on the melodic level he always communicated his musical personality, if only through his instrumental tone, and stamped each performance as his own. In some cases he played without any apparent regard for the accompaniment and achieved considerable intensity of expression. Instances are *Summertime*, *April in Paris* and *East of the Sun*.

During 1950 Parker continued working at clubs like Birdland with his quintet, now with Red Rodney on the trumpet. He also toured Sweden with success in the autumn and recorded with some of the better local modernists. At home he also appeared at a number of clubs, including Birdland, with a string group. Because of its novelty the combination had some commercial appeal, but it was an expensive proposition and could not be booked into the smaller clubs. Parker soon discovered its limitations from his point of view and eventually found the set-up a frustrating one. He was not, in any case, a fit enough man to manage a large unit on tour and it does not reflect favourably on his agents that he was saddled with such responsibilities. While Parker could be very difficult in business negotiations it must always be remembered that he was a sick man for most of his professional life and many people took advantage of his weaknesses. On this point Lucky Thompson has told us,[1] 'The vultures, the cast-out gangsters, and second-rate fight managers who run this game exploit people like Charlie. They used him so long as he was of use to them, but before he died Bird had become an outcast.' This, especially the final sentence, makes it clear that the whole of Parker's story is not likely to be

[1] *Down Beat*, 4 April 1956.

295

told for a long time yet. As far as the string ensemble is concerned he was helped to manage it by Al Haig and it was a further blow when the pianist left and temporarily quit the profession. 'Al used to look after me so well,' he said.

Despite such discouragements he continued to create music of unique distinction whenever he was given the chance, and indeed 1950 was the last year he was to produce a considerable number of wholly representative discs. One session in particular should have been an outstanding one among all modern jazz recordings for it teamed him with Gillespie and Thelonious Monk. Monk is in many respects the most creative modernist after Parker and bringing them together in the recording studio might well have resulted in something exceptional. Once again the date was sabotaged by the inclusion of a musician entirely out of sympathy with the modernists' aims—the drummer Buddy Rich. In the event Monk was simply the pianist on the date. He plays several intriguing introductions, kills most of his solo time with clichés (albeit his own) but chords perceptively behind the horn solos. The music does not show the influence of his personality but it is still not pleasant to hear Rich soloing after Monk. Except on the unenterprising *Melancholy Baby* Parker plays extremely well and with fluency, but his tone is somewhat less ample and expressive than usual.

Rich was also present on two other notable sessions that year, but managed to adapt himself to Parker's way rather better. These were both quartet dates with Hank Jones, piano, and Ray Brown, bass. At the second Coleman Hawkins sat in for one number, *Ballade*. As is to be expected, the partnership is not really a success but the combination of Hawkins's rhapsodic exuberance and Parker's probing intensity is intriguing if not satisfying. It is believed that this and the other track produced at the session, *Celebrity*, were recorded for the sound-track of a film that was never released. Other recordings included a further session with Machito's orchestra, this time to perform Chico O'Farrill's *Afro-Cuban Suite*. This is another unsuccessful attempt at sustained composition in the jazz language that, in the main, manages to reflect the worst of both worlds. As usual Parker remains himself, even in the contexts of O'Farrill's flashy and theatrical scores, and plays with characteristic expressiveness. The bubbling solos in the movements entitled *Jazz* and *Mambo* are easily the work's best moments.

Parker never recorded prolifically again and indeed his career had lost the momentum that, despite all difficulties, it once had. His unreliability increased and he was now working less regularly. He was decidedly not the attraction to club bookers he had once been, not because his box office appeal was substantially less but because no one could be sure he would appear for an engagement. He became careless about the way he dressed and was criticized for arriving at clubs looking like a tramp. In 1951 he began to take bookings to appear as soloist accompanied by local rhythm sections wherever he played. This was a thing he had rarely done before and indicated that the hypercritical musician who had often recorded as many as six takes of a number before being satisfied was already less concerned about his music than formerly. In the past he had made it clear there were comparatively few musicians with whom he actually enjoyed playing. The scope of his capabilities was such that it revealed the limitations of others rather clearly. The change, which was no doubt more gradual than it appears to us now, was duly noted by his fellow musicians. Gigi Gryce said, 'He's got more inside him than any other group of musicians put together. His is a genius you can't fence in with words. But today . . . he just doesn't care.'[1] Dave Brubeck toured with him once and said afterwards, 'He's a giant. But what he blows today isn't as important as three years back. You can't judge his playing now—not because he isn't a good musician but because (for reasons most people know) he can't play; he's an historical figure.'[1]

While these comments were largely justified they were a little too sweeping for a man as unpredictable as Parker. Throughout his life he had brought beautiful music out of chaos and he was still capable of doing so. It happened less often in the recording studio than before, but he had still to make a few records that were fully worthy of his earlier achievements. Of greatest interest were two sessions of January and August 1951. In *Blues for Alice* and *K. C. Blues* he gave us some imaginative blues playing that was as personal as ever and showed that, musically at least, his early roots retained significance for him. Less distinguished, though still effortlessly inventive, were *Back Home Blues* and a remake of the disastrous *Lover*

[1] *Melody Maker*, 19 March 1955.

Man. Perhaps the latter still had unhappy associations for him for this is an unsatisfying performance with a noticeable element of tightness in the alto phrasing. In contrast *Au Privave* contains a great solo that belongs with his best work. *Swedish Schnapps* approaches this quality while both *Si Si* and *She Rote* are excellent.

In 1951 and 1952 Parker had further sessions with Cuban rhythm sections. Unlike his earlier collaborations with Machito these were small group affairs in which the basis was his usual quartet or quintet instrumentation. Despite the more pliable small combo formula these were scarcely more successful. It is true there are polyrhythmic elements in Parker's music that one might expect to be complemented by the patterns of the bongos and conga drum cutting across the rhythmic basis laid down by the other percussion, and theoretically there was no reason why this should not be achieved. In practice, however, such an integration could only be the result of a great deal of work and the musicians concerned working together over a period. As it was they only met on isolated occasions in the recording studios and had little chance to produce anything signi-ficant. Parker's enthusiasm for the Cuban rhythms has already been noted and it is certain these and other such collaborations might have added another facet to jazz. We can only regret that the circumstances of the music and recording business did not allow the full possibilities to be worked out.

La Cucuracha is probably the best of these recordings but in his solos Parker phrases as if he were playing with a conventional rhythm section and without regard to the patterns of the bongos and conga. The same is true of *Mama Inez* and, to a slightly lesser extent, of *Begin the Beguine*. Although the basic material of his improvisations was relatively unimportant to Parker one does feel that, in view of what was being attempted on these sessions, the compositions should have been chosen with some care. Parker sounds discouraged on *My Little Suede Shoes*, and pieces like *Why Do I Love You?* could have been left alone. A satisfying, though not unexpected, aspect of these sessions is the way Parker's tone divests melodies like *La Paloma* and *Estrellita* of their seemingly inherent sentimentality.

THE LAST PHASE

Gradually his unreliability increased. A musician of his reputation could always get work of some kind but, because of his erratic playing and appearances and his much smaller recorded output, he was not so often ac-claimed. Almost as many people wanted to hear him and fellow musicians usually retained their respect but, always sensitive to criticism, he was aware of the change that had taken place. Despite this his position remained in many ways unique. Because of the overwhelming effect of his musical example he had considerable personal influence over other modernists. Although he continued to hold most people at arm's length he was, much of the time at least, well aware of his dual influence and did his best to save others from the errors that had ruined his career. In this connexion the remarks of Sonny Rollins are illu-minating. According to Rollins, 'Bird befriended quite a few guys. Sonny Stitt before me. With us and a few other cats, especially saxophone players, it was like a father thing. When we were hung up personally, we went just to talk to him, just to see him. The purpose of his whole existence was music and he showed me that music was the paramount thing and anything that interfered with it I should stay away from. Later on I was able to take advan-tage of his advice, but he died before I had chance to see him and tell him I had.'[1]

Contacts like this, together with his last wife, Chan, and their children did provide something of the basis for a normal life even at this stage. In the same way that he tried to warn younger musicians of the pitfalls that might lie ahead of them he attempted to protect his family from anything that might possibly constitute an evil influence. Musician friends were not invited to visit his home even if he called on them. He rarely listened to jazz at home and seems to have confined his attention to modern straight music and cowboy films on television! Beneath the bitterness and frustration imposed by his illnesses

[1] *Down Beat*, 28 November 1956.

297

and other personal difficulties Parker remained a man capable of great sensitivity and responsiveness, even if by this time few people were allowed to realize this. In Lucky Thompson's view, 'He was truly one of the warmest guys I ever met. There was no animosity in him. I never heard him say a harsh word about any musician or person. He always seemed sincerely to find out something good in everyone. The only person he ever did harm to was himself.'[1] The singer Annie Ross lived with Parker and his family for a time and said of him, 'I guess I saw Bird at his best—and at his worst. But always, at heart, he was the kindest, the warmest, the most genuine of men.' But by now the curve was inescapably downwards, his family could do little to help him and he was so much of the time a victim to the influences from which he tried to protect others. Some of the letters to his wife—which are very affectionate but end 'Sincerely yours'—indicate the confusion of his mind. Sometimes he would be booked in one town and would be seen that night travelling through another. Altogether the dislocation between the various parts of his life, his music, his family and his professional career, seemed complete.

Yet, as always, he was able to rally himself to the point where his creative faculties were as marvellously integrated as ever. After several unhappy sessions with strings he was recorded in March 1952, with a big band of conventional instrumentation. This group has great power and swing, Don Lamond's drumming being especially inspired, and Parker responds with magnificent playing. His attack is remarkably strong and his tone superb. Although everyone rose to the occasion so well the session cannot be regarded as wholly satisfactory because Joe Lippmann's arrangements, while efficient enough, have no stylistic relation to Parker's work. Thus despite the vitality which infuses everyone's playing the alto solos stand off from the accompaniments rather than being part of the whole. The quartet session of the following December was one of the most consistent of his career. Once again we are struck by the seemingly complete division between this man's life and his music. He was by now in deep distress but surely the dancing lightness of *Kim* cannot be the work of an unhappy man? The truth is probably that while Parker's

work was the product of his life, as with other artists he was able to shut out the miseries of his everyday existence when the need arose so that at the time of creation only the music was real. *The Song is You* is his best up-tempo improvisation on a standard ballad and *Cosmic Rays* is his last great blues record.

Some of the very few recordings to show us Parker in the freer atmosphere of a concert were made in May 1953, when he played at a concert in Massey Hall, Toronto, with Gillespie, Powell, Roach and Charlie Mingus. The ensembles are sketchy but, backed by Mingus's strong bass playing and the alert work of Powell and Roach he once more improvises movingly on every title. Considering the state of his health by this time, he might well have fallen back on remembered patterns, but no—each solo is newly minted and full of fresh ideas even though he had obviously played compositions like *Night in Tunisia* and *Hot House* countless times before. The last session worthy of him took place the following August. Happily Al Haig was at the piano and the date produced the final examples of Parker's unalloyed genius to be preserved. *Chi Chi* has a wonderful variety of phrases, reminiscent of past exuberance. *Now's the Time* is taken at a faster, less suitable, tempo than the original recording but contains a fine solo, as does *I Remember You*. *Confirmation*, written in collaboration with Gillespie so long before in the years of innovation, is the basis of the last great solo he recorded.

It was also in 1953 that Parker's daughter, Pree, died of pneumonia. This seems to have been the final turning-point of his life. Everyone was now saying how bad he looked and the rest of his life seemed to follow a pattern of desperate, resolute self-destruction. With some hesitation Birdland booked him for one week with a string group. On the first night he left home well-dressed and apparently clear-headed. He arrived at the club drunk and led the group for one set without his horn. The musicians tried to leave the stand in their embarrassment but he shouted at them and said he would sack them all. After this he fell asleep on the stand. Later he wandered off into the night and in the small hours of the morning his wife was woken up by his cries of agony. He had drunk iodine in an attempt at suicide.

He was taken to the psychiatric ward of Bellevue Hospital and one doctor took a sympathetic interest in his

---

[1] *Down Beat*, 28 November 1956.

case. When he left he moved to New Hope, Pennsylvania. This was in easy reach of New York and every day he went to the hospital for psychoanalysis. He even stopped drinking and the attempted suicide began to look like a blessing in disguise. At the end of October 1954 he played at a concert at the New York Town Hall. Once again he was as brilliant as ever and, almost miraculously, appeared to have regained complete control. In conversation he spoke like a new man and was full of confidence.

Yet again events followed the course that was, for him, normal. The visits to the hospital gradually came to an end. He spent less time at home and finally broke with his wife. In March 1955 he was again booked to play at Birdland with an all-star group including Bud Powell, Kinny Dorham, Charlie Mingus and Art Blakey. As with his previous Birdland engagement, he did not get beyond the first night. When Mingus announced him he refused to take the stand. Finally he did come on and immediately started an argument with Powell, clearly audible to the audience, about what they were to play. After playing a few disjointed notes he walked off indignantly, but was persuaded to come back and stood there until the end of the set. After Powell had left the stand Parker called his name out loudly over the microphone about a dozen times. The tension can well be imagined. Later in the evening there were other difficulties and a further quarrel with Powell. Mingus had to say to the audience, 'Ladies and gentlemen, please don't associate me with any of this. These are sick people.' To Parker he said, 'If you go on like this you'll kill yourself.' It must surely have been a terrible experience for Mingus, who admired Parker so much, to have to disassociate himself from him publicly.

That was on the fourth of March. On the ninth, at about four in the afternoon he arrived at the apartment of his friend the Baroness de Koenigswarter-Rothschild. He said he was on his way to an engagement at Storyville in Boston but was clearly very ill. A doctor was called who wanted to move him to Bellevue immediately. Parker refused this and it was decided he should stay with the Baroness and her daughter. In the following three days the doctor called several times and warned the Baroness that Parker had advanced cyrrhosis and stomach ulcers and might die at any time. Despite this—there is still time to observe that most things in Parker's life were despite

something—he soon regained his self-possession and optimism and talked freely almost to the last about his future musical plans. He had ideas for an entirely new form involving a big band with some kind of symphonic conception. But he was impatient, he wanted to get on with it rather than talk. On the evening of the twelfth he was watching the Jimmy Dorsey television programme. His laughter turned to a cough and in a moment he was dead.

The Baroness had no idea of Parker's address or his wife's whereabouts. For this reason the death remained a secret until she was traced. When, two days later, it reached the newspapers they were more concerned with the fact he had died in a Rothschild's flat than in the loss that musicians could not at first accept.

If this narrative has had an almost schizoid effect as it alternated between critical discussion of music and accounts of the chaos of Parker's life, it is appropriate. Remembering the nature of much of that life we might have expected his music to be at best tense, disorganized and of little value. Yet, as has been mentioned before, Parker's most obvious achievement was that out of so much misery he created music of wild, impassioned beauty that has the deepest significance for a whole generation of musicians and listeners. The work of a great artist will have varying significance for different people and individuals will read a number of meanings into his work. While remembering that such interpretations are purely subjective it does not seem inappropriate to describe Parker's as a profoundly realistic art. Certainly the escapist will find nothing here for relaxed background listening. Most good artists are too involved in their work to be at all consciously concerned with reflecting the climate of their times, yet this is what many of them do. The intensity of Parker's music derived in part from his own frequently unstable condition, but it is doubtful if the insecurity and anxiety of the post-war world has found more apt and succinct expression than in his work.

Despite the new technical devices it established, it is the content of Parker's music that ensures its durability. Louis Armstrong remains the improvising jazz musician supreme, for in him every quality such an artist needs is found in perfect balance. One cannot say quite so much for Parker, but his amplification of the solo style on melodic, rhythmic and harmonic planes simultaneously has been as widely influential as was Armstrong's desertion of the New Orleans ensemble for the definitive establishment of solo expression. It has been suggested that Parker, a wayward genius, misled jazz into a blind alley. It is true that countless musicians have tried to follow his path by reproducing the letter of his work—that is to say they have copied his phrases—without remotely approaching the inner spirit, but their failure was inevitable. Apart from the fact that none of them has had such important things to say as him it is futile to reproduce music that grew out of another man's experience. We are still too close to Parker to define his influence on the jazz that comes after him but we may be sure that the least significant musicians are those who merely copy him. What may be legitimately sought is the influence of his example. Parker did more for the jazz language than add a set of new technical devices. He left it with a freedom, flexibility and adaptability to experiment that it never had before. In the same way that Armstrong's important contribution was the establishment of the solo, not the actual phrases he played, so the more creative jazz musicians will take advantage of the freedom Parker achieved rather than imitate his phrases. This can already be observed in the playing of Sonny Rollins, perhaps the most gifted soloist of his generation, in isolated figures like Thelonious Monk, and in the Modern Jazz Quartet, a group whose unprecedented experiments remain firmly within the bounds of jazz.

We have seen that, although he was fundamentally a man capable of ready response in his contacts with others and often tried to help musicians younger than himself, much of the time he held people at a distance. Because of this and his inability to achieve a long-term adjustment to reality Parker never realized how widely accepted his work had become. He was aware of his influence among musicians of course but, although he may well have been dismayed at the glibness with which the faithful reproduced his surface mannerisms, he did not realize how vital a figure he was. He always protested that he played just the same as in his Kansas City days and this was perhaps an excuse for not having progressed as much as he thought he ought to have done. Similarly his rather surprising broadmindedness and refusal to make qualitative judgements was probably to some extent a defence in this direction. However the refusal to admit musical boundaries did have some practical basis in his own playing. He told Rollins you could ignore the usual harmonic unities and employ any chords you liked in an improvisation providing only that you 'heard' them, that they were real to you. He was unduly concerned about minor technical lapses in his playing and genuinely believed he was not a very good alto player. All artists are naturally sensitive to criticism, but Parker was more troubled than most because, not realizing how many were moved by his work, he thought only of his opponents, and thus became further alienated from his fellows. He was never able to adopt the urbane attitude of Ellington who could dismiss his critics with: 'Of course, if I started to worry about the people who don't understand . . .' Yet he could always depend on his music; that was the one sure and constant thing in his life, even if he appeared careless of it at times.

Parker's achievements are unique and for a continually sick man almost incredible. It is hard to imagine what he would have accomplished given a long and healthy life. In many ways his admirers got more out of his life than Parker did himself but, in the end, he is not a man to be pitied. On all but his darkest days he experienced the joy of creation that is given few men to know and he enriched the lives of all those who could respond to his work.

DISCOGRAPHY

In view of his vital importance in post-war jazz almost all of Parker's records should be studied by those wishing to gain a full appreciation of the modern idiom. On the following pages, however, is a select discography of the most outstanding titles. Particular attention is drawn to the set of five long playing records Savoy MG12000, MG12001, MG12009, MG12014, and MG12079. They contain almost everything he recorded for Savoy and include in some cases as many as six alternative versions of the same piece. Once one has become reasonably familiar with the general characteristics of Parker's style these are of great interest in demonstrating the several ways in which he arrived at a satisfactory version of a piece. The Savoy takes are not listed in the discography but alternatives recorded for other companies are detailed where they are of special interest. Fantasy records were formerly on the Debut label; Prestige on the Savoy and Guild; Roulette on the Roost; Spotlight (English) on the Dial.

Records that are no longer in the catalogue are marked with an asterisk.

Record Abbreviations:

Apo— Apollo		Rou— Roulette
De — Decca		Spot— Spotlite
Fant— Fantasy		Svy — Savoy
Prst— Prestige		Vrv — Verve

Records marked with an asterisk are not available at the time of this listing. All available items are 12″ long playing records.

Instrument key: (*alt*) alto saxophone; (*bar*) baritone saxophone; (*bo*) bongo(s); (*bs*) string bass; (*bsn*) bassoon; (*clt*) clarinet; (*d*) drums; (*f*) flute; (*fr-h*) French horn; (*g*) guitar; (*mell*) mellophone; (*p*) piano; (*tbn*) trombone; (*ten*) tenor saxophone; (*tpt*) trumpet; (*vib*) vibraharp; (*vln*) violin; (*v-tbn*) valve trombone.

JAY McSHANN AND HIS ORCHESTRA:

Harold Bruce, Bernard Anderson, Orville Minor (*tpt*); Joe Baird (*tbn*); John Jackson, Charlie Parker (*alt*); Harold Ferguson, Bob Mabane (*ten*); Jay McShann (*p*); Gene Ramey (*bs*); Gus Johnson (*d*); Walter Brown (*vcl*).

	Dallas, Texas—April 30, 1941
Swingmatism	De DL5503 *
Hootie Blues	—
Dexter Blues	—

Lawrence Anderson (*tbn*); James Coe (*bar*); Leonard 'Lucky' Ennois (*g*) added; Bob Merrill (*tpt*); Freddy Culliver, Buck Douglas (*ten*); Doc West (*d*) replace Bruce, Ferguson, Mabane and Johnson.

	New York City—July 2, 1942
Lonely Boy Blues	De 79236
Jumpin' Blues	—
Sepian Bounce	—

TINY GRIMES QUINTET:

Charlie Parker (*alt*); Clyde Hart (*p*); Tiny Grimes (*g*); Jimmy Butts (*bs*); Doc West (*d*).

	New York City—September 15, 1944
Tiny's Tempo	Svy MG12001
Red Cross	—

| *I'll Always Love You* | Svy 526 * |
| *Romance Without Finance* | Svy MG9022* |

DIZZY GILLESPIE SEXTET:

Dizzy Gillespie (*tpt*); Charlie Parker (*alt*); Clyde Hart (*p*); Remo Palmieri (*g*); Slam Stewart (*bs*); Cozy Cole (*d*).

	New York City—February 28, 1945
Groovin' High	Prst 24030
Dizzy Atmosphere	—

DIZZY GILLESPIE ALL STAR QUINTET:

Dizzy Gillespie (*tpt*); Charlie Parker (*alt*); Al Haig (*p*); Dillon 'Curley' Russell (*bs*); Sidney Catlett (*d*).

	New York City—May 11, 1945
Shaw 'Nuff	Prst 24030
Hot House	—

RED NORVO AND HIS SELECTED SEXTET:

Dizzy Gillespie (*tpt*); Charlie Parker (*alt*); Flip Phillips (*ten*); Red Norvo (*vib*); Teddy Wilson (*p*) Slam Stewart (*bs*); Gordon 'Specs' Powell (*d*).

	New York City—June 6, 1945
Hallelujah	Spot 101/6
Get Happy	—
J. C. Heard (*d*) replaces Powell	same date
Bird Blues	Spot 101/6
Congo Blues	—

SIR CHARLES AND HIS ALL STARS:

Buck Clayton (*tpt*); Charlie Parker (*alt*); Dexter Gordon (*ten*); Sir Charles Thompson (*p*); Danny Barker (*g*); Jimmy Butts (*bs*); J. C. Heard (*d*).

	New York City—September 4, 1945
Takin' Off	Apo LP103 *
The Street Beat	—

CHARLIE PARKER'S RE BOPPERS:

Miles Davis (*tpt*); Charlie Parker (*alt*); Argonne Thornton (*p*); Curley Russell (*bs*); Max Roach (*d*).

	New York City—November 26, 1945
Billie's Bounce	Svy MG12079
Now's the Time	—
Dizzy Gillespie (*tpt*) replaces Davis	same date
Thriving from a Riff	Svy MG12079
Thornton out; Gillespie plays *tpt* and *p*	same date
Ko-Ko	Svy MG12079
Thornton returns; Gillespie out	same date

Warming up a Riff	Svy MG12079
Meandering	—

CHARLIE PARKER QUARTET/SEPTET:

Charlie Parker (*alt*); Dodo Marmarosa (*p*); Vic McMillan (*bs*); Roy Porter (*d*).

Hollywood—March 28, 1946

Home Cooking	Spot 101/6

Miles Davis (*tpt*); Lucky Thompson (*ten*); Arv Garrison (*g*) added   same date

Moose the Mooche	Spot 101/6
Yardbird Suite	—
Ornithology	—
Night in Tunisia	—

CHARLIE PARKER QUARTET:

Charlie Parker (*alt*); Erroll Garner (*p*); Red Callender (*bs*); Doc West (*d*); Earl Coleman (*vcl* [1]).

Hollywood—February 19, 1947

Dark Shadows [1]	Spot 101/6
Bird's Nest	—
Hot Blues	—
Cool Blues	—

CHARLIE PARKER ALL STARS:

Howard McGhee (*tpt*); Charlie Parker (*alt*); Wardell Gray (*ten*); Dodo Marmarosa (*p*); Barney Kessel (*g*); Red Callender (*bs*); Don Lamond (*d*).

Hollywood—February 26, 1947

Relaxin' at Camarillo	Spot 101/6
Cheers	—
Carvin' the Bird	—
Stupendous	—

Miles Davis (*tpt*); Charlie Parker (*alt*); Bud Powell (*p*); Tommy Potter (*bs*); Max Roach (*d*).

New York City—June, 1947

Donna Lee	Svy MG12001
Chasin' the Bird	—
Cheryl	—
Buzzy	—

CHARLIE PARKER QUINTET:

As last personnel with Duke Jordan (*p*) replacing Powell

New York City—October 28, 1947

Dexterity	Spot 101/6
Bongo Bop	Rou RE105
Prezology	Spot 101/6
Dewey Square	Rou RE105
Superman	Spot 101/6
All the Things You Are	—

Bird of Paradise	—
Embraceable You	Rou RE120
Embraceable You (*alt. take*)	Spot 101/6

Note: *Prezology* is titled *Bird Feathers* on some issues

Same personnel   New York City—November 4, 1947

Schnourphology	Spot 101/6
Klactoveedsedstene	Rou RE105
Scrapple from the Apple	Rou RE120
My Old Flame	—
Out of Nowhere	—
Don't Blame Me	—

CHARLIE PARKER SEXTET:

As last personnel with J. J. Johnson (*tbn*) added

New York City—December 17, 1947

Air Conditioning	Rou RE105
Quasimodo	—
Charlie's Wig	Spot 101/6
Bird Feathers	Rou RE105
Crazeology	—
How Deep Is the Ocean	Spot 101/6

CHARLIE PARKER ALL STARS:

Miles Davis (*tpt*); Charlie Parker (*alt*); Duke Jordan (*p*); Tommy Potter (*bs*); Max Roach (*d*).

Detroit—December, 1947

Another Hair-Do	Svy MG12000
Bluebird	—
Klaunstance	Svy MG12014
Bird Gets the Worm	Svy MG12000

John Lewis (*p*) replaces Jordan

New York City—September, 1948

Barbados	Svy MG12000
Ah-leu-cha	—
Constellation	—
Parker's Mood	—

Same personnel   same date

Perhaps	Svy MG12000
Marmaduke	—
Steeplechase	—
Merry-Go-Round	—

CHARLIE PARKER QUARTET:

Charlie Parker (*alt*); Hank Jones (*p*); Ray Brown (*bs*); Shelly Manne (*d*).

New York City—Autumn, 1948

The Bird	Vrv MGV8001

302

CHARLIE PARKER AND HIS ORCHESTRA:

Kinny Dorham (*tpt*) ; Tommy Turk (*tbn*) ; Charlie Parker (*alt*) ; Al Haig (*p*) ; Tommy Potter (*bs*) ; Max Roach (*d*).

	New York City—April, 1949
Cardboard	Vrv MGV8009
Visa	—
Turk out	New York City—May 5, 1949
Segment	Vrv MGV8009
Passport	—

CHARLIE PARKER QUARTET:

Charlie Parker (*alt*) ; Hank Jones (*p*) ; Ray Brown (*bs*) ; Buddy Rich (*d*).

	New York City—March/April, 1950
Star Eyes	Vrv MGV8009
Blues (fast)	—
I'm in the Mood for Love	—

CHARLIE PARKER AND HIS ORCHESTRA:

Dizzy Gillespie (*tpt*) ; Charlie Parker (*alt*) ; Thelonious Monk (*p*) ; Curley Russell (*bs*) ; Buddy Rich (*d*).

	New York City—June 6, 1950
Bloomdido	Vrv MGV8006
An Oscar for Treadwell	—
An Oscar for Treadwell (alt. take)	—
Mohawk	—
Mohawk (alt. take)	—
Melancholy Baby	—
Leap Frog	—
Leap Frog (alt. take)	—
Relaxing with Lee	—
Relaxing with Lee (alt. take)	—

CHARLIE PARKER QUARTET/QUINTET:

Charlie Parker (*alt*) ; Hank Jones (*p*) ; Ray Brown (*bs*) ; Buddy Rich (*d*).

	New York City—October, 1950
Celebrity	Vrv MGV8002
Coleman Hawkins (*ten*) added	same date
Ballade	Vrv MGV8002

CHARLIE PARKER AND HIS ORCHESTRA:

Miles Davis (*tpt*) ; Charlie Parker (*alt*) ; Walter Bishop (*p*) ; Teddy Kotick (*bs*) ; Max Roach (*d*).

	New York City—January 17, 1951
Au Privave	Vrv MGV8010
She Rote	—
She Rote (alt. take)	—
K. C. Blues	—
Star Eyes	—

Red Rodney (*tpt*) ; Charlie Parker (*alt*) ; John Lewis (*p*) ; Ray Brown (*bs*) ; Kenny Clarke (*d*).

	New York City—August 8, 1951
Blues for Alice	Vrv MGV8010
Si Si	—
Swedish Schnapps	—
Swedish Schnapps	—
Back Home Blues	—
Loverman	—

Jimmy Maxwell, Carl Poole, Al Porcino, Bernie Privin (*tpt*) ; Bill Harris, Lou McGarity, Bart Varsalona (*tbn*) ; Charlie Parker, Harry Terrill, Murray Williams (*alt*) ; Flip Phillips, Hank Ross (*ten*) ; Danny Bank (*bar*) ; Oscar Peterson (*p*) ; Freddie Greene (*g*) ; Ray Brown (*bs*) ; Don Lamond (*d*) ; Joe Lippmann (*arr*).

	New York City—March 25, 1952
Night and Day	Vrv MGV8003
Almost Like Being in Love	
I Can't Get Started	—
What Is This Thing Called Love?	—

THE QUINTET OF THE YEAR:

Dizzy Gillespie (*tpt*) ; Charlie Parker (*alt*) ; Bud Powell (*p*) ; Charlie Mingus (*bs*) ; Max Roach (*d*).

	Massey Hall, Toronto, Canada—May 15, 1953
Perdido	Fant 86003
All the Things You Are	—
Salt Peanuts	—
Wee	—
Hot House	—
Night in Tunisia	—

CHARLIE PARKER QUARTET:

Charlie Parker (*alt*) ; Al Haig (*p*) ; Percy Heath (*bs*) ; Max Roach (*d*).

	New York City—August 4, 1953
Chi Chi	Vrv MGV8005
I Remember You	—
Now's the Time	—
Confirmation	—

CHARLIE PARKER QUARTET:

Charlie Parker (*alt*) ; Hank Jones (*p*) ; Teddy Kotick (*bs*) ; Max Roach (*d*).

	New York City—December 30, 1953
The Song Is You	Vrv MGV8005
Laird Baird	—
Kim	—
Cosmic Rays	—

Bessie Smith

BY PAUL OLIVER

ACKNOWLEDGEMENTS

For their help in the preparation of this book I am greatly indebted to many persons. Sam Benjamin generously loaned me the files he has amassed in his own research on Bessie Smith and I am especially grateful for the opportunity to use the Discography prepared for him by Jorgen Jepsen and checked against the Columbia files, corrected and amended by Walter C. Allen and other collectors. Access to his virtually complete collection of Bessie Smith's recordings was most kindly given me by John Langmead, enabling me to gain a clearer picture of her recorded work. I am most appreciative of the kind assistance of Miss Sheila Metcalf and Staff of the Gramophone Division of Philips Electrical Ltd., and to the Columbia Record Company of America. I was able to learn much of Bessie Smith as a person from Jack Teagarden and the late Big Bill Broonzy whose recollections proved most valuable when this work was undertaken later. To them I am sensible of a great debt. My sincere thanks to Bill Colyer and Brian Davis for the loan of valuable documentary material, and I would like to express my sincere gratitude likewise to the many collectors and authorities who have loaned photographs, given advice and expressed opinions.

INTRODUCTION

'Hold on; let me spit!'

Whilst the recording engineers and the accompanying group of musicians waited, the tall, plump, copper-skinned young woman broke off in the middle of her song and expectorated. Harry Pace, the President of the Pace Phonograph Company which issued Black Swan records, was disgusted and summarily ended the recording test, dismissing the girl on the spot. His offended sensibilities lost him a fortune.

For all her uncouthness on that occasion the girl who was born with the undistinguished name of Bessie Smith was destined to be the greatest Negro recording artist of her day and one of the most outstanding figures in the whole history of American music. Bessie Smith was a complex woman: heavy, truculent, she was coarse in conversation, earthy in her humour, ugly in her manner when she was in her cups. From a squalid background she rose to the pinnacle of her chosen profession, to be admired and acclaimed by all who knew her—rivals no less than friends. Immensely popular as an artist she made a fortune; a near-dipsomaniac, she squandered it, though she was given at times to unpredictable acts of charity and sentimentality. She died in circumstances so bitter that they became a symbol of the tragedy of her race. And a score of years afterwards her artistry remains, with all the changes of fashion and style, the epitome of jazz music.

It seems that no one has unravelled the complexities of her enigmatic personality, and not even those who knew her well and heard her often have successfully explained the deep emotional impact of her vocal art upon her listeners. To have heard Bessie Smith in person was undoubtedly to have shared an experience that transcended that of listening to a great artist expressing himself in his chosen medium; an inexplicable quality remains that has caused many a person who heard her on a single occasion to remark that event as one of major significance in his lifetime. She mesmerized her hearers by the power of her personality and as in all cases where persons have succumbed to hypnosis the impression has never entirely left those that came under her spell. Not only this; the musicians who played with her were either wholly dominated or in a remarkable number of cases they were inspired to performances that were amongst the most brilliant in their careers.

Of jazz enthusiasts only a small number can say today that they saw Bessie Smith. For the majority her recordings are the only real contact that can be made with her artistry and it is fortunate that these were made by means superior to any existing at that time, for within their grooves something of its magic was captured. From these recordings, from personal recollections and from such historical information as exists, it is possible to gain at least an impression of the incomparable, the immortal Bessie Smith.

P.H.O.

1. 'YOUNG WOMAN'S BLUES'

Five miles north of the Tennessee–Georgia State boundary in the Moccasin Bend of the Tennessee River is situated the city of Chattanooga. At the turn of the century it was an important railroad centre where five trunk lines and three subsidiary railways intersected, providing work in the roundhouses and on the sections for a great many Negroes. In 1900 the total population of the city was 30,000; of these more than 13,000 persons were coloured, and the high proportion of Negroes meant that large numbers were without work and hundreds of families lived in conditions of appalling poverty. Even amongst the male populace the rate of illiteracy among Negroes was more than eight times that of whites, and few persons cared about the lack of educational facilities for girls. Into this environment Elizabeth Smith was born to a wretchedly poor and almost anonymous family of Negroes on April 15th, 1898. Coloured children had to learn to fend for themselves and defend themselves in the grim Negro ghetto, and undoubtedly the hard life that Bessie Smith endured as a child in Chattanooga left its indelible impression on her mind and character.

As she learned to assert herself with her sisters, Tinnie, Viola and Lulu and her brother Clarence, Bessie Smith developed a somewhat extrovert, even aggressive personality. Although educational opportunities for coloured girls were so limited she went to primary school, and in school play productions she was able to give early expression to her natural histrionic talents. Whilst still a very young girl she gained confidence in performing before audiences through these class productions. Already possessing a good voice she attracted attention to her singing with such a good effect that at the tender age of nine years

Bessie made her stage début—at the Ivory Theatre, Chattanooga. Proudly she brought home her first week's salary, eight dollars—and more than she was to earn as a professional a few years later. A child at heart, she spent her pay on a pair of roller-skates, only to receive a thrashing from her poverty-stricken mother who was angered at the rashly impractical purchase. Recalling this thirty years later to a *Chicago Defender* reporter, Bessie Smith tried to vindicate to her own satisfaction her childhood purchase by claiming that she went on 'to win the State Roller-Skating Championship'.

Details of Bessie Smith's progression to a professional career are tantalizingly vague and contradictory, as indeed are so many features of her life which in the space of twenty years has assumed the character of a legend. She claimed that a relatively little-known singer, Caro Fisher, whom she may have heard in her home town, was her first inspiration, and that the celebrated blues collector and composer, the late W. C. Handy, was also an early influence. It is known that whilst still a small girl Bessie worked for a brief period in a Memphis choir and it may have been at this time that she gained her inspiration from Handy. Her career seemes to have commenced about 1910 when the Rabbit Foot Minstrels came to Chattanooga. F. C. Woolcott was still touring with a troupe of this most venerable of Minstrel Shows a few years ago, and in its hey-day the 'Rabbit Foot' had several companies on tour. That which came to Chattanooga was managed by Will 'Pa' Rainey, and the star of the show was his young wife, Gertrude, already known as 'Ma' Rainey. Born into Negro show business Gertrude Rainey commenced her career in a manner similar to Bessie Smith when she appeared in a talent show called *The Bunch of Blackberries* at the Springer Theatre, Columbus, Georgia. She was just twelve years older than Bessie but her experience was that of an old trouper. At the age of fourteen she attracted the attention of Will Rainey who had brought his Minstrels to Columbus, and within a year she was married and the principal performer in his show. Her act included songs drawn from every facet of Southern Negro vocal entertainment: from the 'hokum' routines of Minstrel troupes performed to the strum and clatter of banjo and tambourine; from the popular songs of the Vaudeville and Burlesque stage: from the song-and-dance acts of travelling circuses and carnivals, to the traditional songs, the ballads and the blues of the folk.

For close on thirty-five years Ma Rainey toured the South, playing in theatres and barns, and most frequently in the vast marquee which she carried in the long house-trailer made by members of her company which was her vehicle, her dressing-room, her home. Her contact was close with the people; in later life she recalled that she first heard the blues about 1900 and she absorbed the idiom of the folk blues singers into her repertoire. But she brought to the blues a certain professionalism, and reciprocally, she invested much of her more 'legitimate' material with the qualities of expression peculiar to the blues. She was probably the first of the so-called 'classic blues' singers: those who added a conscious artistry to the blues, and she was in many ways the greatest because she was closest to the sources of the music. Professional though she was she retained throughout her career a liking for the jug bands, the fiddle players, the kazoo moaners and swanee whistlers, the barrelhouse pianists and the wandering guitarists who knew and played the blues in its purest folk forms, a partiality that was never shared by Bessie Smith.

Ma Rainey held the attention and affection of her audiences by the warmth of her personality and the bond of sympathy in the form and content of her blues that she shared with them. Rich and warm as a fine wine, her voice was profoundly suited to her material, and like a connoisseur of good wine she savoured her words, rolling them over her tongue and enjoying their flavour to the full. As she moaned, or cried, or hollered her phrases, the shaping of her syllables was full of the qualities of 'blue' feeling that characterize alike the great jazz artist and the folk blues singer. Bessie Smith could not have had a greater tutor.

On one of her seemingly interminable itineraries Ma Rainey came to Chattanooga and whilst there heard the child Bessie singing. In her she recognized a potentially great artist and she took her in her care. During the course of the next few years Bessie Smith was well featured in the 'Rabbit Foot' show as a child singer in short skirts, and she improved all the while. From Ma Rainey she learned the fundamentals of her whole art: her repertoire based on Vaudeville songs and country blues, her dance routines, her dramatic presentation of her material. And, a wise pupil of a great master, in many ways she excelled her teacher.

Maturing both in voice and figure, Bessie Smith in her teens could no longer be featured as a child singer; she was developing as a striking personality on the stage. By those to whom the most conventional forms of beauty most appeal, Ma Rainey has been termed ugly. Certainly she had an impish, Puck-like face, but she had endearing features. If she was 'homely' in the American sense she was also 'homely' in the English sense and her maternal build, her affectionate if perverse regard for young boys, was engaging to her hearers. About her there was a certain primitive barbarism: her wild, uncombed hair was hardly tamed by the beaded band and artificial fringe that she wore; in her ear lobes were rings that held gold coins and a necklace of gold pieces swung in the artificial light as she gestured with a huge fan of ostrich feathers. In contrast, Bessie wore simple dresses that were boldly draped over her splendid figure, her hair was swept back and at her neck she wore a single strand of beads, sufficient to draw attention to the regular beauty of her oval features and her dark, moist eyes. Whereas Gertrude Rainey was short, even squat, Bessie Smith was tall and Junoesque; whereas Ma was homely, Bessie was comely. Long before she came of age she commanded her audiences by her majestic bearing. It was no accident that Gertrude Rainey was known by the affectionate term 'Ma', no accident that she was known throughout the Negro world as the 'Mother of the Blues': she was the maternal archetype, the eternal Mother-figure. Nor was it an accident that Bessie Smith was to be known as the 'Queen of the Blues', as the 'Empress of the Blues', for the power she had to dominate an audience, and the esteem that amounted to virtual worship with which she was held placed her in the ranks of the regal and the unattainable.

As the great New Orleans trumpeter Joseph 'King' Oliver found it impossible to hold at his side indefinitely his brilliant pupil Louis Armstrong, and made no attempt to restrain him after he felt the need to spread his wings, so too, Ma Rainey lost her protégée as Bessie Smith aspired to star in her own right. She did not demur; but it is rather to Bessie's discredit that whilst Armstrong never failed to acknowledge his debt to Oliver, she chose to forget her mentor in later years.

Bessie had no apparent difficulty in securing employment and she was soon a principal singer for Milton Starr's theatre circuit which was governed by his Theatre Owner's Booking Agency—the T.O.B.A. To some Negroes the letters meant 'Tough on Black Artists' for the payment to individual entertainers was often pitifully small owing to the custom then prevalent of booking whole shows. The manager would be paid a sum which he could dispense as he thought fit, and when Bessie joined Pete Werley's Minstrel Show called *The Florida Cotton Pickers* she earned as little as two dollars, fifty cents a week. Clarksdale, Natchez, Pensacola, Birmingham, Jacksonville . . . from town to town the touring road shows travelled, filling theatres for weekly shows or erecting their tents in vacant lots for one-night stands. Bessie generally sang to the playing of an accompanist and for a time she was supported by a pianist from Plaquemine Delta who had been playing in New Orleans for some years, Clarence Williams, a partnership which was to bear fruit in later years.

Seven years passed since Bessie Smith was first heard by Ma Rainey; she worked on the T.O.B.A. circuit and freelanced in Gulf Coast cabarets and 'Darktown' dance halls, in levee camps and water-front dives, her artistry maturing in the bitter school of experience as she performed to audiences of sharecroppers and oilfield workers, turpentine pressers and Piney Woods loggers. Her perambulations took her up the Alabama River from Mobile to the town of Selma and it was there, in a rough, edge-of-town gin-mill that she was heard in 1917 by an aspiring promoter, Frank Walker. She was singing, he remembered, 'the deep moaning blues'—not with the finish of later years but with an intensity of expression that impressed itself on his mind.

By the time she came of age Bessie was commanding a salary of as much as seventy-five dollars a week, which was considered good money. To this could be added almost twice as much again thrown on the stage by enthusiastic listeners and generally a few supporters were deliberately planted in the audience to start throwing the money and encourage this valuable expression of appreciation. As Buster Bailey sagely remarked, singing was a living for Bessie and like other performers in her particular field she would employ the customary devices to make that living a comfortable one. In 1919 she was working at the 91 Theatre on Decatur Street, Atlanta. Admittedly it was a much less attractive theatre than the grander '81' with its sixteen boxes, but it did attract big names. She had her own show called *Liberty Belles* in which a chorus of women as large as Bessie herself were revealed with their backs to the audience and their skirts held high as the curtains opened. Then the 'Belles' turned, and in a rollicking, waddling chorus, shimmied to the footlights singing the hit song of the World War, *Liberty Bell* on which the name of the show was a pun. Bessie sang as leader of a trio and then took over with her own blues and Vaudeville songs. Further up the street at the 81 Theatre, James P. Johnson was appearing with his orchestra and his wife, May Wright, was a featured singer. Together they went to see Bessie and were convulsed by the opening chorus, but somehow Bessie's artistry manifested itself in spite of the burlesque character of the show.

In the course of her formative years Bessie made many connexions that were to be of help to her when she became more established, and the friends that she made at this time were some of the most faithful that she had, for as the passing years tended to make her more difficult to understand only those who had known her when she was young were prepared to stand by her. She disliked people in the entertainment world as a whole and was never present at the gatherings where show people customarily congregated. Even before she became a recording star she resented the presence of any other blues singer on the same bill as herself and she was already sufficiently important to be able to dictate to the managers. When Ethyl Waters appeared on the same bill Bessie made no secret of her irritation. She commanded a private performance of Ethyl Waters' act and insisted that she sang no blues, but in spite of her warnings, her invectives and references to 'Northern bitches' Ethyl did sing *St. Louis Blues* at the request of the audience. Few cared or dared to address Bessie Smith other than as 'Miss Bessie' as Zutty Singleton observed, and Ethyl Waters was careful to do so, for in truth she greatly admired her. Their paths seldom crossed again, but Bessie admitted shortly before her death that 'Long Goody' as she called her, was her favourite singer.

Charles P. Bailey, who managed the '81', was a self-made Georgia impresario who had an unenviable reputation amongst some members of Negro show business. He was strict with his artists, imposed restrictions on their activities and frequently gave vent to an ungovernable temper. As he had successfully negotiated a deal with the T.O.B.A. Negro artists were obliged to perform at his theatre and whilst she was touring the Circuit Bessie was booked there. An argument between the two strong-minded and self-willed persons was almost inevitable and Bailey is alleged to have beaten Bessie across the face until she was nearly insensible. Politically powerful in the Jim Crow town of Atlanta, Bailey had her jailed and none of her supporters dared protest. Shortly after the incident Ethyl Waters was involved in a similar argument with Bailey and was warned that her life was in danger. Escaping from Atlanta she contacted Milton Starr in Nashville, who was already much perturbed at the reports that he had heard and who forthwith terminated the T.O.B.A. contract with the '81'.

Though she was primarily celebrated as a singer, Bessie performed a song-and-dance routine in her shows, high-stepping vigorously in her coloured stockings and strapped, pointed shoes, doing the 'bumps and grinds' with spirit. For a while she loosened her long hair and, following the prevailing fashion, wore it in bangs and heavy waves which threatened to cover her face as she danced. A long chain of beads swung at her neck and she favoured a kimono dress decorated with the currently popular Oriental flower patterns and incongruous fur trimmings at cuffs and hemline. Sometimes, however, she changed into a tuxedo and strutted across the stage, exploiting her strong contralto voice by doing male impersonations.

Early in 1920 Bessie had an opportunity to try her artistry on the more sophisticated coloured audiences of the East, when she received an invitation to entertain at a dance hall in the 'wide open' coastal resort of Atlantic City. For the best part of a year she held the engagement singing to the music of Taylor's band in which Charlie Gaines was the guitarist; to the accompaniment of Charlie Johnson at the piano, or to that of his band—the nucleus of the famous combination that he was shortly to lead at Small's Paradise in Harlem. For several months the celebrated Negro entertainer, Bert Wheeler, was in the show, and the dancer and sometime female impersonator, Frankie 'Half-Pint' Jaxon also performed. A long spell in one location was unsettling for Bessie whose whole career had been spent in continual travelling, playing, packing and travelling again. 1921 found her on the road once more, beating her way through the Deep South to play before the folk whom she called 'her people'. Before she left, however, Bessie made a bid to enter the recording field when she was given an opportunity to record for the Emerson Phonograph Company. On February 12th, 1921, the *Chicago Defender* carried a preliminary announcement: 'One of the greatest of all "blues" singers is Miss Bessie Smith, who is at present making records with the aid of six jazz musicians for the Emerson Record Company. The first release will be made about March 10th . . .' March passed and April too, and the records failed to appear. They were never issued and the identity of the 'six musicians' and the whereabouts of the masters remain mysteries.

Whilst Emerson were debating whether to release Bessie's recordings, the singer herself was working the Gulf Ports from Florida to Louisiana with Clarence Williams to accompany her in her act. Arriving at Pensacola her pianist fell ill, but a substitute was found in a sixteen-year-old girl named Billie Gootson who played for her at the Belmont Theatre. Billie Gootson later moved to New Orleans, in 1930, where she married the trumpeter, Joseph Delacroix, 'Dee Dee' Pierce. When Ida Cox made her last Southern tour a few years ago Billie and Dee Dee Pierce accompanied her singing, and Billie Pierce is herself one of the last singers working in the tradition of Bessie Smith. It was a momentous event for the girl, Billie Gootson, but it was a trifling one for Bessie, accustomed as she was to the vicissitudes of the entertainment business. At the Lyric Theatre, New Orleans, shortly after, she had the whole coloured population at her feet.

Clarence Williams, with whom Bessie had been working, had plans to present her on Broadway and he brought her north again as his preparations for a show matured. He bought her a dress for which he claimed to have paid two to three hundred dollars and he summoned Sidney Bechet from Europe where he was on tour, to take part. Little more than a boy, light skinned and with almond eyes, Bechet was to be cast as a clarinet-playing Chinese character, and Bessie herself was to be the star of the show. Unfortunately, as far as Clarence Williams and his plans were concerned the scheme fell through, but the show did go on, with Gloria Harven as the star singer. Entitled *How Come* it featured Sidney Bechet as a Chinese laundryman—also named 'How Come'. When the show reached Washington Bechet stopped off at the home of singer Virginia Liston, who kept 'open house' and it was there that he met Bessie Smith and heard her sing. Overwhelmed by her splendid voice he successfully arranged for her to replace Gloria Harven and together they toured the principal cities of Ohio and Illinois, during which time Bessie and Sidney enjoyed a somewhat stormy liaison. When at last the show was booked for New York a number of changes were made and Bessie was given totally unsuitable material which brought the show to a rapid close. Whilst they were in New York, however, Clarence Williams arranged a recording session for Bessie Smith with the Okeh Company which was now enjoying remarkable sales returns from the recordings of blues singer, Mamie Smith. James 'Bubber' Miley from Carolina, who had already toured with Mamie, was to play cornet; Sidney Bechet was to play clarinet; Charlie Irvis was selected on trombone and Buddy Christian took the banjo chair. With Armund Piron way back in 1915, Clarence Williams had published their hit tune, *I Wish I Could Shimmy Like My Sister Kate*, and he chose this for Bessie's test piece. In his opinion the test recording was the greatest that she ever made but her style was rough in comparison with that of a singer like Mamie Smith, and Bessie apparently failed the audition. The record was rejected and given to Clarence Williams, who in turn gave it to Bessie as a souvenir. Not surprisingly, she soon lost it.

Shortly after Bessie Smith had another chance when she secured an audition with Harry Pace and the Pace Phonograph Company, but, as already related, her coarse manners proved too much for Pace and once again she was rejected. In a letter to Sam Benjamin over thirty years later his friend, W. C. Handy, recalled, 'Of course Pace "let her go". My daughter Katherine was in the office then and brought the record home, and we used to play it for the amusement it gave us, after Bessie became so well known.'

Though she had been unfortunate with her recording tests to date, and the North was still apparently unwilling to accept her, Bessie was highly popular in the South where the audiences clamoured for her brand of unadulterated blues. Late in 1922 Bessie arrived in Philadelphia where she sang in a cabaret on 13th and South Street. An engagement at 'The Madhouse', situated on 11th and Poplar followed and her reputation in the city spread, winning her an invitation to appear with the Negro entertainers Buzz and Burton at the famous 'Standard Theatre'. It was to be a period engagement and Bessie accepted with alacrity, suspecting perhaps that her 'break' was near. Others were anxious for her to succeed and a local record dealer is reputed to have pawned his watch to pay for her to have an Okeh recording test. This is probably fictitious, but at the offices of the Okeh and Columbia firms changes had been made. Frank Walker was put in charge of the recording of Negro artists for Columbia and Clarence Williams, who had been appointed as 'Race Record Judge' for Okeh, was also acting in an advisory capacity for Walker. Both men had known Bessie Smith and though Walker had not heard her in eight years the impression that she had made then was still vivid. When Williams spoke of her from his recent experience Frank Walker wasted no time. 'Go down there and find her; and bring her back to me,' he instructed the record judge. Williams was cautious and explained that her work had not been liked at her previous tests and that her style was considered uncouth. But Walker knew what he wanted, and he knew his business well.

'You just get her here,' he said.

2. 'AIN'T GOIN' TO PLAY SECOND FIDDLE'

From Philadelphia to New York is a relatively short step and Bessie needed little bidding. When she arrived she still seemed very much of a country girl to Walker who was surprised to see her, 'tall and fat and scared to death'. When she started to sing, however, he knew that the years had matured her as an artist and that his hunch had been wise enough. Nevertheless he established her in New York for some weeks 'to get acclimatized' before he decided to attempt recording her. On February 15th, 1923, she was invited to the studio with Clarence Williams to make a test, and this proving to be good enough she made her first recordings the following day. They have been termed 'the first country blues on record', but it was Bessie's approach rather than her material that betokened the influence of the Southern Country blues, for her first numbers were proven 'hits' drawn from the repertoires of other singers. The first tune was Porter Grainger's *'Tain't Nobody's Bizness If I Do'* which had been recorded the previous November by Sara Martin, and the second was a twelve-bar blues with introductory verse composed by Alberta Hunter and Lovie Austin, *Down Hearted Blues*—a curious choice for it had been sung and recorded by a number of artists and Alberta Hunter's version, which practically initiated the Paramount Race series, had been a best-seller. Perhaps Bessie was nervous that day for her first title was not a success and was rejected, and some five takes were necessary before she made a successful version of the second title. On record, however, it sounds as if Bessie were singing a virgin blues, so warm and personal is her interpretation and the disc with its almost equally celebrated backing, *Gulf Coast Blues*, composed by Williams and recorded the following day, proved to be an outstanding success. With one record Bessie's supremacy as a singer of the 'classic blues' was established beyond challenge and the queues formed outside the disc stores to obtain it until some three-quarters of a million copies were sold.

A contract in her hand, a hundred and twenty-five dollars a side for her records in her wallet and love in her heart, Bessie accepted the proposal of a lean Philadelphia policeman, Jackie Gee, who had been courting her during her engagement at the Standard. It has been rumoured that this was Bessie's second marriage, but if so the identity of her first husband remains a mystery. Jackie Gee and Bessie Smith were married on April 7th, 1923, and spent their honeymoon in New York. Bessie wasted no opportunity: four days after their wedding she was in the recording studio again. Lucille Hegamin had made a best-selling coupling, *Aggravatin' Papa* and *Beale Street Mamma* for Cameo the year before and the same titles were chosen for Bessie's next record. She was accompanied by her 'Down Home Trio', comprising clarinet, banjo and piano, the latter possibly being Clarence Williams who recorded other titles with her later that day. Bessie's voice sounds remarkably mature and her version of *Beale Street Mamma*, a tune not unreminiscent of the traditional *See See Rider*, has a roundness that Lucille Hegamin's thin, though musical voice lacked. Already master of her material she phrases a lead-in with *How Come You Do Me Like You Do* as a lead-trumpeter of the calibre of King Oliver might steer his band into a final chorus.

Clearly Bessie's songs were chosen with a view to 'carving' —or defeating by superior artistry—other recordings made by already established blues singers, though the fact that many of the tunes common to these singers were Clarence Williams compositions may have its significance. Again she tried *'Tain't Nobody's Bizness If I Do* and again she had difficulty, the accepted master being the tenth 'take'. Even more troublesome was *Keeps On A-Rainin'* (*Papa He Can't Make No Time*) also previously recorded by Sara Martin. Bessie attempted it on February 17th, again on April 11th and the accepted master was cut after ten attempts on the 26th, still remaining an item not wholly suited to her style. Of her titles that April, perhaps the most successful was *Baby Won't You Please Come Home Blues* which she takes more slowly than is customary with this popular Clarence Williams composition. She seems to enjoy the enunciation of every word, and as she sings she remodels the melody to such 'blue' effect that it is only on reflection that one realizes that this is done by shading down the top notes—even dropping them an octave, a style which reveals both her limitations and how brilliantly she worked within them.

In the middle of June Bessie made her first recordings with the pianist and band leader, Fletcher Henderson, though a label error on *Outside of That*, on which Clarence Williams' name should have appeared, had implied an earlier meeting. University-educated and academically trained as a musician, Henderson has been criticized for a lack of jazz feeling in his solo work and in Ethyl Waters' words, 'that damn-it-to-hell bass'. His accuracy and simplicity was an ideal foil to Bessie's work and by the effective contrast set off to perfection the subtle inflexions and

313

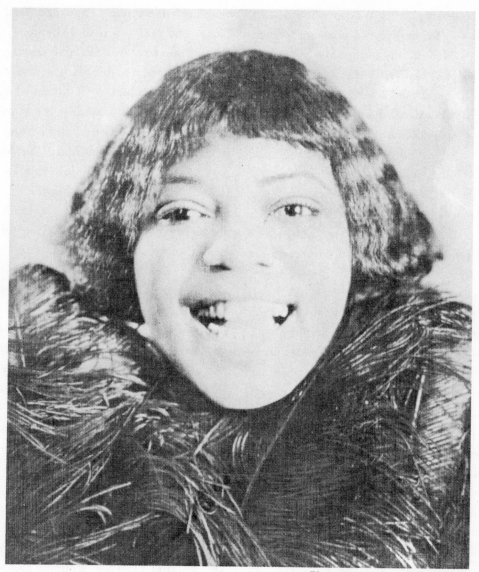

'I've got the world in a jug. . . .'
Bessie Smith in June, 1925

suspensions or anticipations in timing which characterized her singing. With such unexpected studio companions as Eddie Cantor and Frank Crumit, who used the intervening matrices, Bessie made her June 14th date a memorable one. In the trite words of Lovie Austin's *Bleeding Hearted Blues* she invested all the tragedy of loneliness, putting to shame Alberta Hunter's and Edna Hicks' previous versions.

To a certain extent this was the greatest period of Bessie Smith's career; she had not achieved the splendid control that she exhibited at the peak of her fame but she had an instinctive gift for divining the pure gold of her material and though the words were sometimes banal she made them so meaningful that they became vehicles for the expression of her own personality, giving the verses a significance that is scarcely discernible in their texts. Her interpretations were therefore often surprising. An opportunity for a roisterous, swaggering performance lies in the simple boasting song of sexual virtuosity, *Nobody in Town Can Bake a Sweet Jelly-Roll Like Mine* and this is the manner in which it is usually sung. But Bessie sings the bragging lines with a sadness, a poignancy of mood which seems to express a deep regret that the ability to love passionately is gone to waste. She is a young woman yet; in the later years of her exuberance and eventual bitterness she would have sung with greater gusto and insinuation. Playing with economy and sympathy of mood, Henderson is here at his best, contributing his share to one of the singer's greatest records.

During the summer months Bessie went on tour again, reaping the benefit of her initial recordings. Coloured people throughout the South wanted to hear in person the girl whose recordings had transcended those made by her contemporaries and by all who had come before her, and she played to packed houses everywhere. 'Bessie Smith really hits 'em in Nashville,' ran a local newspaper report. 'She knocked all the tin off the theatre. People cried for more and refused to leave. . . .' Three or four times a year she would visit New Orleans to play at Boudreau and Bennett's Lyric Theatre on the corner of Iberville and Burgundy Streets. Until the theatre was destroyed by fire in 1927,

Photograph courtesy Albert J. McCarthy
'I'm a red hot woman, just full of flamin' youth. . . .'
Bessie on stage, *circa* 1928

315

violinist and drummer John Robichaux led its pit orchestra for ten years, and Bessie could depend on him to interpret her musical backgrounds in the manner that she liked. Her arrangements were often written, and when they were lost on one trip, John Robichaux provided new ones. For himself he preferred to order his music from New York publishing houses and he required of his men that whilst they played jazz they should also be reading musicians. Alphonse Picou played clarinet, Johnny Lindsay or Harrison Barnes were favoured trombonists, Arthur Kimball played trumpet and his sister Margaret the piano, whilst on drums would be found Josiah Frazier, or sometimes Zutty Singleton, little more than a boy at this time. Outside, the queues formed long before the opening of the box office and a grateful management would have sea-food suppers on the stage in Bessie's honour after the show. Exploiting the outstanding success of her first records her repertoire included *Gulf Coast Blues, Baby Won't You Please Come Home, Down Hearted Blues* and *Aggravatin' Papa,* and both to demonstrate their making and to encourage sales Bessie toured with a replica of the recording equipment with its horn and cutting apparatus which she had arranged on the stage. After explaining how her records were made she would demonstrate a session and sing her best numbers to a packed and wildly enthusiastic house.

Back in New York in late September she made a number of records with Irving Johns or Jimmy Jones on piano. First of these was *Jail House Blues,* an item which marked a new departure in her recording activities, for until now she had recorded blues that told of the perennial themes of popular music: of love, thwarted, jilted, completed. Now she absorbed the lesson to be learned from Ma Rainey, returning to the subject matter of the folk blues which was largely concerned with other, less attractive aspects of living. Perhaps she was returning too, to the material she had used in earlier days. Though love and sex remained the principal thematic material of her blues, she turned from time to time in ensuing recording sessions to blues concerned with migration, with penury, sickness and death: subjects which were often grim in themselves but which the Negroes who suffered such circumstances liked to buy for the assurance that they gave that others knew and cared, and shared their own privations.

That there were many singing Smiths has been fre-

quently noted: there was Mamie Smith, the first Negro singer to record, whose *Crazy Blues* played such an important part in making the blues a commercial success in the phonograph industry. There was Trixie Smith, who won the first blues-singing contest; Laura Smith, of whom the Okeh Company said, 'she's the gal that jes mops things up wherever she appears' with her 'ragin' blues, can't-be-beat moanin' stuff'. There was Hazel Smith who recorded with King Oliver in 1928 and there was the celebrated red-haired Ada 'Bricktop' Smith who became a Parisian night-club hostess. Bessie even had her namesakes in Elizabeth Smith who also recorded with King Oliver, and in Bessie Mae Smith, known also as Blue Belle and as St. Louis Bessie who was thought by St. Louis Negroes to be *the* Bessie Smith. None of these singing Smiths was related to another, though Bessie's niece exploited her aunt's reputation by calling herself Ruby Smith when she recorded in the 'thirties. Above them all in stature was Bessie's chief rival, Clara Smith, a singer who steadily improved and whose best work represented a serious threat to Bessie's supremacy, sadly and unaccountably forgotten today. Clara Smith had been auditioned in May with Henderson as her accompanist and proving satisfactory she recorded almost as frequently for Columbia as Bessie did herself, the issues of the two singers frequently being released simultaneously and numerically consecutive. She attained her full stature more slowly than did Bessie but she was second only to her and was known as 'The Queen of the Moaners'. On October 4th Bessie made a rare concession by recording two duets with Clara, for she was jealous of sharing vocal honours with anyone. Neither singer was at her best on either *Far Away Blues* or *I'm Going Back To My Used to Be* and on this showing Bessie proved herself Clara's peer. Some years later when they again recorded together the distinction was less marked.

A young saxophonist named Coleman Hawkins had been playing in Mamie Smith's band and now he had an opportunity to record with Bessie Smith. Apparently his playing was not considered good enough for he accompanied her on the first two 'takes' of *Any Woman's Blues* when they met on October 16th, and was dropped for the final, accepted one. There seems to be no great loss, for Bessie, singing with Henderson alone, is superb. Her vocal *glissandi,* her moaning, drawn-out syllables are the quintessence of blues ex-

316

pression as she sings, 'My man ain't actin' right, he stays out late at night. . . .' With marked beat and only occasional treble runs Henderson's piano is simple and in keeping, and as she sings with menacing undertones, '. . . and when I find that gal that tried to steal my pal, I'll get her told, just you wait and see. . . .' Bessie's mellow voice slides over the notes, climbs up to them and shades them down.

With *Chicago Bound Blues* Frank Walker initiated the Columbia 14000 Race series on December 4th, 1923. It was the end of the year and Bessie Smith had been recording with the Company for just ten months. When they closed the books they could thank her for having saved the Columbia Concern from the hands of the official receivers. Apart from the receipts from the records of Clara Smith and other artists the proceeds of Bessie Smith's recordings had made them solvent. As for Bessie herself, she made her home in Philadelphia, brought her entire family from Chattanooga to settle there with her and bought a farm for herself in New Jersey which, for a while at any rate, she worked profitably.

3. 'MONEY BLUES'

'Bessie Smith. Voice N.G.,' wrote Thomas Alva Edison in characteristically laconic terms, against the date April 23rd, 1924, in his 'Talent Audition File'. Bessie Smith's contract with Columbia was an exclusive one, but the day before she had endured an abortive session with banjoist John Mitchell and, perhaps in chagrin, had sought an audition with the great inventor and scientist. Edison was far removed from Negro life and entertainment and though his Edison record catalogue contained the names of a few coloured singers they were of a sweet-voiced variety more calculated to appeal to a white market. For her own part, Bessie had always been loath to play 'the White Time' and like many other coloured singers she rather resented white people as a whole. Hardly ever did she appear before a white audience in New York but her recordings had made her widely known and amongst her admirers were many young white persons who did not share Thomas Edison's opinion of her singing. They were even to be found in the South. After a three-day stint in the recording studios in January, Bessie went on tour once more, terminating this time at the Beale Avenue Palace, Beale 'Street' in Memphis, Tennessee. It was there that she made a new departure in her career when she broadcast in February over the WMC radio network. The orchestra organized by Charles Booker, President of the Yancey and Booker Music Company of Memphis, accompanied her on some numbers whilst the Beale Avenue Palace Orchestra, with whom she was then working, also accompanied her 'on the air'. Included in the songs that she broadcast were *Sam Jones Blues* and *St. Louis*

Gal which she had recorded the previous September and two titles recorded only a couple of months previously, *Chicago Bound* and *Mistreatin' Daddy* which were the rage of the day. Before she left she was persuaded to give a special 11 p.m. performance for white listeners which was enthusiastically received. But white and coloured did not mix.

Early in April she returned to make a number of recordings on which the accompaniment was provided not only by a pianist—Irving Johns—but also by Bob Robbins playing the fiddle, an instrument held in some disrepute by many jazz supporters but one with a long history in Negro folk music. Apparently uninfluenced by the Conservatory, Robbins played in the 'alley fiddle' style of the street musician who plays the instrument at his waist. On *Ticket Agent Ease Your Window Down* his powerful fingers twist the strings as he draws the bow across them, causing them to wail their responses to Bessie's voice. His playing is closer to the folk tradition than the work of any musician whom Bessie had employed to date; closer too, to the kind of support that Ma Rainey cherished. Even the guitar, most favoured of all blues instruments, was used very sparingly on Bessie's records and Harry Reser's contributions a few months before had been singularly undistinguished— though it seems, better than John Mitchell's *Banjo Blues*.

In general, Bessie Smith preferred trained musicians to folk musicians for her accompanists and though Clarence Williams was largely self-taught, he, Fletcher Henderson and James P. Johnson, the three most influential artists

317

who accompanied her, were 'reading' pianists and composers. On them she could rely for an interpretative rendering of her carefully arranged songs. Her approach placed her several steps further from the folk blues than Ma Rainey and closer to the footlights of professional entertainment. Through her the blues underwent a process of urbanization and her treatment brought her closer to jazz music which was undergoing a similar transformation from the folk. But Bessie's roots were bedded deeply in the South and she did not lose her audience by her remodelling of the blues. This was a period of great social change for the Negro and to a certain extent her art symbolized it. Attracted by the prosperity enjoyed by their brothers who had already moved to the northern industrial centres, streams of Negroes from the South continued to pour into Cleveland, Detroit, Chicago and Gary. Retaining some indications of their southern origins and habits, yet trying to assume a new way of life in a strange environment they aggravated the housing problem and were the unintentional cause of many interracial and bi-racial disturbances. Many were homesick, unaccustomed to the teeming cities, the accelerated pace of living and the extreme climate. When they heard that Bessie Smith was in town, a singer who sang the blues and songs of their southern homeland but who was now a part of the urban scene in the Negro north, they flocked to hear her. On Chicago's South Side the concentration of Negroes was considerable and many of them were newly arrived. In May Bessie appeared at the Avenue Theatre there on 31st and Indiana and sang to the hot music of Clarence Jones' Orchestra: the audience shouted and hollered for more, causing a near riot and refusing to let her leave the stage.

Unlike so many of her listeners Bessie was now fully accustomed to life in the cities and was as happy in a vast auditorium as she was in a tent show. She had grown in musical stature and with experience she had gained a mastery of stage technique, winning the confidence and the emotional response of her audiences. Entering from the wings she bore herself with regal dignity as she moved to the footlights, and when she sang, she sang with her whole body—passionately, powerfully, subtly swaying, giving the impression of great strength barely held in control. It was customary at the time for singers to use a megaphone, before the microphone on the stage became generally employed. Bessie eschewed any such device, filling a hall with the volume of her natural voice and showing up the inadequacies of her lesser rivals in the process. With simple, generous sweeps of her full but shapely arms she would emphasize her words; clenching her fists sometimes and striking her palm or wringing her hands in a physical expression of her vocal phrases. As she reached the peak of her blues she would throw back her head and sing full and loud; then she would bow her head till her face was in shadow as she moaned her final choruses. Gone were the days of a hair style of bangs and costume of flowered kimono; now she swept her hair back to a bun as she had when a young girl, so that the beauty of her oval face was not impaired. Simpler dresses uncluttered by needless accessories displayed her well-proportioned if ample figure to advantage. A spray of sequins or a small posy of flowers at her shoulder, a diamanté clip or jewelled clasp at her waist was often all the decoration she required on the striking crimson dresses that she liked to wear. But when she came back for her last appearance—often solely for the last show of a season—she knew and delighted in the intensely dramatic effect of a simply-draped dress in startlingly white satin which reflected the colours projected by an electrician from a spotlight in front of which rotated coloured 'gells'—now mauve, now pink, now blue as her songs. Bessie was the undisputed queen.

Clarence Jones' group at the Avenue Theatre included Eddie Alexander on trumpet and Art Hill on trombone and not infrequently Bessie made use of a pit orchestra at stage performances. Far more conservative on recording dates she had seldom employed a wind instrumentalist, remembering perhaps her ineffectual 'Down Home Trio'. For a couple of titles in September, 1923, she used a clarinet, played, it is rumoured, by George Baquet, though Don Redman is as likely, for he played on a couple of other dates. Bessie did not care for a more positive instrumental voice, but on July 23rd, 1924, Henderson brought with him another member of his band to the studio—his trombonist, 'Long Boy' Charlie Green. Inspired in all probability by her visit to Chicago, Bessie recorded two titles with undoubted social implications, *Workhouse Blues* and *House Rent Blues*, and Green's dolorous notes helped considerably to establish the atmosphere. Encouraged, Henderson brought his lead cornet player, Joe Smith, with him two months later. Not, as has been suggested on more than one occasion, a boy in short pants, Smith was nevertheless only twenty-one years of age though he had gained considerable experience in St. Louis and New York and had developed a bell-like quality of tone of a kind dissimilar to the robust timbre of many of the New Orleans musicians. His improvisations were of great beauty and sensitivity and he had an innate feeling for the blues. Bessie took to her namesake instantly and was delighted in his ability to 'talk' and 'preach' on the cornet. The two sides made on September 26th with Joe Smith, Charlie Green and Fletcher Henderson were amongst the finest in her career.

Weeping Willow Blues commences with three verses of two lines with one-line refrain: in effect a twelve-bar blues, and behind Bessie's infinitely sad voice Joe Smith's beautifully phrased cornet is poignantly mellow; Charlie Green's trombone moans in sympathy. Later the blues changes to a recitative passage of eight lines with a final repeat of the refrain, and through this the group plays a punctuated, repeated melodic phrase—part stop chorus, part riff. Then they break into the blues as the piece closes, with Bessie's voice, now far greater in its range than in former years, soaring an octave higher. Also composed by Paul Carter, *The Bye-Bye Blues* is an exceedingly mournful sessionmate on which the singer's voice is answered by Joe Smith's deeply-felt, muted cornet responses. The historic session marked a new phase in the recorded work of Bessie Smith.

Late in 1924 the pianist, Fred Longshaw, became Bessie's musical director, accompanying her on tours to play in her support or to give the cues and instructions to the pit orchestras so that they could play in accord with her particular taste. On a brief but triumphant return to Chicago, the *Defender* said of Bessie's performance, 'Bessie had them howling long before her first number was half finished. Longshaw accompanied her.' In December, Longshaw made a number of sides with Bessie, sometimes in the company of other musicians. The first few were rejected and remade a few days later, but *Sing Sing Prison Blues* with Don Redman and Buster Bailey playing a clarinet duet was cut on December 6th and issued. For all that it is a curiously tuneless piece and though Bessie was now having more experimental accompaniments the support is colourless. But it could be argued that the lifeless setting and the monotone in which it is sung are suited to the depressing theme. Far more interesting is *Dying Gambler's Blues* made

a week later, a song based on a theme more suited to folk balladry than to Bessie's customary material: the mourning for a dying member of the underworld. An opportunity for Charlie Green to display his virtuosity as a trombonist, it gives him ample scope to make his instrument wail, cry, talk, even utter condolences as he gives expression to Bessie's words when she sings, 'All the women they cry . . . my man said he's so evil . . . they all sympathize. . . .'

A month later two of the greatest figures in the history of jazz music met in the recording studios when Fred Longshaw introduced Louis Armstrong to Bessie Smith. No evidence of disharmony is to be heard on the ensuing records though Bessie is said to have been angry with the choice of Armstrong, having developed a particular liking for Joe Smith's style. As a session it was outstandingly successful for the two brilliant artists inspired each other reciprocally. Though only twenty-five Louis Armstrong was at the peak of his inventive genius and his muted cornet accompaniments to Bessie's singing are models of their kind, probably unsurpassed in jazz; Bessie herself was never greater. There is an essential 'rightness' in the placing of vocal phrase against instrumental line, of answering instrumental passages that amplify and add meaning to all that the singer has to say that is definitive of the jazz-blues performance. If 'Big' Green's use of speech intonation on his instrument is at times a demonstration of his ability rather than a true extension of the content of the blues, in Armstrong's accompaniments the employment of 'vocalized tone' is truly creative with never an unnecessary or superfluous note. Attention must also be paid to Longshaw's part as he plays blue chords perfectly suited to the tunes on an instrument—the organ or harmonium—which scarcely lends itself to such expression. This is especially to be noticed in *Reckless Blues* and in *St. Louis Blues*, of which latter tune, the most recorded in the whole jazz repertoire, this version remains unsurpassed in over thirty years. It is significant that only one take of these sides was considered necessary though in Bessie's career to date four or five takes were far from uncommon.

You've Been a Good Old Wagon, though a vaudeville-styled song, has its roots in the earthy humour of the tent show with its unsubtle but pungent metaphor of the aged lover who has 'done broke down'. Pure Negro folk idiom appears in another of these superb Bessie Smith–Louis

Armstrong recordings in the blues of a penniless man who has 'done gone cold in hand'. Such idiomatic phrases had immediate appeal to the 'back home' market in the South and no doubt it was for this reason that Bessie's recording from her next session of W. C. Handy's celebrated *Yellow Dog Blues* with its now familiar use of Negro folksay was released with alacrity whilst its session-mate *Cake-Walkin' Babies* was rejected as being too far removed from the form of blues with which she had made her name. It was not until the mid-'forties, nearly a decade after her death, that this latter side was finally issued.

Rejected though it may have been, *Cake-Walkin' Babies* was a straw in the wind, for both Bessie's material and the music that accompanied her were changing. That spring of 1925 she appeared at the Paradise Gardens, Chicago, on 35th and Prairie, where many of the young white jazz musicians—the 'Austin High School Gang' and the future 'Chicagoans' heard her for the first time. They preferred the singing of Ethyl Waters for the most part, but Bix Beiderbecke joined the enthusiasts who threw a shower of coins in the customary manner to fall at the feet of the singer—who proudly disdained from picking them up herself. Of all the songs that she sang the one that impressed Beiderbecke most was *I'll See You In My Dreams*—a fact which illuminates the taste of both. A popular melody scarcely representative of the material customarily associated with Bessie Smith, it may well be more characteristic of her stage songs than has been supposed, for the extent to which she included the popular commercial songs of her day in her repertoire has not been determined. Undoubtedly she adapted her style and her material to suit her audience though her recordings must be indicative of the aspects of her work that appealed to the widest section of the community. Every issue of Bessie Smith's was an event, and the *Chicago Defender* carried full-page advertisements to announce each of her latest recordings.

Chicago was a jumping, 'wide-open' city at this time: King Oliver was leading his newly-formed Dixie Syncopators at the Plantation Café with Tommy Ladnier playing second cornet; his past clarinettist, Johnny Dodds, had his own group at Kelly's Stables and his protegé, Louis Armstrong, had briefly returned from his stay with Henderson to play with Erskine Tate at the Vendome Theatre and doubling with his wife, Lil Armstrong, at the Dreamland Café.

Jimmy Wade, Charlie Elgar, Al Wynn, Doc Cook and Dave Peyton—soon to be musical correspondent for the *Defender*—were leading some of the exciting bands playing the most important resorts in the Windy City. Making a regal entry and staying for a suitably short period Bessie Smith visited the ballrooms and theatres. On her return to New York she made her first record with a full jazz band, a group drawn from Henderson's large orchestra and called Henderson's Hot Six in mute acknowledgment of the highly successful Louis Armstrong Hot Five. *Cake Walking Babies* and *The Yellow Dog Blues* were the outcome.

Made at a time when the full orchestra was working from careful arrangements the sides were played in a tradition remarkably evocative of the New Orleans style though only Charlie Green came from the Crescent City. Some four months before Clarence Williams' Blue Five with Charlie Irvis and Louis Armstrong made a remarkable recording of *Cake Walking Babies* taken at a fast tempo with Eva Taylor singing a rapid vocal refrain. Bessie takes the tune at a medium pace and her superiority as an artist is marked. Giving every line its fullest value she drawls the words, 'lifting them up and l-a-y-ing them do-own' with evident delight, whilst behind her a superbly integrated band plays with Joe Smith taking a perfectly timed break. A favourite of the day, W. C. Handy's blues is a classic in the jazz repertoire though Joseph C. Smith's version with its notorious 'laughing trombone' threatened to kill it in infancy. It is superbly introduced by Henderson's Hot Six with a half-chorus played ensemble, Joe Smith's cornet riding clear above the group. A clear stop, and Bessie begins to sing, her stresses falling strongly on the beat and her use of portamento so marked that the first line, 'Ever since Miss Suzie Johnson lost her Jockey Lee . . .' sounds as one extended word. Only part-literate, Bessie had to learn the words of her songs by heart and could not read them. Not infrequently she would make mistakes when singing a popular song or a composition that was not her own. These were sometimes through lack of comprehension, sometimes through lapses of memory and here, Handy's '. . . everywhere that Uncle Sam has even a rural delivery . . .' becomes '. . . everywhere that Uncle Sam is the ruler of delivery'. But at times she reformed the lines deliberately, inserted words or made caesural pauses with a conscious realization of their aesthetic value. Having chosen her words, correct or not, she sings them with wonderful effect, the inflexions of her voice extracting every ounce of music from the often simple melodies.

This session with Henderson's Hot Six was the first at which Columbia used electrical recording methods, and it is possibly the one which became a near fiasco through the enthusiastic theories of the recording engineer. Believing that the result would be acoustically superior he had the artists recording in a tent which was suspended from the ceiling by a single wire. Unfortunately the wire broke, enveloping the entire company in the billowing, collapsing canvas. Frank Walker has recently recalled that Don Redman and Henderson were at the session, but undoubtedly the incident occurred. Afterwards the theories of electrical recording were put on a sounder basis and Columbia proudly announced on the 14000 Race Series labels in sizzling letters the legend 'ELECTRICAL PROCESS'.

Photograph courtesy Sam Benjamin
'Any bootlegger sure is a pal of mine. . . .'
Snapshot *circa* 1934

321

A song about a woman who runs an illicit 'Buffet Flat' and wishes to keep the noise of the revelry from the ears of neighbours and police, *Soft Pedal Blues*, made on May 14th with Green and Henderson, is one of the few—possibly only two—of Bessie's records of which a second master was issued. It demonstrates the thoroughness with which she prepared her recordings and the apparent spontaneity of her recorded work is all the more remarkable when it becomes evident that she rehearsed every turn of phrase and studied every pause. She was a great artist and she knew it; as an artist of stature she realized the great importance of both her material and the means of its expression, finally creating the 'art that conceals art'—the impression that her work was extempore and required neither rehearsal nor practice. Even her exuberant 'hollers' on *Soft Pedal Blues* were virtually identical; a shade more vigorous on the rare first master perhaps. More noticeable than any changes in her presentation are the minor differences in the two accompaniments. But it was only a small technical fault that occasioned the remake.

Louis Armstrong's final sessions with Bessie Smith took place on May 26th and 27th, 1925, when Charlie Green

Photograph by Carl Van Vechten, courtesy Max Jones
'I'm dreary in mind and so worried in heart. . . .'
Bessie Smith at Carl Van Vechten's studio, 1936

322

joined Armstrong and Longshaw to accompany the singer. Green's trombone 'fill-in' phrases gave a firm foundation to *Careless Love* on which Bessie was in exceptionally fine voice. Her every line is picked up on the note by Louis who resolves the phrase with a brilliantly improvised extension. As in the canonical style of the call-and-response work songs at their best, there is often a slight overlap as Bessie leads into the next line, but never once is there a clash; neither does Louis falter in completing it. Between them there was a harmony as rare as any perfect relationship in jazz. Nearly two decades later in January, 1944, interviewer Fred Robbins on Station WHN talked to Louis Armstrong of Bessie's influence upon him. 'Bessie used to thrill me at all times,' said Louis. 'It's the way she could phrase a note in her blues, a certain something in her voice that no other singer could get. . . . She had really music in her soul and felt everything she did.' Possibly Louis himself was a shade too powerful a musical personality for Bessie: she remained more partial to Joe Smith.

In September she had one more date with Clara Smith, now fully developed as a singer. Discussing a mutual lover on the record they might well have been discussing their careers: 'I guess we got to have him on an instalment plan,' says Bessie. And so they seem to have come to a mutual agreement on their recording careers for in their combined output of nearly three hundred items they never duplicated their songs, *Shipwreck Blues*, the one title common to both, being two entirely different items.

That November, Bessie renewed acquaintance with Clarence Williams too, cutting a new version of her first session success in *New Gulf Coast Blues* and attempting her failure from the Okeh test, *Sister Kate*, and faring no better

than before. On the following day when she recorded *At the Christmas Ball* the usually reliable Joe Smith was far from on form and this too was withheld though it was released a score of years later. With the somewhat mysterious Shelton Hemphill, who imitated the surface effect of Louis Armstrong's phrases with some skill, Bessie's last session in 1925 produced only *Lonesome Desert Blues*. So the recording year which witnessed some of Bessie's finest work ended rather lamely; but on the stage she was still at her best.

Late in November, Bessie was appearing at the Orpheum Theatre, Newark, New Jersey, and it was there on the last Thursday of the month—the night of Thanksgiving Day—that Carl Van Vechten first saw her. Van Vechten, a wealthy white author-turned-photographer, was largely responsible for initiating the 'Negro Renaissance' of coloured writers with his novel, *Nigger Heaven*, which influenced such authors as Claude McKay and Jessie Fauset. His sensitive response to Bessie Smith's dramatic personality did much to interest white persons in her artistry. Dressed in a sequin-decorated robe of crimson satin she held the otherwise wholly Negro audience spellbound as she advanced towards them to the wails of muted brass and the beat of a drum. When she sang her blues in 'her plangent African voice, quivering with passion and pain', her audience responded with 'hysterical, semi-religious shrieks of sorrow and lamentation', answering her with 'Amens'. Later, Leigh Whipper, manager of the theatre and incidentally the Crabmeat Man in the first production of *Porgy and Bess*, took his friend Carl backstage to meet Bessie Smith. She received their mumbled words of admiration with regal deference. 'I believe I kissed her hand,' wrote Van Vechten years afterwards. 'I hope I did.'

4. 'LONG OLD ROAD'

'I've got those worst kind of Gin-house blues,' sang Bessie Smith.

There were many who had Bessie's interests at heart who were alarmed at her insatiable demand for gin. She now had the money with which she could afford to indulge in her weakness and neither her manager, Frank Walker, nor her husband could restrain her. Without doubt the back-

ground of extreme poverty, little parental guidance, tours with travelling shows, entertainments in gin-mills and rough taverns in which circumstances she had learned to protect herself, to drink and swear and fight, was now having its effect. Fame had come suddenly to Bessie Smith: a mere decade before she was a toe-dancing prodigy in a Minstrel show working for a dollar a day; now she could demand a thousand, fifteen hundred dollars for an engagement. When one of her records was issued she received an advance royalty of $1,000 and a five per cent royalty on sales after this figure had been passed. During this peak period of Bessie's popularity, assured of sales of 100,000 copies of any record within a week of issue the Columbia company could afford such terms to keep their artist. Pressed on laminations over a graphite and card centre their records were durable and were of superior acoustic quality. They asked and received seventy-nine cents each for them —at a time when other companies were retailing their discs at a third of the figure. Bessie's share of the total receipts meant a considerable income for her.

During 1926 she spent only five days in the recording studio; the rest of the time she was on tour, capitalizing on the success of her records. During the exceedingly bitter months early in the year she was back in Chicago in a package show which included a 'motion picture' entertainment, and the Negro comedian, Stepin Fetchit. But in March she had returned to Harlem, seeking talent for a forthcoming production and taking time off on the 5th to record four titles with Clarence Williams—including an exuberant *Squeeze Me*. Two weeks later she cut her disturbingly autobiographical *Gin House Blues* and a lively *Jazzbo Brown from Memphis Town* accompanied by a 'clarinet hound' playing in the near-hokum manner known as 'gaspipe style', who has been variously identified as Buster Bailey, Lorenzo Wardell and Garvin Bushell. Bessie's material was now altering considerably and she was drawing from novelty songs, jazz tunes and popular songs of the day to which she brought the musical expression of the blues.

Whatever she was singing, her material was the blues to Bessie. Often her songs were in themselves trite and commonplace but she raised them above the mediocrity of their content as she made them valid expressions of her own emotions. In all probability she would not have been as great a singer if she had not experienced so dramatic and bitter a life. As it was, her own perplexity, her dissatisfaction, her inability at times to cope with the change in circumstances of her fortunes sought expression in her singing. Her personal tragedy lay in the complexity of her character and the confusion that wealth and the acclaim of 'her people' had brought her. She knew that she was great; she

knew the responsibilities that she bore for her audiences; she knew she was the Queen, the Empress of the Blues. She bore herself in a manner befitting the title but her regal carriage stemmed fundamentally from her natural dignity and at heart she remained the girl whom Frank Walker had heard in the Selma dive.

There are no stories of Bessie at parties given by the *élite* in Negro entertainment, only stories of her impact upon those to whom and for whom she sang. She did not aspire to mix with show people nor with white persons; she did not marry a dancer, an actor, a singer, a manager but a policeman from the town where she had made her home. Money did not bring her happiness: in six months during 1926 she and her husband dissipated $16,000 but their extravagance created rather than solved problems. Not all Bessie's money was spent on herself and her husband. She was generous in an irresponsible way. She gave coins to the children who clamoured round the stage doors and gave liberally to those who were suffering periods of ill-fortune often out of all proportion to the circumstances. Bessie is credited with having purchased a house and given it to her friends for their use, but some less charitable persons have hinted at a strain of meanness in her character. She claimed to be fond of animals but her love of pets did not interfere with her liking for fur wraps, trimmings and fur coats. As in other fields there are many contradictions in her character. There are hints of a gentler, kinder woman beneath the hard-drinking, tough-talking figure: in the summer of 1926 Bessie was on tour when she heard that Frank Walker's son John was ill. To Frank Walker she was greatly indebted and she promptly suspended the rest of her tour, presenting herself to a surprised Mrs. Walker at her Long Island home, and insisting on acting as servant, maid and nurse until the two-year-old child was out of danger some three weeks later. Then, and only then, Bessie felt herself free to continue her interrupted tour. But even in this act of generosity there is a touch of the extreme which seems to characterize the woman.

On May 4th, Bessie made four recordings with Henderson and Joe Smith. Between the two Smiths there was a remarkable bond of musical sympathy and *Money Blues*, *Baby Doll*, *Hard Driving Papa*, and *Lost Your Head Blues* include some of the finest and most sensitive interpretations that Bessie ever made. The last title exemplifies

Bessie's artistry. A twelve-bar blues of conventional a–a–b verse form, it is fundamentally simple, but at no time does Bessie repeat herself in the handling of her lines. Every repetition of a line in the customary blues form is given an extension of meaning by the shift of emphasis that Bessie places on the words, whilst the melody is subtly remodelled to bring out the full significance of each verse, Joe Smith building instrumental variations on the vocal lines that the singer invents.

In the fall of 1926 Bessie's 'Harlem Frolic' company went on the road: from Ozark in Dale County, Alabama, to Eufala in Barbour County and on to Albany in Dougherty County, Georgia, touring the Deep South. Amongst her troupe were Dinah and Gertrude Scott, entertainers—the latter also acting as stage manager—Clarence Smith, Bessie's brother, and Morris Smith who was apparently no relation. Chief attraction apart from Bessie herself in the total company of forty was the 'bevy of dancing girls' whose bumps and grinds and high-stepping brought roars of appreciation from the country audiences deep 'in the sticks'. 'Professor' Bill Woods led the band which included Alvin Moss, Lorenzo Wardell, Joe Williams and Buster Johnson backing Bessie as she sang in the vast tent which reputedly held 1,500 people. Her tour followed the network of southern railroad lines for she proudly transported her troupe in an eighty-foot Pullman car of the most modern design which had seven state rooms and accommodation for thirty-five other members of the company. And emblazoned on its side was a scroll with the legend 'Jackie Gee' after whom the car was named.

Whilst on tour Bessie may well have witnessed the seasonal floods on the Mississippi, whose constant recurrence is inevitable. Levees are built to control the waters and breaches are made in them to flood certain areas known as 'backwaters' which are considered expendable, in order to relieve the total pressure. In the worst flooding hundreds of people are rendered homeless, and the coloured folk working the bottom-land plantations are among the principal victims. Returning to Chicago in December, Bessie moved on to New York early in 1927 to record on February 17th one of the most moving blues of her career, *Back Water Blues*, which told of the miseries of the floods. Playing on his first session with Bessie the imaginative James P. Johnson creates musical pictures that illustrate her words, rolling the thunder in the bass as she sings of the five days of rain, making an image of the splashing water as she tells of being rescued in a boat and conjuring an impression of the scene when she sings of climbing a hill out of the flooded areas. It is no mere imitation; Johnson's breaks are brilliantly formulated improvisations that perfectly resolve Bessie Smith's blues lines. There was only one 'take' as in nearly all the best products of Bessie's greatest partnerships, and as the blues closes with a moaning humming chorus and Bessie declares that 'there ain't no place for a poor old girl to go' the final notes come crashing into place with terrible finality.

Back Water Blues was strangely prophetic for it anticipated the terrible disaster of 1927, the worst in recorded history, when the arrival of the Ohio floods and the appearance of the Missouri floods at the confluence of the Mississippi coincided. Before they came, however, Bessie also recorded a popular song of the utmost banality, *Muddy Water* which actually expresses a sentimental regard and nostalgia for the swirling waters on the 'Swanee shore'. Between April and June thousands of people were the victims of the floods and according to Big Bill Broonzy the talent scout, Mayo Williams, chartered a boat for a number of blues singers to witness them. Including Lonnie Johnson, Kansas Joe McCoy, Springback James, Sippie Wallace and Broonzy himself the party was joined by Bessie Smith. If his memory served him correctly she did see the worst of the flooding, and some support is found in her *Homeless Blues* of September 28th, in which she specifically refers to it:

> 'My ma and pa was drownded, Mississippi you're to blame, (*twice*)
> Mississippi, I can't stand to hear your name. . . .'

During the year Bessie made a number of sides which showed a trend in her work that was moving away from the blues tradition in spite of these other essentially blues recordings. *Muddy Water* was one of four popular songs which she recorded on March 2nd. Subtitled *A Mississippi Moan* in spite of the 'Swanee shore' reference, it presented a few difficulties for her as the two masters that were issued illustrate, but somehow she managed to introduce some feeling into the singing of the lyrics. Supported by her band, which included Smith, Henderson, Jimmy Harrison and, on certain titles, Buster Bailey and Coleman Hawkins, she sings *After You've Gone* with an *élan* which is not shared by them. On *Alexander's Ragtime Band* they swing in fine style and in response to Bessie's 'Listen to the bugle call!' during the repeat of the chorus Joe Smith plays the hottest bugle call that ever summoned a body of men. He makes a momentary mistake in the selection of the key in the veteran tune of the Spanish-American War, *There'll be a Hot Time in the Old Town Tonight*, but the tune is played and sung with tremendous gusto, Henderson playing a splendid piano lead-in to the ensemble after Bessie's first chorus. Perhaps they did not establish Bessie as a singer of popular songs but these recordings proved her to be unrivalled as a jazz singer.

Next day Green, Smith and Henderson—Bessie's 'Blue Boys'—met to make four more titles, including the rare *Hot Springs Blues* and the rather improbable *Send Me to the 'Lectric Chair*. The first item was a eulogy of Charlie Green's playing as he 'wails and moans, he grunts and groans, he moans just like a cow'. 'His playing would even make a king get off his throne,' says Bessie, 'and he would break a leg I know, doin' the Charleston while you blow . . .' and 'Big' Green responds with vigorous slurs and slides, growling and roaring his way through the tune until Joe Smith takes over with a smooth chorus that is a perfect foil and an equally valid interpretation. Presumably the title of *Trombone Cholly* should have been *Trombone Charlie* but there may well have been a joke amongst the group here, for in Negro slang a 'cholly' is a hobo or tramp. Happy and in splendid form here, this was an ill-fated group. In a car crash only a year after the recording in which all were involved bar Bessie, Henderson was injured in the head suffering damage to the brain that caused him to lose both his sense of responsibility and his ambition. Joe Smith died in a mental asylum a few months after Bessie was killed in a road accident, whilst Charlie Green froze to death on a Harlem doorstep, a starving 'cholly'.

That summer Bessie had a highly successful season in Chicago, playing the 'Big Grand' Theatre at 3110 State Street. Uptown Ethyl Waters was appearing at the Palace Theatre before a white audience who appreciated her sweeter style, but Bessie's audiences were drawn from the throng that paraded the 'hottest stretch in the world' between 31st and 35th on State. She was riding high on a wave of popularity and her best records were selling half a million copies. Her shows were certain successes. During the late 'twenties she had many, though they were often essentially the same show: refurbished, the acts freshened a little, the choruses changed somewhat as the girls became married or were absorbed by others in the highly competitive entertainment world. The 'Scandals', the 'Frolics', the 'Vanities', and the 'Classy, Snappy Novelties' were virtually interchangeable titles which were applied with cheerful liberality to the vaudeville-burlesque-musical shows which Bessie no less than other principal artists organized. These were the days when white 'flapperettes' and 'collegiates' were following Eddie Cantor's lead and were 'Making Whoopee' to the music of coloured and white 'Novelty Jazz Bands'. Recording for Cameo were the 'Whoopee Makers' and Bessie exploited the current fad as she took her 'Whoopee Girls' with a chorus of pretty coloured girls known ironically as 'the clothes-line' through the Southern and Mid-West States.

Returning to New York in September she added another major recording success to her list with *Mean Old Bed Bug Blues*, an extravagant blues which attributed to the bedbug the wit and resource that an older Negro ballad had endowed the boll-weevil. It was backed with Eddie Green's lusty vaudeville song, *A Good Man is Hard to Find* and in Porter Grainger Bessie found another accompanist who could partner her to perfection. Her last session that year was with Ma Rainey's favourite trumpeter, Tommy Ladnier, and it is to be regretted that it was her only date with the footloose musician. A master of instrumental blues, he played with feeling rarely equalled on record when he backed her on *Dyin' by the Hour* and the broad sweep of the singer's majestic phrases and the distress in her voice is echoed in his agonized muted trumpet work.

So 1927 passed. Bessie was at the peak of her fame, adored and admired by the Negro people. But there were many persons who watched her behaviour with trepidation. She was becoming increasingly difficult to please; when she was sober she was agreeable enough, but when she had been drinking she became irascible, temperamental, and her drinking sprees were ever more frequent. Often she was drunk on the stage and she had to be propped against a chair or some other article of stage furniture whilst she sang her blues. When the curtains closed she had to be half-carried from the stage, scarcely hearing in her drunken state the applause of the audience. But she seldom arrived at the recording studio other than coldly sober and if there was a hint that she had been drinking Frank Walker would call off the session rather than have her record in that state. To many, as to May Wright Johnson, 'she was rough'. Eager to shout, to fight, to draw attention to herself, she ex-pended her money wilfully and argued bitterly with Frank Walker when he tried to control her expenditure. Exceedingly fond of her in spite of the arguments Walker encouraged her to buy a house in Philadelphia and to put away $20,000 so that when the crash came, as he believed it would, she would not be a complete victim of her own excesses.

5. 'WOMAN'S TROUBLE BLUES'

It was not until February, 1928, that Bessie Smith was again in the recording studio and by this time the increasingly unpredictable changes in her temper had lost her many friends. She had broken with Fletcher Henderson who was never to accompany her again, whilst her favourite trumpeter stayed with him. Dissatisfied with Frank Walker's careful control over her financial affairs and the material that she used she broke with him likewise. He continued to supervise her recording sessions but he was no longer her manager. Now she elected to choose and write much of her material and her affairs were managed by her husband, the ex-policeman Jackie Gee, whose knowledge of show business was limited to the experience he had gained with her. Of her favourite instrumentalists of former years only Charlie Green remained, though her erstwhile musical director, Fred Longshaw, continued to work with her for a month or two. Green and Longshaw accompanied her on her first session that year and they were joined by a strong trumpet player whose identity has not been satisfactorily established: Henry Mason has been suggested but Deamus Dean seems a more likely accompanist. An undistinguished example in the traditional form, *Thinking Blues* is transformed by the wealth of feeling that Bessie puts into its ordinary lyrics into a blues of some significance. Coming a fractional pause after the conclusion of each line sung, Dean's breaks with their short stabbing thrusts have none of the continuity of emotional sympathy that made the parts played by Smith, Armstrong or Ladnier such brilliant interpretations of the mood that Bessie had created. *I Used To Be Your Sweet Mamma* on the other hand, is played with greater cohesion by the group though the timing is stiff and does not allow the singer the freedom to sing in a cross-rhythm over the riff background, forcing her instead to chop her words into three-beat sections.

During the year Bessie made a number of experimental sides with trio support by piano and clarinets or saxophones, but the support is not always in accord with her singing and these do not constitute her best work. *Spider Man Blues*, for example, is accompanied by Bob Fuller on alto sax and Abraham Wheat on clarinet. The instrumental breaks at the conclusion of the lines have been rehearsed to the point where the instrumentalists play identically and in chorus, leaving no room for spontaneous improvisatory ideas on the theme. Next day, March 20th, Bessie recorded one of her most notable—or notorious—items. Her material had always been of a robust, sometimes even pornographic nature for her Southern audiences, and now she committed such items to wax. It is to the credit of the folk blues that its treatment of sexual themes is frank and uncompromising, avoiding the arch and suggestive insinuations of much popular song that result from the marked puritanical strain that pervades American society. But *Empty Bed Blues* was clearly directed at a market seeking a vicarious satisfaction from pornographic recordings. Its rich but unsubtle imagery does not result from a fundamentally innocent expression of libidinous instincts as may be noticed in many folk blues. Extended over two 'sides' it enjoyed a *succès de scandale* only paralleled by Lizzie Miles's recording of *My Man of War*. Such numbers are known in the entertainment world as 'point numbers', and few must have as many points as those exploited in *Empty Bed Blues*; but it is superbly sung and Bessie's gusto diminishes the offence that it might cause. Grainger stomps his piano accompaniment and Charlie Green's witty comments on trombone add an engaging humour to the record. Altogether it was a roisterous session producing *Put it Right Here (Or Keep It Out There)* a song with similar implications though it purports to be a sharp admonition to a man who fails to provide for his partner, that animals are more faithful—a commonplace comparison which an excess of anthropological enthusiasm has linked with 'African songs of derision'. In an unusual arrangement Bessie even sings one recitative chorus in 'stop time' without instrumental backing, and elsewhere is happy with the support of Green and Grainger, feeling free to take liberties with the tempo against the broad, unerring pace they set.

Though many of the titles she sang still bore the suffix 'blues', there were noticeably fewer items that were truly within the blues vein included in Bessie's repertoire in 1928. *Poor Man's Blues* represented a rare return to social comment and criticism, but it is far from convincing as a blues, tending to sentimentalize the 'poor man who fought all the battles' and would 'do anything for the U.S.A.' Already the threat of the Depression was in the air, but the blues is seldom rhetorical and seldom moralizes; 'If it wasn't for the poor man, Mister Rich Man, what would you do?' strikes a false note. It is Bessie's conviction as she sings that gives *Poor Man's Blues* its strength. Joe Williams, sounding remarkably like Charlie Green, joined Ernest 'Sticky' Elliott, Bob Fuller and Porter Grainger on this date in late August and was with Grainger on her last recording date of the year, the following day. Delighting in her personal vice Bessie sang:

'I don't want no clothes and I don't need no bed, (*twice*)
I don't want no pork chops, just give me gin instead.'

There was little exaggeration in *Me and My Gin* for Bessie was now drinking the liquor by the tumblerful. When she went to a party at Carl Van Vechten's apartment on West 55th Street, New York, she demanded a drink on entering and forthwith downed a glass holding nearly a pint of gin. Porter Grainger took her to the party which was promoted by Van Vechten and Fania Marinoff and to which George Gershwin, Constance Collier and Marguerite d'Alvarez and other persons distinguished in the arts had been invited. 'I attended many of these parties and the "Intellectual Stink" could have been cut with a knife—a dull

knife,' commented the Negro cartoonist, E. Simms Campbell, but he did less than justice to Van Vechten whose sensitivity to Negro thought and whose inspiration to coloured writers was real and informed. Perhaps the invitation of Bessie Smith to the party hints at novelty, but if so, she hardly cared. With Grainger at the piano she sang the blues. 'The real thing: a woman cutting her heart open with a knife until it was exposed for us all to see. . . .' later recalled Van Vechten.

Now she had reason to sing the blues. Still great, and still making her Southern tours with profitable returns she was yet becoming something of an anachronism. The prospect of an engagement on Broadway at Connie's Inn excited her. It lasted three days. A serious blow to her pride, the failure of her performance hurt her deeply. Subtly, insidiously the change was taking place and the phonograph which had aided her popularity also furthered her decline for it brought other, more sophisticated musical forms to the remoter districts. The disparity between the tastes of the South and the arts of the cities became less, and the influence of radio was even more marked. Just as the gramophone reduced the popularity of the piano player and markedly contributed to the decline in ragtime, so radio brought an end to vaudeville. Reducing the great distances to a moment in time the radio brought a slicker, wisecracking humour in place of the vaudeville routines and smoother, sophisticated and sentimental songs replaced those of the past. There remained in the South a certain demand for the 'Down Home' blues of the Southern Country singer and in the cities the brash expression of the urban singers still appealed. But the classic blues singers who had married the blues with the vaudeville stage lost their popularity.

Already Bessie Smith was facing the changing tastes of her public and was beginning to find the battle an unequal one. Her records were no longer selling well and Columbia were slow in summoning her to the studio, an interval of eight months, the longest in her recording career, elapsing before she was again recorded. Porter Grainger was no longer with her but her old companion, Clarence Williams, returned to accompany her, bringing with him a white guitarist who was singular in appearing with a number of 'Race' artists, Eddie Lang. A few days previously he had made his celebrated and much-disputed session with Blind

Willie Dunn's Gin Bottle Four. Recalling the success of *Empty Bed Blues*, Bessie made three sides with Lang and Williams which deliberately exploited their pornographic content. 'Race' terminology appears here and there in *I'm Wild About That Thing*, but such pathetic words as, 'I'm wild about that thing, yell out jing, jing, jing . . .' give the lie to their inclusion. Of similar quality is *You've Got To Give Me Some* with its animal comparisons, whilst the final number, *Kitchen Man*, though distinguished with a better tune is remarkable primarily for the extreme crudity of its metaphors. Though such material has its apologists it is hard to justify the sad stuff of these songs and the methodical manner in which they were bracketed together and purveyed. Did Bessie enjoy recording such material? She was too much of an artist not to give of her best in all she did, however poor the content, but a few weeks later she recorded an item of such poignancy and intensity of expression that her true feelings seem to have been represented in it.

Nobody Knows You When You're Down and Out is one of the outstanding performances on disc of Bessie's career, being a recording of a song that she had learned from the Negro entertainer, Jimmy Fox, when she worked with him many years before on the T.O.B.A. circuit. It is probably true to say that Bessie Smith had innumerable admirers, many worshippers and relatively few friends. Her uncertain demeanour, her unpredictable temper and her tendency to dipsomania made her at best an unreliable friend. Those who had known her for the longest periods: Frank Walker, Clarence Williams, Fletcher Henderson, Joe Smith, Charlie Green and James P. Johnson, who had seen her develop as an artist and had worked with her in lean and in glorious days, were tolerant and understanding when others could not cope with her temperament. As times became harder Bessie grew into an embittered woman. *Nobody Knows You When You're Down and Out* is a song about one who has 'led the life of a millionaire', spending money liberally on her friends, only to find herself friendless when her money has gone and in it is reflected to a disquieting degree the story of Bessie herself. 'It's mighty strange, without a doubt,' she sang, and she remained puzzled and hurt for the rest of her life. She closes the song with a chorus half-hummed, half-sung; a reflective chorus seemingly addressed more to herself than to the listener,

when, one imagines, her eyes were closed and her brow furrowed; a chorus in which her injured feelings are deeply manifest. She received a wholly sympathetic support in the throaty, blue cornet playing of Ed Allen, whilst the deep notes of Cyrus St. Clair's tuba are solemn, even ominous.

In happier frame of mind is *Put it Right Back (Cause I Don't Want It Here)*, a backward-glancing vaudeville song which is in the style of the great entertainers, Butterbeans and Susie, though it is sung solo. In August and October, Bessie made some ten titles with her old associate, the 'Dean of Harlem', James P. Johnson, eight of them being issued. Happy in his company she sang lustily on *He's Got Me Going* and the pianist romps merrily behind her voice. But the tenor of the majority of the titles is somewhat disturbing, hinting at a major crisis in her life. 'Did you ever fall in love with a man that was no good; no matter what you did for him he never understood?' she asks on *Dirty No-Gooder's Blues* and the blues closes with a despairing verse in which she repeats the word 'Lawd' with a dozen different inflexions and as many shades of meaning. The session-mate is virtually a popular ballad but the refrain of *Wasted Life Blues* running, 'Oh me, oh my, wonder what will my end be?' is not without significance. Her mood reached its most morbid in *Blue Spirit Blues*, the grimmest of the constantly recurring items obsessed with death which appeared in her repertoire from her recording of *Cemetery Blues* in 1923. It may not rival Dante's imagery in its description of a dreamed descent into Hell but the 'mean blue spirits' that 'stuck their forks in me, made me moan and groan in misery' are realized in ugly detail. Then, callously, she sings a blues of harsh rejection in *Worn Out Papa Blues* and her confidence is temporarily restored.

Jack Gee had assumed not only the responsibility of being Bessie's husband but that of being her manager too, and proved unequal to the task. There was little left of the considerable fortune that Bessie had made from the sale of eight to ten million records, but together they invested in a new show called *The Midnight Steppers* which Gee managed. Fortunately they had the generous help of James P. Johnson in the presentation of the show and when they took it on the road it proved to be one of the most successful of Bessie's career. Jimmy Johnson had the perspicacity to see the way in which the entertainment industry was

329

developing and it was he who led the band when a film was made of W. C. Handy's *St. Louis Blues.*

A scenario for *St. Louis Blues* had been written by Handy in collaboration with Kenneth W. Adams and this was submitted to the RCA Photophone Company. It was agreed that a two-reel short be made under the production of Dudley Murphy who later made his name as the director of Eugene O'Neill's famous play, *The Emperor Jones.* At a Carnegie Hall concert a year or two before, Handy had directed the orchestra and J. Rosamund Johnson the choir of voices for the first presentation of James P. Johnson's folk opera, *Yamekraw.* The partnership had been a happy one and was renewed for the film, whilst Bessie Smith, who had received early inspiration from Handy and was currently in association with Johnson, was naturally chosen to take the lead part. J. Rosamund Johnson led a mixed chorus of forty-two voices and James P. Johnson led the band which included, to Bessie's delight, Joe Smith on trumpet. Thomas Morris also played trumpet, Happy Cauldwell, tenor saxophone and Kaiser Marshall, drums. A spoken narrative, the large chorus and the use of a crystal microphone did little for Bessie's voice when she sang and the sound recording was poor. Somewhat melodramatic the film showed the singer being struck to the ground, kicked and beaten by a parasitic lover named 'St. Louis Jimmy'— no relation to blues singer, James Clark, who later recorded under this name. In a rich, deep, controlled voice she pleads with her lover to little avail. In a short dress, tight fitting at the hips and top-heavy in its loose, baggy shapelessness across the breast, and wearing an ugly, brimless mob-cap, the singer who could wear clothes so well looks far from at her best in the chosen attire. Something of Bessie's greatness survives the plot, the script, the soundtrack and the presentation, but the film does little justice either to her or to W. C. Handy.

Considered too 'uninhibited' at the time, the film was not released, being rejected by the Hays Office, but its technical limitations may well have accounted for its continued non-release. Forgotten for years, a copy of the film was eventually discovered in Mexico and private showings have since been given at the Museum of Modern Art, New York, the Oakland Rey Theatre, San Francisco and the National Film Theatre, London. A rumour persists that a film was made of James P. Johnson's *Yamekraw* with Bessie taking a leading part, but if this was so, no copy has been found. With all its faults *St. Louis Blues* remains the only visual record of Bessie Smith at work.

6. 'DYIN' BY THE HOUR'

In 1930 Bessie Smith was only thirty-two years of age, but like a professional boxer she had put the best years of her active life behind her. Unlike a boxer, however, she could not accept the fact and she had not budgeted for a decline in her powers or her popularity. Unable to counter the change in popular taste or to meet the devastating effects of the Depression on the entertainment industry, she was left in severe financial straits. 1930 also saw her permanent separation from her husband. Happy enough when Bessie was at the height of popular favour they could not survive together the difficult period into which they had been precipitated, for the incompatibility of their temperaments weakened their ability to fight. Their parting was fortunately made less bitter by the lack of recriminations and harsh words, and they remained good friends until Bessie's death.

Columbia retained Bessie longer on their artist's file than they did many another singer, though Clara Smith's contract with the company lasted four months longer than Bessie's. Just three records of Bessie Smith were issued in 1930; a further coupling was made with Clarence Williams and Charlie Green but it did not appear until a decade after her death. In the company of Johnny Dunn's sideman, Garvin Bushell and the trumpeter, Louis Bacon, who was soon to make his reputation with Chick Webb's band, Bessie made with Charlie Green and Clarence Williams a couple of sides that March. *New Orleans Hop Scop Blues* was written by a pianist from the Crescent City, George Thomas, and on this Louis Bacon plays excellently in a relaxed, open style, clearly influenced by Louis Armstrong. Clarence Williams stomps in chords one moment, plays a boogie eight-to-the-bar chorus and ends with decorative figures that recall Morton. Bessie herself has the warmth of her teacher, Ma Rainey, when singing her *Ma Rainey's Black Bottom* a couple of years before: she shouts and roars her way through the song with a fierce intensity that refuses to believe that all is far from well. Nonetheless she made a rare departure in June when she recorded two pseudo-spirituals with James P. Johnson and the Bessemer Singers, allowing a group to share the vocal honours. Remarking on church 'backbiters' Bessie declares that she wants to know 'what . . . I mean, *who* is biting *me* on the back', making the recording a mockery of a spiritual and disclaiming her alleged devotion to the Church. She sings well but her record does not compare with the remarkable and moving versions of *Livin' Humble* and *Get On Board* that Clara Smith made with Lemuel Fowler and Sisters White and Wallace.

Late in July, Bessie made her final two sides with Ed. Allen who complimented her with his customary sensitivity. Her voice had coarsened somewhat and she produced a growl from her throat which Allen echoed with guttural notes on his muted instrument. Some five years before, Bessie made a recording of *J. C. Holmes Blues* which was based on the ballad of *Casey Jones*; now she remodelled *Stackolee* in the form of *Hustlin' Dan* and in a similar mood of exaggeration which is part of the American folk tradition, parodied a tough mountain community of Paul Bunyans in her *Black Mountain Blues*. Clearly aimed at widely differing markets, the recordings of 1930 failed to recoup any lost ground for Bessie, and Columbia pressed few copies in comparison with the abundant release of her past successes. Even for a disc by Bessie there were now few Negroes who could afford to pay a sum equivalent to two dollars by present-day standards.

There were fewer persons who could afford to hear Bessie sing in person: she was prepared to consider any engagement that was offered. A Negro musical was planned that year for New York's Belmont Theatre and Bessie put in many hours of work on rehearsals. The show folded after the second night. Road shows were scarcely paying their way but Bessie barnstormed her way southwards, shouting her blues in tumbledown theatres and under leaking canvas roofs. Her voice was beginning to crack.

Gin and the Depression had left their mark when Bessie returned to the recording studio on June 11th, 1931. The mellowness of her voice on early recordings was gone: it was harsh now, there was a brittle edge to her words and she used a guttural, throaty intonation that gave a rasping texture to her blues. To many enthusiasts of jazz this grittier quality to her voice is no indication of decline, and they equate it with the 'dirty' tone of the growl trumpet. Such a voice is easier to copy, imparting to a second-rate voice a superficial 'blueness' through its lack of the sweet tones generally associated with the singing of songs more sentimental, less earthy than the blues. Paradoxically the period when Bessie's voice was at its poorest has been the period most admired by her imitators. But there was less music in her voice, less warmth, less light and shade, though the sheer strength and volume, the ferocity and violence of her expression coupled with those inflexions of blues shading that had become second nature to her does impart a compelling power to such recordings as *In the House Blues*. She sings though as one who has a grievance; 'Cain't eat, cain't sleep, so weak I cain't even walk my floor,' she roars in a voice that belies her words. There is conviction in her voice when she sings, 'O-ooh the blues have got me on the go; they run roun' the house and out of my front door.' A 'Novelty Orchestra' comprising Clarence Williams, Charlie Green, Louis Bacon and Floyd Casey is the wildest, the roughest that ever supported her. This is a very different Louis Bacon and an altogether more searing Charlie Green who contribute to an atmosphere that threatens a disintegration which somehow never occurs. It is a group that is perfectly related to Bessie's harassed yet defiant state of mind as she sings 'I got to make it, I got to find the end' of the *Long Old Road*. Disorganization does occur in the last item of the session when a tiring Bessie loses the twelve-bar form and lets the ragged band complete it.

November 20th, 1932, might well have witnessed Bessie's last appearance on record. On that date she was accompanied by an unknown pianist—perhaps Joe Turner, the pupil of James P. Johnson—and the song, *Need a Little Sugar in My Bowl*, was a sadly pornographic number. *Safety Mamma*, which advocated drug addiction as a method of ensuring a man's fidelity, bears evidence of the singer's flagging energies, her voice having lost its strength and her deep breathing being distinctly audible. As it happened, it was not her last session, for a further date was initiated by the young critic, John Hammond, who arranged it as part of a scheme to supply English Parlophone with jazz recordings. Four songs in the true vaudeville tradition were written by Wesley 'Kid Sox' Wilson of the celebrated Grant and Wilson team, whilst another veteran of vaudeville, Buck Washington of 'Buck and Bubbles' playing piano led a mixed coloured and white group which included Frank Newton, Jack Teagarden, Chu Berry, Billy Taylor and Bobby Johnson. Just two years had passed; the date was November 24th, 1933, and Bessie had apparently recuperated to a considerable extent. She revelled in the Harlem slang and racy atmosphere of *Gimme a Pigfoot* and Frankie Newton backed her splendidly, his fiery trumpet emitting sudden bursts of burning notes. For the rest, the accompaniment on the side, which included a totally ineffectual Benny Goodman on clarinet, was turgid and remained so on the other titles except for the moments when Jack Teagarden overcame his awe. Bessie and Newton worked away oblivious to the rest—the singer earning the fifty dollars a side that she was paid.

Thrilled by being in the studio again, Bessie had plans for another recording session and from the repertoire of Grant and Wilson selected *Hot Papa, That's Out*; *Groundhog Blues*, and *Lonesome River Blues* for her numbers. But the session did not materialize and the sadly titled *I'm Down in the Dumps* was the last that the world was to hear on record of Bessie Smith.

'Twenty-five cents? Huh! I wouldn't pay twenty-five cents to go in nowhere!' cried Bessie on *Gimme a Pigfoot*. Doubtless the irony amused her for she was forced to ask the sum at the rent-parties that she was obliged to hold when she was 'cold in hand'. The last half-dozen years of her life were spent in tragic decline. As Joseph Oliver, who was once the 'King', stumbled downhill to eventual misery as a vegetable seller and poolroom attendant, so Bessie Smith, who once was 'Empress', came to selling chewing gum and candy in theatre aisles. She had brief periods of hope: moments when it seemed that success might once more be within her grasp when she was engaged to play in a Harlem Show or at a coast resort. An engagement at Manhattan's Kit Kat Club promised well but turned out to be a failure. Now Bessie was obliged to accept parts in seedy night-club cabarets where, dressed in a long gingham dress, an apron and a kerchief tied about her head to represent that evergreen of American sentiment, the lovable Negro 'mammy', she sang 'coon songs'. At other times she was submerged in the obscurity of cellar clubs to sing porno-

graphic numbers to the *habitués* of 'drag parties', her blues forgotten.

On occasion a barnstorming tour with a travelling show took her far from home; took her to Fort Worth in 1934 where, at the Fat Stock Show the troupe that she was with clashed with the visit of the Haines Carnival which featured no less a person than her mentor of twenty years before, Ma Rainey, temporarily out of retirement and singing to the guitar of Aaron 'T-Bone' Walker. It must have been a meeting of many mixed sentiments.

Back to Harlem and occasional Sunday afternoon visits to jam sessions on 52nd Street when Bunny Berigan would play trumpet behind her, and even in these moments of fading glory, Eddie Condon, Pee Wee Russell, Jack Teagarden or Mezz Mezzrow would listen entranced. A 'Blues and Jazz Concert' at the 'Famous Door' on 52nd Street in February, 1936, brought her, bedecked in furs, before an enthusiastic audience. Half forgotten though her blues may have been her performance was too overpowering for Mildred Bailey who refused to sing after her. 1936 brought her an engagement in a show at Connie's Inn which lasted over six weeks and gave her renewed hope for the future. To a *Defender* reporter she prophesied a change in her fortunes and she was scheduled, she said, for a long tour of De Luxe Theatres for Paramount, Loew and R.K.O. She would retire in 1960. . . .

Apparently the tour did not materialize but prospects seemed brighter as 1937 progressed. Another recording session was being planned; a new film was in the offing; she was invited to star in Winstead's *Broadway Rastus Show*. Late in September she was driven down to join the show in Memphis. Early on Sunday morning of September 26th the automobile was speeding along the highway near Coahoma when it crashed into the rear of a truck parked by the roadside. In the wreckage lay the semi-conscious body of Bessie Smith, her head mutilated and her arm nearly torn from her body. The circumstances of the crash have never been satisfactorily explained and the cruel accident has been the vehicle for much racial propaganda, much sentiment and perhaps much 'whitewashing' too. It has been stated that Bessie died from loss of blood after she had been refused treatment as a Negro at a white hospital. Another version states that she was admitted but died through exposure in a cold waiting-room whilst white injured were treated first. Of a dozen versions perhaps the most likely is the report that a prominent—but unnamed—Memphis surgeon was passing the scene of the accident and stopped to render aid. Whilst trying to lift the 200-lb. body of the singer into his car his own vehicle was struck by oncoming traffic and destroyed. An ambulance summoned by another unknown person arrived a few minutes later and the mortally wounded Bessie was taken to the Negro Ward of the nearest hospital, the G. T. Thomas Hospital at Clarksdale, Mississippi. One of the best surgeons there is said to have amputated her arm, but the severe injuries that she had suffered to her face, head, and internal organs caused her death at a quarter-past noon on the same day. Her body was brought by her brother Clarence to Philadelphia and there interred.

Bitterly tragic in itself, it is shameful that the death of Bessie Smith has been exploited in racial recriminations, but it is understandable. The origins in poverty, the rise to the heights of her profession, the years of success, the search for an elusive happiness, the fall from fame, the final years of hope and disappointment working in squalid shows, the sudden brutal end at the moment when recovery seemed possible: the life and death of Bessie Smith has all the elements of high drama and of great tragedy. As an historic figure alone she has heroic stature, but her importance in jazz music far exceeds the facts of her life. She was the inspiration of almost everyone who heard her and the majestic sweep of her phrases, the grandeur of her singing had the expression commensurate with the creation of great art. Her life was both glorious and hard, but the pleasure and the pain that she experienced in her life ran the gamut of emotions and it was her great gift not only to feel deeply but also to be able to give voice to her feelings, investing her material, whether popular song or twelve-bar blues, with a profundity and universality of meaning that made it as applicable to the lives of her hearers as it was for herself. And her means, her vehicle, was the language of jazz with all its strength, its simplicity, its freedom from orthodoxy. Bessie Smith was Preachin' the Blues to all the world if the world cared to hear. Of the music of 'her people' she said, 'Preach them blues, sing them blues, they certainly sound good to me.' And to those who would listen she sings still, 'Moan them blues, holler them blues, let me convert your soul.'

ABBREVIATED BIBLIOGRAPHY

No book devoted exclusively to the work of Bessie Smith has hitherto existed, and the reports on her career are frequently conflicting in their details. The most valuable source of material in the form of personal recollections of the singer is the September, 1947, issue, No. 58, of *Jazz Record*, which was largely devoted to memories of the singer. The files of the *Chicago Defender* from 1920 until 1937 are another important source and still closer examination may reveal further data. Of currently available literature, George Hoefer's essay on Bessie Smith in *The Jazz Makers* is the most complete account. Principal sources examined during the preparation of the present work are outlined in brief below.

Chicago Defender	*Jazz Music*
Discophile	*Jazz Record*
Downbeat	*Melody Maker*
Hot Notes	*Playback*
Jazzfinder	*Record Changer*
Jazz Journal	*Record Research*
Jazz Monthly	

REFERENCE BOOKS

An Anthology of the Blues by W. C. Handy
Basic Jazz on Long Play by John Lucas
Dictionary of Jazz by Hugues Panassie and M. Gauthier

Encyclopaedia of Jazz by Leonard Feather
Esquire Jazz Book, 1946. Edited by Paul Edward Miller
Father of the Blues by W. C. Handy

Hear Me Talkin' to Ya. Edited by Nat Hentoff and Nat Shapiro

His Eye Is On the Sparrow by Ethyl Waters

Jazz Directory by Albert McCarthy and Dave Carey

Jazzmen by Frederick Ramsey, Jnr. and others

Jazz New Orleans, 1885–1957, by Samuel B. Charters

Really the Blues by Mezz Mezzrow and Bernard Wolfe

Shining Trumpets by Rudi Blesh

The Jazz Makers. Edited by Nat Hentoff and Nat Shapiro

We Called it Music by Eddie Condon and Thomas Sugrue

Bessie Smith Story. Vols 1–4. L.P. recordings. Sleeve notes by George Avakian

SELECTED DISCOGRAPHY OF BESSIE SMITH

It has been said that Bessie Smith never made a bad record and though there was some deterioration in her later sides the truth of the statement remains. All of the following titles are currently available in the five 2-record long-playing Columbia albums that comprise "The Bessie Smith Story":

Any Woman's Blues	G 30126
Empty Bed Blues	G 30450
The Empress	G 30818
Nobody's Blues But Mine	G 31093
World's Greatest Blues Singer	GP 33

All recordings were made in New York City.

Instrument key: (*alt*) alto saxophone; (*bj*) banjo; (*bs*) string bass; (*cnt*) cornet; (*clt*) clarinet; (*d*) drums; (*g*) guitar; (*p*) piano; (*tbn*) trombone; (*ten*) tenor saxophone; (*tpt*) trumpet; (*vln*) violin; (*acc*) accompanied by.

February 16, 1923
acc Clarence Williams (*p*).

Down Hearted Blues	GP 33
(80863-5)	

SEPTEMBER 21, 1923
acc Irving Johns (*p*).

Jailhouse Blues	
(81226-2)	G 30126

APRIL 5, 1924
acc Robert Robbins (*vln*); Irving Johns (*p*).

Ticket Agent Ease Your Window Down	
(81671-3)	G 30450

SEPTEMBER 26, 1924
acc Joe Smith (*cnt*); Charlie Green (*tbn*); Fletcher Henderson (*p*).

Weeping Willow Blues	
(140062-2)	G 30450

JANUARY 14, 1925
acc Louis Armstrong (*cnt*); Fred Longshaw (*harmonium*).

St. Louis Blues	
(140241-1)	G 30818
Reckless Blues	
(140242-1)	G 30818

Longshaw switches to *p*.

Sobbin' Hearted Blues	
(140249-2)	G 30818
Cold in Hand Blues	
(140250-2)	G 30818
You've Been a Good Old Wagon	
(140251-1)	G 30818

MAY 5, 1925
acc HENDERSON'S HOT SIX:
Joe Smith (*cnt*); Charlie Green (*tbn*); Buster Bailey (*clt*); Coleman Hawkins (*ten*); Fletcher Henderson (*p*); Charlie Dixon (*bj*).

Cake Walking Babies	
(140585-2)	G 30818
The Yellow Dog Blues	
(140586-2)	G 30818

MAY 14, 1925
acc Charlie Green (*tbn*); Fred Longshaw (*p*).

Soft Pedal Blues	
(140601-2)	G 30818

MAY 26, 1925
acc Louis Armstrong (*cnt*); Charlie Green (*tbn*); Fred Longshaw (*p*).

Nashville Woman's Blues	
(140625-2)	G 30818

Careless Love Blues
(140626–1)   G 31093

MAY 27, 1925

as last

J. C. Holmes Blues
(140629–2)   G 31093

I Ain't Goin' to Play Second Fiddle
(140630–1)   G 31093

NOVEMBER 18, 1925

acc Joe Smith (*cnt*); Charlie Green (*tbn*); Fletcher Henderson (*p*).

At the Christmas Ball
(141283)   G 31093

MARCH 18, 1926

acc Buster Bailey or Garvin Bushell or Lorenzo Wardell (*clt*); Fletcher Henderson (*p*).

Jazzbo Brown from Memphis Town
(141819–2)   G 31093

The Gin House Blues
(141820–3)   G 31093

MAY 4, 1926

acc Joe Smith (*cnt*); Fletcher Henderson (*p*).

Money Blues
(142146–3)   G 31093

Baby Doll
(142147–2)   G 31093

Lost Your Head Blues
(142149–1)   G 31093

OCTOBER 26, 1926

acc HER BLUE BOYS:
Joe Smith (*cnt*); Buster Bailey (*clt*); Fletcher Henderson (*p*).

One and Two Blues
(142876–2)   G 31093

Young Woman's Blues
(142878–3)   G 31093

FEBRUARY 17, 1927

Back Water Blues
(143491–1)   G 31093

MARCH 2, 1927

acc HER BAND:
Joe Smith (*cnt*); Jimmy Harrison (*tbn*); Buster Bailey (*clt*); Fletcher Henderson (*p*); Charlie Dixon (*bj*).

After You've Gone
(143567–2)   G 31093

Coleman Hawkins (*ten*) replaces Bailey.

Alexander's Ragtime Band
(143568)   G 31093

Buster Bailey (*clt*) added.

Muddy Water (A Mississippi Moan)
(143569–1)   G 30818

Coleman Hawkins out.

There'll Be a Hot Time in the Old Town Tonight
(143570)   G 30818

MARCH 3, 1927

acc HER BLUE BOYS:
Joe Smith (*cnt*); Charlie Green (*tbn*); Fletcher Henderson (*p*).

Trombone Cholly
(143575–3)   G 30818

Send Me to the 'Lectric Chair
(143576–2)   G 30818

FEBRUARY 9, 1928

acc Deamus Dean (*tpt*); Charlie Green (*tbn*); Fred Longshaw (*p*).

Thinking Blues
(145626–2)   G 30818

I Used To Be Your Sweet Mamma
(145628–1)   G 30450

MARCH 20, 1928

acc Charlie Green (*tbn*); Porter Grainger (*p*).

Empty Bed Blues—Part 1
(145785–3)   G 30450

Empty Bed Blues—Part 2
(145786–3)   G 30450

AUGUST 24, 1928

acc Joe Williams (*tbn*); Ernest 'Sticky' Elliott (*clt*); Bob Fuller (*alt*); Porter Grainger (*p*).

Poor Man's Blues
(146895–1)   G 30450

AUGUST 25, 1928

acc Joe Williams (*tbn*); Porter Grainger (*p*).

Me and My Gin
(146897–3)   G 30450

MAY 15, 1929

acc Ed Allen (*cnt*); Cyrus St. Clair (*tuba*); Clarence
Williams (*p*).

Nobody Knows You When You're Down and Out
(148534–3)   G 30126

AUGUST 20, 1929

acc James P. Johnson (*p*).

He's Got Me Goin'
(148902–2)   G 30126

OCTOBER 11, 1929

as last

Blue Spirit Blues
(149134)   G 30126

JUNE 9, 1930

acc BESSEMER SINGERS (*vocal quartet*); James P. Johnson
(*p*).

On Revival Day
(150574)   GP 33

Moan You Mourners
(150575)   GP 33

JULY 22, 1930

acc Ed Allen (*tpt*); Steve Stevens or Clarence Williams (*p*).

Black Mountain Blues
(150658–2)   GP 33

JUNE 11, 1931

acc Louis Bacon (*tpt*); Charlie Green (*tbn*); Clarence
Williams (*p*); Floyd Casey (*d, traps*).

In the House Blues
(151594–1)   Columbia   GP 33

Long Old Road
(151595–)   GP 33

Shipwreck Blues
(151597–)   GP 33

NOVEMBER 24, 1933

acc BUCK AND HIS BAND:
Frank Newton (*tpt*); Jack Teagarden (*tbn*); Leon 'Chu'
Berry (*ten*); Buck Washington (*p*); Bobby Johnson (*g*);
Billy Taylor (*bs*).

Do Your Duty
(152577–1)   GP 33

Benny Goodman (*clt*) added.

Gimme a Pigfoot
(152578–2)   GP 33

Goodman out.

Take Me for a Buggy Ride
(152579–2)   GP 33

I'm Down in the Dumps
(152580–2)   GP 33

Fats Waller

BY CHARLES FOX

I

Fats Waller has always occupied a special place in my affections. He was, you see, the first American jazz musician I ever heard 'live'.

The event took place in the spring of 1939, when I was living in London—on the top floor of a rather grimy house near King's Cross station. By day I attended a foreign travel class at Thomas Cook's head office in Berkeley Street; when evening came I sat down in my little room and swotted up long lists of frontier towns or worked out the fastest route from Osnabrück to Istanbul. I was very serious in those days. Six months later, of course, all that my hard work brought me was the sack—those frontiers were never the same again. And so, looking back at that period of six or seven weeks, I often regret I didn't paint the town red, or at least a gentle pink, instead of mugging up all that useless information. One relaxation I did permit myself, however; that was a weekly visit to the No. 1 Rhythm Club, a highly decorous body which held its meetings at the First Avenue Hotel. The hotel vanished during the blitz, but it stood not very far away from the Holborn Empire, then a flourishing music-hall with gaudy lights outside and the cream of British variety artists to be seen upon its stage.

And it was at the Holborn Empire, I was amazed to see when I glanced at the posters outside one evening, that Fats Waller would be performing! As both my money and time were short I could only go once to see the great man, and the occasion I chose was the first house on the Saturday evening. With me went one of my class-mates, known to everybody as 'Buddy' because of his penchant for American clothes and habits. 'Buddy' professed to like jazz, but I suspected the extent of his commitment when, just about tea-time, he suggested we patronize a George Formby film instead. Our friendship was never quite the same again.

Apart from the Mills Brothers, that wonderful vocal quartet which seemed to be everywhere in London that spring, I cannot for the life of me remember who else was on the programme. Certainly the top billing went to a comedian who could easily have been Max Miller. Fats came on either just before or just after the interval, greeted by vigorous applause from the faithful few, dotted here and there among the audience. I've never kept a diary for more than three weeks, and I rarely keep any record of my reactions to plays or concerts, so my twenty-year-old memory has grown a bit pale and frayed. But I do remember that Fats played *Honeysuckle Rose*, accompanied by a pit orchestra that butchered the tune monstrously, and that he also played and sang *Two Sleepy People* and *Flat Foot Floogie*. At the time I was thrilled, overwhelmed, full of a high and noble ecstasy. And that makes it even more sad that my memories of the occasion only recall what Fats looked like, not how he sounded.

He wore—and I can see it even now—the shiniest evening suit I've ever seen. I was glad, later on, to discover that a gossip columnist in the *Melody Maker* had been as taken aback by it as I was. Then there was the girth, the breadth of the man. He was, I now realize, nothing like the figure of a man that Jimmy Rushing is, lacking that 'fearful symmetry', but at the time his bulk was a marvel to me. How could such a clumsy-looking man, I wondered (and sometimes still do), produce such exquisite, such delicate music? I loved everything, even the bits of byplay: the way Fats sat down very daintily upon the piano stool, then peered round coyly and asked himself, 'Is you all on, Fats?'; the glare he gave his right hand as it rattled off a familiar phrase, the way he shouted 'Come out of that, will you!'

Fats Waller's act can have lasted no more than fifteen minutes. It ended to polite clapping—except, of course, for the frenzied, loyal few—and then the jugglers came on, or it may have been Wee Georgie Wood or Wilson, Keppel and Betty. 'Buddy' seemed to be unmoved; he thought Fats was 'all right' but had enjoyed the comedian even more. For me, however, it was seeing Waller plain that mattered. And in its way, I suppose, the experience was a little like first dipping into Chapman's Homer. Within a couple of months I was to sit a bare eight yards away from Coleman Hawkins for two rapturous hours; in the years that followed I was to see Louis and Duke and Count and Earl. But these post-war glimpses of jazz royalty have never quite lived up to that rich, fulfilling moment when the numbers changed at the side of the stage, a spotlight swung to the curtain's left-hand edge, and Fats Waller—bushy eyebrows puckered and twitching, rather like Robey's—trucked and pranced and swaggered towards the piano.

The performer I saw at the Holborn Empire was the Fats Waller of legend, the gay, irreverent comedian at the piano, a symbol of good fellowship, a kind of latter-day Pickwick with a taste for whisky instead of claret and a decidedly bawdy sense of humour. But the personality which Fats paraded before the public was really a gross over-simplification of the man, as well as something of an obstruction to his work as an artist. To most Britons and Americans, Fats Waller was—indeed he still is, sixteen years after his death—a kind of overgrown baby, lambasting the songs he sang, being uproarious, zestful, lovable, exactly the kind of practical anarchist we all envy in our hearts. The fact that he was also one of the greatest of jazz pianists came, if indeed it occurred to most people at all, only as an afterthought. That Fats himself was aware of this has been emphasized by Gene Sedric, the fine tenor-saxophonist who worked with Waller from 1937 until the pianist's death. 'Nobody who was a personal fan of Waller ever forgot his playing,' Sedric has written, 'but very few got a chance really to hear the finer things he could do on the piano. Through his recordings and picture success the public went for his jive and singing, which to the general public really overshadowed his ability as one of the world's greatest swing pianists. Many times we would be on the job and Waller playing great piano, modern stuff with technique and fine chords, and people would say, "Come on Fats, you're laying down, give us some jive". This at times would be a great drag to him;

he would look at us and say, "You see these people, they won't let me play anything real fine, want to hear all that jive!" But it was the jive instead of fine playing that made him a wealthy man. He was a great comedian, but his only love was music. He loved to study and practise. I personally believe he would have been much happier had his jive not overshadowed his great musical ability.'[1]

Fats Waller, in fact, was not only the prisoner of his personality, a man whose high spirits and gift for showmanship often obscured his brilliance as a musician, he was also a victim of the wide-spread notion that fat men are always funny, a prejudice particularly strong in the world of entertainment. The idea that a fat man can be a sensitive, thoughtful artist still strikes some people as irresistibly comic. For them he must always be the stereotype found in music-hall jokes and on seaside postcards. That professional pessimist, Cyril Connolly, has written a sentence that may already have wormed its way into the dictionaries of quotations: 'Imprisoned in every fat man', observed Connolly, 'a thin one is wildly signalling to be let out.'[2] To some extent that was even true of Fats Waller. Jeff Aldam, who got to know Waller very intimately during his visits to Britain in 1938 and 1939, has pointed out that the pianist certainly had no love for his nickname. 'Those who had more than a passing acquaintance with him', writes Aldam, 'called him "Thomas" or more often just "Tom". I think that, for all his superabundant good humour, he was sensitive about his girth.'[3]

The point I am making is that the conventional image of Fats Waller as a hard-drinking, fun-loving exhibitionist who happened to play the piano rather wonderfully, embodies only one aspect of the man. He did drink too much, he was exuberant, he had no inhibitions about showing his feelings, he could—as we all know—perform miracles upon the piano. But he was also a much more complicated human being than all his *bonhomie* led audiences to suspect. 'America does strange things to its great artists,' wrote John Hammond in his programme notes for Fats Waller's Carnegie Hall concert in January 1942. 'In any other place in the world Thomas Waller might have developed

[1] *The Jazz Record*, March 1945.
[2] *The Unquiet Grave*. Hamish Hamilton, 1945.
[3] *Jazz Music*, January 1944.

340

into a famous concert performer, for when he was eleven he was a gifted organist, pianist and composer. But Waller was not white, and the American concert field makes racial exceptions only for a few singers. Waller's great talent for the piano has never received the acknowledgement that it deserves in this country. It was easier to exploit him as a buffoon and clown than as the artist he is.' Like James P. Johnson, Duke Ellington, Earl Hines, Jelly Roll Morton and many other gifted Negro musicians, Waller became a jazz musician and an entertainer. For those were the days when the two roles were nearly synonymous, the days when Sidney Bechet performed an instrumental 'strip tease', taking his clarinet to pieces while he played it, and when George Brunies used his foot to operate the slide of his trombone. This helps to explain both the strength of Fats Waller's music—its functional quality, its directness and exuberance—and some of the compromises that the pianist had to make during his lifetime. For like his great mentor, James P. Johnson, Waller was at heart a frustrated man. Where Johnson 'ached openly because he could find no audience for his serious compositions,' writes the American critic, John Wilson, 'Waller's desire to find acceptance as a serious musician was buried under a heavy coating of pervasive geniality.'[1]

[1] *The Jazz Makers*, edited by Nat Shapiro and Nat Hentoff. Peter Davies, 1957.

2

Whether heredity plays any part in transmitting a talent, a sympathy for music, is still very debatable. But environment can and does. It did in the case of Fats Waller. Although his grandfather, Adolph Waller, had been a well-known violinist in the southern states during the years which followed the Civil War, a much more important influence upon the boy's development was the fact that his mother, Adeline Locket Waller, possessed a good soprano voice and could play the piano and organ. She and her husband, Edward Martin Waller, had come north from Virginia in the 1890s and settled in New York, living first in Waverly Place, in a downtown area, then on 63rd Street, and finally on 134th Street. Both Adeline and Edward were deeply religious; in fact Edward, after working in a stable and as a trucker, became deacon and later on pastor of the Abyssinian Baptist Church on 40th Street (it subsequently moved to uptown Harlem), a church which is said to attract the largest Protestant congregation in the entire United States. The Wallers, however, were far from prosperous and seldom had as much money as they needed. But then they were quite a large family; twelve children were born altogether, although six of these died while still in their infancy.

Fats was born on 21 May 1904 and christened Thomas Wright Waller. He grew up in a home where a great deal of hymn singing and Bible reading went on but in which there was no piano; that was too expensive a luxury for the Wallers to afford. Ed Kirkeby, who acted as Fats Waller's manager during the late 1930s and early 1940s, has related that when Thomas was very young he was found 'running his fingers over the seats of two chairs which he had pushed together in the semblance of a keyboard—and it turned out that a woman upstairs had allowed him to play her piano and aroused his curiosity'.[1] By the time he was five he could play the harmonium, and a year later, when his brother Robert brought a piano—a Waters upright—into the house, Thomas and his sisters Naomi and Edith were given music lessons. But Thomas, who had already listened to ragtime pianists accompanying the silent films and heard this formal but lilting music drifting out of Harlem cellar clubs, found this conventional approach too tiresome. He began to play by ear, and not until several years later did he learn to read music. By then this liking for ragtime had become apparent to his father, who condemned that style of playing as 'music from the Devil's

[1] *Melody Maker*, 5 March 1955.

workshop'; his mother, however, was much more tolerant and continued to help and encourage him throughout those early years.

In addition to acting as organist in his father's church, Thomas played the piano and organ at school concerts (he was attending Public School 89 in those days) and was a member of the students' orchestra. For a time he even studied the violin and bass viol as well as these other instruments. Edgar Sampson, the well-known jazz arranger, was at school with Waller and has recalled how he would often inject a rhythmic note into his performances, inserting an off-beat here and there in the music. And already, it seems, he was clowning, amusing his class-mates by grimacing and winking as he played. Bulky and heavily built, even as a youth, Waller was fond of reading Nick Carter novels as well as books on musical theory, while to earn his spending money—75 cents a week—he ran errands for a grocery store and pigs' feet stand. When he was eleven his father, who still hoped the boy would enter the church as a minister but who had meanwhile become proud of his son's musical accomplishments, took him to hear Paderewski perform at Carnegie Hall, an experience that only heightened Thomas's determination to become a professional musician. During the next few years, therefore, he studied music under Carl Bohm (as he was to do later on with Leopold Godowsky) while continuing to attend DeWitt Clinton High School. His musical studies eventually began to clash with school work, and when that happened Thomas—naturally enough—decided that music must come first. 'There wasn't any rhythm for me in algebra,' he declared some years afterwards.

Thomas Waller left DeWitt Clinton High School in the spring of 1918. For a time he was employed in a jewel box factory, but he found the work there too dirty. Then he ran errands for Immerman's delicatessen, a store owned by two brothers, Connie and George Immerman, later the proprietors of Connie's Inn, a famous Harlem nightclub. Quite close to the Waller home, however, stood the Lincoln Theatre, a cinema where films were shown to the accompaniment of music from a piano and pipe-organ, the latter a Wurlitzer Grand that had cost the management $10,000. Even while he was still at school, Thomas made a habit of sitting in the front row of this theatre, just behind the pianist, Maizie Mullins, who allowed him to slide under the brass rail and to perch beside her on the piano-stool. Then, if she felt like taking a rest, the boy would play instead. Soon the organist was allowing him similar privileges. He became so adept upon the Wurlitzer, in fact, that when the organist fell ill Thomas deputized for him—at a wage of $23 a week. By a useful coincidence the job suddenly became vacant, so Thomas found himself installed as the Lincoln's regular organist, a position he held until the theatre changed hands several years later.

It must have been around this time that Andy Razaf, who was to write many of the lyrics for Waller's songs, caught his first glimpse of the young musician. (Razaf's real name was Andreamentana Razafinkerifo. Although he himself had been born in Washington, he was actually the nephew of Ranavalona III, the African queen of Madagascar whom the French had deposed in the nineteenth century.) 'He was a chunky little lad', recalls Razaf, 'playing in an amateur pianists' contest at the Roosevelt Theatre in Harlem, on the site where the Golden Gate ballroom stands today. He was maybe 15 years old, and he won the prize, playing a tune by his chief musical mentor, James P. Johnson's *Carolina Shout*.'[1] Waller almost certainly could not have made James P. Johnson's acquaintance by that time, but he must have heard that great pianist perform, or have listened to piano-rolls by him, and already been under his influence. Johnson, a man ten years older than Waller, was, after all, the leading member of the Eastern school of ragtime players, a school that included such remarkable performers as Luckey Roberts and Willie 'The Lion' Smith. Waller, however, does not seem to have entered that musical circle until just after his mother's death, when he was introduced to most of those pianists by Russell Brooks, a friend and fellow musician.

The death of his mother was undoubtedly one of the turning points in Thomas Waller's life, a loss from which he is said never to have completely recovered. Thomas had been the youngest of Adeline Waller's sons and her particular favourite, and for some days after her death he remained almost inconsolable. He left home and was found by Russell Brooks, sitting on the steps outside Brooks's house; for a time, in fact, he stayed with Brooks and his wife. A few weeks later, however, almost as if in

[1] *Metronome*, January 1944.

342

reaction to his mother's death, Thomas married Edith Hatchett, a girl he had known for several years, and after the marriage ceremony was over he went to live with his wife's family on Brook Avenue.

Meanwhile he continued to act as organist at the Lincoln Theatre. It was there that Count Basie (known in those days, quite simply, as Bill Basie) first heard him. 'From then on', says Basie, 'I was a regular customer . . . sitting behind him all the time, fascinated by the ease with which his hands pounded the keys and his feet manipulated the pedals. He got used to seeing me, as though I were a part of the show. One day he asked me whether I played the organ. "No," I said, "but I'd give my right arm to learn." The next day he invited me to sit in the pit and start working the pedals. I sat on the floor watching his feet, and using my hands to imitate them. Then I sat beside him and he taught me. One afternoon he pretended to have some urgent business downstairs and asked me to wait for him. I started playing while he stood downstairs listening. After that I would come to early shows and he let me play accompaniment to the picture. Later I used to follow him around wherever he played, listening and learning all the time'.[1] Soon after this friendship had sprung up, Waller left the Lincoln Theatre for a few weeks to tour with a vaudeville show, playing the accompaniments for an act called 'Liza and her Shufflin' Six'. It was while living in a Boston boarding house that Thomas composed a tune he called *Boston Blues*, and which he originally intended to be a setting of the popular bawdy-house lyric, *The Boy In The Boat*. Waller wanted to publish his composition right away, but he had to wait until 1925, when, with innocent lyrics written by Spencer Williams, it appeared under a new title—*Squeeze Me*. When Waller left Liza and her Shufflin' Six, incidentally, he recommended that Bill Basie should take his place. 'It was', recalls Basie, 'my first trip on the road.'

Back in New York once more, Thomas Waller began building up a small reputation, getting himself known as a pianist as well as an organist. Much of the credit for this must go to James P. Johnson. According to May Wright Johnson, the pianist's wife, 'Right after James P. heard Fats Waller playing the pipe organ, he came home and told me, "I know I can teach that boy". Well, from then on it was one big headache for me. Fats was seventeen, and we lived on 140th Street, and Fats would bang on our piano till all hours of the night—sometimes to two, three, four o'clock in the morning. I would say to him, "Now go on home—or haven't you got a home?" But he'd come every day and my husband would teach. Of course, you know the organ doesn't give you a left hand and that's what James P. had to teach him. Then finally Fats got his first job—it was at Leroy's Cabaret on 135th Street and Fifth Avenue, and I was working there then. Fats was afraid to perform and so I taught him to play for me. That's how he started.'[1]

May Johnson's account of how Thomas Waller came to make his first appearance in New York cabaret is the generally accepted version. Ed Kirkeby, for instance, has related how Willie 'The Lion' Smith got tired of playing at Leroy's and walked out, so the management approached James P. Johnson; he was too busy to take over the job himself, but recommended that Thomas Waller should be given a chance. Willie 'The Lion' Smith's own recollections, however, contained in a set of cheerful reminiscences he recorded in the summer and autumn of 1957, throw a slightly different light upon the role he played in this sequence of events. 'The first time I met Thomas Fats Waller,' says 'The Lion', 'it was right after I came back from the Army. . . . There was a place called Leroy's—internationally known café. I left a kid on my job who could only play in three keys. Naturally he thought he had the job tied down. But when I got back I found that yours truly, Thomas Fats Waller, was working there. Ha! Ha! So naturally I walked in one night with James P. He said, "I want you to hear Filthy play the piano!" I said, "Who do you mean—Filthy?" "Fats," he said. "You know Fats." I said, "Oh, certainly." He said, "Lion, he can play. I want you to hear him play the *Carolina Shout*." This was written by James P. I went in and listened to him play. After I heard him I shook my head. I said, "Watch out, Jimmy, he's got it." ' It was after hearing Waller play, apparently, that 'The Lion' decided the young pianist could join 'the Big Three—Thomas Fats Waller, James P. and myself'.

[1] Programme for Fats Waller Memorial Concert, 2 April 1944.

[1] *Hear Me Talkin' To Ya* edited by Nat Shapiro and Nat Hentoff. Peter Davies, 1955.

'We had a monopoly on the house rent parties. . . . They used to charge one dollar admission—pigs' feet, fried chicken, mashed potatoes. Next room there'd be a card game, next room a dice game—that went on all night.'[1]

During the years just after World War I Harlem experienced a big increase in population. This was caused by the general shift northward of Negroes in the southern states, the movement away from depressed rural areas towards the expanding industrial cities of the north and mid-west. In Chicago the same thing was taking place upon an even larger scale. Accommodation became short, naturally enough, so rents soared high and stayed there. But many Harlemites found their answer to the excessive cost of living by throwing parlour socials, or rent parties—parties for personal profit. A pianist could provide all the music needed, although a drummer was sometimes brought along too. James P. Johnson, Willie 'The Lion' Smith, Luckey Roberts and Thomas Waller were constantly in demand at these parties. Another pianist who moved around with this group for a time was Edward Kennedy

Ellington (better known today as 'Duke' Ellington), who, accompanied by Sonny Greer and Otto Hardwicke, had left Washington for New York in 1922 but returned home again within the year. 'Fats used to follow Jimmy Johnson around', remembers Ellington, 'and the Lion used to say of him, "Yeah, a yearling, he's coming along. I guess he'll do all right." '[1] But Waller met Ellington again the following spring. After taking over Willie 'The Lion' Smith's spot at The Capitol, a nightclub at 140th Street and Lenox Avenue, Waller began touring the burlesque theatre circuit with a band that included the clarinettist and alto-saxophonist Garvin Bushell. Eventually the show reached Washington. Ellington, who was still trying to organize a band, recalls how 'Sitting in my house, eating chickens by the pair, Fats told us that they [his band] were all going to quit; that we'd better come on up to New York and get the job.'[2] Ellington was cautious, however, and with good cause, for within a couple of weeks a telegram arrived from New York saying that Waller and his musicians had decided not to leave.

[1] *The Legend of Willie 'The Lion' Smith.* Grand Award 33-368, Top Rank RX3015.

[1] *Swing*, May 1940.
[2] Ibid., June 1940.

3

The player-piano, that ponderous, many-pedalled contraption, belongs to past history as securely as bead curtains, potted aspidistras and elastic-sided boots. Yet during the early 1920s these player-pianos (or pianolas as they were often called) could be found in the parlours of private homes as well as in saloons and dance-halls. And it was for the player-piano that Thomas Waller made his first recordings, if that term can be used to cover punching holes in a long paper roll. Once again the impetus had come from James P. Johnson. Johnson recommended Waller to the Q.R.S. company, with the result that one day in 1922 (the exact date will probably never be discovered) Waller sat down in the Q.R.S. studios and literally punched out a Clarence Williams tune, *Gotta Cool My Doggies Now.* This was followed, over a period of several years, by eighteen or nineteen more rolls, all labelled 'Thomas Waller' and

bearing a facsimile of his signature, for each of which the pianist received $100. Later on there were also a number of rolls labelled 'Fats Waller', yet actually cut—with Waller's full permission—by another pianist, J. Laurence Cook. Although much of the subtlety of Waller's playing, its individual timing and accenting, got lost in this rather clumsy mechanical process, it is interesting to hear some of those rolls played back today. A number have been transferred to discs, as a matter of fact, and issued on long-playing records; for this rather tricky manœuvre the player-piano was operated—fittingly enough—by J. Laurence Cook. Despite the muffled, slightly robot-like character of these performances, they do demonstrate the great influence that James P. Johnson's playing exerted upon the young pianist in those early days. Waller's first recordings for a gramophone company (*Muscle Shoals Blues* and

Birmingham Blues) were made shortly afterwards, and during the next four years he acted as accompanist on a number of records by blues-singers Sara Martin, Alberta Hunter, Anna Jones, Hazel Meyers, Caroline Johnson, Alta Brown, Bertha Powell and Maude Mills.

By the middle of the 1920s Waller had achieved his first published composition, *Wild Cat Blues*, a tune that was recorded by Clarence Williams's Blue Five, and had made his first broadcast—from the stage of the Fox Terminal Theatre in Newark, New Jersey, sometime in 1923. Meanwhile he continued to double as a cinema organist and a cabaret pianist. The Lincoln Theatre was sold, but Waller moved across to the Lafayette, where he not only received a higher wage but found himself playing a much larger organ. The casual way in which he seems to have taken his duties as accompanist to the silent films can best be demonstrated by repeating an anecdote which Don Redman tells. At the time this incident occurred Redman was playing alto-saxophone with Fletcher Henderson's orchestra, as well as writing many of its arrangements, and he had become very friendly with Thomas Waller, often dropping in to visit him during working hours at the Lafayette. On one occasion Redman sat beside Waller, chatting away animatedly, while a newsreel was being screened up above them. Thomas, he recalls, was playing *Squeeze Me*, his own tune and one that he performed whenever he got the chance. Suddenly Redman happened to glance up and saw, to his horror, that a funeral procession was making its way across the screen. 'Hey, Tom,' he whispered, 'they're showing a funeral. You shouldn't be playing that.' 'Why not?' exclaimed Waller, giving a diabolical grin and continuing to pound away at the keyboard. Then, beckoning to an usher, Waller handed him fifty cents and asked him to slip out and get a pint of gin.

In 1925 Waller travelled up to Chicago to work with Erskine Tate's 'Little Symphony', an orchestra that played a mixture of jazz and light classics at the Vendome Theatre, a popular Chicago cinema. Another member of that band was Louis Armstrong. 'That was in the days of the silent films,' Armstrong has written. 'We used to play for the films, and during the intermission we would play a big Overture and a Red Hot number afterwards. And

folks, I'm telling you, we used to really romp.'[1] Waller's stay with the band produced at least one anecdote that has crept into jazz literature. In those days it was common practice for song-pluggers to take their new material round the theatres, passing it over to the musicians who would then proceed to play it at sight. During one particularly agonizing run-through of a new song by the Erskine Tate band, with the musicians sounding completely at sea, Waller suddenly stopped the music, and leaning down from the piano-stool he asked: 'Pardon me, boys—but what key are you all strugglin' in down there?'

The following year Waller returned to New York. First of all he toured in vaudeville (a popular legend asserts that for a time he acted as accompanist to Bessie Smith), then he got himself a manager—George Raines. Raines introduced him to Bert Lewis, 'The Southern Syncopator', who was then appearing at the Kentucky Club, and the pianist became a part of Lewis's act, swathing his head in a turban and being announced as 'Ali Baba, the Egyptian Wonder'. By now, of course, Waller was not only playing for rent parties up in Harlem but also at downtown parties given by millionaires, people like Charles Schwab, Mrs. Harrison Williams and Otto Kahn. He was beginning, in fact, to be known outside Harlem and the narrow circle of his fellow musicians. But despite the growth of his reputation, Waller remained—as indeed he was to do throughout his whole life—a remarkably uncommercial person. Often he would play at a private party in return for nothing more than a steady supply of whisky, a good cigar and the presence of a handful of people who really enjoyed his music. And it must have been around this period, in the middle of the 1920s, that people began calling him 'Fats', for his figure had been growing plumper and plumper with the years.

There were times, of course, when the 1920s were anything but a gay decade for Thomas Waller. His marriage to Edith Hatchett had gone to pieces very quickly, mainly because he was so seldom at home; in the end Edith kept their son, Thomas Wright, Jr., while Fats moved out of the house. But the situation still remained unsatisfactory, for Waller was as unreliable as he was generous. Once, for

---

[1] Programme for Fats Waller Memorial Concert.

instance, when the pianist was playing with a trio up in Philadelphia, Edith found herself without any money at all and had to borrow from her family and her friends. Even when a settlement had been agreed upon things continued to go wrong as Waller frequently neglected to pay the alimony, with the result that for quite a number of years the pianist was constantly being chased by process servers, often having to disappear for several days at a time. Ed Kirkeby has told, 'as gospel truth', of how a process server once caught up with Fats and forced him to spend some days in jail, and yet how reluctant Fats was to leave those guarded premises. When some of his friends eventually arrived to bail him out, he explained that he was sharing a cell with a millionaire, who was daily stocking the place with all the pleasures of life—including a piano, so there seemed little point in abandoning these amenities too hastily.

Thomas Waller met Anita Rutherford in 1924. He fell in love with her and they got married, making their first home at the house of Anita's grandparents. The marriage turned out to be a very happy and successful one, but for the first few years Thomas and his wife were often very short of money, and Waller's attempts at raising funds often took a sadly uneconomical turn. Once, for instance, he offered to sell an entire folio of his manuscripts to the Q.R.S. company for as little as ten dollars, but luckily for him the proposal was rejected. On another occasion he tried to persuade Don Redman to buy every song he had for the same amount. Several years later he actually sold his rights in *Ain't Misbehavin'*, *Black and Blue*, and seventeen other songs to a well-known music publisher for a total of $500. There was also the time when he spent an evening with Fletcher Henderson and a group of the musicians from Henderson's band and they all went into a hamburger bar. Fats quickly gobbled down nine hamburgers and then confessed that he had no money. His proposition was simple. If Fletcher would pay the bill, Fats, in return, would present him with nine tunes. The bandleader accepted this offer, so Waller immediately sent out for manuscript paper and within a very short time had roughed out a set of tunes that included *Top and Bottom* (later called *Henderson Stomp*), *Thundering Stomp* (better known as *Hot Mustard*), *Variety Stomp*, *St. Louis Shuffle* and *Whiteman Stomp*. Henderson, however, very properly

insisted upon paying Fats ten dollars for each composition, instead of the hamburger which the pianist had demanded. But this practice of trying to rob himself was one that Waller kept up throughout a large part of his life; because of it a great many of his compositions have been published under the names of other men.

Towards the end of the 1920s Fats Waller and Andy Razaf began working together as a song-writing partnership, Waller composing the music and Razaf writing the lyrics. 'One of the first things we did as a team', recalls Razaf, 'was to cash in on a vogue for West Indian songs. As soon as we got broke all we had to do was grind out two or three West Indian numbers, take them up to Mills or some Broadway office and get a nice sum for them. Around that time there was a heavy demand for cabaret-type songs, with blue lyrics. We did hundreds of those. Sometimes Fats worked with other lyric-writers and composers; there was a bunch of us who pulled around together, including James P. Johnson, J. C. Johnson, Spencer Williams, and a kid named Bud Allen, who was Fats's permanent sidekick, helping to keep him on time for dates, get him home and generally look out for him. The first big show score we wrote together was 'Keep Shufflin'; the hit songs were *How Jazz Was Born* and *My Little Chocolate Bar*. Then Connie and George Immerman sent for us to write a Connie's Inn show, and things really started humming.'[1]

Keep Shufflin' was produced in 1928. In addition to the songs mentioned by Andy Razaf it also contained *Willow Tree*—one of Waller's most delightful melodies, *Labour Day Parade*, *Everybody's Happy in Jimtown*, and the show's theme tune, *Keep Shufflin'*. Waller and James P. Johnson performed at two pianos ('the two best left-hands in the jazz business playing together'[2]) and the pit orchestra included the trumpet-player, Jabbo Smith. The following year saw Waller and Razaf start work upon their score for *Hot Chocolates*, a revue which opened at Connie's Inn and eventually doubled between that nightclub and the Hudson Theatre on 46th Street. Connie's Inn, of course, was located at the corner of 131st Street and Seventh Avenue, not just an ordinary corner but 'a whole atlas by itself— the crossroad of the universe', to quote Mezz Mezzrow's

[1] *Metronome*, January 1944.
[2] Bennie Paine in *Jazz Journal*, May 1952.

346

ecstatic description. Next door stood the Lafayette Theatre while immediately outside the entrance was the legendary Tree of Hope, 'Harlem's Blarney Stone', that totem pole which gamblers would touch for luck on their way to a game of cards or dice. *Hot Chocolates* was staged by Leonard Harper, who produced most of the shows at Connie's Inn during the 1920s, and its cast included Louis Armstrong, Jazzlips Richardson, Jimmy Baskette, Eddie Green, Baby Cox, Thelma and Paul Morres, Edith Wilson, Margaret Simms and the Jubilee Singers. Mary Lou Williams, who arrived in New York from Kansas City around this time, remembers visiting Connie's Inn during the rehearsals and

dancing.'[1] Mezz Mezzrow also met Waller for the first time while the pianist was working on this score and he remembers how Fats and Razaf would sit side by side on the stage, Razaf sometimes changing the lyrics but when he did so always singing the new version 'in a very pleasant voice'. 'I asked Fats why they didn't take a part in the show as a team', writes Mezzrow, 'and Andy chimed in and said, "Yeah, Mezz, I've been telling him the same thing for a long time." But Fats answered, "Mezz, you know, I am a musician and not an actor." '[2]

For *Hot Chocolates* Fats Waller and Andy Razaf wrote a string of fine songs, including *That Rhythm Man*, *What*

From the files of Melody Maker

Fats Waller and his Rhythm at a recording session (probably 11 March 1938). *Left to right*: Slick Jones, Herman Autrey, Fats Waller, Cedric Wallace, Albert Casey, Eugene Sedric

noticing how casually Fats Waller worked. 'He sat,' she recalls, 'overflowing the piano stool, a jug of whisky within easy reach. Leonard Harper, the producer, said, "Have you anything written for this number, Fats?" and Fats would reply, "Yeah, go on ahead with the dance man." Then he composed his number while the girls were

Did I Do To Be So Black And Blue, *Dixie Cinderella*, *Can't We Get Together*, *Sweet Savannah Sue* and *Say It With Your Feet*. But the hit of the original show was Margaret Simms's performance of *Ain't Misbehavin'*. 'From the first time

[1] *Hear Me Talkin' To Ya.*
[2] Ibid.

Fats Waller and his Rhythm (with the Deep River Boys vocal quartet in the foreground) at a recording session (13 July 1942). *Left to right:* Eugene Sedric, Cedric Wallace, Albert Casey, John Hamilton, Arthur Trappier, Fats Waller. The man standing at the back of the studio with a pipe in his mouth is Ray Durant, the regular pianist with the Deep River Boys

I heard it', writes Louis Armstrong, 'that song used to "send me". I wood-shedded it until I could play all around it. . . . I believe that great song, and the chance I got to play it, did a lot to make me better known all over the country'.[1] Andy Razaf's account of how *Ain't Misbehavin'* got written is revealing. 'I remember one day going to Fats's house on 133rd Street', he writes, 'to finish up a number based on a little strain he'd thought up. The whole show was complete, but they needed an extra number for a theme, and this had to be it. We worked on it for about 45 minutes and there it was—*Ain't Misbehavin'*.'[2] Suitably enough, the melodic line of *Ain't Misbehavin'* sounds very suggestive of Louis Armstrong playing a blues chorus, but an even odder coincidence is that the tune popped up again several years later, in an almost identical form, as a theme in the first movement of Shostakovich's Seventh Symphony.

After their success with *Keep Shufflin'* and *Hot Chocolates*,

Fats Waller and Andy Razaf worked on many shows together—not only for Connie's Inn but also for floor shows at the Everglades, the Silver Slipper and other New York nightclubs. But it was often very hard to tie Waller down to a job and Razaf sometimes bribed him to stay at the Razaf home in Asbury Park, New Jersey, by getting his mother to cook up some particularly tempting meals. It was at Asbury Park, incidentally, that another famous tune was composed, and once again in a typically off-hand way. 'We were working on a show called "Loads of Coal" for Connie,' recalls Razaf, 'and had just done half the chorus of a number when Fats remembered a date and announced: "I gotta go." I finished the verse and gave it to him later on the telephone. The tune was *Honeysuckle Rose*.'[1] At that single session, a session lasting just under two hours, the two men also composed another two songs—*Zonky* and *My Fate Is In Your Hands*. 'Fats was the most prolific and fastest writer I ever knew,' says Razaf. 'He could set a melody to any lyric and he took great pains working on it, getting the

---

[1] *Swing That Music.* Longmans, 1937.

[2] *Metronome*, January 1944.

[1] Ibid.

exact mood and phrasing until the melody would just pour from his fingers. I used to say he could have set the telephone book to music. He took great pride in doing an accurate, perfect job with every note in the right place, so much so that even if he finished a whole piano copy in half an hour, it could be sent right down to the printer's without any changes. . . . Fats and I had many hits together

—*Concentratin', Gone, If It Ain't Love, My Fate Is In Your Hands, Aintcha Glad, Keepin' Out Of Mischief Now, Zonky, Blue Turning Grey Over You, How Can You Face Me*—but we never realized our ambition of getting a big break in Hollywood as a team.'[1]

[1] *Metronome*, January 1944.

4

'The organ is the favourite instrument of Fats Waller's heart,' wrote Ashton Stevens, the music critic of the *Chicago American*, 'the piano only of his stomach.' It was a true enough comment and one that Fats himself endorsed. 'Well, I really love the organ,' he once said, 'I can get so much more colour from it than the piano that it really sends me. . . . And next to a grand organ there's nothing finer than a magnificent symphony orchestra.' An organ was installed in the Wallers' apartments on Morningside Avenue and at 133rd Street; later on—after the pianist and his family had moved out to St. Albans on Long Island—a built-in Hammond electric organ stood alongside the Steinway grand piano. When Fats was working in Chicago, a local music store often sent along a Hammond organ for him to play up in his hotel room, and there he would sit—playing spirituals, hymns and pieces by Bach and other classical composers as well as jazz. Tommy Brookins recalls going up to a hotel room in Chicago at five o'clock one morning and hearing Fats play the organ for over three hours, ending up with what Fats described as 'my favourite piece—*Abide With Me*.' Another musician with memories of Waller's disconcerting habit of getting up at five or six in the morning to perform on the organ is Snub Mosely, the slide-trumpet player. 'He'd have an inspired moment', says Mosely, 'and maybe play a little loud, you know? Sure enough the super in the building started raising hell and so Fats had to go out and buy himself a house.'[1]

What fascinated Fats Waller about the organ was its capacity to produce rich, colourful textures, as well as its

[1] *Hear Me Talkin' To Ya.*

sonority and depth of tone. These were qualities that, as far as the instrument would allow it, he also introduced into his piano playing. By far the most important characteristics of the 'stride piano' style (sometimes called 'Harlem piano') which he and James P. Johnson created during the 1920s was the way it thickened the harmonies and extended the emotional scope of ragtime, giving that highly formal, rather brittle idiom something of the expressiveness to be found in the blues. But then it should never be forgotten that Waller started out as an organist, and that for a number of years he played the organ night after night at either the Lincoln or Lafayette theatres. What was more natural, therefore, that as soon as he began recording regularly under his own name he should choose to perform on the pipe-organ? In the autumn of 1926 he made two such recordings—*St. Louis Blues* and *Lenox Avenue Blues*, and during the following year he actually recorded no fewer than twenty-five organ solos, although only about half of them were ever issued. One session for the Victor company found him playing versions of Rimsky-Korsakof's *Flight of the Bumble Bee*, Bach's Fugues in B Minor and D Minor, Liszt's *Liebestraum*, Moszkowski's *Spanish Dance No. 1* and Rudolph Friml's *Spanish Days*. None of these recordings has been released, but it is believed that Waller first played each item in a legitimate fashion, then improvised upon it. And in addition to accompanying two singers— Juanita Stinette Chappelle and Bert Howell—upon the organ, he also played the instrument on some band recordings with Thomas Morris's Hot Babies, blending very piquantly with the front-line of trumpet and trombone. During 1926 and 1927 Fats also played both piano and organ on two sessions by Fletcher Henderson's orchestra. In 1928, however, he took part in only two recording sessions altogether, on one of which he accompanied a singer, Johnny Thompson, at the piano, while the other was a very successful partnership with James P. Johnson (Waller playing the organ, Johnson the piano) in a group called The Louisiana Sugar Babes.

The first session by Fats Waller's Buddies—the name Waller gave to his early recording bands—took place in March 1929 and resulted in four classic sides, two of them piano solos (*Handful of Keys*, *Numb Fumblin'*), the other two band performances (*The Minor Drag*, *Harlem Fuss*). Eddie Condon, who had arrived in New York from Chicago only ten months earlier, has given a very amusing account of this session in his autobiography, *We Called It Music*. He was approached a few days beforehand by the Southern Music Company, which as well as being a subsidiary of Victor Records acted as Fats Waller's publisher and had a financial interest in the success of his recordings. They were, it appears, familiar with Waller's lackadaisical behaviour and wished to circumvent it. Condon was offered seventy-five dollars if he would ensure that the pianist arrived at the studio on time and with a band that had been properly rehearsed. The banjoist had never met Waller before, so he went down to Connie's Inn, where rehearsals were going on for *Hot Chocolates*, and introduced himself, explaining: 'Earl Hines told me to look you up.' 'Ol' Earl,' replied Fats. 'Well, that's fine. How's ol' Earl? I'm so glad to hear about him. Sit down and let me get a little gin for you. We'll have to talk about Earl.' 'He was so amiable,' writes Condon, 'so agreeable, so good-natured, that I felt almost ashamed of my mission; but I performed it. I asked Fats about making a record. A recording date? He'd be delighted, he'd be proud; just any time. In four days! Fine. At Liederkranz Hall? Wonderful! At noon? Perfect!'[1]

During the next three days Condon occasionally tried to get Fats to discuss the subject of the recording session. 'After we get the band together, what shall we play?' he asked. 'Why, we'll play music,' Fats replied.

Charlie Gaines, the trumpet-player, has told how Waller and Condon called to see him at Connie's Inn the night before the session: 'They wanted to talk more about it so waited till I finished at four. By then, Fats, who had been drinking gin, was in wild shape. . . .'[1] The next morning found Condon and Waller sleeping off the effects. 'It's half past ten,' cried Condon, terrified. 'We're due at the studio at noon.' Fats was calm, unshaken, completely serene. He stretched his arms, yawned, and then smiled. 'That's fine! That's wonderful! That's perfect!' he said. 'Now we got to see about a band. Look around for some nickels, so I can make the telephone go.' As a result of his telephoning three musicians presently arrived—Charlie Irvis, the trombonist, Arville Harris, who played clarinet and alto-sax, and Charlie Gaines. Fats, it seems, was not bothering about getting a drummer or bassist; presumably he could rely upon the power of his own left hand. Anyway, he announced—much to Condon's astonishment, that Eddie would be playing banjo with them. In the taxi on the way to Liederkranz Hall Fats hummed a simple little pattern, a blues in a minor key, and explained what each musician was supposed to do. At exactly ten minutes to twelve the five men walked into the hall, where a delighted executive of Southern Music congratulated Condon upon getting everybody there so punctually. 'Well, Mr. Waller,' he said, turning to the pianist. 'What is it to be this morning?' 'I think we'll start with a little thing we call *The Minor Drag*,' replied Fats. 'It's a slow number. Then we got a little ol' thing for the other side we call'—he paused for a moment—'*Harlem Fuss*.' The session went very smoothly after that. 'An excellent example of the wisdom of planning and preparation,' the executive told Condon later. The only trouble came when the record was issued, for the company had reversed the titles, *Harlem Fuss* being labelled *The Minor Drag* and vice versa.

During 1929 Fats Waller recorded some of his very finest piano solos—among them *Smashing Thirds*, *Gladyse*, *Sweet Savannah Sue*, *Valentine Stomp* and *My Feelings Are Hurt*, as well as *Numb Fumblin'* and *Handful Of Keys*. He also played on a session by The Little Chocolate Dandies, a recording group organized by Don Redman, and on three sessions with McKinney's Cotton Pickers, in addition to making two sides—*You've Got To Be Modernistic* and *You Don't Understand*—with a James P. Johnson group

---

[1] *We Called It Music*. Peter Davies, 1948.

[1] *Hear Me Talkin' To Ya*.

that included King Oliver on cornet. In the company of his Buddies, Fats cut six more titles for Victor and just as he had used Eddie Condon on the earlier session he now had two white musicians—Jack Teagarden and Gene Krupa—playing alongside Henry Allen, Charlie Gaines, Al Morgan and Otto Hardwicke. On 30 September 1929, this band—like its predecessor, one of the earliest mixed groups ever to record[1]—made *Look'n Good But Feelin' Bad* and *I Need Someone Like You*, while about ten weeks later a very similar band, but with J. C. Higginbotham, Happy Caldwell, Albert Nicholas, Pops Foster and several other musicians added, recorded *When I'm Alone, Ridin' But Walkin', Lookin' For Another Sweetie* and *Won't You Get Off It, Please?*

The only recordings Fats Waller made during 1930 were two piano duets with Bennie Paine—*St. Louis Blues* and *After You've Gone*. 'The record was made quite by chance,' writes Bennie Paine. 'Someone at Victor had the idea of turning out a double-sided piano record, with one side played by a real old-time jazz pianist, and the reverse featuring swing piano ... but the other guy didn't show up. I was hanging around, so Fats grabbed me for the date, "just for a little rent money", as he put it. But our styles of playing were so similar [that] they teamed us up on two pianos. ... It was a pity in a way that the other fellow didn't show up, as I think the Victor people had an interesting idea in that contrasting style stunt. The other player, by the way, was to have been a New Orleans pianist by the name of Jelly Roll Morton.'[2]

Why Fats Waller made only two recordings during the whole of 1930 is difficult to understand. Perhaps the depression had something to do with it; perhaps his alimony troubles reached a new peak; perhaps he was just too busy composing and rehearsing shows. Yet it was also around this time that he got a regular broadcasting spot on a CBS programme, Paramount On Parade, sandwiching it in between his appearances at the Hot Feet Club in Greenwich Village, where he was working with Otto Hardwicke's band. This group included, at various times, Garvin

Bushell, Theodore McCoy and Wayman Carver, as well as a young and still quite obscure tenor player named Chu Berry. This must also have been the year when Fats started singing. At first, if one can judge from recordings, he sang in a relatively straightforward fashion, only gradually inserting the facetiousness and grotesqueries that almost became the trademark of his act half a dozen years later. On the label of his 1931 solo recordings of *I'm Crazy 'Bout My Baby* and *Draggin' My Heart Around*, Fats is described as 'Singing to his hot piano'. Much more amazingly, however, he contrived to sing on a record session sponsored and attended by Ted Lewis, that top-hatted guardian of traditional hokum. On that occasion Lewis's band contained Muggsy Spanier, George Brunies, Bud Freeman and Benny Goodman as well as Fats Waller, and its performances of *Dallas Blues, Royal Garden Blues, Egyptian Ella* and *I'm Crazy 'Bout My Baby* were conspicuously robust and satisfying. That autumn Fats was again the only Negro member of an otherwise all-white band when he played piano and sang on four recordings (*You Rascal You, That's What I Like About You, Chances Are* and *I Got The Ritz From You*) by Jack Teagarden's orchestra. He took part in yet another mixed session, one that produced a set of exciting but flamboyant performances, in July 1932, when *I Would Do Anything For You, Mean Old Bed Bug Blues, Yellow Dog Blues* and *Yes Suh* were recorded. Calling itself, quite simply, The Rhythmakers, this group consisted of Henry Allen, the clarinettist Jimmy Lord, Pee Wee Russell (playing tenor-sax), Fats Waller, Eddie Condon, Jack Bland, Pops Foster and Zutty Singleton, with Billy Banks singing the vocal choruses.

As well as writing songs in collaboration with Andy Razaf, Fats Waller had also been working on some songs with Spencer Williams. Within the space of only a few days, according to Ed Kirkeby, Fats and Spencer Williams now turned out twenty-seven[1] different songs, and with the money earned by this concentrated labour they set out for Europe. The discographers reveal that Fats recorded *Old Yazoo* with Baron Lee and the Mills Blue Rhythm Band on 17 August 1932, which means that he must have sailed

---

[1] In an interview with Fats Waller printed in the *Melody Maker* (20 August 1938) Leonard Feather asserts that the pianist recorded with Roy Gorman, Chester Hazlett, Buddy Christian, the banjoist Cali and other white musicians earlier in the 1920s. No discographer, however, seems to have traced any of these items.

[2] *Jazz Journal*, May 1952.

[1] In *Eddie Condon's Treasury of Jazz* (Peter Davies, 1957), Al Silverman suggests that the figure was nearer a hundred.

aboard the *Ile de France* within a day or two of that session. Hugues Panassié, the distinguished French jazz critic, maintains that it was sometime around the middle of August when he first heard that Waller was in Paris. 'I leapt into the air,' recalls Panassié and he goes on to relate how he rushed excitedly from club to club, hoping to run into the pianist. But he was unlucky that night and had to wait until the next morning. At his hotel in the rue Pigalle, Waller handed Panassié a letter of introduction given him by John Hammond, already a very influential jazz critic and impresario. Fats also explained that he and Spencer Williams were only on holiday in Paris; they had no engagements there, although they were due to perform in London[1] a few weeks later.

Panassié had plenty of chances to hear Fats Waller play at informal sessions during the time he was in Paris. 'I found almost as much pleasure in watching him as in listening to him,' he has written. 'His appearance when he played was a complete reflection of his style. The body leant slightly backwards, a half-smile on the lips which seemed to say, "I'm really enjoying myself; wait a bit, now listen to that, not bad, eh? . . ." He only raised his hands a very little from the keyboard. Thus the incredible power of his playing proceeds not so much from the rapidity of his attack as from its heaviness. Its force is not nervous at all, but muscular. . . .'[2] At Waller's last meeting with Panassié in Paris he assured the French critic that he would see him in about a fortnight, after the engagement in London. 'The next day', writes Panassié, 'I learned from Spencer Williams that Fats had indeed taken a boat— but for America.' Two explanations have been offered for Waller's precipitate departure. The first, and most commonly accepted, is that he suddenly became homesick; the other was given by John Hammond in the *Melody Maker*[3] only a couple of months later when he wrote: 'I am distressed to learn that he [Fats Waller] did not get to England after all because of some consular difficulty'.

Apocryphal anecdotes and dubious legends have gained plenty of credence with jazz historians. Some may even have been perpetuated in these very pages. One that until quite recently was certainly accepted as being genuine concerns Waller's stay in Paris, and tells how Fats and the celebrated French organist, Marcel Dupré, clambered up to the organ loft of Notre-Dame cathedral. There, as Fats put it, 'First he played on the God box, then I played on the God box.' The French pianist, Eddie Bernard, who knew how partial Waller was to tongue-in-the-cheek humour, once asked Panassié if the story was true. 'Yes, Fats told me all about it the same evening,' replied the French critic. 'Marcel Dupré invited him there. Unfortunately at the time it happened, Fats didn't inform me.' After making a few investigations, however, Bernard eventually discovered that none of Waller's acquaintances in Paris had witnessed this incident at Notre-Dame. He set out, therefore, to interview M. Dupré, now the organist at the Church of Saint Sulpice, and was admitted to the presence of Madame Dupré. 'As soon as I mentioned the words "Jazz Hot" ', writes Bernard, 'I had the feeling that I had offered a drink of whisky to a Moslem. "Sir", said Mme Dupré, "my husband abhors jazz." '[1] After explaining why he had come, Bernard was told that between the years 1927 and 1937 M. Dupré had never set foot in Notre-Dame (he was not, it appears, on speaking terms with Louis Vierne, the organist there during that period) and Fats Waller had certainly never visited Saint Sulpice. Louis Vierne had died in 1937, but Bernard managed to contact a friend of his, only to find that she too knew nothing about a meeting between either Dupré or Vierne and Fats Waller. At last Bernard called upon Pierre Cocherau, the present organist at Notre-Dame. Cocherau was charming. 'Oh yes,' he said, 'Fats Waller *did* play on the Notre-Dame organ.' But then it was discovered that the musician Cocherau was thinking of had actually been a white American, and that that incident took place in 1937. Finally Bernard went back to Cocherau and begged him to search his memory for the name of the person who had told him about Waller playing the cathedral organ. 'It was my assistant, Moreau,' said Cocherau eventually. Eddie Bernard spoke to Moreau, who quickly answered: 'Of

---

[1] This was probably to have been at the Kit-Kat Club.

[2] *Douze Années de Jazz*. Corrêa, Paris, 1946. An extract—*Fats Waller In Paris*—was translated and published in *The P.L. Yearbook of Jazz*. Nicholson & Watson, 1946.

[3] October 1932.

[1] *Jazz Hot*, c. 1958. An extract was translated and reprinted in *Metronome*, December 1958.

course Fats Waller played on the Notre-Dame organ in 1932!' But when Moreau was asked how he knew this, he thought hard for a moment, then replied: 'I read it on the sleeve of a Fats Waller record.'

5

'Mr. Waller, what is swing?' asked the American matron. 'Lady, if you got to ask, you ain't got it,' replied the pianist, twitching an eyebrow at his questioner. This riposte—pithy, truthful, characteristic—has become the most-quoted utterance by any jazz musician. It also serves as a good introduction to the last ten years of Fats Waller's life, a decade that also happens to be known in the jazz world as 'the swing era'. From being a music that appealed only to the Negro population, economically always the poorest segment of American society, and to a small minority of whites, the original 'jazz buffs', jazz suddenly became commercial. 'It don't mean a thing if it ain't got that swing,' sang Ivie Anderson with Duke Ellington's orchestra back in 1932, a year when 'swing' was still a verb, a name for the quality that distinguished a good from a bad jazz performance. When, six years later, Billie Holiday sang 'Once they called it ragtime, now they call it swing', the change was not only a matter of semantics, it also expressed the truth about the music itself. 'Swing' had turned into a noun, a smart new name for jazz, an identifying trademark for a thing, a product, which could be bought and sold very profitably. And the result, surprisingly enough, was a revolution in taste, a revolution which, despite all its attendant vulgarity and debasement, raised the general level of American popular music. It also provided jobs for a lot of jazz musicians who until then had been faced with the alternatives of going hungry or playing rubbish.

But all this still lay in the future when Fats Waller sailed back to New York in the autumn of 1932. One of the first things he did after landing was to engage a manager, Phil Ponce, who promptly arranged for him to do a series of programmes—Fats Waller's Rhythm Club—over radio station WLW at Cincinatti. It was while working on this show, incidentally, that the pianist first became known as 'the harmful little armful' ('the cheerful little earful' seems to have been a later variant). A student at the Cincinatti Conservatory of Music, Kay C. Thompson, who used to play the piano over WLW, remembers most vividly her first meeting with Fats: 'As I was concluding the final number of one of my regular stints,' she has written, 'I chanced to look up, and there he was, making faces at me through the studio window.... Instinctively I made faces in return. Such, then, were the beginnings of our friendship.'[1] Fats Waller's Rhythm Club became so popular that it later toured as a vaudeville act on the RKO theatre circuit, yet Waller himself, so Miss Thompson avers, got far more satisfaction out of playing WLW's Wurlitzer organ on a late-night programme, Moon River. This programme consisted entirely of classics, light classics and ballads, so Waller always performed on it anonymously, although his identity was occasionally betrayed by the embellishments he added to some of the compositions.

In 1934 Fats was busy in New York once more, appearing at a number of clubs, including Adrian's Tap Room, a club operated by the bass-saxophonist and vibraphone player, Adrian Rollini. His radio commitments, however, were beginning to interfere with cabaret work. Soon he was doing a couple of broadcasts on his own each week (one was yet another version of Fats Waller's Rhythm Club) as well as making guest appearances on such programmes as Saturday Revue, Morton Downey's House Party, The Columbia Revue and Harlem Serenade. Side by side with all this activity came the chance to make a series of records for the Victor company. Not only had Fats not recorded at all during 1933, but he had recorded nothing under his own name since the spring of 1931. Phil Ponce, however, secured him a new contract and on 16 May 1934 the first of over fifty sessions by Fats Waller and his Rhythm took place. This rise to success began at a time when another great pianist and bandleader, Jelly Roll Morton, was suffering a fall from popularity. During the late 1920s

[1] *Jazz Journal*, May 1951.

Victor had advertised Morton's Red Hot Peppers as 'The Number One Hot Band', but soon after R.C.A. took over the company in 1930 Morton found himself being looked on as old-fashioned. It was just another indication of the way that jazz was changing. Jelly Roll made a few half-hearted attempts at enlarging his group and playing big-band swing, but eventually his contract was allowed to lapse. Although Duke Ellington recorded for Victor he was never their exclusive artist for very long, so it was Fats

out the next nine years. Fats would play the opening chorus on piano and then sing the second chorus (or vice versa), after which there would be a solo on the trumpet or tenor-saxophone. The final chorus would be sung, or else 'jammed' by the band. 'I divide Wallerism into three classes—the Riotous, the Mildly Irresponsible, and the Blues,' wrote Leslie Barnard,[1] and his light-hearted definition came very near the truth. Most of the recordings Fats Waller made with 'his Rhythm' were either exuberant,

Max Jones

A convivial group in Paris (1932). *Left to right:* Louis Coles, Ivan Browning, Grant Fisher, unidentified member of the Kentucky Singers, Fats Waller, Spencer Williams, Bricktop

Waller who virtually took over Morton's old position. And where Jelly Roll had failed to make his jazz commercial enough to satisfy the audience of those Depression years, Waller, by an ironic twist of events, owed much of his fame to the brutality with which he burlesqued and lampooned the more banal of the songs he was asked to perform.

The performances at that first session in the spring of 1934 set a pattern which remained almost unaltered through-

noisy performances or else slow and gentle, perhaps with Fats playing the celeste very delicately, yet often with mockery lurking behind the reticence. Hugues Panassié once described the records by this group as possessing an ease and abandon rarely found elsewhere; they were, he declared, 'almost the only records on which the musicians play exactly as they would in a nightclub.'[2] Although there were fine soloists in the band, quite apart from

[1] *Melody Maker*, 21 May 1938.

[2] *The Real Jazz*. Smith & Durrell, New York, 1946.

354

In England (1938)

Duncan Schiedt

Waller himself, the merits of the performances lay quite as much in this element of relaxation as in the brilliance of individual performers. But then this group, with its personnel almost unchanged for years on end, made so many records that the musicians must have developed a nonchalant attitude to the whole business. Four titles were cut on that first session—*A Porter's Love Song To A Chambermaid, I Wish I Were Twins, Armful of Sweetness,* and *Do Me A Favour,* the last-named being a particularly outstanding performance—with a band consisting of Herman Autrey (trumpet), Ben Whittet (clarinet and alto-sax), Waller himself at the piano, Albert Casey (guitar),

Billy Taylor (bass) and Harry Dial (drums). When a second session was made, three months later, however, Whittet was replaced by that fine tenor-player, Eugene Sedric.

Casey, Sedric and Autrey all played with Fats Waller throughout the 1930s and were the key men in his band, yet neither Casey nor Sedric—the two best soloists—have ever really been given the praise they deserve. This is particularly true of Casey, who must be one of the finest guitarists that jazz has known. When that first session was recorded he was only nineteen and still going to music school, and by an odd coincidence, although actually born

355

in Louisville, Kentucky, he had attended DeWitt Clinton High School. A guitarist who mixes single-string work with rich chords and subtle changes, Casey has always imparted a remarkable swing to his solos and there is strength as well as resilience in his playing. It is interesting, therefore, to discover that because so much of his solo work has been concentrated upon the first string of his guitar, he eventually started using a B (second) string in the first string position to give extra power. Casey is featured at length in the 1941 recording of *Buck Jumpin'* and takes a great many short solos on other records, notably in *Georgia May, Do Me A Favour, Mandy, Black Raspberry Jam, Paswonky, What's The Reason, Dust Off That Old Piano* and *I Ain't Got Nobody*. Most of these solos are played in an expansive, chorded style, but his single-string work can be heard at its finest in *Fats Waller's Original E Flat Blues*. And as well as being a superb soloist, Casey also performed imaginatively within the ensemble, often improvising a counter-melody behind Waller's singing; a good example of this can be found during the first part of the vocal chorus in *Dream Man*.

When Eugene ('Honeybear') Sedric began recording with Fats Waller he had just returned from a tour of Europe with Sam Wooding's orchestra, and before working regularly with Waller he played in the bands of Fletcher Henderson and Don Redman. Born in St. Louis, Missouri, where his father, Paul Sedric (known locally as 'Can-Can'), had been a well-known ragtime pianist, Eugene Sedric had played as a youth aboard Mississippi riverboats with Charlie Creath and Fate Marable, and this background of New Orleans music was reflected in his supple, lyrical phrasing on the clarinet. But it is as a tenor-saxophonist that Eugene Sedric is at his best, and Fats Waller once called him 'God's gift to the tenor-sax'. In the 1930s he was also something of an exception among tenor-players, for his style did not derive directly from that of Coleman Hawkins, a musician whose influence upon tenor-saxophonists during that decade was almost as complete as Armstrong's upon trumpet-players. Sedric, indeed, possessed a more vehement manner than Hawkins, at the same time very direct and much less baroque; yet he could also play with extreme delicacy and warmth, and always displayed exceptional inventiveness. Among the best of the many solos he recorded with Fats Waller are those in *Don't Let It Bother You, Baby Brown, Bye Bye Baby, Boo Hoo, Oh! Frenchy, Hallelujah! Thing Looks Rosy Now, Something Tells Me, 'Tain't Nobody's Bizness* and *Pantin' In The Panther Room*.

Although Herman Autrey was always a much more erratic soloist than either Casey or Sedric, his playing nonetheless possessed a fiery, impetuous quality that fitted in excellently with the general character of the band. Like the other two musicians he was a Southerner, coming from Alabama, and he had played with the bands of Charlie Johnson and Fletcher Henderson before working regularly with Fats Waller. The muted half-chorus in *Don't You Know Or Don't You Care* is perhaps the best solo he ever recorded with Waller, but he also played very satisfyingly in *Let's Pretend There's A Moon, Twelfth Street Rag,* and *Yacht Club Swing*.

For his third session, made in September 1934, Waller brought in two white Chicagoans—the trombonist, Floyd O'Brien, and the clarinettist, Mezz Mezzrow. The result was an exceptionally good set of performances: *Serenade For A Wealthy Widow, How Can You Face Me, Sweetie Pie, Mandy, Let's Pretend There's A Moon* and *You're Not The Only Oyster In The Stew*. Two months later he recorded again with his usual group, except that Bill Coleman, a very lyrical trumpet-player, took the place of Herman Autrey, producing three outstanding sides in *Honeysuckle Rose, Believe It Beloved* and *Dream Man*. A week later Fats rounded off the year by recording four piano solos— *African Ripples, Clothes Line Ballet, Alligator Crawl* and *Viper's Drag*, all of them to be ranked among his very best work.

With his Rhythm, Fats Waller made seven sessions for the Victor company during 1935, the most notable performances being of *Baby Brown, I Ain't Got Nobody, Because Of Once Upon A Time, I'm Gonna Sit Right Down And Write Myself A Letter* (probably the most popular of all his recordings), *Twelfth Street Rag* and *Sweet Sue*. There was, in addition, a curious session which found the regular Waller group augmented by side-men from Don Redman's orchestra, including Redman himself, but only two sides were ever issued off this date—*Functionizin'* and *I Got Rhythm*. Fats also recorded thirty-one titles, playing the piano and singing, for Muzak-Associated, a company which supplied material to broadcasting stations. Luckily all those recordings, together with similar ones made four years later, have been issued commercially during the past few years. The late summer and autumn of 1935, however, found Fats Waller out in Hollywood, taking part in two films—*Hooray For Love* and *King of Burlesque*, the former starring Ann Sothern and Gene Raymond and with dancing and singing by Bill 'Bojangles' Robinson; the cast of the latter was headed by Warner Baxter, Jack Oakie, and Alice Faye, and the film included a sequence in which Fats sang and played *I've Got My Fingers Crossed*. These film appearances, of course, were yet another indication of the way that Waller's personality—his personality much more than his piano-playing—with its atmosphere of *bonhomie* and gentle leg-pulling, joined to the melodic impudence of his singing, were becoming widely popular among the American public.

This popularity was once more reflected in the fact that during 1936 Fats Waller made more recordings than in any previous year. There were eight sessions altogether, the resulting performances including such fine sides as *Christopher Columbus, You're Not The Kind Of A Girl For A Boy Like Me, Bach Up To Me, Paswonky, It's A Sin To Tell A Lie, S'posin', Tain't Good, Hallelujah! Things Look Rosy Now, I'm Sorry I Made You Cry, Until The Real Thing Comes Along, Swingin' Them Jingle Bells, One In A Million* and *Nero*. And by now Waller was touring, playing at dance-halls as well as in vaudeville, with a regular orchestra—Charlie Turner's Arcadians—that included all the musicians who appeared on his records. Charlie Turner, of course, was the bass player who had taken over from Billy Taylor at the beginning of 1936. Fats was now beginning to earn really good money and a token of this new prosperity was the fact that he bought and rode about in a $7,000 Lincoln De Luxe automobile. But his success as a touring bandleader was constantly being jeopardized by his unpredictability. Despite the loyalty of Eugene Sedric, who declares he never saw Fats late at a job or unable to play, other reports suggest that he failed to turn up at several engagements, and rumours of unreliability spread very quickly among agents and band bookers. Meanwhile the records continued to pour out in a steady stream, eight sessions in 1937 producing such fine sides as *San Anton', The Meanest Thing You Ever Did Was Kiss Me, Sweet Heartache*, the boisterous

The Joint Is Jumping and twelve-inch versions of *Honeysuckle Rose* and *Blue Turning Grey Over You*. Fats also recorded five piano solos (*Keepin' Out Of Mischief Now, Stardust, Basin Street Blues, Tea For Two* and *I Ain't Got Nobody*) and took part in the all-star *Jam Session at Victor*, playing *Honeysuckle Rose* and *Blues* in the company of Bunny Berigan, Tommy Dorsey, Dick McDonough and George Wettling.

The winter of 1937-8 saw some changes take place in Fats Waller's personal and musical affairs. For some time Phil Ponce had been in bad health and now he handed over the management of the pianist and his band to Ed Kirkeby, previously an Artists and Repertoire executive with several major record companies. And it was also around this time that Buck and Bubbles (Buck Washington and John Sublett), the Negro variety act, took over leadership of Charlie Turner's Arcadians and Waller began using Don Donaldson's orchestra instead, while retaining, of course, all the key-men from his recording group. The full personnel of the touring band in the spring of 1938 consisted of John Hamilton, Courtney Williams and Herman Autrey (trumpets); John Haughton and George Robinson (trombones); Lionel Simmons, William Allsop, Freddy Skerritt, James Powell and Eugene Sedric (reeds); Fats Waller and Don Donaldson (pianos), Albert Casey (guitar), Cedric Wallace (bass) and Slick Jones (drums). With this group Waller set off early in 1938 on a series of one-night stands in the South. The tour, however, was something of a disaster. For one thing Fats's habit of missing engagements had become too well known, with the result that bookers were growing chary of using him; and for another, many of the engagements at which he did turn up were hardly worth the journey, as on the occasion when the band arrived in a small Mississippi town to find a dance-hall built on stilts and without any piano. It was probably on this tour, as well, that anti-Negro hoodlums slashed the tyres of Waller's car and poured sand into its crankcase.

In between tours, however, Waller continued to record prolifically, although more and more he was being given unsuitable material, pop-songs of the very cheapest kind. Leonard Feather, at that time a regular features writer and record reviewer for the *Melody Maker*, visited New York in the spring of 1938 and his account of a recording session he attended emphasizes this point. First of all, however, he commented upon the surprisingly sober nature of the session, the scene lacking completely that abandon which characterized the finished records. 'The musicians', he wrote, 'sat calmly in their places, scarcely even talking, except to confirm details with Fats as he hastily sketched out a routine for the number.'[1] Each man was provided with a skeleton arrangement, usually little more than a set of chord sequences. Then Fats played little phrases on the piano, his suggestions for background riffs, to Eugene Sedric and Herman Autrey, after which the band started recording. Feather goes on to describe the pressure put on Waller to record a song he had never heard before, a pop-song of very indifferent quality. Waller tried again and again, struggling with the unfamiliar melody and lyrics, but each time unsuccessfully. 'Then', writes Feather, 'he started strumming the recently popularised Harlem hymn to marijuana, *If You're A Viper*. Sedric and Autrey worked out a grand riff to carry right through the record. Fats played a wonderful chorus on the celeste with his right hand, accompanying himself on the piano with his left. Everyone could see that *If You're A Viper* was going to be a killer; everyone, that is, except those in charge of the session, who still insisted that Fats record the pop tune. After further verbal engagements, to appease Mr. Waller a wax was used on *If You're A Viper*, after which the pop was again insisted upon and Fats struggled through it, though with such difficulty that he did not even attempt to play piano during his vocal.'[2] The following week Feather inquired what had happened to *If You're A Viper*, adding that he felt sure it would be Fats's best record in many months. He was told that the master had been destroyed, and that the pop tune would be used instead.

[1] *Melody Maker*, 30 July 1938.
[2] *Melody Maker*, 30 July 1938.

When one remembers the commercial pressures under which Fats Waller had to work, the large quantity of mediocre songs he was forced to record, the apathy of most Artists and Repertoire men to what was really worthwhile in his music, it seems all the more amazing that he should have created so many fine recordings. During the first seven months of 1938, for instance, he recorded three sessions, producing such excellent sides as *Something Tells Me*, *The Sheik Of Araby* (this one with the full Don Donaldson orchestra), and *If I Were You*. In May of that year he also made a broadcast to Britain, one of a series of relays of American jazz bands that the B.B.C. was running at the time; Edgar Jackson, who in those days reviewed radio programmes for the *Melody Maker* under the pseudonym of 'Detector', praised the broadcast highly, describing Fats as 'the Peter Pan and the Little Audrey of jazz rolled into one'.

But Fats Waller's life during this period was growing more and more harassed and difficult. The tour of the South had been a complete failure and he was also being chased again for payment of alimony to his first wife. And after enjoying three years of popularity there now seemed to be a slump, a decline in his drawing power; or perhaps it was merely that the band bookers were just being cautious. At any rate Ed Kirkeby was faced with the problem of keeping Waller not only in good spirits but also in work. He knew that the pianist enjoyed a big reputation in Europe and conceived the idea of sending him on a continental tour. 'Send a wire', he told Tommy Rockwell, the head of a major American booking agency, 'and find out if there's any demand for Fats—at $2,500 a week.' 'Are you crazy?' Rockwell is supposed to have retorted. 'Send the wire anyway,' said Kirkeby. They received an answer the same day. It read: INTERESTED STOP WHEN CAN HE START.

6

When Fats Waller, his wife Anita, and Ed Kirkeby strolled down the gangplank of the *Transylvania* at Greenock one July afternoon in 1938, they were greeted by some very familiar sounds. Billy Mason's Empirex Orchestra, with Duncan Whyte blowing plenty of Armstrong phrases on his trumpet, welcomed the American visitors by playing

Waller's best-known tune, *Honeysuckle Rose*. The following Monday night, at the Glasgow Empire, the reception was even more overwhelming. It was, Fats assured the jubilant audience, the greatest reception he had ever had in his life. He responded to it by sitting down again at the piano, with a plaid beret perched on top of his head, and playing *Loch Lomond*—dead straight. Only when a man high up in the gallery shouted 'Hey, Fats, swing it!' did the pianist unbend and start twisting the melody to his own ends.

A week later Fats arrived in London. 'The mighty atom, Fats Waller, shook the Palladium to its foundations,' wrote Dan Ingman. 'On a tastefully draped stage was a white grand piano and a white celeste. Fats started off with *Marie*. Then followed *I'm Gonna Sit Right Down*, *St. Louis Blues*, *Handful of Keys*, *Ain't Misbehavin'* ("introduced to England by my little friend Louis Armstrong") and finishing up with *Flat Foot Floogie*. . . . He had to rely on the pit orchestra, and very little support did he get. Not only was the accompaniment so loud as to drown most of Fats' vocalisms, but it actually dragged one beat behind for a whole chorus until Fats played a miraculous nine-beat break to put it right.' After saying that the jazz fans in the audience were obviously delighted by Waller's performance, Ingman went on to point out that Fats did not get all the applause he deserved. 'Perhaps', he concluded, 'the answer lies in the fact that Elsie and Doris Waters were also on the bill, and undoubtedly brought hundreds of their supporters to the house.'[1] It is reassuring, by the way, to turn to the following week's *Melody Maker* and to find that the puritan streak in British jazz collectors—a streak that nowadays becomes inflamed at the antics of Louis Armstrong, Lionel Hampton and even Duke Ellington—was already in evidence. 'We are quite sure that if Fats had done the Indian rope trick Ingman's enthusiasm would have known no bounds', said a letter from two young Scots, A.M.B. and G.T.V. of Dumbarton, who complained that they found Waller's 'ridiculously vulgar act . . . nauseating in the extreme.'

A second week at the Palladium was followed by bookings at the Stratford, Holborn and Finsbury Park Empires and then at the Leeds Empire. It was at the Finsbury Park Empire, recalls Jeff Aldam, that Waller discovered

a trombonist in the pit orchestra who could actually play jazz. He was so good, apparently, that Fats insisted he improvise behind his vocal choruses. That trombonist's identity, alas, remains shrouded in mystery. Meanwhile Waller was enjoying himself. Not only did he renew his friendship with Spencer Williams, who had stayed in Europe in 1932 and now lived at Sunbury-on-Thames, he also met scores of young jazz collectors who could talk for hours about his records. In fact his only moments of disquietude occurred when he travelled by car; as a man accustomed to driving on the right-hand side of the road, Waller shrank back in terror whenever he saw a Green Line coach hurtling toward him.

Leonard Feather had approached H.M.V. with a suggestion that Fats Waller should record with a pick-up group of British musicians, and that session took place at H.M.V.'s Abbey Road studios on a Sunday afternoon, 21 August. Some of the musicians really went out of their way to be present. The West Indian trumpeter, Dave Wilkins, travelled down from Glasgow and immediately after the session hurried off to Liverpool, where he was due to work with Ken 'Snakehips' Johnson's orchestra, while the trombonist, George Chisholm, became probably the first musician ever to interrupt a honeymoon for a recording date; he flew over from Jersey on the Sunday, then flew back again the following morning. Also taking part were Alfie Kahn, playing tenor-sax and clarinet; Ian Shepherd, a Scottish musician who doubled on violin and tenor-sax; yet another Scot, the guitarist Alan Ferguson; Len Harrison on bass; and behind the drums a West Indian who in those days performed regularly at the Nest Club— Edmundo Ros. Six sides were recorded by the band: *Don't Try Your Jive On Me* (a Leonard Feather composition), *Ain't Misbehavin'*, *Flat Foot Floogie*, *Pent Up In A Penthouse*, *Music Maestro Please* and *A-Tisket, A-Tasket*. In addition Waller played some solos, nearly all of them of Negro spirituals, on H.M.V.'s Compton organ, and used the same instrument to accompany the singer, Adelaide Hall, in *That Old Feeling*, and *I Can't Give You Anything But Love*.

Adelaide Hall, although she was now living in Britain, had been a member of the *Blackbirds* show and had recorded with the Duke Ellington orchestra. She had also been responsible for bringing Art Tatum to New York

[1] *Melody Maker*, 13 August 1938.

as her accompanist at a time when that pianist was completely unknown. And now, as well as recording together, she and Fats Waller took part in a fifteen-minute broadcast which was relayed by the B.B.C. to the United States. Soon afterwards Waller left for the Continent, spending a fortnight touring Denmark, Sweden and Norway. He returned to Britain on 28 September for a one-night engagement at Sherry's in Brighton and to broadcast with Jay Wilbur's band on the following evening. That was, however, a week of crisis, with Germany invading Czechoslovakia and the world poised on the brink of a second world war. Because the Regional wavelength was needed for news broadcasts to foreign countries, Waller's programme, originally scheduled to go out on that wavelength at 8 p.m., was transferred without previous warning to five o'clock in the afternoon on the National wavelength. Because of this many listeners missed the broadcast altogether. Two days later, while Neville Chamberlain was busy negotiating the Munich agreement, Fats Waller sailed back to New York.

During Fats Waller's absence in Europe, most of his musicians had been working with other bands. Herman Autrey, for instance, had joined the Claude Hopkins orchestra. As soon as he arrived back, however, Fats got his men together again and started playing at the Yacht Club on 52nd Street. Decorated in the style of a pleasure yacht, its ceiling sprinkled with glittering artificial stars, this club stood only a few yards away from the Famous Door, where Count Basie's orchestra was making a name for itself. Waller's stay at the Yacht Club was the longest he ever made at one place, and when he left in January 1939 it was to fulfil engagements at the Apollo Theatre in Harlem and the Howard Theatre, Washington. Before that, however, he became involved in a melodramatic episode which was reported by Leonard Feather in the *Melody Maker*.[1] Early in December, with the New York pavements covered in ice, Fats and his brother Edward left a nightclub at about five in the morning. They were about to enter a taxi when two white girls ran up to ask Fats for his autograph. Two men, who were with the girls, came across and tried to drag them away, cursing and beating

them, and when Fats's brother protested one of the men— a twenty-two-year-old convict named Kehoe—drew a gun and fired two shots into Edward Waller's chest and legs. Kehoe was then battered into unconsciousness by the infuriated Fats, with the help of several bystanders.

Between his arrival back in the United States and his departure for a second tour of Europe in March 1939, Fats Waller and his Rhythm made five recording sessions, producing such excellent sides as *Two Sleepy People*, *You Look Good To Me*, *Yacht Club Swing*, *Good For Nothing But Love*, *Step Up And Shake My Hand* and *Undecided*. In addition Fats recorded six titles for the Martin Block radio show as a member of an all-star band that also comprised Louis Armstrong, Jack Teagarden, Bud Freeman and probably Al Casey and Zutty Singleton. When he finally travelled back to Europe, it was aboard the same boat as the four Mills Brothers, for the two acts were being booked together on a fourteen-week tour of British theatres. Ed Kirkeby had tried hard to get the Ministry of Labour to allow Fats to bring his own band with him this time, but the Ministry, no doubt advised by the Musicians' Union, refused to permit this.

When Fats Waller performed at the Holborn Empire (with the Mills Brothers on another part of the same programme) the *Melody Maker* reviewer was a little harsher than before. 'They [the fans] got more for their eyes than their ears,' he began. 'The necessity of playing from the stage to an audience which seems to expect to see Fats wriggle his scalp and roll his eyes at the antics of an active right hand, seems to take the 15-minute programme into the field of an exhibition rather than a jazz recital. . . .'[1] No doubt A.M.B. and G.T.V. of Dumbarton agreed with him. The tour, however, was notable for the fact that Fats was spurred into producing a batch of new compositions. Four of these were written with Spencer Williams and included *Cottage In The Rain*, a song inspired by a wet week-end at Williams's house beside the Thames. Another song was born in Sheffield, where Waller woke Ed Kirkeby up at six o'clock one morning. 'Tiny and I [Tiny was Waller's chauffeur],' said Fats, 'we've been walkin' in the botanical gardens, and the birds played me a song. Come on down.' When Kirkeby got downstairs Fats was in his

[1] 17 December 1938.

[1] *Melody Maker*, 25 March 1939.

dressing-gown, playing the piano and drinking sherry. 'Let's have a libation first,' he proposed, then started playing a melody. Kirkeby listened for a time in silence. 'I got it,' he said suddenly. 'When we came over on the *Queen Mary* and you were talking to that gushy woman, you said "Honey, hush". That's it—"Honey Hush".' Two hours later *Honey Hush* had been completed and Kirkeby crept back to bed again.

But the most important work which Waller did during this visit was to record his *London Suite*, a set of six piano solos. What actually happened was that Waller and Ed Kirkeby went along to Billy Higgs's studios at the beginning of April,[1] and while Kirkeby gave rapid verbal sketches of Piccadilly, Chelsea, Bond Street, Soho, Limehouse and Whitechapel, Fats—assisted by Johnny Marks on drums—improvised a separate solo for each thoroughfare or locality. According to Kirkeby the entire suite was composed and recorded within an hour. At the same time Waller recorded three of his new songs—*You Can't Have Your Cake And Eat It, Not There—Right There*, and *Cottage In The Rain*; the first two sides have been issued by Tempo, but the third—a very attractive tune, yet so far unpublished—has only appeared on the semi-private Ristic label.

Sunday 2 April was another eventful day in British jazz history. The afternoon found Coleman Hawkins playing in a jam session at the Phœnix Theatre, while that evening Geraldo presented the first of his Sunday Night Swing Club Concerts at the St. Martin's Theatre. The Heralds of Swing, a newly formed, short-lived orchestra, dedicated to playing jazz and composed of star British musicians like George Chisholm and Tommy McQuater, acted as the

house band, Eddie Pola and Sam Browne were the compères, while the guest artists included Una Mae Carlisle (an American girl pianist who sounded remarkably like Fats), Don and Jimmy Macaffer, George Shearing, the Radio Revellers and Fats Waller. The evening was musically a success, despite the fact that the theatre was only two-thirds full (a significant indication of how poorly jazz concerts were supported in London during the pre-war years). Later that night Waller played blues for half an hour at the Nest Club, his piano backed up by George Chisholm's trombone and Tiny Winters's string bass.

Fats Waller did not leave Britain until 14 June, and the day before he sailed he went to the H.M.V. studios to make commercial recordings of his *London Suite*. The results, however, were far from satisfactory (Waller, it seems, was disgusted with the studio drummer, who failed to produce any kind of beat). The recordings were not issued at the time, and during the war the masters were destroyed. Not until eleven years later did shellac pressings of five of the solos turn up; the sixth was discovered lying in a London publisher's office by Ed Kirkeby himself, when he visited Britain with the Deep River Boys in 1950. In this way the entire set was eventually assembled, dubbed and released commercially.

Before Waller went into the H.M.V. studios he had spent some weeks touring Scandinavia. At one point it was necessary for him to travel through Germany to get to Sweden, but he refused to make the trip unless his compartment was sealed. At Hamburg, however, he was forced to change trains, and the first thing he saw after leaving his compartment was a detachment of Nazi Storm Troopers goose-stepping outside the station. Three months later, when Fats Waller was back in America, these men and their deluded comrades brought war to Europe.

---

[1] The date of 12 June, usually given for the original recording of the *London Suite*, is patently false. A full account of the session, together with a photograph, appeared in the *Melody Maker* on 8 April 1939.

7

'We were on the road a lot,' recalls Eugene Sedric, writing about his touring days with Fats Waller, 'and while we were on the road there was no chance to record, so we'd

need a hit when we did. It's a funny thing that out of the hundreds of great hits Fats made on records, most of all the largest hits were numbers he didn't care about making, but we'd just go into it spontaneously, and some of the ones we didn't like and thought no good turned out to be the greatest hits.'[1]

Leaving things to chance was almost the guiding principle of Fats Waller's life, except where his piano-playing was concerned. When he returned to America in the summer of 1939 he was thirty-five years old, yet he showed no signs of steadying up as he crept closer to middle age. He grew more and more audacious, if anything, sometimes inserting the most outrageous ad-libbed remarks into his performances. A typical image of Waller at that time would probably have had him sitting at the piano, his derby hat tilted on one side, winking and leering at his audience as he butchered yet another sentimental lyric with a chuckle and some salty innuendo. But not all of Fats's wisecracks were bawdy. 'I wonder what the poor people are doing tonight?' he once remarked, almost quizzically, to a particularly prosperous gathering of socialites at a smart New York nightclub.

As soon as he got back to the United States, Waller took his band into the Famous Door on 52nd Street; then, on 12 August, they opened in the Panther Room of the Hotel Sherman in Chicago, playing opposite a group which was just making its début—Muggsy Spanier's Ragtimers. During the next few months Fats and his band covered a lot of territory; one week appearing at the Southland in Boston, the next at the Famous Door; now filling an eight-weeks engagement at the College Inn in Chicago, now working in variety at the Apollo Theatre or the Harlem Opera House (better known in Harlem as the 'Uproar House'). Within a week of his arrival in New York, after the trip to Europe, Fats was busy in the Victor studios, and between June and December 1939 the band played on three recording sessions, making such excellent sides as *Squeeze Me*, *Darktown Strutters' Ball* and the slyly boisterous *Your Feet's Too Big*. Four sessions held during 1940 produced, among other good performances, *Swinga Dilla Street*, *Oh! Frenchy*, *Mighty Fine*, *The Moon Is Low*, *Too Tired*, *My Mommy Sent Me To The Store*, *Dry Bones*, *Hey, Stop Kissin' My Sister*, and *'Tain't Nobody's Bizness If I Do*. By this time John Hamilton had begun to play trumpet with the group, instead of Herman Autrey, but

[1] *Jazz Record*, March 1945.

otherwise the personnel stayed unchanged. Fats also recorded some transcriptions for broadcasting, both as a soloist and with the band, most of which have now been released commercially. In addition he played with Max Kaminsky's orchestra when it accompanied the singer Lee Wiley on a handful of titles, and he also sat in alongside Marty Marsala, George Brunies and Pee Wee Russell on a session for the Commodore label under Eddie Condon's leadership. As Fats was under contract to the Victor company he displayed untypical prudence by using a pseudonym—in this case the name of his son, Maurice. Finally, to round off 1940, Fats and his Rhythm appeared in four short films: *Ain't Misbehavin'*, *Honeysuckle Rose*, *Your Feet's Too Big*, and *The Joint is Jumpin'*.

The seven recording sessions which took place in 1941 produced such oustanding performances as *Pantin' In The Panther Room*, *You're Gonna Be Sorry*, *Chant Of The Groove* (this one by the big band) and *Buck Jumpin'* (featuring Albert Casey), as well as five piano solos. And commercially, of course, Waller was in equally good form, playing to enthusiastic audiences everywhere; physically, however, he was beginning to feel the strain of years devoted to hard work and heavy drinking. By 1942 his doctor was warning him that he must take things more easily, and for a couple of months Fats stopped drinking. Earlier that year his tippling had almost ruined an event which should have been a landmark in his career—the concert he gave at Carnegie Hall on 14 January before an audience of over 2,800. The first half consisted of piano and organ solos, without any singing, and this went off passably well. During the interval, however, so many old friends dropped in backstage to wish him luck that Fats was more than a little bemused when he returned to the platform. He began by playing a medley of Gershwin tunes, including *Summertime*, and after that everything he attempted kept turning into *Summertime*. Perhaps the most memorable music created during that erratic evening was Albert Casey's long guitar solo in *Buck Jumpin'*.

Fats recorded only a couple of sessions with his band before the American Federation of Musicians imposed its ban on recording in the summer of 1942, a ban which stayed in force until the following year. Then, in the winter of 1942–3, he travelled to Hollywood to appear in the all-Negro musical film, *Stormy Weather*. Lena Horne,

Bill 'Bojangles' Robinson and Cab Calloway's orchestra were all featured in that film, but the most enduring sequence was a scene in a gin-mill where Fats bandies lines with the blues-singer, Ada Brown, in a song called *That Ain't Right.* The pianist was also heard performing *Ain't Misbehavin'* and *Moppin' and Boppin'* with a group that included Benny Carter (trumpet), Alton Moore (trombone), Gene Porter (clarinet and tenor-sax), Irving Ashby (guitar), Slam Stewart (bass) and Zutty Singleton (drums). One critic wrote of the film: 'Fats Waller lifted his eyebrow and really stole the picture.'

But in spite of his air of continual, almost relentless *bonhomie,* Fats was really a sick man. He finally disbanded his orchestra in May 1943 and the musicians proceeded to find themselves other jobs. Eugene Sedric got a small group of his own together and took it into The Place, a club in Greenwich Village; Herman Autrey and Slick Jones began working with Una Mae Carlisle; Cedric Wallace found himself a very comfortable and well-paid job playing bass at the fashionable Ruban Bleu Club. Only Albert Casey, the best musician of them all, failed to land on his feet; for quite a long time he was working for a very small wage at George's Tavern, one of the less fashionable clubs in the Village. Meanwhile Fats himself was busy composing the score for a new Broadway musical, *Early To Bed,* and later that year he recorded a selection of the songs, including *Slightly Less Than Wonderful, There's A Gal In My Life,* and the delicious *This Is So Nice It Must Be Illegal,* for V-Discs, the records which were distributed among the U.S. Armed Forces. *Early To Bed* turned out to be a great success, so much so that at the time of Waller's death Richard Kollman, the show's producer, was negotiating for Fats to write another musical, to be performed by an all-Negro cast.

Autumn moved into winter, the year was growing old. Fats Waller had to play three engagement—the first in Omaha, the second in Los Angeles, the last, at the beginning of December, in Hollywood, at the Florentine Gardens. Then he would travel home to New York to spend the Christmas holiday with his family. He got through the Omaha and Los Angeles dates successfully, but arrived in Hollywood suffering from a bad attack of influenza. At the end of the engagement there was an all-night farewell party, after which Ed Kirkeby loaded the pianist aboard the Santa Fé Chief at the railway station. Just as the train pulled out Fats sat down and said, 'Oh, man, I can't take this much longer.' Kirkeby agreed with him, saying that Fats must give up doing one-night stands. There was enough money coming in from records and other royalties for the pianist to take things easier. They walked into the club car, where Fats was at once surrounded by a crowd of people, and soon another party had got going. The next day Waller slept on until the evening, an event which was not at all unusual. At about two o'clock the next morning, however, Kirkeby opened the door of the room and a gust of cold air hit him in the face. 'Jesus, it's cold in here,' he said, and Fats replied: 'Yeah, Hawkins is sure out there tonight.'[1] 'About five that morning,' Kirkeby has related, 'I woke up and heard a choking sound. I saw Tom over there in bed, trembling all over. I shook him, thinking he was having a bad dream, but he didn't wake. The train was stopped at the time in Kansas City and I rushed to find a porter to get a doctor. Finally the doctor came and examined Tom. Then he said to me, "This man is dead".'[2]

Fats Waller died on 15 December 1943. An autopsy later diagnosed the cause of his death to be bronchial pneumonia. The effect upon musicians and jazz *aficionados* all over the world was quite stunning. James P. Johnson is said to have been so broken up by Waller's death that he could not touch a piano for several days afterwards. In Britain the B.B.C. carried the news in its nine o'clock bulletin, the first time it had ever done so for a jazz musician.

As might have been expected, Fats Waller's funeral was both large and expensive. The service took place at the Abyssinian Baptist Church, the same church at which Waller's father had been the pastor many years before. Not only was the church itself completely filled, but thousands of people waited in the streets outside. Hazel Scott played *Abide With Me* on the organ, and her husband, the Rev. Adam Clayton Powell, conducted the service. The pall-bearers included Count Basie, Don Redman, Claude Hopkins, Andy Kirk, Andy Razaf, J. C. Johnson, and

---

[1] He was referring, of course, to Coleman Hawkins's blustering style of tenor playing.

[2] Quoted by Al Silverman in *Eddie Condon's Treasury of Jazz.*

James P. Johnson. A memorial programme later took place at Café Society Downtown, where James P. Johnson performed his *Blues For Fats.*

Four months later, on 2 April 1944, a memorial concert was held at Carnegie Hall. Teddy Wilson went on first, with his little band; then James P. Johnson revived some old Waller tunes; Count Basie brought his band along, together with his blues-singer, Jimmy Rushing; Duke Ellington, Earl Hines and Mary Lou Williams all played solos, and Willie 'The Lion' Smith once more performed his *Echoes of Spring.* If only Art Tatum and Nat 'King' Cole had been in New York at the time, the list of jazz pianists would have been nearly complete. But the significant thing about this concert is that it was a gay affair. Backstage everybody started remembering uproarious incidents from the past in which Fats had been involved, and soon the dressing-room was filled with laughter and the loud slapping of hands upon knees. As Louis Armstrong put it: 'Every time someone mentions Fats Waller's name, why you can see the grins on all the faces, as if to say, "Yea, yea, yea, yea, Fats is a solid sender, ain't he?" '[1]

[1] Programme notes for Fats Waller Memorial Concert.

8

When Ronald, Fats Waller's youngest son, was asked at school what his father did for a living, he replied: 'He drinks gin.' In later years, of course, gin was replaced by whisky; four fingers immediately after rising, four more after shaving—that was Waller's 'liquid ham and eggs', his start to the day. Fats Waller, it cannot be denied, lived in an outsized way. Not only was he large physically (he normally weighed around twenty stone), but he also drank prodigiously and ate enormously. Yet it would be mistaken to think of him as a drunkard or glutton, a dissolute, self-pitying man. Food and drink were looked on rather as ways of renewing his energy, of enlarging his zest for life. He was a gentle man, too, compassionate, generous, and devoted to Anita and their two sons and adopted daughter. They all lived together in a modern brick house at St. Alban's, Long Island, in a street that could easily have been called Piano Row. James P. Johnson owned the house on one side, Clarence Williams that on the other, while only a few yards away lived Hank Duncan, another New York pianist and a protégé of Fats.

'One never knows, do one?' This favourite remark of Waller's, a phrase he was fond of tagging on to the end of a record or slipping into a broadcast, somehow expressed the puzzled tolerance, the sceptical kindliness of the man. At the peak of his career he had been earning as much as $72,000 a year, yet when he died he left no more than $20,000. But then he was a man to whom money meant very little, and anyone with a hard luck story always found him to be a 'soft touch'. Edith, his first wife, survived her former husband by eleven years, but Anita still lives in that house in St. Alban's, overlooking the park, with its built-in Hammond organ and Steinway grand piano.

A man whose favourite poets are Longfellow and Andy Razaf, whose heroes are Lincoln, Bach, Theodore Roosevelt and George Gershwin, shows himself to possess very eclectic tastes. And just as Waller embraced these opinions about literature and history, his music was equally catholic and broadly-based. Although the primary influence upon his playing was that of James P. Johnson, it would be foolish to overlook the difference between the two pianists. Johnson had started out playing ragtime, under the instruction of his mother, and his style grew out of that background. Waller, on the other hand, received an orthodox classical training before he began to play ragtime or jazz with any regularity. He brought to those idioms, therefore, a self-sufficient technique, whereas Johnson's instrumental ability was conditioned, to a large extent, by the music he played. As a result of this, Waller's playing was often lighter, and possessed more symmetry, than Johnson's. Both men, however, although Johnson's was the dominating contribution, helped in creating the stride piano style (sometimes called 'Harlem piano'), a direct descendant of ragtime but with heavier chords and a much more flexible and expressive technique.

'When I pointed out [to a musician] that some of Fats Waller's piano solos swing far more than many orchestral recordings,' writes André Hodeir, 'he answered aptly, "That's because Fats uses his left hand to suggest the presence of a bass fiddle".'[1] It is this power, this sense of solidity and purpose in Waller's playing that makes the strongest and most immediate impression. 'I remember [my father] emphasizing the use of tenths in the bass', recalls Maurice Waller, 'and he used to tell me that a piano man without a left hand is a very weak pianist. He also told me never to let the body, the richness get out of the piano. A pianist should be rich with sound and cover a distance too. I mean by that he should really play open chords—tenths, elevenths, etc.'[2] But perhaps the most distinctive aspect of Waller's piano style was his use of off-beats, always placed forcefully, never impetuously. He was fond, as well, of playing a walking bass, or of switching the melodic line to the left hand, sustaining the rhythm in the treble. Many of his bass figures were simple enough, but the relationship created between the heavy, left-hand tenths and the after-beat chords was subtle and delicately balanced, although lacking the complexity one finds in the work of some boogie-woogie pianists. But then Waller, like many Harlem pianists of his generation, was openly contemptuous of boogie-woogie playing ('Why? Because it's too monotonous—it all sounds the same'). According to the *New York Times* his contracts even contained a special clause forbidding any association of that style with his name.

As a soloist, Waller could play the blues magnificently, sometimes even better than James P. Johnson. He was also capable of transforming the melodies of popular songs as deftly and with the same kind of understanding that a singer such as Billie Holiday displays in twisting their lyrics and meaning. Fats was, however, sometimes criticized for falling back too frequently upon his own clichés —'Wallerisms' is the term usually employed; in this, of course, he resembled a soloist like Louis Armstrong or Sidney Bechet, both of whom use a variety of stock phrases. The technique seems legitimate enough when a performer has sufficient artistry to deploy these phrases intelligently and imaginatively, so that they spring from the pattern of his solo in a completely natural and spontaneous fashion. Fats was also fond of 'worrying' a passage, repeating a phrase again and again in order to increase tension, a device he seems to have passed on to Count Basie, a pianist who during his earlier years was strongly influenced by Waller.

Hugues Panassié once suggested that jazz pianists could be divided into two categories—'fat' and 'thin', the former playing the piano as if it were a miniature orchestra, using very full harmonies, the latter treating it as a solo instrument, concentrating upon a springing melodic line.[1] Oddly enough this division works out very successfully, for it is undeniable that the leading pianists of the 'fat' school (James P. Johnson, Fats Waller and Willie 'The Lion' Smith) have all been inclined to corpulence, while their opposite numbers (Earl Hines and Teddy Wilson, say) are much more slimly built. And whatever the fallacy underlying the physical analogy (and Erroll Garner tends to upset things a little), the musical distinction seems sound enough. The basis of the 'fat' style, of course, is the stressing of the strong beat with a powerful bass, a technique which gives force and solidity to a performance. It was this power in the left hand that made Waller perhaps the most stimulating of all ensemble pianists, one of a select company which also includes Jelly Roll Morton, Duke Ellington and Count Basie. But where these other musicians have been remarkable more for the way they 'fed' their soloists or sections, or controlled the dynamics of their orchestras, Waller's ensemble playing was outstanding because of its sheer rhythmic force. His presence within a band was equal to that of a complete rhythm section.

To some extent, of course, this expansive, orchestral style of Waller's must have been nourished by his long experience as an organist. And where playing jazz upon the organ is concerned, Fats remains completely unique; no one has come anywhere near equalling his performances on that instrument. Perhaps he was helped, as Mezz

---

[1] *Jazz: Its Evolution and Essence.* Secker & Warburg, 1956.
[2] *Hear Me Talkin' To Ya.*

[1] *The Real Jazz.*

Mezzrow suggests, by the fact that he possessed such enormous 'pedal extremities'. 'To watch those twenty pound feet moving delicately and sensitively over the keyboard of the bass of the immense organ in the Paramount studios', writes Mezzrow, 'was one of the most amazing sights imaginable.' Sometimes, when Fats wanted to change many stops in the organ (and there were hundreds of them), he would use his feet to produce the two or four bars between the chorus, for this gave him a chance to obtain the exact tone he wanted. 'He could play different passages in very fast tempo,' concludes Mezzrow, 'hardly giving time for the mechanism to work on the reeds of the organ. He played as though it were a piano.'[1]

[1] *Jazz Journal*, May 1953.

Since his death Fats Waller has been kept alive not only by his many recordings, but through the playing of pianists as diverse as Joe Sullivan, Johnny Guarnieri, Ralph Sutton, Art Tatum and Erroll Garner. Tatum, especially, was very proud of his musical origins: 'Fats, man, that's where I come from', he always used to say. Yet Waller's style of playing has also had its impact, although in an oblique rather than a direct sense, upon the work of musicians possessing a very different conception of jazz, pianists like Thelonious Monk and Bud Powell, for instance. But then Fats Waller, like all great jazz musicians, cannot be contained within any era or school of jazz. 'Some little people has music in them,' said James P. Johnson, shortly after Waller's death, 'but Fats, he was *all* music—and you know how big he was.'

DISCOGRAPHY

The following is a list of all Fats Waller LPs available in the United States at the time this book went to press.

JAZZ PIANO ANTHOLOGY
Muscle Shoals Blues (solo).
Columbia KC 32355

FATS WALLER AND HIS RHYTHM—'34/'35
Don't Let It Bother You, If It Isn't Love, Serenade for a Wealthy Widow, Black Bottom Blues (solo), *Mandy, You've Been Taking Lessons in Love, Numb Fumblin'* (solo), *(Oh Suzanna) Dust Off That Old Pianna, Somebody Stole My Gal, Breakin' the Ice, I Ain't Got Nobody, Goin' About* (solo), *Dinah, Whose Honey Are You?, Blue Because of You, 12th Street Rag.*
RCA Victor LPV 516

FATS WALLER AND HIS RHYTHM—VALENTINE STOMP
Got a Bran' New Suit, Thief in the Night, Let's Sing Again, Valentine Stomp (solo), *Sweet Thing, I've Got My Fingers Crossed, Spreadin' Rhythm Around, Black Raspberry Jam, Why Do I Lie to Myself About You?, Sugar Blues, I've Got a Feeling I'm Falling* (solo), *I Got Rhythm, The Girl I Left Behind Me, Love Me or Leave Me* (solo), *Sing an Old Fashioned Song, The More I Know You.*
RCA Victor LPV 525

FATS WALLER AND HIS RHYTHM—FRACTIOUS FINGERING
The Curse of an Aching Heart, S'posin', 'Taint Good, Nero, I'm Sorry I Made You Cry, Floatin' Down to Cotton Town, Fractious Fingering, La-De-De La-De-Da, Bye Bye Baby, I'm at the Mercy of Love, Please Keep Me in Your Dreams, Who's Afraid of Love?, Swingin' Them Jingle Bells, Gladyse (solo), *My Feelin's Are Hurt, Sweet Savannah Sue.*
RCA Victor LPV 537

FATS WALLER AND HIS RHYTHM—SMASHING THIRDS
Smashing Thirds (solo), *Waitin' at the End of the Road, Turn on the Heat, Beat It Out, What Will I Do in the Morning?, Boo-Hoo, You've Got Me Under Your Thumb, How Ya Baby?, Honeysuckle Rose, Spring Cleaning, She's Tall She's Tan She's Terrific, How Can I?, I'd Rather Call You Baby, Sweet Heartache, You're My Dish, Blue Turning Grey Over You.*
RCA Victor LPV 550

FATS WALLER AND HIS RHYTHM—AFRICAN RIPPLES
You Look Good to Me, Something Tells Me, In the Gloaming, If I Were You, Shame! Shame!, Every Day's a Holiday, Patty Cake, Hold My Hand, Fair and Square, I Love to Whistle, Tell Me with Your Kisses, Let's Break the Good News, Yacht Club Swing, African Ripples (solo), *My Fate Is in Your Hands, Baby Oh Where Can You Be?*
RCA Victor LPV 562

Following Fats Waller albums are no longer available:

Riverside RLP12-103—Young Fats Waller
Riverside RLP12-109—The Amazing Mr. Waller

RCA Victor LPM 1246—Ain't Misbehavin'
RCA Victor LPM 1502—Handful of Keys
RCA Victor LPM 1503—One Never Knows, Do One?
Camden CAL 473—The Real Fats Waller